The Birth of
CHRISTIANITY

The Birth of
CHRISTIANITY

DISCOVERING WHAT HAPPENED IN THE YEARS IMMEDIATELY AFTER THE EXECUTION OF JESUS

John Dominic Crossan

HarperSanFrancisco

A Division of HarperCollinsPublishers

HarperSanFrancisco and the author, in association with The Basic Foundation, a not-for-profit organization whose primary mission is reforestation, will facilitate the planting of two trees for every one tree used in the manufacture of this book.

A TREE CLAUSE BOOK

HarperCollins Web Site: http://www.harpercollins.com

HarperCollins®, ▄®, and HarperSanFrancisco™ are trademarks of HarperCollins Publishers Inc.

Design by Interrobang Design Studio
FIRST EDITION

Library of Congress Cataloging-in-Publication Data
Crossan, Dominic.
The birth of christianity : discovering what happened in the years immediately after the execution of Jesus / John Dominic Crossan. —1st ed.
p. cm.
includes bibliographical references and indexes.
ISBN 0–06–061659–8 (cloth). ISBN 0–06–061660–1 (pbk.)
ISBN 0–06–061672–5 (int'l)
I. Title.
BR129.C75 1998
270.1—dc21 97-32526
CIP

98 99 00 01 02 RRD(H) 10 9 8 7 6 5 4 3 2 1

In memory of
my younger brother,
Daniel Joseph Crossan, Jr.

CONTENTS

PREFACE

The Lost Years

If they do not listen to Moses and the prophets, neither will they be convinced even if someone rises from the dead.

Luke 16:31

This book is about the lost years of earliest Christianity, about the 30s and 40s of the first century, about those dark decades immediately after the execution of Jesus. Those years are cloaked in a silence similar to that shrouding Jesus' own early life. Where did Jesus go, it is sometimes asked, in those decades before he emerged to public life as a follower of John the Baptist? He went, it is sometimes answered, to India and learned wisdom. I no more believe that story than that he went to Ireland and learned Gaelic. Be that as it may, there is, for earliest Jesus and earliest Christianity, a parallel period of empty years and darkened decades. But it is more surprising to have such lost years for a social movement than for an individual person. It is not at all unusual that the ancient record of a personal life should begin at full maturity. The emperor Augustus, who died on August 19 of 14 C.E., left his autobiography to be inscribed on bronze tablets in front of his mausoleum in Rome. That story began with the words "at the age of nineteen." Neither does Luke 2:46–47 pierce the lost years of Jesus with any historical information. At the age of twelve, Jesus was found by his parents "in the temple, sitting among the teachers, listening to them and asking them questions. And all who heard him were amazed at his understanding and his answers." Josephus records a similar precocious situation for himself in his *Life* 9: "While still a mere boy, about fourteen years old, I won universal applause for my love of letters; inasmuch that the chief priests and the leading men of the city used constantly to come to me for precise information on some particular in our ordinances."

But how does it happen that the early years of Christianity are so shrouded in silence? The obscurity of the 30s and 40s can be emphasized by the comparative brilliancy of the 50s. For that later decade we have the letters of the apostle Paul. From them we know about Christian communities in four Roman provinces, Galatia and Asia in central and western Turkey, and Macedonia and Achaia in northern and southern Greece. From them we learn about urban churches in Philippi, Thessalonica, and Ephesus. From them, with sociological analysis wedded to theological exegesis, we can almost fill a small library on the personalities and problems of the Corinthian congregation alone. From them we catch glimpses of past events in the 30s and 40s at Damascus,

Antioch, and Jerusalem. From them we catch glimpses of future plans for the 60s in Italy and Spain. From them, above all else, we receive the temptation to gloss speedily over the 30s or 40s and move swiftly to those better-documented 50s. This book intends to resist that temptation and to ask instead these questions: What forms of Christianity were present in the 30s for Paul the persecutor, before he became Paul the apostle, to persecute? What forms of Christianity were present before Paul, without Paul, and even if Paul had never existed?

There is an obvious objection. Do we not have precious information in what we call the Acts of the Apostles about those lost years of the 30s and 40s? We do indeed, but with several difficulties. First, it is hard, without independent vectors, to separate history from theology and tradition from redaction in that writing. Second, Luke gives us a very general picture. It is like a summary of 1944–1945 asserting that the Allies landed on the beaches of Normandy and pushed eastward to Berlin. That is absolutely true, but—apart from omitting details such as Bastogne—it says nothing about the Russians pushing westward toward the same destination. It describes the past in a way that renders the future incomprehensible. Luke's Acts of the Apostles moves Christianity on the westward Jerusalem-to-Rome axis with nothing said about northward Syriac or southward Coptic Christianity. Third, you would know from that text about Christianity in Jerusalem, but you would know nothing about Christianity in Galilee. In fact, when you put together Luke and Paul on the 30s and 40s, you would conclude that Christianity operated exclusively from Jerusalem. This book intends to give *equal* attention to Christianity in both Galilee and Jerusalem. It also refuses to replace the old ascendancy of Jerusalem with a new one of Galilee. *Both,* then, not *either.*

There are no documents from those 30s and 40s dated as Paul's letters are to the 50s. How, then, is reconstruction possible or anything new worth saying about those decades? It is a question of new method and new material. My new *method* is an interdisciplinary combination of anthropological, historical, archeological, and literary disciplines. It establishes the sharpest possible context before any Christian text is studied within that matrix. My new *material* is obtained from the earlier strata or larger sources of Christian texts we already have available to us. It is especially significant where two independent early Christian texts share common traditions that must, therefore, be earlier than either of them. But no matter what sources or texts I am using, they are always used to illumine the Christianity of the 30s and 40s in the Jewish homeland. That is what this book is about.

My title is *The Birth of Christianity,* and that requires two explanations. First, about the word *birth.* Conceptions are usually more private and hidden than births. Christianity's conception was the kingdom-of-God movement as Jesus and his first companions lived in radical but nonviolent resistance to Herod Antipas's urban development and Rome's rural commercialism in Lower Galilee of the late 20s. Christianity's birth was in that movement's continuation as those same companions wrestled not only to imitate Jesus' life but also to understand Jesus' death. This book is about that birth. It presumes conception but does not go on to growth or maturity. Birth, in other words, is the 30s and the 40s. Now about the word *Christianity.* If you can hear that term only as a religion separate from or even inimical to Judaism, you are not hearing it as intended in this book. I use *Christianity* to mean Christian Judaism, just as I use *Essenism, Pharisaism,* or *Sadduceeism* to mean Essene Judaism, Pharisaic Judaism, or Sadduceean Judaism. They are all divergent, competing, and mutually hostile options *within* the Jewish homeland as it struggled to withstand Greek cultural internationalism and Roman military imperialism. What was Christian Judaism before Paul and without Paul?

I conclude with Luke 24:13–33, which summarizes in a single paragraph what it will take me a whole book to develop. Two Christians travel from Jerusalem to Emmaus on Easter Sunday. One is named and male; his companion, unnamed, is presumably female, given the protocols of Mediterranean patriarchy. The risen Jesus joins them on their journey. But the road to Emmaus is not the road to Damascus. This is an apparition without blinding light or heavenly voice. This is a vision without slow demonstration or immediate recognition. Even when Jesus explains the scriptures about the suffering and glorification of the Messiah, the travelers do not know who he is. But then they invite the stranger to stay and eat with them. *He* does not invite *them*. *They* invite *him*.

> As they came near the village to which they were going, he walked ahead as if he were going on. But they urged him strongly, saying, "Stay with us, because it is almost evening and the day is now nearly over." So he went in to stay with them. (Luke 24:28–29)

You will notice how that invitation is emphasized. The pair have presumably arrived at their village home and, but for the invitation, the stranger would have passed on and remained unrecognized. The pair are, in terms to be used later in this book, itinerants who become householders, but it is invitation that leads to meal that leads to recognition. "Then their eyes were opened, and they recognized him; and he vanished from their sight," as 24:31 puts it. Resurrected life and risen vision appear as offered shelter and shared meal. Resurrection is not enough. You still need scripture and eucharist, tradition and table, community and justice; otherwise, divine presence remains unrecognized and human eyes remain unopened. That is exactly what this book is about.

PROLOGUE

The Content of Your Vision

"Gnosis" or "Gnosticism" is [a] ... form of religion in late antiquity.... A clear-cut definition of this "religion of knowledge" or of "insight", as the Greek word *gnosis* may be translated, is not easy, but should at least be briefly suggested at the very outset. We shall not go far wrong to see in it a dualistic religion, consisting of several schools and movements, which took up a definitely negative attitude towards the world and the society of the time, and proclaimed a deliverance ("redemption") of man precisely from the constraints of earthly existence through "insight" into his essential relationship, whether as "soul" or "spirit",—a relationship temporarily obscured—with a supramundane realm of freedom and of rest. [It] spread through time and space, from the beginning of our era onwards, from the western part of the Near East (Syria, Palestine, Egypt, Asia Minor).... One can almost say that Gnosis followed the Church like a shadow; the Church could never overcome it, its influence had gone too deep. By reason of their common history they remain two—hostile—sisters.

Kurt Rudolph, *Gnosis*, pp. 1–2, 368

It all began with the vision of a dead man, a dead man still bearing the wounds of an execution as horrible as hate could devise and contempt accomplish. And it happened outside the city walls, where dogs and crows waited for an unburied body. There was also a story. It told of a community, conceived in heaven but born on earth. It told of a kingdom standing in opposition to the other kingdoms of the world. It told of an individual, Peacemaker and Lord, Savior and Son of God, who proclaimed that kingdom's advent as gospel, good news for all the earth.

If you had heard that vision and that story in the early first century, would you have believed it? If you heard that vision and that story in the late twentieth century, would you believe it? And what, in first or twentieth century, would such belief entail?

The Vision of a Dead Man

The souls of the dead could certainly interact with the living and with each other, in ways exactly analogous to normal life. Instances abound in which the dead were touched and touched others. . . . The souls of the dead, though described as impalpable, seem not to notice this minor modification; they live and act exactly as do the living, even alongside the living. . . . Any Semitic or Greco-Roman soul could appear to the living, still bearing the recognizable form of the body. Any soul could pass through closed doors, give preternatural advice, and vanish. Did Jesus appear to and instruct his disciples after his crucifixion? So Patroklos appeared to Achilles, Samuel to Saul, the elder Scipio to his grandson, as did numerous others to their survivors. Did the resurrected Jesus eat broiled fish, and a meal with his disciples? Any soul could, and often did, eat with friends and relatives in the repasts of the cult of the dead, a practice perhaps especially common among Christians.

Gregory J. Riley, *Resurrection Reconsidered*, pp. 58, 67

The story that began with a vision of a dead man was heard as choral hymn, read as national epic, and seen as marble frieze within the Roman Empire. But the inaugural vision that began the story took place over a thousand years earlier, on the night the Greeks burned Troy to the ground. In book 22 of Homer's *Iliad*, Achilles slew the Trojan hero Hector, and other Greek warriors stabbed his naked corpse. Achilles had taunted the dying Hector that "the dogs and birds will maul you, shame your corpse. . . . [T]he dogs and birds will rend you—blood and bone." After he died, Achilles brought Hector's body back to the Greek encampment as described in Robert Fagles's translation (554–555):

Piercing the tendons, ankle to heel behind both feet,
he knotted straps of rawhide through them both,
lashed them to his chariot, left the head to drag
and mounting the car, hoisting the famous arms aboard,
he whipped his team to a run and breakneck on they flew,
holding nothing back. And a thick cloud of dust rose up
from the man they dragged, his dark hair swirling round
that head so handsome once, all tumbled low in the dust—
since Zeus had given him over to his enemies now
to be defiled in the land of his own fathers.

Only the abject pleas and supplicant humility of Hector's father, Priam, king of Troy, moved Achilles to surrender the body for honorable burial by its own people. And that is how the *Iliad* ends: with the lament of Andromache, Hecuba, and Helen, the three women closest to Hector; with funeral pyre, golden ossuary, and deep, hollow grave; and with, in the poem's last lines, "a splendid feast in Hector's honor." But where Homer's *Iliad* ends, Virgil's *Aeneid* begins.

Julius Caesar was assassinated in March of 44 because aristocratic republicans thought he planned autocracy. Octavius, his nineteen-year-old adopted son and legal heir, deified Caesar in January of 42, defeated Antony and Cleopatra in September of 31, and was declared Augustus in January of 27 B.C.E. Octavius was also Peacemaker, Benefactor, Savior, and Son of God. He was even Lord of time itself, so that his birthday on September 23 would become New Year's Day in the Roman province of Asia Minor, because, in the words of that calendrical decree (Danker 217), "the birthday of our god signalled the beginning of good news (*euaggelion*) for the world because of him." That, however, was thirty years after the crucial exchange in 27, when Octavius gave the senate back most of the provinces and they gave Augustus back most of the legions. He was now what Caesar might have been, supreme autocrat, even if called by whatever name one chose to disguise that obvious fact. But neither deity nor power had been enough to protect Caesar from assassination. What Augustus needed (to solidify the legions and power he now had) was artists and propaganda. Virgil's *Aeneid* is superb poetry. It is also superb propaganda.

It tells the story of the Roman people, especially the story of the Julian clan up to and including Caesar, Augustus, and their families. It all begins long before that, though, with the Trojan male Anchises and the Greek goddess Aphrodite. Aeneas is the human-divine or mortal-immortal child of that union, and it is to him that Hector appears with the Greeks already inside the walls of the doomed city. This is that vision, from book 2 of the *Aeneid,* in Robert Fitzgerald's translation (43):

> In sleep, in dream, Hector appeared to me,
> Gaunt with sorrow, streaming tears, all torn—
> As by the violent car on his death day—
> And black with bloody dust,
> His puffed-out feet cut by the rawhide thongs.
> Ah god, the look of him! How changed
> From that proud Hector who returned to Troy
> Wearing Achilles' armor, or that one
> Who pitched the torches on Danaan ships;
> His beard all filth, his hair matted with blood,
> Showing the wounds, the many wounds, received
> Outside his father's city walls.

Aeneas, "child of the goddess," flees Troy, taking with him his father Anchises and his son Julus. They eventually arrive in Italy, and the rest is, if not exactly history, at least magnificent poetry. Virgil's great poem, unfinished at his death in 19 B.C.E. after ten years of work, celebrated "the Trojan Caesar. . . . Julius [Caesar] his name, from Julus handed down" (13), linked heaven and earth, connected Troy and Rome, and gave the Roman people and the Augustan principate a divine origin and a mythic destiny.

Those preceding paragraphs make a very simple point. The general Mediterranean culture would find nothing impossible about that vision of Hector to Aeneas. Nothing in that story would have raised a first-century eyebrow. The dead existed in the realm of Hades or Sheol and could reappear thence to the living. Thus, although Hector's body had flamed to ashes on a Trojan funeral pyre, his "body" was still visible and recognizable to Aeneas. That the dead could return and interact with the living was a commonplace of the Greco-Roman world, and neither pagans nor Jews would have asserted that it could not happen. That such interaction could generate important processes and events, as with Hector saving Aeneas to found the Roman people and the Julian ascendancy, was also a commonplace. You did not expect the dead to return from Hades simply to say hello. You could easily say that such a return did not happen this time or that time. You could *not* say that it never happened anywhere or could never happen at all. That is a first pointer toward the core problem of this book. Now on to a second pointer.

Visions Then, Visions Now

Others, too, are visited. [Dale Murphy's] mother looks out the bedroom window one day and sees Murph ambling down their street in huge deck boots. Someone else spots him in traffic in downtown Bradenton. From time to time Debra dreams that she sees him and runs up and says, "Dale, where've you been?" And he won't answer, and she'll wake up in a cold sweat, remembering.

Sebastian Junger, *The Perfect Storm*, p. 214

Not only were visions and apparitions an accepted and even commonplace possibility in the early first century, they are also an accepted and even commonplace possibility in the late twentieth century. In a paper presented to the 1995 spring meeting of the Jesus Seminar, Stacy Davids summarized recent psychiatric literature on grief and bereavement. "Review of well-conducted studies of the past three decades shows that about one-half to eighty percent of bereaved people studied feel this intuitive, sometimes overwhelming 'presence' or 'spirit' of the lost person. . . .

These perceptions happen most often in the first few months following the death but sometimes persist more than a year, with significantly more women than men reporting these events. . . . The American Psychiatric Association, author of *The Diagnostic and Statistical Manual of Mental Disorders–IV*, considers these phenomena (when 'one hears the voice of, or transiently sees the image of, the deceased person') as non-pathological. They are viewed as common characteristics of uncomplicated grief, and not attributable to a mental disorder. . . . Part of the work of grief entails repeated, monotonous recalling of the events leading up to the death, as the mourner undergoes a restless need to 'make sense' of what happened, to make it explicable, and to classify it along with other similar events. . . . During this process, accurate recording and telling of the dead person's life is of utmost importance to the bereaved" (3–6).

As I write this Prologue, Sebastian Junger's powerful elegy for those who go down at sea is deservedly high on the *New York Times* best-seller list for nonfiction. It centers on the *Andrea Gail,* a seventy-two-foot steel swordfisher out of Gloucester that disappeared with all hands off Sable Island east of Nova Scotia, October 28, 1991, in waves one hundred feet high. "If the men on the *Andrea Gail* had simply died, and their bodies were lying in state somewhere, their loved ones could make their goodbyes and get on with their lives. But they didn't die, they disappeared off the face of the earth and, strictly speaking, it's just a matter of faith that these men will never return" (213). That comment and the epigraph above tell us what can happen today in contemporary America after any death— but especially after a sudden, tragic, or mysterious one—as intimates mourn their beloved dead. There are dreams and there are visions. Dale Murphy, who disappeared on the *Andrea Gail,* left a three-year-old son, an ex-wife, and a mother behind him. His son "wakes up screaming in the middle of the night" because "Daddy's in the room. . . . Daddy was just here. . . . Daddy was here and told me what happened on the boat" (214).

Hopes and fears, dreams and nightmares, visions and apparitions are not the same as delusions and hallucinations. If you wake up screaming because a giant figure is ready to attack you, that is a nightmarish dream. Your spouse reassures you, saying it is just a bad dream, urging you to go back to sleep. And you do. But if you call 9-1-1 that night to report an intruder and summon ADT the next day to put in a security system, you are moving from dream into delusion. It is part of reality to know which is which. If you come down from the mountaintop and report a revelation from the Archangel Michael, you have seen an apparition. If you keep insisting that Bigfoot-with-Wings is up there and that everyone should go to see it, you are beyond vision and into hallucination. It is part of reality to know which is which. The present discussion is not about delusions and hallucinations, about losing touch with reality, and neither is it about tricks and lies, about losing touch with honesty. Trance and ecstasy, vision and apparition are perfectly normal and natural phenomena. Altered states of consciousness, such as dreams and visions, are something common to our humanity, something hard-wired into our brains, something as normal as language itself. They were recognized as common possibilities in the early first century, and they are still recognized as such in the late twentieth century. And only when their human normalcy is accepted can a proper response be offered. That response should not be, We deny the *fact* of your vision. It should be, Tell us the *content* of your vision. And then we will have to judge, not whether you had it or not, but whether we should follow it or not.

By now the problem at the heart of this book should be clear. Asked about the birth of Christianity, most people might say something like this: Jesus' followers thought that he was the Messiah, but then he was executed and buried. Later his tomb was found empty and he appeared to his former companions as risen from the dead. Christianity was born on Easter Sunday, the seventeenth day of the month Nisan in the year 30 C.E. It is the resurrection of a dead man that explains the power of Christianity's birth and growth, spread and triumph, across the Roman Empire. Here, however, is the problem. Why, against that early-first-century context, does vision, apparition, or resurrection explain anything, since such events were not considered absolutely extraordinary let alone completely unique? And why, in this late-twentieth-century context, do they explain anything if things are still the same? There *was* an easier time when anti-Christian secularists could claim that visions and apparitions of the dead were simply lies at worst and delusions at best. There *was* an easier time when pro-Christian fundamentalists could respond that there was only this one unique case in all of human history where a human being had risen from the dead. Both sides admitted the abnormality of such events: one side said these events could never happen; the other side said they had happened only once. They were twin sides of the same rationalist coin.

That first century lacked not only a clear separation of church and state, it also lacked a clear separation of heaven and earth. Turn for a second from the end to the beginning of Jesus' life. Christianity said, according to Luke 1:26–38, that Jesus was born of Mary and the Holy Spirit, of a human mother and a divine Father. Paganism could not respond in rebuttal that such was quite impossible. Pagans knew, after all, of the birth of Aeneas from a divine mother and a human father. Closer to home, there was the claim that Augustus himself was conceived from a divine father and a human mother. Atia spent the night in Apollo's temple, the god visited her in the guise of a snake, and "in the tenth month after that Augustus was born and was therefore regarded as the son of Apollo," according to Suetonius's *The Lives of the Caesars: The Deified Augustus* 94:4 (Rolfe 1.267). Against such a background, the best paganism could offer to refute Luke was this, from Celsus's late-second-century *On the True Doctrine*: "Are we to think that the high God would have fallen in love with a woman of no breeding?" (Hoffmann 57–58). Not, *It could not happen,* but *It could not happen to a peasant woman.* In a world where gods and goddesses, spirits and immortals regularly interacted physically and sexually, spiritually and intellectually with human beings, the conception of a divine child and the vision of a dead person are neither totally abnormal nor completely unique events. So how do visions and apparitions, even if factual and historical, explain the birth of Christianity?

You could *and should* object that it is not as simple as all that. In his first letter to the Corinthians, Paul explains the resurrection of Jesus as the beginning of the general resurrection at the end of the world. As a Pharisee, Paul believed in such an apocalyptic resurrection and concluded that it had *already begun* with Jesus. We often say that for Paul the end of the world was imminent. It is more accurate to say that for Paul the end had already begun; only its final consummation was imminent. That is why, in 1 Corinthians 15, he can argue quite logically that Jesus' resurrection and the general resurrection stand or fall together.

If there is no resurrection of the dead, then Christ has not been raised. . . .
For if the dead are not raised, then Christ has not been raised. . . . But in fact
Christ has been raised from the dead, the first fruits of those who have died.
(1 Corinthians 15:13, 16, 20)

It never occurs to Paul that Jesus' resurrection might be a special or unique privilege given to him because he is Messiah, Lord, and Son of God. It never occurs to Paul that Jesus' case might be like the case of Elijah, who was taken up individually to live with God but without any wider, communal, or cosmic effects. Risen apparitions are, for Paul, not about the vision of a dead man but about the vision of a dead man who begins the general resurrection. It is, in other words, an apparition with cosmically apocalyptic consequences. All of that is quite correct, but it only serves to intensify the question: Why, against that first-century background, did the vision of a resurrected Jesus make Paul and other Christians conclude that this was the beginning of the end and not just a personal gift for Jesus alone?

There are other problems with the standard understanding of the birth of Christianity offered above. I mention them here but do not think any of them is as significant as the one I have been emphasizing. They all arise only on the presumption that we are reading literal rather than symbolical, and historical rather than theological, descriptions of the risen Jesus. First, it is difficult to reconcile Paul's list of people to whom Jesus appeared after the resurrection (1 Corinthians 15:5–8) with those of the evangelists as they conclude their gospels. Second, it is difficult to reconcile those gospel accounts among themselves with regard to time, place, and content. Third, it is quite likely that none of those gospel accounts is describing visions at all. What happened to Paul was certainly a vision, but those gospel accounts are more about establishing an authority than about receiving an apparition. Finally, the gospel accounts indicate very serious theological disagreements between each other on the necessity or validity of such visions. In an earlier preparation for his own resurrection visions, Luke 16:31 gave this solemn warning: "If they do not listen to Moses and the prophets, neither will they be convinced even if someone rises from the dead." Those problems are all important ones and I do not disregard them, but they are not the major one that haunts this book.

If we were to say that visions and apparitions, divine conceptions and bodily resurrections do not ordinarily happen, then we could conclude that the gospels record typical human delusions about things that never happen *or* that they record unique divine accounts of events that happened only once. But my problem going into this book is that such arguments are *certainly* invalid for the early first century and *probably* invalid for the late twentieth century. Visions of risen corpses or apparitions of resurrected bodies are not uniquely special. The question, then, is what is special about any given one? What is the content of *your* vision, the challenge of *your* apparition?

Dualism and Inconsistency

There is no longer Jew or Greek, there is no longer slave or free, there is no longer male and female; for all of you are one in Christ Jesus. . . . In the one Spirit we were all baptized into one body—Jews or Greeks, slaves or free— and we were all made to drink of one Spirit.

Paul, Galatians 3:28 and 1 Corinthians 12:13

Some Christians (whether Jewish or Gentile) could declare that there is no Greek or Jew, no male or female. No rabbinic Jew could do so, because people are bodies, not spirits, and precisely bodies are marked as male or female, and also marked, through bodily practices and techniques such as circumcision and food taboos, as Jew or Greek as well.

Daniel Boyarin, *Carnal Israel*, p. 10

I begin this book, then, with a problem or, if you prefer, a presupposition. It is not a religious or a theological presupposition but an anthropological and an historical one. It is not enough to say that the vision of a dead man birthed Christianity, because that, at least in the first century and probably in every century since, is not special enough of itself to explain anything. Neither is it enough to say that the vision of a dead man was interpreted as the start of the general resurrection and that interpretation birthed Christianity. That only rephrases the problem: Why was this man's resurrection, as distinct from any and all other ones, understood as such a beginning? From that problem as presupposition I draw this hypothesis: the birth of Christianity is the interaction between the historical Jesus and his first companions and the continuation of that relationship despite his execution. This book, therefore, attempts an historical reconstruction of that interaction, that continuation, and the reasons that one led to the other. Its focus is on birth not growth, on those years before and especially after Jesus' crucifixion, on those who were with him beforehand and continued within him afterward. It is about the years before Paul; in other words, it concerns what was there for Paul to persecute. And that last point requires some careful consideration.

I include Paul not in the birth of Christianity but rather in its growth and development. That is neither a deliberate insult nor a calculated disparagement. My decision is based on four factors, of which the last is the crucial one. First, I do not think Paul was as important theologically or historically in the first Christian century as he was in the sixteenth Christian century, and that later importance often blocks our ability to assess his original significance. Second, we tend to move much too swiftly from the historical Jesus in the 20s (where we have no contemporary texts) to the historical Paul in the 50s (where we *do* have contemporary texts). What happened in the 30s? What do we *imagine* happened in the 30s? Third, I sense profoundly different results between those who start with Paul and then go back (or refuse to go back) to the historical Jesus, and those who start with Jesus and then go on (or refuse to go on) to Paul. I put it as a challenge: *If you begin with Paul, you will interpret Jesus incorrectly; if you begin with Jesus, you will interpret Paul differently.* The reason for that belief lies in my fourth (and most basic) point, which I write in dialogue with the fascinating and provocative work of Daniel Boyarin, as summarized in the above epigraph to this section.

When a traditional society is confronted with imperial modernization, it can choose rejection or assimilation. But it can never take either option absolutely. It is always a case of where, when, what, and why to renounce or accept that alien intransigence. It is always a case of what is superficial and what is basic, of what is negotiable and what is intolerable. It is always a case of *who* decides that difference and *how* that difference is decided. By the first common-era century, ancient traditional Judaism was under increasing pressures not just from Roman commercial exploitation in the age of Augustus but from Greek cultural domination since the age of Alexander the Great. Modernization for many *then* was Hellenization—Greek internationalism—just as modernization for many *now* is Americanization. Is that a matter of jets, computers, communications? Is it a matter of sex, drugs, violence? Is it a matter of freedom, democracy, justice? Is it a matter of materialism, individualism, secularism, capitalism? How exactly can a venerable traditional society negotiate acceptance *and* rejection when faced with social, economic, and military domination? But, especially, how can it withstand overwhelming *cultural* imperialism: Paul speaks, in Galatians 3:28, of "Jew and Greek," not of "Jew and Roman."

In a 1994 book Daniel Boyarin labeled Paul "a radical Jew" and summarized his purpose like this: "[1] Paul was motivated by a Hellenistic desire for the One, which among other things produced an ideal of a universal human essence, beyond difference and hierarchy. [2] This universal humanity, however, was predicated (and still is) on the dualism of the flesh and the spirit, such that while the body is particular, marked through practice as Jew or Greek, and through anatomy as male or female, the spirit is universal. [3] Paul did not, however, reject the body—as did, for instance, the gnostics—but rather promoted a system whereby the body had its place, albeit subordinated to the spirit" (7, my numbers). Later, the first two points of that thesis are repeated verbatim, but there is a different final point: "[4] The strongest expression of this Pauline cultural criticism is Galatians and especially 3:28–29" (181). Those are, in other words, the four major and sequential points of his powerful thesis. Watch, now, as Judaism and Hellenism clash deep in Paul's sensibility, and—without condescension at this safe distance—judge which you think is winning on the issue in question.

That dualism of flesh and spirit derived from a pervasive Platonism in Paul's contemporary culture. "Various branches of Judaism (along with most of the surrounding culture) became increasingly platonized in late antiquity. By platonization I mean here the adoption of a dualist philosophy in which the phenomenal world was understood to be the representation in matter of a spiritual or ideal entity which corresponded to it. This has the further consequence that a hierarchical opposition is set up in which the invisible, inner reality is taken as more valuable or higher than the visible outer form of reality. In the anthropology of such a culture, the human person is constituted by an outer physical shell which is non-essential and by an inner spiritual soul, which represents his *[sic]* true and higher essence" (59, *sic* original). That hierarchical dualism of spirit over flesh formed a spectrum from bodily neglect through bodily denigration to bodily rejection. The flesh could be to the spirit as its distracting mansion, its nomadic tent, its decrepit abode, or its filthy prison cell. Those were all points, however, along the same dualistic scale. Paul was not as radically dualistic as were the Gnostics, but he had "as thoroughgoing a dualism as that of Philo," the contemporary Jewish philosopher from Alexandria—that is, "the body, while necessarily and positively valued by Paul is, as in Philo, not the human being but only his or her house or garment" (59). Boyarin insists that Paul's dualism *does not imply a rejection of the body*" (59) and "does not abhor the body" (64); it "makes room for the body, however much the spirit is more highly valued" (185). Paul stands, however, on a very slippery Hellenistic slope.

That dichotomy between a monism of necessarily enfleshed spirit and a dualism of accidentally enfleshed spirit needs some precise descriptive terminology. If we are talking only about Christ, it underlies the distinction between incarnational and docetic Christology. The former gives Jesus a full, normal, human body; the latter gives him only an apparent body (*dokein*, means "to seem" in Greek). It is, as it were, a body for the job, like those assumed by the Greco-Roman gods and goddesses for business purposes on earth. If we are talking only about Christianity, it underlies the distinction of Gnostis against Church cited from Rudolf in this Prologue's epigraph. It also underlies the more accurate distinction of Gnostic Christianity against Catholic Christianity, which emphasizes at least that both are options *within* Christianity. But that latter formulation has become so contaminated by apologetics and polemics, by accusations of heresy and claims of orthodoxy, that it is no longer helpful except for name-calling. That underlying dichotomy is, in any case, far older and wider than Christianity. It was there between traditional and Hellenistic Judaism before Christianity ever existed. And it is here today wherever flesh is separated from spirit, flesh is then sensationalized, spirit is then sentimentalized, and both are thereby dehumanized. I call that monism of enfleshed spirit *sarcophilia* and that dualism of flesh against spirit *sarcophobia*, from the Greek roots for flesh (*sarx*), love (*philia*), and fear (*phobos*). The terms are created on the analogy of *sarcophagus*, the marble coffin of antiquity, from flesh (*sarx*) and eat (*phagein*). We are dealing, therefore, with a profound fault-line in Western consciousness, with the great divide between a sarcophilic and a sarcophobic sensibility.

Boyarin understands correctly that none of this has to do with "a Hellenistic Judaism which is somehow less pure than a putative 'Palestinian' Judaism" (6). It is not as if all of Palestinian Judaism was sarcophilic and all of Hellenistic Judaism was sarcophobic. It was a difference not in geography but in ideology. It depended, wherever you lived, on whether you accepted or rejected that Platonic dualism and in what form or to what degree you did so. Boyarin parallels Paul with Philo, but in case you think that dualistic ideology is only for Diaspora Jews, I insert an example from Josephus, a Palestinian contemporary.

It is a rather stunning example of Platonic dualism, of the spirit's transcendence over the body, and of the flesh's irrelevance to the soul. It is a speech placed by Josephus on the lips of Eleazar, leader of the besieged rebels atop Masada at the end of the First Roman-Jewish War in 74 C.E. The Romans under Flavius Silva had built up a huge ramp against the isolated mesa-like rock fortress, and the end was now in sight. The defenders decided to kill their families and then themselves. Eleazar encouraged them to prefer death to slavery:

> For it is death which gives liberty to the soul and permits it to depart to its own pure abode, there to be free from all calamity; but so long as it is imprisoned in a mortal body and tainted with all its miseries, it is, in sober truth, dead, for association with what is mortal ill befits that which is divine. . . . But it is not until, freed from the weight that drags it down to earth and clings about it, the soul is restored to its proper sphere, that it enjoys a blessed energy and a power untrammelled on every side, remaining, like God Himself, invisible to human eyes. (*Jewish War* 7.344, 346)

That speech is not Eleazar speaking to his fellow rebels, of course, but Josephus speaking to his fellow Romans. But it is hard to find a more precise formulation of the superiority of soul over body and of spirit over flesh. The question, for first-century Jews, was not whether you lived in Palestine or the Diaspora or whether you spoke Greek or Aramaic, but whether you had absorbed ideologically that Hellenistic dualism, as had Philo, Paul, and Josephus.

How does that apply, for Boyarin, to Paul's three distinctions of ethnicity, class, and gender, negated for Christians in Galatians 3:28 ("There is no longer Jew or Greek, there is no longer slave or free, there is no longer male and female")? Against such a dualistic background those three negated distinctions could apply to the person-as-soul rather than to the nonperson-as-flesh. They could apply to ritual present or heavenly future but not to contemporary society or social reality. You could easily imagine a Platonizing or Hellenizing Paul asserting that such physical or material disjunctions had nothing whatsoever to do with the soul, the spirit, the true human being. They were as irrelevant before God or in Christ as the color of one's hair or the shape of one's toes. That is the way Boyarin explains Paul. "What drove Paul was a passionate desire for human unification, for the erasure of differences and hierarchies between human beings, and . . . he saw the Christian event, as he had experienced it, as the vehicle for this transformation of humanity" (106). But if that was all Paul had done, if he had been consistently

Hellenistic, we would still be yawning. His Jewish and Hellenistic genes fought not to a compromise but to an inconsistency. A compromise might have said that the flesh is to be kept in its inferior place but is never to be totally rejected. An inconsistency is something else, and that is what happens to Paul.

This is it. *He takes that first distinction of Jew and Gentile out of the soul and puts it onto the body, out of the spirit and onto the flesh.* He takes ethnicity-negation out into the streets of the Roman cities, but he does not take class-negation or gender-negation outside in the same way. He does not say for ethnicity, as he does for class and gender, that it is irrelevant before God religiously and spiritually but should be maintained physically and socially. *The contradiction is not that he took all three spiritually but that he took one physically as well as spiritually.* If the Jew/Greek distinction were taken spiritually, it would mean that inside both were equal and that outside neither was significant. It would make no difference, then, to be circumcised Jew or uncircumcised Greek. It would make no difference, *one way or the other.* To be not circumcised would be no better or worse than to be circumcised. But, to put it bluntly and practically, if Paul had had a son, he would not have circumcised him. Even though Galatians 5:6 and 6:15 insist that "neither circumcision nor uncircumcision" is important, not to circumcise *was* important for Paul. Circumcision is caustically termed mutilation in 5:12. Paul had earlier broken with James, Peter, Barnabas, and everyone else over minimal kosher observance so that Jewish Christians and pagan Christians could eat together at Antioch in Galatians 2:11–14. Boyarin is quite right that Paul has compromised between his Judaism and his Hellenism by adopting not a radical (rejection of flesh for spirit) but a moderate Platonic dualism (subordination of flesh to spirit). It is not that *compromise* I emphasize but the *inconsistency* with which he applies it to Galatians 3:28.

What is needed, from Paul then or Boyarin now, is to meditate on the *difference between those three differences.* And in that meditation, the presence of the class distinction is crucial. You could, for example, preserve difference without hierarchy in the case of ethnicity and gender. But not in the case of class. For class, difference *is* hierarchy and hierarchy *is* difference. The rich are *different* from the poor: they have more money. The free are *different* from the slaves: they have more power. Had Paul negated *all three* distinctions physically and materially in the urban streets of Roman cities, his life would have been as short as that of Jesus. Boyarin does not see that inconsistency in Paul. It is an inconsistency that allows Paul to negate Jew/Greek to the fullest *physical* extent concerning circumcision and kosher practice while negating slave/free and male/female in a far more *spiritual* manner. The inconsistency on those three distinctions in Paul is matched by a similar one in Boyarin himself.

In my above epigraph from his 1993 book, *Carnal Israel,* Boyarin mentions only the first and last of Paul's three distinctions from Galatians 3:28. He cites *ethnicity* and *gender* but omits *class*. That could have been just a passing emphasis and omission were it not for what happens in his 1994 sequel, *A Radical Jew,* which is a total interpretation of Paul based on Galatians 3:28, which he calls "my key for unlocking Paul" (23). In that second book he repeatedly, consistently, and without excuse or explanation omits the middle term *class* to concentrate exclusively on *ethnicity* and *gender*. The distinction of *class* is singled out for emphasis once—"there is no slave or free in Christ" (5)—with specific regard to Paul's letter to Philemon about his runaway slave Onesimus. All three distinctions are mentioned together a few times—for example, "in baptism, all the differences that mark off one body from another as Jew or Greek, . . . male or female, slave or free, are effaced" (23), or again, "Behind Paul's ministry was a profound vision of a humanity undivided by ethnos, class, and sex" (181), and again, "In Galatians Paul seems indeed to be wiping out social differences and hierarchies between the genders in addition to those that obtain between ethnic groups and socioeconomic classes" (183). But that is about all there is on the class distinction in a book that discusses brilliantly those of ethnicity and gender. I emphasize that point, for both Paul and Boyarin, because if you think about *the difference between those three differences,* and you think about *the difference between difference and hierarchy,* you will have to face these questions: If you can have differences of ethnicity and gender without hierarchy, can you do the same for class? How is class different from ethnicity and gender?

Despite that reservation, however, Boyarin's Pauline thesis has one other very telling critique, one other very impressive proposal. Because that "common dualist ideology . . . has characterized western thought practically since its inception," there "is . . . nothing striking in claiming that Paul was such a dualist; if anything the bold step that I am making is to claim that the Rabbis (as opposed to both earlier Hellenistic Jews and later ones) *resisted* this form of dualism" (85). Boyarin uses the term *rabbis* or *rabbinic Judaism* "only with regard to the second century and onward" (2), and the resistance of these rabbis to Platonic dualism is what he means by a "rejectionist" rather than an "assimilationist" reaction to Hellenization (7). "Of course," he says, "the Rabbis also believed in a soul that animates the body. The point is, rather, that they identified the human being not as a soul dwelling in a body but as a body animated by a soul, and that makes all the difference in the world" (278 note 8).

I agree with those statements and admit that my own personal sensibility also rejects human dualism in any shape or form it may take. On this point I stand with Judaism and against Hellenism. I do not find compromise feasible in this case because, while radical and moderate Platonism may differ in theory, they usually result in the same effects in practice. We are, for me, self-conscious flesh that can, paradoxically, negate not only the legitimacy of its flesh but even the validity of its self-consciousness. But we nonetheless remain self-conscious flesh. I find Platonic dualism, be it radical or moderate, to be ultimately dehumanizing. I admit this openly, because both author *and reader* have to answer for their own sensibility before continuing this discussion. Where are *you* on this point?

This is why I want to be very careful about Jesus and Paul. Boyarin knows that "Paul's entire gospel is a stirring call to human freedom and autonomy" (199). And Stephen Patterson has recently written about "the continuity between Paul and the sayings tradition [in the gospels] precisely in terms of the tradition of social radicalism they both share" (1991:35). I agree with both those statements. That is not my criticism of Paul. And my objection is not just to Paul's blazing inconsistency in taking the first of his three distinctions, ethnicity, but not the other two, class and gender, all the way down to the depths and all the way out to the streets. It is this: the Platonic dualism that had influenced Philo, Paul, and Josephus had not so influenced John the Baptist, Jesus, and James, nor, I imagine, the Essenes and the Pharisees before the rabbis. Start with Paul and you will see Jesus incorrectly; start with Jesus and you will see Paul differently. In this book, therefore, I bracket Paul to concentrate on a Christianity that had to be born before he could notice its existence and persecute its presence.

The Bodily Resurrection of Jesus

The Gospel stories mention a gentle enshrouding, a magnanimous laying out, and a loving tombside vigil; but a limed pit is much more probable. . . . Lime eats the body quickly and hygienically. Therefore we find virtually no skeletal remains of the thousands crucified outside Jerusalem in the first century. . . . The hungry little ones, always with the church, are the reason why the resurrection of Jesus must be affirmed as bodily, absolutely, for Christian faith. There is no room for the nice wedge of metaphor to slip in between them, who are the body of the Risen Lord, and the real Jesus.

Marianne Sawicki, *Seeing the Lord,* pp. 180, 275

Two points from the preceding section are still relevant for this one. First, Paul's compromise. I agree with Boyarin that Paul worked out a *compromise* between traditional Judaism and modern Hellenism on cosmic dualism. The flesh is to be subordinated to but not rejected by the spirit. In practice, however (even if not in theory), radical and moderate dualism may look very much alike. Second, Paul's inconsistency. There is an *inconsistency* in Paul's application of that compromise to the three distinctions of ethnicity, class, and gender. In this section, that compromise creates another inconsistency.

(I do not use terms such as *compromise* or *inconsistency* with any sense of superiority or condescension, by the way, because they designate what, for Paul, were powerful and generative forces created by swimming hard in the riptides of history. We should not, however, simply repeat those processes but should develop further their profoundly human challenge.)

Paul is still at Ephesus in the early 50s C.E., but now he is writing westward to the city of Corinth rather than eastward to the region of Galatia. Some of his Corinthian converts are proper Platonic dualists who have no problem with Jesus as resurrected soul or immortal spirit. But how can he possibly have a body, and why would he want one in any case? Why tell a prisoner he will get back his cell for all eternity? Who needs an immortal burden? Soul yes, body no. Spirit yes, flesh no.

In 1 Corinthians 15 Paul begins by enumerating all the apparitions of the risen Jesus. But, having recited them in 15:1–11, he never mentions them again throughout the rest of the argument in 15:12–58. The reason is quite clear. The Corinthians know all about visions and apparitions and would not dream of denying their validity. Of *course* the shades return from below with visible and even tangible bodies. Of *course* the immortals, born of human and divine parents and assumed among the gods and goddesses after death, return from above with visible and even tangible bodies. Of *course* the gods and goddesses assume bodies to contact mortals, to make love, to make war, to make conversation. But those are seeming-bodies, play-bodies, in-appearance-only bodies. They are not made from flesh and blood but from ether and air. Notice, by the way, that we use *body* and *flesh* more or less interchangeably but that a Hellenistic sensibility could easily concede that divinities, immortals, or spirits had bodies but not flesh. It is somewhat like our special-effects movies today. Sometimes we see body but not flesh, as it were. Those dinosaurs do not digest. In what follows, Paul is trying to hold on to something clearly important for him—but watch, once again, how compromise begets inconsistency.

The question could not be clearer, in 15:35: "But someone will ask, 'How are the dead raised? With what kind of body do they come?'" Paul interweaves two answers, one fairly conventional, the other more challenging. The conventional one claims that there are lots of different body-types. The stars, for example, move, so they are perceived by those in Paul's day as living beings with bodies. But their bodies are immortal, unlike our own. There is even, Paul claims, such a thing as "a spiritual body." Most Hellenistic hearers would consider the bodies of apparitional divinities as "spiritual" rather than "physical" ones, to be hung up like clothes, as it were, at the end of the operation. New ones, different ones, vegetable, animal, or mineral ones, were created as needed. But, as you read Paul's response, watch also for another answer, the metaphor of sowing:

> Fool! What you sow does not come to life unless it dies. And as for what you sow, you do not sow the body that is to be, but a bare seed, perhaps of wheat or of some other grain. But God gives it a body as he has chosen, and to each kind of seed its own body. Not all flesh is alike, but there is one flesh for human beings, another for animals, another for birds, and another for fish. There are both heavenly bodies and earthly bodies, but the glory of the heavenly is one thing, and that of the earthly is another. There is one glory of the sun, and another glory of the moon, and another glory of the stars; indeed, star differs from star in glory. So it is with the resurrection of the dead. What is sown is perishable, what is raised is imperishable. It is sown in dishonor, it is raised in glory. It is sown in weakness, it is raised in power. It is sown a physical body, it is raised a spiritual body. If there is a physical body, there is also a spiritual body. (1 Corinthians 15:36–44)

The metaphor of multiple body-types emphasizes only difference, but the metaphor of sowing emphasizes *both* continuity and divergence. What is sown is both absolutely the same and completely different from what is reaped. You do not sow a fish and reap a bird. You sow a seed and reap a specific ear of grain. That is the present inconsistency that I see arising from Paul's Platonic compromise. There is, of course, spiritual continuity between the earthly Jesus and the heavenly Christ. Nobody at Corinth is debating that. But is there bodily continuity—that is, physical and material continuity—between them? Paul wavers in response. If you focus on those different body-types, the answer is no: Jesus once had a physical body; Jesus now has a spiritual body. If you focus on the seed metaphor, the answer is yes: Jesus is now both totally the same and absolutely different. The Corinthians probably focused on that "spiritual body" and understood it as meaning a body, air-woven as it were, like those that divinities, immortals, and shades assumed for human contacts. They would have been reassured of that interpretation when Paul concluded with this comment:

> What I am saying, brothers and sisters, is this: flesh and blood cannot inherit the kingdom of God, nor does the perishable inherit the imperishable. (1 Corinthians 15:50)

There might be different types of *bodies,* but there was only one type of *flesh-and-blood* body. It was flesh and blood that bothered the Platonic dualist; spiritual bodies were quite acceptable. In all of that, I can hold on only to Paul's seed

metaphor, because there, for a moment, the compromise is negated and his traditional Judaism speaks aloud. The seed that is sown and the grain that is produced
are both same and different and are in unbroken material and physical continuity.
But that is only a passing Jewish-Jewish inconsistency in a generally Hellenistic-
Jewish explanation. Nevertheless, since I myself find Platonic dualism, in any
degree and by whatever name, to be fundamentally dehumanizing, I hold on to
that inconsistency and ask what else, besides such dualism, is at work in Paul.

The epigraph to this section combines two statements from Sawicki. One
suggests that a limed pit was the most likely fate of Jesus' crucified *body*. The
other insists that the *bodily* resurrection of Jesus is an absolute for Christian faith.
I agree with her that Joseph of Arimathea is most likely a fervent hope for the
best rather than an historical description of what happened. But I also agree with
her on that second statement. I am not totally sure I understand all she implies
by it, however, so I formulate it here as I see it.

The earthly Jesus was not just a thinker with ideas but a rebel with a cause.
He was a Jewish peasant with an attitude, and he claimed that his attitude was
that of the Jewish God. But it was, he said, in his life and in ones like it that the
kingdom of God was revealed, that the Jewish God of justice and righteousness
was incarnated in a world of injustice and unrighteousness. The kingdom of God
was never just about words and ideas, aphorisms and parables, sayings and dialogues. It was about a way of life. And that means it was about a body of flesh
and blood. Justice is always about bodies and lives, not just about words and
ideas. Resurrection does not mean, simply, that the spirit or soul of Jesus lives on
in the world. And neither does it mean, simply, that the companions or followers
of Jesus live on in the world. *It must be the embodied life that remains powerfully efficacious in this world.* I recognize those claims as an historian, and I believe them
as a Christian. There is, then, only one Jesus, the embodied Galilean who lived a
life of divine justice in an unjust world, who was officially and legally executed
by that world's accredited representatives, and whose continued empowering
presence indicates, for believers, that God is not on the side of injustice—even
(or especially) imperial injustice. There are not two Jesuses—one pre-Easter and
another post-Easter, one earthly and another heavenly, one with a physical and
another with a spiritual body. There is only one Jesus, the *historical* Jesus who
incarnated the Jewish God of justice for a believing community committed to
continuing such incarnation ever afterward.

With that understanding, I accept Paul's seed metaphor as very helpful.
From seed to grain is a combination of something absolutely the same and yet
totally different. So too with resurrection. It is the same Jesus, the one and only
historical Jesus of the late 20s in his Jewish homeland, but now untrammeled by

time and place, language and proximity. It is the one and only Jesus, absolutely the same, absolutely different. He is trammeled, of course—then, now, and always—by faith. Bodily resurrection has nothing to do with a resuscitated body coming out of its tomb. And neither is bodily resurrection just another term for Christian faith itself. Bodily resurrection means that the *embodied* life and death of the historical Jesus continues to be experienced, by believers, as powerfully efficacious and salvifically present in this world. That life continued, as it always had, to form communities of like lives.

In the light of all that, the title of this section should be not "The *Bodily* Resurrection of Jesus" but "The *Fleshly* Resurrection of Jesus." I tend to use those words interchangeably, but Paul most certainly did not—and it is now clear why he *would* not. When, therefore, he says that "flesh and blood" cannot enter the kingdom of God, a gulf in sensibility opens up between him and Jesus (and between him and me, to be honest). For Jesus, *anyone* incarnating divine justice on earth was "flesh and blood" entering the kingdom of God. Paul is also in contradiction to the declaration in John 1:14 that "the Word became *flesh* and lived among us." The "Word"—*Logos,* in Greek—is the intelligibility of the world, the rationality of the universe, the meaning of life, as revelation of the Divine Mind. And John says that Word became not just body but flesh, not just the special-effects *body* of standard Greco-Roman divine visitations, but the one and only flesh and blood of full and normal human existence. The *Word* became *flesh;* that is to say, the divine meaning of life is incarnated in a certain human way of living.

The Plan of This Book

Detailed investigation of economic conditions lie beyond the scope of this book, though we shall consider a few points . . . in connection with the cost of maintaining the temple and the priesthood. . . . The general assessment of economic conditions lies outside the range of this book, but I shall discuss taxes, since otherwise we misunderstand the place of religious dues in the entire system.

E. P. Sanders, *Judaism*, pp. 120, 159

The preceding sections indicate a very basic question that pervades this book. It is always there between the lines or behind the scenes. How do *you* understand a human being? Is it as enfleshed spirit, self-conscious flesh, a monistic interaction that can be distinguished but not separated? Or is it spirit *against* flesh, spirit *over* flesh, a dualistic separation with flesh at best a distraction and at worst an imprisonment? My own sensibility accepts, as I told you, that former option, although *accepts* is too weak a word for something over which I have so little control. I do not know whether it comes from being Irish or being Roman Catholic or being both. It is, in any case, irrevocably there. It is also a sensibility that I find in traditional Judaism when it is not influenced by Hellenistic dualism. One result of that monism is that, just as you cannot separate spirit from flesh, neither can you separate religion and politics, justice and society, theology and economics. What is wrong with the above epigraph, for example, is not that Sanders's book explains religion well but neglects economics. It is that he *cannot* explain religion without economics—unless, of course, religion is about a ritual and a ceremonial that has forgotten what it symbolizes or celebrates. But the Jewish God is a god of justice and righteousness in a covenant, under a law, in a land, with a people of justice and righteousness. You cannot explain the "practice and belief" of such a Judaism separated from its "economic conditions." If you try, you will have a book about Judaism in the period dated "63 B.C.E.–66 C.E."—that is to say, a hundred years of a religion—that does not prepare you for three terrible revolts against the Roman Empire in the next hundred years. The traditional Judaism that begot both the historical Jesus and earliest pre-Pauline Christianity did not separate spirit from flesh or flesh from spirit. Neither, therefore, did it separate religion from politics, ethics from economics, or divinity from humanity. They interpenetrated one another and were understood only in that interaction. You could distinguish, of course, but you could not separate.

My original name for this book was *Life After Jesus*—a title suggested by my wife, who had her own personal interpretation of what it meant. I liked it very much because, apart from Sarah's meaning, I saw two others appropriately interwoven within it. The first meaning of *after* was temporal and chronological. The book is about how those who were there with Jesus before his execution continued with him after it. What happened in the interaction between Jesus and his first companions that even Roman crucifixion could not terminate forever? Josephus said their love continued. Tacitus said their contagion spread. Why? What in that original interaction made continuation from *before* to *after* possible or even inevitable? The second meaning of *after* is paradigmatic and unitive. What does it mean to go *after* Jesus or to follow *after* Jesus? Does he have some monopoly on the kingdom of God so that he alone can enter? Or is it about a way of life that he has shown as possible and invited all to continue? My editor, John Loudon, thought that title too enigmatic, and I agreed with him that *The Birth of Christianity* was clearer in intention and communication. But I would ask you, as you read this book with that new title, to remember the old one as well. The birth of Christianity is about life *after* Jesus in *both* those senses.

The present title needs very careful explanation. When most people see the term *Christianity,* they think about a religion quite separate from Judaism. That is an accurate description of the present situation, but it is hopelessly wrong for the early first century. I could speak of the kingdom-of-God movement, the Jesus movement, or the Christ movement, or I could use some other term that would be historically accurate and would keep us from thinking of a religion separated from Judaism, but none of these options would face the core problem. Whenever I use the words *Christian* or *Christianity* in this book, I intend a sect within Judaism. I refer to Christian Judaism just as I might refer to Pharisaic Judaism, Sadduceean Judaism, Essene Judaism, apocalyptic Judaism, or any other of the manifold sects and factions in that first-century Jewish homeland as it struggled to maintain its ancient traditions against Greek cultural internationalism and Roman economic commercialization. No matter what those groups said about one another or did against one another, no matter how imperial and economic pressures from the outside splintered national and religious cohesion on the inside, theirs was an intra-Jewish debate. No matter what any group said about another group (or even *all* other groups), no matter how people criticized their fellow Jews for following any group but theirs, the confrontation was never an attack on Judaism from outside but an attack on other Jews from inside.

It is not even accurate to say that Christianity eventually broke away from Judaism. It is more accurate to say that, out of that matrix of biblical Judaism and that maelstrom of late Second-Temple Judaism, two great traditions eventually emerged: early Christianity and rabbinic Judaism. Each claimed exclusive continuity with the past, but in truth each was as great a leap and as valid a development from that common ancestry as was the other. They are not child and parent; they are two children of the same mother. So, of course, were Cain and Abel.

That other word in my subtitle, *birth,* is equally important. I distinguish *birth* from *growth* in order to focus on that earliest continuation from before to after the execution of Jesus. It is easier to move on swiftly to expansion, to the Pauline letters and cities of the 50s where we have dated texts and contemporary sources. But we are then, as Boyarin correctly claimed above, into a Judaism Hellenized by Platonic dualism, and we may not even have noticed the transition from a Judaism not so Hellenized. I repeat that there is no clear distinction between Palestinian Judaism and Hellenistic Judaism. *All* Judaism in the first century was Hellenistic Judaism. But, although that older geographical distinction was never valid, another more ideological one is *always* valid. Who rejected and accepted Hellenization? And, since that is much too big a question, I repeat it in the limited context established by Boyarin. Where within first-century Judaism was the Hellenistic dualism of flesh and spirit accepted and followed, and where was it rejected and resisted? In focusing on the *birth*, I intend to emphasize that as the underlying question of this book. Earliest Christianity, as I reconstruct it in the villages of Galilee and the streets of Jerusalem, is not Hellenized into Platonic dualism. That is the deep structure of this book.

Its surface structure is organized around four key questions for reconstructing the continuity from the historical Jesus to earliest Christianity, for describing the birth of Christianity itself. The first question, in Part I, is *why* do it at all? Why not simply accept the basic story given in the last chapters of the canonical gospels—Matthew, Mark, Luke, and John—and the first chapters of the Acts of the Apostles? The second question, in Parts II and III, is *where* do I find my sources? If I am not writing a synthesis of those intracanonical sources, what other sources do I have? Where do I get my data? I surely do not have new documents dated to the 30s or 40s that nobody else knows about, so where do I derive my information? The third question, in Parts IV and V, is *how* do I do it? Granted that *why* and that *where,* what method do I use and what is the methodological justification for that approach rather than some other one? The fourth question, in Parts VI through X, is *what* do I find when my method is applied to the materials available? One of the most striking results is a distinction between two great inaugural traditions, the Life Tradition in Parts VI through VIII and the Death Tradition in Parts IX and X. The Life Tradition, with its emphasis on the sayings of Jesus and on living within the kingdom of God, is centered in Galilee and goes out from Galilee. The Death Tradition, with its emphasis on the resurrection of Jesus and on lives lived in expectation of his return, is centered in Jerusalem and goes out from Jerusalem. Although that latter tradition was often elevated to ascendancy in the past and the former tradition hardly recognized at all, the present challenge is not to reverse that discrimination but to emphasize both traditions equally. Another major challenge is to see what they have in common and to recognize the Common Meal Tradition as basic to them both. Christianity's birth, in other words, took place in two different locations, but there is only a single mother, the meal whose communal sharing renders the Jewish God of justice present on earth.

PART I
Continuation and Reconstruction

A candid but rational inquiry into the progress and establishment of Christianity may be considered as a very essential part of the history of the Roman empire. While that great body was invaded by open violence, or undermined by slow decay, a pure and humble religion gently insinuated itself into the minds of men, grew up in silence and obscurity, derived new vigour from opposition, and finally erected the triumphant banner of the Cross on the ruins of the Capital. . . . But this inquiry, however useful or entertaining, is attended with two peculiar difficulties. The scanty and suspicious materials of ecclesiastical history seldom enable us to dispel the dark cloud that hangs over the first age of the church. The great law of impartiality too often obliges us to reveal the imperfections of the uninspired teachers and believers of the Gospel; and, to a careless observer, *their* faults may seem to cast a shade on the faith which they professed. But the scandal of the pious Christian, and the fallacious triumph of the Infidel, should cease as soon as they recollect not only *by whom,* but likewise *to whom,* the Divine Revelation was given. The theologian may indulge the pleasing task of describing Religion as she descended from Heaven, arrayed in her native purity. A more melancholy duty is imposed on the historian. He must discover the inevitable mixture of error and corruption which she contacted in a long residence upon earth, among a weak and degenerate race of beings. Our curiosity is naturally prompted to inquire by what means the Christian faith obtained so remarkable a victory over the established religions of the earth. To this inquiry an obvious but satisfactory answer may be returned; that it was owing to the convincing evidence of the doctrine itself, and to the ruling providence of its great Author. But as truth and reason seldom find so favourable a reception in the world, and as the wisdom of Providence frequently condescends to use the passions of the human heart, and the general circumstances of mankind, as instruments to execute its purpose, we may still be permitted, though with becoming submission, to ask, not indeed what were the first, but what were the secondary causes of the rapid growth of the Christian church? . . . In the course of this important, though perhaps tedious, inquiry, I have attempted to display the secondary causes which so efficaciously assisted the truth of the Christian religion. . . . It was by the aid of these causes—exclusive zeal, the immediate expectation of another world, the claim of miracles, the practice of rigid virtue, and the constitution of the primitive church—that Christianity spread itself with so much success in the Roman empire.

Edward Gibbon, *The Decline and Fall of the Roman Empire,* vol. 1, pp. 382–383, 430

When the Jewish historian Josephus and the pagan historian Tacitus described Christianity, they noted four consecutive points: *movement, execution, continuation,* and *expansion.* My earlier books *The Historical Jesus* and *Who Killed Jesus?* were about, respectively, that movement and that execution. This is the next step, and it is strictly limited to *continuation;* it is not about *expansion.* It is about the *birth* of Christianity, not the *growth* of Christianity. It is about, in Gibbon's terms, "the dark cloud that hangs over the first age of the church" and not about "the triumphant banner of the Cross on the ruins of the Capital." But Gibbon knows a fifth point not dreamed of by either Josephus or Tacitus—namely, Christianity's final *domination* over the Roman Empire. Gibbon writes with clenched teeth about Christianity and bared teeth about Judaism. From those five points, *movement, execution, continuation, expansion,* and *domination,* I focus in this book, as I said, on *continuation,* on the linkage between the historical Jesus and earliest Christianity that is for me the birth of Christianity. It is, of course, a *continuation* of a *movement* after and despite an *execution.*

Part I indicates my strictly limited focus for this book. It explains the continuation I address and discusses *why* it is worth considering. (Afterward will come the *where* of sources in Parts II and III, the *how* of methods in Parts IV and V, and the *what* of results in Parts VI through X.) Part I has two chapters.

Chapter 1 establishes the continuation that I intend in Part I's title. It is that of Jesus' first companions from before to after his crucifixion. (By *companions* I mean not so much named individuals as their communal structures and organizational systems.) What happened afterward to those who were there from the beginning? What can we say about that earliest possible and closest discernible continuation? In addressing those questions, Chapter 1 does not look at the historical Jesus alone or at the first Christian communities alone; rather, it seeks to probe the earliest interfaces between them.

When I wrote *The Historical Jesus* in 1991, I did not think it necessary to defend the validity of that enterprise. I considered historical Jesus research an established part of the scholarly landscape. I concentrated there on the *how* of methods and the *what* of results. Granted the scholarly consensus that Jesus materials are original, traditional, and evangelical, all together in glorious undifferentiation, *how* do you distinguish those strata with some academic integrity? And, granted that methodological *how, what* do you get as the end result? I never asked the *why* question. I ask it here and now in Chapter 2. *Is historical Jesus research necessary for Christian faith?* I do not ask, Is the historical Jesus necessary to Christian faith? That could mean the "real" Jesus known only to God or the "gospel" Jesus known only to faith. I ask instead, Is the Jesus reconstructed by scholarly integrity necessary for Christian faith? My answer in Chapter 2 is: for Monastic and Sacrophilic Christianity yes, for dualistic and sarcophobic Christianity no.

CHAPTER 1

VOICES OF THE FIRST OUTSIDERS

Chronologically the first pagan to mention Christians was Pliny in 111, after him Tacitus in 115 and then Suetonius after 122. From among these three Pliny describes a situation in 111 A.D., and Tacitus deals with the fire of Rome in 64 A.D. But Suetonius in addition to Nero's persecution [in A.D. 64], refers to an incident [in A.D. 49] which is interpreted by some as having to do with Christianity prior to the fire of Rome.

Stephen Benko, "Pagan Criticism of Christianity During the
First Two Centuries A.D.," ANRW 2.23, p. 1056

Three pagan Roman authors, writing within a few years of one another at the start of the second century, agreed completely and emphatically on the nature of the Christian religion. Pliny was a correspondent of Tacitus and a friend of Suetonius, the former both imperial governors from the highest echelons of the aristocracy, the latter an imperial secretary from its middle reaches. They concurred that Christianity was a "superstition" and differed only on the most appropriate negative adjectives to accompany that pejorative term. These are their considered judgments:

"a depraved and excessive superstition" (*superstitio prava, immodica*)
"this contagious superstition" (*superstitionis istius contagio*)
Gaius Plinius Caecilius Secundus, Letters 10.96

"pernicious superstition" (*exitiabilis superstitio*)
Publius Cornelius Tacitus, Annals 15.44.3

"a new and mischievous [*or*: magical] superstition" (*superstitio nova et malefica*)
Gaius Suetonius Tranquillus, Lives of the Caesars: Nero 16.2

For those first pagan outsiders, Christianity was, cumulatively, a depraved, excessive, contagious, pernicious, new, and mischievous superstition. *Religion,* to put it bluntly, was what aristocratic Romans did; *superstition* was what others did—especially those unseemly types from regions east of Italy.

A Depraved Superstition

Cicero is generally thought to be the most representative of the great writers of the late Republic, and his letters provide the most revealing information about his times. It is 150 years before the Empire has its letter-writer in Pliny. He has left a more faithful and less prejudiced picture of Rome as he knew it than did any of his contemporaries, and in him we can see best how a Roman of his class lived and thought at the turn of the first century.

Betty Radice, *The Letters of the Younger Pliny*, p. 12

Among aristocratic Roman writers, we learn most about earliest Christianity from Pliny the Younger, so called to distinguish him from his uncle, Pliny the Elder, commander of the western Mediterranean fleet, who died during Vesuvius's eruption in 79 C.E. The emperor Trajan sent the younger Pliny as his emergency legate to Bithynia-Pontus on the Black Sea's southern coast, a disturbed province that had brought official charges against its two preceding governors. He arrived there in the late summer of 111 but was dead, business unfinished, within two years.

In the midst of his tour he encountered accusations against the Christians in a city of northern Pontus. These attacks were probably put forward by pagans whose temples and sacrifices were economically damaged by Christian monotheism. The reversal of that social situation is, at least, the good result Pliny reports from his actions (Radice 1969:2.404–405).

'Tis certain at least that the temples, which had been almost deserted, begin now to be frequented; and the sacred festivals, after a long intermission, are again revived; while there is a general demand for sacrificial animals, which for some time past have met with but few purchasers. From hence it is easy to imagine what multitudes may be reclaimed from this error, if a door be left open to repentance. (Pliny, *Letters* 10.96)

I cite in great detail the report he sent back to Trajan about that situation, as well as the imperial reply to his queries. It is an extraordinary interchange. In reading it, recognize that this is the moment when pagan Rome chose the official program of reaction that would eventually lead to Christian victory.

Pliny's actions developed over two stages. First, those Christians who had been denounced to him were brought before his tribunal (Radice 1969:2.401–403).

I interrogated them whether they were Christians; if they confessed it I repeated the question twice again, adding the threat of capital punishment; if they still persevered, I ordered them to be executed. For whatever the nature of their creed might be, I could at least feel no doubt that contumacy and inflexible obstinacy deserved chastisement. There were others also possessed with the same infatuation, but being citizens of Rome, I directed them to be carried thither. (Pliny, *Letters* 10.96)

Those first trials were probably of the more obvious leaders, more distinguished members, or more aggressive proponents of local Christianity. The impression is left that these all confessed and died as martyrs. And their accusers were apparently named and known individuals. But then something happened that moved the process to a second and more serious stage (Radice 1969:2.402–403).

These accusations spread (as is usually the case) from the mere fact of the matter being investigated and several forms of the mischief came to light. A placard was put up, without any signature, accusing a large number of persons by name. Those who denied they were, or had ever been, Christians, who repeated after me an invocation to the Gods, and offered adoration, with wine and frankincense, to your image, which I had ordered to be brought for that purpose, together with those of the Gods, and who finally cursed Christ—none of which acts, it is said, those who are really Christians can be forced into performing—these I thought it proper to discharge. Others who were named by that informer at first confessed themselves Christians, and then denied it; true, they had been of that persuasion but they had quitted it, some three years, others many years, and a few as much as twenty-five years ago. They all worshipped your statue and the images of the Gods, and cursed Christ. (Pliny, *Letters* 10.96)

At this point Pliny was doubly alarmed. The numbers involved were very large, and interrogations, even under torture, had produced nothing of a criminal nature. There was no evidence of magic, orgy, incest, cannibalism, or any of those evils usually attributed to deviant cults by mainstream pagan religion. It was time to refer the whole matter to Trajan and his advisers back in Rome. Pliny asked three questions. Rome gave three answers—but not exactly to the same three questions. There was also one question that Pliny did *not* ask but Trajan answered, rebuking him implicitly and somewhat condescendingly in the process (Radice 1969:2.400–407, numbers added).

Pliny to Trajan: Having never been present at any trials of the Christians, I am unacquainted with the method and limits to be observed either in examining or punishing them. [1] Whether any difference is to be made on account of age, or no distinction allowed between the youngest and the adult; [2] whether repentance admits to a pardon, or if a man has been once a Christian it avails him nothing to repent; [3] whether the mere profession of Christianity, albeit without crimes, or only the crimes associated therewith are punishable—in all these points I am greatly doubtful. . . . I therefore adjourned the proceedings, and betook myself at once to your counsel. For the matter seemed to me well worth referring to you,—especially considering the numbers endangered. Persons of all ranks and ages, and of both sexes are, and will be, involved in the prosecution. For this contagious superstition is not confined to the cities only, but has spread through the villages and rural districts; it seems possible, however, to check and cure it. . . . [M]ultitudes may be reclaimed from this error, if a door be left open to repentance. (Pliny, *Letters* 10.96)

Trajan to Pliny: The method you have pursued, my dear Pliny, in sifting the cases of those denounced to you as Christians is extremely proper. It is not possible to lay down any general rule which can be applied as the fixed standard in all cases of this nature. [1] No search should be made for these people; when they are denounced and found guilty they must be punished; [2] with the restriction, however, that when the party denies himself to be Christian, and shall give proof that he is not (that is, by adoring our Gods) he shall be pardoned on the ground of repentance, even though he may have formally incurred suspicion. [3] Informations without the accuser's name subscribed must not be admitted in evidence against anyone, as it is introducing a very dangerous precedent, and by no means agreeable to the spirit of the age. (Pliny, *Letters* 10.97)

That description by Pliny is rather extraordinary. If I had read it in a Christian writing, I probably would have attributed it to missionary exuberance or numerical propaganda. Christian numbers are said to be large enough to damage pagan economy and society. They are also spread across rank, age, sex, and location.

But that is also a quite extraordinary imperial reply. Trajan's first response is an indirect reply to Pliny's third question. It implicitly responds that the very name of *Christian* is itself a crime, like being a member of an illegal group. But, on the other hand, these "criminals" are not to be searched out. Trajan's second reply is a direct response to Pliny's second question. Christians are to be pardoned if they repent and recant. Finally, Trajan gives no reply to Pliny's first question, instead implicitly rebuking him for moving at all on anonymous accusations. Christianity, clearly, is a very special sort of crime! That imperial reply established three principles that would guide 150 years of official imperial policy toward Christianity. Do not go searching for Christians. Do not punish them if they repent. Do not accept anonymous accusations. When, in the middle of the third century, that policy was changed to investigative persecution, it was far too late for Roman paganism. But, in any case, with human decency triumphing over legal logic, it shows us Pliny, Trajan, and Rome at their best.

In the process of explaining to Trajan that he had found absolutely no evidence of evil acts within Christian assemblies (in fact, the reverse), Pliny gives us this precious description of at least one local form of that religion within a hundred years of the death of Jesus (Radice 1969:2.402–405).

[The accused Christians] were in the habit of meeting on a certain fixed day before it was light, when they sang in alternate verses a hymn to Christ, as to a god, and bound themselves by a solemn oath, not to any wicked deeds, but never to commit any fraud, theft or adultery, never to falsify their word, nor deny a trust when they should be called upon to deliver it up; after which it was their custom to separate, and then reassemble to partake of food—but food of an ordinary and innocent kind. Even this practice, however, they had abandoned after the publication of my edict, by which, according to your orders, I had forbidden political associations. I judged it so much the more necessary to extract the real truth, with the assistance of torture, from two female slaves who were styled *deaconesses* but I could discover nothing more than depraved and excessive superstition. (Pliny, *Letters* 10.96)

I take two points from that description. First, those two unnamed deaconesses were tortured presumably to death, for, since they had nothing evil to admit, how, short of death, would the torturers know when to stop? But Pliny was, among Roman aristocrats, as decent as you could imagine and, among Roman governors, as good as you could find. "Several humble people," notes Betty Radice, "had reason to be grateful to him: his old nurse for a small farm, . . . a school-friend of Comum for a substantial sum to raise his social status, . . . a friend's daughter for a dowry, . . . and a valued freedman for holidays abroad in search of better health"; and he was ready "to reduce his tenants' rents when times were bad . . . and make concessions to the contractors who stood to lose when the grape harvest was a bad one, . . . and [he] once seriously considered introducing the experiment of rent payment by share of produce" (1963:23, 24). The deaconesses were dispatched summarily and are mentioned in Pliny's letter only to prove the accuracy of his information. That torture in pursuit of information was carried out by as humane a Roman governor as we have on record. Remember Pliny and those deaconesses, therefore, whenever you think about Pilate and the peasant Jesus. Jesus was not much above these women's status in official eyes, and, in any case, Pilate was no Pliny.

The second point is more to my present concern. In the above account any reader would easily conclude that Christians took their name from Christ. The account gives vital information about Christian life and liturgy from at least one corner of the Roman Empire in the early second century, but it does not tell us who this Christ is, where he came from, or how Christians were connected to him. We do not get that information from Pliny, the first of our three pagan outsiders, and neither do we get it from Suetonius, the third one. For the identity of Christ and the connection from Christ to Christians, we depend, among those three authors, on Tacitus alone.

A Spreading Contagion

For Tacitus, in certain respects an utter fool, only the few thousands of his own circle really existed.

Ramsay MacMullen, *Roman Social Relations: 50 B.C. to A.D. 384*, p. 58

Tacitus may have been the greatest of the Roman historians and the last great mind of Roman paganism.

Ronald Mellor, *Tacitus*, p. 163

First came the full moon of mid-summer; then came the fire, in the night between July 18 and 19 of 64 C.E. The fire started among the shops, stores, and taverns at the west end of the Circus Maximus and surged down that great race-course, like four-horse chariots out of their holding stalls, funneled through timbered tiers and open spaces along the valley between the Palatine to the north and the Aventine to the south. At the east end of that valley the fire turned northward through another valley, this time between the Palatine and the Celian, and was finally stopped after six days by a deliberate firebreak at the foot of the Esquiline. Then it broke out again in a separate area north of the Capitoline hill and for three days threatened but did not penetrate into the open spaces of the Campus Martius, whose public buildings housed the terrified homeless of Rome's inner city. After those nine days, only four of Rome's fourteen regions were left unharmed, three had been totally destroyed, and the other seven had been severely damaged. But the great temples on the Capitoline, the ancient buildings in the Forum, and possibly the tenemented slums of the Subura were all untouched. In describing this fire, Tacitus mentions the Christians, and in explaining them tells us about Jesus.

Tacitus saw clearly the open and more superficial evil in persons and individuals but not the hidden and more profound evil in structures and systems. And because of that he sought the roots of Roman decline not in her empire but in her emperors, never recognizing the latter as but the former's personification. In his *Histories*, written in the first decade of the second century, he had chronicled the decline and fall of the Flavians, Rome's second imperial dynasty, from

Vespasian to Domitian between 69 and 96. In his *Annals,* written in the following decade, he repeated that process for the Julio-Claudians, Rome's first imperial dynasty, from Tiberius to Nero between 14 and 68. In the former account he never mentioned Jesus and summarized the state of Palestine between 14 and 37 by commenting, in *Histories* 5.9.2, that "under Tiberius all was quiet." But in the latter account, while discussing Nero in *Annals* 15.44.2–3, he mentioned Rome's great fire in July of 64. The terrified population looked for a scapegoat and found one in Nero himself, absent from Rome at coastal Antium (now famous as Anzio) when the fire started. Nero himself immediately passed the blame on to "a class of men, loathed for their vices, who the crowd styled Christians," *possibly* because those Christians were most heavily concentrated in two swampy valley areas left untouched by the fire, inside Trastevere off the Via Aurelia to the west and outside Porta Capena off the Via Appia to the southeast. Tacitus explained who Christians were in terms of their connection to Jesus, in *Annals* 15.44 (Jackson et al. 4.282–283, my numbers and headings):

[1. *Movement*] Christus, the founder of the name, [2. *Execution*] had undergone the death penalty in the reign of Tiberius, by sentence of the procurator Pontius Pilatus, [3. *Continuation*] and the pernicious superstition was checked for the moment, only to break out once more, [4. *Expansion*] not merely in Judaea, the home of the disease, but in the capital itself, where all things horrible or shameful in the world collect and find a vogue.

First, the *movement*. Tacitus was rather laconic on this first point, so it is not totally clear from that sentence alone whether Jesus himself founded the movement before his death or his supporters did so after it.

Next, the *execution*. In the course of six campaigns at coastal Caesarea, seat of the Roman occupation authorities in the Jewish homeland, an Italian archeological expedition discovered in 1961 a relocated and reused dedicatory block of local limestone containing those same two imperial names in Latin. Even in its present very damaged condition, the first line mentions a "Tiberiéum," apparently some edifice dedicated to that emperor, the second and third lines name "[Po]ntius Pilate" the "[pre]fect of Judaea" as the dedicator, and the fourth, obliterated line must have had some verb like *made, gave,* or *dedicated.* Tacitus simply retrojected the title of *procurator,* current from the time of the emperor Claudius between 41 and 54, back onto Pilate, who was actually *prefect* at that earlier period.

Then, the *continuation*. That third phrase clarifies his preceding sentence. The execution of Jesus was intended to stop a movement *already begun by him,* but it failed to do so. For Tacitus, continuation was like the progression of a disease thought to have been eliminated by medicine. Execution had failed its purpose, but that made Christ founder of the name of *Christian*.

Finally, *expansion*. Tacitus let his distaste and contempt for Christianity display itself here most openly. Not only did the movement continue in Judaea, but it spread all the way to Rome itself, where everything rotten arrives eventually. And there, had Tacitus but known it, lay the future. In *Finnegans Wake* James Joyce, playing with the expression *to make a long story short* and thinking of Tacitus on Ireland rather than on Christianity, called him "our wrongstory-shortener." Exactly.

Tacitus, alone among those first three pagan outsiders, tells us briefly but clearly about Christ, his movement, and his execution, and how, despite that sentence, the movement not only continued but expanded all the way from Judaea to Rome itself. Those same four points were also noted even before the end of the first century by another outsider, not pagan this time but Jewish, the historian Flavius Josephus.

An Unbroken Love

Flavius Josephus, or Joseph ben Matthias . . . [is] certainly the single most important source for the history of the Jewish people during the first century C.E.
Harold W. Attridge, "Josephus and His Works," p. 185

Josephus . . . can invent, exaggerate, over-emphasize, distort, suppress, simplify, or, occasionally, tell the truth. Often we cannot determine where one practice ends and another begins.
Shaye J. D. Cohen, *Josephus in Galilee and Rome*, p. 181

Both Tacitus and Josephus were aristocratic historians, one from the Roman consular nobility, the other from the Jewish priestly elite. Both lived to their early sixties, but Cornelius Tacitus, born around 55, was the younger contemporary of Flavius Josephus, born around 37. Both remained profoundly faithful to their origins—Tacitus to the senatorial ideals of the Roman republic, Josephus to the sacerdotal ideals of the Jewish theocracy. But both could have been accused of collaboration with imperial tyranny, and both would have replied that such was preferable to suicide. For, when others die for speech, those who live through silence must at least remember and record. So Tacitus: "We should also have lost our memory along with our voice, had it been as easy to forget as to keep silence" (*Agricola* 2). And Josephus: "Never may I live to become so abject a captive as to abjure my race or to forget the traditions of my forefathers" (*Jewish War* 6.107).

They could even have met at Rome, because there, between the 70s and 90s under the new Flavian dynasty, Tacitus's career was just beginning and Josephus's was coming to a climax. If they had met, they would probably not have liked one another, even if the demands of aristocratic honor and the dictates of imperial patronage made polite respect much wiser than open contempt. Tacitus, with both general ethnocentrism and specific anti-Semitism, claimed that "toward every other people they [the Jews] feel only hate and enmity" (*Histories* 5.5.1). But Josephus defended his people for having "laws . . . that . . . teach not impiety, but the most genuine piety, . . . [which] invite men not to hate their fellows, but to share their possessions" (*Against Apion* 41). They were, however, in complete agreement on one small item concerning Jesus, with about forty words in Tacitus's Latin and sixty in Josephus's Greek: there was a *movement,* there was an *execution,* there was a *continuation,* and there was an *expansion.* But that Jesus item is given in passing, with each writer primarily interested in larger imperial events and broader historical horizons.

Tacitus's interest was in dynastic degeneration, imperial corruption, and how "the souls of tyrants . . . show bruises and wounds . . . [from] cruelty, lust, and malice" (*Annals* 6.6). Josephus's interest was in procuratorial misgovernment, popular reaction, and how those disturbances led eventually to open revolt against Rome in the Jewish homeland. But both of them made the same four points about Jesus, and that is my present concern. Two preliminaries prepare for a look at that Josephan text.

First, overlap. Josephus's two major works—*Jewish War,* written in the late 70s and early 80s of the first century, and *Jewish Antiquities,* written in its early 90s—overlap on the history of the period from the mid-160s B.C.E. to the early 70s C.E. They give, in other words, two versions of events in the Jewish homeland during most of that first century. Absences, changes, and divergences between those twin accounts must always be assessed carefully to understand bias, prejudice, and purpose. In the section about Pontius Pilate in *Jewish War* 2.169–177, he notes only two popular disturbances brought on by his misgovernment. Nothing at all is said about Jesus. In retelling that same period in *Jewish Antiquities* 18:55–89, Josephus makes two major changes, and these are significant for the context of his Jesus story.

Second, context. He first enlarges the Pilate disturbances to three, closing with a new one that cost Pilate his job and could well have cost him his life if the emperor Tiberius had not died before he reached Rome for judgment. That set of three Pilate disturbances is similar in that the authorities involved are all to blame for the troubles. But then Josephus inserts, between those older two items in 18.55–64 and the newer final one in 18.85–89, three more disturbances in 18.63–64, 65–80, and 81–84. This second set is also similar, but in the opposite way to the first set. Now it is not the authorities but the protagonists who seem more to blame for the disorders. The first in this new set concerns Jesus, and that is quite appropriate since he appeared under Pontius Pilate. But the next two inserts are quite strange. They both involve disturbances, to be sure, but in Rome rather than Jerusalem. In one story priests of the Egyptian goddess Isis assist a libertine aristocrat in seducing a high-born Roman matron named Paulina. The guilty priests are crucified and their temple is destroyed as a punishment. In the other story "a certain Jew, a complete scoundrel, who had fled his own country because he was accused of transgressing certain laws and feared punishment on this account" (18.81), conspired to defraud an aristocratic Jewish proselyte named Fulvia of gifts designated for the Temple at Jerusalem, and the result was that "the whole Jewish community" (18.83) was ordered to leave Rome as punishment. The juxtaposition of Pilate disturbances and Rome disturbances, of those criminal fraud stories and the Jesus story, gives the latter a rather negative context. Was that Josephus's purpose and design? Is the story of Jesus to be judged by association with the two incidents that follow it? Jesus, the Isis priests, and the Jewish "scoundrel" may well have been, for Josephus, three warnings of how public disturbances and official punishments may be caused by individual religious malfeasance.

Third, text. Even if the context has been deliberately arranged to cast some negative reflection on the Jesus story, the text itself, in *Jewish Antiquities* 18.63–64, is quite carefully neutral. But, above all, notice those same four elements found earlier in the Tacitus summary:

[1. *Movement*] About this time there lived Jesus, a wise man, *if indeed one ought to call him a man.* For he was one who wrought surprising feats and was a teacher of such people as accept the truth gladly. He won over many Jews and many of the Greeks. *He was the Messiah.* [2. *Execution*] When Pilate, upon hearing him accused by men of the highest standing amongst us, had condemned him to be crucified, [3. *Continuation*] those who had in the first place come to love him did not give up their affection for him. *On the third day he appeared to them restored to life, for the prophets of God had prophesied these and countless other marvellous things about him.* [4. *Expansion*] And the tribe of the Christians, so called after him, has still to this day not disappeared.

Josephus's account is more detailed than Tacitus's, but notice the sentences I have italicized above. They are so patently Christian that some scholars explain the entire section on Jesus as a later Christian insertion. However, even if Christian editors delicately inserted those italicized phrases later to make the description more positive, the basic content of the passage is most likely original. Once the questionable phrases are omitted, what remains is in a style and language characteristically Josephan. That remaining description is so studiously neutral that I wonder if Josephus wrote with a careful eye on Christians and Jews in his contemporary Rome more than on their predecessors of over sixty years earlier. That possibility arises not just from the impartiality of his description but from that mention of "many Jews and many Greeks." That surely bespeaks the historical situation of the Roman 90s rather than of the Palestinian 20s.

I turn now to the four components of Josephus's description. First, the *movement*. Jesus is named and termed a "wise man," as were, earlier in *Jewish Antiquities* 8.53 and 10.237, both Solomon, "a wise man endowed with every virtue," and Daniel, "a wise man and skilful in discovering things beyond man's power and known only to God." Jesus' wisdom was manifest, for Josephus, in both deeds and words, in both actions and teachings. The sequence of that duality, with actions first, is probably worth noting. Josephus describes Jesus' actions with a Greek phrase translated here as *surprising feats*. Those are the same Greek words used in *Jewish Antiquities* 9.182 to describe the activities of the prophet Elisha: "He was a man renowned for righteousness and one manifestly held in honour by God; for through his prophetic power he performed astounding and marvellous deeds [*or:* surprising feats], which were held as a glorious memory by the Hebrews." I take as an example of such surprising feats or marvelous deeds the immediately subsequent story told by Josephus, more or less from 2 Kings 13:20–21: "Some robbers threw into the grave of Elisha a man whom they had murdered, and when the corpse came into contact with his body, it was restored to life . . . [for] after death he still had divine power. . . ." Josephus also describes Jesus as a "teacher of such people as accept the truth gladly." That audience is qualified ambiguously, since the Greek word translated as "gladly" could also be translated as "easily" in the sense of "much too easily." Josephus used that same Greek word earlier in *Jewish Antiquities* 17.329 for the gullible followers of a man masquerading as Herod the Great's executed son Alexander: "They willingly [*or:* gladly, eagerly] believed his stories." All in all, however, Josephus offers a much more helpful summary than Tacitus's laconic comment.

Next, the *execution*. Josephus adds important new information here as well. That phrase, "men of the highest standing" (*literally:* the first men among us), could, in itself, refer to either the priestly or lay aristocratic leadership in the Jewish homeland, but in this case it *may* lean slightly toward that priestly possibility. In *Jewish Antiquities* 18.120–123 Vitellius, the pagan governor of Syria, accompanied by Herod Antipas, the Jewish tetrarch of Galilee and Perea, was going to march with the Syrian legions through "the land of Judaea." They were entreated not to do so by "men of the highest standing" since their military standards bore offensive pagan images. Vitellius agreed and even went up himself to sacrifice at Jerusalem. In that particular case, at least, "men of the highest standing" must surely mean the high-priestly authorities. But in itself the term simply designates aristocrats, leaders, authorities. In the Arabic *Book of the Title,* a history of the world written around the middle of the tenth century by Agapius, Melkite bishop of Phrygian Hierapolis in Asia Minor, there is a citation of this text from Josephus, but all it says is this: "Pilate condemned him to be crucified and to die." That is, however, more likely a paraphrase of the fuller version rather than an independent, more original, and more accurate one. Thus, for Josephus, there was a conjunction, on the highest level, of Jewish aristocratic accusation and Roman imperial execution.

Then, the *continuation.* Josephus's description of the third step is, once again, quite neutral and impartial after you remove, as I do by italics, those later Christianizing interpolations. He explains the continuation not as a spreading contagion but as an undying love.

Finally, the *expansion.* Tacitus noted that Christians are so called after Christ. Josephus says they are so called after "him"—that is, after "Jesus," the only name he had already mentioned. Maybe, of course, he just expects his readers to know that Jesus was called by his followers the Anointed One—*Christ* in Greek, *Messiah* in Hebrew or Aramaic. There is also another possibility. Later, in *Jewish Antiquities* 20.200, Josephus tells how,

> he [Ananus, the high priest] convened the judges of the Sanhedrin [in 62 C.E. during the interregnum between the prefects Festus and Albinus] and brought before them a man named James, the brother of Jesus who was called the Christ, and certain others.

In that text he says that Jesus *"was called* the Christ." That is a neutral, not a credal, statement. It is possible, therefore, but not much more, that he had used a similar expression in the opening phrases of his earlier mention of Jesus in 18.63–64 and that Christian interpolation had changed "He *was called* the Christ" into the confessional assertion "He *was* the Christ." *Maybe,* at best.

Among those four earliest outsiders, Pliny and Suetonius tell us about Christians but not about Christ. Only Josephus and Tacitus tell us about Jesus or Christ and the continuation from him to Christianity. That continuation is what this book is about. But it is about very special and precise forms of continuation.

A Focus on First Continuation

The most startlingly idiosyncratic of all the followers of Jesus known to us came from a world that barely touched at any point on the experiences of those who preached in the cramped and explosive countryside of Palestine. Paul of Tarsus was a Greek-speaking Jew of the Diaspora. He was even, apparently, a Roman citizen. His missionary journeys took him to cities deep in the hinterland of western Asia Minor. In the early 50s, he lingered, for periods of years at a time, in the great pagan cities of the Aegean—Ephesus, Thessalonica, Philippi, and Corinth. He was executed at Rome, in the faraway capital of the Empire, around 60 A.D.

Peter Brown, *The Body and Society,* p. 44

On one perfectly valid level all two thousand years of Christianity, all of Christian cult and culture, history and theology are a continuation of Jesus confessed as the Christ. On another perfectly valid level the first three hundred years in that preceding epigraph are a continuation of Jesus confessed as the Christ. On a final perfectly valid level that first century summarized above by Josephus and Tacitus is a continuation of Jesus confessed as the Christ. But this book is not an account of two thousand, three hundred, or even one hundred years. It is, instead, *a probe of the earliest and closest continuation discernible, the continuation from before to after crucifixion, the continuation that includes both those moments and focuses on their connection.* It asks, What happened to Jesus' first companions in the days and weeks, months and years immediately after his execution? It asks, What happened to believers in the kingdom of God when the God of that kingdom did not prevent Jesus' crucifixion? It asks, What was there before Paul or what was there for Paul to persecute? And that focus demands a word about Paul himself.

This book does not include a study of Paul, although it certainly includes elements from his life, his letters, and especially his pre-Pauline traditions. That lack is quite deliberate, but I do not intend it as an indirect attack on Pauline theology. I am completely convinced that his thought represents *a* perfectly valid and very early continuation from Jesus to Christianity in a very different context from that of the historical Jesus. But I have programmatically omitted him from this book for two reasons. One reason is that I seek to focus disciplined reconstructive imagination on those who started with Jesus before his death and continued with Jesus after his execution. *It is the continuity of Jesus' companions from before to after Calvary that is my concern.* What strands of tradition, I ask, among all the available ones, show that precise continuation? Another reason is that the secure presence of Paul's authentic letters seduces historians to skip rather hastily over the early 30s and move much too swiftly into the late 30s, 40s, and 50s, the decades for which those texts are extremely precious witnesses. Let me give two examples of that last phenomenon, because it was they, more than anything else, that persuaded me to reimagine the Christianity that was there before Paul, without Paul, and apart from Paul; that persuaded me to investigate what was there for Paul to persecute, what would have been there had he never existed, and what continued into the future as though he never had. My two examples, taken from recent books on early Christianity, were chosen not because they are bad but because they are very, very good books.

The first book is by Wayne Meeks, *The First Urban Christians: The Social World of the Apostle Paul,* published in 1983. "Paul was a city person," he asserts in opening his first chapter. "The city breathes through his language. Jesus' parables of sowers and weeds, sharecroppers, and mud-roofed cottages call forth smells of manure and earth, and the Aramaic of the Palestinian villages often echoes in the Greek. When Paul constructs a metaphor of olive trees or gardens, on the other hand, the Greek is fluent and evokes schoolroom more than farm; he seems more at home with the clichés of Greek rhetoric, drawn from gymnasium, stadium, or workshop. . . . In those early years, then, within a decade of the crucifixion of Jesus, the village culture of Palestine had been left behind, and the Greco-Roman city became the dominant environment of the Christian movement" (1983:9, 11). I leave aside for now the fact that newly spread manure in the countryside probably smelled much better and certainly did far less damage to human health than the fetid stench of unsewered city tenements and alleys. I concentrate instead on the swiftness of that passage from Aramaic to Greek and from Palestinian village to Roman city. My question is this: How did *that* happen, and happen so swiftly—within a decade of Jesus' death? The problem is not how Christianity spread from one Roman city to another but how it moved from Galilean villages to Roman cities at all. How, in other words, did it ever get out of those villages? My point is not that Meeks should have faced that problem of the transition from village to city. I emphasize only that it is still there as a problem and that it is the one that concerns me in this book.

The second book is by Rodney Stark, *The Rise of Christianity: A Sociologist Reconsiders History,* published in 1996, which establishes a powerfully clear distinction between sects and cults. "*Sect* movements . . . occur by schism within a conventional religious body when persons desiring a more otherworldly version of the faith break away to 'restore' the religion to a higher level of tension with its environment. . . . *Cult* movements, on the other hand, are not simply new organizations of an old faith: they are *new faiths,* at least new in the society being examined" (33). Furthermore, *sects* appeal especially to those "if not the dispossessed, at least of lower social standing than those who stick with the parent body," but *cults* "must draw upon the more privileged for their recruits" (33, 34).

Those preceding distinctions are preparatory to this passage: "During his ministry, Jesus seems to have been the leader of a sect movement within

Judaism. Indeed, even in the immediate aftermath of the Crucifixion, there was little to separate the disciples from their fellow Jews. However, on the morning of the third day something happened that turned the Christian sect into a cult movement. Christians believe that on that day Jesus arose from the dead and during the next forty days appeared repeatedly to various groups of his followers. It is unnecessary to believe in the Resurrection to see that because the apostles believed in it, they were no longer just another Jewish sect. Although it took time for the fact to be recognized fully (in part because of the immense diversity of Judaism of this era), beginning with the Resurrection Christians were participants in a new religion, one that added far too much new culture to Judaism to be any longer an internal sect movement. Of course, the complete break between church and synagogue took centuries, but it seems clear that Jewish authorities in Jerusalem quickly labeled Christians as heretics beyond the boundaries of the community in the same way that Moonies are today excluded from Christian associations" (44–45).

You will notice the qualifications needed to support that instant sect-to-cult transformation: "it took time for the fact to be recognized fully" and "the complete break between church and synagogue took centuries." But the core question is this: Did any such instant transformation happen? Since all those involved were Jewish sectarians, were they not experiencing or describing something within their normal range of Jewish presuppositions? Is it not just as likely that Christianity's double appeal (and double nonappeal) was as a *sect* inside Judaism but as a *cult* outside paganism? Eventually it had to settle for one or the other, but that happened slowly and diversely, at different times and places, in divergent steps and processes. Once again we are moving much too swiftly, as with Meeks from village to city, so now with Stark from sect to cult. My point, once again, is not that Stark should have faced that problem of transition from sect to cult. I emphasize only that it is still there as a problem and that it is the one that concerns me in this book.

Those two cases help me to see my own question more clearly. It is this: *What continuation can we discern between the companions of Jesus before and after his execution?* What was it like for those who were there before the crucifixion to be there after it? What was it like for *them* in the early 30s? What traces have they left for us to discern in later texts? What trajectories have they created for us to examine in later documents? That is what I mean by *first continuation*. It is the continuation from before to after, the continuation of both before and after. I could also state the problem in a more personal way. This book is the closest possible sequel I can imagine and the closest possible continuation I can create to my earlier work, *The Historical Jesus: The Life of a Mediterranean Jewish Peasant*. It is not concerned with the historical Jesus alone or with Christian origins alone but with their interface, with the continuation from one to the other for Jesus' first companions. The objection, however, is obvious. How can I say anything at all about those earliest years? Is it not wiser to move, with Meeks, Stark, and most others, swiftly and smoothly on to Paul and the late 30s, 40s, or 50s? Why even try to reconstruct that primordial continuation? *Why?*

CHAPTER 2

RECONSTRUCTING EARLIEST CHRISTIANITY

I shall assume that there were 1,000 Christians in the year 40. . . . 40 percent per decade (or 3.42 percent per year) seems the most plausible estimate of the rate at which Christianity grew during the first several centuries. . . . So long as nothing changed in the conditions that sustained the 40-percent-a-decade growth rate, Constantine's conversion would better be seen as a response to the massive exponential wave in progress, not as its cause. . . . The projections reveal that Christianity could easily have reached half the population [almost 34 out of 60 million people] by the middle of the fourth century without miracles or conversions en masse. The Mormons have, thus far, traced the same growth curve, and we have no knowledge of their achieving mass conversions.

Rodney Stark, *The Rise of Christianity*, pp. 5, 6, 10, 14

The above epigraph offers one way of reconstructing early Christianity, at least in terms of its numerical expansion. The reconstruction depends, of course, on those earliest numbers being fairly accurate. It also uses comparative sociological data to double-check the expansion in terms of contemporary parallels. Whether those figures are correct or not I leave for others to decide. I cite them here simply as an example of reconstruction. But no matter how done or how validated, it is an example of historical reconstruction, and that raises, especially today, the following question: *Why* is the historical study of Christianity's birth possible, valid, and necessary?

History and Story

A young woman named Ann described how she recovered in therapy memories of terrible satanic ritual abuse at the hands of her parents, and also discovered that she harbored multiple personalities. Family videotapes and photos showed Ann, prior to therapy, as a vibrant young woman and a budding young singer. . . . "I don't care if it's true," asserted Ann's therapist, Douglas Sawin. "What's important to me is that I hear the child's truth, the patient's truth. That's what's important. What actually happened is irrelevant to me." Asked about the possibility that a client's report is a delusion, Sawin did not flinch: "We all live in a delusion, just more or less delusionary."

Daniel L. Schacter, *Searching for Memory*, pp. 262–263

Forget for a moment about the historical Jesus, Christian origins, the first continuation from one to the other, or companions' lives from before to after Jesus' execution. Think instead of that preceding epigraph. It is a particularly horrible example, to be sure. It is bad enough if such abuse happened to Ann; it is worse if it happened and no redress was possible. But it is surely worst of all—for herself, for her family, for her society—if her therapist finds the distinction between fact and fiction, fantasy and history, of no importance whatsoever. In telling that incident from the recent "memory wars" in the United States, Schacter footnoted that "objective or 'historical truth' . . . becomes important when, as in Ann's case, a multimillion dollar law suit is filed against the alleged perpetrators" (344 note 28). But surely, even for therapy (or *especially* for therapy), and apart from potential or actual lawsuits, there is a supreme difference between actual and delusional stories. And it is necessary to decide which is which. History *matters*. And history is possible because its absence is intolerable.

History is not the same as story. *Even if all history is story, not all story is history.* Imagine this purely hypothetical case. In the courtroom, faced with a man accused of double murder, the defense and the prosecution tell very different stories. In one the man is a murderer who must be condemned. In the other he is an innocent who has been framed. Both attorneys are highly competent and entertaining storytellers, but only one of the two stories they share in that courtroom is *history*. The other is mistake, fiction, invention, lie. At the end, when the man walks out of the courtroom, he is either a freed murderer or a framed innocent. He cannot be both. Maybe we will never know for sure which version is history-story and which is story-story. But we know that only one version is *correct*. And our decency, morality, and humanity demand that we *never* say it is all relative, perspective, hype, and spin, or that, since we cannot know for sure, it does not matter at all.

This is my working definition of history: *History is the past reconstructed interactively by the present through argued evidence in public discourse.* There are times we can get only alternative perspectives on the same event. (There are *always* alternative perspectives, even when we do not hear them.) But history as argued public reconstruction is necessary to reconstruct *our* past in order to project *our* future.

I return now, but against that background, to the historical Jesus and Christian origins. Here the objection is more pointed. We have, leaving aside other materials, four accounts of the historical Jesus from Matthew, Mark, Luke, and John. And all of them tell us about continuation from before to after crucifixion (at least for the first few days). Likewise we have four accounts of the historical Tiberius, the imperial ruler under whom Jesus was crucified—accounts by Velleius Paterculus, Tacitus, Suetonius, and Dio Cassius. The canonical stories are all by anonymous authors, none of whom knew Jesus personally but all of whom wrote before the end of the first century. The imperial accounts are by one first-century historian who slogged with Tiberius through his German and Pannonian campaigns and by three who wrote in the second or third centuries. If one emphasizes how different Jesus appears in Mark and John, it could be countered that Tiberius is equally different in Paterculus (who worshiped the ground he walked on) and in Tacitus (who hated the air he breathed). Furthermore, for Christian origins we have the Acts of the Apostles, which describes earliest Christianity from the 30s to the 60s. There, surely, is the history I seek, and all I have to do is read it carefully and thoughtfully.

The problem is that, slowly but surely across the past two hundred years of scholarly research, we have learned that the *gospels* are exactly what they openly and honestly claim they are. They are not history, though they contain history. They are not biography, though they contain biography. They are gospel—that is, good news. *Good* indicates that the news is seen from somebody's point of view—from, for example, the Christian rather than the imperial interpretation. *News* indicates that a regular update is involved. It indicates that Jesus is constantly being actualized for new times and places, situations and problems, authors and communities. The gospels are written for faith, to faith, and from faith. We have also learned that Matthew and Luke used Mark as a source. So we can now see, by comparing Matthew and Luke with their Markan source, the sovereign freedom with which the evangelists adopted and adapted, added and omitted, changed and created the very words and deeds of Jesus himself. And if, as many scholars now think, John is dependent on those three synoptic authors, that creative freedom is almost as great as we could possibly imagine. That term *synoptic,* by the way, indicates how easily Matthew, Mark, and Luke can be placed in parallel columns and seen synoptically—that is, at a single glance. Furthermore, what we presently separate as the gospel of Luke and the Acts of the Apostles was first written as twin volumes of the same gospel. Together—and they *must* be read together—they tell how the Holy Spirit first moved with Jesus from Galilee to Jerusalem and then moved with the apostles from Jerusalem to Rome. The good news, for Luke-Acts, is that the Holy Spirit moved headquarters from Jerusalem to Rome. The Holy Spirit, apparently, did not cross the Euphrates to the north or the Nile to the south but only the Mediterranean to the west. Each of those twin volumes, and one no more or less than the other, is theology rather than history. It is *our* problem if we wanted journalism. We received gospel instead. But it is all that hard-won understanding of the nature of gospel in general and the relations between gospels in particular that raises the historical problem. What do we know about Jesus and earliest Christianity through historical reconstruction—that is, through evidence arguable as public discourse?

As I noted earlier, when I wrote *The Historical Jesus* in 1991 I did not think it necessary to defend the validity of that enterprise. I considered such a study an established part of the scholarly landscape. I still do, of course, but now it is also necessary to give reasons. After more than twenty-five years of study, I see three reasons why historical research is necessary both into the life and death of Jesus and also into those first days, weeks, months, and years of earliest Christianity.

The Historical Reason

It indeed seems that the recent wave of attempts to recover the historical person of Jesus of Nazareth unwittingly mirrored a movement that reached its apex in Newt Gingrich's "Contract with America." There is a considerable movement from the very guarded steps, taken by German scholars in the first two decades after World War II, to the confidence of the last fifteen years, especially in the United States, the victorious leader of the capitalist world. It is perhaps no accident that almost all the major recent works on the historical Jesus have been produced by American scholars.

Helmut Koester, "The Historical Jesus and the Cult of the *Kyrios Christos*," p. 14

The first reason is historical, and I propose it in debate with recent articles by Dieter Georgi and especially Helmut Koester. It is the Mallory principle, but applied to historical figures rather than high mountains. People climb Everest because it is there; people study Jesus because he is there. Jesus and his first companions are historical figures and can be studied historically by anyone with the appropriate competence. That says no more or less about those early Christians than could be said about Socrates and his opponents or about Julius Caesar and his assassins.

There is always, of course, a general difficulty when contemporary present looks at distant past. It is not that *we* are that different from *them,* as if all of *us* were a single unified *we* and all of *them* a single unified *they*. There is probably as much divergence among modern-us as there ever was among ancient-them. Two individuals from different locations in our present contemporary world may be far more distant from one another than two individuals from different times in ancient and modern worlds. That is not the problem. The problem is that *we* know what happened, *we* know how it all turned out, at least from then to now. *We* know the future of *their* past. How, for example, could we reconstruct the crucifixion of Jesus *as if* we did not know gospel descriptions, artistic visualizations, musical celebrations, and two thousand years of Christian worship? What makes it all even, of course, is that we do *not* know the future of our *own* present. As we internalize our predecessors' ignorance of past-to-present, we become aware of our own ignorance of present-to-future. But that is nothing more than the general problem and general gift of any ancient history.

There is also a special problem when religious belief or disbelief, commitment or distaste, love or hate is involved. Writing almost a century ago when the search for the historical Jesus was already in mid-course, Albert Schweitzer divided researchers into *haters* and *lovers*, "for hate as well as love can write a Life of Jesus" (1969:4). He first described the Jesus-haters and their work: "The greatest of them [the Lives of Jesus] are written with hate. . . . It was not so much hate of the Person of Jesus as of the supernatural nimbus with which it was so easy to surround Him, and with which He had in fact been surrounded. They were eager to picture Him as truly and purely human, to strip from Him the robes of splendour with which He had been apparelled, and clothe Him once more with the coarse garments in which He had walked in Galilee. And their hate sharpened their historical insight. They advanced the study of the subject more than all the others put together" (1969:4). He is speaking especially of Hermann Samuel Reimarus, who lived from 1694 to 1768 but was published anonymously only after his death. He is also speaking of David Friedrich Strauss, who lived from 1808 to 1874 and was published at the start of his university career—an achievement that immediately ended it. Schweitzer next described the Jesus-lovers: "But the others, those who tried to bring Jesus to life at the call of love, found it a cruel task to be honest. The critical study of the life of Jesus has been for theology a school of honesty. . . . It was fortunate for these men that their sympathies sometimes obscured their critical vision, so that, without becoming insincere, they were able to take white clouds for distant mountains" (1969:5). Are hate and love, polemics and apologetics, the inevitable alternatives for historical Jesus research, and, if so, does not each option prejudice the evidence in equal but opposite directions? Jesus was received by both belief and disbelief, by both acceptance and indifference, by both worship and crucifixion. Is it not possible to bracket either response today and reconstruct what it would have been like to bracket it two thousand years ago? What did he say and do that begot such divergent responses?

Those twin difficulties do not make reconstructions invalid. They only make them hard. But strange things happen to historians when the subject is Jesus. One example will suffice. I cite it to emphasize that, if historical reconstruction is often a minefield, historical *Jesus* reconstruction is all mine, no field.

In a 1992 article Dieter Georgi applied to biblical exegetes the same sort of historical criticism that we ourselves apply regularly to our ancient texts. He argued that Reimarus's concerns, for example, were not just personal or emotional idiosyncrasies but were driven by social and historical forces beyond not only his control but even his knowledge. That all began, however, long before

Reimarus "in the southern and western Europe of the eleventh and twelfth centuries." From those inaugural moments, "life of Jesus theology developed further in close interplay with the socioeconomic and ideological evolution of the European bourgeoisie, as one of its motors as well as its conscience. The formation of conscientious and responsible burghers called for an ideal that was able to inspire and direct individuals who would represent and shape the new societal vision. The evolving life of Jesus theology would provide that germinal stimulation" (56). And that social impetus continued right into the middle and late twentieth century. "The origin of the so-called New Quest [for the historical Jesus] in the early 1950s, its rather explosive spread, not only in Germany but also worldwide, and its continuing life were and still are a complete surprise for the historian at least on the surface. There were no new methods or truly new methodological insights, no new texts or any other new historical evidence that had direct bearing on the problems of historical authenticity of the Jesus tradition. . . . For the New Quest the kingdom of God remains central—the theme that since the Middle Ages had remained so fertile for the development of bourgeois consciousness. . . . I observe the main cause in the continuous social and historical situation of the whole quest for the historical Jesus, that is, its location within the evolution of bourgeois consciousness, not just as an ideal but as an expression of a socioeconomic and political momentum. The contemporaneity of the New Quest with the end of the New Deal and the restoration of the bourgeoisie in the United States and Germany after World War II and within the confines of a burgeoning market-oriented Atlantic community is not accidental" (80, 82, 83).

Two immediate comments. First, I do not know how such a sweeping thesis could be verified or falsified. It has the advantage of being beyond disproof, the disadvantage of being beyond proof. But, in any case, even if it were absolutely true, it simply shows that socioeconomic factors and religious emphases interpenetrate one another. And that is surely correct. Second, Georgi's analysis remains descriptive rather than prescriptive. Whatever he himself thinks about the rise of the Euro-American middle-class bourgeoisie or the development of scholarly research on the historical Jesus, his review is neutral in tone and impartial in depiction. I presume that, even if his analysis is totally correct, description is not indictment.

Helmut Koester has accepted Georgi's argument and extended it beyond description toward indictment. First, he cites Georgi's conclusion and concurs with it: "The return of interest in the life of Jesus after World War II can therefore be seen as the consequence of the restoration of the bourgeois establishment, in which the life of an important individual provides the role model for either its moral justification or its, albeit revolutionary, criticism" (1995:14; compare 1994b:539). By the way, if historical Jesus research furnishes a life that can *both* morally justify *and* radically criticize middle-class values, it is surely well worth investigating how such a contradiction is possible. To pursue that question would probably tell us a lot about the historical Jesus and earliest Christianity, about ourselves as historians or Christians, and about everything else in between. Second, Koester, in the text that serves as epigraph to this section, expands Georgi's review of historical Jesus research up to its contemporary North American context. I am not sure I understand that application, but the association with Newt Gingrich and the "Contract with America" does not seem a compliment. Finally, Koester concludes another recent article like this: "Political, social, and environmental problems of our age will not be cured through the ever renewed search for the exemplary personality of Jesus and his wisdom, in order to legitimize the individual's search for perfection and success. A new paradigm that defines the perimeters of a new world that is not exploitative and that also includes the voices of people outside of the Western world may eventually liberate us from the quest for the historical Jesus. It may appear then that the comparison of Paul's proclamation of God's failure in the world of human affairs as the turning point of the ages in comparison with the success of Augustus's eschatological imperialism is a more worthwhile topic than the quest for the historical Jesus" (1994b:544–545).

That is clear enough and quite correct about Paul's proclamation. Rome had officially crucified Jesus under a governor's legally mandated and imperially approved right-to-execute. But the Jewish God of cosmic justice was on the side of Jesus and therefore against Rome, despite all its utopian propaganda about Augustus's divine descent, his personal divinization, and his establishment of Roman fertility, prosperity, and peace. Divergent eschatological visions were at war with one another, Christian gospel at war with Roman gospel. Koester is perfectly right about that. But why set the historical Paul against the historical Jesus? What if historical Jesus research is not about the "individual's search for perfection and success" or about Jesus' own "exemplary personality" but is about the "new world" of the Jewish God incarnated as human justice opposing the pagan God incarnated as Roman imperialism? Why set the historical Jesus, because we have to reconstruct him, against the historical Paul, as if we did not have to reconstruct him?

In making those comments, however, I am deeply aware of divergent sensibilities between Koester and myself. I am Irish and Roman Catholic; he is German and Lutheran. Furthermore, we lived in very different worlds in the 1940s, and I was in the far safer (but not necessarily the more honorable) location, the protected lee of a rejected empire. That does not make either of us right and the other wrong, but it gives us different religious, political, and autobiographical sensitivities. I do not undertake historical Jesus research as a quest for "the great human or even superhuman personality" (1992:13) or for the "'uniqueness' of Jesus' words and ministry" (1994b:541). Nor do I see, as Koester does, the specter of Hitler inevitably haunting such study. As an example, he rejects the term "Jesus movement" with this explicit comparison: "The word 'church' seems to have very negative connotations; 'movement' seems to be preferable today. I cannot help but remember that Hitler and the National Socialists called their endeavor a 'movement' (1992:6 note 14). And again later, but even more pointedly: "The term 'movement' has problematic political overtones—one may recall the [Nazi movement]. . . . E. Schüssler Fiorenza . . . uses the designation 'Jesus movement' throughout her book [In Memory of Her] and characterizes it as 'an inner-Jewish renewal movement'" (1994a:544, and note 19). I ask, for others less involved to answer, Is that association of Nazi *movement* and Jesus *movement* a fair or even decent comment?

I admit, finally, to suspecting those who insist that Jesus cannot be reconstructed historically. And I am equally suspicious whether that assertion is made openly and initially or is the implicit conclusion to listing all the difficulties involved. Why is Jesus, alone of all historical figures, so covered by a cloud of unknowing and a cloak of protective invisibility? That assertion of historical agnosticism seems but a negative way of asserting unique status and transcendental dignity. If Jesus is but a figure like Zeus, historical reconstruction is quite obviously absurd. If Jesus is but a figure like Hamlet, historical reconstruction is equally absurd. The former lives only in myth, the latter only in literature. Jesus may live in both those realms too, but he also lived in history. Or that, at least, is the first historical question to be asked about him.

The Ethical Reason

What the historian or exegete cannot hope to do by historical research is to resolve what are really philosophical questions (e.g., whether miracles do take place) or theological questions (e.g., whether God has indeed acted in this particular "miracle," thus calling people to faith). Such questions, while important, simply go beyond the realm of history proper.

John P. Meier, *A Marginal Jew: Rethinking the Historical Jesus,* vol. 2, p. 220

The second reason is ethical, and I propose it in debate with the ongoing multivolume work of John Meier on the historical Jesus. This ethical reason operates on two different but connected levels. One level concerns how we reconstruct, as historians, and it focuses on the present. The other concerns how we believe, as Christians, and it focuses on the past. Together they concern the ethics of public interpretation of the past.

If gospel were parable, with Jesus challenging our faith as does the Good Samaritan, this reason would not hold. If gospel were theology, with Jesus speaking as divine wisdom from the throne of God, this reason would not hold. But Christianity has always claimed an historical basis, so this reason presses. When, in our gospels, are *the evangelists* making and *we* reading historical statements, and when are *they* making and *we* reading theological ones? Those italicized words underline the twin aspects of my ethical reason for historical Jesus research.

I give one example, concerning the divine conception of Jesus, as a case study to raise the general problem. John Meier concluded, concerning the historicity of that account that, "by itself, historical-critical research simply does not have the sources and tools available to reach a final decision on the historicity of the virginal conception as narrated by Matthew and Luke. One's acceptance or rejection of the doctrine will be largely influenced by one's own philosophical and theological presuppositions, as well as the weight one gives Church teaching. Once again, we are reminded of the built-in limitations of historical criticism. It is a useful tool, provided we do not expect too much of it" (1.222). I am more uneasy than I can say with that serene disjunction. To say that Jesus is divine or Son of God is theologically beyond historical proof or disproof. That seems to me absolutely correct. It is a matter of faith—that is, of the theologically based interpretation of history's meaning. But to say that he had no earthly father and that Mary conceived him virginally is an historical statement open, in principle, to proof or disproof. Those are matters of fact and open to historical discussion.

The conception of Jesus is told by the evangelist Luke writing in the 80s of the first century. It is a miracle of divine and human conjunction, a child conceived from a divine father and a human mother. It occurs without the participation of any human father.

In the sixth month the angel Gabriel was sent by God to a town in Galilee called Nazareth, to a virgin engaged to a man whose name was Joseph, of the house of David. The virgin's name was Mary. And he came to her and said, "Greetings, favored one! The Lord is with you." But she was much perplexed by his words and pondered what sort of greeting this might be. The angel said to her, "Do not be afraid, Mary, for you have found favor with God. And now, you will conceive in your womb and bear a son, and you will name him Jesus. He will be great, and will be called the Son of the Most High, and the Lord God will give to him the throne of his ancestor David. He will reign over the house of Jacob forever, and of his kingdom there will be no end." Mary said to the angel, "How can this be, since I am a virgin?" The angel said to her, "The Holy Spirit will come upon you, and the power of the Most High will overshadow you; therefore the child to be born will be holy; he will be called Son of God." (Luke 1:26–35)

That text makes claims that are historical, that are empirically verifiable, at least in part and in principle. It does not speak just of God but of a woman, Mary, who belongs to this earth and to its history. How does the historian respond? One reaction is to insist that any negation is just as theological as affirmation and that neither is historically acceptable. Historical reconstruction must stand mute before such transcendental claims. They are beyond historical verification or falsification, and the proper reaction is to bracket them historically without either affirming or denying them. The other reaction is to contend that there has never been adequate empirical proof for such claims throughout past or present history and that the story, and others like it, should not be taken literally. This reaction also asserts certain physical consistencies for which exceptions would have to be publicly proved rather than privately asserted. Hold any decision between those two positions and read this second story.

The conception of Octavius, Augustus-to-be, is recorded by the Roman historian Suetonius in his *Lives of the Caesars,* written during the first quarter of the second century. This divine conception took place over half a century before that of Jesus. As he prepares to narrate the emperor's death, Suetonius pauses to record the omens that indicated his great destiny in birth and life as well as death. This is how his mother, Atia, conceived him (Rolfe 1.264–267):

> When Atia had come in the middle of the night to the solemn service of Apollo, she had her litter set down in the temple and fell asleep, while the rest of the matrons also slept. On a sudden a serpent glided up to her and shortly went away. When she awoke, she purified herself, as if after the embraces of her husband, and at once there appeared on her body a mark in colors like a serpent, and she could never get rid of it; so that presently she ceased ever to go to the public baths. In the tenth month after that Augustus was born and was therefore regarded as the son of Apollo. (*The Deified Augustus* 94.4)

Augustus came from a miraculous conception by the divine and human conjunction of Apollo and Atia. How does the historian respond to that story? Are there any who take it literally or even bracket its transcendental claims as beyond historical judgment or empirical test? Classical historians, no matter how religious, do not usually do so. That divergence raises an ethical problem for me. Either all such divine conceptions, from Alexander to Augustus and from the Christ to the Buddha, should be accepted literally and miraculously or all of them should be accepted metaphorically and theologically. It is not morally acceptable to say directly and openly that our story is truth but yours is myth; ours is history but yours is lie. It is even less morally acceptable to say that indirectly and covertly by manufacturing defensive or protective strategies that apply only to one's own story.

This, then, is my problem, and I repeat that it is an ethical one. Anti-Christian or direct rationalism says that certain things cannot (or, more wisely, *do* not) happen. They are so far beyond the publicly verifiable or objectively provable consistencies of our world that, whatever their value as myth or parable, fable or story, they are not to be taken as fact, event, or history. It is easy, of course, to mock that attack, but we all live by it every day, especially where others are involved. (Where are you on aliens or Elvis?) Pro-Christian or indirect rationalism admits that those same types of events *usually* do not occur but insists that in one absolutely unique instance they did. A divine conception or a bodily resurrection, for example, has happened literally only once in the whole history of the world. To Jesus. When Christians *as historians* bracket from discussion or quarantine from debate those specific events but not all other such claims, past and present, they do something I consider unethical. But that raises the second aspect of my ethical problem.

We know from the above examples, and dozens like them, that the earliest Christians lived in a world not yet bedeviled by either direct or indirect rationalism, a world where divine conceptions were quite acceptable, where, in fact, divine and human, eternal and temporal, heaven, earth, and Hades were marvelously porous and open to one another. *They* could never have argued that Jesus was uniquely singular because divine conception had happened to him alone in all the world. They could not and they did not. That is the second and more fundamental aspect of the ethical problem. When *we* read *them* as saying that the historical Jesus is uniquely unique and that such events happened only to him, *we* are misreading *them*. But let me be very clear, they *were* making claims for their Jesus, and those claims *were* comparative over against all other such claims. That was precisely their point. Where, they asked, do *you* find the divine especially, particularly, or even uniquely present? Is it, for example, in Augustus, a Roman emperor backed by fabulous colonial wealth and massive military power, or in Jesus, a Jewish peasant child poor enough to be born in somebody else's stable? Where do *you* find your God? Choose.

We cannot live without group ideology (or, if you prefer, theology), but we must be able to keep it in dialectic with public evidence—if, that is, we make claims to such data. My own position as an historian trying to be ethical and a Christian trying to be faithful is this: I do not accept the divine conception of *either* Jesus *or* Augustus as factual history, but I *believe* that God is incarnate in the Jewish peasant poverty of Jesus and not in the Roman imperial power of Augustus.

The Theological Reason

If it can be demonstrated that Jesus did two different things, it is not therefore legitimate to understand those things in light of each other, as though
they were mutually interpretive. The reason for this is clear: we lack knowledge of all the other things Jesus said and did that provide the only real context for the interpretation of specific deeds and sayings.

Luke Timothy Johnson, *The Real Jesus*, p. 130

The third reason is theological, and I propose it in debate with Luke Timothy
Johnson's 1996 book, *The Real Jesus*. But, precisely to respond to that book, I offer
it as a Christian to a fellow Christian and within the specific model of the New
Testament gospels themselves. This dispute, however, is also of interest to anyone who has absorbed enough individual dualism to think of spirit-soul residing in body-flesh as in a lovely distracting house, a rundown motel room, or a
ghastly prison cell. This is for me the most important reason why historical Jesus
research is necessary. I offer it as a challenge within Christian faith, within the
Christian canon, and within Christian theology. It is based quite deliberately and
conservatively on the nature of the *canonical* gospels.

Luke Timothy Johnson's book *The Real Jesus* argued, as its subtitle said, that
the "quest for the historical Jesus" was "misguided" and that it denied the "truth
of the traditional gospels." Johnson claimed, first, that the "real" extended far
beyond the "historical" and could never be fully or properly grasped by history's
limited strategies. That is absolutely true, but—being true of everyone in general—it is irrelevant for anyone in particular. At a televised debate from New
York's Trinity Institute on May 1, 1996, for example, Johnson said that his own
wife exceeded as real what he could know about her as history. Of course, we do
not even know our own "real" selves in that omniscient sense. But the term *real*
comes from advertising, not scholarship—Coke is the real thing—and it is calculated to make debate impossible. So, with the stipulation that the reality of *any*
human being far exceeds what can be known publicly or argued historically, I
prefer to retire the phrase *"real* Jesus" and revert to what scholarship has always
discussed: the *"historical* Jesus"—that is, *the past Jesus reconstructed interactively by
the present through argued evidence in public discourse.*

Johnson claimed, next, that "good historical method" could establish "that
Jesus existed as something more than a fictional character—the sheer production
of ancient literature interpreting him and referring to him suffices to show that—
but we can have confidence about such fundamental issues as the time and place
of his activity and the manner of his death, as well as some clues as to the character of his activity" (117, 126). But Johnson then denies validity to "pushing past

the framework" he has just advocated and, in the process, negates the possibility not only of historical Jesus reconstruction but, in effect, of all past and even present history. Take that quite representative sentence cited in the epigraph above. It denies the validity not only of historical reconstruction but of everything else as well, from ordinary everyday knowledge to crucial juridical decision. In historical reconstruction, you present your best public argument that certain words, deeds, events, or happenings can or must be legitimately connected in order to understand what happened. (The accused said that he would kill the deceased, was seen leaving his house after his death, had blood in his car. . . .) That is true for scholars reconstructing a past event just as it is for jurors deciding a present guilt. And no amount of epistemological uncertainty can preclude the ethical necessity of such judgments. We never know it all, not of the past and not of the present, not of others and not even of ourselves. Yet we have no choice, even (or especially) amidst such uncertainty and insecurity, but to reconstruct the past that will serve as basis for our preconstructed future.

Since, however, Johnson argues as a Christian and a Roman Catholic, I respond to him ultimately not just with those preceding generalities, but also with a three-step theological and canonical counterproposal.

A FOURFOLD TYPOLOGY OF GOSPELS

I ask you, first, to consider four different types of gospels, four different ways of telling the Jesus story within early Christianity. It is not a case of four different gospels—Matthew, Mark, Luke, and John—within the present New Testament canon. Rather, it is a case of four different *types,* with those four canonical gospels as but one single type. Three preliminaries: First, I deliberately use a rather vague term, *types,* rather than a more precise term, *genres,* because there may be several different genres involved in a given type. Second, this typology places an emphasis not just on content but even more especially on form, and indeed on the point where form becomes content, where the medium becomes the message. Finally, it is not significant for my present concern whether or not a given text explicitly calls itself a gospel. What is important is what type of text is used to tell the story of Jesus as good news. I give each type a descriptive title.

Sayings Gospels.

The first type, *sayings gospels,* includes collections primarily of the words of Jesus. These consist generally of aphorisms, parables, and short dialogues. Incidents, insofar as they are present, emphasize the word rather than the deed. There are, for example, few miracle stories, no birth tales, no passion narratives, and no risen apparitions. The classic examples from the middle of the first century (about which much, much more later) are the *Q Gospel* and the *Gospel of Thomas.* The former is a *hypothetical written source* discovered during the last century in the gospels of Matthew and Luke. The latter is an *actual written document* discovered during this century in the sands of Egypt.

Biography Gospels.

The second type, *biography gospels,* is represented by the four canonical gospels. I emphasize not only that there are four but that all belong to the same single type. In this set Jesus is located back in the late 20s of his first-century Jewish homeland, but he is also updated to speak or act directly and immediately to new situations and communities in the 70s, 80s, and 90s. There is an absolute lamination of Jesus-then and Jesus-now without any distinction of Jesus-said-then but Jesus-means-now. In Mark, for example, Jesus confesses and is condemned while Peter denies and is forgiven, but those specific events—dated, say, to the year 30—speak directly and were created precisely for a persecuted community in the year 70. *You should have behaved like Jesus,* the message reads, *but even if you behaved like Peter, there is still mercy and forgiveness from Jesus himself.* This lamination explains why the four canonical gospels could turn out so different even though they were copying from one another. Indeed, one might well wonder why the early Christians kept all four, given that anyone could see the quite obvious differences. The reason becomes clearer, however, when we consider the next type.

Discourse Gospels.

The third type, *discourse gospels,* begins where the preceding type ends. While *biography gospels* detail the life of Jesus and end with his resurrection, *discourse gospels* begin after the resurrection and go on from there. Jesus appears to the disciples, and the narrative continues in a mix of monologue and dialogue, of questions and answers between them and him. Two examples will suffice.

The first example is the late-first-century or early-second-century *Apocryphon of James* from a codex discovered at Nag Hammadi (I,2) in 1945 (*NHLE* 30–37).

> The twelve disciples [were] all sitting together and recalling what the Savior had said to each one of them, whether in secret or openly, and [putting it] in books—[But I] was writing that which was in [my book]—lo, the Savior appeared, [after] departing from [us while we] gazed after him. And five hundred and fifty days since he had risen from the dead, we said to him. . . . But Jesus said. . . . They all answered. . . . He said. . . . [etc.] (*Apocryphon of James* 2.9–29)

In *discourse gospels* it is the risen Jesus who speaks and the disciples, especially Peter and James in this case, who ask questions. But the striking feature is not just that dialogue or discourse phenomenon but the fact that it all takes place after the resurrection.

The second example is similarly set after the resurrection, but now the questioners are Bartholomew, Mary, Matthew, Philip, and Thomas. It is *The Sophia of Jesus Christ*, also from Nag Hammadi (III,4) and dated to the latter half of the first century (*NHLE* 222–223):

> After he rose from the dead, his twelve disciples and seven women continued to be his followers and went to Galilee onto the mountain. . . . [T]he Savior appeared, not in his previous form, but in the invisible spirit. And his likeness resembled a great angel of light. . . . And he said: "Peace be to you! My peace I give to you!" And they all marveled and were afraid. The Savior laughed and said. . . . Philip said. . . . The Savior said. . . . [etc.] (*The Sophia of Jesus Christ* 90.14–92.6)

If *biography gospels* give us twenty chapters before the resurrection, *discourse gospels* give us twenty chapters afterward.

Biography-Discourse Gospels.

The title given to the fourth and final type, *biography-discourse gospels*, emphasizes its polemically hybrid aspect. Once again two examples will suffice. But the content of those two examples is very different. The first example is the *Epistula Apostolorum* (or *Epistle of the Apostles*). The discourse part of this document is far longer than its biography part, but the epistle tries, as it were, to subsume discourse within biography. The second example is *John's Preaching of the Gospel*. The biography part of this document is slightly longer than its discourse part, but it tries, as it were, to subsume biography within discourse.

The mid- to late-second-century Greek *Epistula Apostolorum*, extant now only in fairly early Coptic and very late Ethiopic translations (*NTA* 1.252–278), devotes nine of its fifty-one present units to biography: *Epistula Apostolorum* 3–12a summarize in swift outline the canonical gospel accounts of Jesus' words and deeds, life and death, burial and resurrection. This outline is actually a catalogue of miracles. It begins with the virginal conception and Bethlehem birth, mentions Jesus studying letters but knowing them already, and then goes on to recount the stories of the wedding at Cana, the woman with a hemorrhage, the exorcism of Legion into the swine, the walking on the waters, and the multiplication of loaves and fishes. It concludes with the crucifixion under Pontius Pilate and Archelaus (Antipas?), the burial, the women at the tomb (and Jesus' appearances to them), the disbelief of the disciples, and, finally, Jesus' appearance to them, despite the doubts of Peter, Thomas, and Andrew. In these few sections, the life and death of Jesus is swiftly summarized.

But all the rest—*Epistula Apostolorum* 13–51—is a postresurrectional dialogue with repeated interchanges between the risen Jesus ("he said") and the apostles ("we said"). Here, in 12a, is the point where *biography gospel* converts smoothly into *discourse gospel* (NTA 1.256):

> But we [touched] him that we might truly know whether he [had risen] in the flesh, and we fell on our [faces] confessing our sin, that we had been [un]believing. Then the Lord our redeemer said, "Rise up, and I will reveal to you what is above heaven and what is in heaven, and your rest that is in the kingdom of heaven. For my [Father] has given me the power to take up you and those who believe in me. . . . We answered. . . . Then he answered. . . . We said. . . . [etc.] (*Epistula Apostolorum* 12)

Jesus even foretells, in *Epistula Apostolorum* 31–33, that Paul would persecute the church and be converted to become apostle to the pagans. The entire discourse section is between Jesus and the disciples as a choral "we," without any individuals singled out as questioners.

The second example of this hybrid type is an early-second-century source usually called *John's Preaching of the Gospel*, now embedded in the *Acts of John* 87–105 (NTA 2.179–186). It is a beautiful text that merges those twin types in an extraordinary way.

In the first part, *Acts of John* 88b–96, the earthly life of Jesus is summarized, but with an emphasis on the unreality of his body. This unreality is shown by four points, each of which is mentioned twice (NTA 2.180–181). First, Jesus' body is polymorphous and ever-changing. The sons of Zebedee see Jesus on the shore, but at first James sees a "child" and John sees a "man . . . handsome, fair, and cheerful-looking." Later, as they beach their boat, John sees Jesus as "rather bald-(headed) but with a thick flowing beard," while James now sees "a young man whose beard was just beginning." Second, John "never saw Jesus' eyes closing, but always open." One night, in fact, while John was faking sleep, he saw "another like him coming down" to Jesus. Third, Jesus' body was both small and huge. "He sometimes appeared to me as a small man with no good looks, and then again as looking up to heaven." Thus, for example, on the Mount of Transfiguration, Jesus' "head stretched up to heaven," but when he turned about he "appeared as a small man." Fourth and finally, Jesus' body "had another strange (property); when I reclined at table he would take me to his own breast, and I held him (fast); and sometimes his breast felt to me smooth and soft, but sometimes hard like rock." And again, a second time, "I will tell you another glory, brethren; sometimes when I meant to touch him I encountered a material, solid body; but at other times again when I felt him, his substance was immaterial and incorporeal, and as if it did not exist at all."

The second part, *Acts of John* 97–101, takes place at the crucifixion itself. And in this gospel, consequent on that bodily unreality, it is not the reality of Jesus who suffers and dies, except, as John insists, in symbol (*NTA* 2.184–185):

And so I saw him suffer, and did not wait by his suffering, but fled to the Mount of Olives and wept at what had come to pass. And when he was hung (upon the Cross) on Friday, at the sixth hour of the day there came a darkness over the whole earth. And my Lord stood in the middle of the cave and gave light to it and said, "John, for the people below in Jerusalem I am being crucified and pierced with lances and reeds, and given vinegar and gall to drink. But to you I am speaking, and listen to what I speak. I put into your mind to come up to this mountain so that you may hear what a disciple should learn from his teacher and a man from God. (*Acts of John* 97)

That sounds like the postresurrectional Jesus beginning a standard discourse-type gospel, but, in this instance, pre-Easter and post-Easter have no meaning since there is only one Jesus who both *is* and *is not* ever embodied. Jesus' explanation insists on this paradox (*NTA* 2.186):

You hear that I suffered, yet I suffered not; and that I suffered not, yet I did suffer; and that I was pierced, yet I was not wounded; that I was hanged, yet I was not hanged; that blood flowed from me, yet it did not flow; and, in a word, that what they say of me, I did not endure, but what they do not say, those things I did suffer. (*Acts of John* 101)

There are, Jesus explains, two crosses: the Cross of Wood, on which his unreality suffered, and the Cross of Light, on which his reality continues to suffer. The former is the transient passion of body. The latter is the permanent passion of God. God has been, as it were, dismembered, and his parts, like fragments of light, scattered within bodies here on earth. Until all those members return home, God is in suffering, impaled, as it were, on a Cross of Light.

The third part, *Acts of John* 102–104, begins with the ascension of Jesus: "[H]e was taken up, without any of the multitude seeing him." John then concludes with a commentary of his own. His basic interpretive principle is this: "I held this one thing fast in my (mind), that the Lord had performed everything as a symbol and a dispensation for the conversion and salvation of man." Hence those stunning paradoxes above: Jesus did not really suffer on the Cross (of Wood) but he always suffers on the Cross (of Light). And the former is the symbol of the latter. Similarly, says John, the present persecution of our bodies is important as symbol for the persecution of our spirits; the former may place us on a Cross of

Wood, but we are always, with God, on a Cross of Light. We are always part of the passion of God. Hence this profoundly beautiful and terribly poignant conclusion (*NTA* 2.186):

> (Let us worship) him who was made man (apart from) this body. And let us watch, since he is at hand even now in prisons for our sakes, and in tombs, in bonds and dungeons, in reproaches and insults, by sea and on dry land, in torments, sentences, conspiracies, plots and punishments; in a word, he is with all of us, and with the sufferers he suffers himself, (my) brethren . . . being the God of those who are imprisoned, bringing us help through his own compassion. (*Acts of John* 103)

That preceding gospel version might strike a contemporary reader as exceedingly strange, but that very strangeness reveals most clearly what is at stake in the fourfold typology.

A WAR OF GOSPEL TYPES

That fourfold typology is not a placid inventory of gospel possibilities but a war of gospel types. Understanding that war, at the center of which is the clash between *biography gospels* and *discourse gospels,* requires some background knowledge of an even more basic and ancient debate.

First, there was a profound fault line in much of ancient thought between, on the one hand, body, flesh, or the material world, and, on the other, soul, spirit, or the immaterial world. There is an immediate problem with establishing proper *terms* for that disjunction, for the views of those who accepted it and for the views of those who rejected it. In what follows, therefore, I insist on the primary importance of *concepts* rather than just *terms*. But as you will recall, I proposed the terms *sarcophobia* and *sarcophilia* for those opposing sensibilities when this subject was first mentioned in the Prologue. The anti-body viewpoint, body-against-spirit disjunction, or sarcophobic sensibility involved a spectrum from the flesh as irrelevant or unimportant for the spirit, through the flesh as an impediment or distraction for the spirit, to the flesh as inimical or evil for the spirit. At one end of that spectrum was a philosophical anthropology negating flesh as the clinging distraction or degrading downfall of spirit. At the other end of the spectrum was a mythical cosmology negating flesh as the stultifying narcosis or evil opponent of spirit. The pro-body viewpoint, body-and-spirit conjunction, or sarcophilic sensibility opposed that spectrum at whatever point was appropriate for debate.

Second, there was another presupposition built upon that preceding one. Some moderns may live in a world where immortal and mortal, heavenly and earthly, divine and human are rather transcendentally separated from one another. Not so, in general, for the ancients. Their world was filled with gods, goddesses, and spirits who assumed divergent shapes and figures, who assumed and changed bodies as we assume clothes and change styles. Gods and goddesses, for example, could appear in any material, animal, or human form appropriate for the occasion. But all such bodies were not *really* real. They were only *apparently* real. They were like the interchangeable puppets of a single puppeteer. Could and did gods or goddesses become incarnate? Of course. They did so regularly, differently, and realistically, so that mortals could not recognize the unreality of those apparitional, illusional bodies. But did they *really* become incarnate? Of course not!

The irrelevance of human flesh, on the one hand, and the unreality of divine flesh, on the other, presented earliest Christianity with a serious and profound problem concerning Jesus. Those believers were poised on that giant fault line in the ancient world, a fault line that involved the whole material world and all humans in it but was now focused on Jesus. We might think to ourselves, Of *course* Jesus was human, but was he divine? They had the opposite problem. If they believed that Jesus was divine, the question became, How could he be human? How could his body be real rather than apparitional and illusional? Was it not just a seem-to-be body?

There was no point in responding that people saw, heard, or even touched his body. For all those things could be arranged, as it were, by resident divinity. One obvious answer has been brilliantly explored by Gregory Riley (1998). Jesus could be explained not as *god* or *spirit* but as *hero,* as the offspring of a divine and human conjunction, himself therefore half-human and half-divine but really and truly each half. He could, as such, ascend after a real and true death to take his place among the heavenly immortals. But if one of the ancients wished to move beyond Jesus as hero to Jesus as spirit or Jesus as god, the unreality of his flesh and the apparitional illusion of his body would have seemed inevitable concomitants.

If Jesus was divine, was his body real and incarnational in the sense of fully and validly enfleshed, or was his body unreal and apparitional, only seemingly enfleshed, a docetic body (from Greek *dokein,* "to seem")? One way of describing that clash of interpretation is to speak of incarnational as against docetic Christianity. Another way is to speak of catholic as against Gnostic Christianity but, as we saw earlier in this book's Prologue, it is probably wiser not to use those terms because they are now laden with too much historical controversy and too little descriptive accuracy.

But there existed then and still exists today a specific dichotomy that must be named as accurately as possible. Only then is it possible to know on which side do ancient authors *and* modern readers stand. That great fissure in Western consciousness cuts through paganism, Judaism, and Christianity, and it extended its powerful dichotomy from time past to time present, from the ancient world to our contemporary culture. Because of its importance, then and now, this book's Prologue gave it a special name. It is the disjunction of monastic and sarcophilic sensibility where the human being is flesh-spirit conjunction as against dualistic and sarcophobic sensibility where the human being is flesh-spirit separation. That disjunction is as present today as it was two millennia ago. That disjunction contains a spectrum of options from one extreme to its opposite. And that disjunction about the reality and importance of Jesus' flesh, that is, about the importance of the historical Jesus, best explains the clash of gospel types.

It explains how *biography gospels,* the programmatic gospels of sarcophilic Christianity, and *discourse gospels,* the programmatic gospels of sarcophobic Christianity, opposed one another. It also explains how *sayings gospels,* which were earlier and could have moved in either direction, were doomed by that very ambiguity. They would end up incorporated into either of those opposing types, with the *Q Gospel* moving in one direction and the *Gospel of Thomas* moving in the other. It explains, finally, those hybrid *biography-discourse gospels.* On the one hand, the *Epistula Apostolorum* "mimics a form of revelation literature which was popular among many gnostics attempting to combat its opponents with their own theological weapons," as Ron Cameron put it (132). If, in other words, sarcophobic Christians used *discourse gospels,* sarcophilic Christians could respond with *biography-discourse gospels.* On the other hand, the *Acts of John* 87–105 had the earthly or biographical Jesus as unreal and docetic, albeit as symbolically significant, as one could imagine.

When, therefore, the canon has four examples of the *biography gospel* type, it makes normative not only those four but that very type. *Biography gospels* insist on the utter embodied historicity of Jesus while *discourse gospels* find that emphasis radically misplaced. By the way, in case you still find this all very strange, let me ask you a question. If you were guaranteed five minutes with Jesus but had to choose between five from history long ago or five from heaven right now, which would you choose?

THE CANONICAL GOSPELS AS NORMATIVE TYPE

Before proceeding, a short time-out for confession is required. I admit immediately that my own religious sensibilities are irrevocably within sarcophilic Christianity rather than within sarcophobic Christianity. I prefer, in other words, *biography gospels* over against either *discourse gospels* or *biography-*

discourse gospels. But I can make that admission without denying Christian status to sarcophobic Christians, without describing them unfairly or unjustly, and without thinking that persecution is the best form of persuasion. I will also admit that the history of Christian theology often seems to me but the long, slow victory of sarcophobic over sarcophilic sensibility.

My challenge, however, is a theological one from within canonical normativity. How exactly are those *four gospels as a single type* normative for Christians who invoke their authority and seek to live within that heritage? It is not just their *content* that is normative but especially their very *form*. They are not simply four discourses by the risen Jesus, each giving absolutely orthodox and officially approved doctrines. Such texts, no matter how unimpeachable their content, were not canonically acceptable, and that decision was a fateful one for Christianity's future and my present concern with the birth of Christianity. Each of those canonical gospels goes back to the historical Jesus of the late 20s in his Jewish homeland, but each of them has that Jesus speak directly to its own immediate situation and community. In every case, as I noted before, there is a dialectic of then-and-now, of then-as-now—that is, of the historical Jesus then as the risen Jesus now. It is not the historical Jesus alone then and not the risen Jesus alone now, but the two as one within a contemporary faith. It is always that same process, but always with slightly or massively divergent products. Think, for example, of how different the Agony in the Garden appears in Mark 14, which has no garden, and in John 18, which has no agony. But still that dialectic of then and now continues to hold. My proposal is that *the canonical gospel type is normative primarily as that dialectical process*. Those gospels created an interaction of historical Jesus and risen Jesus, and that interaction must be repeated again and again throughout Christian history.

I take the canonical gospels as normative model for all subsequent Christian discourse—that is, for the dialectic of Jesus-then as Jesus-now. They are normative not only as product (what they do) but even more profoundly as process (how they do it). They always go back to the one and only historical Jesus, the Jesus of the late 20s in his Jewish homeland. That one Jesus may be experienced as risen Jesus through divergent modes, through justice and peace, prayer and liturgy, meditation and mysticism, but it must always be *that* Jesus and no other. There is, in other words, ever and always only one Jesus.

The Easter issues of *Newsweek*, *Time*, and *U.S. News & World Report*, April 8, 1996, all had cover stories on the historical Jesus. *Newsweek* had the caption "Rethinking the Resurrection: A New Debate About the Risen Christ." It was written across a picture of Jesus rising heavenward, arms uplifted, hands facing outward. What struck me immediately as strange was the complete absence of any wounds on those clearly visible hands and feet. I failed to realize that they had mistakenly taken Jesus from a transfiguration instead of a resurrection painting. There were, of course, no wounds on that Vatican work by Raphael, because it depicted an event before the death of Jesus. *U.S. News & World Report*, on the other hand (no pun intended), had a correct picture. Its cover had the caption "In Search of Jesus: Who was he? New appraisals of his life and meaning?" written across Jesus as depicted in a Bellini painting of the resurrection with the wound in Jesus' right hand clearly visible.

There is, I repeat, ever and always only one Jesus. For Christians that is the historical Jesus *as* risen Jesus. And the test is this: Does the risen Jesus still carry the wounds of crucifixion? In Christian gospel, art, and mysticism, the answer is clearly yes. But those wounds are the marks of history, and to understand them you have to know about his death. But to understand the death, you have to know about his life. Unless you know otherwise, Jesus might have been a criminal meeting appropriate sentence, or his executioners might have been savages operating from sheer random brutality. With those canonical gospels as inaugural models and primordial examples, each Christian generation must write its gospels anew, must first reconstruct its historical Jesus with fullest integrity and then say and live what that reconstruction means for present life in this world. History and faith are always a dialectic for sarcophilic Christianity. Put otherwise, its insistence on the resurrection of Jesus' body is my insistence on the permanence of Jesus' history. But then, now, and always it is a history seen by faith.

Our Own Faces in Deep Wells

Others taunt me with having knelt at well-curbs
Always wrong to the light, so never seeing
Deeper down in the well than where the water
Gives me back in a shining surface picture
Me myself in the summer heaven, godlike,
Looking out of a wreath of fern and cloud puffs.
Once, when trying with chin against a well-curb,
I discerned, as I thought, beyond the picture,
Through the picture, a something white, uncertain,
Something more of the depths—and then I lost it.

Robert Frost, "For Once, then, Something" (91)

There is an oft-repeated and rather cheap gibe that historical Jesus researchers are simply looking down a deep well and seeing their own reflections from below. I call it *cheap* for three reasons. First, those who use it against others seldom apply it to themselves. Second, it is almost impossible to imagine a reconstruction that could not be dismissed by the assertion of that gibe. Your Jesus is an apocalyptic: you are bemused by the approaching millennium. Your Jesus is a healer: you have been hearing Bill Moyers. Your Jesus is an ecstatic: you are interested in brain chemistry. What could anyone *ever* say that would not fall under that ban? Third, those who repeat the taunt so readily must never have looked down a deep well or heeded Emily Dickinson's warning (3.970, no. 1400):

What mystery pervades a well!. . .
But nature is a stranger yet;
The ones that cite her most
Have never passed her haunted house,
Nor simplified her ghost.

Imagine two alternative and opposite modes of historical reconstruction, one an impossible delusion, the other a possible illusion. The possible illusion is *narcissism*. You think you are seeing the past or the other when all you see is your own reflected present. You see only what was there before you began. You imprint your own present on the past and call it history. *Narcissism* sees its own face and, ignoring the water that shows it up, falls in love with itself. It is the first of the twin images in Frost's poem. It is when,

the water
Gives me back in a shining surface picture
Me myself in the summer heaven, godlike,
Looking out of a wreath of fern and cloud puffs.

The impossible delusion is *positivism*. It imagines that you can know the past without any interference from your own personal and social situation as knower. You can see, as it were, without your own eye being involved. You can discern the past once and for all forever and see it pure and uncontaminated by that discernment. *Positivism* is the delusion that we can see the water without our own face being mirrored in it. It thinks we can see the surface without simultaneously seeing our own eyes. It is the second of the twin images in Frost's poem. It is when, even if only once, uncertainly, possibly, and vaguely,

I discerned, as I thought, beyond the picture,
Through the picture, a something white, uncertain,
Something more of the depths—and then I lost it.

But, I would ask, *if the poet's face is white,* how did it see "through the pic-ture" of itself "a something white" that was also "beyond the picture"? *Maybe what it saw was its own face so strangely different that it did not recognize it.* That introduces a third image not given but provoked by Frost's second image.

There is, therefore, a third alternative, and I'll call it *interactivism,* which is, incidentally, the way I understand postmodernism. The past and present must interact with one another, each changing and challenging the other, and the ideal is an absolutely fair and equal reaction between one another. Back to the well: you cannot see the surface without simultaneously seeing, disturbing, and distorting your own face; you cannot see your own face without simultaneously seeing, disturbing, and distorting the surface. It is the third image begging to be recognized behind the two overt ones in Frost's poem. What the poet saw was his own face so strangely different that he did not recognize it as such. It was, indeed, "something white" and "something more of the depths." But it was not "beyond the picture" or even "through the picture." It was the picture itself changed utterly. That is the dialectic of interactivism and, as distinct from either narcissism or positivism, it is both possible and necessary. Two examples, both reviewing classical scholarship, may help as illustrations and warnings.

The first example concerns the historical reconstruction of the Roman emperor Augustus. Ronald Mellor frames his book on Tacitus with these com-ments about four great interpretations of Rome's transition from republican to imperial rule: "The greatest Roman historians of the last two centuries—Gibbon, Mommsen, Rostovzteff, and Syme—wrote with passion as they saw connections between Rome and their own times. . . . Edward Gibbon, a child of the French Enlightenment which affected his views of religion, was issued in 'Bowdlerized' editions in Victorian England; Theodor Mommsen, the only professional histo-rian to win the Nobel Prize for literature, wrote a passionate, multi-volume *History of Rome* in which Caesar became the inevitable solution to republican Rome's dilemma as Mommsen himself yearned for a strongman to resolve the chaos of nineteenth-century Germany; Michael Rostovzteff brought his flight from revolutionary St. Petersburg to bear on his *Social and Economic History of the Roman Empire* (1926)—a glorification of the Roman municipal bourgeoisie; and Sir Ronald Syme's *The Roman Revolution* (1939) looked at the rise of Augustus through the spectacles of a liberal who saw on his visits to Italy the names and trappings of Augustan Rome used by a new *dux,* Benito Mussolini, and wished to expose in a very Tacitean way the thuggish similarities between the two regimes" (45, 164). In all those cases powerful sociopersonal interactions between past and present resulted in towering achievements, works we call *classical* in both senses of that term. And, of course, their multiplicity serves as a corrective each on the other.

The second example concerns the historical reconstruction of earliest Christian art. Thomas Mathews discusses "how the Emperor Mystique came to be the controlling theory for explaining the development of Christian imagery," and he asserts that "the need to interpret Christ as an emperor tells more about the historians involved than it does about Early Christian art. The formulation of the theory can be traced to three very bold and original European scholars in the period between the wars; the medievalist Ernst Kantorowicz, a German Jew of a well-to-do merchant family; the Hungarian archaeologist Andreas Alföldi, son of a country doctor; and art historian André Grabar, a Russian emigré, whose senatorial family held important posts under the last Czars. . . . If there is a single common thread uniting the life and work of these three great scholars, it is nostalgia for lost empire. The three imperial states in which they were raised, and which they fought valiantly to defend, they saw crumble ignominiously in the horrible chaos of the First World War and its consequences. The glory of the czars, the might of the Prussian and Austro-Hungarian emperors, could never be restored" (16, 19). Mathews judges that interaction of present and past to have misinterpreted early Christian art and then draws an explicit analogy between his own corrective reconstruction and the "quest for the 'historical' Jesus, an enterprise that verged on reducing him to the product of wishful thinking on the part of his first disciples. Since Christ wrote nothing himself, the historian is necessarily limited to sifting through the distorted impressions of a circle of people who were very deeply affected by their experience of him. The Christ of Early Christian art is quite as elusive as the 'historical' Jesus. As in the written sources, so in the visual monuments Christ has many guises, depending on who is visualizing him. We are faced, then, with the difficult task of understanding as far as possible the impression Christ made on people when they, for the first time, were seeking to represent him. Hitherto he had existed only in the hearts of believers, in the visions of mystics, in the words of preachers; now he has to have a life in stone and paint" (21–22). Historical reconstruction is always interactive of present and past. Even our *best* theories and methods are still *our* best ones. They are all dated and doomed not just when they are wrong but even (and especially) when they are right. They need, when anything important is involved, to be done over and over again. That does not make history worthless. We ourselves are also dated and doomed, but that does not make life worthless. It just makes death inevitable. I have two corollaries from that understanding of interactivism.

A first corollary concerns the term *search* or *quest*. You may have noticed that I do not speak of the *search* for the historical Jesus or of the *quest* for Christian origins. Those terms seem to indicate a positivistic process in which we are going to attain an answer once and for all forever. That is not how I now imagine the process. I speak instead of *reconstruction,* and that is something that must be done over and over again in different times and different places, by different groups and different communities, and by every generation again and again and again. In order to emphasize that viewpoint, I talk hereafter only of reconstructing the historical Jesus as best one can at any given place and time.

Recently N. Thomas Wright spent very many pages distinguishing three quests for the historical Jesus. The First Quest lasted from Reimarus to Schweitzer, in round numbers from 1700 to 1900. The Second or New Quest was proposed by Ernst Käsemann in 1953 as a reaction to the bracketing of the historical Jesus in the work of his teacher, Rudolf Bultmann. But I think it fair to say that no New Quest ever took place, no Second Search ever followed that manifesto. Wright proposes, however, that many contemporary scholars, including myself, are simply on a "renewed 'New Quest.'" We are, therefore, part of the discarded past. The Third Quest is actually composed of about twenty scholars, including Wright himself. He invented that title just for that group because that "is where the real leading edge of contemporary Jesus-scholarship is to be found" (1996:84). Unable to decide whether that cartography is amusing impertinence or annoying arrogance, I limit myself to two brief comments. Positivist delusions haunt such terms as *search* or *quest.* The historical Jesus, like the Holy Grail, is to be found once and for all forever. That is not how I see it. Furthermore, I wonder why Wright does not simply put people like myself into a Third Quest and his group into a Fourth Quest. Or, put another way, does Wright imagine a Fourth Quest for the future, and then a Fifth, and a Sixth, etc., etc., etc.? Positivist delusion also haunts the term *third?* In Indo-European folklore, the third time is closure, finish, completion. The hero may fail twice but will succeed the third time. That happens, unfortunately, only in folklore and fairy-story.

A second corollary concerns method. I insist that Jesus reconstruction, like all such reconstruction, is always a creative interaction of past and present. But what keeps that dialectic of *us* and *them* as even and honest as possible? Method, method, and once again method. Method will not guarantee us the truth, because nothing can do that. But method, as self-conscious and self-critical as we can make it, is our only discipline. It cannot ever take us out of our present skins and bodies, minds and hearts, societies and cultures. But it is our one best hope for honesty. It is the due process of history. And that brings me back once again to Wright. I think that we are in agreement on what he calls "critical realism" and I call "interactivism," but we differ on how that concept works in practice. My answer is by developing a method that protects your subject not from conversation but from violation, not from discussion but from disfigurement. That is why, for example, I gave *my* complete inventory of the Jesus tradition broken down in terms of independent attestation and stratigraphic location as appendix to *The Historical Jesus*. Wright, however, finds that "despite the postmodern tone which predominates in the book, the massive inventory of material is bound to look like a thoroughly modernist piece of work, appearing to lay firm, almost positivist, foundations for the main argument of the book" (1996:50). A postmodern sensibility—that is, an equal awareness of your own and your subject's historicity—does not *preclude* but *demands* attention to method. As due-process keeps the legal interaction of defense and prosecution fair, so due-method keeps the historical interaction of past and present honest. But there is not in my work any presumption that the historical Jesus or earliest Christianity is something you get once and for all forever. And that is not because Jesus and Christianity are special or unique. No past of continuing importance can ever avoid repeated reconstruction.

This, then, is my challenge. sarcophilic as distinct from sarcophobic Christianity is a dialectic between history and faith. That dialectic has its normative model in the canonical gospel-*type* and its paradigmatic instances in those four gospel-*texts*. They show, across the 70s, 80s, and 90s of that first century, how Jesus-then becomes Jesus-now, how the historical Jesus becomes the risen Jesus, and how, while you can have history without faith, you cannot have faith without history. In every generation, the historical Jesus must be reconstructed anew, and that reconstruction must become by faith the face of God for here and now. If that seems too strange, consider this parallel situation.

Within Christianity the Bible is the Word of God made text, just as Jesus is the Word of God made flesh. It would have been quite possible for Christian tradition to have declared some one, single, given manuscript of the Bible to be official and canonical. Imagine that had happened, for example, to the Codex Vaticanus, a fourth-century vellum copy of 759 leaves, three columns per page, 42 lines to the column. Imagine that had been declared to be the immutable and inspired Word of God with its three-column pages manifesting forever the mystery of the Trinity. There might have been discussion on what to do about the indignant scribe who added in the left-hand margin of Hebrews 1:3 this succinct comment on an earlier colleague's work: "Fool and knave, can't you leave the old reading alone, and not alter it" (Metzger 1981:74). But it would have made no difference what tattered fragments or total texts survived from earlier times in the Egyptian sands. It would have made no difference what academic scholars or textual critics thought was historically a more accurate original text. The Codex Vaticanus would have been *it*, once and for all forever. The Word of God made text would have been safe from the vagaries of history, the excavations of archeologists, and the surprise discoveries of peasants or shepherds.

Instead of that option, I have on my desk the fourth revised edition of *The Greek New Testament*, published by the United Bible Societies in 1993. It gives the closest a committee can come to the original text with the alternative readings in footnote apparatus. It grades any disputed reading from A to D "to indicate the relative degree of certainty in the mind of the committee for the reading adopted as the text." Bruce Metzger explains the committee's grading as follows: "The letter {A} signifies that the text is virtually certain, while {B} indicates that there is some degree of doubt concerning the reading selected for the text. The letter {C} means that there is a considerable degree of doubt whether the text or the apparatus contains the superior reading, while {D} shows that there is a very high degree of doubt concerning the reading selected for the text. In fact, among the {D} decisions sometimes none of the variant readings commended itself as original, and therefore the only recourse was to print the least unsatisfactory reading" (1971:xxviii). I believe, as a Christian, in the Word of God, not in the words of specific papyri or the votes of specific committees. But fact and faith, history and theology intertwine together in that process and cannot ever be totally separated.

As with the Word of God made text, so also with the Word of God made flesh. Historical reconstruction interweaves with Christian faith, and neither can substitute for the other. I insist, however, that it did not have to be that way. It is sarcophilic as distinct from sarcophobic Christianity that gave out hostages to history. It is now too late for it to repent, and I, for one, would not want it to do so. But I also wonder about this: Is the history of Christianity and especially of Christian theology the long, slow victory of sarcophobic over sarcophilic Christianity?

PART II
Memory and Orality

The "Great Events" of the past are designated as such by people external to most local societies, and certainly all peasant societies. . . . Just because historians regard Napoleon as worth remembering and discussing, other people are not required to think in the same way, or, indeed, to commemorate any Great Events at all. (This is certainly true as far as peasants are concerned, for . . . they tend to stress their social identity through images of resistance to the state, which are peculiarly unlikely to get into Great Events history.) There is a more specific reason why such choices are important, too: they show that these differences in commemorations are internal to communities, and not imposed from outside, whether by literature or schooling or the media, which would all have made memories more homogeneous, and would scarcely have failed to stress the Revolution and Napoleon. This cannot be repeated too often: however much a novel or a schoolteacher's story can affect the *content* of a memory of an event held by an individual or even a social group, it will have much less effect on which *sorts* of events social groups will characteristically choose to commemorate, which are linked to deeper patterns of identity. . . . Peasants do not, unfortunately, spend most or even much of their time revolting. But revolts are useful for our purposes, if for no other reason than that it is at such times that outside observers (particularly before this century) bother to write down anything peasants actually *say*. What they say about the past at such times tends to fall into certain broad types. One is the commemoration of past local resistance itself, most notably resistance against the state (revolts against landlords—which were anyway often smaller in scale and more temporary—do not seem to produce the same long-term resonance and narrative force in local societies). Another is the remembrance of a Golden Age of just royal rule over the country concerned, in the name of which the peasants are resisting present rulers who are less just. A third is the more legendary nobility . . . which can serve as an image of absolute justice, much more divorced from time and place. A fourth, still more distant, is the millenarian image of divine justice at the very beginning of time, set against which no human society can ever be wholly legitimate.

James Fentress and Chris Wickham, *Social Memory,* pp. 96, 108–109

Parts II and III are a tandem set picking up from Part I and preparing for another tandem set in Parts IV and V. That preceding Part I explained the earliest continuation that I intended to reconstruct between the historical Jesus and Christian origins—namely, the continuation of Jesus' companions from before to after his execution. It also explained the *why* of that focus, why I considered that study worth undertaking despite all its obvious difficulties. After *why* comes *how,* but in between comes *where.* *How* has to do with methodology—that is, with the logic of my method, with the reasons behind my use of this rather than that method. But it is *where* I get my materials and the type of materials I get that determine my method. So I move from *why* in Part I through *where* in Parts II and III to *how* in Parts IV and V.

The materials or data appear as either the memories of oral tradition or the texts of scribal transmission, and that duality corresponds to my distinction between this Part II and the next Part III. Part II concerns memory, orality, and the delicate interaction between orality and literacy in a premodern society that is millennia away from universal orality in the past, but also millennia away from universal literacy in the future.

Part II has four chapters. Chapter 3 looks at recent claims about peasant memory and oral transmission in the earliest Jesus tradition and focuses on implicit presuppositions that are neither theoretically justified nor methodologically verified. Chapter 4 considers memory itself, especially in terms of experimental psychology. Is memory recollection or reconstruction? Is it based on actual facts, personal desires, or social patterns? Is it most accurate when it is most certain, when it has visual images to collaborate its recall, when it can remember more and more details to fill in the general scenario? If, in other words, you claim that what Jesus said or did was *remembered,* what theory of memory do you presuppose? Chapter 5 moves from memory into orality and literacy based on classical studies from the 1930s. How, on the one hand, does the memory of epic poetry work for illiterate but traditional bards? How does it actually *work?* How, on the other hand, does the memory of short narratives work for literate but modern students? How does it actually *work?* Chapter 6, finally, is a short concluding section that proposes delicate interface rather than yawning chasm between orality and literacy in societies where there is only, say, 3 to 5 percent literacy. For, in the whole history of the world, there have been human societies without literacy, but there have been none without orality. The choice, therefore, is not between orality or literacy, but between orality without literacy or orality with literacy.

CHAPTER 3

THE MYSTIQUE OF
ORAL TRADITION

Perhaps illiterate people have particularly good memories to compensate for being unable to write things down, just as the blind are popularly believed to have especially keen ears or sensitive fingers. Such arguments must be rejected. . . . And while it would be logically possible to argue that literacy and schooling make memory worse, the fact of the matter is that they don't. On the contrary: cross-cultural studies have generally found a positive relation between schooling and memory. . . . Skilled performances by oral poets are found only in nonliterate societies because the concept of poetry itself changes when literacy appears. . . . Literal, verbatim memory does exist, nevertheless. It makes its appearance whenever a performance is *defined* by fidelity to a particular text.

Ulric Neisser, *Memory Observed*, pp. 241–242

How were Jesus materials transmitted in the forty years that elapsed from the death of Jesus to the writing of Mark's gospel in 70 C.E.? How did they continue to be transmitted thereafter until the canonical foursome became normative within Catholic Christianity after the middle of the second century? The standard answer is oral tradition, and comparative examples are then cited to affirm its existence and influence, its possibility and accuracy. Here is one recent example of that answer.

"The overwhelming probability is that most of what Jesus said, he said not twice but two hundred times with (of course) a myriad of local variations," according to N. Thomas Wright. That seems quite reasonable and unexceptionable. Therefore, Wright continues, "the only thing standing in the way of a strong case for Jesus' teaching being passed on effectively in dozens of streams of oral tradition is prejudice" (1992:423). He amplifies that theme later by suggesting that "this provides a window on a world of which, perhaps surprisingly, Crossan says nothing, for all his repeated emphasis on Jesus and his early followers as coming from peasant stock. It is the world of *informal but controlled oral tradition*. . . . It enables us to explain, without as yet having recourse to complex theories either of synoptic relationships or of a freely expanding tradition, the way in which again and again the story comes out slightly differently, but the *sayings* remain more or less identical. . . . Ironically, therefore, by agreeing with Crossan upon the vital importance of setting Jesus in his Mediterranean peasant culture, we have reached a conclusion which radically undermines Crossan's own historical reconstruction" (1996:134–136). If, for example, we have divergent versions of an aphorism in the four canonical gospels, it could be explained as four divergent Jesus-tellings of the same saying. It *could*, of course. But it could also arise from a single stream of dependent and developing tradition—from, in other words, Matthew and Luke developing Mark, and John further developing that triple synoptic tradition. Nothing at all is achieved by calling that latter suggestion a prejudice; and, once the scribal dependence suggestion has been proposed, argued, and accepted by a vast majority of scholars, opponents cannot simply ignore or deride it. They must take it on frontally and disprove it. Scribal dependence *could* be wrong, but then so could the opposite explanation of oral independence.

Any study of the transition from the historical Jesus to earliest Christianity must, therefore, face this question of oral tradition, and that is where I begin this reconstruction. I bring to this question, however, certain presuppositions about the distinction between oral tradition, oral transmission, and oral sensibility, which I can best describe initially through autobiographical background.

Tradition, Transmission, Sensibility

Oral tradition was a fickle mistress with whom to flirt. But scholars could call in to their help the "fantastic memories" so "well attested" of illiterate people. They felt that a text could remain from one generation to another unaltered, or altered only by inconsequential lapses of memory. This myth has remained strong even to the present day. The main points of confusion in the theory of those scholars . . . arose from the belief that in oral tradition there is a fixed text which is transmitted unchanged from one generation to another.

Albert Bates Lord, *The Singer of Tales,* pp. 9–10

When I was in grammar school, my family lived in Naas, about twenty miles west of Dublin. During the Second World War petrol was restricted to professional necessity, so our Vauxhall car spent six years with its wheels removed and its axles on upturned butter-boxes in the garage. In those carless days when I was about nine or ten years of age, my father and I went for long walks along the main Dublin road. He recited poetry to me, and I learned it by heart. It was not *great* poetry, but the going price for Kipling's "Gunga Din"—whole, entire, and correct by the end of the walk—was sixpence. My father is gone now; so is the sixpenny piece, and so is the Naas-Dublin road as once it was. But I still recall large snatches of that poem, and with its recital come back the houses and fields of that road, the voice, smile, and walking-stick of my father.

Though the poem stays with me, what I experienced on those walks was not oral tradition, however. It was only oral transmission. My father and I both presumed a written text, a scribal tradition. It was in a book at home, and both our versions were certified against that archetype. Any disputes could be checked against that original, uniform version. The process was scribal tradition transmitted orally and received aurally. Both of us operated within scribal, not oral, sensibility. If we had operated within a scribal register but with an oral sensibility, we would have considered that written version to be just another performance comparable with our own (and in no way normative for it). But the words on the page controlled absolutely our remembrances and our repetitions. It was scribal tradition transmitted orally and received aurally within a scribal sensibility.

When I was eleven my family moved to Donegal as my father became manager of Ballybofey's Hibernian Bank (now gone also). I went to a centrally located boarding school, St. Eunan's College in Letterkenny, which had a large component of native speakers of Irish. All our classes (except English) were in Irish, and nonnative speakers like myself who wanted to improve our Irish went to certain regions around the west coast of Donegal in the summers to live with Irish-speaking families. It was still possible in those days to find individuals, illiterate in both Irish and English, who had received orally and passed on orally the ancient epic tales of Ireland. Such a process was, in the fullest sense of the word, oral tradition. It was the tradition repeated in creative performance by individuals who had learned their craft not as students from books but as apprentices from masters. There was no single archetypal or uniform version, but a multiform or pluriform performance from a traditional narrative matrix.

Meanwhile, back at school we learned by heart at least ten lines of Irish poetry and ten lines of English poetry or Shakespearean soliloquy for each day's class. Memorization was the presupposition of discussion, since we were trained to argue not from the book but from what we knew by heart. When we took the country-wide and government-set intermediate or final high school exams, for instance, we were expected to argue for or against propositions concerning that poetry, "quoting freely" from memory. That was marvelous education, but it had nothing whatsoever to do with oral tradition. We gave, in class, the oral rendition of what we had memorized from written text, and we gave, in examination, the scribal rendition of that same memorization. Oral tradition in which the tradition is received orally and transmitted orally (often by illiterates) within the discipline of creative performance is a different world from scribal tradition transmitted orally within the discipline of exact (as best we could!) memorization.

Those experiences left me with a very great respect for oral tradition. We, after all, traveled to listen to those storytellers; they did not travel to listen to us. But I learned early the difference between oral tradition and oral transmission and between scribal and oral sensibility. I also learned early that tradition is not just gossip, rumor, or even memory. But terms must be used carefully and exactly. What those native Gaelic speakers on Donegal's Atlantic coast retained and performed was oral tradition. You could call any given enactment the oral transmission of that oral tradition. The poetry I memorized on walks with my father was the oral transmission of a scribal tradition: he had read and memorized from a book, he repeated it to me orally, and I memorized it from his voice. The poetry and soliloquies I memorized in high school were the scribal transmission of a scribal tradition. Those native speakers operated within oral tradition, transmission, and sensibility. Neither I, my father, nor my teachers did. Correct, for us, was what the book said. Correct, for them, was how the tradition operated. It is possible, of course, to imagine someone operating within a scribal tradition but having an oral sensibility. Such a person would treat a written version as just another performance of the poem or story, and, even as they were memorizing or transcribing it, they could perform it anew.

Is it correct, then, to describe the earliest transmission of Jesus materials as *oral "tradition"*? How exactly did such a *tradition* work? And, if *oral tradition* is not the best name for the process, how did any of the historical Jesus' words and deeds survive into earliest Christianity (if, in fact, they did)?

Evidence of Orality

Some more recent scholarship reflect[s] a way of viewing early Christianity and the gospel traditions that takes it as highly probable that traditions originally existed in oral form, and the writing down of the synoptic, or canonical gospels, did not exhaust them. . . . The problem in making such a claim is that it cannot be demonstrated, as likely as it may seem. Oral tradition, as real as it may have been, is uncontrollable and ephemeral unless it survives to us in written form.

Dwight Moody Smith, "The Problem of John and the Synoptics," pp. 152–153

It is hard for me to imagine more confusion and misinformation than accompanies current presuppositions about memory, orality, and literacy in connection with the Jesus traditions and the gospel texts. I choose two examples from a recent and massive study on *The Death of the Messiah* by Raymond E. Brown to indicate some of those presuppositions. But first a word of background.

There are five early versions of the passion of Jesus still extant, in the gospels of Matthew, Mark, Luke, John, and Peter. Those first four have always been available in complete accounts within the New Testament, but the last one was only discovered in fragmented papyri from Egypt within the last hundred years. My examples concern the interaction of memory, orality, and literacy in determining the relationship between those five texts.

The first example involves the dependence of Matthew and Luke on Mark. A large consensus of gospel scholarship agrees that Matthew and Luke used Mark as one of their main literary sources and that they did so independently of one another. In terms of *our* but not *their* world, they copied or plagiarized from him. That explains why the *order* of their accounts follows his sequence of events and why the *content* of their accounts develops his version of events. That hypothesis, in other words, explains why, when, and where they agree together with Mark. But what about those places where they agree together *against* Mark? What about those cases where Matthew and Luke are copying from Mark but both contain an element not present in Mark? Scholars call those cases *the minor agreements of Matthew and Luke against Mark,* and they are an objection (but not an insurmountable one) to that general theory of Matthean and Lukan dependence on Mark. Here are two instances of such minor agreements from the account of Jesus' trial before the Jewish authorities.

One instance records what happened to Jesus after he was declared guilty and was being abused by those around him:

Matthew 26:67	Mark 14:65	Luke 22:63
Then they spat in his face and struck him; and some slapped him, saying,	Some began to spit on him, to blindfold him, and to strike him, saying to him,	Now the men who were holding Jesus began to mock him and beat him; they also blindfolded him and kept asking him,
"Prophesy to us, you Messiah! *Who is it that struck you?"*	"Prophesy!"	"Prophesy! *Who is it that struck you?"* They kept heaping many other insults on him.
	The guards also took him over and beat him.	

Matthew and Luke each make their own separate changes on their Markan source, and that represents no theoretical problem. But how does one explain those italicized words, representing verbatim the same five words in Greek, found in both Matthew and Luke but not in Mark?

Another instance records what happened to Peter after his triple denial of Jesus as he recalled the prophecy of Jesus:

Matthew 26:75	Mark 14:72	Luke 22:61
Then Peter remembered what Jesus had said:	Then Peter remembered that Jesus had said to him,	Then Peter remembered the word of the Lord, how he had said to him,
"Before the cock crows, you will deny me three times." *And he went out and wept bitterly.*	"Before the cock crows twice, you will deny me three times." And he broke down and wept.	"Before the cock crows today, you will deny me three times." *And he went out and wept bitterly.*

Once again, Matthew and Luke each make their own separate changes on their Markan source, and that represents no theoretical problem. But how does one explain those italicized words found in both Matthew and Luke but not in Mark? And once again we are dealing with verbatim the same five words in Greek. Even that word *wept,* which is in all *three* texts, has the same case in Matthew and Luke but a different one in Mark.

My present interest is not in the solution to the minor-agreements problem in general (or even to those instances in particular). I ask only whether oral memory has anything to do with solving the problem, and, more important, whether claiming such a solution betrays a misunderstanding of memory, orality, and literacy.

In *The Death of the Messiah,* Brown solved those preceding cases by proposing oral tradition. Matthew and Luke, in other words, knew not only Mark's written text (which they had in front of them) but also an oral tradition of the same events—a tradition that contained the italicized words (44–45, 784, 857). Thus the solution to "Who is it that struck you?" is "the oral approach . . . [as] the key to important agreements between Matt and Luke who scarcely worked on texts totally isolated from the way these stories continued to be narrated orally among Christians" (579). And that is also the solution to "And he went out and wept bitterly," because "even after drawing upon Mark, in a popular narrative like this which was surely told and retold, both evangelists were influenced by oral tradition, and in that tradition an emotional phrase like this was already fixed" (609, 611 note 43). This presumes that oral versions of an event (if such existed) were so syntactically fixed that they could override the syntactically fixed written versions. It presumes, in other words, that those oral versions were so verbally precise that they could add a five-word verbatim sequence at one point in a scribally copied version without otherwise disturbing its original content.

I find that proposal very unlikely for two reasons, which I give here as theses to be developed in what follows. First, memory is creatively reproductive rather than accurately recollective. Second, orality is structural rather than syntactical. Apart from short items that are retained magically, ritually, or metrically verbatim, it remembers gist, outline, and interaction of elements rather than detail, particular, and precision of sequence. "Even in cultures which know and depend on writing but retain a living contact with pristine orality, that is, retain a high oral residue, ritual utterance itself is often not typically verbatim," as Walter Ong noted. "The early Christian Church remembered, in pretextual, oral form, even in her textualized rituals [words of the Last Supper], and even at those very points where she was commanded to remember most assiduously" (65). That is a very striking example: the words of eucharistic institution from the Last Supper are not cited word-for-word the same within the New Testament itself.

All of this will require much more explanation in what follows. But, for now, I ask, On what general theories or empirical studies of oral memory are Brown's conclusions based? On what general theories or empirical studies of the interaction between orality and literacy are Brown's conclusions based? Where did they come from?

The second example intensifies those questions. It involves the dependence of the *Gospel of Peter* (*GPet* in the quotes that follow) on the canonical or New Testament gospels as proposed, once again, by Brown (1994). I return to this subject in Chapter 25, but it is of such importance that I cite four different assertions of it here. A first example: "*GPet* . . . draws on the canonical Gospels (not necessarily from their written texts but often from memories preserved through their having been heard and recounted orally)" (1001). A second example: "*GPet* may have heard a reading of Matt or of Mark and have written from memory of that oral communication rather than from a written copy" (1057). A third example: "*GPet* is best explained in terms of the author's knowing the canonical Gospels (perhaps by distant memory of having heard them)" (1306). A fourth example: "*GPet* had [no] written Gospel before him, although he was familiar with Matt because he had read it carefully in the past and/or had heard it read several times in community worship on the Lord's Day, so that it gave the dominant shaping to his thought. Most likely he had heard people speak who were familiar with the Gospels of Luke and John—perhaps traveling preachers who rephrased salient stories—so that he knew some of their contents but had little idea of their structure. . . . I see no compelling reason to think that the author of *GPet* was directly influenced by Mark. . . . Intermingled in the *GPet* author's mind were also popular tales about incidents in the passion, the very type of popular material that Matt had tapped in composing his Gospel at an earlier period" (1334–1335). A fifth and final example: "*GPet* . . . was not produced at a desk by someone with written sources propped up before him but by someone with a memory of what he had read and heard (canonical and noncanonical) to which he contributed imagination and a sense of drama" (1334–1336).

I have argued against this sort of interpretation in earlier books (1988, 1995), and, for now, I wish only to emphasize its presuppositions about memory, orality, and literacy. It claims that, having heard or read the gospels of Matthew, Luke, and John, but working from "distant memory" rather than direct scribal copying, the author of the *Gospel of Peter* produced the text we discovered so very recently.

In an earlier formulation of that position, Brown was quite aware of the problems it might raise. "[T]he phenomena visible in GP [the *Gospel of Peter*] seem to demand ... oral dependence of GP on some or all of the canonical Gospels. . . . If the objection is raised that this introduces the uncontrollable into the discussion of dependence, so be it. Too often scholars transfer their desk situation with Gospel copies propped up before them into the ancient church" (1987:335). That position—that the author of the *Gospel of Peter* was dependent on the canonical gospels, but only from "distant memory"—is not, however, "uncontrollable." You can still ask questions. What theory of memory, for example, lies behind that position? Memory is often impossible to predict beforehand but usually quite possible to explain afterward. Since we have the texts of Matthew, Luke, and John available to us, we should be able to explain how the *Gospel of Peter* remembered as it did. Why, then—at least in general—did it retain this, omit that, and change something else?

An example may clarify my objection. During Senate Watergate hearings in 1973, John Dean testified that he had met Herbert Kalmbach in the coffee shop of the Mayflower Hotel in Washington, D.C., and thence gone directly to his room upstairs. But the hotel register did not record Kalmbach's presence on the day in question. Maybe, Dean responded, he used a false name? But, as it turned out, Kalmbach was registered that day at the Statler Hilton Hotel in Washington, and it had a coffee shop called the Mayflower Doughnut Coffee Shop (Loftus and Doyle 30). Although we may not always be able to explain the vagaries of memory so neatly as in that case, we must be ready to offer *some* explanation for the *Gospel of Peter*'s somewhat strange and even perverse memory of those passion narratives heard or read in the past. I recall this comment from James Fentress and Chris Wickham's *Social Memory*: "Memories have their own specific grammar, and can (must) be analysed as narratives; but they also have functions, and can (must) also be analysed in a functionalist manner, as guides, whether uniform or contradictory, to social identity" (88). What, then, is the logical coherence, narrative grammar, and social function of *Peter*'s memory in Brown's hypothesis?

Brown compounds that difficulty when he offers the following "contemporary comparison" in support of his theory about the origins of the passion story in the *Gospel of Peter*. "Let me suppose that we selected in our own century some Christians who had read or studied Matt in Sunday school or church education classes years ago but in the interim had not been reading their NT. Yet they had heard the canonical passion narratives read in church liturgies. Also they had seen a passion play or dramatization in the cinema, on TV, or on the stage, or heard one on the radio; and they had attended a church service where preachers were using imagination to fill in PN [passion narrative] lacunae and were combining various Gospel passages, e.g., a Good Friday three-hours or Seven-Last-Words service. If we asked this select group of Christians to recount the passion I am certain that they would have an idea of the general outline, but not necessarily be able to preserve the proper sequence of any particular Gospel. . . . They would remember some catch phrases . . . one or two of his sayings ('words') on the cross . . . the more vivid Gospel episodes . . . characters like Pilate, Herod, and the high priest. . . . There would be a tendency to portray more hostiley the enemies of Jesus. . . . And amid the remembrances of the passion from the Gospels there would be an admixture of details and episodes not in the Gospels. . . . In other words, we would get from our test group of Christians modern parallels to *GPet*" (1336). In other words, the *Gospel of Peter*'s remembrance of things past would be exactly like that of any ordinary group of Christians chosen more or less at random and asked to recall the passion narrative.

That assertion cries out for experimental testing. As a minimal but unscientific test, write out your own remembrance of the passion story and see if it reads at all like the *Gospel of Peter*. As a maximal but still unscientific test, I once asked my undergraduates in a general-education class at DePaul University to write me their recollections of Jesus' passion story, including the arrest, trial, execution, and burial. I told them that it was an experiment that I would explain more fully after they had completed it. They were promised five final-grade points no matter what they wrote but were asked to guarantee me in writing that they would not ask anyone for help or look up any biblical sources. They were simply to write me that story as they remembered it.

I received about thirty-two summaries. There were some rather amusing details. Quite a few spoke about "Pontius Pilot," and one mentioned "the trader Judas." One student remembered "something about Jesus descending into hell to check it out," and another said that, in the Garden of Gethsemane, Jesus asked God "if there was any other way to go about his pretty morbid situation. The answer by Almighty God was, nope." There were also a few understandable transpositions. One said that the dying Jesus "told Peter (?) to be a son to his mother (Mary)," and another said that "Mary cleaned the body and wrapped it in clean linens." Here is one complete example, chosen both for brevity and some interesting details:

Even though I have been educated at a Catholic Grammar School, High School, and now College, I can honestly say I do not remember much. I will though try to recall the Arrest, Trial, Execution, and Burial of Jesus in as much detail as possible.

What I do remember about the Arrest of Jesus is that Judas betrayed Jesus. Judas was one of Jesus' disciples and betrayed him anyway. He came to a town one day where Jesus was preaching and healing people and arrested him in front of the whole crowd. Judas and some men captured Jesus and took him away to what is known as the trial.

The Trial of Jesus was quite short from what I remember. They took Jesus into a room and questioned him about his identity. Some priest asked Jesus if he really was the Son of God, and Jesus replied "yes" and that did it. The crowd was shouting "crucify him", they thought he was an impostor. Their decision was to kill him which led to the Execution of Jesus.

I remember the Execution of Jesus as being very sad. I was taught that Jesus was stripped of his clothes, and hung on a cross with nails pounded through his hands and his feet. Also, they placed a crown of thorns on his head and beat him. I do not remember who tortured him, but I do remember that he was horribly abused. They did this in order to see if God would rescue his Son.

One of Jesus' disciples had buried him in a tomb. The people in the town had guards watching the tomb, because Jesus proclaimed that he would rise from the dead. Sure enough he did rise from the dead and the whole town was shaken up. Not many believed he was the Son of God, until now.

Neither in that summary nor in any other one did anybody come up with anything even remotely resembling the passion version of the *Gospel of Peter*. Nobody said anything about a crucifixion under Herod Antipas rather than Pontius Pilate or about one conducted by Jewish people rather than Roman soldiers. And nobody said anything about a resurrection taking place clearly and visibly before Jewish authorities and Roman soldiers. I would, in fact, challenge Brown to produce any such contemporary remembrances of the passion as he proposed to explain the strange memories in the *Gospel of Peter*. And that brings me back to my core objection: What theory of memory or remembrance undergirds those claims by Brown? Put another way, how should they be tested?

The answer is very obvious, but it involves combining social-scientific criticism with older methods such as historical and literary criticism in studying biblical texts. That is the only way to discipline claims about the intersection of memory, orality, and literacy based on assumed common sense, personal intuition, or hypothesis unaccompanied by either theoretical foundation or experimental confirmation. What, in other words, do we learn about the intersection of memory, orality, and literacy from oral fieldworkers operating inductively, or from social psychologists operating experimentally? It is time to confront the mystique of the oral Jesus tradition with some hard and inductive data from checked experience and controlled experiment.

CHAPTER 4

DOES MEMORY REMEMBER?

Experiments have shown that simply repeating a false statement over and over leads people to believe that it is true. Likewise, when we repeatedly think or talk about a past experience, we tend to become increasingly confident that we are recalling it accurately. Sometimes we are accurate when we recount frequently discussed experiences. But we are also likely to feel more confident about frequently rehearsed experiences that we remember inaccurately. Retrieving an experience repeatedly can make us feel certain that we are correct when we are plainly wrong. The tenuous correlation between a person's accuracy and confidence is especially relevant to eyewitness testimony. Witnesses who rehearse their testimony again and again in interviews with police officers and attorneys may become extremely confident about what they say—even when they are incorrect. This consequence of rehearsal is especially important because numerous studies have shown that juries are powerfully influenced by confident eyewitnesses.

Daniel L. Schacter, *Searching for Memory,* p. 111

Almost everything that common sense tells us about memory is wrong. And recently in North America ruined reputations, shattered lives, and destroyed families have been the price of that common sense. Nowhere has our misunderstanding of memory been so clearly and terribly demonstrated as in what we now call "false memory syndrome" but should always have known as "ordinary memory syndrome." Memory is as much or more creative reconstruction as accurate recollection, and, unfortunately, it is often impossible to tell where one ends and the other begins. We usually work from either or both with the same serene and implacable confidence.

Common sense tells us that, apart from deliberate lying, eyewitnesses are the best proof of guilt; and the more closely involved they are, the better their witness. It tells us that traumatic events, and especially those of maximum personal involvement, are hardest to forget, are most indelibly recorded in memory. It tells us that everything is recorded somewhere in memory even though we may not be able to find it easily or ever. Here, then, are three situations of memory at work, given to offset common sense's confidence. They are all derived from sources cited or experiments conducted by Elizabeth Loftus, a professor of psychology at the University of Washington and an expert witness in court cases on the dangerous deceits and confident inaccuracies of memory. My point in what follows is not that we remember some things and forget other things, or that we remember the important things and forget the unimportant things, or that we remember the main events and forget the specific details, or that we remember the core but forget the periphery (who determines which is which?). Those features of memory are understood in theory if not always properly assessed in practice. My point is how much fact and fiction, memory and fantasy, recollection and fabrication are intertwined in remembering. And how nobody, including ourselves, can be absolutely certain which is which, apart from independent and documented verification. Not even when we ourselves are remembering about ourselves.

Fact Becomes Non-Fact

> The laboratory evidence makes it plain that emotion aids memory for some sorts of material within an event, but undermines memory for other sorts of material.
>
> Daniel Reisberg and Friderike Heuer, in *Affect and Accuracy in Recall,* p. 183

The first situation of memory that we will address involves the move from *fact* to *non-fact*. It is a process we all know about but whose theoretical implications we seldom face. We remember an event and mistake the details. It happens all the time. But we may recite those details just as securely as we record the event.

Case 1.

Jack Hamilton was pitching for the California Angels against Tony Conigliaro of the Boston Red Sox on August 18, 1967, in Fenway Park. At the age of twenty, some three years before that game, Conigliaro led the American League with thirty-two homers. At twenty-two he was the youngest batter to reach one hundred homers. But at twenty-three he was hit by a first-pitch fastball from Hamilton that crushed the left side of his face, fractured his cheekbone, dislocated his jaw, and so damaged his vision that it eventually terminated his career. It was a Friday-night game, the first of four in the Angels' last visit to Boston for that season. Conigliaro was batting sixth in the Red Sox lineup and it was the fourth inning, no score, two out, nobody on. When Tony Conigliaro died of kidney failure in 1990 after round-the-clock nursing care since a heart attack in 1982, Dave Anderson of the *New York Times* interviewed Jack Hamilton about that fateful pitch (Tuesday, Feb. 27; p. B9). Hamilton remembered it as a day game because "I tried to go see him in the hospital late that afternoon or early that evening but they were just letting the family in." He also remembered his manager leaving it up to him whether to accompany the team for its next series in Boston that same season. (He said he went.) And he remembered that "it was the sixth inning when it happened. I think the score was

2–1, and he was the eighth hitter in their batting order. With the pitcher up next, I had no reason to throw at him."

There is, of course, no question about the *fact* of that accident. But, even though Hamilton admitted that "I've had to live with it; I think about it a lot," he got five details wrong in his recollection of what happened. It was a night not a day game; it was the Angels' last time in Boston that season; the batter was sixth not eighth in the lineup; the score was 0–0 not 2–1; and it was the fourth not the sixth inning. All of those are, of course, very minor and quite typical memory mistakes. But notice three features of that example. Even (or especially) in such a traumatic experience, the details are not protected by the indelible nature of the event itself. Further, there is no clear distinction in Hamilton's memory between correct and false details, even though, in this case, we have the independent ability to check and make that distinction for ourselves. Finally, there may be a logic to those mistakes in memory. Hamilton denied motivation twice in the interview: "I know in my heart I wasn't trying to hit him" and "I had no reason to throw at him." In general, his memory mistakes tended to support those claims, exonerating him from any suspicion of malice rather than accident. Hamilton also remembered details that shifted blame elsewhere: "He'd been hit a lot of times," Hamilton said. "He crowded the plate."

As Hamilton remembered and "had to live with it," Conigliaro's injury and his own innocence fused not just to recollect the event accurately but to reproduce the event appropriately. "The general principle," as Daniel Schacter wrote recently, "that memories are not simply activated pictures in the mind but complex constructions built from multiple contributions . . . also applies to emotionally traumatic memories" (209).

Case 2.

People, we are told, can recall with great accuracy where they were and what they were doing when they first heard the news of President Kennedy's assassination on November 22, 1963, or the space shuttle *Challenger*'s explosion on January 28, 1986. Those cases enlarge that individual memory of a traumatic pitching accident to a general remembrance of a traumatic national disaster. In 1977 two experimental psychologists, Roger Brown and James Kulik of Harvard University, coined the term "flashbulb memories" for recollections of "the circumstances in which one first learned of a very surprising and consequential (or emotionally arousing) event" (73). A flashbulb memory is "very like a photograph that indiscriminately preserves the scene in which each of us found himself when the flashbulb was fired" (74) and is "fixed for a very long time, and conceivably permanently, varying in complexity with consequentiality but, once created, always there, and in need of no further strengthening" (85). They even claimed a special biological mechanism for the specially vivid and detailed clarity of such specially imprinted memories. Thus, for example, thirteen years after President Kennedy's assassination, only 1 percent of their respondents had forgotten the circumstances in which they first heard about it. Unfortunately, however, there was no way to test the detailed accuracy (as distinct from the detailed imagery) of those memories. No baseline of memory had been immediately established against which later memories could be tested for inconsistency.

The morning after the *Challenger* explosion, the 106 students in Psychology 101 ("Personality Development") at Emory University filled out questionnaires on how they had first heard of the disaster. That established a baseline for their memories within twenty-four hours of the event itself in January of 1986. Then, in October of 1988, the forty-four of 106 students still at Emory were requestioned (only 25 percent remembered the original questionnaire!) and their two answers compared. Finally, in March of 1989, follow-up interviews were given to the forty students willing to participate in the final phase of the experiment. Here is one example of two questionnaire answers from the same subject:

Report of Memory After 24 hours (Jan. 1986)	Report of Memory After 2 ½ years (Oct. 1988)
I was in my religion class and some people walked in and started talking about [it]. I didn't know any details except that it had exploded and the schoolteacher's students had all been watching which I thought was so sad. Then after class I went to my room and watched the TV program talking about it and I got all the details from that.	When I first heard about the explosion I was sitting in my freshman dorm room with my roommate and we were watching TV. It came on a news flash and we were both totally shocked. I was really upset and I went upstairs to talk to a friend of mine and then I called my parents.

That case, as the researchers explain, was not unusual: "[N]one of the enduring memories was entirely correct, and . . . many were at least as wide of the mark. . . . [T]hose questionnaires revealed a high incidence of substantial errors" (Neisser and Harsch 9, 12). One other student, for example, who later recalled hearing the news from a girl who ran screaming down her dorm corridor, had actually heard it in the cafeteria and been too sick to finish her lunch. Another student later thought she had been at home with her parents when it happened, although she had actually been on campus.

When those second versions were compared with the first ones for accuracy and graded on a 0–7 scale for major *(location, activity, informant)* and minor *(time, others)* attributes of the event, "the mean was 2.95, out of a possible 7. Eleven subjects (25%) were wrong about everything and scored 0. Twenty-two of them (50%) scored 2 or less; this means that if they were right on one major attribute, they were wrong on both of the others. Only three subjects (7%) achieved the maximum possible score of 7; even in these cases there were minor discrepancies (e.g., about the time of the event) between the recall and the original report. What makes these low scores interesting is the high degree of confidence that accompanied many of them" (18).

Confidence in the inaccuracy is surely much more disquieting than the inaccuracy itself, and the visual vividness with which the inaccuracy was recalled was even more disquieting. The mean for accuracy was 2.95 out of 7, as I noted; the mean for confidence was 4.17 out of 5, and the mean for "*visual* vividness" was 5.35 out of 7! In the instance given above, for example, the subject rated the confidence of her 1988 memory at a 5 ("absolutely certain") for *location, activity, informant, others* and at a 4 for *time* (2:00 or 3:00 P.M., rather than 11:39 A.M. EST). Its actual rating was 0 on all counts.

In the follow-up interviews after the twin questionnaires had been compared, the researchers made another significant discovery. The subjects' memories for their second-version accounts remained "remarkably consistent" between October of 1988 and March of 1989, and when the researchers tried to help the subjects recover their first-version accounts, they found that "none of [their] procedures had any effect at all" (Neisser and Harsch 13). Even when subjects were shown their own original reports, they never "even pretended that they now recalled what was stated on the original record. On the contrary, they kept saying, 'I mean, like I told you, I have no recollection of it at all' or 'I still think of it as the other way around.' As far as we can tell, the original memories are just gone" (21). Flashbulbs illuminate but also blind: at least in this one case where checking was possible, neither visual vividness nor confident assertion bore any strong relationship to accuracy.

Fiction Becomes Fact

A healthy distrust of one's memory, and of memory in general, is not a bad idea. When all is said and done, memory is selective; the memory machine is selective about what gets in and selective about how it changes over time. . . . We seem to have been purposely constructed with a mechanism for erasing the tape of our memory, or at least bending the memory tape, so that we can live and function without being haunted by the past. . . . The malleability of human memory represents a phenomenon that is at once perplexing and vexing. It means that our past might not be exactly as we remember it. The very nature of truth and of certainty is shaken. It is more comforting for us to believe that somewhere within our brain, however well hidden, rests a bedrock of memory that absolutely corresponds with events that have passed. Unfortunately, we are simply not designed that way.

Elizabeth F. Loftus, *Memory,* pp. 147, 190

The next situation involves the move from *fiction* to *fact*. In the examples cited for the preceding situation, the core phenomenon was always factually certain. Hamilton struck Conigliaro and effectively terminated his career. President Kennedy died, the *Challenger* exploded, and people heard about those events. The details got lost and were replaced by mistakes. Confidence exuded illegitimately from core to periphery. But at least the central events actually took place and were remembered. In the following examples, however, a fictional story is transmuted by memory into a factual one.

Case 1.

There is a very famous footnote in one of Jean Piaget's books on childhood. Piaget is discussing why we have no memories of our very earliest years, and in that context tells the following story: "There is also the question of memories which depend on other people. For example, one of my first memories would date, if it were true, from my second year. I can still see, most clearly, the following scene, in which I believed until I was about fifteen. I was sitting in my pram, which my nurse was pushing in the Champs Elysées, when a man tried to kidnap me. I was held in by the strap fastened around me while my nurse bravely tried to stand between me and the thief. She received various scratches, and I can still see vaguely those on her face. Then a crowd gathered, a policeman with a short cloak and a white baton came up, and the man took to his heels. I can still see the whole scene, and can even place it near the tube station. When I was about fifteen, my parents received a letter from my former nurse saying that she had been converted to the Salvation Army. She wanted to confess her past faults, and in particular to return the watch she had been given as a reward on this occasion. She had made up the whole story, faking the scratches. I, therefore, must have heard, as a child, the account of this story, which my parents believed, and projected into the past in the form of a visual memory, which was a memory of a memory, but false. Many real memories are doubtless of the same order" (187–188 note 1). Notice that last bit: reconstruction, visualization, and even newly "remembered" details do not guarantee accuracy. Lie had become memory; fiction had become fact.

Case 2.

A scene from the 1944 movie *A Wing and a Prayer* focused on the three-man crew of a navy torpedo bomber in the South Pacific. As the crippled plane plunged downward and the gunner prepared to parachute, the pilot said to his wounded and immobilized radioman, "We'll take this ride together." In a byline from "A Flying Fortress Base, England, Feb. 1, 1944," Jack Tait recorded a similar story in the *New York Herald Tribune*, but now it was one gunner who stayed with another trapped gunner: "Take it easy, we'll take this ride together." He admitted that he could not verify the story except as one "circulating at this base that has almost become a legend." That qualification was omitted when the *Reader's Digest* condensed the story in its issue of the following April.

Ronald Reagan told that story as an historical fact during his 1976 and 1980 presidential campaigns and then repeated it, on December 12, 1983, to the annual convention of the Congressional Medal of Honor Society in New York City. The story involved the pilot and ball-turret gunner of a B-17 over the English Channel: "He took the boy's hand and said, 'Never mind, son, we'll ride it down together.' Congressional Medal of Honor, posthumously awarded."

That last point, however, was open to verification, and when Lars-Erik Nelson, Washington bureau chief of the *New York Daily News,* checked the 434 Medal of Honor citations from World War II, he found no such act of heroism recorded anywhere. Presidential spokesman Larry Speakes, when questioned about the story's accuracy, said, "If you tell the same story five times, it's true." President Reagan, who had seen *A Wing and a Prayer* and was a regular follower of *Reader's Digest,* claimed that he recalled "reading a citation" recommending a medal for such a heroic act while he was himself in the army (Cannon 58–60).

It is unnecessary to claim that Reagan could not tell fiction from fact or propaganda from history. What happened in his memory was not as unusual as we might like to think. Fiction had become fact and was thereafter impervious to criticism. Who could prove there had been no such citation recalled from Reagan's army days? But, on the other hand, who believes there *was* one?

Non-Fact Becomes Fact

Could it be that Eileen's memory [allegedly repressed for twenty years, of her father, George Franklin, having murdered her best friend Susan Nason in Foster City, near San Francisco, on September 22, 1969] was put together by an overactive, fantasy-prone imagination, with bits and pieces of the factual story supplied by newspaper reports, television accounts, and numerous conversations that took place over the years?
Elizabeth F. Loftus and Katherine Ketcham, *The Myth of Repressed Memory,* p. 93

This third situation involves the move from *non-fact* to *fact.* It concerns not invented details of an event but the invention of an event itself. It is clearly the most disquieting of the three instances, but it does no more than bring those preceding ones to their logical conclusion.

Case 1.
Elizabeth Loftus describes another psychologist's experiment on remembering classmates from high school—an experiment that continued for many sessions over days and even months. "The longer they tried to remember, the more

names they came up with. The graph opposite shows one person's progress at remembering her classmates" (1980:130). That graph plotted the "number of recall sessions" (=10) against the "number of [correct] names recalled" (=220). That is extremely impressive: 220 correct names out of a possible 600, after ten hours of trying. But the graph also showed the number of "fabrications" (=100). "The subject who kept recalling more names with each attempt also produced more false constructions or fabrications. Many times the fabrication was the name of an actual person, but from a different class or different part of the woman's life. A substantial number of the names people remembered were fabrications. In this study, by the tenth hour of recall almost half of the newly generated names were false" (1980:133). In a controlled experiment such as this, with a documented database, it was possible, of course, to verify memory and to record 220 right and 100 wrong out of 600. In ordinary life, however, such fabrications are non-facts that easily became facts.

Case 2.

Loftus also describes an experiment of her own—one that she devised to assess the possibility of creating in children a whole, traumatic, false memory and having it taken thereafter as fact. To avoid any ethical impropriety, the traumatic incident had to be temporary and have a happy ending: "Would it be possible to make someone believe that they were lost in a shopping mall as a child when, in fact, they had never been lost in a shopping mall?" (Loftus and Ketcham 1994:96). The experiment, which was but a preliminary probe for a more scientifically controlled one to follow, involved five people, aged from eight to forty-two, who were told by a family member that they had been lost at around five or six years of age in some large building complex. In all cases the false memory was accepted as true and embellished immediately with newly invented details. "The subjects' willingness to expand on the memory and provide details that were not even hinted at in the initial suggestion seemed to indicate that the memory was very real indeed" (99). One example will suffice.

An older brother presented his fourteen-year-old sibling with a single-paragraph description of four childhood events, three true and one false. He was asked to write about all four events every day for five days and record anything he could remember about each. If he could not remember, he was simply to record that fact. Here is the false memory followed by the boy's comments on it for each of the five days:

> It was 1981 or 1982. I remember that Chris was five. We had gone shopping at the University City shopping mall in Spokane. After some panic, we found Chris being led down the mall by a tall, oldish man (I think he was wearing a flannel shirt). Chris was crying and holding the man's hand. The man

explained that he had found Chris walking around crying his eyes out just a few moments before and was trying to help him find his parents.

Day 1: I remember a little bit about that man. I remember thinking, "Wow! He's really cool!"

Day 2: That day I was so scared that I would never see my family again. I knew that I was in trouble.

Day 3: I remember Mom telling me never to do that again.

Day 4: I also remember that old man's shirt.

Day 5: I sort of remember the stores.

Chris also recalled a conversation with the man—"I remember the man asking me if I was lost"—and remembered that he had had balding hair and glasses. Chris freely embellished his memory of the false event (even though, about one of the *true* events, he kept saying for five days, "I still can't remember"). Chris's mother, on the other hand, consistently maintained over the five days that she could not recall the event. On the fifth day, for example, she said, "For some reason I feel guilty about this, that I can't remember" (97–99).

Memory Against Mystique

Studies of the Jesus tradition within the New Testament, which spans decades only and not generations and which is the cherished property of only a minority . . . would . . . fall within the realm of *oral testimony* and not of *oral tradition*.

Øivind Andersen, in *Jesus and the Oral Gospel Tradition*, p. 17

I do not suggest that we never remember anything correctly. That would be absurd. Neither do I suggest that memory is but another name for imagination, or that we make it all up under the influence of suggestion and society. That would also be absurd. But all those preceding cases serve, first, to mitigate the serene complacency of common sense about memory and, second, to warn us that, while we do certainly remember, we remember by a reconstructive process. That reconstructive process mixes recollected facts from an actual happening with ones seen, heard, or imagined from similar happenings. That reconstructive process recalls gist rather than detail, core rather than periphery—and somebody must then decide which is which. (In an eyewitness identification of a murderer, for example, is a beard gist or detail, core or periphery?) That reconstructive process often claims equal accuracy and veracity for what we actually recall and for what we creatively invent.

But what is most important for here and now is to place this chapter on memory, on what experimental psychology can show and cognitive neuro-science can explain, in tension with Chapter 3, "The Mystique of Oral Tradition." Recall Brown's use of oral tradition to explain those minor agreements of Matthew and Luke against Mark in the passion narratives. Recall also his explanation of the *Gospel of Peter* as memory of hearing or reading the New Testament gospels in the distant past. On what theory of memory can you claim that a writer using a written source overrides that written version with a syntactically precise recollection from oral tradition? On what theory of memory can you explain the differences between Peter and either Matthew, Mark, Luke, or John as Peter's inexact recollections? How and why did that reconstruction come out as it did?

Take another example. James Dunn, writing about the multiplication of the loaves and fishes, notes that "in every case where a *number* is given, there is precise agreement between all four Gospels—2,000 denarii . . . 5 loaves and 2 fish . . . 5000 men . . . 12 baskets of fragments" (363). From that perfectly correct observation, he draws the following conclusion: "The fixed points seem to have been the numbers; the other details of agreement are mostly contingent on them and would almost inevitably be involved in the unfolding of a story round these details. But this is precisely what we would expect in oral tradition—fixed points of detail which the Christian retelling the story would elaborate in his own words, so that while language and other detail might diverge, and diverge quite markedly . . . the substance of the story remained constant" (364). But do human memory and oral tradition operate by recalling such numbers exactly and recreating the story around them, or by remembering the story's core, gist, or outline and recreating those numbers in performance? And if the latter case is more likely, the absolute persistence of those specific numbers in both intra- and extra-canonical versions must indicate very early ritualization of the story.

Maybe, however, a group unable to write and therefore much more dependent on oral tradition has different or better memories than we have. All those cases cited above were contemporary ones from within a scribal culture. Since the culture of Jesus was between 95 and 97 percent illiterate, memory and orality may have interacted in ways quite different from the modern world. It is necessary, next, to look at the intersection of memory, orality, and literacy. But I always presume in what follows that this chapter has warned us to be very, very careful about memory, even when it is most sure of itself. I do not think that eyewitnesses are always wrong; but, for example, if eyewitness testimony is a prosecution's *only* evidence, there is always and intrinsically a *reasonable doubt* against it. *Always.* As John Bohannon and Victoria Symons put it, "In studies of eyewitness testimony, the most favorable estimates of the correlation between confidence and accuracy are about .40" (67).

CHAPTER 5

A TALE OF TWO PROFESSORS

It was my privilege to study with Milman Parry [1902–1935] during the period, so prematurely cut short, when he was teaching Classics in Harvard College. . . . No one who knew Parry is likely to forget his incisive powers of formulation or to underrate the range and depth of his cosmopolitan mind. He has been appropriately hailed, by an eminent archeologist, as the Darwin of oral literature.

Harry Levin, in the Preface to Albert B. Lord, *The Singer of Tales,* n.p.

It was from Cambridge [University] that [Sir Frederic C.] Bartlett launched his quixotic challenge to the memory establishment of the 1920s and 1930s. He was convinced that his contemporaries understood neither the purpose nor the nature of memory, and that standard laboratory procedures just obscure its real characteristics. His challenge went almost unheard for 40 years, from the publication of *Remembering* (1932) until this decade [the 1970s], but it is unheard no longer.

Ulric Neisser, *Memory Observed,* pp. 3–4

This chapter is about two professors who published profoundly important research on the intersection of memory, orality, and literacy in the early 1930s. But, as the above epigraphs note, Parry's theories and experiments generated a major academic industry from the very beginning, while Bartlett's theories and experiments went mostly ignored until very recently. I pair them here, however, to establish and emphasize the parameters of that intersection between memory, orality, and literacy.

Homer in a Balkan Coffeehouse

The human accomplishment of lengthy verbatim recall [fifty words or more] arises as an adaptation to written text and does not arise in cultural settings where text is unknown. The assumption that nonliterate cultures encourage lengthy verbatim recall is the mistaken projection by literates of text-dependent frames of reference.

Ian M. L. Hunter, in *Progress in the Psychology of Language,* p. 207

I first met Homer in a classical high school in Ireland between 1945 and 1950. We read him in Greek, cribbed him in English, and translated him into Gaelic (there were no cribs or ponies in Gaelic). And we knew, with adolescent precision, how to translate so that the teachers could never be sure whether it was the Greek we did not know or the Gaelic. Certain set phrases, repeated with predictable if not numbing regularity, remain with me to this day. I recall none of them in Gaelic, some of them in Greek, and all of them in English. Maybe they seemed less strange and memorable in Greek or Gaelic—languages that were somewhat strange to us in any case. For example: the Homeric heroes were "the well-greaved Greeks"; the morning was "the rosy-fingered dawn"; the Aegean was "the wine-dark sea." But even if Greek warriors wore good bronze leg-guards and so were always "well-greaved," surely the dawn of a Greek mid-winter is not always "rosy-fingered" and the sea of a Greek mid-summer is not always "wine-dark." Why are those set and repeated phrases so typical of Homeric poetry?

That question was the focus of Milman Parry's master's thesis at the University of California (Berkeley) in 1923 and his major and minor doctoral theses at the University of Paris (Sorbonne) in 1928. Parry spoke of such phrases as "traditional epithets" or "formulae" and studied them in terms of Homeric meter and style. In that same year, 1928, Matija Murko gave three lectures for the Sorbonne's Institute of Slavic Studies on contemporary popular epic poetry in Yugoslavia. Parry's son Adam, who edited all his father's work in one 1971 volume, has noted that "it may have been Murko and his work that first suggested to Parry the possibility of finding in a living poetry an observable analogue to the poetry of Homer" (xxiv). In any case, it was the creative juxtaposition of ancient Homeric style and modern Balkan technique that led Parry to his basic conclusion that both phenomena arose from popular epic poetry performed orally by a traditional "singer of tales." Parry's fieldwork in Yugoslavia during 1934–35 brought back to Harvard over 12,500 texts—songs by singers and talks with singers taken either through dictation or on over 3,500 twelve-inch aluminum phonograph records. He had just begun a book called *The Singer of Tales* when an accidental gunshot brought life and research to an end.

Albert Bates Lord, who had studied with Parry at Harvard and accompanied him to Yugoslavia in 1934–35, chose that same title, *The Singer of Tales,* for the 1960 publication of his own 1949 doctoral dissertation in the Department of Comparative Literature at Harvard. He also extended the Balkan fieldwork into Albania in 1937, Yugoslavia again in 1950–51, and Bulgaria in 1958–59. The Parry-Lord contention, in comparing ancient Homeric and modern Slav tradition, is "that a comprehension of oral poetry could come only from an intimate knowledge of the way it was produced; that a theory of composition must be based not on another theory but on the facts of the practice of the poetry," as Lord put it in the Foreword of his own book. Specifically, how does the Serbo-Croatian tradition of epic song by illiterate performers, a tradition still alive in the 1920s and 1930s, actually work? And, when Parry and Lord transcribed their performance into written format, was that what somebody else had done long ago for Homer? More generally, how do illiterate poets produce thousands upon thousands of lines on demand? How do they remember? Do they recall thousands of lines *verbatim?* How do they compose?

PERFORMING THE TRADITION

In the beginning is the tradition. It gives performers three structural elements with which they work creatively, dynamically, and interactively. First of all, it gives them the general *stories,* the overall narratives. Bosnian Muslims tell, for example, "of the olden times, of the deeds of the great men of old and the heroes on both sides in the time when Sulejman the Magnificent held empire. Then was the empire of the Turks at its highest. Three hundred and sixty provinces it had, and Bosnia was its lock, its lock it was and its golden keys, and a place of all good trust against the foe" (Parry 1974:13). Next, it gives them the *themes,* which can be mixed and matched into those story frames. Standard themes, for example, are the ruler's council, the army's muster, or the wedding's guests. Finally, and most especially, it gives them hundreds of *formulae,* set phrases that can also be mixed and matched to form those themes and thence those stories. A formula, in Parry's definition, is "a group of words which is regularly employed under the same metrical conditions to express a given essential idea" (Lord 30). But lest this all sound mechanistic and automatic, here is a set of variations on a formula about *mounting one's horse,* culled from various places (52–53):

> Then he mounted his winged horse.
> Then he mounted his bedouin mare.
> Well, she mounted her white horse.
> Then they mounted their horses in the courtyard.
> They mounted two post horses.
> With a cry to Allah, he mounted and departed for Budim.
> Ðulić mounted his brown horse.
> They mounted their ready horses.

The formula, with its rhythms carved deep below conscious memory, is the heart of traditional oral epic poetry. But once again, lest this sound like mechanical juxtaposition rather than creative virtuosity, here are twin versions of the same moment in the same story by the same singer recorded fifteen years apart (Lord 62):

Halil Bajgorić recorded in 1935	Halil Bajgorić recorded in 1950
A dark Arab heard of this	A black Arab heard of this
Across the dark blue sea, the deep,	Across the sea, dark blue, deep,
And he mounted his bedouin mare,	That Stočević Alija had died,
Black as a raven she was.	And he secured himself and his mare.

Recall, also, that those fluid patterns in Serbo-Croatian epic are supported by using the *gusle,* a one-stringed mandolin-like instrument played on one's lap with a bow. The gusle supplies the rhythmic beat for ten-syllable lines into which those fluidly set formulae can be swiftly inserted while composing at about ten to twenty lines a minute. Two cases will serve as illustrations and prepare an understanding of what "ten thousand lines verbatim" means in traditional oral performance for illiterate epic bards.

Case 1.

Petar Vidić, of Stolac in Hercegovina, was, according to Lord, "no more than an average singer . . . the type of singer who must carry the brunt of the transmission of the art" (Lord 113). He is, in other words, a typical rather than an extraordinary example. The Parry collection at Harvard now contains four full versions of *Marko and Nina of Kostur* from that artist, as follows (71, 236–241):

1. Parry no. 6: dictated August, 1933, with a total of 154 lines
2. Parry no. 805: dictated December 7, 1934, with a total of 234 lines
3. Parry no. 804: recorded December 7, 1934, with a total of 279 lines
4. Parry no. 846: recorded December 9, 1934, with a total of 344 lines

Those divergent line-totals warn us immediately that the same story even from the same singer is not the same each time. And, for comparison, two versions of it were recorded from another singer, Halil Bajgorić, as follows:

5. Parry no. 6695: recorded (disc) in 1935, with a total of 464 lines
6. Lord no. 84: recorded (wire) in 1950, with a total of 209 lines

A detailed comparison is even more interesting. Besides those four full versions noted above, Petar Vidić did two shorter trial runs (Parry nos. 803a, 803b) of the first twenty lines in preparation for the recording in Parry no. 804. Here are those six versions of the story's opening stanzas (Lord 74–75):

Parry #6 [8 lines]	Parry #803a [9 lines]	Parry #803b [7 lines]	Parry #804 [7 lines]	Parry #805 [6 lines]	Parry #846 [5 lines]
Marko Kraljević	Marko Kraljević arose early In his white well-built tower In Prilip the white city, He arose and drained his coffee,	Marko Kraljević arose early In his white well-built tower, Before dawn and white day.	Marko Kraljević arose early In his white tower of stone.	Marko Kraljević arose early In Prilip in his white tower,	Marko Kraljević arose early In his white tower of stone,
is drinking wine	And began refined brandy;		He arose, began his brandy, And Marko drained the brandy.		
With his old mother,	With him was his old mother, His old mother it was,	Next to him his old mother,	Next to him his old mother,	And next him his old mother,	And next him his old mother,
And with his true love,	And next the mother Kraljević's wife,	Next to his mother his true love,	Next his mother his true love,	And next the mother his true love,	And next his mother his true love,
And with his only sister.	And next his wife the well-adorned Anđelija.	And next to his love, the well-adorned Anđelija. This was his true sister.	And next his love, the well-adorned Anđelija.	And next his love his sister Anđelija.	And next his love his true young wife [mistake for sister]
When Marko had drunk his wine, Then Marko brimmed the glass To the health of his old mother, And his love and his only sister.				He toasted them in clear brandy	

These openings, varying from five to nine lines, indicate quite clearly how the formulaic possibilities appear and reappear creatively. But even nos. 803a and 803b, dictated in preparation for 804 on the same day, show no attempt to memorize in what we would call verbatim fashion.

Case 2.

If Petar Vidić was an ordinary singer, Abdullah (or Avdo) Međedović was an extraordinary one. Nikola Ivanov Vujnović, Parry's field assistant from 1933 to 1935, said of him in 1939, "When Avdo is no longer among the living, there will be no one like him in singing." After Međedović died in 1955 at about age eighty-five, Lord agreed with that assessment: "It may well be that he was the last of the truly great epic singers of the Balkan Slavic tradition of oral narrative song" (Parry 1974:11–12). If Homer was the ancient Greek Singer of Tales, Avdo Međedović "is our present-day Balkan Singer of Tales" (Lord, Foreword). He was born around 1870 and had followed his father into butchering animals and singing songs by the time he was fifteen. He picked up Turkish during nine years in the army but never learned to read or write in any language. His superiority as a performer was a thing of both quantity and quality.

Quantity. Međedović had a repertoire of fifty-eight epics. In 1935, when he considered himself somewhat past his peak, he recited nine epics for Parry and Lord with a total of 44,902 lines recorded and 33,653 dictated. In 1950–51, when Lord returned to Bijelo Polje, Međedović recorded three more epics with a total of 18,168 lines. That brings his transcribed songs to just below 100,000 lines. Furthermore, two of the longest songs in the Slavic tradition of oral epic are transcribed from his repertoire in 1935, one at 12,323 and another at 13,331 lines. "Avdo could sing songs of about the length of Homer's *Odyssey*. An illiterate butcher in a small town of the central Balkans was equaling Homer's feat, at least in regard to the length of song" (Parry 1974:8).

Quality. In 1935 Lord deliberately set up an experiment with Međedović. Another singer, Mumin Vlahovljak of Plevlje, performed a song of 2,294 lines that the listening Međedović had never heard before. Then Parry, without warning, asked Međedović if he could repeat the performance. He addressed his version courteously to his "colleague Muminaga," but his repetition ran to 6,313 lines (Parry 1974:11). That almost-three-fold expansion is exemplified in the twin descriptions of the tale's hero, Bećiragić Meho, as those original full versions are summarized by Lord (223):

Bećiragić Meho by Mumin Vlahovljak [description of Meho: 11 lines in original full version]	*Bećiragić Meho* by Avdo Međedović [description of Meho: 34 lines in original full version]
The poor orphan Meho was at the foot of the assembly, near the door.	Near the poor of the tavern sat a sad young man.
He wore only cotton pants and shirt, but he had a fine sash and two beautiful golden pistols.	He did not wear breastplate or helmet with plumes, but only cotton trousers and a silk shirt; over his fine sash was an arms belt in which were two golden pistols. (They are described.) He hung his head and gazed at the *aghas*.
Nobody in the assembly offered him coffee or tobacco or a glass. He gazed sadly at the company.	Nobody spoke to him nor offered him a glass. His heart was wilted like a rose in the hands of a rude bachelor.

A somewhat similar difference appeared in two versions of *The Wedding of Smailagić Meho*, performed by Međedović himself, as transcribed first for Parry in 1935 and then, with no intervening performance, for Lord in 1950. The story of Mehmed (or Meho), son of Smail, ran to 12,323 lines in the former but only 8,488 lines in the latter version. By 1950 Međedović was much older, sicker, and weaker. Nonetheless, as Lord noted, that length was still "a prodigious undertaking which few, if any, younger men could have accomplished" (Parry 1974:11).

PERFORMER MEETS RECORDER

It is clear from the preceding cases that before a Homer and a Međedović found a literate transcriber, they operated in a medium that was traditional in story, theme, and formula, structural and rhythmic in composition, and creatively multiform in presentation. But here is a very interesting postscript on the subject of verbatim repetition, of word-for-word and line-for-line accuracy, at that very intersection of memory, orality, and literacy. In the four following examples, watch how literate scribe and illiterate poet talk past one another on that subject. Watch how the very words *same* and *not different* are *not the same* but *different* for each speaker. Watch, especially, a certain nervousness or even truculence as the singer wrestles with the writer. He recognizes his doom.

Case 1.

The singer, Đemó Zogić, told Nikola Vujnović, Parry's research assistant in the Balkans, that one Ramadan he had heard another singer, Sulejman Makić, sing a song he had never heard before and that he had been able to repeat it himself the very next night (Lord 27):

N: Was it the same song, word for word and line for line?

Đ: The same song, word for word and line for line. I didn't add a single line, and I didn't make a single mistake. . . .

N: Tell me this: If two good singers listen to a third singer who is even better, and they both boast that they can learn a song if they hear it only once, do you think that there would be any difference between the two versions? . . .

Đ: There would. . . . It couldn't be otherwise. I told you before that two singers won't sing the same song alike.

You can already see in the contradiction between those interchanges the clash of oral and scribal imagination: "word for word and line for line" has changed meaning from the illiterate Đemó to the literate Nikola. And that last line sounds mildly truculent, as if Đemó knows that "the same" is a different concept for each speaker. Actually, both Makić's and Zogić's versions were recorded by Parry and, as Lord underlines, "they are recognizable versions of the same story," but "they are not close enough . . . to be considered 'exactly alike'" (28). Of course not. But Zogić was not lying, because, for him, *verbatim* simply meant *traditional*. A literate actor can memorize and perform thousands of lines of epic poetry. An illiterate singer can also memorize and perform thousands of lines of epic poetry. Both may claim exact and even verbatim fidelity. But between them stands the presence of written text, and thereby memorization, performance, and exactitude take on different meanings in each case.

Case 2.

In another instance, Avdo Međedović was discussing with Nikola Vujnović two singers from whom he had heard the same story (Parry 1974:73):

A: ... [T]here wasn't any difference between them that I could tell.
N: They sang it just the same?
A: They sang it exactly alike.
N: You mean everything exactly alike?
A: Everything. No more than ten words' difference in the whole thing.
N: But I'll bet the decoration of the song was different, now wasn't it—the things that they dressed up in the song?
A: That's just what I mean—it wasn't.
N: Nothing different at all?
A: Nothing, so help me, no more, no less.
N: Is it at least possible that you do it a bit more amply than they did?
A: Well, maybe I decorate it better.

At this stage, and even without the transcript evidence of those two other singers' version, we can take it absolutely for granted that the differences exceeded ten words. But in all such discussions, it is necessary to remember Međedović's announced principle that "whichever is the better is the true one" (Parry 1974:60).

Case 3.

Although many illiterate Balkan bards were operating in a purely oral tradition at the time of Parry and Lord's research, writing was, of course, a fact of life all around them. Lord warned of this problem: "The collector even in a country such as Yugoslavia, where published collections have been given much attention for over a century, some of which have become almost sacrosanct, must be wary; for he will find singers who have memorized songs from these collections" (Lord 14). Once you memorize from a written text, you are no longer an oral artist but a scribal artist performing orally. Here, however, there is a very delicate interface between the oral and the scribal, and it brings us back to Avdo Međedović and *The Wedding of Smailagić Meho*. How did he first hear this story of treachery by the Christian vizier of Buda against the Muslim sultan of the Turkish empire in the middle of the sixteenth century? The questioner, as usual, is Nikola Vujnović (Parry 1974:74):

N: How about *The Wedding of Smailagić Meho*?
A: Let's see—did I tell you about how I heard it from a songbook?
N: From a songbook?
A: Yes.

N: I believe you did. Who read it to you?

A: Hivzo Džafić. There was a lad here in the slaughter house, who got it from somewhere. . . .

N: How many times did he read it to you?

A: Five or six times.

N: Did you ever hear anyone sing it to the *gusle*.

A: No.

N: Are you sure you never heard it sung by anyone at all?—yes.

A: No, I didn't.

But Međedović treated the scribal version heard orally just as if it were another oral version. He informed his questioner that his rendition was longer, "yes, more, by at least twice"; and, as Lord emphasized in praising the originality of his adaptation, "magnificence is the keynote of Avdo's expansion" of the published text (Parry 1974:13).

A week or so later, in August of 1935, Nikola Vujnović went on to question Hivzo Džafić about the songbook he had read to Avdo Međedović The subject once again is "same" and "different," but watch the respondent's hesitations (Parry 1974:77):

N: Did he [Međedović] sing it just the way it was in the poem, or did he sing longer than that?

H: No, no, ah—so to speak, he, uh—, he sang it all exactly as it is in the book, but what I mean to say is that it got to be quite long by the time he was through with it because you see, it uh—, it doesn't take as much time to read it as it does to sing it.

N: Of course. But do you suppose there was possibly some difference, that he might have added something here or there?

H: Oh, I couldn't judge that at all.

N: So there wasn't anything added?

H: On my word of honor, I didn't notice anything to criticize. . . . [I]t's the same way in the book as it is when he sings it. If I were to take the book, and open it like this while he was dictating, I'd see exactly the same thing there with my eyes as he'd said.

It is as if the respondent were saying, "The singer is good. If to be good means it's the exact same version, then that it is; if to be good means it's different, then *that* it is. What do you want me to say?"

Case 4.

Finally, in an earlier conversation in July of 1935, Nikola Vujnović was again questioning Avdo Međedović about his art. "One of the lads" read *The Siege of Osjek* to him "several times" from a songbook. He then sang it before a large crowd in the coffeehouse (Parry 1974:66):

> When I had finished the song, the waiter brought me a cup of tea and a dime. I asked him: "Who ordered this?" He said: "The lieutenant over there wishes to honor you with the tea." And sure enough, there he was sitting up by the chimney. "And the dime is so you can buy tobacco." I said: "Give him my thanks." He called to me from where he sat: "Old fellow, are you literate?" All this happened only year before last. "No, I'm not." "So you don't read the newspapers?" "No." "Bravo! I'm here all the way from Lauž, and here's the songbook with this song in it. The way I read it, you haven't made a single mistake."

There the stage is fully set for the eventual triumph of literacy over orality. At a first stage, with Homer, for example, there was only the tradition of rhythmic epic narrative, and while it was, of course, traditional in story, theme, and formula, it was pluriform in composition, combination, and performance. At a next stage, writing and literacy have entered the picture, but the oral poet still treats a written text as just one among many possible performances. But ambiguities now abound, and intrusive scribal questioners ask not whether that performance is better or worse but whether it is verbatim or not. Finally, writing triumphs, and even oral creativity defends itself as verbatim exactitude. There is something terribly sad about Avdo Međedović's pride in recounting a compliment that dooms his craft to inevitable irrelevance. But, of course, there would be sadder events than that in store for the Balkans and for the town of Sarajevo, where Hivzo Džafić bought his songbooks.

Memory in a Cambridge Laboratory

Oral stories in their written form may be unusually schematic or even summarized versions of any given retelling. The schema only preserves the overall form of the story while allowing an individual narrator to elaborate details according to individual interests and purposes.

Jean M. Mandler and Nancy S. Johnson, "Remembrance of Things Parsed," p. 113, note 1

I turn now from Milman Parry to Frederic Bartlett in this tale of two professors studying memory inductively in the early thirties of this century. What Parry discovered about the memories of illiterate singers operating in an oral, epic, and rhythmic tradition has, for all practical purposes, nothing whatsoever to do with the memories of illiterate peasants operating within the Jesus tradition. In fact, the very term "oral tradition" cannot be used of the two transmissions without inviting serious misunderstanding and misapplication. To propose that Jesus and his first companions, precisely because they were illiterate peasants, would have shared special memory capacities akin, for example, to Parry's Balkan bards, is to ignore the presence of centuries-old tradition in the Balkan case and of total new-ness in the Jesus case. If, on the other hand, the traditions about Jesus had stayed alive for centuries primarily among illiterate Galilean peasants, their transmission might well have developed procedures analogous to those used by a Homer or a Međedović. In this case, however, Bartlett's experiments may be more useful than Parry's in assessing correctly the role of memory in the transmission of Jesus materials. And, with Bartlett, I return once more to a severely critical assessment of memory's accuracy, even (or especially) when it is most emphatic, assured, cer-tain, and secure of itself.

Bartlett's experiments involved the recall of eight different stories either by various subjects after differing lengths of time, which he termed *repeated repro-duction,* or by various subjects who had transmitted the story from one to another, which he termed *serial reproduction.* The story used as his main example "was adapted from a translation by Dr. Franz Boas of a North American folk-tale" (Bartlett 64). I went back, however, to check Bartlett's source in Boas and found two interesting details. Boas's original publication attributes the story to Charles Cultee of Bay Center, Washington, speaking in Kathlamet, the dialect of Upper Chinook used farthest down the Columbia River, and it summarizes the story like this (Boas 161):

> Two men are met by a canoe, the occupants of which invite them to join in a war expedition. One of them refuses, the other one goes, and in combat is wounded, though he does not feel any pain. The people carry him home and he discovers that they are ghosts. The next morning he dies.

But here is a very interesting detail ignored by Bartlett. "In order to ascertain the accuracy of his mode of telling," records Boas, "I had ['The War of the Ghosts'] . . . which he [Cultee] had told in the summer of 1891 repeated three and a half years later, in December, 1894. . . . They show great similarity. . . ." (Boas 5). We have, therefore, for that story, twin versions from 1891 and 1894 (Boas 182–184, 185–186). That allows us not only to compare Boas's twin versions with one another but also to compare both of them with Bartlett's transcription. Since my subject here is the interface between memory, orality, and literacy, I found that comparison quite interesting. Here are the endings of Boas's 1891 and 1894 versions and of Bartlett's 1932 transcription, which never mentions that duality. The section describes the death of the man who went with the ghosts.

"The War of the Ghosts" (1891)	**"The War of the Ghosts" (1894)**	**"The War of the Ghosts" (1932)**
He told it all, and then he became quiet.	Then he told them about it.	He told it all, and then he became quiet.
When the sun rose, he fell down.	Daylight came in the house. Then he fell down dead.	When the sun rose he fell down.
Something black came out of his mouth and blood came out of his anus.	*Blood came out of his mouth, and something black came out of his anus.*	*Something black came out of his mouth.*
His face became contorted. He was dead.		His face became contorted.
The people jumped up and cried.		The people jumped up and cried.
He remained dead.		He was dead.
	It looked like salal berries. His friend was well. He did not die, because he did not accompany the ghosts.	

Notice two minor details in the section I italicized. The changes between 1891 and 1894 are typical oral variations. The *structure* persists in memory: something comes out at both ends. But the *elements* can be freely organized in performance: black/mouth and blood/anus become blood/mouth and black/anus. One could also imagine two other equally valid performances of that same structure: blood/anus and black/mouth or black/anus and blood/mouth. Those changes are performatory variations, the free play of elements (black, blood, mouth, anus) within a fixed structural pattern (something comes from both ends of the human body). But look now at Bartlett's version. That is not the free variation of oral performance but the deliberate change of scribal copying. Call it hermeneutical not performatory variation, the effect of deliberate change rather than random performance. I presume, in other words, that it represents a gesture of delicacy, a minor censoring of the story's transmission, a decision that the anus has no place at Cambridge. But the oral difference between 1891 and 1894 as well as the scribal change between Boas and Bartlett are further warnings of how delicate is that place where memory, orality, and literacy intersect.

REPEATED REPRODUCTION

In this first set of experiments, twenty subjects—thirteen women and seven men—initially read the story through twice at their normal reading rates (Bartlett 65, 79). They were then asked for written reproductions almost immediately, and for consequent reproductions at divergent intervals of hours, weeks, months, and years. Bartlett, of course, gives not only the full narrative of "The War of the Ghosts" but also complete versions of his subjects' several reproductions. You can read fully, for example, how Subject P reproduced the story immediately and then after a fortnight, a month, two months, and, finally, two and a half years. But the extreme parameters of this experiment are established by two individuals.

Subject W had not reproduced the story after his first or immediate version until he tried it again six and a half years later. He wrote the story from long-distance memory using brief numbered items in such a way that one can see his actual process of recall and reconstruction, invention and rationalization. "This is a brilliant example of obviously constructive remembering," Bartlett comments. "The subject was very pleased and satisfied with the result of his effort, and indeed, considering the length of the interval involved, he is remarkably accurate and detailed. There is a great deal of invention, and it was precisely concerning his inventions that the subject was most pleased and most certain. The totem, the filial piety, the pilgrimage—these were what he regarded as his most brilliant re-captures, and he was almost equally sure of the black forest, once it had come in. . . . It will be noticed that the story as he constructed it is full of rationalisations and explanations, and most of the running comments of the subject concerned the inter-connexion of the various elements and were directed to making the whole narration appear as coherent as possible" (78). I am not sure if "remarkably accurate" is remarkably accurate. Totem, filial piety, pilgrimage, and dark forest are all pure inventions, and what Subject W does is brilliantly create a totally different story based on his recall of canoe, war party, and two "brothers" (in the original story they were "two young men"), one dying with "something black from mouth." It is hard to give a more classic example of *accurate remembrance* as *creative transformation*.

Subject C involved an even longer timespan: ten years. In the original story the two young protagonists were from "Egulac" and they went "up the river to a town on the other side of Kalama." But, as Bartlett records, "Sooner or later, the proper names dropped out of all the reproductions, with the single exception of the one in which they seemed, after ten years, to be the only readily accessible detail. As a rule, before they entirely disappeared, they suffered change. Egulac became Emlac, Eggulick, Edulac, Egulick; Kalama became Kalamata, Kuluma, Karnac, to give only a few of the variations. . . . The subject (C) read the story in the spring of 1917. In 1919 she unexpectedly saw me pass her on a bicycle and immediately afterwards found herself murmuring 'Egulac', 'Kalama'. She then recognised me, and remembered reading the story, and that these names were a part of the story. In the summer of 1927 she agreed to try definitely to remember the tale. She wrote down at once 'Egulac' and 'Calama', but then stopped and said that she could do no more. Then she said that she had a visual image of a sandy bank and of two men going down a river in a boat. There, however, she stopped" (82, 78).

Subjects W and C are beautifully extreme cases. One remembers a few details and constructs a totally different but very detailed and coherent plot from that residue. The other remembers almost nothing but the twin place names, which everyone else changes or omits. That serves to warn us that, with regard to individual memory, scientific prediction is impossible beforehand even if plausible explanation is possible afterward. I think, for example, that I could not have predicted, but I can probably explain, how Egulac became Eggulick.

From those experiments in repeated reproduction, Bartlett gives fourteen conclusions, two with subdivisions (93–94). They are too long for full citation, so I offer here those items that are the most important for my present purpose. First of all, "accuracy of reproduction, in a literal sense, is the rare exception and not the rule." Second, "with frequent reproduction the form and items of remembered detail very quickly become stereotyped and thereafter suffer little change," but "with infrequent reproduction, omission of detail, simplification of events and structure, and transformation of items into more familiar detail, may go one indefinitely, or so long as unaided recall is possible." Third, "in all successive remembering, rationalisation, the reduction of material to a form that can be readily and 'satisfyingly' dealt with, is very prominent." Bartlett also emphasizes that "several of the factors influencing the individual observer are social in origin and character. . . . [M]any of the transformations . . . were directly due to the influence of social conventions and beliefs current in the group to which the individual subject belonged" (118). I conclude with this permanent warning on memory as creation: "An observer who had completed one of his reproductions [after six weeks] casually remarked: 'I've a sort of feeling that there was something about a rock, but I can't fit it in'. He gave the matter slight consideration and finally rejected the notion. Two months later, without a word of comment or explanation, the rock took its place in the story. There was no rock in the original" (91).

SERIAL REPRODUCTION

As you would probably expect, matters do not get better in moving from repeated to serial reproduction. As the story was passed along one chain of ten subjects, for example, details that did not fit expectations were regularly omitted, and others were rationalized until they *did* fit expectations. By the end, on the level of the general story, "no trace of an odd, or supernatural element is left: we have a perfectly straightforward story of a fight and a death." By the end, on the level of specific detail, Egulac became Malagua, Momapan, Mombapan, and, finally, the Bay of Manpapan (120–125).

Here is another example along that tenfold chain. In the original story the young man who had fought alongside the war party of ghosts was wounded, returned home, and told everybody about the fight. In Bartlett's 1932 transcription, the tale concluded: "When the sun rose he fell down. Something black came out of his mouth. His face became contorted. The people jumped up and cried. He was dead" (65). The story, in other words, began "one night" and ended "when the sun rose." But this is how that terminal incident was transformed as it passed from one recounter to another along a chain of ten individuals (127, my numbers):

1. When the sun rose he fell down. And he gave a cry, and as he opened his mouth a black thing rushed from it.
2. When the sun rose he suddenly felt faint, and when he would have risen he fell down, and a black thing rushed out of his mouth.
3. He felt no pain until sunrise the next day, when, on trying to rise, a great black thing flew out of his mouth.
4. He lived that night, and the next day, but at sunset his soul fled black from his mouth.
5. He lived through the night and the following day, but at sunset his soul fled black from his mouth.
6. He lived during the night and the next day, but died at sunset, and his soul passed out from his mouth.
7. Before the boat got clear of the conflict the Indian died, and his spirit fled.
8. Before he could be carried back to the boat, his spirit had left this world.
9. His spirit left the world.
10. ("Nonsense," said one of the others, "you will not die.") But he did.

Those examples of serial reproduction result in this inevitable judgment from Bartlett: "Serial reproduction normally brings about startling and radical alterations in the material dealt with. Epithets are changed into their opposites; incidents and events are transposed; names and numbers rarely survive intact for more than a few reproductions; opinions and conclusions are reversed—nearly every possible variation seems as if it can take place, even in a relatively short series. At the same time, the subjects may be very well satisfied with their efforts, believing themselves to have passed on all important features with little or no change, and merely, perhaps, to have omitted unessential matters" (175).

In studying Bartlett's experiments with either repeated or serial reproduction of "The War of the Ghosts" and other stories, it is hard to avoid his basic conclusion about "the constructive character of recall" (176), and I emphasize that his term *constructive* clearly means "creative" or "inventive." "Human remembering is normally exceedingly subject to error. It looks as if what is said to be reproduced is, far more generally than is commonly admitted, really a construction, serving to justify whatever impression may have been left by the original. It is this 'impression', rarely defined with much exactitude, which most readily persists. So long as the details which can be built up around it are such that they would give it a 'reasonable' setting, most of us are fairly content, and are apt to think that what we build we have literally retained" (175–176).

I have now come full circle to where this chapter began. From students at Cambridge University in the first quarter of this century to students at Emory University in the last quarter of this century, experiments agree in warning us that memory is much less accurate than we think and that it *may be least accurate when it is most secure.* Do we conclude, then, that memory is a radical failure? Memory is a totally flawed human system? Memory is a pure delusion? Not at all. On the one hand, its function is to link us with the past in such a way that we can survive the present and project the future. It does that admirably. On the other hand, were a memory to retain everything it had heard or seen, our human system might shudder into immobility. And were it not programmed to organize and reorganize the past, to recreate and reinvent the past, we would probably be frozen in time and place forever. "Our memory systems," as Daniel Schacter sums them up, "do a remarkably good job of preserving the general contours of our pasts and of recording correctly many of the important things that have happened to us. We could not have evolved as a species otherwise. . . . Yet our stories are built from many different ingredients: snippets of what actually happened, thoughts about what might have happened, and beliefs that guide us as we attempt to remember. Our memories are the fragile but powerful products of what we recall from the past, believe about the present, and imagine about the future" (308).

None of that argues against the existence of mnemonists, of individuals otherwise normal or abnormal who can perform feats of extraordinary memory (which can be checked only against a fixed or scribal archetype, of course). The Latvian mnemonist whom cognitive psychologists call VP read Bartlett's transcription of "The War of the Ghosts" and then (having been given no warning that he would be asked to repeat it), reconstructed it, when asked, after one hour, then after six weeks, and finally after one year. His last two recalls correctly retained 55 percent of the nouns and 49 percent of the verbs from the original (Neisser 1982:392, 396–398). Exceptions, however, prove the rule. But there is, as we have seen, a profound difference between ten thousand lines performed from oral tradition and ten thousand lines memorized from written transcription.

CHAPTER 6

CHASM OR INTERFACE?

> It would seem that the discovery of the psychodynamics of primary oral cultures produced in some contemporary Western intellectuals an orality bias rather than a chirographic bias. . . . One appropriates the concept of primary orality from cultures with no knowledge whatsoever of writing, and transfers it all too easily to biblical Israel and Qumran, early Christianity and rabbinic Judaism, thus gratuitously introducing into those milieus the figment of a gaping dichotomy between oral tradition and written transmission. This procedure stands in need of revision.
>
> Shemaryahu Talmon, in *Jesus and the Oral Gospel Tradition*, p. 149

Where does all of that leave us? It leaves us with the need to go very, very carefully. If the transition from historical Jesus to earliest Christianity depends primarily on memory, we need to indicate clearly what theory of memory we are using in our analysis and what practice of memory we are observing in our evidence. If we invoke oral *tradition,* we need to explain in detail how the Jesus materials became a *tradition* and what evidence we have for the controls that make a tradition more than gossip, rumor, hearsay, or even memory. If we speak of oral *transmission* and/or aural reception, we need to be precise about what the ear retained from hearing texts read or words spoken. But, against all of that background, two distinctions will be especially important throughout the rest of this book.

A first distinction is between *matrix* and *format.* An example may help to clarify that distinction. As I ask you three questions, answer them to yourself before you read on, but watch your mind at work as you do so. First question: Do you remember somebody saying something about fearing fear? Second question: Do you recall whether the speaker was for or against fearing fear? Final question: What exactly and precisely did that person say? *Matrix* is that unphrased structure in memory that tells you President Franklin Delano Roosevelt warned a Depression-devastated America (in his first inaugural address, I think) that only fear itself was to be feared. But notice that even to describe that matrix I had to formulate it sequentially and syntactically. In our heads we have, as it were, a whirling concomitance or simultaneous dance of (no order!): do not fear, Roosevelt, fear itself, Depression. You might even lose Roosevelt and the

Depression but still recall somebody, sometime, warning against fearing fear itself. *Format,* on the other hand, is the exact and individual formulation. Which, if any, of the following did Roosevelt actually say?

> The only thing there is to fear is fear itself.
> Fear itself is the only thing there is to fear.
> There is nothing to fear but fear itself.
> Fear alone is all there is to fear.

Those options could, of course, be multiplied. For "there is" you could put "you have" or "we have," and so on. What was actually said is, "The only thing we have to fear is fear itself." That is the *scribal uniform,* the only correct quotation of Roosevelt's challenge. But, for an oral tradition, there is no uniform, there is only *oral multiform.* There are multiple, equally valid ways of saying and resaying that phrase. A single matrix or core structure gives us a performatory multiform. But, note well, a formulation that asserts one *should* fear fear itself is not another multiform but a simple goof—oral, scribal, or whatever.

I give another example, but now from the Jesus tradition. In oral discourse Jesus makes a conjunction that his hearers remember as a strange and disturbing equation of *children* and *kingdom.* Think of that conjunction, in whatever order, as the matrix. Jesus may have said it a dozen different ways or a dozen different times. But each time would have demanded an acceptable syntactical sequence, not just the utterance of two isolated words in whatever order. Think of that plurality as *multiform.* The hearers' memory, however, is not of a syntactically sequential phrase but of a structurally interactive relationship. It is a matrix, not a saying, that is recalled. Notice, of course, that even to articulate it in minimal format I had to decide which term came first. In memory, however, the twin terms could stay simultaneously present. But to articulate them, either in speech or in writing, one must choose a specific sequence. Here are a few examples:

Choose *children* first:	"Children fill the kingdom."
Choose *kingdom* first:	"The kingdom contains only children."
Choose negative format:	"Unless you are a child, you will not enter the kingdom."
Choose positive format:	"Children are those who enter the kingdom."
Choose main verb:	"Enter" or "obtain" or "possess" or "receive."
Choose opening:	"Whoever" or "Those who" or "If anyone."

The concept of matrix helps explain all the variant formats of this saying (and others) now present in our gospels. Orality retains a matrix based on that surprising conjunction of *children* and *kingdom* and formulates its articulation anew each time (though, of course, one formulation may become habitual for a given individual). Then literacy writes it down and checks all future formats against that established original format.

None of that justifies the presumption that there could be a multiform without some controlling structure, that there could be oral multiform without traditional matrix. In discussing my book *The Historical Jesus,* Werner Kelber, for example, comments on that example: "The fourfold independent attestation of the saying on 'Kingdom and Children' suggests an underlying 'central and shocking' metaphor that goes back to Jesus" (Crossan 1991:269). The question is whether we can *grope* our way through tradition to the *mind* of Jesus by reconstructing a core complex. Must not any such reconstruction remain *speculative?* . . . To collect and place side by side all written versions of a dominical saying and to trace a trajectory back to the core structure, will give us something that had no existence in oral or textual form. Even if we managed to extract a pattern common to all existing versions of a saying, we would have succeeded merely in conjuring a *structuralist stability* that by oral, historical standards is a fictional construct" (1994:149). (I italicized the rhetorical moves in that passage.)

I agree that we end up with a fictional construct, of course, but so what? Even in an absolutely pure oral culture (with writing not yet invented), there must be some way of recognizing versions of the same theme, plot, or story as distinct from different themes, plots, or stories. Call that *structuralist stability,* if you wish, but it is simply how we recognize another version of a joke we know as distinct from a brand-new joke. And it certainly does exist in memory as matrix for the variants uttered orally or recorded scribally. I can imagine a dozen versions of the Greek epic about the Trojan War and also a dozen versions of the Gaelic epic about the Tain Bo Cuailnge, but none of the former is a variant of the latter (or vice versa). You can talk, no doubt, at some transcendent degree of abstraction, about a common demand for the return of one's claimed possession, about a Greek king named Menelaus demanding the return of his beautiful wife and an Irish queen named Medb demanding the return of her magnificent bull. I admit to some interest in comparing epics so diversely engendered, but, for here and now, I ask something more simple: What identifies one oral *multiform* from another? How does one pay equal attention to the *multi* and the *form?* How does one distinguish the tradition from the performance? How does one recognize the performance of this traditional unit from the performance of that traditional unit? There has to be a matrix or core structure that makes, for example, the *Iliad* not a multiform of the *Odyssey,* the kingdom/children saying not a multiform of kingdom/violence.

A second distinction is between *chasm* and *interface.* Is the relationship between oral and scribal culture best seen as chasm or as interface? There is, of course, a certain therapeutic necessity and strategic benefit in shocking us out of our scribal prejudices by asserting a forceful orality-versus-literacy rift, a great divide between oral culture and written culture. Werner Kelber, for example, admits that if the "emphasis in [his 1983 book] fell on that division, it was because a novel approach requires a strong thesis" (1994:159). The same purpose and justification might also be offered, I suppose, for that preceding emphasis on performatory multiform to the almost total exclusion of traditional matrix. Be that as it may, the great divide—understanding of orality versus literacy will not work because, while there have been oral cultures without literacy, there have been no literate cultures without orality. The divide, great or gradual, is not oral versus literate but *oral alone* versus *oral and literate* together. That point has been asserted in several very important studies across the last decade. Here are four recent examples.

The first example is from Brian Stock in 1983: "There is in fact no clear point of transition from a nonliterate to a literate society. . . . The change [is] not so much from oral *to* written as from an earlier state, predominantly oral, to various combinations of oral *and* written" (9). The second example is from Brian Street in 1984: "[As distinct from an 'autonomous' model] an 'ideological' model of literacy . . . concentrates on the overlap and interaction of oral and literate models rather than stressing a 'great divide'" (2–3). The third example is from Jack Goody in 1987: "It is a mistake to divide 'cultures' into the oral and the written: it is rather the oral and the oral plus the written, printed, etc. This being the case, for the individual there is always the problem of the interaction between the registers and the uses, between the so-called oral and the written traditions" (xii). The final example is from James Fentress and Chris Wickham in 1992: "The mere fact that a society has acquired the ability to represent its knowledge in written forms does not mean that that society has ceased to be an oral culture as well. We remain an oral society, and the ways in which we pattern our social memory continue to reflect, albeit in altered forms, the same practices and thought processes of preliterate cultures. Writing may absolve us of the need to learn complex mnemotechniques; it does not absolve us of the need to speak" (46).

Throughout this book, therefore, I will be working not with chasm but with interface, not with a great divide between oral and scribal worlds but with their manifold interaction and with the delicacies required by that dialectic.

I conclude with an example of what I mean by oral-scribal interface, from a world both distant and close to that of Jesus and his contemporaries. In *Angela's Ashes,* a boyhood memoir of luminous horror, Frank McCourt recalls the last days of his friend Patricia Madigan. They meet in Limerick's Fever Hospital, where he is recovering from typhoid at ten and she is dying from diphtheria at fourteen. They talk back and forth from one room to the other, and "she reads me part of a poem which I have to remember so I can say it back to her early in the morning or late at night when there are no nuns or nurses around." They are working day by day, stanza by stanza through the poem's suspenseful narrative about "the highway man" who came riding "up to the old inn-door." But before they are finished, the nurse moves Frank upstairs because "diphtheria is never allowed to talk to typhoid." Patricia dies two days later, and Frank wonders how the poem ended. Seamus, who sweeps out the wards, "doesn't know any poetry at all especially English poetry. . . . Still he'll ask the men in the local pub where there's always someone reciting something and he'll bring it back to me." Later Seamus reports that a "man in his pub knew all the verses of the highway-man poem and it has a very sad end. Would I like him to say it because he never learned how to read and he had to carry the poem in his head. He stands in the middle of the ward leaning on his mop and recites" the concluding stanzas. "Now if you want to know any more poems, Frankie, tell me and I'll get them from the pub and bring 'em back in my head" (196–201). That is one way the delicate interface of oral and scribal transmission operates. This book is about some other ways.

PART III
Gospels and Sources

As regards the parables and the sayings . . . there is . . . no reason to suppose that each story was told on one occasion only. On the contrary, it seems most likely that they were repeated over and over again—sometimes in identical words, sometimes with variations. (Thus the parables of the Great Supper and the Marriage of the King's Son have every appearance of being the same story, varied to suit the occasion; the parables of the Talents and the Pounds offer a similar "doublet", as do the similes of the Improvident Builder and the Improvident King.) We need not imagine that the appearance of the same story in different contexts argues any inaccuracy or contradiction, or that the version of one Evangelist is more authentic than that of another. The teacher who thought of such a story as that of the Good Samaritan or the Prodigal Son would be foolish indeed to confine it to a single audience. He would repeat it over and over, till his disciples knew it by heart in all its variations. . . . It must be remembered that, of the four Evangels, St. John's is the only one that claims to be the direct report of an eye-witness. And to any one accustomed to the imaginative handling of documents, the internal evidence bears out this claim. The Synoptists, on the whole, report the "set pieces", it is St. John who reports the words and actions of the individual, unrepeated occasion, retrieving them from that storehouse of trained memory which, among people not made forgetful by too much pen and ink, replaces the filed records and the stenographer's note-book. . . . All through, in fact, the Gospel of St. John reads like the narrative of an eye-witness filling up the gaps in matter already published, correcting occasional errors, and adding material which previous writers either had not remembered or did not know about. . . . In modern memoirs written by real people about another real person we should expect just that sort of diversity which we find in the Gospels. . . . Take, for example, the various accounts of the Resurrection appearances at the Sepulchre. The divergences appear very great on first sight. . . . But the fact remains that *all* of them, without exception, can be made to fall into place in a single orderly and coherent narrative without the smallest contradiction or difficulty, and without any suppression, invention, or manipulation, beyond a trifling effort to *imagine* the natural behaviour of a bunch of startled people running about in the dawnlight between Jerusalem and the Garden.

Dorothy L. Sayers, *The Man Born to Be King*, pp. 26–29

Parts II and III are a tandem set looking at the materials, the *where* that connects the *why* of Part I to the *how* of Parts IV and V. Part II was concerned with memories and oral tradition. Part III is concerned with manuscripts and scribal transmission. What about the written gospels as sources for reconstructing the historical Jesus, Christian origins, and especially the closest interface discernible between them?

Part III has three chapters. Chapter 7 looks at the inevitable need for historical judgments about the nature, number, contents, and relationships of the extant gospels as preparation for doing historical reconstruction on Jesus and earliest Christianity. What are my present presuppositions from the past history of scholarly research on the gospels?

Chapter 8 considers dependent and independent gospels and looks at how we can determine dependence or independence between two gospels. It also considers extracanonical as well as intracanonical gospels—that is, those outside as well as inside the official or canonical New Testament. Should both be used for historical reconstruction? Should either be privileged over the other? What are my own answers to those questions?

Chapter 9 acknowledges that the preceding questions have become increasingly controversial and that debates about them have become increasingly polemical. Is there any relatively objective evidence indicating how gospels now inside or outside the canon were seen before there ever was a definitively closed canon? There are three aspects that cut across our inside/outside distinction, and two of those aspects point toward a centralized authority with both intracanonical and extracanonical gospels falling under that unified control. Those twin aspects are the very early Christian preference for the codex over the scroll, and the equally early Christian use of abbreviations for certain key theological expressions.

I chose the epigraph to Part III carefully and deliberately. It was written over fifty years ago by someone who was a scholar, a novelist, and a playwright. Because it breathes common sense in every line, even suggesting an alternative interpretation seems to indicate the eccentricity of scholarship seeking to overthrow the normalcy of intelligence. Allow me, however, two more autobiographical details before proceeding.

For most of my adult life, as I mentioned before, I taught primarily undergraduate, required, general-education classes at DePaul University in Chicago. Whenever we touched on the four gospels, which was usually at some speed and in passing, the students found biblical research on the source relationships *between* the gospels blissfully unbelievable. Why not take them more or less as Dorothy Sayers did in that epigraph? You have four versions of the same event, and all you have to do is integrate them into a synthetic whole. Or, conversely, you have different versions of the same event because the speaker said the same thing in different ways at different times. Why do *I* not take the gospels like that?

What separates my presuppositions about the gospels from those of my students, or my conclusions about the gospels from those of a Dorothy Sayers?

I spent the 1960s poring over the four gospels in parallel columns, word after word and unit after unit, day after day and year after year. I was studying the scholarly hypothesis that some of those gospels had used others as their sources—in other words, I was doing *source-criticism*—and in the end I found it absolutely convincing. I was also, presuming that first hypothesis, testing out a second one: you could get a very good glimpse into the heart and mind of an author by watching how a source was edited or redacted—that is, by doing *redaction-criticism*. (I know, by the way, that others had more interesting times in the sixties, but I spent them in a monastery, where alternative activities were somewhat curtailed.) In any case, those two processes—source-criticism and redaction-criticism—were the twin sides of the same coin. They stood or fell together; they confirmed or disconfirmed one another. Another term, *tradition-criticism*, could be used to describe the fuller process in which they fitted. If Unit A (the *source*) was used by Unit B (the *redaction*), a continuing *tradition* was developing. The basic validity of that double process is the major presupposition to be outlined in this section. If it is wrong, any historical reconstruction of Jesus and his followers built upon it is methodologically invalid. Ditto, of course, for any alternative hypothesis. It is the scholarly conclusions of *tradition-criticism*, hard won by gospel scholarship over the last two hundred years (but also confirmed by my own personal study), that separates me from the simplicity of common sense that here, as elsewhere, can become *uncommon nonsense*.

CHAPTER 7

ADMITTING GOSPEL
PRESUPPOSITIONS

The much-vaunted "normal critical tools", particularly form-criticism, are being tacitly (and in my view rightly) bypassed in the search for Jesus; enquiry is proceeding by means of a proper, and often clearly articulated, method of hypothesis and verification. . . . [M]uch of the impetus for form-critical and redaction-critical study came from the presupposition that this or that piece of synoptic material about Jesus *could not* be historical; in other words, that an *historical hypothesis about Jesus could already be presupposed* which demanded a further tradition-historical hypothesis to explain the evidence. If, however, a viable alternative historical hypothesis, whether about Jesus or about the early church, is proposed, argued out, and maintained, the need for tradition-criticism within the search for Jesus (to say nothing about its undoubted value in other historical enterprises) could in principle be substantially reduced and altered in shape. . . . [A]ll sorts of things in the gospels which, on the Bultmannian paradigm, needed to be explained by complex epicycles of *Traditionsgeschichte* [tradition-criticism] turn out, after all, to fit comfortably within the ministry of Jesus.

N. Thomas Wright, *Jesus and the Victory of God*, p. 87

First, presuppositions are not, as used in this section, dogmatic or theological acts of faith. They are simply historical conclusions reached earlier but taken for granted here. Fuller argumentation about them has already been done on previous occasions and is publicly available from such earlier study. No reputable scholar uses such presuppositions without at least rechecking them. They are necessary, however, because without them one would have to start from scratch every time on every thing.

Second, nobody can avoid presuppositions, although you can avoid *these* in favor of *those*. You can refuse mine and choose your own. In historical Jesus research, nobody can avoid presuppositions about the gospels—about their number, their nature, and their relationships. And nobody can dismiss another's presuppositions using the grounds that they are just that. Presuppositions can be rejected only by judgments of inadequacy, illegitimacy, or invalidity. They will then be replaced by other presuppositions, which will be argued as more adequate, legitimate, and valid.

Third, if there is a large consensus about certain aspects of the gospels, you can check, accept, and presume that majority opinion. A majority opinion is not necessarily right, of course, but, if you disagree with it, you should argue against it and not just ignore it. It is not sufficient simply to accuse it of bias, prejudice, paranoia, or delusion.

Fourth, superstructures are built on top of foundations. Conclusions and decisions about the historical Jesus are built, *by everyone,* atop their presuppositions about the gospels. Mistakes about foundations can bring superstructures tumbling down either partially or totally. But, on the other hand, one way to test foundations or presuppositions is to build atop them as heavily as possible and watch for the cracks to appear. Presuppositions are being constantly tested by the structures built on top of them. Wrong presuppositions, wrong conclusions. Same judgment for me, you, and everyone else.

All historical Jesus research, I repeat, works within certain presuppositions about the gospels—about their number, nature, and relationships. But whatever they are, let this be absolutely clear: a little Egyptian child playing tomorrow on the edges of the Libyan desert could dig up a papyrus-filled jar that would make all those presuppositions obsolete and force scholarship to start all over again. In the meanwhile, and pending such little-child leadership, this section lays out presuppositions about the gospels that will be important for what follows about *text* in Parts VI through X of this book. My purpose in this section, then, is to emphasize the inevitability of presuppositions by looking at the work of N. Thomas Wright on the historical Jesus as summarized in that preceding and the two succeeding epigraphs.

On Bypassing Previous Scholarship

Schweitzer said that Jesus comes to us as one unknown. Epistemologically, if I am right, this is the wrong way around. *We* come to *him* as ones unknown, crawling back from the far country, where we have wasted our substance on riotous but ruinous historicism. But the swinehusks—the "assured results of modern criticism"—reminded us of that knowledge which arrogance had all but obliterated, and we began the journey home.

N. Thomas Wright, *Jesus and the Victory of God,* p. 662

Wright speaks in those two epigraphs of "the much-vaunted 'normal critical tools'" and of the "'assured results of modern criticism,'" and his quotation marks prepare you for their dismissal. That is his first point. There are three main historical procedures involved, and I mentioned two of them in my preceding section. *Source-criticism* seeks to determine if and what genetic relationships exist between texts. Who used what as a source? *Redaction-criticism,* reversing that process, seeks to determine the authorial development of such sources. What omissions, additions, and changes were involved in the redaction of an earlier source by a later author? *Form-criticism* seeks to determine the forms in which oral units were transmitted and to correlate them with the situations that produced and used them. A form, for example, might be an aphorism, a parable, a dialogue, a debate, and so on. All those procedures come together under the general heading of *tradition-criticism* (or *transmissional analysis*), which attempts to trace the genetic relationship and historical trajectory of large and small units of tradition about Jesus. That synthetic work is based, of course, on combined conclusions about forms, sources, and redactions. Can a scholar bypass all that previous work and the presuppositions it developed about the gospels? You could certainly oppose it, argue against it, and declare publicly and accurately your own alternative conclusions as new presuppositions. I do not think, however, that you can *bypass* it.

Wright's second point is that those procedures are all illegitimate because they presume a prior hypothesis about Jesus. That is flatly incorrect. Many earlier scholars thought that such procedures would bring them back directly and automatically to the historical Jesus. That did not and never will work. If Matthew used Mark, it does not follow that Mark gives you the historical Jesus. But it does follow that, in those places where he is copying Mark, Matthew gives you the historical Mark and not the historical Jesus. Those analytical procedures stand or fall by themselves. They do not stand or fall by the intentions or expectations, theological visions or historical programs of those who invented or first used them. They cannot be "bypassed," and neither can they be dismissed as based "on the presupposition that this or that piece of synoptic material about Jesus *could not* be historical." The former is unwise. The latter is untrue.

A third point proposes an alternative to building on such tradition-criticism. Wright proposes to offer a major hypothesis about the historical Jesus and then verify it by determining how well it explains all the data available. I return to see how this might work below, but, for now, let us look at how it would discriminate between the following two reconstructions. Ed Sanders announces the principle that "the synoptic gospels are to be preferred as our basic source of information about Jesus" (1993:73). Wright does not announce a similar hypothesis in theory but seems to use it in practice. The "Index of Ancient Sources" at the back of his book has twenty-five columns of references to the three synoptic gospels but only one column of references to John. I think that emphasis is correct, but, on Wright's new model of hypothesis and verification bypassing prior historical conclusions about the gospels, why should it be followed? Why not hypothesize that John had it historically correct, that Jesus spoke in long discourses making absolutely transcendental claims about himself, and that the synoptics broke that all down into safer, simpler, smaller forms and contents? That is, after all, the equally plausible hypothesis of Dorothy Sayers in the epigraph to Part III. I do not think that the latter claim works as a hypothesis—it has already failed in testing for most scholars—but it is certainly a *possibility*. Or again, what about Stevan Davies's recent hypothesis that Jesus was an ecstatic healer who taught others how to meet God in ecstasy (1995)? Jesus himself spoke Johannine-like when in ecstasy and synoptic-like when not in ecstasy. That explains both those traditions as equally primitive and also explains that wide swath of Spirit-possessed trance in the primitive church. It is easy to mock that theory by laughingly claiming that it gives new meaning to the phrase "kingdom on high." But what is wrong with it as hypothesis and verification?

The final point is rather supremely ironic. The single name most associated with those historical methods and analytical procedures just mentioned, with what is known in German as *Traditionsgeschichte* and in English as tradition-criticism, is Rudolf Bultmann. But he is even more famous for the theological positions and historical overviews that he built over, under, around, and through those procedures. For example, he interpreted mythological or eschatological language as existential challenge or personal decision, and he privileged the words of Jesus to the almost total exclusion of his deeds. Many scholars, myself included, accept those analytical procedures but reject the wider theological or even historical frameworks in which they are imbedded. Wright rejects it all as one composite and contaminated whole. Therein lies a supreme irony. Bultmann was a Lutheran Protestant who looked in the gospels and found tradition. Wright is a Anglican Catholic who looked in the gospels and found scripture. I think Bultmann was correct. Tradition was there before, in, and after the gospels. You cannot bypass it.

Hypothesis and Verification

Nobody grumbles at a book on Alexander the Great if, in telling the story, the author "harmonizes" two or three sources; that is his or her job, to advance hypotheses which draw together the data into a coherent framework rather than leaving it scattered.

N. Thomas Wright, *Jesus and the Victory of God*, p. 88

Wright's alternative proposal is hypothesis and verification, but without any prior judgments about sources and traditions. "It is vital that this point of method be grasped from the outset. . . . [T]he task before the serious historian of Jesus is not in the first instance conceived as the reconstruction of traditions about Jesus, according to their place within the history of the early church, but the advancement of serious historical hypotheses—that is, the telling of large-scale narratives—about Jesus himself, and the examination of the *prima facie* relevant data to see how they fit." He uses the example in the epigraph above to show what he means, and he footnotes the following comment from the historian J. Michael Wallace-Hadrill: "I believe that the literary sources exaggerate when I can catch them out, but otherwise I give them the benefit of the doubt. . . . One should not approach any of them in a spirit of resistant scepticism" (1996:87–88). "Otherwise," as Wright adds later, "'critical history' becomes mere paranoia, insisting on conspiracy theories and unable to see the way that the real evidence is pointing" (105). All of that sounds, as did Sayers's words earlier, quite sanely obvious and quite obviously right. Divergent versions of the same saying or parable, event or incident, are explained by Wright on the perfectly plausible presumption that Jesus would have said and done the same things in slightly different ways in different places and on different occasions. Here is an example, however, to complicate matters.

Remember, from Chapter 2 of this book, that just as we have four biographies of Jesus from Matthew, Mark, Luke, and John, we have four biographies of the emperor Tiberius, under whom Jesus was crucified, from Velleius Paterculus, Tacitus, Suetonius, and Dio Cassius. Imagine, now, classical historians reconstructing the life of Tiberius from those sources. They would, as Wright notes for Alexander, work out a critical but synthetic harmonization of all four accounts. But imagine, next, a complicating situation. Suppose that some, many, most, or all classical historians came to the following scholarly conclusions: First, Velleius Paterculus was not a contemporary of Tiberius but wrote in the very early 70s. Second, Tacitus and Suetonius both copied rather massively from Paterculus but changed, omitted, and added to his accounts for their own quite discernible purposes. Third, Dio Cassius copied from all three of his predecessors, using those last two sources even more radically than they used the first one. That would certainly change everything. If the analysis of *source* and *redaction* came up with that stream of *tradition*, then any form of harmonization would be ruled out completely. A unit found in all four sources, for example, would be valueless as an historical datum in the last three and could be studied only in its first appearance. Each author could, of course, have other independent sources available for other details. But, in such a situation, their massive dependence on a single source would underline their historical limitations. Let me emphasize two side issues before continuing. If that were the actual situation with those four classical historians, I would not *presume* that they were all cheats or liars. Maybe that was the way they thought history should be written—as a genetically linked stream of tradition, with later historians rewriting earlier ones. And neither would I presume that the final version was valueless. Even if it had only copied data and absolutely no new facts of its own, it might still produce an interpretation more persuasive than all those preceding ones put together.

That imaginary classical scenario is an actual biblical one. A vast majority of scholars in this century considers that Mark was used by Matthew and Luke as a major source, and an equal majority in this century has swung from one side to the other and back on those three synoptic gospels as the major source for John. For those scholars, among whom I include myself, there is no possibility of ignoring sources, redactions, and traditions in the gospels. Decisions about them must be made, and those decisions then become presuppositions for later research on the historical Jesus and the birth of Christianity. It does not actually make any difference what paranoia or suspicion, what motivation or prejudice, what theological position or even historical presumption may have led to those conclusions. The only question finally is, Are they valid? If I hated Tacitus and intended to destroy his reputation by showing that he had copied massively from Paterculus, that actually is irrelevant. If I detested classicists and wanted to show that they were all misguided fools, that also is irrelevant. In the final analysis, there is only one important point: Are we or are we not dealing with genetically independent versions? You understand, of course, that this is not some legal plagiarism case, but an attempt to discern where we have independent attestations and where we have dependent traditions. Nothing, therefore, that Wright says, often quite correctly, about the specific theological motivations or even the general historical overviews of those who first advocated or now use gospel sources, redactions, and traditions can invalidate those processes in themselves.

Presuppositions about gospel materials, therefore, will crucially dictate and control one's method for research on both the historical Jesus and earliest Christianity. Those presuppositions will touch on the nature and function of the gospels but also on the contacts and relationships between them. Just imagine, in conclusion, three very different models for such functions and contacts. Imagine that you were hearing about the gospels for the first time and had, as yet, no conclusions about them. Any one of the following might be your initial hypothesis, to be tested against the data, and no one of them could be invalidated at the start just because it is a hypothesis.

First, the gospel authors are like *four witnesses giving legal testimony*. All are doing their level best, as if in a court of law, to tell you exactly what happened as fully as they can remember it. There may be slight divergences, but that only proves the normal vagaries of memory. The described phenomenon is surest where all four agree. In this model, the reconstruction of the historical Jesus should depend on that *consensual stratum,* that fourfold agreement, for its most secure data. Threefold, twofold, or single attestation would supply the successively less secure data.

Second, the gospel authors are like *four scholars doing basic research.* Each author goes back to the data in the past and, while not ignoring earlier work, seeks each time to write a brand-new and more accurate report. In that model, the later the writer, the more historical the account will be. On that understanding of the four gospels, the *latest stratum* would give the most secure data about the historical Jesus.

Third, the gospel authors are like *four historians conducting oral interviews.* If, in this oral history, their subject played variations on certain themes in different times and places, the collectors would end with different versions not just from vagrant memories but from parallel occasions. On that understanding of the four gospels, all versions are equally correct. Diversity simply indicates that Jesus said or did the same thing in slightly different ways.

Fourth, the gospel authors are like *four evangelists rewriting earlier tradition.* There are two separate points to that description, *gospel* and *tradition.* I have already touched on that first point twice before, but it bears repetition because it is basic to this book. An evangelist is someone with *good news* to impart. *Good* indicates that the news is seen from somebody's point of view, from the Christian Jewish rather than the Roman imperial interpretation. *News* indicates that a regular update is involved. It indicates that Jesus is constantly being actualized for new times and places, situations and problems, authors and communities. But that second point is equally important. We are dealing with a continuing and a developing tradition, but it is a continuing or developing tradition *that seems to swallow whole its predecessors.* Later gospels totally absorb the earlier one that they used as sources. They absorb them, redact them, and thereby transform them. For example, the Common Sayings Tradition, about which much more later, is absorbed into the *Q Gospel* and the *Gospel of Thomas.* The *Q Gospel* and Mark are absorbed into Matthew and Luke. The synoptics are absorbed, partially or totally, into John. If that is your view of the gospels—and it *is* mine—the problem of the historical Jesus pushes you back and back along that absorptive path to the earliest stratum of the tradition.

My point in all of this, I repeat, is not to debate these specific presuppositions but, first, to emphasize that one must have some set of gospel conclusions and, second, to show you what my own are and why I hold them. If you take the intracanonical gospels as four independent witnesses to the historical Jesus, you will act one way on that presupposition. If you take the intracanonical gospels as basically a linked stream of tradition, you will act differently on that presupposition. Any work done on a wrong presupposition will be seriously weakened or even totally vitiated. Granted all that, then, what are my own presuppositions about the gospel traditions, and how do those presuppositions justify my methodological focus on the *earliest* layer of that tradition for historical Jesus research?

CHAPTER 8

RELATING GOSPEL CONTENTS

Crossan's insistence that all Jesus traditions—from apocryphal as well as canonical writings—must be put on an even footing appears as simple fair-mindedness and intellectual rigor: he will demand that every strand of tradition prove itself! But closer examination suggests that the game is fixed. Crossan's remarkably early dating for virtually all apocryphal materials, and his correspondingly late dating for virtually all canonical materials, together with his frequent assertion that the extracanonical sources are unaffected by the canonical sources and therefore have independent evidenciary value, rests on little more than his assertions and those of the like-minded colleagues he cites. He never enters into debate with those who do not share such views. The position, in other words, is presumed, not proved.

Luke Timothy Johnson, *The Real Jesus,* p. 47

As you can see from that epigraph, the use of *both* intracanonical (canonical) and extracanonical (apocryphal) gospels is rather controversial. The charge of having "fixed" the evidence is the most serious accusation one scholar can make against another. That indictment serves to introduce the problem of relating gospel contents, assessing gospel relations, deciding whether any gospels are, in whole or part, dependent on other gospels, and comparing intracanonical and extracanonical gospels. I repeat, once again, that you must decide your presuppositions about gospel traditions before reconstructing either the historical Jesus or earliest Christianity. Everyone must. Everyone does.

Dependent and Independent Gospels

My guess would be that we have two versions of the great supper parable, two versions of the talents/pounds parable, and two versions of the beatitudes, not because one is adapted from the other, or both from a single common written source, but because these are two out of a dozen or more possible variations that, had one been in Galilee with a tape-recorder, one might have "collected". Anyone who suggests that this is not so must, I think, either be holding on doggedly to the picture of the early church which I criticized in the first volume [*The New Testament and the People of God*], or be in thrall to a highly dogmatic view of scripture, or simply have no historical imagination for what an itinerant ministry, within a peasant culture, would look like.

N. Thomas Wright, *Jesus and the Victory of God*, p. 170

That epigraph tells us that Wright does not accept the existence of what other scholars call the *Q Gospel* as the best explanation for the twin but divergent versions of the three "units" (cited above) found in Matthew 22:1–10 = Luke 14:16–24 (the parable of the great supper), Matthew 25:14–30 = Luke 19:12–27 (the parable of the talents/pounds), and Matthew 5:3–4, 6, 11–12 = Luke 6:20b–26 (the beatitudes). He has, in other words, different presuppositions about gospel sources and redactions. I intend these three examples and what follows not as debate on those presuppositions but rather as an indication of how gospel presuppositions necessarily dictate methods and models for research on the historical Jesus and earliest Christianity.

The first question concerns *dependent and independent gospels*. How can you tell if one gospel is or is not dependent on another? What happens, for example, if you have twin texts that are too similar in order and/or content for coincidence to serve as an explanation? There are four possible explanations why two texts might be too similar for sheer coincidence. The first two involve a common source (oral or scribal) used independently of one another by later authors. The second two involve literary dependence (direct or indirect) of a later author on an earlier one.

Common Oral Matrix.

One explanation is that they are both actualizations of a common oral matrix. Here is a classic example of that possibility involving a gospel and non-gospel text:

Luke 12:35 (RSV)	Didache 16:1
Let your loins be girded and your lamps burning.	Let your lamps be not quenched and your loins be not ungirded.

The core of the oral matrix is those twin symbols of readiness in no set order. Actualizations must then choose either lamps/loins or loins/lamps as sequence, and either positive ("be") or negative ("be not") as formulation. I prefer that explanation to direct dependence of either text on the other.

Common Literary Source.

Another explanation for such twin texts is that they are both dependent on a common literary source. Here is a classic example of that possibility:

Matthew 3:7–10	Luke 3:7–9
But when he saw many Pharisees and Sadducees coming for baptism, he said to them, "You brood of vipers! Who warned you to flee from the wrath to come? Bear fruit worthy of repentance. Do not presume to say to yourselves, 'We have Abraham as our ancestor'; for I tell you, God is able from these stones to raise up children to Abraham. Even now the ax is lying at the root of the trees; every tree therefore that does not bear good fruit is cut down and thrown into the fire."	John said to the crowds that came out to be baptized by him, "You brood of vipers! Who warned you to flee from the wrath to come? Bear fruits worthy of repentance. Do not begin to say to yourselves, 'We have Abraham as our ancestor'; for I tell you, God is able from these stones to raise up children to Abraham. Even now the ax is lying at the root of the trees; every tree therefore that does not bear good fruit is cut down and thrown into the fire."

That indictment by John the Baptist, over sixty words in Greek, is verbatim the same in Matthew and Luke except for four very minor changes (all subject to textual debate). Those twin versions are not the independent actualizations of an oral matrix but the very, very faithful reproductions of a written source. That source, about which more below, is the *Q Gospel*. Notice, of course, the divergent introductions that precede the attack.

But what if some common source, be it oral matrix or written text, is not an adequate explanation? What if one text is dependent on the other? How do you tell when that is so and which one has used the other? What, for example, has convinced a vast majority of scholars that Mark was used by Matthew and Luke rather than any other explanation of their remarkably similar order and content? Those three gospels, to repeat an earlier statement, are so similar that they can easily be placed in parallel columns and seen *at a glance*—hence their usual title of the *synoptic* gospels. There are certainly no easy answers to that question (as if the shorter or longer were always first, or the better-written or worse-written were always first). The process is much more complicated in theory and much more controversial in practice.

Direct Literary Dependence.

This explanation must be supported by two mutually supportive arguments: one is *genetic relationship* and the other is *redactional confirmation*. *Genetic relationship* means that certain elements of order and content that are characteristically Markan are found in Matthew and Luke. We are not talking of general tradition common to all three gospels but of specific editorial aspects of Markan sequence or style whose presence in those other two texts indicates copying. What we are seeking, as it were, are Markan literary fingerprints or Markan theological DNA present within the gospels of Matthew and Luke. Here is a classic example of that possibility.

One of the most peculiarly distinctive Markan compositional devices has been called an *intercalation* or *sandwich*. The device has two elements. First, literary presentation: Event A begins (A¹), then Event B begins and finishes (B), and finally, Event A finishes (A²). Second, theological meaning: the purpose of the intercalation is not mere literary show; it presumes that those two events—call them the "framing event" and the "insert event"—are mutually interactive, that they interpret one another to emphasize Mark's theological intention. It is this combination of literary structure *and* theological import that makes those intercalations peculiarly if not uniquely Markan.

There is fairly wide agreement on the following six cases as examples of Markan intercalations:

A¹:	3:20–35	5:21–24	6:7–13	11:12–14	14:1–2	14:53–54
B:	3:22–30	5:25–34	6:14–29	11:15–19	14:3–9	14:55–65
A²:	3:31–35	5:35–43	6:30	11:20–21	14:10–11	14:66–72

Several scholars agree on those six instances but add others as well. For example, Frans Neirynck gives seven examples (1972:133), John Donahue also seven (42 note 2, 58–59), and James Edwards nine (197–198). "The Evangelist," as Tom Shepherd summarizes Mark's purpose from those six cases, "has brought two stories together and yet held them apart in contrast to one another to produce an interpretation." In 14:53–72, for example, there is a supremely ironic contrast: "Jesus gives a faithful confession of his Messiahship and receives the sentence of death [A¹ + A²]. Peter denies his Lord three times and saves himself from suffering [B]" (523, 532).

What reassures me that the device does not move from either Matthew or Luke into Mark but vice versa is the fact that, as Edwards notes, "of Mark's nine sandwiches, Matthew retains Mark's A-B-A pattern five times and Luke retains it four times" (199). It is probably fair to say that both Matthew and Luke consider it a rather strange phenomenon and often eliminate it quite ruthlessly. Take, for example, the way Mark intercalates the Temple's symbolic destruction in 11:15–19 within the fig tree's cursing in 11:12–14 and withering in 11:20–21. That structure tells us how Mark interprets Jesus' somewhat enigmatic Temple action. It is a symbolic destruction of the Temple, just as the cursing of the fig tree is a real one. It is a case of destruction not cleansing, according to Mark. Luke, however, omits the whole fig tree incident; and Matthew, who includes it, has cursing and withering happen together in 21:18–19 ("And the fig tree withered at once"), but after the Temple action in 21:12–13 and separated from it by the intervening events in 21:14–17. It is the presence of such specific, personal, or compositional elements, be they order or content, topic or style, that is the surest evidence of the dependence of one text upon another.

Two footnotes. First, the presence of such individual components of one gospel in another must be checked carefully in case after case so that the argument is finally cumulative. Second, no conclusions on dependence are absolute or beyond debate, since all such decisions are, in effect, working hypotheses or operational theories. But, in effect, you cannot *not* have them, for that is itself but another working hypothesis!

Redactional confirmation supports *genetic relationship*. It is not really a second *proof* but a way of testing some postulated genetic relationship. If, for reasons such as those given in the preceding example, you postulate Matthean and Lukan dependence on Mark, you should be able to explain every omission, addition, or alteration in Matthew and Luke over their Markan source. Because, of course, we still have Mark. For many scholars, including myself, it was the success of such endeavors in redaction-criticism that served retroactively to confirm the historical primacy of Mark. Joseph Fitzmyer, for example, noted over twenty-five years ago that this argument from successful usage is "a valuable, but extrinsic, criterion for judging the worth of this hypothesis" (1970:134; 1981–1985:65).

But now a problem starts to appear. It has to do with the difference between proving a positive as against proving a negative, the difference between arguing for dependence as against arguing for *in*dependence. Go back to that Markan intercalation example. What if Matthew and Luke had so disliked that device that they had both removed it completely? Where would we be then? Because the texts *do* include intercalation, we have an argument for their dependence on Mark. But if they did *not* have it, would we have an argument for their *in*dependence from Mark? It is quite often taken for granted that the genetic relationship argument works equally for positive and negative situations. But it cannot do so with equal security, just as physical evidence can prove guilt but its lack cannot prove innocence. What happens when, unlike that synoptic situation, we have two texts too close for sheer coincidence or simple divergent performance but lacking specific traits of one in the other?

Indirect Literary Dependence.

That question presses because recently Raymond Brown has questioned whether the synoptic model of *direct literary dependence* should be the unique or even dominant model for dependency relations. In that model, we can imagine Matthew and Luke working with Mark's text *directly* before them, whether on their writing desk or read to them by slave, servant, or colleague. It is precisely because Matthew and Luke copied Mark rather closely that we have been able to obtain a massive scholarly consensus on their dependency. But what if, as Brown suggests, an author had heard or read another text and wrote it from memory many years later? As we saw earlier, that is how he judges the *Gospel of Peter* to be dependent on the gospels of Matthew, Luke, and John. It depends on those canonical versions, "not necessarily from their written texts but often from memories preserved through their having been heard and recounted orally"—that is, by "distant memory of having heard them"; in other words, the *Gospel of Peter* was not produced "at a desk by someone with written sources propped up before him" (1994:1001, 1306, 1336). Let me call that a case of *indirect literary dependence.* Remembrance of a text heard or read years before would most likely lack any peculiar, individual, or personal identifying traits found in the original—such as the Markan intercalations. Somebody today, for instance, rewriting Mark from memory and not knowing about the importance of the intercalations, would probably not even recall their presence. That would make impossible an argument from genetic relationship even where such existed. Are we at an impasse in such a case? Not exactly. We still have that second argument mentioned above, that of *redactional confirmation.* If we postulate an author writing from distant memory of a text heard or read, we should still be able to do redaction-criticism on that presumption. How and why did that author remember in that way? What theory of memory explains the production? What literary and/or theological purposes explain the final composition? I return to this difficulty in Chapter 25.

Intracanonical and Extracanonical Gospels

The earliest gospel traditions and gospel writings contain the seed of both . . . later heresy as well as later orthodoxy. For the description of the history and development of gospel literature in the earliest period of Christianity, the epithets "heretical" and "orthodox" are meaningless. Only dogmatic prejudice can assert that the intracanonical writings have an exclusive claim to apostolic origin and thus to historical priority.

Helmut Koester, *Ancient Christian Gospels,* p. xxx

[I am not] sympathetic to a simplistic tendency to regard extracanonical works as the key to true Christianity as contrasted with a narrow-minded censorship represented by the New Testament.

Raymond E. Brown, *The Death of the Messiah,* p. 1347

I am deliberately using neutral terms to describe two sets of gospels. I use *intracanonical* and *extracanonical* rather than more judgmental ones such as *canonical* and *apocryphal* or *orthodox* and *heretical.* This is not a question of which gospels I or anyone else accepts as more religiously significant or theologically valid. It is simply an attempt to handle all the historical evidence fairly and accurately. To study the *Gospel of Thomas,* for example, and to decide that it contains canonically independent but heavily redacted early Jesus tradition, does not mean, *for me at least,* that it is somehow better or more normative than any one of the intracanonical gospels, which also contain early Jesus tradition and are also heavily redacted. It is simply there and must be investigated. You may get, however, a sense of how controversial this discussion is by noting the tone of those preceding epigraphs. When terms like "dogmatic prejudice" and "narrow-minded censorship" enter the discourse, any hope for useful academic debate is long gone.

PRESUPPOSITIONS ABOUT THE INTRACANONICAL GOSPELS

I have (and would like to summarize here) three presuppositions concerning relations between the intracanonical gospels. By *presuppositions* I do not mean positions beyond current debate or even future change. Neither do I mean theological commitments. Rather, I mean historical judgments based on present evidence and requiring constant future testing against new theory, method, evidence, or experience. I have learned these presuppositions from scholarly tradition, have studied them internally, have tested them externally, and have found them consistently more persuasive than their alternatives. But if they are wrong, then everything based on them is questionable; and if they are *proved* wrong, then everything based on them will have to be redone. In the meanwhile, I *must* take a position on questions of gospel sources and relations in order to do historical study, because not to do so is simply to do so differently.

First Presupposition.

In 1789–1790 the German scholar Johann Jakob Griesbach explained the genetic relationship between the three synoptic gospels by proposing that Matthew came first, Mark copied from Matthew, and Luke copied from them both. That theory is still accepted today by scholars such as Hans-Herbert Stoldt in Germany and William Farmer in the United States. But in 1835 Karl Lachmann argued for a different genesis: Mark came first, and both Matthew and Luke copied from him (but independently of each other). That theory is held today by a fairly massive (but by no means total) consensus of contemporary critical scholarship. My first presupposition, then, is the validity of Markan priority, the theory that Mark was used by Matthew and Luke as the first of their major consecutive sources. I presume, of course, that scholars working within a consensus study the data, check the evidence, and confirm the conclusions for themselves. I also presume that adopting an hypothesis means continuing to test it against one's continuing research. But it is probably fair to say that Mark's genetic priority within the synoptic tradition is the consensus basis for modern historical criticism of the gospels. To claim chronological or even genetic priority is not, of course, to claim religious or theological priority. Furthermore, I make no argument that consensus must be right or that the lone dissident is thereby wrong. I simply say that one must make a decision, *one way or the other,* on Markan priority and then work on that presupposition. Wrong there, wrong thereafter.

Second Presupposition.

In 1838, Christian Hermann Weiße developed some earlier ideas of Friedrich Schleiermacher and suggested that Matthew and Luke used another major consecutive source besides Mark. Then, in 1863, Julius Holtzmann gave this source a name or designation: Λ, short for Λόγια, the Greek word for "sayings [of Jesus]." Finally, in 1890, Johannes Weiss, writing about the Beelzebul controversy in Matthew 12:22–32 = Luke 11:14–26, argued that they had not derived that incident from Mark 3:22–27 but from another common source (source is Quelle in German), namely Q, for short, as cited by Frans Neirynck (1982:686).

It is, however, rather demeaning to call Q simply a source, as if it had no integrity, continuity, or theology of its own. It is hardly correct to define something by its later usage rather than by its primary purpose. Imagine, for example, calling our second intracanonical document not the gospel of Mark but the Synoptic Narrative Source. Thus, "in recent years," as Frans Neirynck has observed, "some North American scholars have suggested introducing the term 'gospel' in the designation of Q with its full name: the Sayings Gospel Q" (1995a:421). I belong to that group but, since the *Gospel of Thomas* is also a sayings gospel, I prefer to call Q the *Q Gospel.* That serves to respect its textual and theological integrity (Q as gospel) but also to remind us that we know it only by scholarly reconstruction (Q as source).

An aside. The point here is not what certain texts name themselves. The Q document does not call itself a gospel—but then, neither do Matthew, Luke, and John. The point is what *scholars* name such texts. Is there bias in privileging our first four canonical texts as gospels even when they lack that same title but refusing it to others even when they contain the same content? Is there bias, on a more prosaic level, in never italicizing the titles for the intracanonical gospels—those of Matthew, Mark, Luke, and John—but in always doing so for the extracanonical gospels, such as the *Gospel of Thomas* or the *Gospel of Peter?* The only neutral way to control scholarly bias that I can think of is to accept Helmut Koester's double suggestion. Put positively, we should include within "gospel literature . . . all those writings which are constituted by the transmission, use, and interpretation of materials and traditions from and about Jesus of Nazareth." Put negatively, we should exclude documents that "are not related to or constituted by the continuing development of sources containing materials from or about Jesus of Nazareth" (1990a:46, 47). Back, in any case, to the *Q Gospel.*

The *Q Gospel,* therefore, is a hypothetical document whose existence is persuasively postulated to explain the amount of non-Markan material found with similar order and content in Matthew and Luke. That postulate does not have the massive consensus that Markan priority has, but it is certainly a major scholarly conclusion. Even within that shared conclusion, however, there is a growing difference between those who regard the *Q Gospel* as a major gospel text and those who accept its existence and contents but not its significance and implications. John Meier, for example, accepts its presence in Matthew and Luke but concludes, "I cannot help thinking that biblical scholarship would be greatly advanced if every morning all exegetes would repeat as a mantra: 'Q is a hypothetical document whose exact extension, wording, originating community, strata, and stages of redaction *cannot* be known'" (1994:2.178, my italics). But how does he know that those things *cannot* be known unless he has entered into detailed debate with the alternative quarter-century of scholarship that runs, for example, from Robinson (1971) to Kloppenborg (1990) and extends into both the Society of Biblical Literature's Q Seminar and the International Q Project? Furthermore, there is another and even more basic mantra that those same exegetes should utter each morning on rising: "Hypotheses are to be tested." And you test them by pushing, pushing, pushing, until you hear something crack. Then you examine the crack to see how to proceed. Q was quite acceptable as long as it was nothing more than a source to be found within the safe intracanonical confines of Matthew and Luke. But now the *Q Gospel* is starting to look a little like a Trojan horse, an extracanonical gospel hidden within two intracanonical gospels. If certain scholars have held all noncanonical gospels to be late and dependent, what will they do with a noncanonical gospel that is not only early and independent but on which two intracanonical gospels are themselves dependent? My second presupposition, then, accepts the existence of the *Q Gospel*, the theory that it was used by Matthew and Luke as the second of their major consecutive sources. I also take very seriously and am profoundly indebted to all of that recent Q scholarship. If it is wrong on Q, then so am I on the historical Jesus and earliest Christianity. The same applies, of course, to those who deny the *Q Gospel*'s existence in theory or ignore its significance in practice. We all build on our presuppositions and we all stand or fall on their validity.

Third Presupposition.

My third presupposition, which is more complicated, concerns the relationship of John to the three synoptic gospels. This is a problem on which scholarship has oscillated strongly from one alternative to the other within this century. Dwight Moody Smith has given a very thorough review of that process, and this is his summary: "At the beginning of the century, the exegete or commentator could safely assume John's knowledge of the Synoptics. We then passed through a period of a quarter of a century or more (1955–1980) in which the opposite assumption was the safer one: John was perhaps ignorant of the Synoptics, certainly independent of them. We have now reached a point at which neither assumption is safe, that is, neither can be taken for granted" (1992a:189). Adelbert Denaux, introducing the published papers of an international meeting on John and the synoptic gospels at Belgium's Leuven University in 1990, claimed, more strongly, that there was now "a growing consensus that the author of the Fourth Gospel was related to and/or in one way or another dependent upon one or more of the Synoptic Gospels" (viii).

My own position presumes both independence and dependence. That is not just a silly attempt to have it both ways but a necessary conclusion from my own research. In the early 1980s, working on the aphorisms of Jesus for *In Fragments,* I found those in John to be independent of the synoptic gospels (1983:x), but in the late 1980s, working on the passion and resurrection of Jesus for *The Cross That Spoke,* I found the opposite to be true (1988:xii–xiv). I consider that John's gospel developed over certain major stages. First, there was an independent collection of miracles and aphorisms that were creatively integrated so that the miracle-signs represented as physical events (bread, sight, etc.) what was announced by the aphorism-dialogues as spiritual events ("I am the bread, light," etc.). Second, pressure from groups accepting the synoptic gospels as the dominant Christian model resulted in the necessity of adding John the Baptist traditions at the start and passion-resurrection traditions at the end of a gospel which, left to itself, would have begun with that magnificent hymn at the start in John 1:1–18 (without the Baptist, of course) and concluded with that equally magnificent discourse of Jesus at the end in John 14–17. Third, pressure from groups accepting Peter as the dominant Christian leader necessitated the addition of John 21. Is all of that absolutely secure and definite? Of course not. But once again, a scholar has to decide and to wager the general validity of future work on that decision, whatever it is and whichever way it is taken.

Take the passion narrative in John as seen by two major scholars for a specific example of that preceding problem. Raymond Brown judges that John is independent of the synoptic gospels: "John did not use any of the Synoptic PNs [passion narratives] in writing his own account." He then builds his magisterial passion commentary on that presupposition and explicitly acknowledges the importance of his independence hypothesis: "Since Mark and John wrote independently of each other, the agreement of their PNs is often an important indicator of preGospel order and stories" (1994:92–93). Maurits Sabbe, on the other hand, in a series of articles just as finely detailed and fully documented as Brown's book, concludes that the combination of direct dependence and literary creativity is the best explanation for John's relationship to the other three gospels (1991:385, 513; 1995:219). On the death of Jesus in John 19:16b–42, for example, he argues that "the hypothesis of a direct dependence upon the Synoptists, combined with a certain amount of Johannine literary creativity, appears to be the most probable explanation for the similarities and dissimilarities between the Fourth and the antecedent Synoptic Gospels" (1994:34).

I agree with Sabbe rather than Brown on the dependence of the passion-resurrection sections of John but am *not yet* convinced about the dependence of the miracle-discourse sections, and I leave them aside for now. Why with Sabbe rather than Brown? For two reasons—one negative, one positive. Brown mocks "the picture of the Johannine evangelist working directly on the written Marcan PN [passion narrative], making dozens of inexplicable changes of order and words, and thus producing the very different PN that appears in John" (1994:83). But since, as we just saw, he himself introduced the possibility of *indirect* rather than *direct* literary dependence, he cannot any longer presume that John's only mode of synoptic usage must be direct (desktop) copying. It could be literarily dependent but filtered through distant memory, repeated liturgy, profound meditation, literary and theological creativity, or all of the above.

That is the negative aspect of this issue, but the positive is more important for me. Recall those Markan intercalations given above (p. 106) and focus on the last example in that list. What Mark did was intercalate Jesus' confession under trial in 14:55–65 (=B) between the beginning in 14:53–54 (=A^1) and ending in 14:66–72 (=A^2) of Peter's denials. Since Mark's community is repeatedly warned about persecution, the point of that sandwiched juxtaposition is very clear. Take Jesus as your model for brave and open confession of the truth under trial. But, if you deny Jesus under pressure and even curse him to prove your innocence, there is still hope for repentance and forgiveness. Surely a very consoling double message *about* Christians who died bravely through confession and *for* Christians who survived safely through denial.

That A^1-B-A^2 inclusion of Mark 14:53–72 is retained in Matthew 26:57–75 but eliminated in Luke 22:56–71, where Peter's denials in 22:54–62 simply precede Jesus' confession in 22:63–71. But here is the important point: John not only presents the same A^1-B-A^2 pattern, he intensifies it by having one denial precede (18:13–18) and two others follow (18:25–27) Jesus' confession (18:19–24). His purpose was probably not just to contrast Jesus and Peter, as Mark did, but also to contrast Peter and "the other disciple":

Simon Peter and another disciple followed Jesus. Since that disciple was known to the high priest, he went with Jesus into the courtyard of the high priest, but Peter was standing outside at the gate. So the other disciple, who was known to the high priest, went out, spoke to the woman who guarded the gate, and brought Peter in. The woman said to Peter, "You are not also one of this man's disciples, are you?" He said, "I am not." (John 18:15–17)

It is significant that nothing is said about *that other disciple* who is presumably the same as the Beloved Disciple, denying Jesus! The transference of that peculiarly or even uniquely Markan literary-theological structure from Mark 14:53–72 into John 18:13–27 persuades me to accept, at least as a working hypothesis, the dependence of John's passion account on Mark's.

Hence my third major presupposition about the intracanonical gospels is that John is dependent on the synoptic gospels *at least and especially* for the passion narratives (here I agree with Maurits Sabbe [1991: 355–388, 467–513; 1994; 1995]) and for the resurrection narratives (with Frans Neirynck [1982: 181–488; 1991: 571–616]). Once again, if that is wrong, everything I build on it is invalid. And again, the same goes for the opposite position.

PRESUPPOSITIONS ABOUT THE EXTRACANONICAL GOSPELS

Exactly the same principles used in determining relations between the intracanonical gospels are used for those between intracanonical and extracanonical gospels. For *direct literary dependence:* in this situation, *genetic relationship* is established by finding specific stylistic traits of one gospel within another gospel and using *redactional confirmation* to explain why that latter version used the former as it did. In the absence of such traits giving evidence of direct literary dependence in either direction, independence may be hypothetically proposed. For *indirect literary dependence:* in this situation, where no specific stylistic traits of one gospel are present in another, *redactional confirmation* is the only method available to argue in either direction. Those principles will be exemplified in what follows, but an even more basic problem must first be faced.

Fixing the Evidence?

Why is it necessary to make a distinction here between intracanonical and extracanonical gospels if exactly the same principles establish dependence or independence among them all? Go back and read the epigraph to this section, a passage from Luke Johnson's book *The Real Jesus,* with its accusations that my method is "fixed"; that I have given an early date and independent status to "virtually all apocryphal materials" and a correspondingly late date and dependent status to "virtually all intracanonical materials"; and that my only arguments are citations from "like-minded colleagues." Something clearly happens to collegial courtesy, scholarly integrity, and academic accuracy when extracanonical gospels enter the debate. But, since principles and not just polemics are concerned in that indictment, let me use it to review my methodology.

First, it is very, very serious to charge that another scholar has "fixed" his research methodology. Our only integrity as scholars is not to be right and correct but to be honest and public. "Fixing" data entails a deliberate intention to deceive. When one scholar accuses another of fixing the evidence, somebody has lost his integrity. Others will have to decide whether it is Johnson or myself.

Second, I do not give a "late dating for virtually all intracanonical materials." I date them all just as everyone else does (within, of course, those three presuppositions mentioned above). There is a full inventory of the Jesus tradition in Appendix 1 to *The Historical Jesus,* and, where applicable, Paul is always in first place since his authentic letters are most securely dated to the 50s. Paul, therefore, ends up in fourteen out of the twenty-nine units with more than triple independent attestation in my earliest stratum (1991:434–436). I also date the *Q Gospel* to those same 50s, which I take to be the consensus position of experts on that text, as revealed in this example: "The entire development of Q . . . must be dated within the first three decades after the death of Jesus" (Koester 1990:170).

Neither do I give a "remarkably early dating for virtually all apocryphal materials." In fact, I don't even address more than a small fraction of them: the Apocrypha is a huge body of material, and I left the vast majority of it aside, having judged it to be either dependent on or aware of the intracanonical gospel texts. Here, almost at random, are four examples of such dependence: the *Epistula Apostolorum,* the *Infancy Gospel of Thomas,* the *Protoevangelium of James,* and the *Gospel of the Nazaroeans.* But I also singled out four extracanonical gospel texts that I judged to be crucially important for understanding the Jesus tradition. Three were independent of the intracanonical texts: the *Gospel of Thomas,* the *Egerton Gospel,* the *Secret Gospel of Mark.* The fourth text, the *Gospel of Peter,* is dependent on the intracanonical texts but also contains an independent source, which I termed the *Cross Gospel* (like the *Q Gospel* within Matthew and Luke). Because of the importance of those four gospels for my historical Jesus research, I published *Four Other Gospels* in 1985 and explicitly argued my position on dependence or independence for each one of the four. I cannot, however, claim originality for any of those assertions; though controversial, to be sure, they have been around ever since those documents were discovered in 1945, 1934, 1958, and 1886–1887 respectively.

Dwight Moody Smith, for example, cautiously summarized the situation concerning those four gospels in 1992 by saying that "in each case, the arguments for independence from, as distinguished from priority over, the intracanonical gospels have a certain plausibility, and Crossan is by no means the first or only scholar to advance them." He found in current research on the extracanonical gospels "a tilting in the direction of affirming their traditional and churchly roots as giving them an equal standing with the intracanonical gospels, which, so to speak, won out over them in the struggle that gave birth to the New Testament canon. Despite reservations about specific positions taken, I believe that this effort to see the origins of the intracanonical and apocryphal gospels together, as one process, is a useful one" (1992b:151–152).

In any case, by the time I had finished *Four Other Gospels,* I knew that the proposed *Cross Gospel* in particular, and the larger *Gospel of Peter,* was so important for understanding the development of the passion and resurrection stories that it would need a book all to itself. In 1988, *The Cross That Spoke* presented a scholarly defense of my position on the relationship of the extracanonical *Gospel of Peter* to the intracanonical passion-resurrection narratives. (When I need to establish a position, I write a book, not a footnote.) But it is rhetorical overkill, putting it mildly and kindly, to describe an early dating of those four texts (or, in the case of the *Gospel of Peter,* of a source within it) as an "early dating for virtually all apocryphal materials." Scholarly debate must continue, of course, on all those positions.

Third, I do, of course, quote from "like-minded colleagues." I am, for example, profoundly indebted to experts on the *Q Gospel,* from Robinson to Kloppenborg, as mentioned above, and to experts on the *Gospel of Thomas,* from Koester to Patterson, just to mention colleagues in this country. If their work is basically wrong, then so is mine.

Assessing the Evidence.

As an illustration, and because the *Gospel of Thomas* is so important for what immediately follows, I focus on it here as an example of how I assess (not fix) the evidence. My position on it represents a fourth major presupposition about the gospel sources available for reconstruction of the historical Jesus and earliest Christianity.

The *Gospel of Thomas* is, first of all, not a hypothetical necessity (as the *Q Gospel* is) but an extant document available partially in Greek (in fragments from three different manuscripts) and fully in Coptic (in a translation from a single manuscript).

The Greek fragments were discovered by Grenfell and Hunt in 1896–1897 and 1903–1904 at ancient Oxyrhynchus (1897; 1898; 1904ab). What they found, without anyone then knowing it, was fragments from the *Gospel of Thomas* in its original Greek. These are the three papyri with their van Haelst catalogue numbers and dates:

#593: Papyrus Oxyrhynchus 654 = *Gos. Thom.* Prologue and 1–7
#594: Papyrus Oxyrhynchus 1 = *Gos. Thom.* 26–33 (with 77b attached to 30)
#595: Papyrus Oxyrhynchus 655 = *Gos. Thom.* 24 and 36–39

P. Oxy. 654, now in London's British Library, is a single fragment from a reused scroll, dated to the middle of the third century. P. Oxy. 1, now in Oxford's Bodleian Library, is a single fragment from a codex, dated to the start of the third century. P. Oxy. 655, now in Harvard's Houghton Library, is eight fragments from a papyrus scroll, dated to the start of the third century. The dates, of course, are for the time the manuscripts were copied and not for the time the gospel itself was composed.

Grenfell and Hunt gave very decisive conclusions about the text contained in their P. Oxy. 1. They did not know, of course, that it was part of the *Gospel of Thomas,* but I cite their summary because, in my judgment, it is absolutely accurate for that gospel as a whole. They made "four points: (1) that we have here part of a collection of sayings, not extracts from a narrative gospel; (2) that they were not heretical; (3) that they were independent of the four Gospels in their present shape; (4) that they were earlier than A.D. 140, and might go back to the first century" (1898, 2; see 1897, 16–20). I emphasize that those fragments were from three *different* copies of the *Gospel of Thomas,* which indicates a fairly high popularity for that text (at least in second-century Egypt).

The Coptic translation was discovered in 1945 by a group of Egyptian peasants digging for nitrate-rich fertilizer at the base of the Jabal al-Tarif cliff near modern Nag Hammadi, about 250 miles south of Oxyrhynchus, also on the western bank of the Nile. It was part of what became known as the Nag Hammadi Library, twelve full codices and part of a thirteenth containing fifty-two tractates in all. The *Gospel of Thomas,* for example, is tractate 2 of codex 2, and the name is given not within the tractate's own prologue but separately, at the end (Robinson 1979). It is now preserved in the Coptic Museum in Old Cairo. (*Coptic* designates the Egyptian language as eventually written with the Greek alphabet and several other special letters. But it also designates Egyptian Christianity, without whose venerable antiquity all those intracanonical and extracanonical papyri would never have existed, been buried, to be but recently discovered.)

Second, here is why I judge it to be independent of the intracanonical gospels (1985:35–37 = 1992:17–19). If it were in direct literary dependence—that is, if the author of the *Gospel of Thomas* had had the intracanonical gospels available when writing—you would expect some influence from their individually specific order and content in the *Thomas* composition.

On order: In 1979 Bruno de Solages placed the sayings in the *Gospel of Thomas* in one column in its order, and their equivalents as they appear in each of the intracanonical gospels (as well as Q) in other columns in their order. He then drew lines between the equivalent versions of the same saying. What resulted was a total mess of lines showing absolutely no common order anywhere.

On content: In 1966 John H. Sieber's doctoral dissertation at Claremont Graduate School focused not on common traditional materials in the *Gospel of Thomas* and the synoptics but on individually specific stylistic or redactional details in the synoptics, to see if those items appeared in *Thomas.* He concluded that "there is very little redactional evidence, if any, for holding that our Synoptic Gospels were the sources of Thomas' synoptic sayings. In the great majority of cases there is no such evidence at all" (262). The same conclusion, reached via a similar rigorous methodology, appeared in another Claremont dissertation—that of

Stephen J. Patterson in 1988. He concluded that, "while Thomas and the synoptic texts do in fact share a large body of common material, there is neither a consistent pattern of dependence of one text upon the other, nor a substantial amount of agreement in the way each text ordered the material they share" (1993:16).

But what if one raises the possibility of indirect literary dependence—that is, the possibility that the author of *Thomas* created a collection of sayings after having heard or read the synoptic gospels in the distant past? Then the emphasis shifts, of course, from *Thomas*'s lack of any redactional order or content derived from synoptic sources to *Thomas*'s own redactional intention and composition. Why did the author choose *those* sayings rather than all the others available for inclusion? Why, to give a specific example, did the author manage to hear or read that *set* of beatitudes in Matthew and Luke and remember them as the discrete ones given in the *Gospel of Thomas* 54 (poor), 68–69:1 (persecuted), and 69:2 (hungry)?

The *Gospel of Thomas* is fairly unique among extracanonical gospels proposed as canonically independent because it is not a fragmentary but a complete text. One who is not persuaded of its independence will hardly be persuaded of the independence of any other extracanonical text presently available. In 1978 the late George MacRae concluded that "it now appears that a majority of scholars who have seriously investigated the matter have been won over to the side of 'Thomas' independence of the intracanonical Gospels, though these scholars hold a variety of views about the actual history of the composition of the 'Gospel of Thomas'" (152). Be that as it may, the theory of *Thomas*'s intracanonical independence is now strongly enough supported by experts that one can begin to build on it and thereby to test it further. That is what I have done in the past and intend to do in even greater detail below.

Method and Debate.

In conclusion, the debate has never been, despite Johnson's exaggeration, that some scholars, myself included, take "virtually all" of the extracanonical Jesus traditions as early and independent, and "virtually all" of the intracanonical texts as late and dependent. The fact is that a very *small* number of extracanonical gospel sources have been proposed as canonically independent by some scholars, myself included, while opposing scholars declare *all* extracanonical texts to be late and canonically dependent. Apart from detailed arguments in specific cases, I have one initial problem with that general conclusion.

Once certain scholars—for example, Neirynck in Belgium (1989) or Meier (1991–1994:1.114–139) in the United States—have declared *every* extracanonical gospel so far discovered to be canonically dependent, on what principles might any future discovery be assessed differently? My own principles for judging *direct literary dependence* are these: *genetic relationship* is established by the presence of individually specific order or content from independent into dependent text, and *redactional confirmation* is established by showing where, how, and why the dependent text changed the independent one. *Indirect literary dependence* is, of course, much more difficult for arguments in either direction, since genetic relationship is generally precluded in this case. All that is left is *redactional confirmation* of whatever option is chosen. Thus, for example, if there is some sort of indirect literary relationship between the *Gospel of Peter* and our intracanonical gospels, be it in one direction as source (Crossan 1988; 1995) or in the opposite direction as digest (Brown 1987; 1994), one must be able to explain by redactional confirmation how an author got from the independent to the dependent one(s). This, then, is my challenge: On what principles might *any* future extracanonical text be judged as canonically independent by those who have thus far refused that position to all past ones? Put another way: How could your position ever be falsified? My own theory on the *Gospel of Peter,* for example, could be falsified to my satisfaction if somebody could explain an author who knew the intracanonical passion-resurrection accounts and came up with *that* version of them.

I have mentioned four separate source presuppositions in this chapter, and two more will be added in Chapters 21 (the *Didache*) and 25 (the *Gospel of Peter*). But for ease of reference I give you all six of them immediately. These six crucial decisions about sources form the foundation of this book. Here they are in summary:

Presupposition 1: The Priority of Mark. Mark is a major source used by both Matthew and Luke. This is the basis for all modern critical gospel research, because we can compare all three texts and thence understand processes of gospel composition, tradition development, and "history" creation.

Presupposition 2: The Existence of the Q *Gospel.* The *Q Gospel* is the other major source used by both Matthew and Luke. It is a gospel in its own right, with textual, generic, and theological integrity, and not just their source. It is also possible to discern redactional layers within its compositional history.

Presupposition 3: The Dependence of John. John is dependent on the synoptic gospels for its initial narrative frames about the John the Baptist and for its terminal frames about the passion and resurrection of Jesus. It also has an independent tradition of sayings and miracles, in which the physical miracles become signs of spiritual realities.

Presupposition 4: The Independence of the Gospel of Thomas. The *Gospel of Thomas* is independent from any and all of the four intracanonical gospels. It was composed originally without their use (before their existence?), but there may be minor traces of their influence during later transmission and transcription.

Presupposition 5: The Independence of the Didache. This is not a gospel but a community rule, and it presents a fascinatingly different insight into an early Christian community quite different from those glimpsed in the letters of Paul. I consider it to be *entirely* independent of any one or all of our four intracanonical gospels.

Presupposition 6: The Existence and Independence of the Cross Gospel. There exists within the present *Gospel of Peter* a consecutive source, which I term the *Cross Gospel* for convenience (the name is irrelevant; call it Source X, if you prefer). The *Cross Gospel* is a passion-resurrection narrative quite different from that in Mark.

Of these six crucial presuppositions about sources, three concern intracanonical texts and three concern extracanonical texts. Some we have just seen, and some are still to come. None of them is original, and none is infallible. In general, they get more controversial as you descend the list. But no scholar who works on the reconstruction of the historical Jesus or earliest Christianity can avoid making a decision on each of those items. Wrong anywhere there, wrong everywhere thereafter. And that holds for *everyone*.

CHAPTER 9

COMPARING GOSPEL
MANUSCRIPTS

There are two stigmata of Christian texts . . . the early and consistent use of
the codex and the *nomina sacra*. . . . It is not at all surprising that some of our
earliest Christian manuscripts should be of the Old Testament. What is surprising is that the format in which they are written should be the codex and
not the roll; this startling break with Jewish tradition implies, I think, that
these early manuscripts of the Old Testament had been preceded by specifically Christian works with which the new format originated. . . . *Nomina
sacra* as a term in Greek and Latin paleography denotes a strictly limited
number of words, at most fifteen, the sacral character of which, intrinsic or
contextual, is emphasized by abbreviating the word in question, normally by
contraction [first and last letters], occasionally in the earliest period by suspension [first letters]. A horizontal line is placed above the abbreviation as a
warning that the word cannot be pronounced as written, as it was in documents with numerals, and where, as is usual, contraction is used, the treatment of the end of the word is governed by strict rules.
    Colin H. Roberts, *Manuscript, Society, and Belief in Early Christian Egypt,*
pp. 19, 20, 26

Prior to any reconstruction of the historical Jesus or the birth of Christianity,
historians must have already made their own historical judgments about the
relationships among *all* the early gospels, about dependence and independence
between them, and about possible sources hidden within them. Granted that
necessity, and granted also the polemical tone of current scholarly discussion, is
there any relatively objective evidence that might be introduced into the debate?
Can we catch a glimpse of what is now divided into intra- and extracanonical
before any such division existed? (In what follows, by the way, note carefully the
difference between writing *materials,* such as plant papyrus or animal parchment,
and writing *formats,* such as roll-like scroll or book-like codex.)

There are three common aspects of the earliest gospels that cut across that
later distinction. Gospels, both inside and outside the present canon, show
equally early dates for extant manuscripts, equally clear preferences for papyrus
codices, and equally set usages for sacred abbreviations. Those last two points
will require fuller explanation as we proceed, but they are extremely important,

because together they indicate that some centralized authority controlled the creation of those earliest gospel manuscripts.

Common Early Dates

> The distinction between Biblical and non-Biblical texts would not have been so obvious to the users of these as it is to us, and both the Egerton Gospel and the *Shepherd* of Hermas might have been regarded as indistinguishable from the canonical books of the New Testament. . . . The distinction between Biblical and non-Biblical works is, at any rate in the second century, to some extent anachronistic.
>
> Colin H. Roberts and T. C. Skeat, *The Birth of the Codex*, p. 42

The term *papyrus*, which appears repeatedly in these chapters, names a writing material made from pressed plant pith. T. C. Skeat offers this succinct description of how the substance was manufactured: "The plant grows with its roots submerged in water, from which the jointless stem, triangular in section, rises to a height of 10–15 feet, ending in a tuft of flowers. For the manufacture of papyrus the plant was cut down and the stem was divided into sections, the length of which determined the height of the papyrus roll which was to be made. From these sections the outer rind was stripped off, and the soft pith, while still fresh, cut lengthwise into thin strips. These strips were laid side by side, slightly overlapping, on a hard surface, and a second layer was laid over them, the strips running at right angles to those in the first layer. The two layers were then consolidated by hammering and pressing, and then dried. The sheet thus formed was then trimmed, and the surface smoothed with pumice and burnished with rounded polishers of shell or ivory. Finally, a number of sheets were pasted together with flour paste to make long lengths which were then rolled up for storage or transport" (1969:55). In a more recent article on the price of papyrus, Skeat estimated that "papyrus left the factories in standard rolls of 20 sheets," about 12 inches high by 136 inches long; and while "the daily wage of a labourer in the 1st century A.D. very rarely exceeded 1 drachma," the price of such a scroll was "2 drachmas in the mid 1st cent. A.D." (1995:88–89).

EXCAVATING RUBBISH DUMPS

At the end of the third century, Oxyrhynchus, 250 miles south of Alexandria, west of the Nile, on the edge of the Libyan desert, was a walled city with five gates, a theater that seated 11,200 spectators, and the honorific title of "illustrious and most illustrious." At the end of the nineteenth century, Oxyrhynchus—modern El Bahnasa—was, in the words of Eric Turner, "a waste of rubbish mounds and deep-blown sand . . . [a] pillaged and wrecked site, where buildings had been quarried for stone down to their foundations and their position was marked, if at all, by no more than lines of chips in the sand" (1952:80). To this site in 1896 the newly created Graeco-Roman Account of London's Egypt Exploration Fund sent two Oxford University archeologists, Bernard Pyne Grenfell (1869–1926) and Arthur Surridge Hunt (1871–1934), in very deliberate search of papyri. They dug trenches twenty-five feet deep through those ancient rubbish dumps and excavated for six seasons, one in 1896–1897, the rest between 1903 and 1907. The vast hoard of papyri they discovered, among them fragments from three different Greek copies of the *Gospel of Thomas,* is still under slow but steady publication in volumes of *The Oxyrhynchus Papyri,* now numbering over fifty and counting.

They were racing against other diggers, the Egyptian peasants who used that papyrus-enriched earth to fertilize their gardens and fields. Fifty years later and another 250 miles south along the Nile, such diggers found the Nag Hammadi codices in a sealed jar buried beneath the Nile-side cliffs. That race between scholar-diggers and farmer-diggers has been amusingly described by the British poet and dramatist Tony Harrison in a 1988 play titled *The Trackers of Oxyrhynchus.* One of the Grenfell and Hunt papyri contained about half of a lost comedy by Sophocles called *The Trackers.* Harrison remade those four hundred broken lines creatively for a one-performance world premiere in the stadium at Delphi in Greece. He did so by writing Grenfell and Hunt, trackers of papyri, and the Egyptian fellaheen, trackers of fertilizer *(sebakh),* into the fragmented play about the satyrs, trackers of Apollo's lost lyre. He put these words on Grenfell's lips (1990:10):

> Papyri! Insects gnaw them. Time corrodes
> and native plants get potted in a mulch of Pindar's Odes!
> Horrible to contemplate! How can a person sleep
> while Sophocles is rotting on an ancient rubbish heap?
> Our fellaheen, though, are not entirely sure
> if Menander's not more use to them as manure!
> They ferret for fertilizer, and Hunt and I track
> for philosophy and drama in nitrogenous *sebakh.*
> Spinach now flourishes from the pulped-up roll
> that held still hidden secrets of Sappho's soul.

All diggers and trackers have, no doubt, their own integrity and validity, but the "crate after crate" and "load after load" that Grenfell and Hunt shipped back to England may stand here as introduction and background to my present focus on format and style in the earliest Christian papyri. It would, by the way, take massive opposing evidence to change the general picture that has emerged so far.

CHRISTIAN PAPYRI

The earliest manuscripts of the New Testament are all on papyrus, and scholars count them to date as Papyrus 1 to Papyrus 99 or $\mathfrak{P}^1$ to $\mathfrak{P}^{99}$. Since that number may well be out of date by the time you read its assertion, you should check it against the updated data available through the Electronic New Testament Manuscript Project on the Internet at *http://www.entmp.org*. We await not just new discoveries but the completed publication of older ones.

New Testament papyri may also have another title, apart from those $\mathfrak{P}$ numbers, derived from the place where they were found, the person who obtained them, the fund that purchased them, or the museum where they are now located. $\mathfrak{P}^{90}$, for example, is also Papyrus Oxyrhynchus (or P. Oxy.) 3523, published only in 1983 from Grenfell and Hunt's huge store of rescued rubbish. It is a single codex sheet with a single column of text on both sides. Badly mutilated, it is dated by its editor, T. C. Skeat, to the second century. It contains John 18:36–19:7 (*NDIEC* 7.242–243). That serves to remind us that among discovered gospel papyri, the score at the moment is John with 22, Matthew with 18, Luke with 8 (Acts with 13), and Mark with 3 papyri examples (*NDIEC* 7.257). A numbered papyrus may be either a tiny fragment, as is $\mathfrak{P}^{52}$ (Papyrus Rylands, Greek 457), dated to the early second century but containing only parts of John 18:31–34, 37–38; or a full gospel, like $\mathfrak{P}^{66}$ (Papyrus Bodmer II), dated to the second century but containing almost all of John.

The *recto* is the side of a papyrus sheet with horizontal fibers; the *verso* is the side with vertical fibers. A scroll is usually written only on its recto side, but a codex is written on both sides. That is why even a tiny fragment, such as $\mathfrak{P}^{52}$ above, can be identified clearly as a codex and not a scroll. The original codex of which only $\mathfrak{P}^{52}$ survived was a bound book an inch thick containing 110 7-by-8¼-inch pages, according to Skeat's calculations (1994:264). A scroll can, of course, be reused on its verso side for a new text. Known as an *opisthograph,* a scroll seeing double duty is not calculated as a genuine choice of scroll over codex for the new and secondary text.

EARLY GOSPEL MANUSCRIPTS

I focus here on papyrus gospels up to the start of the third century, as listed in Abbé Joseph van Haelst's invaluable catalogue of Jewish and Christian literary papyri (1976:209, 409–410). The point is not that he is infallible or even complete but that he is a neutral and consistent source. Here is that list, with van Haelst's suggested dates and catalogue numbers, each text's $\mathfrak{P}$-number in the ongoing roster of New Testament papyri, the general (but often very fragmentary) content of each, and an identification as either c (codex) or s (scroll):

Early 2nd century:	(1)c	#462	℘52	John
2nd century:	(2)c	#426	℘66	John
	(3)c	#586	*Egerton Gospel*	Stories about Jesus
2nd/3rd centuries:	(4)c	#336 + #403	℘67 & ℘64 & ℘4	Matthew & Luke
	(5)c	#372	℘77	Matthew
	(6)c	#406	℘75	Luke & John
	(7)s	#592	P. Oxy. 2949	*Gospel of Peter*
Start 3rd century:	(8)c	#594	P. Oxy. 1	*Gospel of Thomas*
	(9)s	#595	P. Oxy. 655	*Gospel of Thomas*
	(10)c	#1065	P. Rylands, Greek 463	*Gospel of Mary*

I have three preliminary comments on that list. First, eight of those ten items are from codices; only two (7 and 9) are from scrolls. On the one hand, those two cases are extracanonical gospels; on the other hand, there are three cases (3, 8, and 10) where extracanonical gospels are on codices. There are no intracanonical gospels on scrolls in that list, however; there is, in fact, only one current example of such a case (#459, ℘22 or P. Oxy. 1228, containing two tiny fragments from John 15–16, dated to the third century).

Second, it is debated whether #403 (℘4) (see the fourth item in the above list) is part of the same codex as #336 (℘67+ 64). They both have two columns per page, but their discoloration is quite different. Abbé van Haelst called it "probably the same codex" (1976:146), while Colin Roberts asserted that "there can in my opinion be no doubt that all these fragments come from the same codex" (1979:13; see also 1962:58–60). More recently, T. C. Skeat, having restudied all three fragments, argued that they were from the same late-second-century codex and proposed that it was the earliest four-gospel codex now extant (1997:30–31). Philip Comfort, on the other hand, concluded that the three texts were not from the same codex but only from the same scribe. "I cannot confidently make an absolute identification of the three manuscripts as having belonged to the same codex. What I can suggest is that the same scribe produced all three of these manuscripts, perhaps copying Matthew's Gospel some time prior to Luke's Gospel—using a different stylus (a blunter one for Matthew than for Luke)" (1995:51). But, for my present purpose, I leave that list at those ten items.

Third, notice how small most of the items are. Apart from the Bodmer Papyri in #426 and #406, the rest are mostly fragments from a single or at best a few sheets (with, of course, two sides or pages per sheet). The great, post-Constantinian full-Bible codices of the fourth and fifth centuries have, in contrast, between 730 and 820 sheets extant. Also, as another instance of the vagaries of preservation, that #336/#403 duo was reused and thus survived as binding material for a work by the early-first-century Jewish philosopher Philo of Alexandria.

When you read down the contents in the chart above, note the interesting comparison between what we *now* call intracanonical and extracanonical gospels. Up to the start of the third century, we have evidence for three intracanonical gospels: John (three cases), Matthew (two cases), and Luke (two cases). But we also have evidence for four extracanonical gospels: *Egerton* (one case), *Peter* (one case), *Thomas* (two cases), and *Mary* (one case). In other words, of the ten items, five pertain to eventual intracanonical, five to eventual extracanonical gospels. From that point on, the ascendancy of the intracanonical gospels becomes more and more clear in the numerical record. I do not intend to press that comparison too far. I simply want to make this point: if we knew nothing about intracanonical and extracanonical distinctions or about orthodox and heretical judgments but knew only those inventoried discoveries up to around 200, we would probably conclude that *all* seven of those gospels were of early Christian significance.

Nothing that I have said is intended to deny the eventual ascendancy of the fourfold gospel in Catholic Christianity. But historical reconstruction demands the acknowledgment that, looking just at the papyri record to the start of the third century, we would be unable to decide which gospels are "intracanonical" and which are "extracanonical." I see, therefore, those earliest papyri gospels as one relatively objective indication that our clear distinction between extracanonical and intracanonical gospels is not historically useful in studying them both.

Common Papyrus Codices

Three distinct types of writing materials, papyrus, parchment, and wooden tablets, contributed, though in very different ways, to the formation of the Christian book, and all were in common use in Palestine and most of the Near East during the first century A.D. . . . . The Dead Sea caves and elsewhere in the Judaean desert . . . have now produced fragments . . . of nearly 800 manuscripts. . . . All, where ascertainable, are in the form of rolls, and the great majority are on skin or parchment. . . . When, however, we turn to Christian literature, the position is entirely different . . . [and] the contrast with pagan literature is, if anything, even more sharply drawn. . . . In the past, all sorts of reasons have been put forward to explain the Christian preference for the [book-like] codex [over the roll-like scroll].

T. C. Skeat, "Early Christian Book-Production," pp. 54, 64, 69

Colin Roberts listed fourteen items as the earliest manuscript evidence for Christian literature. By "earliest" he meant "those texts which in the general judgment of palaeographers are assigned to the second century." He himself would omit, for example, #426 ($\mathfrak{P}^{66}$ or P. Bodmer II of John) from my list above. This is his list, with van Haelst inventory numbers, papyrus names, and general contents (which can, of course, be very fragmentary) (1979:13–14):

2nd century:	(1) #462	$\mathfrak{P}^{52}$	John
	(2) #33	P. Baden 4.56	Exodus & Deuteronomy
	(3) #12	P. Yale i.1	Genesis
	(4) #52	P. Chester Beatty VI	Numbers & Deuteronomy
	(5) #179	P. Ant. i.7	Psalms
	(6) #224	P. Lips. 170	Psalms
	(7) #151	Bodl. MS. Gr. bibl.g.5(P)	Psalms
	(8) #336 + #403	$\mathfrak{P}^{67} + \mathfrak{P}^{64} + \mathfrak{P}^{4}$	Matthew, Luke
	(9) #534	$\mathfrak{P}^{32}$	Titus
	(10) #372	$\mathfrak{P}^{77}$	Matthew
	(11) #586	*Egerton Gospel*	Stories about Jesus
	(12) #657	P. Michigan 130	Hermas, *Shepherd*
	(13) #594	P. Oxy. 1	*Gospel of Thomas*
	(14) #671	P. Oxy. 405	Irenaeus, *Against Heresies*

All items save two on that list are from codices. Of those two, his twelfth item is "written on the verso of a roll carrying a documentary text of the third quarter of the second century" (1979:14), evidencing use of available waste papyrus rather than a true choice of roll format. His fourteenth item is the only true scroll choice in the presently extant Christian works of the second century.

Roberts and Skeat give that same list with the addition of one more example—a text that Skeat had recently edited, the P. Oxy. 3523 text of John 18:36–19:7, known as New Testament $\mathfrak{P}^{90}$ (1983: 40–41; *NDIEC* 7.242–244). It too is a papyrus codex, so the point remains the same. The future would belong, if not to that material, at least to that format.

WHY THE CHRISTIAN CODEX?

The Christian preference for the papyrus codex is very striking when its ratio of scroll to codex is contrasted with the ratio for pagan Greek literature in discoveries dated before the year 400 C.E., as given by Roberts and Skeat (1983:38–44; *NDIEC* 7.251). For pagan Greek literature, the ratio of scroll to codex is eight to one. For early Christian literature, it is almost the reverse. There the ratio of scroll to codex is one to seven. It is only in the 300s that the ratio of scroll to codex finally and irrevocably reverses itself in favor of the book format in Greek literature (scroll to codex is one to three). But even in the 200s that Christian ratio of scroll to codex was one to thirteen. That victory of codex over scroll happened only slowly and late for Greek literature but almost instantly and early for Christian literature. But "by adopting the codex format the early church appears to have opted for an inferior quality of production . . . a second-class status in comparison with its contemporary rival, the roll," and hence this question: "If the gospels were committed first to rolls, as is frequently assumed from a consideration of their lengths, what were the reasons which led to their change of format?" (*NDIEC* 7.254, 256). Why did Christians move so swiftly to the codex format, turning thereby against both Greco-Roman and Jewish tradition, which favored the scroll for literary works?

Several reasons have been suggested for that Christian change to codex (or possible Christian invention of codex); but while one or all of them may be correct, none is totally compelling, as Roberts and Skeat have shown (1983:45–53). Reasons adduced include economy, compactness, capacity, convenience, and ease of reference. But all of those are questionable as fact, and even if true may be more evident for us, to whom the codex format is natural, than for those who grew up with scrolls as a given.

Skeat proposed a new reason in two recent articles. He suggested that the codex was chosen over the roll because it could easily hold all "four Gospels." Even though "it is certainly true that most of the earliest Gospel fragments come, or appear to come, from single-Gospel codices . . . these single-Gospel codices are in fact evidence for the existence of the four-Gospel codex . . . [because] the four-Gospel codex was already in existence and had thus set the standard for manuscripts of individual Gospels" (1994:264). He repeated that proposal later, explaining that "the reason why the Christians, perhaps about 100 A.D., soon after the publication of the Gospel of John, decided to adopt the codex was that only a codex could contain all four Gospels. . . . [T]he motivation for this decision was the desire to ensure the survival of the four best-known and most widely accepted Gospels, and at the same time to prevent the accretion of further Gospels which could not be expected to contain authentic information but might rather seek to propagate doctrines which the Church had rejected" (1997:31). That, however, is surely a very strange argument and a very perverse reading of the evidence: single-gospel codices, for which we have earlier documented evidence, are derived from four-gospel codices, for which we have only later documented evidence.

In Graham Stanton's reference to Skeat's proposal, the strangeness of its argumentation is again quite obvious: "[Skeat] accepts that single gospels circulated as codices, but only as 'spin-offs', so to speak, of the four-Gospel codex. . . . If (as Skeat suggests) the four-Gospel codex preceded the circulation of single-gospel codices, it must have been adopted soon after the beginning of the second century, for we have in 𝔓52 (usually dated to c. 125 A.D.) a single-gospel codex. But a date soon after the turn of the century is difficult to square with the ways written

gospels and oral gospel traditions were used at that time" (337, 338). Stanton concludes, following the extant evidence, that "Christian scribes first experimented
with single-gospel codices" and that "their general counter-cultural stance would
have made them more willing than their non-Christian counterparts to break with
the almost unanimous preference for the roll and experiment with the unfashion-
able codex" (338, 339). Even if this "counter-cultural stance" is not *a* (let alone *the*)
reason for the choice of papyrus codex, it is in any case significant in its own right.

A DOCUMENTARY BACKGROUND?

Papyri, in general, are either *documentary* or *literary*. Documentary papyri are
those thousands upon thousands of letters and records, bills and loans, rents and
contracts, pleas and suits that have made the everyday life of ordinary people in
ancient Egypt come alive so clearly and powerfully. Literary papyri range from
the oldest texts of Homer, the Greek classic found most frequently in ancient
Egypt, to the oldest text of Virgil, a tiny fragment from the *Aeneid* 4:9, left by one
of the Roman conquerors who stormed the Jewish fortress on Masada in 73–74
C.E. They also include most of the Dead Sea Scrolls, both biblical and sectarian
texts, and some of those writings on Roberts's fourteen-item list of the earliest
Christian papyri seen above. There is, of course, a clear difference between the
competent but primarily functional style of the documentary scribe and the calligraphic or deliberately elegant style of the literary copyist.

Roberts described the authors of the items on his list as "far from unskilled,"
but, with the exception of those who produced items 8, 10, and 14, they were "not
trained in calligraphy and so not accustomed to writing books, though they were
familiar with them; they employ what is basically a documentary hand but at the
same time they are aware that it is a book, not a document on which they are
engaged. They are not personal or private hands; in most a degree of regularity
and of clarity is aimed at and achieved. Such hands might be described as
'reformed documentary'. (One advantage for the paleographer in such hands is
that with their close links to the documents they are somewhat less difficult to
date than purely calligraphic hands)." The result is, for example, a clear "contrast
between the hieratic elegance of the Graeco-Jewish rolls of the Law and the
workaday appearance of the first Christian codices (whether of the Old Testament or of early Christian writings). . . . Their writing is based, with some
changes and with a few exceptions, on the model of the documents, not on that
of Greek classical manuscripts nor on that of the Graeco-Jewish tradition. . . .
Behind this group of papyri it is not difficult to envisage the men familiar to us
from the documentary papyri in the Arsinoite or Oxyrhynchus; tradesmen, farmers, minor government officials to whom knowledge of and writing in Greek was
an essential skill, but who had few or no literary interests" (1979:14, 19, 20, 21).

Competent styles for handling documentary papyri do not look exactly like calligraphic styles for copying literary classics. Roberts gives several examples that betray the documentary heritage of those second-century scribes. An obvious case is using numerals for numbers rather than writing them out in full—for example, 12 rather than *twelve*. But this is also "documentary with a difference," since these early texts often contain reading aids and marks: the texts are intended to be read in public; they are for communal use (1979:21).

The scribal conservatism that rendered Greco-Roman paganism so slow in adopting the codex for literary works may have been far less operative with writers coming out of a primarily functional background in letter-writing and record-keeping. The codex was what they were used to; the codex was therefore what they used. "Economic and social factors as well as religious were at work and," as Roberts concludes, "the business-like hand of the early texts mirrors the character and circumstances of the communities that used them" (1979:20). In a more recent review of the whole question, Harry Gamble traces the dominance of the codex for early Christian literature back to Pauline usage. But once again, the reason he finds is pragmatic: "The codex, whether of parchment or of papyrus, would have been familiar to a small businessman like Paul and to the circles in which he moved. . . . [I]t is conceivable that [his letters] were written in small codices" (64). Of the seventeen second-century *non-Christian* texts on codices, one-third are what Gamble terms "professional manuals," and even some of the other, literary texts may have been intended for similar "educational use" (65). The early Christians chose the codex over the roll immediately and overwhelmingly not for any theological, exegetical, economic, or polemical reason. Theirs was "an essentially utilitarian attitude": "the early Christians adapted a familiar, practical medium for a new but still practical purpose. Christian texts came to be inscribed in codices not because they enjoyed a special status as aesthetic or cult objects, but because they were practical books for everyday use: the handbooks, as it were, of the Christian community" (65–66).

Common Sacred Abbreviations

The Christian scribes wished to give graphic expression to the theological equation already present in the earliest apostolic preaching, in which *kyrios* [LORD], the name for the God of Israel, was used as a title for Jesus Christ. In other words, the four nouns [LORD, GOD, JESUS, CHRIST] which are universally accorded special treatment in the early papyri of the New Testament are not simply *nomina sacra* [sacred names] but rather *nomina divina* [divine names].
        Schuyler Brown, "Concerning the Origin of the *Nomina Sacra*," p. 19

The second major difference between the earliest Christian and other Jewish or Greco-Roman literary texts is equally striking. It is the use of what are called *nomina sacra*, a term taken from the title of Ludwig Traube's pioneering work in 1906. They are *sacred names* or, more precisely, standard abbreviations for certain sacred names. The term, in Roberts's description, "denotes a strictly limited number of words, at most fifteen, the sacral character of which, intrinsic or contextual, is emphasized by abbreviating the word in question, normally, by contraction, occasionally in the earliest period by suspension." A horizontal line is placed above the abbreviation as a warning that the words cannot be pronounced as written" (1979:26). If the name JESUS appears as J̄E, using the first two letters, that is abbreviation by suspension. If it appears as J̄S, using first and last letters, that is abbreviation by contraction.

Almost forty years ago Anton Paap surveyed all Christian manuscripts up to the year 500 and outlined the evidence for usage of the fifteen sacred words. I focus, just as an example, on his data for the earliest texts, those dated by their editors up to ±200 (1959:6–11; #3–#15A). Ten of the words had already appeared by that date with these percentages:

GOD is abbreviated in 8 out of 14 texts = 57%

LORD is abbreviated in 8 out of 14 texts = 57%

JESUS is abbreviated in 6 out of 14 texts = 43%

SPIRIT is abbreviated in 5 out of 14 texts = 36%

FATHER is abbreviated in 4 out of 14 texts = 29%

MAN is abbreviated in 3 out of 14 texts = 21%

CHRIST is abbreviated in 3 out of 14 texts = 21%

SON is abbreviated in 2 out of 14 texts = 14%

ISRAEL is abbreviated in 1 out of 14 texts = 7%

CROSS is abbreviated in 1 out of 14 texts = 7%

But the other five—HEAVEN, DAVID, JERUSALEM, SAVIOR, and MOTHER—had not yet been abbreviated by the year 200. I cite these statistics here (even though they need revamping and updating from discoveries and publications since the 1950s) to let the list of names reverberate as the condensed or concentrated theology of those Christians who used the abbreviations. Their overlining is like our underlining, an emphasis on certain key words elevated out of the ordinary level even in texts already sacred in general.

Another (but newer) example from within that same period is the P. Oxy. 3523 manuscript of John 18:36–19:7 mentioned above (𝔓⁹⁰). Lines 35–36 of the fragment's mutilated verso contain John 19:5, and there is a definite sacred abbreviation of Jesus' name: "So J̄S [came] out, wear[ing] the crown [of th]orns [and the pur]ple robe." That word JESUS appears as only its first and last letter with a flat stroke above them. A similar abbreviation must be restored for Jesus' name in two cases on the recto's equally mutilated side. Line 6 is John 18:36 with ["J̄S̄ answered"] and line 24 is John 19:1 with "Pil[ate took J̄S̄]." Restoration to J̄S̄ rather than to JESUS is aided by stichometry, the relatively regular number of letters per line in columns of text on scroll or codex, but one can never, of course, be absolutely certain in such cases.

That same sacred abbreviation is found not only in the Greek fragments of the *Gospel of Thomas* but in the Coptic translation, where "JESUS [as J̄S̄] said" starts a great majority of its sayings. Another and even more striking example is the extracanonical *Egerton Gospel,* cited in both the lists above. (It is, by the way, so called from the fund that endowed its purchase.) Its nine different sacred abbreviations are anomalous both in the ones that are used and in the ways they are shortened.

Three sacred names are present without any particular surprises: ḠD̄ for GOD, L̄D̄ for LORD, and J̄S̄ for JESUS. According to Paap's data, out of eighty-seven sources mentioning Jesus in the first five Christian centuries, JE is used by 8 percent, JES (contraction, not suspension) by 28 percent, and J̄S̄ by 64 percent. The actual total, not by sources but by instances, is, respectively, 5, 15, and 80 percent (1959:108). The future belonged to abbreviation by contraction.

A fourth unsurprising abbreviation in the *Egerton Gospel* is FER for FATHER. Using one or more of the initial or terminal letters seems characteristic of this gospel's mode of contraction. A fifth abbreviation used in the *Egerton Gospel* is very rare; it appears only in two other, much later texts. It cannot be adequately expressed in English translation. The question to Jesus about taxes "to Caesar" in Mark 12:14 is here expressed as taxes "to kings," which is a ten-letter Greek word abbreviated in the *Egerton Gospel* to its first two and last six letters. A strange way to do it—and maybe even stranger to do it at all. It is not, after all, a very sacred name, and hardly like Jesus himself as King of kings.

Finally, there are the four cases unique to this gospel. One is MO for MOSES (on the analogy of JE for JESUS), using abbreviation by suspension rather than contraction. Another is ISAĦ, abbreviating ISAIAH by using its first two and last two letters, a combined suspension and contraction admixture. Yet another is P̄R̄O̅P̄H̄S̄ for PROPHETS, using the first four and last two letters of an eight-letter Greek word. The final case is P̄R̄O̅P̄H̄IED for PROPHESIED, using the first five and last three letters of a twelve-letter Greek verb form. All those words have lines above them indicative of abbreviation.

There are certain rather obvious conclusions we can draw about the system of abbreviations in this specific extracanonical gospel. The writer seems caught between suspension and contraction (sometimes using both for the same word) and ends up with abbreviations almost as long as the original words themselves.

Furthermore, as Jon Daniels says in his extremely helpful doctoral dissertation on the *Egerton Gospel,* "it is reasonable to suppose that prophetic figures of Jewish history and tradition held special place for Egerton's scribe or the tradition in which s/he was trained" (1990:7). Finally, speaking of that prophetic emphasis-by-abbreviation, Roberts concludes that "both the early date and the connectedness of this group set them apart. It seems to represent an experimental phase in the history of the system when its limits were not clearly established, though the basic words were. . . . By the end of the second century the list had been pruned and effectively closed" (1979:39). It is no wonder that H. I. Bell and T. C. Skeat, the British Museum's manuscript curators and the *Egerton Gospel's* official editors, dated the document to "the middle of the second century," describing that date as "highly probable and . . . likely to err, if at all, on the side of caution, for there are features in the hand which might suggest a period yet earlier in the century" (1935a:1).

How and why sacred names were invented and used in earliest Christianity is about as controversial as how and why papyrus codices were adopted (or invented) in earliest Christianity. Ludwig Traube and Anton Paap thought the practice of sacred names derived directly from Jewish usage in writing the name of God, but Schuyler Brown has argued for a much more indirect connection. In unpointed or unvocalized Hebrew script, the sacred name of God looks like any other word. In order to give its sanctity appropriate emphasis, Jewish tradition spoke it with a special pronunciation, wrote it with an archaic script, or decorated it with gold leaf. Maybe, then, that practice gave Jewish Christians the *idea* of treating certain names as uniquely special to them. Notice, therefore, this severely qualified conclusion by Colin Roberts: "The ineffability of the name of God, expressed when the Law was read in Hebrew by replacing the vowels proper to it by those of Adonai ('Lord'), is directly or indirectly the psychological origin of the *nomina sacra*" (1979:29).

What must be emphasized, in any case, is that we are faced with two huge jumps of imagination in earliest Christianity. One giant leap was from casual parchment notebooks to sacred papyrus codices. The other was from the unique case of a single sacred name (YHWH) as one that could be written normally but not pronounced normally to a set of sacred names that could be pronounced normally but not written normally. *No amount of debate about the exact how or why should obscure the fact that both those jumps had taken place as early back as material remains let us go.* What does that dual phenomenon say about central authority and scribal tradition in earliest Christianity?

Central Manuscript Control?

We may perhaps imagine the invention as originating with some leading figure in the early Church, who, whatever the ultimate source of his inspiration, succeeded both in devising a distinctive format for Christian manuscripts of the Scriptures, differentiated equally from the parchment roll of Judaism and the papyrus roll of the pagan world, and in imposing its use throughout the Church. . . . [T]he introduction of the *nomina sacra* seems to parallel very closely the adoption of the papyrus codex. . . . It is no less remarkable that they seem to indicate a degree of organization, of conscious planning, and uniformity of practice among the Christian communities which we have hitherto had little reason to suspect, and which throws a new light on the early history of the Church.

> T. C. Skeat, "Early Christian Book-Production," pp. 72–73

Common early dates, common papyrus codices, and common sacred abbreviations are three aspects that cut across our distinction of intracanonical and extracanonical gospels in the earliest manuscript evidence currently available. I now focus especially on those last two aspects because, as that epigraph mentions, their ubiquity demands some centralized uniformity and some unified authority. But that centralized authority controlled alike both the gospels we now have inside the canon and those we have outside it.

It is possible, of course, that the creation of papyrus codices and the use of sacred abbreviations were quite separate inventions of different early Christian communities. But their antiquity and ubiquity seem to demand some central authority and organized control from a common base, some communal Christian consensus that moved against contemporary habits and norms, whether from Jewish or pagan scribal traditions. But what created and controlled that unusual and almost immediate consensus? Scholars have proposed either a centralized authority or a dominant model, be it the Pauline letter or the Markan gospel (Horsley [Llewelyn and Kearsley] 7.257).

Where would such an authoritative center have existed in earliest Christianity? Rome is one obvious possibility, and was proposed as such by Joseph van Haelst (1989:35), but the earliest Christian Latin manuscripts do not seem at home with the system. Roberts proposed Jerusalem, "probably before A.D. 70" (1979:46), but later, in a work co-authored with Skeat, he preferred Antioch, capital of the Roman province of Syria, while acknowledging that "it is, however, not necessary to think of Jerusalem and Antioch as mutually exclusive. Owing to the close links between them, either or both of these innovations might have taken place through joint consultation between the two Churches" (1983).

We have, indeed, one example from around the middle of the first century when James and Jerusalem, even according to the somewhat different accounts in Galatians 2 and Acts 15, gave orders to Antioch and were obeyed by that community. Paul disagreed, lost, and left. The issue was whether a mixed community of Jewish and Gentile Christians had to observe together certain minimal purity regulations. In Paul's account they all disagreed with him and were wrong. In Luke's account they all agreed together and were right. But in both accounts it was James and Jerusalem that ultimately decided the issue and gave the conclusion as hierarchical command to Antioch. When, by contrast, the Roman community wrote the letters known as 1 *Clement* to the Corinthians toward the end of that century about an "unholy sedition" created by "a few rash and self-willed persons," they argued rather than commanded, and their language does not seem merely polite rhetoric thinly veiling flat command.

In that first century, it seems to me, only Jerusalem had the authority, be it exemplary or peremptory, to establish such striking novelties as papyrus codices and sacred abbreviations widely across the Christian communities. That system, in other words, may have passed from Jerusalem to Antioch, but it must have *started* with Jerusalem, and that pushes the process back before 70 C.E. My present point, however, depends not on how one explains that consensus but simply on its factual existence. The authority of that consensus, be it from dominant model or authoritative place, works alike for intracanonical and extracanonical gospels without distinction.

The Egyptian desert, below the delta and above the water table, did not make any distinction between intracanonical and extracanonical gospels. Whatever the origins of the above-discussed consensus about the usage of the papyrus codex and the presence of sacred abbreviations, those early gospels came from a time when that consensus was accepted by all strands of the Christian scribal tradition presently available on papyrus manuscripts. Distinctions of intracanonical and extracanonical would come later and destroy that consensus forever. Thus, for instance, by the fourth century, we have, as mentioned earlier, twenty-two papyrus manuscripts of John's gospel and eighteen of Matthew's gospel but still only those three of the *Gospel of Thomas* and one of the *Gospel of Peter*.

PART IV
Methodology and Anthropology

Dug in upon the back of a stony hill are about a hundred one-story houses, irregular and misshapen, blackened by time and crumbling away from wind and rain, their roofs ill covered by tiles and rubbish of every kind. Most of these hovels have only one opening, which serves as doorway, window, and chimney flue. In the unfloored interior with its dry walls live, sleep, eat and procreate together on the straw matting men, women, and their children, donkeys, pigs, goats and chickens. . . . The same sky, the same earth, the same rain, the same snow, the same houses, the same feast days, the same food, the same poverty: poverty handed down from fathers, who had inherited it from their grandfathers, who had received it from their forefathers. The life of men, beasts and earth always seeming shut in a motionless circle, closed away from the changes of time. Closed in a natural circle of its own. First would come the sowing, then the weeding, then the pruning, then the sulphuring, then the reaping, then the harvest. And then? Then, once again. Sowing, weeding, pruning, sulphuring, reaping, harvest. Always the same thing, unchanging. Always. Years passed, years piled up behind, the young grew old, the old died, and they sowed, weeded, pruned, sulphured, reaped, and harvested. And then what? The same thing. And after that? Ever the same thing. Each year like the year before it, each season like the season before it. In bad weather months they arranged family affairs. That is, they quarreled about them. There are not two families . . . that are not related to each other. In little villages usually all the families are related to each other. For that reason all the families quarrel with each other. Always the same squabbles, endless squabbles, passed down from generation to generation in endless lawsuits, in endless paying of fees, all to decide who owns some thornbush or other. The bush might get burned but they would keep right on quarreling. There was no way out of it. They could put aside twenty soldi a month, thirty soldi a month, even up to a hundred soldi in summer, and these might come in a year to make as much as thirty lire. But then some sickness would come along, or some other accident, and the savings of ten years would be eaten up. And then it would begin all over again, twenty soldi, thirty soldi, a hundred soldi a month. And then all over again.

Ignazio Silone, *Fontamara*, pp. vii–x

Part I considered the *why*, the reasons for this book. The tandem set of Parts II and III studied the *where*, the sources for this book. And now another tandem set, Parts IV and V, continues with the *how*, the methods to be used in this book.

Presuming, from Parts II and III, the situation of oral and written traditions, of intracanonical and extracanonical gospels, of independent and dependent texts, what method should be used to focus on that first continuation from before to after the execution of Jesus? Since gospels openly and honestly proclaim themselves as written from faith to faith for faith, how can I do historical reconstruction without it becoming either apologetics or polemics, without it turning history into theology, or turning history against theology? That is the problem of the *how*, of the *method*.

As I just mentioned, Parts IV and V are a linked pair. Part IV looks at the problem of methodology and then begins presentation of my own interdisciplinary method based on cross-cultural anthropology. Part V continues that presentation, building atop the anthropological basis with, first, Judeo-Roman history and, then, Lower Galilean archeology. I emphasize in those two parts how the three interdisciplinary layers lock together at the point of Roman urbanization and rural commercialization in early-first-century Lower Galilee.

Part IV has two chapters. Chapter 10 is about methodology—that is, about the logic of my method. Why do I use this one rather than some other? I remind you, with an example at the start, about the nature of a gospel and about the need for any method to proceed from decisions about the nature of our sources. Finally, I end that chapter with an introductory outline of my own method.

Chapter 11 establishes the basic substratum of that interdisciplinary method in cross-cultural anthropology. What can we say about agrarian empires and peasant societies, about class and gender, about resistance and leadership, from cultural and social anthropology? What general expectations can anthropology establish, within which particular historical forces and individual archeological discoveries must be located and processed?

A word about the epigraph on early-twentieth-century Italian peasants. It describes only the good times. It does not mention the bad times of famine and disease, invasion and war. The Jewish peasants who lived from one hundred years before to one hundred years after Jesus, from the 60s B.C.E. to the 130s C.E., knew bad times more often than good.

CHAPTER 10

THE PROBLEM OF
METHODOLOGY

In my opinion, research aiming to be innovative should not be bound by
strict, predetermined rules. Indeed, although the claim coming from someone born in Hungary, educated in Belgium and France and citizen of the
United Kingdom by naturalization only, may strike a faintly amusing note, I
pride myself on being a true *British* pragmatist. Methodology, no doubt irra-
tionally, makes me see red perhaps because more than once I have been
rebuked by trans-Atlantic dogmatists for illegitimately arriving at the *right*
conclusion, following a path not sanctioned by my critics' sacred rule book.

Geza Vermes, *The Religion of Jesus the Jew*, p. 7

In the sentence before the quoted passage, Vermes mentions the "grandilo-
quent, but highly fashionable, label of *methodology*." There is, however, nothing
particularly strange about methodology in either term or concept. *Method* is *how*
you do something. *Methodology* is *why* you do it that way rather than some other
way. Methodology is simply the theory or logic of your method. It is the normal
due-process of public discourse.

I have been publishing on the historical Jesus since 1969. In all that time, I
have worked on two fronts simultaneously, studying both materials and methods. On materials, I have studied parables and aphorisms as well as intracanonical and extracanonical gospels. On methods, I started with historical criticism,
next incorporated literary criticism, and finally added macrosociological criticism
to form an integrated interdisciplinary model. When I finally published *The Historical Jesus* in 1991, I intended not just to present another reconstruction of Jesus
but to inaugurate a full-blown debate on methodology among my peers. I spent
no time debating other views of Jesus because, without methodology, method,
and inventory, one view was as valid as the other. If you can pick what you
want, you will get what you need. There still is no serious discussion of methodology in historical Jesus research, and the same applies to the birth of Christianity. That does not make me very proud of myself and my scholarly colleagues.
Lest that seem a little extreme, I offer one immediate example of that avoidance
of methodological discussion.

In 1994 Bruce Chilton and Craig Evans edited a massive and very useful survey of current research on the historical Jesus. It ran to over six hundred pages and, published by Brill of Leiden, cost around $175. It covers every obvious subject with very helpful discussion and very complete documentation. It covers every obvious subject, that is, except one: there is no chapter on method or methodology. I am not certain whether that lack indicts the volume or current scholarship. There is, after all, very little methodological scholarship in historical Jesus research to evaluate or survey. But might it have been better to have a chapter discussing that failure?

The Necessity of Stratification

How are the Gospels to be used as sources for constructing an image of the historical Jesus? . . . The Gospels are literally the voices of their authors. Behind them are the anonymous voices of the community talking about Jesus. And embedded within their voices is the voice of Jesus, as well as the deeds of Jesus (for some of the stories were about deeds). Constructing an image of Jesus—which is what the quest for the historical Jesus is about— involves two crucial steps. The first step is discerning what is likely to go back to Jesus. The second step is setting this material in the historical context of the first-century Jewish homeland.
　　Marcus J. Borg, "The Historical Study of Jesus and Christian Origins," p. 144

If you and I intended to debate Paul's Epistle to the Romans, for example, we would have exactly the same text in front of us. We would use the latest edition of the United Bible Societies' *The Greek New Testament*, complete with the major textual variants and the editorial committee's judgments on those divergent readings. And so with any other book of the New Testament. The *inventory*, let us call it, is already done, and we can move immediately to *interpretation*. We might have, of course, strong disagreements on interpretation, but at least we would be disagreeing about the same text. That is not—emphatically *not*—the position for research on either the historical Jesus or the birth of Christianity. This difference must be emphasized to understand the absolute importance of methodology for that special type of study.

In the above epigraph, Borg summarizes the standard scholarly view on gospel stratification. It flows, in fact, necessarily and legitimately from the very nature of *gospel* as *good news* (a nature discussed several times already). All the gospel texts, whether inside or outside the canon, combine together three layers, strata, or voices. There is, as the earliest stratum, "the voice of Jesus." There is, as the intermediate stratum, "the anonymous voices of the community talking about Jesus." There is, as the latest stratum, "the voices of their [the gospels'] authors." But all three voices are integrated together as a single choir. They are cited as if all of them were the voice of Jesus himself. If you are interested in the historical Jesus, as I am, or in the earliest communal continuation from that Jesus, as I am, the problem is establishing the specific strata appropriate to those interests. The *methodical* challenge is how to do it, and why to do it *that* way and not some other way.

We cannot act here as if we all had the same inventory of materials—the same "text," as it were—in our hands or on our desks. And of course our results and conclusions will be different when we start with different data-bases or inventories of first-stratum materials. There is no point, therefore, in scholars debating result and conclusion until after they have debated theory and method. I give one example, lest this get too abstract.

Imagine that we are debating the passion of the historical Jesus and that your inventory is Mark 14–15 while mine is John 18–19. (Please allow the oversimplification.) Look at how those accounts diverge, for example, at both the start and the finish.

They both begin in the Garden (John) of Gethsemane (Mark), across the Kidron valley (John) on the Mount of Olives (Mark). But thereafter their descriptions diverge quite radically, even when they are recording the same events. I focus especially on three elements—ground, cup, and flight—to emphasize how differently each writer interprets the same details.

Ground.

Who is prostrate on the ground? For Mark it is Jesus himself. But for John it is the arresting *cohort*—that is, the full complement of about six hundred pagan auxiliary troops protecting Jerusalem. We call that event the Agony in the Garden; however, as noted earlier, for Mark there is agony without garden, while for John there is garden without agony:

> [Jesus] . . . began to be distressed and agitated. And said . . . "I am deeply grieved, even to death." . . . And going a little farther, he threw himself on the ground. (Mark 14:33–35)

> Jesus, knowing all that was to happen to him, came forward and asked them, "Whom are you looking for?" They answered, "Jesus of Nazareth." Jesus replied, "I am he." . . . When Jesus said to them, "I am he," they stepped back and fell to the ground. (John 18:4–6)

Cup.

For both Mark and John, Jesus is, of course, obedient to the will of God. But in Mark he prays for the cup of suffering to pass him by if at all possible, while in John there is no such hesitation. Others may have a problem with that destiny, but, for John, Jesus does not:

[Jesus] prayed that, if it were possible, the hour might pass from him. He said, "Abba, Father, for you all things are possible; remove this cup from me; yet, not what I want, but what you want.". . . But one of those who stood near drew his sword and struck the slave of the high priest, cutting off his ear. (Mark 14:35–36, 47)

Then Simon Peter, who had a sword, drew it, struck the high priest's slave, and cut off his right ear. The slave's name was Malchus. Jesus said to Peter, "Put your sword back into its sheath. Am I not to drink the cup that the Father has given me?" (John 18:10–11)

Flight.

All the disciples abandon Jesus and flee off into the night in Mark. But in John they leave at Jesus' command in order to fulfill the scriptures. And that command is given not to them but to Jesus' captors:

All of them [the disciples] deserted him and fled. A certain young man was following him, wearing nothing but a linen cloth. They caught hold of him, but he left the linen cloth and ran off naked. (Mark 14:50–52)

[Jesus] asked them, "Whom are you looking for?" And they said, "Jesus of Nazareth." Jesus answered, "I told you that I am he. So if you are looking for me, let these men go." This was to fulfill the word that he had spoken, "I did not lose a single one of those whom you gave me." (John 18:7–9)

Two radically different interpretations of the same event. Mark describes the Son of God almost out of control, arrested in agony, fear, and abandonment. John describes the Son of God in total control, arrested in foreknowledge, triumph, and command.

Death.

If we turn to the ending of the passion in Mark and John, we find exactly the same process. The moment is the same in each, the last words of Jesus on the cross just before his death:

Jesus cried out with a loud voice, "Eloi, Eloi, lema sabachthani?" which means, "My God, my God, why have you forsaken me?" When some of the bystanders heard it, they said, "Listen, he is calling for Elijah." And someone ran, filled a sponge with sour wine, put it on a stick, and gave it to him to drink, saying, "Wait, let us see whether Elijah will come to take him down." Then Jesus gave a loud cry and breathed his last. (Mark 15:34–37)

After this, when Jesus knew that all was now finished, he said (in order to fulfill the scripture), "I am thirsty." A jar full of sour wine was standing there. So they put a sponge full of the wine on a branch of hyssop and held it to his mouth. When Jesus had received the wine, he said, "It is finished." Then he bowed his head and gave up his spirit. (John 19:28–30)

In Mark the bystanders mistake Jesus' last words by taking "Eloi" for "Elijah" and derisively attempt to keep him alive for a few extra minutes to see if the prophet comes to his aid. The drink is their own mocking idea. In John, of course, there is no cry of desolation and no mockery, and the drink is Jesus' idea and brought at his command. For Mark, the passion of Jesus starts and ends in agony and desolation. For John, the passion of Jesus starts and ends in control and command. Both speak, equally but divergently, to different times and places, situations and communities. Mark's Jesus speaks to a persecuted community and shows them how to die. John's Jesus speaks to a defeated community and shows them how to live.

Neither of those accounts is *history* of what actually happened. Each is *gospel*—but for different situations and communities. But my point is this. If you and I are debating the historicity of Jesus' passion but you use Mark while I use John (as I would not), or you use both while I use neither (as I would), we are not just ships that pass in the night, we are ships that pass on different nighttime oceans. We have radically divergent inventories. Thus *inventory precedes interpretation* and *method precedes inventory*. We must always begin by asking: What texts are you using to understand the birth of Christianity, and why those rather than some others?

Criteria Are Not Method

The Semitic minds behind a good part of our biblical literature were not overly troubled by our Western philosophical principle of noncontradiction. . . . The ancient Semitic mind, not unlike the outlook of many third-world people today, was not overly concerned with the principle of noncontradiction, however revered the principle may be by Western logic. . . . The problem of logical consistency that the Western mind may raise with regard to the systematic writings of a Spinoza may be beside the point when dealing with an itinerant Jewish preacher and miracle-worker of 1st-century Palestine. Our concern about the principles of noncontradiction might have been greeted with a curious smile by the Nazarene and his audience.

John P. Meier, *A Marginal Jew*, vol. 2, pp. 11, 399, 452

John Meier begins his work with an explicit list of primary criteria that represents his serious attempt at disciplined method. Meier details his five primary criteria in the first volume of his ongoing multivolume study of the historical Jesus (1991:168–177), and he summarizes them again at the beginning of the second volume (1994:5). The first criterion is *embarrassment,* which "pinpoints Gospel material that would hardly have been invented by the early church, since such material created embarrassment or theological difficulty for the church even during the NT period." The second criterion is *discontinuity,* which "focuses on words or deeds of Jesus that cannot be derived either from the Judaism(s) of Jesus' time or from the early church." The third criterion is *multiple attestation,* which "focuses on sayings or deeds of Jesus witnessed in more than one independent literary source . . . and/or more than one literary form or genre." The fourth criterion is *coherence,* by which "other sayings and deeds of Jesus that fit in well with the preliminary 'data-base' established by the other criteria have a good chance of being historical." The fifth and final criterion is *rejection and execution,* which "looks at the larger pattern of Jesus' ministry and asks what words and deeds fit in with and explain his trial and execution." It must be admitted immediately that all of those criteria have been around for quite some time, and their employment has not created any consensus on anything. That piece of prior knowledge is probably influencing my reaction to them. Why have they not worked to create even the vestige of consensus so far? The basic question I ask is whether a list of criteria—*any* list of any criteria—represents a method? Are criteria the *same* as method? That basic question has three parts.

First, how are those five criteria theoretically based? Two examples. Let's start with that first criterion. There is a lot of very embarrassing material in Mark about the disciples and relatives of Jesus, including, for example, the sworn denial of Jesus by Peter at his trial. Is that material historical from Jesus' time or editorial from Mark's purpose? Did Mark, in other words, polemically create that embarrassment for Peter and Jesus' main disciples? On to the second criterion. How do we know, before we begin, that there is a double discontinuity between Jews and Judaism, on the one hand, and Jesus and Christianity, on the other? Is that not a conclusion rather than a criterion? Furthermore, since Jesus was Jewish, would not whatever the Jewish Jesus said and did be already within the early first century's Judaism(s)? If, to give a silly example, Jesus said that God had two heads, must we not conclude that a two-headed God was an option for at least one person within first-century Judaism?

Second, how are those criteria operationally organized? Do you simply use now one, now the other; here this one, there that one? I leave aside the fourth criterion, since it is subordinate to some or all of the others. If Meier argued, for example, to a primary inventory established from materials where *all four* of those remaining criteria were met, we would have the start, admittedly rather wooden and mechanical, of a move from criteria to method. But with multiple criteria all operating independently, it becomes too easy to slide from one to the other.

Third, are those criteria publicly usable? If a group of scholars accepted them and applied them to the gospel traditions, would those scholars come up with a reasonably common inventory? If not (and I am suggesting they *would* not because they *have* not), those criteria are too general, broad, or vague for common use. In summary, *criteria,* no matter how good, do not constitute a *method* unless they are organized on some theoretical basis into some operational system that can be used by anyone.

Finally, the weakness or vagueness of those criteria on the methodological level shows up eventually in Meier's interpretation of Jesus' eschatology. And this is my most serious criticism of them. Moving backward and forward from one of those criteria to the other, Meier concludes that the historical Jesus taught about "the future, definitive, and imminent arrival of God's kingly rule" but also that "*in some way* the kingdom of God had already arrived—however partially and symbolically—in his own words and actions" (2.398). That phrase I italicized reappears again and again in various forms: as "in some way" (2.450), as "somehow" (2.429), and especially as "in some sense" (2.398, 399, 400, 403, 423, 429, 454). Is it not part of an interpreter's job to define that "somehow" as closely as possible and not simply to repeat, as if repetition were *somehow* explanation.

It is certainly possible to reconcile a here-now *and* still-imminent kingdom, because that is precisely the position of Paul, and it is quite clear why he holds to it. Believing already as a Pharisee in the general resurrection at the end of time, he came to believe that the resurrection of Jesus had begun that process. Jesus was "the first fruits of those who have died," as he said in 1 Corinthians 15:20. He was the beginning of the apocalyptic harvest, the start of the end (but not the end itself). By divine mercy, to leave time for Gentile repentance and salvation, the eschaton was not an abrupt instant but a short period. Paul's theology of an end already started but not yet completed is perfectly clear and consistent. What, then, is Jesus' understanding of the end as already here but still imminent?

Meier is very much aware that "somehow" is not enough and that he owes his readers at least an attempted explanation. He offers three excuses, and I find their tone as significant as their content. He is more and more truculent as he moves across these three refusals to explain Jesus' coming-soon-but-here-already eschatology.

First, "the kingdom of God that [Jesus] proclaims for the future is in some sense already present. How this coheres—or whether it coheres—with what Jesus says about the kingdom soon to come remains an open question. But that further problem should not lead us to suppress or twist some of the evidence that creates the problem, all for the sake of a neat systematization that was not a major concern of Jesus" (2.423).

Second, Meier claims that Jesus saw an "organic link between his own ministry in the present and the full coming of God's eschatological rule in the near future." But, he continues, "in my view this is all that we can say. To go beyond this minimal explanation of the kingdom present yet future is to leave exegesis and engage in systematic theology" (2.453).

Third, Meier advances three times the excuse or explanation that I take as the primary one: the excuse used as the epigraph for this section. I find it not only unconvincing but condescending. The three repetitions he offers are shown here in fuller context. A first time: "Recently some critics have objected that a kingdom both future and present is an intolerable contradiction in terms. One might reply that the Semitic minds behind a good part of our biblical literature were not overly troubled by our Western philosophical principle of noncontradiction" (2:11). A second time: "[T]he kingdom that [Jesus] promised for the near future was paradoxically, in some strange way, already present in his work. To some modern minds such a paradox may seem an intolerable contradiction. . . . The ancient Semitic mind, not unlike the outlook of many third-world people today, was not overly concerned with the principle of noncontradiction, however revered the principle may be by Western logic" (2.399). A final time: "The problem of logical consistency that the Western mind may raise with regard to the systematic writings of a Spinoza may be beside the point when dealing with an itinerant Jewish preacher and miracle-worker of 1st-century Palestine. Our concern about the principles of noncontradiction might have been greeted with a curious mile by the Nazarene and his audience" (2.452).

I hope I am as open to mystery and paradox as anyone around. A kingdom of God both here-already and coming-soon can be explained quite easily in, for example, the case of Paul (as I noted above). That is not the problem. But those varied excuses indicate Meier's knowledge of a serious problem in his reconstruction. All of those defenses may be needed only because Meier's criteria are not methodological enough to discriminate accurately between the various layers of the tradition. He ends up honestly unable to combine what are not only divergent but even opposing strata of the Jesus tradition. And this underlines my challenge. Without method, there will be no self-critical inventory of texts for the historical Jesus level or for the earliest-communities level. But with a proper method, even the interpretation of that inventory will be much more disciplined.

An Interdisciplinary Method

The hard fact is that we do not have the choice of whether we will use models or not. Our choice, rather, lies in deciding whether to use them consciously or unconsciously. . . . The most immediate benefit conferred by the use of cross-cultural models is that of inducing a form of "culture shock" in the user. . . . Models should have the effect of expanding rather than inhibiting one's sense of the possible in research. . . . The best one is whichever gets the best results from a particular set of data for a particular problem. Models are only as good as their results.

Thomas F. Carney, The Shape of the Past, pp. 5, 16, 37

First, my method is interdisciplinary, applying anthropology, history, archeology, and literary criticism to the same subject. Second, it is interactive, involving the reciprocal interaction of those disciplines with one another. Third, it is hierarchical, moving upward, as it were, from the first to the last of those four disciplines. Fourth, and above all, it involves three stages that I code with the words *context, text,* and *conjunction.* Finally, my method begins not with *text* but with *context,* as shown in this outline of the process:

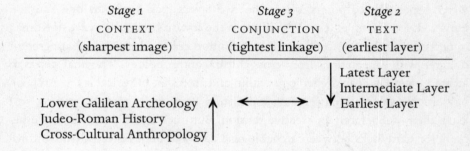

The first stage establishes the sharpest possible reconstruction of the context. The second stage establishes the earliest possible layer of the tradition. The third stage establishes the tightest possible linkage between that context and that text. In this book Parts IV and V are about the context, Parts VI through X are about the text, and the whole book is about their conjunction. But first a few preliminary observations.

Context.

Why begin with context? The sequence is crucial, although also a little artificial. It presumes, of course, some general or preliminary text/context basis. I do not start, for example, with nineteenth-century Dublin as context. I know that I cannot eliminate text from my mind or even from context. (How, without text, would I even know what context Jesus belongs in?) But, for a while, I place it in brackets, as it were, and turn to context. The main reason is that, when I turn later to text, I will be taking elements out of their present contextual positions in, say, the *Q Gospel,* the *Gospel of Thomas,* Mark, John, or wherever. There must be some validly established context into which I relocate them, or they may become meaningless words and deeds. There will have to be, eventually, an interaction of context and text, but the context must be there first.

The next question is *what* context? By *context* I mean the *sharpest possible reconstruction of the 20s in Lower Galilee.* I do not mean the Mediterranean world in general, the Roman Empire in general, Judaism in general, or even the Jewish homeland in general. All of that is important, but I need, as context, the most detailed available image of that very specific place and time.

The final question is *how* to obtain that context? I do so by building up three ever more specific and detailed layers of data, one on top of the other. But remember, this process is both interdisciplinary and interactive. I begin with the widest and most general framework given by cross-cultural anthropology. What, for example, does such macrosociological analysis conclude about agrarian empires and peasant societies viewed across time and place? The next step is to place history within or atop that general anthropological framework and to watch especially for points where the two layers lock hard into one another. How did, for example, Jewish tradition in the Jewish homeland react to Roman imperialism in the first century of the common era? And how did that agree or disagree with expectations from cross-cultural anthropology? The final step is to locate Lower Galilean archeology within and atop that historical layer. Archeology emphasizes material remains and history emphasizes textual remains, so I leave them deliberately in creative tension. But once again, I am looking especially for hard locks between archeological data and both historical and anthropological data. An example, though I jump ahead of myself, may help.

Cross-cultural anthropology indicates that peasant unrest and resistance escalates as agrarian empires increase their commercializing activities and take peasant land (not just peasant surplus). History concludes that the Roman Empire in the first common-era century was in an economic boom (insofar as ancient economies could boom) under Italian peace and Augustan prosperity. But history also details steady and increasing peasant unrest in the Jewish homeland of that same period. Is that due to commercialization? And, finally, was there commercialization in Lower Galilee by the 20s, or was that region a forgotten backwater stagnating outside the economic boom?

The result from that first or context stage is the *sharpest reconstruction possible of the late 20s in Lower Galilee obtained by the hierarchical overlay of those three disciplines.* That process allows, of course, for added disciplinary layers, for divergent disciplinary views, and for different disciplinary interactions in future research. What it does *not* allow for is the exclusion of anthropology and sociology or the avoidance of archeology.

Text.

I do not think, after two hundred years of experimentation, that there is any way, acceptable in public discourse or scholarly debate, by which you can go directly into the great mound of the Jesus tradition and separate out the historical Jesus layer from all later strata. You can, as mentioned above, do so if you have already decided who Jesus was. That works, of course, but it is apologetics rather than research. Recall, for example, that criterion of *discontinuity* mentioned above in the discussion of John Meier's work. That criterion presumes that Jesus is different from all other Jews. Then it argues that no other Jew says or does some specific word or deed in the text. Therefore, it concludes, that word or deed is from Jesus. But that is a vicious circle rather than an interpretive spiral.

You can, however, with academic integrity, argue to what is the earliest discernible stratum of the tradition. That, in effect, is what the last two hundred years of gospel research has been doing. But any such stratification presumes a whole range of decisions about sources and relationships. You might be wrong on any or all of those decisions, but then so might your opponent. There is, in any case, no way to avoid making decisions and risking error. But that argument from stratification makes one very important presupposition. Why earliest and not latest? Why earliest and not commonest? Why earliest and not all? My answer presumes what was seen in Part III. Gospel tradition, from the general scholarly consensus of two hundred years of research (as profiled in Chapter 9), is a highly genetic process. It is because, for example, the *Q Gospel* and Mark are absorbed massively into Matthew and Luke that those earlier texts receive special emphasis. If all the gospels were mutually independent texts, the earliest might be of no significance at all.

Conjunction.

This method asks, finally, whether there is a tight linkage between that sharpest image of context and that earliest layer of text. If there is, that is the best reconstruction of the historical Jesus and his companions presently available. Does that earliest layer speak from and to the situation of the 20s in Lower Galilee? If it does, that is the best reconstruction of the historical Jesus and his companions presently available.

One final comment. A model is a conceptual map, a conscious framework that, because it *is* conscious, can itself be changed, abandoned, or replaced, and, as framework, can organize, interpret, and even predict the data it contains or imagines. Our choice with models is not whether to use them or not but whether to use them self-consciously and self-critically or to let them use us willingly or unwillingly. The value of a multicultural, cross-cultural, or comparative model is that it helps us discipline the inevitable tendency to take one's own perfectly valid but particular experiences and erect them all too swiftly into human universals.

CHAPTER 11

CROSS-CULTURAL ANTHROPOLOGY

One fact impresses itself on almost any observer of agrarian societies, especially on one who views them in a broadly comparative perspective. This is the fact of *marked social inequality*. Without exception, one finds pronounced differences in power, privilege, and honor associated with mature agrarian economies.

Gerhard E. Lenski, *Power and Privilege*, p. 210 (his italics)

Lenski's . . . agrarian societies include societies where merchants have become so powerful that they are no longer purely *traditional* but *commercialized* or more or less modern, like the late Roman empire. . . . I distinguish *traditional* aristocratic empires from more or less 'modern' *commercialized*, colonial, and industrial societies.

John H. Kautsky, *The Politics of Aristocratic Empires*, pp. 20, 21 (my italics)

In this chapter I explain the basic anthropological template that undergirds my interdisciplinary model. This is the first step in the first stage of the method. It has three equally important components: an anthropology of class, of gender, and of resistance. In my earlier research for *The Historical Jesus*, I used only an anthropology of class, but an anthropology of gender and of resistance must be included as well. Marianne Sawicki, for example, noted that Lenski's model has nothing at all about gender (1994a:12 note 6). That is absolutely correct; it is a model for social class. But I do not intend to lose what I learned from it (Lenski) in developing an equal emphasis on gender (Rogers) and on resistance (Kautsky).

Anthropology of Class

Class, then, essentially a relationship, *is* above all the collective social expression of the *fact of exploitation* (and of course of resistance to it): the division of society into economic classes is in its very nature the way in which exploitation is effected, with the propertied classes living off the non-propertied. I admit that in my use of it the word "exploitation" often tends to take on a pejorative colouring; but essentially it is a "value-free" expression, signifying merely that a propertied class is freed from the labour of production through its ability to maintain itself out of a surplus extracted from the primary producers, whether by compulsion or by persuasion or (as in most cases) by a mixture of the two.

G.E.M. de Ste. Croix, "Karl Marx and the History of Classical Antiquity," p. 26

I use the term *social class* as de Ste. Croix does in that epigraph, and as Norman Gottwald did in his 1992 presidential address to the Society of Biblical Literature: "Social classes may be said to exist whenever one social group is able to appropriate a part of the surplus labor product of other groups. In such a situation of exploitation, wealth and power accrue disproportionately to those who are able to claim and dispose of what others produce. Those who have this power of economic disposal tend also to have political predominance and ideological hegemony" (1993:4).

My basic paradigm for a cross-cultural anthropology of class is what I call the Lenski-Kautsky model. This model combines two equally important elements. One is Gerhard Lenski's typology of human societies based on ecology and technology and locating agrarian society on a continuum that moves from gathering-hunting to industrial societies. Another is John Kautsky's distinction, within Lenski's agrarian societies, between traditional and commercializing types (the Roman Empire being an example of the latter type). I take those two elements one at a time below—but first a rather obvious objection.

Is the choice of this model a prejudicial option? Is there some other model that would force me in a totally different direction? I considered one other macrosociological study as a possible alternative model to the Lenski-Kautsky synthesis, but it would not have changed anything significant for this book. That alternative is Shauel Noah Eisenstadt's recently reissued volume on *The Political Systems of Empires*. Eisenstadt is "concerned with one major type of political system, namely, with the centralized historical bureaucratic empires or states" among whose "most important examples" are "the Roman and Hellenistic empires" (11). But his focus is especially on political relationships among the upper levels of social stratification; the lower levels are mentioned almost in passing. He knows, of course, that in a state such as the Roman Empire, "agricultural producers" are divided into different strata: "(1) the aristocracy and gentry; (2) independent peasants; and (3) various types of tenants and semi-servile, dependent rural classes controlled by the lords and gentry" (34). He also knows, of course, in terms of stratification, that "lowest of all come the peasantry" (82), that "numerically, the middle and lower peasant groups were the largest part of the rural population," and that "the peasantry carried the greatest burden of taxation and of military mobilization" (207). Nevertheless, in an extremely detailed seven-page Table of Contents at the start of his book, those peasants are mentioned only once, under the rubric "The Place of the Peasantry in the Political Struggle." (They are placed last in a list of eight similar titles describing "The Place of" bureaucracy, army, aristocracy, religious and cultural groups, professional elites, the urban economic and social group, and the gentry "in the Political Struggle" [x].) In the book itself, the peasantry receives only four pages (207–210). Is that all one need say about the peasantry, the vast majority of the world's population in recorded history? But I do not find anything in Eisenstadt's macrosociology of Rome among political empires that disagrees, for my purposes, with Lenski's macrosociology of Rome among agrarian empires or Kautsky's of Rome among commercializing empires. I return, therefore, to consider the twin components of that Lenski-Kautsky model.

MARKED SOCIAL INEQUALITY

Gerhard Lenski's typology has several powerful advantages, especially within the ecology-technology matrix of which it is a part (189–296). First, Lenski is primarily concerned with the distributive process, with who gets what and why, in the various types of societies human ingenuity has devised. Second, that focus on how the material surplus is handled lets him balance the twin warring emphases of functional and conflictual analysis within the social sciences. Functionalists emphasize common interests, common advantages, consensus, and cooperation; conflictualists emphasize dividing interests, domination, exploitation, and coercion. Lenski synthesizes both approaches, and surely both together are more accurate than either one alone. Third, he divides human societies, on the basis of ecology and technology, into gathering-hunting, simple horticultural, advanced horticultural, agrarian, and industrial societies. Within that typology, for example, the Roman Empire was an agrarian society, characterized by the wheel, sail, iron plow, harnessed animal power, basic metallurgy, and (to repeat from the epigraph to this chapter) "marked social inequality" (210). Agricultural productivity increased, elite appropriation of peasant surpluses increased, and inequality between the producers and the takers increased. That increase in social inequality was facilitated by three distinctive features. The first one was urbanization: "[T]he normal pattern in reasonably mature agrarian societies involves a multiplicity of fairly large and relatively permanent urban centers" (199 note 30). The second feature was monetization: "[W]ith the development of monetary systems, debts could be extended further and money-lending could provide yet another instrument for controlling the peasants and separating them from the surplus they produced" (207). The third feature was scribalization: "[W]riting also served to widen the traditional gulf between the ruling classes and the common people by introducing a major cultural distinction between the literate minority and the illiterate majority. In agrarian societies *limited literacy* was the rule" (208). Finally, the model is not built up deductively from theoretical presuppositions but inductively from historical studies and detailed analyses of empirical societies. It is those four features that give the Lenski model its tremendous descriptive and persuasive power.

The model divides agrarian societies into upper and lower strata, and these are the classes proposed by Lenski on either side of that great divide:

Ruler
Governing Class   Peasant Class
Retainer Class   Artisan Class
Merchant Class   Unclean and Degraded Class
Priestly Class   Expendable Class

He comments, concerning the Ruler and the Governing Class, "On the basis of available data, it appears that *the governing classes of agrarian societies probably received at least a quarter of the national income of most agrarian states, and that the governing class and the ruler together usually received not less than half*. In some instances their combined income may have approached two-thirds of the total" (228). In other words, 1 to 2 percent of the population took 50 to 65 percent of the agricultural productivity.

The Retainer Class contained those military and bureaucratic hierarchies whose primary purpose was to support and defend the Governing Class. Without the assistance of the retainers, that tiny minority Governing Class could hardly have controlled the vast majority on whose extracted surplus they lived in luxury. Though retainers represented only about 5 percent of the population, through sword and pen they rendered the whole surplus-appropriation process possible. Collectively they were indispensable, individually they were expendable, and (even if the pen was mightier than the sword) it was only from the military rather than the scribal retainers that the Ruler and Governing Class were ever really threatened.

The Merchant Class probably evolved upward from the Peasant Class. Depending more on market than authority relations, merchants could often outflank those in the Governing Class to acquire considerable wealth and even power. Even when they were at their most successful, however, their wealth was usually translated back into land. That meant that the Merchant Class retreated back, whenever possible, into the Governing Class. As a result, merchants never became an actual middle class in antiquity.

The Priestly Class, "last but not least among the privileged elements in agrarian societies," owned, for example, 15 percent of the land of Egypt in the twelfth century B.C.E. and 15 percent of the land of France in the eighteenth century C.E. (256–257). I return to this class later in my discussion of resistance and its leadership.

The Peasant Class, that vast majority of the population, was held "at, or close to, subsistence level" (271) so that their appropriated surplus could support elite conspicuous consumption. Those appropriations could reach cumulatively as high as "two thirds of the total crop" (267). But "the religions of the East, especially Hinduism and Confucianism, were compatible with extremes of exploitation in a way that Judaism and Christianity were not; the former left the peasantry more defenseless than the latter" (276–277).

The Artisan Class "was originally recruited from the ranks of the dispossessed peasantry and their noninheriting sons and was continually replenished from these sources. Furthermore, despite the substantial overlap between the wealth and income of the peasant and artisan, the median income of artisans apparently was not so great as that of the peasants" (278). Peasant artisans were lower, not higher, than peasant farmers in social class.

The Unclean and Degraded Class is the term Lenski uses for groups such as, for example, the "untouchables" in Hindu society. This class included those who, like porters, miners, and prostitutes, "had only their bodies and animal energies to sell and who were forced to accept occupations which quickly destroyed them" (281). It is, in fact, hard to distinguish them from the next-lowest group, the Expendable Class, except where they performed functions at once "necessary" as well as "obnoxious or offensive," such as tanning (280).

The Expendable Class is the terrible title given by Lenski to the very bottom of this social structure. It "included a variety of types, ranging from petty criminals and outlaws to beggars and underemployed itinerant workers, and numbered all those forced to live solely by their wits or by charity" (281). Why was this class maintained, and what was its structural purpose in society? The explanation is as terrible as the title: "Despite high rates of infant mortality, the occasional practice of infanticide, the more frequent practice of celibacy, and adult mortality caused by war, famine, and disease, agrarian societies usually produced *more people than the dominant classes found it profitable to employ*" (281–282). What was the origin of those in the Expendable Class? They "were seldom able to maintain normal marriages, and owing to infanticide, malnutrition, disease, and deprivation, seldom reproduced themselves," but such "high death rates were usually offset by the steady stream of new recruits forced into [their] ranks from the classes immediately above [them]. These recruits were largely the sons and daughters of poor peasants and artisans who inherited little more than the shirts on their backs and a parental blessing" (282–283). What did expendables do? "It seems safe to say that illegal activity was the best hope of those who fell into this class, and for the poorest peasants as well" (282). What was their number? "The best estimate . . . is that in normal times from 5 to 10 per cent of the population found itself in this depressed class, with the figure rising as high as 15 per cent on some occasions and falling almost to zero on others" (283).

One final point. You will notice how much space I gave to the Expendable Class. The reason is that that class is the *systemic* price required to hold as much as possible of the peasantry at subsistence level. Some will rise above that level; more must fall below it. At the end of his two chapters on agrarian societies Lenski appended a two-page "note on distributive justice." I quote at length from those pages because they indicate different forms of evil that, however inter-twined and interactive, must be kept distinct: "On the whole, agrarian societies give the impression of gross injustice in the distributive realm. As we have seen, a small number of individuals enjoyed immense luxury, consuming in a single day goods and services sufficient to support large numbers of the common people for a year. At the same time a considerable portion of the population was denied the basic necessities of life and was marked out by the social system for a speedy demise. It does not take much imagination to conceive of a more equitable method of distribution. However, when the demographic factor is introduced into the analysis, we suddenly discover that the problem was never so simple as it sometimes seems to those of us who live in the comfort of a modern industrial society. Despite the ravages of war, famine, plague, and other disasters, and despite the influences of infanticide, abortion, monasticism, and prostitution, those segments of the population which were at, or above, the subsistence level continued to produce more offspring than could be employed except by a steady reduction in privilege. Thus, barring an effective method of controlling fertility, which no agrarian society ever discovered, there seems to have been no alterna-tive to the existence of a class of expendables, as harsh as such a statement may sound to modern ears. The most that could have been achieved, had the elite per-mitted it, was the temporary elimination of this class for the short time it would take population growth to eliminate the economic surplus" (295).

In case that is all too abstract, I give an example from Charles Morris's recent summary description of Ireland's Great Famine in his book *American Catholic*. "For a brief time early in the nineteenth century, life may have approached the idyllic even for Irish-speaking peasants. . . . Irish prosperity touched off a frightening rural population explosion. Between 1779 and 1841, largely because of the improved, potato-based countryside diet, Ireland's popula-tion increased by an almost incredible 172 percent, and Irish peasant life came to be dominated by a desperate scrabble for plots of land to grow potatoes. . . . Careful estimates are that 2.5 to 3 million Irish were in a state of semistarvation most years before the Great Famine" (31, 32). Then came the potato blight of the late 1840s, the "coffin-ships" to Canada with a general record of one-third dead in passage and another third dead after arrival, and continued immigration in the next decades. On the eve of the Great Famine there were 9 million people in Ireland. By the end of the century Ireland's "population stabilized at 4 million, or about the same as in 1750" (36). *Ecological* evil does not excuse the *systemic* evil of colonial misrule that made disaster inevitable and restoration impossible. *Systemic* evil does not excuse the *personal* evil of Lord Palmerston of Sligo, who paid passage for all his two thousand peasants, dumping them (many naked, starving, and diseased) on the docks of New Brunswick, and thereby got his lands back for grazing and his welfare assessments vastly reduced.

I imagine, from all of that, three widening circles of evil. The first circle is personal and individual. An example is a master brutalizing a slave, an owner beating, raping, or killing a slave. The second circle is structural and systemic. An example is a whole society built on slave labor and considering the entire process ideologically appropriate or even natural. The existence of that second circle does not justify anything in the first one. Systemic evil does not excuse personal evil. But neither does personal goodness obliterate systemic evil. No amount of private almsgiving can excuse the public injustice that necessitates it. The third circle is ecological or cosmic. It is what Lenski described in explaining the Expendable Class. Without exploitation and oppression by the Roman Empire, there would have been ecological disaster in the Mediterranean basin. Does that justify the oppression? This book will argue that Jesus is concerned primarily with systemic rather than individual evil, but that third specter of ecological disaster will always be there in the background.

AGRARIAN COMMERCIALIZATION

John Kautsky distinguishes two different subtypes within Lenski's agrarian empires: "Lenski's . . . agrarian societies include societies where merchants have become so powerful that they are no longer purely *traditional* but *commercialized* or more or less modern, like the late Roman empire. . . . I distinguish *traditional* aristocratic empires from more or less 'modern' *commercialized*, colonial, and industrial societies" (20, 21, my italics). For Kautsky, "ancient Athens and Rome . . . are commercialized" agrarian empires (25 note 31).

I accept Kautsky's distinction of *traditional* or *commercialized* as a friendly amendment to the Lenski model of *agrarian* societies or empires. Put bluntly: in a traditional agrarian empire, the aristocracy takes the *surplus* from the peasantry; in a commercializing agrarian empire, the aristocracy takes the *land* from the peasantry. The former devours the industry and productivity of the peasantry, the latter their very identity and dignity. Commercialization moves them in increasing numbers down the terrible slope from small freeholder to tenant farmer to day-laborer to beggar or bandit.

In discussing traditional agrarian empires, Kautsky repeats over and over again, like a definitional drumroll, that aristocrats "live off" peasants (4, 6, 18, 24). This is, of course, the proper relational or interactional understanding of the term *peasant,* which is not simply a romantic or nostalgic word for "farmer," let alone a polite term for "rustic," "yokel," or "country bumpkin." A peasant is, quite simply, an *exploited* farmer. Kautsky is not persuaded by claims of mutuality. It is "a very one-sided relationship: the aristocrat takes and the peasant gives. . . . [G]enerally there is no reciprocity in the relationship between peasant and aristocrat" (110, 113). But aristocracies usually mask exploitation as reciprocity, claiming law, order, peace, and protection as returns for the peasantry's appropriated surplus. They seldom say, We are bigger and stronger than you. Therefore, we will take your surplus and prevent others from doing so. Do you have a problem with that?

The major advantage of Kautsky's distinction has to do with peasant revolts, rebellions, uprisings, and revolutions. His thesis is that such events pertain much more to commercialized than to traditional agrarian or aristocratic empires. In traditional empires, the peasantry and aristocracy lived almost in different worlds; apart from expropriation of surplus as rents, tolls, taxes, or labor demands, the latter interfered but little in the lives of the former. In commercializing empires, the incidence of resistance rises steadily, and the reason is not difficult to understand. The aristocracy can raise taxes only to a certain point, can push peasants below subsistence levels only to a certain volume, before insurrection occurs. But what if the aristocracy could take over the peasant lands and reduce the peasants to tenants or laborers on lands they once owned as their family inheritance? Not just increased taxation but increased indebtedness would lead inevitably to land expropriation as debtors became insolvents and mortgages became foreclosures. Hence Kautsky's major and repeated thesis: "Statements in the literature asserting or implying that peasant revolts occurred or were even common in aristocratic empires are typically the result of a failure to distinguish clearly between traditional aristocratic empires and societies subject to some commercialization . . . [for] such revolts break out only in the aftermath and presumably as a consequence of commercialization. . . . [Peasant] rebellions begin to occur in the early stages of commercialization. . . . [They] seem to break out within a century or two of the transition from traditional aristocratic empire to commercialization . . . [but] remain relatively rare . . . even in commercialized societies" (280, 281, 288, 289, 291).

The primary index that he gives for this move from traditional to commercializing empires is the alienability of land. "Land becomes alienable and a commodity only under the impact of some commercialization, as happened in Greece, in Rome, in the Chinese empire, and in medieval Europe" (273); and again, "the alienability of land . . . [means that] landless peasants may develop, dependent on and exploited by those who acquired their land . . . [as a] consequence of commercialization . . . [and this] is deeply upsetting to peasants formerly engaged in subsistence agriculture on their own land" (291). In a traditional agrarian empire, land is a familial inheritance to be retained by the peasantry. In a commercializing agrarian empire, land is an entrepreneurial commodity to be exploited by the aristocracy. Rural commercialization, land expropriation, and peasant dispossession are more or less synonymous. And as they increase, so also does the incidences of peasant resistance, rebellion, or revolt.

In the steady-state operation of a traditional agrarian empire, the peasants see the aristocracy as something like a natural evil. Drought and flood, disease and disaster, death and taxes, subsistence living and appropriated surplus seem part of a natural cycle that one need not like but cannot change. A too brutal local expropriation may, of course, result in an equally brutal local reaction, but that outcome is usually both defensive and desperate. Commercialization, on the other hand, makes it terribly clear that things *can* change, and are, in fact, changing—*for the worse*. But, peasants then ask, if things can change for the worse, can they not also change *for the better*?

That explains why peasant reactions to commercialization are, as Kautsky notes, "typically also characterized by chiliasm and utopianism, involving far-reaching demands for equality and the end of aristocratic exploitation" (308). Peasants who have accepted subsistence living and appropriated surplus for centuries smell the whiff of doom in commercialization and reach not just for the restoration of traditional exploitation but for radical, utopian, and egalitarian visions of an ideal world. "Only the changes to which commercialization subjects peasants makes them capable of believing that they can bring about social change. Having suffered adverse changes, they can demand favorable ones, and these may now go far beyond the restoration of older forms of exploitation all the way to communistic utopias" (318). Those are, of course, visions of revolution rather than just rebellion, visions of a world without any exploitation and oppression rather than one simply restored to former and traditional levels of each.

Anthropology of Gender

Ranking society is characterized by inequalities in production, distribution, exchange, and consumption, although these are not as marked as in stratified society. . . . What caused ranking to develop? The existence of egalitarian relations in some societies precludes the pop-science answer that inequalities arise from the competitiveness of human nature. . . . One line of reasoning followed by many anthropologists is that the beginnings of hierarchical organization must have had something to do with population growth. . . . An alternative hypothesis for the development of ranking, and the more likely one in our view, is that the growth of trade was critical. . . . This did not mean the disappearance of egalitarian traditions, but it did mean an unequal access to important resources that undermined the economic structure of egalitarianism. . . . Egalitarian gatherer-hunter bands and communal village horticulturalists all engaged in some trade, but critical to the development of ranking would be the point when such trade became important enough to lead to specialization and the consequent reorganization of production relations.

> Mona Etienne and Eleanor Leacock, Introduction to *Women and Colonization*, p. 13

There is always the danger that anthropological observers will unconsciously impose their own cultural presuppositions on the society they are observing and describing. There is also the complementary danger that informants will cooperate in such delusions by telling questioners what they want to hear. If, for example, male anthropologists from male-dominated societies look at and ask about female-male relations in other societies, will they see and hear only what they take to be humanly normative?

WOMEN IN PREINDUSTRIAL SOCIETIES

To discern such bias it is often necessary to read between or behind the lines of male descriptions of female-male relations. Here are two examples of such counter-reading, both involving the Montagnais-Naskapi of eastern Canada's Labrador Peninsula, as cited by Eleanor Leacock (26–27, 39–40).

The first two reports, one from the 1630s and the other from the 1890s respectively, agree closely on the jobs undertaken by the women and judge them as servile drudgery:

The women . . . besides the onerous role of bearing and rearing the children, also transport the game from the place where it has fallen; they are the hewers of wood and drawers of water; they make and repair the household utensils; they prepare food; they skin the game and prepare the hides like fullers; they sew garments; they catch fish and gather shellfish for food; often they even hunt; they make the canoes, that is skiffs of marvelous rapidity, out of bark; they set up the tents wherever and whenever they stop for the night—in short, the men concern themselves with nothing but the more laborious hunting and the waging of war. . . . Their wives are regarded and treated as slaves.

The sexes have their special labors. Women perform the drudgery and bring home the food slain by their husbands, fetching wood and water, tanning the skins, and making them into clothing. The labor of erecting the tents and hauling the sleds when on their journey during the winter falls upon them, and, in fact, they perform the greater part of the manual labor. They are considered inferior to men, and in their social life they soon show the effects of the hardships they undergo.

Those two reports must be read alongside these other accounts from, respectively, the same times and sources. They indicate accuracy in description despite prejudice in understanding:

Women have great power. . . . A man may promise you something and if he does not keep his promise, he thinks he is sufficiently excused when he tells you that his wife did not wish him to do it. . . . The women know what they are to do, and the men also; and one never meddles with the work of the other. . . . Men leave the arrangement of the household to the women, without interfering with them; they cut and decide and give away as they please without making the husband angry. I have never seen my host ask a giddy young woman that he had with him what became of the provisions, although they were disappearing very fast. . . . The choice of plans, of undertakings, of journeys, of winterings, lies in nearly every instance in the hands of the housewife.

An amusing incident occurred within a stone's throw of Fort Chimo. An Indian had his clothes stripped from him by his enraged wife. She then took the tent from the poles, leaving him naked. She took their property to the canoe, which she paddled several miles upstream. He followed along the bank until she relented, whereupon their former relations were resumed, as though nothing had disturbed the harmony of their life. The man was so severely plagued by his comrades that for many days he scarcely showed his head out of the tent.

But the phrase "their property" is precisely the problem. As Leacock comments, "Translating the incident into the terms of political economy, women retained control over the products of their labor. These were not alienated, and women's production of clothing, shelter, and canoe covering gave them concomitant practical control and influence; despite formal statements of male dominance that might be elicited by outsiders" (40). If the description is accurate, it can be read against the presuppositions of the male describer and even used to disconfirm them.

The preceding quotations are from a set of feminist studies on women and colonization focusing on gathering-hunting societies but including some advanced horticultural groups as well. They "illustrate the reality of female-male complementarity," as editors Mona Etienne and Eleanor Leacock explain, and they "document the clash between this egalitarian principle and the hierarchical organization that European colonization brought about in many parts of the world" (10).

About twenty years ago Martin King Whyte reported the results of a controlled-sample investigation of ninety-three preindustrial societies that set out "to examine in a general cross-cultural study how a wide range of aspects of the status of women relative to men varies, and then try to explain why the status of women is higher in some societies and lower in others" (12). Of those preindustrial societies, about one-third were nomadic gathering-hunting cultures, another one-third were "peasant communities within complex agrarian civilizations," and a final one-third were in between those other two types (5). Here are three major conclusions from that five-year research project (167, 170, 172–173):

The first conclusion denies the claim that male-over-female domination is universal. "We do not find a pattern of universal male dominance, but much variation from culture to culture in virtually all aspects of the position of women relative to men. Our findings do lead us to doubt that there are cultures in which women are totally dominant over men ... [but] there is substantial variation from societies with very general male dominance to other societies in which broad equality and even some specific types of female dominance over men exist."

The second conclusion denies that there is a single, unitary status of women. "One can no longer assume that there is such a thing as *the* status of women cross-culturally. Nor can one assume that a favorable position for women in any particular area of social life will be related to favorable positions in other areas. Nor can one search for *the best* indicator of the status of women, or for *the key* variable that affects the status of women. ... In other words, each aspect of the status, roles, and relationship of women relative to men must be examined and explained separately, unless further research shows a cross-cultural reality that is very different from the patterns we have discovered."

The third conclusion compares women in simple and more complex preindustrial societies and "shows the strongest and most consistent results. In the more complex cultures, women tend to have less domestic authority, less independent solidarity with other women, more unequal sexual restrictions, and perhaps receive more ritualized fear from men and have fewer property rights, than is the case in the simpler cultures. At the same time women in these more complex cultures tend to have more informal influence and perhaps somewhat more joint participation with males. ... On balance, and even with allowance for the fact that not all of our scales have clear status implications, the lot of women would seem to be somewhat better in the simpler societies in our sample than in the more complex ones." The preindustrial spectrum of simple to complex societies is specified in these words: "Both preliterate hunting bands and communities in settled agrarian empires are included."

Since my present interests concern women in first-century Galilee—that is, women in "peasant communities within complex agrarian civilizations"—I am led to wonder what can be said about their precise situation. How, in other words, do class and gender intersect one another as equal variables in the specific case of peasant women?

WOMEN IN PEASANT SOCIETIES

Susan Carol Rogers has proposed a theory of peasant power distribution and peasant sexual differentiation based on field experience in a French peasant village for six months in 1971 (with short returns in 1972 and 1973) and on feminist anthropological literature about similar situations.

In a first article, in 1975, she focused on two different types of power distribution within peasant society. One is overt, direct, symbolical, and formal. The other is covert, indirect, real, and informal.

Rogers argued that "although peasant males monopolize positions of authority and are shown public deference by women, thus superficially appearing to be dominant, they wield relatively little real power. Theirs is a largely powerless authority, often accompanied by a felt sense of powerlessness, both in the face of the world at large and of the peasant community itself. On the other hand, within the context of peasant society, women control at least the major portion of important resources and decisions. In other words, if we limit our investigation to the relative actual power of peasant men and women, eliminating for the moment those sources of power from the outside world which are beyond the reach of either peasant men or women, women appear to be generally more powerful. At the same time, the 'symbolic' power of men should not be underestimated, nor can it be left unexplained" (1975:728–729).

Think, for example, of two aspects of peasant society. Men, let's imagine, have public-political responsibility and women, let's imagine, have private-domestic responsibility. But peasant society has, by definition, no public-political power within itself for men to exercise, and domestic activity, far from private, "is of primary economic, political, and social importance so that a woman's power in this sphere extends to the village at large" (1975:733). Rogers concludes that "what we see operating in peasant society is a kind of dialectic, a delicately balanced opposition of several kinds of power and authority: overt and covert, formal and informal, direct and indirect. For this reason, I would suggest that the model of one sex group in a 'primary' or dominant role and the other in a 'secondary' one is specious and ignores the complexity of the situation" (1975:746). It may well be precisely because peasant men are relatively powerless that peasant women accord them public deference and formal respect. Peasant women have actual power-as-control. Peasant men have "mythical" power-as-status.

In a second article, in 1978, Rogers built on that former one. She now focused on two different types of sexual differentiation within peasant society. The first, *behavioral* differentiation, has to do with gender-specific roles, jobs, and responsibilities. Some of those differences come from nature, some come from culture, some come from the delicate interface of nature and culture, and most come from where the culture masquerades as nature. The second is *ideological* differentiation, which concerns not just separation of roles and responsibilities but, more profoundly, separation of the sexes themselves into almost twin species. Behavioral differentiation means women and men have different jobs. Ideological differentiation means women and men are different species. Apples and oranges, let us say, are both behaviorally and ideologically different. Which, then, is better than the other? Apples, no doubt, think apples are better. Oranges, ditto.

Rogers proposes that *behavioral* sexual differentiation, in which "each sex acts out different roles, participates in different activities, and so on," is "evidently universal." Not so with *ideological* sexual differentiation, by which "males and females view themselves as fundamentally different from each other, e.g. as separate entities or species. Where they are ideologically differentiated, each sex may be expected to have its own perception of the universe, values, goals, and so on (within the overarching basic values of the society). . . . That is, women, for example, will consider some male-controlled resources relatively unimportant, and value highly their own, while men hold the opposite valuation"; or "male resources may be publicly recognized as most important by both sexes, and privately belittled by one or both" (1978:154–155). That distinction is important because, in the contemporary North American ideal, we tend to deny the validity of *both* differentiations and therefore may not bother to distinguish or even acknowledge them. Be that as it may, it is especially difficult for us to understand, for example, societies where both those differentiations are forcibly and openly present. But it is precisely such societies that are Rogers's main concern.

It is when there is a combination of both behavioral and ideological differentiations that "a balance of power is most likely to occur . . . [since] the two groups . . . are perceived as two different things . . . related dialectically, at once opposed to each other, and equally dependent upon each other. . . . That first pattern . . . is the most common cross-culturally, and the one in which a dominant/subordinate relationship between the sexes is least likely to occur." The second pattern involves behavioral without ideological differentiation, and here "a hierarchical relationship between the sexes—with a clear imbalance of power—becomes more probable. Here, it is believed that males and females are fundamentally the same.... The resources controlled by one group, however, are likely to be more highly valued by both. Because differential access to control of resources is not firmly grounded in differential ideology, behavioral differentiation may be perceived as unjust, immoral, or illegal, at least by the sex group without access to highly valued resources" (1978:155–156).

Rogers finds that first combination present "in traditional European peasant societies" and also "in pre-colonial West African societies," but "evidence of a transformation to the second pattern may also be found in these two world areas" (1978:157). The change from first to second pattern—that is, from dialectical to hierarchical female-male relationships—was especially associated with "colonization in West Africa and industrialization in Europe." Obviously that change was not in women's favor, but Rogers makes the same very interesting qualification in each case.

With regard to colonization in West Africa: "Although economic growth induced by colonization initially upset the balance of power in women's favor, there is some indication that with integration into wider economic systems, men may take over and surpass women in the control of formerly feminine resources. They may thus attain a more powerful position than women." With regard to industrialization in Europe: "As industrialization takes over the countryside, peasant men lose control of their resources, or these are devalued by the group as a whole, with a subsequent rise in the relative value of women's resources, and a power imbalance favoring women. Male control resurfaces, with new resources, most notably those relating to integration in a larger group" (1978:158–159). *Initially* and *temporarily,* then, peasant women confronted with foreign or domestic commercialization may be slightly better off than peasant men. That, by the way, is the point where anthropology of class and gender intersect most forcibly for my present concerns. The Lenski-Kautsky model indicates commercialization (as in the first-century Roman Empire) as regular prelude to peasant resistance and rebellion. But colonization as well as industrialization are simply forms of commercialization, the former both ancient and modern, the latter a relatively contemporary type. If Rogers's analysis is correct, the initial stages of colonial commercialization in Lower Galilee, for example, would have left peasant women in a temporarily better position than peasant men. That fact would be very important to our understanding of the peasant women companions of Jesus.

Anthropology of Resistance

Inasmuch as peasants have a sharp appreciation of their relations with rural elites, they have no difficulty in recognizing when more and more is required of them and less and less is given in return. Peasants are thus not much subject to "mystification" about class relations; they do not need outsiders to help them recognize a pattern of growing exploitation which they experience daily. This does not mean outsiders are inconsequential. On the contrary, they are often critical to peasant movements, not because they convince peasants that they are exploited but because, in the context of exploitation, they may provide the power, assistance, and supralocal organization that helps peasants *act*. It is thus at the level of collective action that the typically small scale of peasant social life constitutes a disability, not at the level of assessing relations.

James C. Scott, *The Moral Economy of the Peasant*, pp. 173–174

The Lenski-Kautsky model indicates that peasant resistance escalates as rural commercialization encroaches on the traditional peasant way of life, breaches the safety net of kinship relations and village contacts, and changes the land from inalienable family inheritance to negotiable business commodity. But in that model, and also in the Eisenstadt citations given above (as well as in every other cross-cultural anthropologist I have read), the problem of leadership arises as soon as peasant resistance is mentioned. It arises especially in terms of leadership from classes above the peasantry, from the "outsiders" mentioned in the above epigraph from James Scott. In many or even most cases, those scholars are thinking of military revolts and of leadership from dissident retainer or aristocratic classes. I want, however, to broaden the question of resistance and leadership to include ideology as well as army, scribal as well as martial situations. What if priests, prophets, scribes, bureaucrats, or retainers, acting institutionally or charismatically, instigate an *ideological* revolution? As you read the following quotations on peasant resistance and outsider leadership, do not imagine only military retainers leading peasant armies.

RESISTANCE AND LEADERSHIP

My first quotation is from Kautsky himself. "The lack of suitable leadership among the peasants of the traditional villages [is] another reason for the absence of organization and hence of revolts reaching beyond at most a few neighboring villages. . . . Townspeople, given their different environment and experience, may have developed such attributes, like skills in communicating with and organizing strangers, and they may have the requisite material resources to practice these skills. For uprisings to spread widely and to maintain themselves, such skills and resources of outside leaders are required to overcome the localism of peasants. . . . It appears that all peasant revolts that spread beyond local confines in societies undergoing commercialization or modernization from without did so under nonpeasant leadership or in alliance with nonpeasant movements. . . . If peasant revolts could spread only because of nonpeasant leadership, then the absence of such leadership in traditional aristocratic empires may be a major reason for the virtual absence of peasant revolts transcending local confines in such empires. Commercialization and, more recently, modernization from without are followed by peasant revolts not only because they affect the conditions under which peasants live but also because they produce revolutionary groups in the towns, bring the peasants in contact with them, and make them available as the peasants' leaders" (304, 306).

That makes a very interesting point. Commercialization (and all that comes with it) disturbs not only traditional peasant life but also traditional town or even city life. What if, for example, it relativizes the importance of *our* priests, negates the value of *our* temples, changes the validity of *our* laws, customs, and morals? What if I am a lower-order scribe whose livelihood has been endangered by a change in the dominant language to facilitate international commerce—a change, say, from Aramaic to Greek? Dissident priests or scribes may become leaders for dissident peasants or artisans. And that is a rather dangerous combination. Once again from Kautsky: "[T]he outsiders who can formulate more far-reaching programs and demands on behalf of peasants, who can visualize achieving a world different from the existing one, who can lead a proactive movement are themselves a product of commercialization and modernization" (309). That is a very important point, and I underline its structural implications. The systemic dislocations created by commercialization both create an environment conducive to peasant resistance or rebellion and supply the dissenting retainers who will become its leaders.

The second quotation is from Eisenstadt. Notice how it envisages various forms of resistance leadership, even if only in passing: "The peasantry became politically active only rarely. Even when it did, it did not usually become active independently, but mostly in conjunction with other groups and strata, like the army or religious movements. . . . [The peasants] often took part in rebellions, and sometimes even inaugurated them, under the leadership either of their own people or of alienated bureaucrats, gentry, or religious leaders" (207–208). Once again the dangerous combination is an alienated peasantry with leadership not just from itself but from alienated retainers, be they scribes or priests.

The last quotation is from Eric Robert Wolf's classic study of peasants: "The emergence of a common myth of transcendental justice often can and does move peasants into action as other forms of organization cannot, but it provides only a common vision, not an organizational framework for action. Such myths unite peasants, they do not organize them. If sometimes the peasant band sweeps across the countryside like an avalanche, like an avalanche, too, it spends itself against resistance and dissolves if adequate leadership is not provided from without" (108).

All of the above quotations focus on how peasant resistance or revolt can break out of localism and regionalism, usually under nonpeasant leadership.

INTERLUDE FOR AN EXAMPLE

Lest those multiplied quotations seem too abstract, I pause to give one concrete example of what they are talking about. I do not, by the way, find anything romantically wonderful about peasant revolt or rural terrorism. But neither do I find anything romantically wonderful about the imperial exploitation that breeds those acts. Brutality brutalizes.

The case is taken from Michael Beames's fascinating study of *Peasants and Power*. The time and place is early-nineteenth-century Ireland in the decades between the end of the Napoleonic Wars and the start of the Great Famine. In those years there was "a gradual process by which external pressures were forcing the Irish peasantry onto smaller and more insecure holdings with the eventual threat of descent into a rural lumpenproletariat" of beggary and/or banditry (127). That external pressure was commercialization or land-jobbing. "'Land jobbers' viewed land as a commodity to be acquired and held according to commercial criteria. Whiteboys [rural rebels], on the other hand, regarded it not only as an essential means of subsistence but the resource around which peasant social relationships were based and thus something over which the peasantry had a right to exercise control" (137–138). The response to that external pressure, across the country, was rural terrorism involving various groups with different names in different places; but the term *Whiteboys* became the generic name for violent resistance involving, first, warning or threat, and then, if that failed, arson or assassination.

Ireland was, in those years, a legally constituted part of Great Britain, so various British commissions were assigned to solve that situation. We thus have the records of diverse individuals giving testimony about those events and can actually hear the voices of the peasantry itself. The following statements from three different people (recorded by the *Royal Commission to Inquire into the Condition of the Poorer Classes in Ireland* in 1836 and cited in Beames [126–127]) give a glimpse of their sense of moral outrage:

> [A County Galway laborer named Ward:] And it's that that makes men disturbed and unlawful when they see themselves, and them that are about them, turned adrift in the world; it is that that brings "Terries" [Whiteboys]

into the country. They may as well take my life when they have taken my land; what's an existence without a place (i.e. a holding).

[*A County Galway laborer named Byrne:*] About three years ago a man who had held a farm eight or nine years, and had paid his rent up to the last farthing, was turned out, though he offered the same rent, as the man that was put in his place. The "Terries" [Whiteboys] came (they would come from Clare for revenge) and swore the newcomer to give up the land; he didn't keep his oath; in a week's time a man came at twelve o'clock in the day; he sent into the house for Flanagan, and when he came out to him, where three or four of his own labourers were standing, the strange man drew out a pistol and shot him.

[*A Queen's County dispossessed tenant:*] The poor would rather lose their lives, when driven to such desperation, than quietly submit to be ejected from their lands, for they have no other means of living, and if they once give up their land, they would be starving wanderers through the world, as even their relations and former friends would turn their backs upon them, considering them as an encumbrance; when the poor ejected tenant applies to them, and tells them of his misfortune, they turn a deaf ear to him, unless it is to urge him to revenge himself upon his oppressors.

The government knew, of course, exactly what was at stake in such resistance—especially in the peasants' moral claims about social justice. Lord Norbury, for example, had spelled it out with admirable clarity twenty-five years earlier, as cited by Beames (138):

[The principle of laissez-faire economics] is the first principle in a commercial country and the first consequence of national prosperity, that property should be in a state of perpetual transfer and circulation. To check this natural progress, to avert this perpetual motion in the great machine of human society, no legislature, however strong or powerful has been ever rash or strong enough to attempt; and whatever the wisest of men and best of governments would tremble to undertake as practicable, and would reject as undesirable, these mob legislators and banditti reformers have announced as the law of their association, and enforce the observance of that law by torture and murder. Land they say, shall never rise, and property shall never change its possessor. To all ranks are their mandates equally directed, to the rich and to the poor.

An aristocracy for whom land is an entrepreneurial commodity clashes fiercely and profoundly with a peasantry for whom land is an inalienable livelihood.

Given that clash in early-nineteenth-century Ireland, who offered leadership to the peasants in those years of rural terrorism? Not dissident aristocrats, rebellious gentry, or recalcitrant clergy, but village schoolmasters—which in those days meant "hedge" schoolmasters, who taught in the open air. I quote once again from Beames (61):

> The hedge schoolmasters were independent of control by state, church or local squire, they were reliant upon the support and goodwill of the peasantry. To an extent the "people" controlled their own education. . . . Whether or not these schoolmasters actually participated in the Whiteboy movements is perhaps less important than the fact that they provided an alternative focus, a different source of authority and education for the peasantry from landlord, priest and parson. Given their close involvement with and dependence on the peasant community, it seems highly probable that they acted as a catalyst for the articulation of peasant grievances. At the very least, their contribution to Whiteboyism must have been to teach the authors of threatening letters how to write.

Though a hedge schoolmaster, even one recalling the Celtic tradition of the itinerant poet-scholar, was fairly low among the Retainer Class, the combination of dissident teacher and dissident peasants is always dangerous, especially on the ideological level.

THE PRIESTLY CLASS REVISITED

I return, in the light of those considerations of leadership, to look in more detail at what Lenski says about the Priestly Class. This serves both to conclude this chapter on cross-cultural anthropology and to create a hard lock with the next one on Judeo-Roman history.

Lenski's division of the Retainer Class and the Priestly Class needs to be reconsidered for use in this present study. The reasons are both internal and external. On the internal side, there is a slight but significant warning of difficulty as one moves from Lenski's description of those classes in his text to their depiction in his visual model. In the description they are clearly differentiated from one another as "the Retainer Class" (243–248) and "the Priestly Class" (256–266), but in the model they appear together as "retainers and priests" (284).

On the external side, recent scholars of earliest Christianity, using Lenski's classification, seem to have sensed this same problem. In 1991 David Fiensy adapted the Lenski model to "the social structure of Palestine in the Herodian period." Fiensy's diagram places the high-priestly families among the Governing Class, and "bailiffs, tax farmers, and government bureaucrats" among the Retainers (158). That adaptation is accepted, with population percentages added, in

Dennis Duling's 1994 edition of Norman Perrin's New Testament introduction (56). Lenski's Priestly Class seems to have disappeared (except, of course, for those few priestly aristocrats at the very pinnacle of power within the Governing Class). But, in that process of evolution, something more important than a category was lost. What was lost was the potential for the Priestly Class, as defined by Lenski, to initiate ideological revolt against aristocracy or royalty in the name of divinity itself.

It is necessary to consider in very great detail what Lenski means by the Priestly Class. "Strictly speaking, this term refers only to those who mediate relations between God, or the gods, and men through the performance of sacrificial rites. I shall use the term more broadly, however, to include monks, ministers, rabbis, imams, and all other religious leaders whose livelihood and status in society were dependent primarily on their leadership role in the religious system. The nature of the priestly class varied considerably from one agrarian society to another. . . . Because of all these variations, it is extremely dangerous to generalize about the role of the priestly class. It may even be that the nature of this class was the most variable feature of importance in agrarian societies, when viewed from the standpoint of the distributive process" (256–257). In other words, the Priestly Class involved anyone who, institutionally or charismatically, officially or popularly, claimed *religious* authority and leadership in an agrarian society. Why is the Priestly Class so disparate and difficult to contain even in typological generalization?

On the one hand, it was very much to the advantage of Ruler and Governing Class that the Priestly Class legitimated their authority "to separate the common people from the major part of what they produced" (260), and it was very much to the Priestly Class's advantage to have the political elites protecting their rights, embellishing their temples, and even paying their salaries. On the other hand, there was always "the fact of divided authority" (261). That is the root of the problem. The Priestly Class claimed a divine mandate even without any force, coercion, or violence; and the Ruler or Governing Class, even when also claiming a divine mandate, did so with the army standing always at the ready. No matter how agrarian societies may differ in handling that division (or even in attempting totally to negate it—say, with priest-rulers or temple-states), it is always present, like a giant fault line in the authority structure. And it is along fault lines that earthquakes occur.

For Lenski, therefore, the Priestly Class, unlike the Retainer Class, is defined not by service to the Ruler or Governing Class but by service to the divine or transcendental mandate that they claim to have and to fulfill. But what if that divine mandate involves a concern for social justice and human compassion? Without in any way denying the extent to which the Priestly Class has been co-opted or compromised even in traditions recognizing such a mandate, Lenski asserts that these religious leaders "played a unique role among the privileged classes in agrarian societies. In a type of society in which men of power saw to it that there was a massive flow of goods and services from the many to the few, some members of the priestly class managed to slow this movement and even to stimulate a small flow in the opposite direction. *In this respect, the priestly class tended to function as the preserver of the ancient Redistributive Ethic of primitive societies, where the accumulation of goods in private hands had served as a form of communal insurance rather than as private property.* The extent to which the priestly class performed this important function varies considerably from religion to religion, and within religions from century to century and area to area. Of all the factors responsible for this variation, the most important seems to have been the actual content of a faith and the degree to which God was believed to be concerned with social justice" (266). The Priestly Class means *religious* leadership, whether we are dealing with priest or prophet, visionary or teacher, institutional or charismatic individual, official or popular personage—*as long as the claimed authority is transcendental or divine.*

Lenski's Priestly Class covers all those who claim to be religious leaders in an agrarian society, all those whose assertion of authority is not intrinsically dependent on Governing Class or Ruler, all those whose loyalty to aristocratic exploitation is always a little suspect (at least in a society where religion is concerned with social justice). In the first-century Jewish homeland, then, Sadducees, Pharisees, Essenes, John the Baptist, and Jesus all belonged to Lenski's Priestly Class—a result so confusing that a modified classification is clearly needed.

My proposal is to keep the term *Retainer Class*—since, in general, the retainer's role is to support the Governing Class—but to envisage three groups within it. (In all three cases, watch the ambiguity necessitated by that support of those in power: If the Governing Class needs the Retainer Class, why are the retainers not the governors?) The first subgroup is *military retainers,* including all those skilled in violence, and ranging from army to police to enforcers. The danger connected with this group is obvious: What if they rebel or attempt to usurp governing prerogatives? But of course, whenever they do it, they must also reveal the naked force and coercion by which the entire system is sustained, whatever its moral justification. The second subgroup is *religious retainers,* including all those skilled in divinity, ranging from priests to prophets, from ordained ministers to popular charismatics. The danger, once again, is obvious: What if, in the name of their sacred power, they turn on Ruler and Governing Class? What about, in Lenski's apt phrase, "the fact of divided authority" (161), of a loyalty split between earth and heaven? The third subgroup is *scribal retainers,* including all those skilled in literacy or accountancy, ranging from bureaucrats to lawyers. Any danger from them will probably arise in conjunction with one of those other two subgroups—unless, of course, they move to claim the status of military or religious retainers in their own right.

The point in these modifications is not to establish little taxonomic boxes but to emphasize the structural ambiguity, first, of the entire Retainer Class as such and, second, that of the military, scribal, and religious subgroups always interacting within it. In all of this I am primarily interested in systemic fault lines, and I especially do not want to lose Lenski's emphasis on the fault lines within what he termed the Priestly Class. He himself noted that "on many occasions, especially in the Judaic-Christian tradition, though not there alone, the priestly class opposed tyranny and injustice and supported the needs and interests of the weaker elements of society," and did so from "the tradition embodied in the Western religions that God is above all a God of justice and that His awesome power will be used to punish the unjust" (263).

One final point. This is another case where the Lenski-Kautsky model and the Eisenstadt model are in complete agreement, but as usual the latter is much more general than the former. Eisenstadt notes that "in most of the societies studied, the value systems of the major religions were sufficiently differentiated to contain a strong ingredient of universalistic and/or transcendental orientations. They thus constituted potential sources of autonomous orientations, of change, and of dissent. . . . The latent predilection for change that characterized some of the religious institutions, orders, and groups explained their frequent participation in 'radical' social and political movements—e.g., in peasant uprisings, and in urban movements and conspiracies" (190). A transcendent mandate can often justify a political or social situation. But it can also turn it upside down. Clergy and aristocracy, however named, differentiated, or combined, represent divergent sources of power, and that social fault line cannot be eliminated without eradicating either religion or politics. Probably not even then.

PART V
History and Archeology

Governments, Theocracies and Armies are, of course, stronger than the scattered peasants. So the peasants have to resign themselves to being dominated, but they cannot feel as their own the glories and undertakings of a civilization that is radically their enemy. The only wars that touch their hearts are those in which they have fought to defend themselves against that civilization, against History and Government, Theocracy and the Army. These wars they fought under their own black pennants, without military leadership or training and without hope, ill-fated wars that they were bound to lose, fierce and desperate wars, incomprehensible to historians. . . . But the myth of the brigands is close to their hearts and a part of their lives, the only poetry in their existence, their dark, desperate epic. Even the appearance of the peasants today recalls that of the brigands: they are silent, lonely, gloomy and frowning in their black suits and hats and, in winter, black top coats, armed whenever they set out for the fields with gun and axe. They have gentle hearts and patient souls; centuries of resignation weigh on their shoulders, together with a feeling of the vanity of all things and of the overbearing power of fate. But when, after infinite endurance, they are shaken to the depths of their beings and are driven by an instinct of self-defense or justice, their revolt knows no bounds and no measure. It is an unhuman revolt whose point of departure and final end alike are death, in which ferocity is born of despair. The brigands unreasonably and hopelessly stood up for the life and liberty of the peasants against the encroachments of the State. By ill luck they were unwitting instruments of History, and History, quite outside their ken, was working against them; they were on the wrong side and they came to destruction. But through the brigands the peasants defended themselves against the hostile civilization that never understands but everlastingly enslaves them; instinctively they looked on the brigands as heroes. The peasant world has neither government nor army; its wars are only sporadic outbursts of revolt, doomed to repression. Still it survives, yielding up the fruits of the earth to the conquerors, but imposing upon them its measurements, its earthly divinities, and its language.

Carlo Levi, *Christ Stopped at Eboli*, pp. 137–140

The general conclusion from Part IV was that peasant dislocations created by rural commercialization increase the possibility or inevitability of resistance, rebellion, and even revolution. Building directly on that preceding Part IV, Part V considers Jewish tradition and Roman history on a collision course at that precise point of incipient rural commercialization in the first century. What happens when Roman urbanization and its concomitant ruralization finally reach Lower Galilee?

Part V has two chapters. Chapter 12 probes what went so terribly wrong between imperial Roman policy and traditional Jewish religion in the first two hundred years of their interaction. The constitutional traditions of Judaism involved a God of justice and righteousness in covenantal relationship with a people of justice and righteousness under a law of justice and righteousness in a land of justice and righteousness. That God *could* not be other, and that people *should* not be other. God's Law was not a matter simply of divine will or divine command but of divine nature and divine character. In sacred law, in prophetic critique, and in scribal wisdom, this God stood against oppression and exploitation, against indebtedness, enslavement, and dispossession, against everything that increased inequality and destroyed equality. Land, as the basis of life, was not just a commodity for normal entrepreneurial manipulation: the land belonged to God; God's people were all tenants on divine property. Then along came Roman imperialism, which sought land for commercial exploitation as well as territorial expansion. Jewish tradition clashed predictably with that Roman policy. And it clashed not only because peasants usually resist rural commercialization but also (and especially) because Jewish peasants had a long and sacred tradition of such resistance.

Chapter 13 places the third and final layer on my interdisciplinary model for context. Granted those anthropological and historical layers, there is still a further question. Was Galilee simply a Roman backwater of no value for urbanization or commercialization? Archeology indicates precisely what was happening in Lower Galilee in the first twenty years of the first common-era century. Herod Antipas was moving to urbanize Lower Galilee as his father, Herod the Great, had done earlier in Judaea and Samaria. The rebuilding of Sepphoris and the creation of Tiberias represented centers for rural commercialization, and with their advent, anthropology, history, and archeology came together at the precise point where resistance could be expected. The time and place were now ready for the baptism-in-the-Jordan movement of John and the kingdom-of-God movement of Jesus.

CHAPTER 12

JUDEO-ROMAN HISTORY

The notion of social justice was deeply rooted in the commandments and the oral law as they had developed over 1200 years, whatever might be the differences of interpretation among the Jews, differences that tended to derive from the class origins of the interpreters. . . . The basic problem of moral values and practices that the Jewish people had evolved over the centuries, and their close union of morality and common identity produced a national consciousness that far exceeded that of its neighbors in solidarity and roots. An important part of Jewish legislation, moreover, regulated such vital matters as local government, slavery, land ownership, cultivation, Sabbath, debt, and contributions to the central shrine—all of which had economic implications. . . . It is well to note that the organized resistance that became the driving force of the Jewish revolution of 66–74 was generated by a strongly religious and ethical conception—that the earth belonged to the Divinity—the first protestant declaration of faith. This faith evoked resistance to an unjust economic situation, and the resistance intensified the confiscation and eviction and the growth of the landless, which composed the greater part of the active resistance movements.
  Shimon Applebaum, "Josephus and the Economic Causes of the Jewish War,"
  pp. 237–238, 256–257

The phrase *Judeo-Roman* in the title of this chapter is not exactly a standard one. But I want, in this discussion, to focus as closely as possible on the interaction between Roman imperialism and traditional Judaism in the Jewish homeland. The general background is the Hellenistic world, the cultural cosmopolitanism and economic internationalism resulting from Alexander's conquests of the eastern Mediterranean toward the end of the fourth century B.C. But I focus here especially on Judeo-Roman relations in the Jewish homeland.

That land had been under pagan imperial domination since the sixth century B.C.E. The Romans were not its first imperial overlords. What, then, went so utterly wrong between Roman policy and Jewish tradition? Think about these round numbers: Within the first four hundred years of foreign control, under the Persian Empire and its Greek replacements, there was only a single revolt, at the very end of that period. But within the first two hundred years of Roman control there were three major revolts, one under Nero and Vespasian in 66–74, another under Trajan in 115–117, and a final one under Hadrian in 132–135. In more detail:

Under Persian Empire	208 years (539–331 B.C.E.)	no revolts
Under Alexander and generals	29 years (331–302 B.C.E.)	no revolts
Under Greco-Egyptian Empire	104 years (302–198 B.C.E.)	no revolts
Under Greco-Syrian Empire	31 years (198–167 B.C.E.)	one revolt
Under Roman Empire	172 years (63 B.C.E.–135 C.E.)	three revolts

The three terrible wars against the Roman Empire resulted, respectively, in the burning of the Temple, the destruction of Egyptian Judaism, and the paganization of Jerusalem. The first and last revolts took place in the Jewish homeland itself. The middle one spread from Egypt and Cyrene to Cyprus, Palestine, and even as far as Mesopotamia. There are always several reasons for widespread revolt leading to all-out war, but why did Jewish relations with Rome—*specifically* with Rome—deteriorate so badly and end up so disastrously?

The basic stratum of cross-cultural anthropology from the Lenski-Kautsky model emphasized how commercialization provoked peasant resistance in agrarian empires. It also considered Rome as an example of such commercialized agrarian empires. The next step is to establish a hard lock between anthropology and history within my method's interdisciplinary design. That hard lock is *rural commercialization,* which the Roman Empire accepted as manifest imperial destiny and much of Jewish tradition rejected as divinely forbidden injustice. In this chapter, then, I look first at the general social structure of the Roman Empire and then at Jewish traditions about rural commercialization.

Better Slave Than Peasant?

The Roman Empire was the most complete preindustrial system that has ever existed with the possible exception of dynastic China.
Stephen L. Dyson, "A Classical Archaeologist's Response to the 'New Archaeology,'" p. 10

The most oppressed social strata in the Roman empire were the fairly poor and impoverished sections of the rural population. Among those sectors those who suffered worst were not the slaves on the *latifundia* [plantations], who were of value to their masters and were at least regularly fed, but the mass of nominally "free" peasants, who were without means of support and who, in the provinces, often also lacked the privileged status of a Roman citizen. For example, the life of the "free" country-dwellers of Judaea or Egypt was far worse than that of the slaves on [an Italian] estate.
Géza Alföldy, The Social History of Rome, pp. 145–146

Géza Alföldy has given a specific historical model of the Roman Empire's social structure (1985:146), and it can easily be superimposed on the general anthropological model of Gerhard Lenski seen earlier (1966:284). One advantage of Alföldy's historical model is its clear distinction of the upper and lower classes. There was no middle class in antiquity. There was, of course, a spread of wealth across the entire spectrum from very high to very low, but middle *wealth* did not entail middle *class*. The clear dividing line was, in agricultural terms, between those who possessed land that others worked for them and those who worked their land for themselves (even if the working family could also afford seasonal help or permanent slaves).

Another advantage of this model is its delineation of the distinctions and anomalies in the upper classes of the early Roman Empire. There, indeed, were latent the seeds of disaster, not so much in the distinctions as in the anomalies. Rome began its imperial existence while still a republic governed by two consuls replaced annually. Think of them as *twin kings for a year*, with all the advantages of *kings*, and with the disadvantages mitigated by *twin* and *for a year*. But the writing was already clearly on the wall in the 80s B.C.E., when Lucius Cornelius Sulla returned from the conquest of Greece and Asia Minor with enough booty to pay one million legionnaires for one year. That gave a new meaning to the term *for one year*. How could consuls control such warlords, and what was to stop consuls or ex-consuls becoming warlords themselves? The choice was between permanent civil war or established monarchical rule (but without that adjective!). By the late 30s, Octavius, adopted son and designated heir of Julius Caesar, was ready to become *Princeps* and *Augustus*, less than king in name and more than king in fact.

Some idea of ancient monetary values is helpful in appreciating what follows. The best way to understand those values is by looking at costs and prices from the period in question, rather than attempting to translate ancient monies into contemporary currencies. Listed below are a few examples (culled from Sperber 190; Duncan-Jones 10–11, 208, 349–350). Amounts are all given in sesterces. Bear in mind that four Roman sesterces were the equivalent of one Roman denarius, or one Greek drachma, or a quarter Jewish shekel.

Normal salary for a day-laborer:	1–3 sesterces a day
Cost of maintaining an urban slave:	350–500 sesterces a year
Price for an unskilled slave:	600 sesterces (minimum)
Stipend for a freed slave:	850–1,000 sesterces a year
Salary of a Roman soldier:	900 sesterces a year
Salary of a major provincial governor:	1,000,000 sesterces a year

Pliny the Younger, with a capital of about 20 million sesterces, left donations for freed slaves that would have produced between 850 and 1,000 sesterces for each one per year. That may be taken, therefore, as a basic subsistence allowance for one year.

At the very apex of the Alföldy model were the emperor and his dynastic family. Immediately below him was the Senatorial Order, whose 600 members, distinguished by the broad purple stripe on their togas, had to have a *minimum* capital of 1 million sesterces (which, at 6 percent, would have produced 600,000 sesterces annually).

Below the Senatorial Order was the Equestrian Order, so called because originally their cavalry horses were subsidized by the state. This order was distinguished by the narrow purple band on its togas, and each of the 20,000 members had to have a capital of at least 400,000 sesterces. Their wealth and power depended, as did that of the senators, on civil and military appointments, on the ownership of land, and on money-lending; especially for them, wealth and power also depended on various commercial, industrial, fiscal, and business operations. Therein lay a first anomaly: equestrians could end up far more wealthy than senators, for whom, in theory at least, those last occupations were beneath their dignity. And a second anomaly: Would the emperor, who might well be from the Equestrian Order himself, prefer to trust them more than the senators, who retained, after all, some nostalgic memories of their own lost power?

Beneath the Equestrian Order as such (but often identical with it in specific cases) was the Councilor or Decurion Order. This was not an empire-wide order but simply the separate elites of each city, usually involving about 100 members of the council and the magistrates. There were probably between 100,000 and 150,000 decurions across the 1,000 or so cities of the Roman Empire, and the capital requirements to hold that position ranged anywhere from 20,000 to 100,000 sesterces. Remember numbers, however: "If we add up the number of senators, *equites,* and decurions without equestrian status, we arrive at a total of no more than 200,000 adult males: these, together with their wives and children, amount to no more than 1 per cent of the total population of the empire" (147). So Alföldy's "upper strata" (the three orders described above) and "lower strata" represent, respectively, 1 percent and 99 percent of the Roman Empire.

I have already drawn attention to one anomaly in the Alföldy model: the topmost equestrians could be far wealthier than the lower senators. There are two other even more anomalous social categories: Caesar's Family and Freed Slaves. The emperors managed the empire as if it were an extended household, so that the enslaved and freed members of "Caesar's Family" often achieved enormous power and wealth. Even if you belonged to the Senatorial, Equestrian, or

Councilor Orders, your access to the emperor might well be through financial, legal, or political departments controlled by enslaved or freed bureaucrats. Such a situation could but decrease aristocratic loyalty to the new imperial system.

Even apart from that anomaly, the very possibility of people who were *rich but freed* created a social problem, not of course for them but for the elite orders theoretically above them. It must be remembered that Roman conquests had produced hordes of slaves as intelligent, cultured, and educated as their captors—and often far more so. Imagine conservative Roman landowners who knew that much money could be made in business ventures but did not want to dirty their hands, risk their reputations, or display their ignorance by trying to make that money. They owned smart slaves, captured in the East, who were well versed in commercial operations. They gave them *peculia,* amounts of money with which they could trade and bargain as if they were their own, but all profits had to be split between slave and master. (Obviously masters could order the slaves to transact business for them with no *peculia* agreement, but carrots work better than sticks in such circumstances.) Finally, when the slaves had made enough profit of their own, they could buy freedom for an agreed price. This usually happened at about 30 years of age, the bad news being that the average adult age at death was then 38.8 years for a man and 34.2 for a woman (Morris 74), a statistic badly skewed by the fact that about one-third of live births were dead by 6 and two-thirds by 16 (Carney 88).

Freedom or manumission from a Roman citizen conferred Roman citizenship on the freed slave. Only about 25 percent of the Roman Empire's members were citizens in that early first century of the common era, and it has been suggested that freed citizens might have been as high as 80 percent of that body. Freed slaves would always be designated as *freed* rather than *freeborn* and would always owe certain duties to the patronal household that had granted freedom, but any children born after manumission would be freeborn Roman citizens. No wonder that, as Alföldy said in the epigraph to this chapter, it was often better to be a Roman household slave than a free Jewish peasant. But once again, the social anomaly of the rich freed people whose wealth exceeded their power and whose power exceeded their status cast shadows all over the theoretical distinctions of the Roman aristocratic elite. It was, of course, a very good situation for enslaved and freed, but could a system long survive when it had mortgaged the loyalty of those it still kept at its pinnacle?

That, in briefest summary, was the Roman social system. One general comment about it before turning to the Jewish homeland. Stephen Dyson has done very thorough research on native revolts against Roman imperialism. Because he is primarily interested in the tribal societies of the West rather than the ancient societies of the East, he does not address such areas as Greece or Judaea. He concludes, however, that "the process of Romanization produced severe social and economic tensions which drove the native populace to repeated expressions of rebellion. . . . The tensions produced by the contrast of different economic life styles were a major factor in rebellion throughout Roman history" (1975:171). Roman imperialism meant not just taxation of an economy already in place but the commercialization of the local economy for more taxes and revenues in the future. How would that program fit with the Jewish tradition in the Jewish homeland?

A Thirst for Divine Justice

We can see a tension within the attitudes toward land tenure in the ancient Near East. On the one hand, there was the recognition that land was a unique resource that must receive special regulation in order to prevent the ruin of the people. On the other hand, there was a movement toward greater individual freedom in the use and disposal of the land, allowing for the possibility of latifundism [agribusiness] and the pauperization of masses of people. It appears that the ancient Near East was pulled in the latter direction, and it was in such a context in which Israel came into being.

Jeffrey A. Fager, *Land Tenure and the Biblical Jubilee*, p. 27

I begin with a few preliminary points. There are three elements in this section that cannot be separated from one another, although we often try to do so. Divine righteousness, social justice, and ritual purity are interwoven in Jewish tradition like three strands of one and the same rope. No matter which term is used, all three are presumed. Terms like *righteousness, justice,* or *purity* are biblical words whose repetition may have numbed us to their meaning. That numbing (or even dumbing) of our minds will be the major problem in this section. Throughout it I will emphasize how words and ideas that we may hear as exclusively religious or theological were originally such, but were economic, political, and social as well—all those many aspects intertwined together. To emphasize that conjunction, I did not entitle this section "A Thirst for Social Justice," which would have been a perfectly valid heading, but "A Thirst for Divine Justice," which is an even more accurate one. The subject is the justice of God for this earth. And how does one know that God is just? Because God stood against the Egyptian Empire to save some doomed slaves. God does not simply prefer Jews to Egyptians. God does not simply prefer slaves to masters. The only true God prefers justice to injustice, righteousness to unrighteousness, and is therefore God the Liberator. That very ancient Jewish tradition was destined to clash profoundly and fiercely with Roman commercialization, urbanization, and monetization in the first-century Jewish homeland.

Another preliminary point. I concentrate in what follows on biblical texts, on the constitutive and normative documents of Judaism itself. I realize, of course, that those texts can beget violently conflicting interpretations and that *class*, for instance, plays a crucial difference in how one interprets and applies God's justice on this earth. On the one hand, it is rather easy to be in favor of justice and righteousness. Few individuals, groups, or divinities proclaim themselves against such virtues or in favor of injustice and unrighteousness. But, on the other hand, the biblical texts indicate repeatedly what exactly such justice entails. And the logic behind that divine justice is human equality, a radical egalitarianism that shows itself not in abstract manifestos but in specific laws. Let me explain exactly what I mean through a comparison between Athens and Jerusalem, between Greek philosophy and Jewish theology.

Forty years ago Karl Polanyi wrote that the Greek philosopher Aristotle, who lived between 384 and 322 B.C.E., must "be seen as attacking the problem of man's livelihood with a radicalism of which no later writer on the subject was capable—none has ever penetrated deeper into the material organization of man's life. In effect, he posed, in all its breadth, the question of the place occupied by the economy in society" (66). Not all economic historians would agree with that judgment. Joseph Schumpeter, in a work published just before Polanyi's accolade, found Aristotle full of "decorous, pedestrian, slightly mediocre, and more than slightly pompous common sense" (57). Be that as it may, Aristotle taught that justice meant *in*equality. Moses Finley summarizes his idea of justice like this: "The distribution of equal shares among unequal persons, or of unequal shares among equal persons, would be unjust. The principle of distributive justice is therefore to balance the share with the worth of the person" (1970:29). Or, to put it more bluntly, from Finley quoting Marx: "'Greek society was founded upon slavery, and had, therefore, for its natural basis, the inequality of men and of their labour power'. That natural inequality is fundamental to Aristotle's thinking is beyond argument: it permeates his analysis of friendship in the *Ethics* and of slavery in the *Politics*" (1970:38). Slavery was natural. Therefore, *in*equality was natural. And, therefore, distributive justice demanded inequality.

Come back, now, from the philosophers of Greece to the theologians of Israel. You will not find in the Hebrew Bible any manifestos announcing that all people or even all Jews are equal. Neither will you find assertions that slavery is unnatural or against the will of God. But you will find there decrees and decisions, threats and promises that make sense only on the presumption that the justice of God strives insistently against inequality among God's people. If indebtedness, enslavement, and dispossession are simply the vagaries of life, as natural as drought, disease, and death, why does God seek to curtail indebtedness, control enslavement, and reverse dispossession? Why is the thrust toward equality and egalitarianism some sort of fundamental ideal?

Again, the Hebrew tradition did not proclaim philosophical manifestos about equality. But without that as its deep presumption, its words and deeds against the growth of inequality make no sense. The problem is, of course, that when God is revealed by freeing doomed slaves from imperial control, the future is set on a collision course with domination, oppression, and exploitation—even when those actions are exercised by a people on itself. In the biblical texts, accusations of injustice are made against the rich and powerful within Judaism itself. That is because Jews were then in charge of their own people and land. In the postbiblical texts, accusations of injustice are made against the pagan nations, the great empires, and the imperial gods. That is because they were then in charge of the Jewish people and the Jewish land. But what is always at stake is the Jewish God of justice, who stands against injustice, against unjust individuals, against unjust empires, and against unjust gods. Justice as equality is demanded not just by God's decree but by God's character, and it is up to human beings to figure out how that works in practice.

A final preliminary point. Many scholars now talk about Judaisms in the plural rather than the singular. Such a term rightly emphasizes the plurality and diversity of that religion in the first common-era centuries. It also reacts appropriately against the tendency to retroject later norms of orthodoxy back onto a much more variegated earlier period. On the other hand, there must have been something that held those several Judaisms together, something within which opposition to one another made sense. For my present purpose, I do not want to argue for or against a term such as *Judaisms*. What I describe below may be common or basic Jewish identity in the Jewish homeland, or it may be just one strand among many. It is, in any case, the strand that concerns me, and it does not seem to be marginal, peripheral, or idiosyncratic. It comes from deep within the constitutional documents of the Jewish people.

THE ANCIENT NEAR EAST

It is emphatically clear, from Léon Epsztein in 1986 to Moshe Weinfeld in 1995, that the ancient Near East's presuppositions about divine, royal, social, and popular justice are the background for certain ancient Jewish traditions. "Thanks to the discoveries of the last two centuries," says Epsztein, "it is possible to demonstrate from the texts the existence of a general aspiration towards justice extending over the various regions of the ancient Near East. . . . The quest for justice which appears in Israel has analogies to that which appeared among its neighbors. The Hebrew notion of justice can be compared with Maat [in Egypt] . . . the deity, daughter of the sun god, Re, symbol of good order, of the true state of nature and society as it has been fixed by the creative act. . . . We find distant antecedents for the biblical word-pair *mishpat/tsedeqa* [justice/righteousness], which is not an abstract formula but a notion profoundly bound up with the specific life of the people of Israel . . . in Babylon and among the western Semites" (45). Similarly, Weinfeld's study of "the practice of *righteousness and justice* in the socio-political realm" argues that it "refers primarily to acts on behalf of the poor and less fortunate classes of the people . . . carried out by means of social legislation, initiated by the kings and the ruling circles." He can therefore compare "the performance of justice and righteousness . . . by the rulers of Israel with the establishment of . . . righteousness in Mesopotamia and the proclamation of 'freedom' in Egypt. These social institutions were usually introduced by the kings when they ascended the throne or at other decisive times in the history of the nation" (8–9). In the following texts, from Mesopotamia through Ugarit into Egypt, there is, for example, an explicit mention of justice for widows and orphans, of special divine and therefore royal protection for those no longer protected by paternal linkage into kinship safety nets. A similar emphasis appears in all three sections of the Hebrew Bible: for example, in the Law (at Exodus 22:21–24), in the Prophets (at Zechariah 7:9–10), and in the Writings (at Job 24:3, 9).

In Mesopotamia, in the first centuries of the second millennium B.C.E., the Prologues to the ancient law codes mention how the gods and goddesses called the king to be protector of justice. Lipit-Ishtar, in the first half of the nineteenth century B.C.E., was "called . . . to the princeship of the land in order to establish justice in the land," and he "established justice in Sumer and Akkad . . . caused righteousness and truth to exist; brought well-being to the Sumerians and Akkadians." A century and a half later, Hammurabi of Babylon was "named . . . to cause justice to prevail in the land, to destroy the wicked and the evil, that the strong might not oppress the weak . . . that justice might be dealt the orphan (and) the widow . . . to give justice to the oppressed" (*ANET* 159, 161, 164, 178).

In Ugarit, immediately north of Israel-to-be in the fourteenth century B.C.E., there is a poem about one Yassib the Lad, who determines to usurp the throne of his father, Keret the Noble. In "The Legend of King Keret," he announces the good news to his father (*ANET* 149, slightly modified):

> Hearken, I pray you, Keret the Noble!
> > Listen and incline your ear. . . .
> You have let your hand fall into mischief.
> You judge not the cause of the widow,
> > Nor do you adjudicate the case of the wretched;
> > You drive not out them that prey on the poor;
> You feed not the fatherless before you,
> > The widow behind your back.

Having become a brother of the sickbed,
    A companion of the bed of suffering,
Descend from the kingship—I'll reign;
    From your authority—I'll sit enthroned.

The text breaks off soon after that proposal, with Keret praying that the god break Yassib's head, the goddess his pate. (You can see, by the way, where the Bible got its traditions of poetic parallelism.)

In Egypt there is one particularly interesting parabolic story from the Middle Kingdom of the twentieth to the eighteenth centuries B.C.E. Called "The Protests of the Eloquent Peasant," it describes how a peasant named Khun-Anup obtained justice directly from the chief steward of Egypt. He had been beaten and despoiled of his produce-laden donkeys by one Thut-nakht, who tricked the beast into eating a mouthful of standing grain. Thut-nakht was an important personage, vassal of the chief steward, Rensi, so he ignored the peasant's pleas. But Khun-Anup went directly to Rensi himself, upbraiding the chief steward for his slowness in response (*ANET* 408–409):

Because you are the father of the orphan, the husband of the widow, the brother of the divorcee, and the apron of him that is motherless. Let me make your name in this land according to every good law: a leader free from covetousness, a great man free from wrongdoing, one who destroys falsehood and brings justice into being, and who comes at the cry of him who gives voice. . . . Do not plunder of his property a poor man, a weakling as you know him. His property is the (very) breath of a suffering man, and he who takes it away is one who stops up his nose. You were appointed to conduct hearings, to judge between two men, and to punish the brigand, (but) behold, it is the upholder of the thief which you would be. One trusts in you, whereas you are become a transgressor. You were appointed to be a dam for the sufferer, guarding lest he drown, (but) behold, you are his flowing lake.

Rensi eventually gives in, arrests Thut-nakht, confiscates his property, and gives it all to Khun-Anup as restitution.

CREATION, EXODUS, ESCHATON

None of those Mesopotamian, Ugaritic, or Egyptian parallels diminishes in any way the far, far more serious way in which righteousness and justice, especially as protective of the widows and the orphans, the poor and the wretched, were taken in the Bible. There it was the righteousness of the one and only covenantal God that was at stake. There it was the justice of Israel's continued existence in God's land that was at stake. And it all began as early as this text:

For I have chosen him [Abraham], that he may charge his children and his household after him to keep the way of the Lord by doing righteousness and justice; so that the Lord may bring about for Abraham what he has promised him. (Genesis 18:19)

Righteousness and justice come from God to Abraham, and the divine promises to his progeny are contingent on establishing and maintaining that righteousness and justice on earth.

Twice, once at the start and again at the end of his book, Moshe Weinfeld summarizes God's establishment of righteousness and justice on three special occasions: at the Creation, at the Exodus, and at the Eschaton. "The appearance of God to judge with righteousness in the past, present and future thus signifies: (1) the redemption of the earth and all its creatures during the Creation; (2) the redemption of Israel from the enslavement of Egypt, the granting of the Law at Sinai (social redemption), and the salvation of Israel from its enemies in Canaan; (3) the redemption of Israel and the nations in the eschatological future" (21). Here are examples of those three paradigmatic moments, all from the Psalms:

The word of the Lord is upright, and all his work is done in faithfulness. He loves righteousness and justice; the earth is full of the steadfast love of the Lord. By the word of the Lord the heavens were made, and all their host by the breath of his mouth. He gathered the waters of the sea as in a bottle; he put the deeps in storehouses. (Psalm 33:4–7)

Mighty King, lover of justice, you have established equity; you have executed justice and righteousness in Jacob. . . . He spoke to them in the pillar of cloud; they kept his decrees, and the statutes that he gave them. . . . The Lord works vindication and justice for all who are oppressed. He made known his ways to Moses, his acts to the people of Israel. (Psalms 99:4, 7; 103:6–7)

Let the heavens be glad, and let the earth rejoice; let the sea roar, and all that fills it; let the field exult, and everything in it. Then shall all the trees of the forest sing for joy before the Lord; for he is coming, for he is coming to judge the earth. He will judge the world with righteousness, and the peoples with his truth. (Psalm 96:11–13)

Weinfeld reverts to that summary in conclusion: "God, the ruler of the universe, proclaims 'freedom' and 'liberation'—that is performs [righteousness and justice]," first, at the dawn of Creation, then at the exodus from Egypt, and, finally, "in the [messianic] future, when He shall reign over the entire earth" (205–206). It is hardly possible to overemphasize that central tradition. The Jewish people were in covenant with a God who had delivered them from oppressive slavery and imminent extermination under Pharaoh in Egypt. That God was, therefore, a divinity that freed the oppressed—unlike foreign gods and goddesses, who were divinities that had enslaved them. Had God intended but to relocate slavery and injustice? Had God effected a primordial deliverance only to allow a later one equally intolerable? Under another Pharaoh? Even under a Pharaoh from among their own people?

THE LAW

It is often claimed, especially in Christian commentaries, that the prophets spoke for the inner spirit and for justice but that the priests held for the external law and for worship. Some Jews, no doubt, failed to live up to covenantal righteousness, but it was not simply the prophets who did and the priests who did not. Indeed, as Norman Gottwald put it, "Law and Prophets were to become two separate and firmly delimited collections of authoritative writings, constituting the first and second divisions of the three-part Hebrew Bible. Despite the division between the two collections, it is nonetheless evident that these two sets of traditions interacted intimately within the institutional life of Israel over approximately eight centuries from ca. 1050 to 250 B.C.E." (1985:458). But what is especially important in what follows is that when the priests articulated traditional law, *they did not substitute holiness and purity for justice and righteousness, they combined them both together.* Indeed, that combination of justice and purity in the Holiness Code at Leviticus 25 contains one of the most radical proposals for social equality anywhere in the entire Bible (or anywhere else?).

We are dealing with three main legal collections, and they can be correlated with the periods of prophetic criticism in the succeeding unit. One is the Covenant Code in Exodus 20:22–23:19, which derived from the northern half of the Jewish homeland in the ninth century, the period of socioeconomic injustice attacked by Elijah and Elisha. Another is the Deuteronomic Code in Deuteronomy 12–16, which was brought southward after the destruction of that northern half at the end of the eighth century. It was then adapted for the surviving southern half of the Jewish homeland in the seventh century, around the time of Jeremiah. A final text is the Holiness Code in Leviticus 17–26, which derives from priestly circles in that southern half in the same seventh-century period. I focus on four major points from those law codes, noting especially how those points reach their climax under priestly control and emphasis in the Holiness Code. It is there that we can see most clearly how righteousness and justice combine with holiness and purity. One could always debate, then or now, what should be placed in the category of justice-purity, but such debates do not validate the separation of justice from purity or the reduction of justice-purity to purity alone. The four points to be studied are rest, indebtedness, enslavement, and dispossession.

Establishing Rest

I place this element first because it is somewhat striking in its unexpectedness. It concerns the sabbath day and the sabbath year. The idea of sacred days set aside for divine worship, communal celebration, and special festivals is utterly ordinary and completely common to both pagan and Jewish tradition. But the idea that every seventh day must be set aside as sacred rest is distinctively and uniquely Jewish. It derives from the rest of God as completion and climax of creation. It is not due to any human designation and is therefore beyond human control. But why should rest be so important: Rest from what? Rest for what?

The sabbath day is mentioned in the Covenant Code and again in Deuteronomy, but not within the Deuteronomic Code itself. Watch the results and thereby infer the reasons for that day of sabbath rest.

Six days you shall do your work, but on the seventh day you shall rest, so that your ox and your donkey may have relief, and your homeborn slave and the resident alien may be refreshed. (Exodus 23:12)

Observe the sabbath day and keep it holy, as the Lord your God commanded you. Six days you shall labor and do all your work. But the seventh day is a sabbath to the Lord your God; you shall not do any work—you, or your son or your daughter, or your male or female slave, or your ox or your donkey, or any of your livestock, or the resident alien in your towns, so that your male and female slave may rest as well as you. Remember that you were a slave in the land of Egypt, and the Lord your God brought you out from there with a mighty hand and an outstretched arm; therefore the Lord your God commanded you to keep the sabbath day. (Deuteronomy 5:12–15)

The sabbath day represents a temporary stay of inequality, a day of rest for everyone alike, for animals and humans, for slaves and owners, for children and adults. Why? Because that is how God sees the world. Sabbath rest sends all alike back to symbolic egalitarianism. It is a regular stay against the activity that engenders inequality on the other days of the week.

The sabbath year is to years as the sabbath day is to days. Every seventh year is also special. It represents another stay against inequality. Notice, once again, how its reason is formulated in that earliest Covenant Code.

For six years you shall sow your land and gather in its yield; but the seventh year you shall let it rest and lie fallow, so that the poor of your people may eat; and what they leave the wild animals may eat. You shall do the same with your vineyard, and with your olive orchard. (Exodus 23:10–11)

Leaving land periodically fallow to have minerals replenished by animal pasturing and organic manuring is not particularly unusual. But what exactly is imagined in *that* law? Léon Epsztein suggests that the land "could not have been left fallow. It was cultivated, but once the harvest was reaped, it was not taken in; the corn was left spread on the ground to be there for those who needed it. . . . [I]t is improbable that this measure was applied to all Israel at the same time; it is more probable that each farmer adopted the measure at regular intervals in rotation" (132). Norman Habel claims, to the contrary, that "the land sabbath, unlike the fallow law, applies to all arable land during the sabbath year; every seven years all agriculture is to cease in the land" (103). That seems a more correct reading of the law, especially since Josephus records the following decree of Julius Caesar in 47 B.C.E. concerning taxes from the Jewish homeland:

> Gaius Caesar, Imperator for the second time, has ruled that they shall pay a tax for the city of Jerusalem, Joppa excluded [included?], every year except in the seventh year, which they call the sabbatical year, because at that time they neither take fruit from the trees nor do they sow. (*Jewish Antiquities* 14.202)

I leave aside exactly *how* the sabbath year was done, emphasizing instead the reason given for *why* it should be done. Cereal, olives, and grapes belonged, as it were, not just to their owners but to the indigent poor and even the wild beasts. The land belonged to God and therefore fundamentally to all residents alike.

The formulation of sabbath year rest in the Holiness Code is even more striking. It repeats what was said in the Covenant Code but adds and emphasizes something else in first place. The land *itself* deserves a rest. This is not a question of human fallowing but of divine hallowing.

> When you enter the land that I am giving you, the land shall observe a sabbath for the Lord. Six years you shall sow your field, and six years you shall prune your vineyard, and gather in their yield; but in the seventh year there shall be a sabbath of complete rest for the land, a sabbath for the Lord: you shall not sow your field or prune your vineyard. You shall not reap the aftergrowth of your harvest or gather the grapes of your unpruned vine: it shall be a year of complete rest for the land. You may eat what the land yields during its sabbath—you, your male and female slaves, your hired and your bound laborers who live with you; for your livestock also, and for the wild animals in your land all its yield shall be for food. (Leviticus 25:2b–7)

Rest puts everything, even the land itself, back in a state of stasis, equity, equality. There is one interesting corollary to that emphasis. *The poor have rights not just to alms or handouts but to the land and its produce.* Here is another example from the book of Deuteronomy, outside the code section proper. It is also in the Holiness Code.

> When you reap your harvest in your field and forget a sheaf in the field, you shall not go back to get it; it shall be left for the alien, the orphan, and the widow, so that the Lord your God may bless you in all your undertakings. When you beat your olive trees, do not strip what is left; it shall be for the alien, the orphan, and the widow. When you gather the grapes of your vineyard, do not glean what is left; it shall be for the alien, the orphan, and the widow. (Deuteronomy 24:19–21)

> When you reap the harvest of your land, you shall not reap to the very edges of your field, or gather the gleanings of your harvest. You shall not strip your vineyard bare, or gather the fallen grapes of your vineyard; you shall leave them for the poor and the alien: I am the Lord your God. (Leviticus 19:9–10)

The untouched corner, the dropped produce, and the seventh-year yield belong to the poor by right. In the words of Léon Epsztein, the Holiness Code offers the poor "a chance of sharing in the very act of production" (113), not just in the act of consumption. They get a right and a share not just an alms and a handout.

The rest that indicates ideal equality and temporarily reverts everyone to that egalitarian moment has three great opponents: indebtedness, enslavement, and dispossession. Remission for all three of those problems was well known in the ancient Near East on the occasion, for example, of a new king or a new dynasty ascending the throne. What is of importance here is how those occasional remissions were ordained regularly in Israel and were deeply imbedded there in the covenant relationship between God, Law, People, and Land. There the implementation was not left to human decision or timing but was established by divine command based on the very nature of Israel's God.

Controlling Indebtedness

The stasis or rest of equality could be broken and inequality developed through debt. Whether through laziness or incompetence, drought or famine, disaster or death, one family occasionally needed to borrow from another. The law codes tried to control if not eliminate the inequality of growing indebtedness in several ways, including the forbidding of interest, the controlling of collateral, and the establishment of remission.

Let's look at the first of these, the forbidding of interest. Interest was forbidden on loans to Jewish neighbors and to the resident alien poor but not to foreign merchants or investors. Since the latter took interest on Jewish loans, interest could be taken from them in return. "When Israelites borrow from foreigners whose civil legal codes permit interest taking . . . the borrowers suffer 'damages' from the standpoint of Mosaic law," according to Barry Gordon. "It would be equitable and just, then, that equivalent compensation for those damages is taken when Israelites assume the role of lender" (412). The injunction is stated succinctly in the Covenant Code and in Deuteronomy (but outside the Deuteronomic Code):

If you lend money to my people, to the poor among you, you shall not deal with them as a creditor; you shall not exact interest from them. (Exodus 22:25)

You shall not charge interest on loans to another Israelite, interest on money, interest on provisions, interest on anything that is lent. (Deuteronomy 23:19)

But that injunction is greatly expanded in the Holiness Code. That code also makes explicitly clear that the interest forbidden includes both pre-interest, due when the loan is given out, and post-interest, due when the loan is paid back:

If any of your kin fall into difficulty and become dependent on you, you shall support them; they shall live with you as though resident aliens. Do not take interest in advance or otherwise make a profit from them, but fear your God; let them live with you. You shall not lend them your money at interest taken in advance, or provide them food at a profit. (Leviticus 25:35–37)

It was, of course, very easy, even in the absence of interest, to get more and more deeply in debt. Hence the next step was at least some control over creditors and what they could do with pledges given as collateral.

The second step, then, was the controlling of collateral to avoid oppressive or vengeful actions. The Covenant Code is, as usual, quite succinct. Its formulation is expanded in Deuteronomy (but again not in the Deuteronomic Code itself).

If you take your neighbor's cloak in pawn, you shall restore it before the sun goes down; for it may be your neighbor's only clothing to use as cover; in what else shall that person sleep? And if your neighbor cries out to me, I will listen, for I am compassionate. (Exodus 22:26–27)

No one shall take a mill or an upper millstone in pledge, for that would be taking a life in pledge. . . . When you make your neighbor a loan of any kind, you shall not go into the house to take the pledge. You shall wait outside, while the person to whom you are making the loan brings the pledge out to you. If the person is poor, you shall not sleep in the garment given you as the pledge. You shall give the pledge back by sunset, so that your neighbor may sleep in the cloak and bless you; and it will be to your credit before the Lord your God. (Deuteronomy 24:6, 10–11)

The third step, finally, was the remission of debts. The Deuteronomic Code took the idea of the seventh-year rest and, in a somewhat extraordinary move, applied it to debt. Remitting debt followed the same pattern as forbidding interest. It did not apply to the foreign merchant from whom, since he demanded interest of you, you could demand interest in return. It was not present in the Covenant Code but was invented by the Deuteronomic Code as part of the sabbath year liberation.

Every seventh year you shall grant a remission of debts. And this is the manner of the remission: every creditor shall remit the claim that is held against a neighbor, not exacting it of a neighbor who is a member of the community, because the Lord's remission has been proclaimed. . . . If there is among you anyone in need, a member of your community in any of your towns within the land that the Lord your God is giving you, do not be hardhearted or tight-fisted toward your needy neighbor. You should rather open your hand, willingly lending enough to meet the need, whatever it may be. Be careful that you do not entertain a mean thought, thinking, "The seventh year, the year of remission, is near," and therefore view your needy neighbor with hostility and give nothing; your neighbor might cry to the Lord against you, and you would incur guilt. Give liberally and be ungrudging when you do so, for on this account the Lord your God will bless you in all your work and in all that you undertake. Since there will never cease to be some in need on the earth, I therefore command you, "Open your hand to the poor and needy neighbor in your land." (Deuteronomy 15:1–2, 7–11)

I leave aside, once again, how that was all arranged—or even if it was ever applied in practice. Martin Goodman, however, has pointed to evidence that it was applied in the first century. He cites the institution of the *prosbul*, which was connected to Hillel in that century. This was "a public declaration before a court by a man seeking a loan that he would accept his legal duty to repay the money even after the advent of the Sabbatical Year." There also seems to be reference to the sabbatical year "within one of the loan agreements of the early second century A.D. found in the Judaean desert" (1987:57–58). In any case, once again, I emphasize the legal ideal regardless of the actual practice.

Liberating Enslavement

Individuals or families could sell themselves into slavery or be enslaved by their creditors when debt became too desperate. We are still talking about indebtedness, in other words—but now at an extreme. Freedom of slaves was ordained for the sabbath year in the Covenant Code. A difference was made between male and female enslavement because the female as concubine required special protection.

> When you buy a male Hebrew slave, he shall serve six years, but in the seventh he shall go out a free person, without debt. . . . When a man sells his daughter as a slave, she shall not go out as the male slaves do. If she does not please her master, who designated her for himself, then he shall let her be redeemed; he shall have no right to sell her to a foreign people, since he has dealt unfairly with her. If he designates her for his son, he shall deal with her as with a daughter. If he takes another wife to himself, he shall not diminish the food, clothing, or marital rights of the first wife. And if he does not do these three things for her, she shall go out without debt, without payment of money. (Exodus 21:2, 7–11)

No such distinction is made in the Deuteronomic Code, which imagines release for slaves of either gender in the sabbatical year. But this code also ordains forms of severance payment for the released slave and warns against stinginess:

> If a member of your community, whether a Hebrew man or a Hebrew woman, is sold to you and works for you six years, in the seventh year you shall set that person free. And when you send a male slave out from you a free person, you shall not send him out empty-handed. Provide liberally out of your flock, your threshing floor, and your wine press, thus giving to him some of the bounty with which the Lord your God has blessed you. . . . Do not consider it a hardship when you send them out from you free persons, because for six years they have given you services worth the wages of hired laborers; and the Lord your God will bless you in all that you do. (Deuteronomy 15:12–15, 18)

That phrase "male slave" is simply "him" in Hebrew and should be taken inclusively to include male or female.

Reversing Dispossession

We are again talking about indebtedness as it creates a desperate situation—this time not enslavement but dispossession, the loss of that land, which was the ultimate guarantee for loans. One's ancestral inheritance from God was never to be permanently alienated. One's land was not a commodity available for a fair exchange or a good price. Deuteronomy, for example, warns against any change of ancient boundary lines or markers:

You must not move your neighbor's boundary marker, set up by former generations, on the property that will be allotted to you in the land that the Lord your God is giving you to possess. (Deuteronomy 19:14)

"Cursed be anyone who moves a neighbor's boundary marker." All the people shall say, "Amen!" (Deuteronomy 27:17)

But what if dispossession *did* happen? It should not happen, but what if it did? The Holiness Code established something that is as special to it as the remission of debts is to the Deuteronomic Code. It ordains a sabbath of sabbath years, a super-sabbath, a special Jubilee Year in the fiftieth year after seven sets of seven years.

You shall count off seven weeks of years, seven times seven years, so that the period of seven weeks of years gives forty-nine years. Then you shall have the trumpet sounded loud; on the tenth day of the seventh month—on the day of atonement—you shall have the trumpet sounded throughout all your land. And you shall hallow the fiftieth year and you shall proclaim liberty [*deror*] throughout the land to all its inhabitants. It shall be a jubilee for you: you shall return, every one of you, to your property and every one of you to your family. That fiftieth year shall be a jubilee for you: you shall not sow, or reap the aftergrowth, or harvest the unpruned vines. For it is a jubilee; it shall be holy to you: you shall eat only what the field itself produces. In this year of jubilee you shall return, every one of you, to your property. . . . The land shall not be sold in perpetuity, for the land is mine; with me you are but aliens and tenants. (Leviticus 25:8–13, 23)

The idea of *proclaiming liberation* is not at all unique to Israel. It fits once again into the ancient Near Eastern background. As Moshe Weinfeld noted, the announcement of "'liberation' *(andurāru)* during the Neo-Assyrian period entailed the return of exiles to their homes, the restoration of towns and temples, the release of prisoners, etc. In Egypt, as well, 'release' was expressed in the liberation of convicts, rebels and various other guilty parties, and in particular in the return of exiles to their homes" (12). But there is, as always, a striking difference with Israel. In his recent study of the Jubilee Year, Jeffrey Fager comments that "kings often proclaimed a 'release' that included the manumission of slaves, the cancellation of debts and the return of lost land. How often or with what regularity such edicts were proclaimed is still unknown, and there is no evidence that they occurred with the automatic regularity called for by the biblical jubilee" (25). But what is especially important for the biblical ideology is that last sentence in Leviticus 25:13: "The land shall not be sold in perpetuity, for the land is mine; with me you are but aliens and tenants." That sets Israel apart from the liberation practices of either Mesopotamia or Egypt. Once again these stand or fall together: God, Law, People, and Land (and the Covenant binding them), and a ceaseless pull toward equality resulting at least in *a ceaseless pull* against *increasing inequality*. There are, however, two major questions about that text.

First, what was the purpose of the Jubilee Year? And notice, by the way, that it started on the Day of Atonement. Here, at least, the answer is quite clear. From Léon Epsztein: ". . . in order to restrict the creation of *latifundia*, [that is,] to prevent the concentration of rural properties." From Norman Habel: "The policy provided a mechanism for deterring in the short term and preventing in the long term land monopolies of latifundialization, the process of land accumulation in the hands of a few landowners to the detriment of peasant farmers" (105). From Jeffrey Fager: "It attempted to restrict the latifundism which was prevalent in the ancient Near East in order to keep the means of production evenly distributed among independent families" (88). Or, as Isaiah 5:8 said, it was intended to defeat "you who join house to house, who add field to field, until there is room for no one but you, and you are left to live alone in the midst of the land!" It wanted to stop the transformation of multiple peasant smallholdings into single large landownerships, to deter the eradication of the family farm and the creation and extension of latifundism or agribusiness. That, of course, put divine tradition on a collision course with rural commercialization.

Second, was the Jubilee Year ever implemented? This is a more delicate and difficult question than the preceding one. One could answer in the negative and still miss the entire point. Léon Epsztein, for example, says that "it is not certain that the Jubilee Year was ever applied in Israel" (134). Both Norman Habel and Jeffrey Fager agree, but with much more nuanced responses. Norman Habel concludes that "there is no clear evidence that the jubilee program was ever implemented on a regular basis according to the agenda outlined in Leviticus 25. This lack of historical evidence, however, does not negate the significance of the jubilee as an ideological symbol of a radical land reform program promoting the rights of the peasant" (107–108). Fager makes a similar point, emphasizing it repeatedly. He rejects the choice of *either* actual practice *or* utopian ideal and insists that the jubilee was described as *something that could be done in this world even if it never were*. "The jubilee can be seen not so much as a utopian concept of another world (even though its regulations may be economically impractical), but as a statement that proper distribution of land can be attained and maintained within the confines of this world. . . . The priests did not spiritualize the law so much that it became a mere abstraction; land was to be distributed equally among the people and maintained in that way. However, the jubilee was seen as a catalyst to that process, not the process itself; it was a signal to the people, leading them towards a proper relationship with the land. . . . The jubilee as we now have it occupies a 'middle ground' between practical regulation for everyday existence and idealistic vision of a world that does not exist" (80–81, 111, 115).

If the priests who created that legislation had wanted merely to set up a utopian ideal, they would hardly have made the Jubilee Year occur only every fifty years. For utopia, why not every seven years? And neither would they have made this striking qualification:

> If anyone sells a dwelling house in a walled city, it may be redeemed until a year has elapsed since its sale; the right of redemption shall be one year. If it is not redeemed before a full year has elapsed, a house that is in a walled city shall pass in perpetuity to the purchaser, throughout the generations; it shall not be released in the jubilee. But houses in villages that have no walls around them shall be classed as open country; they may be redeemed, and they shall be released in the jubilee. (Leviticus 25:29–31)

The point is clear. We are to protect peasant farms and rural villages, though we may do as we please with the commercialized real estate of walled cities. *The Jubilee Year may be utopian ideal, but it is so formulated as to be actually possible.* Josephus, in fact, records how to do it with three examples that have no biblical basis:

> [When the Jubilee Year arrives] the vender and the purchaser of the site meet together and reckon up the products of the site and the outgoings expended upon it. Then if the proceeds are found to exceed the outgoings, the vendor recovers the estate; but if the expenditures preponderate, he must pay a sufficient sum to cover the deficit or forfeit the property; if, lastly, the figures for revenue and expenditure are equal, the legislator restores the land to its former possessors. (*Jewish Antiquities* 3.283–284)

That too may all be dreaming. But it is not derived from the biblical text and it at least imagines how contracts might be handled at the Jubilee. It could be done. It *should* be done. So what happened when it was not done?

THE PROPHETS

I have deliberately put this section in second place to the preceding one. It is almost a cliché that the biblical Jewish prophets demanded social justice as covenantal responsibility. They did not suggest it as a nicer way to live together. They did not propose it to create a kinder, gentler country. Social justice was for them the human face of divine justice. "If," as Léon Epsztein insists, "they had been asked whether they considered themselves primarily to be religious reformers or social reformers, they would probably have protested violently against the distinction" (92). They would have been right. The one and only God, the God of righteousness and justice, made a covenant with a people of righteousness and justice to live in a land of righteousness and justice under a law of justice and righteousness. The Jewish prophets were not, in other words, inventing something new and transient. They were demanding something old and permanent in new circumstances.

A Tradition of Relentless Criticism

As soon as the Jewish people had a king of their own, they had a prophet to invoke the justice of the covenantal God as charter for that monarch's rule. The prophet Samuel warned the people before Saul was anointed as their first king:

> He will take the best of your fields and vineyards and olive orchards and give them to his courtiers. He will take one-tenth of your grain and of your vine-yards and give it to his officers and his courtiers. He will take your male and female slaves, and the best of your cattle and donkeys, and put them to his work. He will take one-tenth of your flocks, and you shall be his slaves. And in that day you will cry out because of your king, whom you have chosen for yourselves; but the Lord will not answer you in that day. (1 Samuel 8:14–18)

All of that was but the normalcy of royal privilege in the ancient Near East. But, as God informed Samuel, accepting that style of rule meant rejecting God's style of rule. You could not have a monarch of injustice and inequality under a God of justice and equality. "They have rejected me from being king over them," as God said to Samuel in 18:7. They have chosen injustice and oppression over justice and liberation. It was, of course, utterly possible to oppose that anti-monarchical ideology with a pro-monarchical one. In Psalm 2, for example, the ruler can be called by God to be both king and emperor, to be anointed as Son of God and King of Zion. But, despite such defenses, prophetic criticism would not go away.

Food and Life.

Recall the widows, orphans, poor, and afflicted who were supposed to be the special concern of divinity and monarchy from Mesopotamia through Ugarit into Egypt. In the northern part of the Jewish homeland during the ninth century B.C.E., the prophets Elijah and Elisha opposed foreign gods and royal injustices as twin sides of the same coin. But they did not simply *talk* about widows and orphans, they *did* something about them. And their deeds, not just their words, were remembered. Recall in what follows that in a patriarchal society "widows and orphans" are a fixed pair. Both are systematically vulnerable as lacking normal male protection—the widow lacking a husband, the "orphan" lacking a father.

In 1 Kings 17:8–16 a poor widow with a single orphan son is dying of hunger. Elijah miraculously and continuously replenishes the widow's meal and oil. Then, in 17:17–24, her son dies and Elijah miraculously raises him to life again. A similar but much more developed set of miracles is recorded of Elijah's successor, Elisha. In 2 Kings 4:1–7 a poor widow with only some oil in her house is about to lose her two children as slaves to creditors. Elisha miraculously fills every jar she can find with oil and she pays her debts. Then, in 4:8–37, he promises a son to a wealthy but barren woman and later raises him from the dead when he dies of sunstroke. But those two prophets not only helped widows and orphans, they also ruthlessly opposed the local pagan god Baal and toppled a Jewish dynasty that had accepted his worship. All of that went together, from their viewpoint. The Jewish god Yahweh was a divinity demanding traditional righteousness and justice. The pagan god Baal presumed a far less egalitarian society. Different divinities begat different monarchies, and those begat different rights and justices.

There is, however, one very significant story where foreign divinity and domestic injustice come clearly together. The Jewish king Ahab was married to a Phoenician princess named Jezebel, and as part of what he considered sensible foreign relations, he combined the worship of God, the covenantal deity of his people, with that of Baal, the fertility-bringing deity of the local pagans. In 1 Kings 21:2 King Ahab asks Naboth for his vineyard, "that I may have it for a vegetable garden, because it is near my house; I will give you a better vineyard for it; or, if it seems good to you, I will give you its value in money." That might seem fair enough to us. The king does not exercise royal right or eminent domain; he does not simply take it. Instead, he offers either exchange or money for it. Naboth replies, in 21:3, "The Lord forbid that I should give you my ancestral inheritance." Ahab dejectedly gives in, but Jezebel has Naboth accused of cursing God and the king. After he is stoned to death for that crime, his vineyard becomes a royal possession. The fundamental clash in that episode is between land as commodity to be sensibly bought and sold or land as ancestral inheritance never to be alienated from the family. The former is Jezebel's pagan presupposition; the latter is Naboth's Jewish tradition. Selling land is right and just among pagans, under Baal; holding land is right and just among Jews, under God. But what, then, about business as usual?

Poor and Needy.

Around 760 B.C.E. the prophet Amos was appalled by the widening discrepancy between rich and poor in the booming prosperity of Jeroboam II's thirty-year reign over the northern half of the Jewish homeland. In the following quotations, notice the word-pairs he uses (my italics): righteous and needy, poor and afflicted, needy and poor. It is for those people that he demands that other word-pair, justice and righteousness.

Thus says the Lord: For three transgressions of Israel, and for four, I will not revoke the punishment; because they sell the *righteous* for silver, and the *needy* for a pair of sandals—they who trample the head of the *poor* into the dust of the earth, and push the *afflicted* out of the way; father and son go in to the same girl, so that my holy name is profaned; they lay themselves down beside every altar on garments taken in pledge; and in the house of their God they drink wine bought with fines they imposed. (Amos 2:6–8)

Ah, you that turn *justice* to wormwood, and bring *righteousness* to the ground! . . . They hate the one who reproves in the gate, and they abhor the one who speaks the truth. Therefore because you trample on the *poor* and take from them levies of grain, you have built houses of hewn stone, but you shall not live in them; you have planted pleasant vineyards, but you shall not drink their wine. For I know how many are your transgressions, and how great are your sins—you who afflict the *righteous,* who take a bribe, and push aside the *needy* in the gate. (Amos 5:7, 10–12)

Hear this, you that trample on the *needy*, and bring to ruin the *poor* of the land, saying, "When will the new moon be over so that we may sell grain; and the sabbath, so that we may offer wheat for sale? We will make the ephah small and the shekel great, and practice deceit with false balances, buying the poor for silver and the needy for a pair of sandals, and selling the sweepings of the wheat." The Lord has sworn by the pride of Jacob: Surely I will never forget any of their deeds. (Amos 8:4–7)

Notice the very specific details of those indictments. They are not generalities about practicing justice or about protecting those lacking the normal defenses of family relations and village connections. They get down to commercial transactions in which "smart" landowners or merchants can defraud "dumb" peasants or workers with false weights and measures.

The Critique Continues.

Amos was not alone in those accusations. In the 250 years from around 750 to 500 B.C.E., powerful imperialistic states moved westward from Mesopotamia against the Jewish homeland. The resurgent Assyrian Empire destroyed the

northern half of the country under Sargon II in 721 B.C.E. After the Assyrians suc-
cumbed to the Babylonian Empire, the southern half of the Jewish homeland
was destroyed by Nebuchadnezzar in 587 B.C.E. and its leadership taken into exile
around Babylon. But then the Persian Empire captured Babylon in 539 B.C.E. and
sent the exiled Jewish aristocracy back to restore their country, capital, Temple,
and ancestral law. It is against that long imperial background that we hear the
relentless drumbeat of prophetic demand for social justice—that is, for divine
justice on earth. The tradition extends from Hosea, Isaiah, and Micah in the second half of the eighth century, through Jeremiah at the end of the seventh century, into Ezekiel and Zechariah at the start and end of the sixth century. Here is
a single instance from each of those prophetic voices. Notice that the attack is
always from God. The speaker claims not personal viewpoint but divine mandate, based, of course, on covenantal relations and ancient traditions.

A trader, in whose hands are false balances, he loves to oppress. Ephraim has
said, "Ah, I am rich, I have gained wealth for myself; in all of my gain no
offense has been found in me that would be sin." I am the Lord your God
from the land of Egypt; I will make you live in tents again, as in the days of
the appointed festival. (Hosea 12:7–9)

The Lord enters into judgment with the elders and princes of his people: It is
you who have devoured the vineyard; the spoil of the poor is in your
houses. What do you mean by crushing my people, by grinding the face of
the poor? says the Lord God of hosts. (Isaiah 3:14–15)

They covet fields, and seize them; houses, and take them away; they oppress
householder and house, people and their inheritance. . . . Should you not
know justice?—you who hate the good and love the evil, who tear the skin
off my people, and the flesh off their bones; who eat the flesh of my people,
flay their skin off them, break their bones in pieces, and chop them up like
meat in a kettle, like flesh in a caldron. (Micah 2:2; 3:1b–3)

Thus says the Lord: Act with justice and righteousness, and deliver from the
hand of the oppressor anyone who has been robbed. And do no wrong or violence to the alien, the orphan, and the widow, or shed innocent blood in this
place. . . . Woe to him who builds his house by unrighteousness, and his upper
rooms by injustice; who makes his neighbors work for nothing, and does not
give them their wages. . . . Did not your father eat and drink and do justice
and righteousness? Then it was well with him. He judged the cause of the
poor and needy; then it was well. Is not this to know me? says the Lord. But
your eyes and heart are only on your dishonest gain, for shedding innocent
blood, and for practicing oppression and violence. (Jeremiah 22:3, 13, 15b–17)

Thus says the Lord God: Enough, O princes of Israel! Put away violence and oppression, and do what is just and right. Cease your evictions of my people, says the Lord God. You shall have honest balances, an honest ephah, and an honest bath. The ephah and the bath shall be of the same measure, the bath containing one-tenth of a homer, and the ephah one-tenth of a homer; the homer shall be the standard measure. The shekel shall be twenty gerahs. Twenty shekels, twenty-five shekels, and fifteen shekels shall make a mina for you. (Ezekiel 45:9–12)

Thus says the Lord of hosts: Render true judgments, show kindness and mercy to one another; do not oppress the widow, the orphan, the alien, or the poor; and do not devise evil in your hearts against one another. (Zechariah 7:9–10)

That consistent tradition, from around 750 to 500 B.C.E., repeats the same themes over and over again. It is not the eccentric vision of an individual here or there but the constant vision of a tradition involving this God, this people, this land, this justice.

The Prophets as Bleeding Heart Liberals.

Morris Silver has written a fascinating counter-indictment of the biblical Jewish prophets. He claims that they were inventing a new religion of social justice. Furthermore, "just as love for social justice can be accompanied by hatred of human beings, so universalism can be transformed into corrosive self-hate. Both tendencies are evident in the writings of Israel's classical prophets" (129). Finally, this is his concluding summary: "By the beginning of the eighth century, Israel and Judah [the separated northern and southern parts of the Jewish homeland] had been projected into a glittering era of prosperity and power. . . . Since an appreciable number of Israelites became men of means, it is not surprising that the eighth and seventh centuries reverberated with the call for social justice. . . . However, as an economist and social scientist, I can testify that whatever its presumed moral virtues, the advice of the classical prophets was destructive from the standpoint of economic affluence and political strength" (246–248). The classical prophets, in other words, brought on by their policies the destruction they prophesied. They said, in effect, If you do not establish justice, you will be destroyed. But the people were destroyed because they did.

Two major points, in reply. First, it is easy and tempting to dismiss Silver's claim as an indirect attack on the American welfare system. In speaking of Amos, for example, he draws explicit attention to the fact that "the central image is one familiar to modern Americans, namely the blight of poverty amid affluence" (124). Next, "Modern liberalism . . . is the closest contemporary analog to the program of the prophets," and "not unexpectedly, the prophets opposed expansionist militarism and patriotism" (129). Finally, he admits to "some trepidation, for it is predictable that some of you will angrily slam this book closed and accuse me of such as 'importing the twentieth century into ancient Israel' or engaging 'not in historical scholarship, but in a conservative polemic against liberal social reformers'" (134). But, be all that as it may, and apart from presuppositions and intentions, what about arguments and conclusions?

Second, then, is that a good case against classical Jewish prophecy? One objection. The prophetic message was utterly traditional and deeply rooted in covenant faith and Jewish monotheism. The prophets were not radical liberals but, if anything, conservative traditionalists. Another objection. A 250-year-long insistence indicates that their message was not exactly accepted, followed, or widely practiced. A final objection. Nothing anyone could have done or not done in the Jewish homeland would have deterred imperial foreign policy coming out of the Mesopotamian plains or the Nile delta. But if the Jewish homeland was almost certainly destined for imperial domination in any case, it may have been more important to have a tradition for which people would live and die, a tradition that insisted that such imperial domination was not right and not just. That is how a people survives not just in the short run but over the long haul.

Why Set Justice Against Ritual?

There is one element in that 250-year prophetic tradition demanding justice in the name of covenantal monotheism that needs special attention. It has often been misinterpreted, especially since the Reformation. Protestant scholars sometimes insisted on the prophetic statements against cult and ritual as an equivalent to their own opposition to Roman Catholicism. I give you here examples from five of the prophets mentioned above. Once again, notice that it is God who is rejecting ritual in the absence of righteousness and dismissing worship in the absence of justice. The prophets speak for God.

Hear this word, you cows of Bashan who are on Mount Samaria, who oppress the poor, who crush the needy, who say to their husbands, "Bring something to drink!" . . . Come to Bethel—and transgress; to Gilgal—and multiply transgression; bring your sacrifices every morning, your tithes every three days; bring a thank-offering of leavened bread, and proclaim freewill offerings, publish them; for so you love to do, O people of Israel! says the Lord God. . . . I hate, I despise your festivals, and I take no delight in your solemn assemblies. Even though you offer me your burnt offerings and grain offerings, I will not accept them; and the offerings of well-being of your fatted animals I will not look upon. Take away from me the noise of your songs; I will not listen to the melody of your harps. But let justice roll down like waters, and righteousness like an everflowing stream. (Amos 4:1, 4–5; 5:21–24)

For I desire steadfast love and not sacrifice, the knowledge of God rather than burnt offerings. (Hosea 6:6)

Hear the word of the Lord, you rulers of Sodom! Listen to the teaching of our God, you people of Gomorrah! What to me is the multitude of your sacrifices? says the Lord; I have had enough of burnt offerings of rams and the fat of fed beasts; I do not delight in the blood of bulls, or of lambs, or of goats. When you come to appear before me, who asked this from your hand? Trample my courts no more; bringing offerings is futile; incense is an abomination to me. New moon and sabbath and calling of convocation—I cannot endure solemn assemblies with iniquity. Your new moons and your appointed festivals my soul hates; they have become a burden to me, I am weary of bearing them. When you stretch out your hands, I will hide my eyes from you; even though you make many prayers, I will not listen; your hands are full of blood. Wash yourselves; make yourselves clean; remove the evil of your doings from before my eyes; cease to do evil, learn to do good; seek justice, rescue the oppressed, defend the orphan, plead for the widow. (Isaiah 1:10–17)

"With what shall I come before the Lord, and bow myself before God on high? Shall I come before him with burnt offerings, with calves a year old? Will the Lord be pleased with thousands of rams, with ten thousands of rivers of oil? Shall I give my firstborn for my transgression, the fruit of my body for the sin of my soul?" He has told you, O mortal, what is good; and what does the Lord require of you but to do justice, and to love kindness, and to walk humbly with your God? (Micah 6:6–8)

For if you truly amend your ways and your doings, if you truly act justly one with another, if you do not oppress the alien, the orphan, and the widow, or shed innocent blood in this place, and if you do not go after other gods to your own hurt, then I will dwell with you in this place, in the land that I gave of old to your ancestors forever and ever. (Jeremiah 7:5–7)

That last example from Jeremiah is particularly striking and can serve as a fitting summary and climax. Here is the context.

In the year 609 B.C.E., with the Assyrian Empire in its death throes, Jeremiah went into the Temple of Jerusalem and announced that God would abandon that place if the people persisted in social injustice:

Will you steal, murder, commit adultery, swear falsely, make offerings to Baal, and go after other gods that you have not known, and then come and stand before me in this house, which is called by my name, and say, "We are safe!"—only to go on doing all these abominations? Has this house, which is called by my name, become a den of robbers in your sight? You know, I too am watching, says the Lord. (Jeremiah 7:9–11)

You think, says Jeremiah in the name of God, that you are safe, no matter what foreign god you worship or what social injustice you practice, as long as you make it regularly to the Temple in Jerusalem. You feel secure, he says, like robbers who have made it safely back to their den. (An aside. In terms of Jesus and the Temple much later in history, please note that a den of robbers is not where robbers rob others but where they run for safety when they have robbed others elsewhere.) The threat is clear: use my Temple to avoid social justice and I will destroy my Temple. That oracle, by the way, almost cost Jeremiah his life. Priests and prophets accused him, in 26:11: "This man deserves the sentence of death because he has prophesied against this city, as you have heard with your own ears." But the royal officials and "all the people" answered them, in 26:16: "This man does not deserve the sentence of death, for he has spoken to us in the name of the Lord our God."

But why is there that alternative of ritual *or* righteousness, of cult *or* justice? Commentators usually insist that this is prophetic hyperbole, that the prophets actually demand *both* worship *and* social justice, rather than one *or* the other. That is certainly true, but still the question presses. Why not put it that way: God demands both/and rather than either/or? But notice that while there is no problem in finding biblical prophetic statements in which God rejects worship in the absence of justice, there is not a single biblical statement in which God rejects justice in the absence of worship. There is more involved here than both/and. What is it?

Worship, ritual, cult, and Temple are not just the celebration of the covenantal God but the celebration of that God as liberator from oppression and domination, slavery and death in Egypt, into a land where opposites reign, a land of righteousness, justice, and freedom. The Jewish cult celebrates *that* God of *that* justice. And such a God is worthy of liturgy and worship, worthy of feast and celebration. But such celebration in the absence of social justice is sheerest hypocrisy. You cannot say: your ritual is right but you must add on your righteousness. In Jewish tradition, ritual ritualizes justice, worship worships the God of justice. Of course, as that God insists, justice is paramount, and without it ritual is hypocrisy.

And what of justice without ritual? Can that be? The bond between ritual and justice is tightly woven indeed. Those who diminish or abandon ritual must guard against weakening or losing justice at the same time. When much, much later Christianity left aside Jewish ritual, did it also leave aside Jewish justice and, thereby, the Jewish God?

THE WRITINGS

I begin with an example from the book of Job written at some time between the early sixth and late fifth centuries B.C.E. As you read this single verse, watch what *content* you are imagining in your mind. Job himself is speaking in 29:14:

> I put on righteousness, and it clothed me;
>   my justice was like a robe and a turban.

Those two lines are in poetic parallelism. Just as "put on . . . clothed" parallels "a robe and a turban," so also "righteousness" parallels "justice." "Righteousness" and "justice" are two different words for the same reality; and as seen earlier, they appear repeatedly in the Bible as a tandem set. What are you imagining as the content of that twin set? What does it mean?

At the start of the book God acknowledges, in 1:8, that Job has "no one like him on earth, a blameless and upright man who fears God, and turns away from evil." Later, in the present context, Job is describing how it was before calamity befell him and how he was revered by young and old, honored by nobles and princes. Why? Because, in 29:12–17,

> I delivered the poor who cried,
>   and the orphan who had no helper.
> The blessing of the wretched came upon me,
>   and I caused the widow's heart to sing for joy.
> I put on righteousness, and it clothed me;
>   my justice was like a robe and a turban.
> I was eyes to the blind,
>   and feet to the lame.
> I was a father to the needy,
>   and I championed the cause of the stranger.
> I broke the fangs of the unrighteous,
>   made them drop their prey from their teeth.

The fuller context gives us the content of *righteousness* and *justice* in this passage. You may judge for yourself whether Job's acts were what you had imagined. Notice, of course, that they are *acts,* not ideas, and that we might call them acts of social justice, that is, of divine justice for earth.

What is right and what is just are covenantal commands for Israel and are therefore divine imperatives for the entire creation. Morris Silver argued, as you will recall, that the prophetic demand for social justice ruined the economic prosperity, social strength, and military power of ancient Israel. But he also found "that the social-justice theme penetrated the literature of prayer and wisdom" (178). It is found, to put this all more broadly, not only in the Law and the Prophets but in the Writings as well. In other words, it is in all three major divisions of the Hebrew Bible.

In the book of Proverbs the poor are sometimes mentioned as a category to be played off against the rich in a proverbial rather than an ethical mode—for example, in 10:15; 13:7; 15:15; 18:23; 19:4; 19:22. But there are also texts like these:

Do not rob the poor because they are poor, or crush the afflicted at the gate; for the Lord pleads their cause and despoils of life those who despoil them. (Proverbs 22:22–23)

Do not remove an ancient landmark or encroach on the fields of orphans, for their redeemer is strong; he will plead their cause against you. (Proverbs 23:10)

In the Psalms you find, of course, that tandem mention of justice and righteousness. It is, first and above all, the attribute of God, in Psalms 33:5; 89:14; 96:13; 97:2; 99:4. But thence it is supposed to be an attribute of the earthly king as God's representative, in Psalm 72:1, 7. Finally, it must be an attribute of everyone, in Psalms 106:3; 112:5–6. Here is one example from each of those three cases:

[O Lord,] righteousness and justice are the foundation of your throne; steadfast love and faithfulness go before you. (Psalm 89:14)

Give the king your justice, O God, and your righteousness to a king's son. May he judge your people with righteousness, and your poor with justice. May the mountains yield prosperity for the people, and the hills, in righteousness. May he defend the cause of the poor of the people, give deliverance to the needy, and crush the oppressor. (Psalm 72:1–4)

Happy are those who observe justice, who do righteousness at all times. (Psalm 106:3)

You also find mention of the orphan and the oppressed in Psalm 10:18, of the poor and the needy in Psalms 12:5 and 72:12, of interest and bribery in Psalm 15:5, of the weak and the orphan in Psalm 82:3, and of the widow, stranger, and orphan in Psalm 94:6. There is one magnificent psalm that can serve as climactic summary of those preceding ones. God is seated amid the divine council of the gods. He accuses them of divine malpractice in not establishing justice on earth, demotes them from the level of immortal gods to that of mortal princes, and takes over control of the universe. I cite the entire Psalm 82:1–8:

God has taken his place in the divine council;
   in the midst of the gods he holds judgment:
"How long will you judge unjustly
   and show partiality to the wicked?
Give justice to the weak and the orphan;
   maintain the right of the lowly and the destitute.
Rescue the weak and the needy;
   deliver them from the hand of the wicked."
They have neither knowledge nor understanding,
   they walk around in darkness;
   all the foundations of the earth are shaken.
I say, "You are gods,
   children of the Most High, all of you;
   nevertheless, you shall die like mortals,
   and fall like any prince."
Rise up, O God, judge the earth;
   for all the nations belong to you!

That, finally, is most clear. It is not that Israel's God is one among many or even one *over* many gods. Israel's God is the one true God of all the earth and all the nations because this alone is a God of justice and righteousness for those systemically vulnerable, for the weak, the orphan, the lowly, the destitute, and the needy. This God stands against injustice and wickedness because that is the nature and character of this God. The gods and their nations have failed the wretched of the earth.

CHAPTER 13

GALILEAN ARCHEOLOGY

Archaeology, of course, has been fascinated by empire since the very beginning of the discipline's history, as research into the Assyrian, Aztec, Inca or Roman cases, among many others, serves to demonstrate. Yet for most of this history, it has been the élite, palace-based cultures, with their 'Great Traditions,' which have dominated archaeological attention: royal iconography, imperial architecture and prestige goods as specific objects of curiosity and connoisseurship. Today, instead of focusing upon the perquisites of the victor, archaeologists are engaging with the effects of imperialist expansion upon subject peoples, generating a new kind of 'archaeology of imperialism.' A battery of archaeological techniques is being turned upon issues such as shifting levels of exploitation, changes in economic and social behavior, acculturation, and resistance. Settlement studies, often made possible for the first time as a result of archaeological survey, have in many cases proved particularly crucial indicators of the life of a conquered population.

Susan E. Alcock, Graecia Capta, p. 5

Consider where we are at the moment in this discussion of my interdisciplinary method for establishing *context* as sharply as possible. I have outlined the basic or anthropological layer with an emphasis on class, gender, and resistance. The major conclusion is that peasant resistance tends to develop more and more intensely as agrarian empires become more and more commercialized. In other words, the variables of rural commercialization and peasant rebellion are correlative. Such was the status of the Roman Empire at the time of Augustus's peace and prosperity. It was commercializing rather than traditional. It was interested not just in holding territory and taking taxes but also in developing territory and increasing revenues. Upon that general anthropological basis, I superimposed the more specific tradition of Judaism, with its insistence on a God of justice and righteousness holding a people to justice and righteousness by a law of justice and righteousness in a land of justice and righteousness. Anthropology and history lock hard together at the point of rural commercialization, since Romans see land as entrepreneurial commodity and Jews (some? all?) see it as divine gift. I understand, even at this point in the discussion, why relations between imperial Romans and colonial Jews in and around the Jewish homeland might become both desperate and disastrous.

That conjunction of anthropological and historical data explains not only the three great revolts between 66 and 135 C.E. but, preceding them, the frequency of disturbances detailed so well in the work of Richard Horsley (1985). From the death of Herod the Great in 4 B.C.E. until the first revolt, there were constant signs of lower-class resistance to Roman imperial power in the Jewish homeland. *Protesters* gathered, again and again, to make unarmed pleas before the second-rank Roman prefect of Palestine or the distant but first-rank Roman governor of Syria. Sometimes they were effective in their protests; sometimes they were slaughtered. *Prophets* gathered large groups of followers and led them out into the desert so that they could cross the Jordan into that land, which God would then give back to them from the Romans as of old from the Canaanites. Since they were expecting divine deliverance and not human violence, these prophets and their followers were usually unarmed. Always they were slaughtered. *Bandits* increased in number as farmers were forced off their lands through debt or disaster and chose the option of banditry in the hills rather than beggary on the roads. *Messiahs* arose, invoking the ancient ideal of David and proclaiming war against Rome in the name of God.

My next and final step is the superimposition of archeology, and especially Lower Galilean archeology, on those two previous strata. Anthropology has indicated for us the general conditions within which peasant resistance or rebellion may arise, and it has shown, in the specific case of the commercializing Roman empire, that such conditions were present. But were those conditions actually and particularly present *in early Roman Galilee?* What if everything just cited from peasant anthropology and Jewish tradition were true, but there was neither the slightest evidence of commercialization in Galilee in the first third of the first century nor the slightest changes in Galilean culture in the hundred years from the arrival of Herod the Great to the First Roman-Jewish War? What if all the evidence showed Galilee as a rural backwater which neither the Roman Empire nor the Herodian dynasty had found worthy of exploitation? How does the early Roman culture look to Galilean archeology, *especially when that data is superimposed on the cross-cultural anthropology of agrarian empire and peasant society?*

It is a very good time to ask such questions. In his doctoral dissertation, Jonathan Reed summed up the present situation of Galilean archeology by noting, "During the past decade there has been an explosion of new excavations in and around Galilee. In the past few years the spade has been set to the ancient cities of Tiberias, Bethsaïda, Gaba, and Caesarea Philippi. Other excavations on their initial phase are being conducted at Hippos and Jotapata. Several major sites have also been re-excavated using modern field methods: Capernaum, Sepphoris, and Scythopolis. The Galilean villages of Gush Halav, Kefar Hananya, Khirbet Shema', Meiron, and Nabratein have also been examined for the first time. The archaeological record of Hellenistic and Roman Galilee has finally reached a critical mass that New Testament scholarship must address" (1994a:6–7). But there is one initial problem to be faced before I can use Galilean archeology—a problem that will continually complicate the process of interdisciplinary integration in this chapter.

Options in Archeology

Archaeology, we contend, is an interpretative practice, an active intervention engaging in a critical process of theoretical labour relating past and present. It is entirely misleading to pose the problem of understanding and explaining the past in terms of either a purely factual representation tied to the past and purged of subjective "bias", or a presentist quest for liberation from the dogmatic burden of the archeological record through unrestrained fictionalizing and mythologizing. Interpretation is an act that cannot be reduced to the merely subjective. Any archaeological account involves the creation of a past in a present and its understanding. Archaeology in this sense is a performative and transformative endeavour, a transformation of the past in terms of the present. This process is not free or creative in a fictional sense but involves the translation of the past in a delimited and specific manner. The facts of the case become facts only in relation to convictions, ideas and values. However, archaeology would amount to an exercise in narcissistic infatuation if it *only* amounted to a deliberate projection of present concerns onto the past. The archaeological record itself may challenge what we say as being inadequate in one manner or another. In other words, data represents a network of resistances to theoretical appropriation. We are involved in a discourse mediating past and present and this is a two-way affair.
  Michael Shanks and Christopher Tilley, *Re-Constructing Archaeology*, pp. 103–104

That is a rather long and involved epigraph. Here are a few aphoristic summaries of its thesis. Ian Hodder put it this way, in the book's Foreword: "All archaeological texts re-present the world of today in the past" (xvi). Shanks and Tilley themselves rephrased it in a later book in these words: "Archaeology, as cultural practice, is always a politics, a morality," and again, "Archeology is nothing if not critique" (1988:212, 213).

That understanding of archeology is identical to my own understanding of history at the start of this book. And that, of course, is no coincidence. Both are attempts to wrestle closely and honestly with postmodernism's correct assertion that the object known is changed by the subject knowing it. How, then, do we chart a course between objectivism and subjectivism, between historicism and relativism, between positivism and narcissism? My own answer, as you already know, is that the present must reconstruct the past in openly admitted interaction so that each will challenge and change the other. And we must conduct that interaction by argued evidence in public debate. It is that public debate rather than any prior confession (I am white, European, male, heterosexual, Christian, allegedly living, etc.) that counts. All of that, as you know by now, comes down for me to *method,* to making one's method as self-conscious and self-critical as possible and to displaying it in a manner that makes debate as pointed and precise as possible. Be that as it may, the view of archeology in that epigraph is the last of three current methodological options outlined by Marianne Sawicki in a very provocative recent article:

The first and oldest type is called classical, historical, or pre-processual archeology. At its worst it tended toward cultural looting—taking, but thereby sometimes saving, ancient artifacts from colonial or Eastern countries for imperial or Western museums. But even its best it was often "text-driven," so that its "outcomes tend to corroborate whatever version of the past has come down in the texts," although "it has sometimes corrected the historical texts that inspired it." The most serious problem, however, is that "this kind of archeology is not critical of its own assumptions," according to Sawicki (1994:319, 320).

The next type is processual archeology, the so-called new archeology of the 1960s and 1970s. Its focus was especially on prehistory, where, by definition, no texts were available to be confirmed or denied. "In the university, this archeology became one of the branches of anthropology rather than of classics or history." Although worked out especially for textless prehistory, it was used as well for texted history, allowing material remains to offer checks and balances to verbal remains. But this above all: "It also opens access to the material remains of the vast majority of people who did not leave us any texts" (1994:320). That is crucially important. "Because the texts represent the élite sectors of society, 'prehistory' lasts until the present for most women and many other non-élite groups. The reconstruction of the lives of eighteenth-century factory workers, for instance, employs many of the same excavation techniques that are used for reconstructing the lives of ancient hunter-gatherers" (1994:334). This new style of archeology emphasizes empirical, material causality operating within integrated systems or processes (hence the name *processual*). Sawicki's example is also a criticism: "On this interpretation, the 'because' of the existence and location of a great city such as Sepphoris would be given in terms of food supply and climate. All other social and creative factors would ultimately reduce to those physical conditions" (1994:322).

The third type, post-processual archeology, has been, since the early 1980s, a deliberately critical or corrective reaction to that preceding type. "Postprocessualists assert that historical agency and self-interested strategy are the key terms in archeological understanding. Moreover they insist that today's scientific strategies are comparable to and interactive with the very social strategies of the past that are under investigation. Archaeologists' own social statuses—determined, for example, by the gendered assignment of their labor or by their political organization—are in play whenever those archaeologists are at work. Thus 'science' is subjective, and only through its subjectivity is its objectivity achieved" (1994:322). Any reconstruction of the past is interactive with the present. Our own personal and individual, social and cultural positions in terms of race, color, creed, gender, class, and everything else as well, are at play in such reconstruction. "The post-processuals . . . argue [that] archaeology is an ideological enterprise done in the present to serve present interests. . . . The dimensions chosen for mapping the past are the very ones that are significant, and therefore hotly contested, in today's societies. . . . Reconstruction of the past is a component of the social construction of the present. . . . So-called subjective factors are not 'noise on the line' for archaeological data transmission; they are the line itself" (1994: 323, 330).

I consider that to be absolutely correct. But where does one go from there? Is it enough to preface all work with an autobiographical confession? Sawicki sees the problem all too clearly. She has three conclusions. One is that "the differences between processual and post-processual archaeology matter little in the field or in the lab, but become significant at the point when a synthetic account of a past society is attempted." (But that is exactly the point where I am now. How can Lower Galilean archeology build an overall image of that past place and time?) Another conclusion is that "post-processualism does not offer an internally coherent theory and does not seem able on its own to escape a debilitating relativism" (1994:323). That is, of course, the moral black hole threatening all of postmodernism. A final conclusion offers a theoretical solution. That three-way debate leaves archeology in a state of theoretical unrest, but Sawicki suggests that "it is moving toward *a chastened realism,*" which she describes very aptly as "planting both feet firmly in scientific processual archaeology while bending into the wind of post-processualism" (1994:323, 324). One minimal aspect of such chastened realism would be for archeologists to pay at least some attention to cross-cultural anthropology, even if not to postmodern epistemology. But what does all of that have to do with Lower Galilean archeology on the 20s of the first century as the third layer of my own interdisciplinary model for obtaining the sharpest possible context for the historical Jesus and the birth of Christianity?

First of all, I am working with a general model for context because, without one, I can interpret data almost at will. Second, all three levels of my model are interactive with one another and potentially corrective of each other. Third, within that interaction I still presume a certain hierarchy of stratification: from anthropology, through history, to archeology. Both history's textual remains and archeology's material remains are located for me within general anthropological or macrosociological matrixes. Fourth, I have one major problem in this chapter. As I read the published results of recent Galilean archeology, I find a strange phenomenon. Scholars do not simply describe what they have found but also give interpretive social commentary on that data. That commentary is often somewhat caustically critical of what someone like myself might say about the historical Jesus. But where does *their* wider social matrix come from? Where did *they* get it?

Let me give an example. Suppose we agree that there was extensive urbanization in Lower Galilee in the first quarter of the first century? How do you decide, in general, whether that was good or bad news for the local peasants? And, be it good or bad, was it so for most, many, or only some of them? How would you answer that question archeologically? And, if you do not know how to answer it by specific archeology, should you answer it by general anthropology? Should you, at least, know that such general answers exist and must be presumed pending specific objection?

Watch very carefully, therefore, what I do in this chapter. I choose three basic emphases of recent Galilean archeology. In each case I use an epigraph from the Lenski-Kautsky model—that is, from anthropology—that should, at least, sensitize the archeologist to possible general interpretations of the data discovered. Next, I look at their general interpretation of that data and especially at the social conclusions they announce after it or presume before it. Finally, my overarching point is that what the archeologists have discovered fits very well, often despite their own assertions, with the Lenski-Kautsky model of commercialization precipitating resistance.

A final comment. I am not a field archeologist. I lived for two years between 1965 and 1967 at the French Biblical and Archeological School just north of the Damascus Gate of Jerusalem's Old City. I visited as part of my studies all the major archeological sites not only in Jordan and Israel but from Lebanon and Syria to Iraq and Iran, from Greece and Turkey to Morocco, Tunisia, and Egypt. I am deeply grateful for the difficult work of Near Eastern archeologists and appreciate, as an outsider, their financial, logistical, and especially political problems. I respect their archeological conclusions, which I often have time to read only in popular summary and which I accept on the level of straightforward data. My present disagreements are with their social conclusions, which seem to contradict general anthropological ones and which would therefore need specific arguments and proofs to substantiate them.

Countryside and City

Another important characteristic of agrarian societies was the regular and widespread occurrence of urban communities . . . [which] never constituted more than 10 per cent of the total [population of an agrarian empire], and in some instances accounted for less than 5 per cent. . . . [But] despite this fact, the residents of urban centers usually dominated agrarian societies politically, economically, religiously, and culturally.

Gerhard E. Lenski, *Power and Privilege*, pp. 198, 200

My first example concerns the general relationship of city and countryside within the Lenski-Kautsky model for ancient agrarian as distinct from later industrial or postindustrial societies. That model warns us against presuming that the term *peasants* is simply an archaic and nostalgic term for farmers or that peasants were isolated rural cultivators in those societies.

It is possible, in reaction to the rural romanticism of Ernest Renan's *The Life of Jesus,* which situated him "in the midst of [the] green hills and clear fountains" of his "beloved Galilee" (118), to situate him instead in an equally romantic urban environment. In *Jesus and the Forgotten City,* Richard Batey describes how "Sepphoris rises like a shining Camelot" (80) and imagines Jesus over there for regular attendance at its theater. But in between those equally unreal extremes, what do we know of rural-urban relations in the time and place of Jesus and, more pointedly, what do we know about peasants and cities, then and always?

Think, first of all, about cities. James Strange has been leading one of the expeditions digging at Sepphoris in Lower Galilee for over a decade. In a methodologically programmatic essay, he uses a startlingly benign term for Roman urbanization in Galilee. He calls it an "urban overlay" (1992a:31), but he also mentions "the city as a symbol of power" (1992a:53 note 41). He is extremely clear on the fact that "material culture is a product of the conceptual and symbolic world from which it springs" (1992a:29) and that "the symbols of specifically Roman culture, sometimes on a co-opted Hellenistic base, include *baths,* hippodromes, theaters, amphitheaters or circuses, odeons, nymphaea, figured wall paintings, statues, triumphal monuments, temples (Augustea, Tiberia), etc." (1992a:33, my italics). Consider, however, that first item, baths, especially in its Roman cultural symbolism. Andrew Wallace-Hadrill, introducing a series of 1987 consultations between archaeologists and historians on city and country in the ancient world, notes the symbolic interaction of water, aqueduct, and bath: "The relationship [of town and country] is more visible if we picture the tentacles spread out by the Roman town into its hinterland in the form of aqueducts [rather than roads]: symbolically siphoning off . . . the resources of the land into the urban centre, to feed the public baths where the imported water acts as a focus of sociability, and as a symbol of the 'washed' and civilised way of life that rejects the stench of the countryman. Implicit in the aqueduct is a dynamic of power, flowing between country and town; and if we wish to represent the dynamic as exploitative, we may extend our picture to the sewers to which the water eventually flows . . . as an image of the wasteful consumption of the city" (x). Even if the peasants did not miss that water, the high material visibility and great cost of aqueducts underlined another flow from country to city, that of taxes and supplies. In an essay from that same 1987 consultation, Mireille Corbier adds, "Among the images which evoke the way cities siphoned off resources from their territory, we may briefly recall two centripetal movements: the channelling of water and the stockpiling of grain" (222). Symbols represent something other than themselves. So which, one might ask, was the better symbol of ancient rural-urban interaction, the apparently two-way road or the clearly one-way aqueduct?

Think, next, about peasants. It is important never to confuse a general term such as *rural* or *isolated* or *farmer* with a technical term such as *peasant* since, for cross-cultural anthropology, an isolated or absolutely rural peasant is a contradiction in terms. I explained quite clearly what the term *peasant* means in my book on *The Historical Jesus: The Life of a Mediterranean Jewish Peasant* (125–128) and again in *Jesus: A Revolutionary Biography* (25). *Peasant* is an interactive term for farmers who are exploited and oppressed—a definition presuming that somewhere there must be exploiters and oppressors. That definition is contained within the Lenski-Kautsky model as well. Note the epigraph to this section and recall Kautsky's insistence, mentioned earlier, that aristocrats "live off" peasants. Granted that they so live *off*, where, then, did they *live* off? In cities, of course. In agrarian empires, peasants and elites imply, in other words, peasants and cities. A peasant without a city is simply a happy farmer. To rephrase Kautsky: *cities* "live off" peasants. And the exceptions, as usual, prove the rule: "There are," as Lenski notes, "a few instances of agrarian societies in which urban communities were wholly or largely absent, as in parts of early medieval Europe, when the breakdown in the political system led to the near disappearance of urban life" (199 note 30). Theoretically, of course, *castle* aristocrats could "live off" peasants just as well as *city* aristocrats could, but those castles would simply end up fighting one another, so a city would be needed as the place where elites could congregate to compete with one another in conspicuous consumption rather than in continual warfare.

But what about peasants in Galilean archeology? James Strange argues, at the start of the essay just mentioned, against the proposition that "Galilee was especially suited to a rural or peasant style of life" (1992a:28) and insists, at the end, that "it is no longer possible to affirm the extreme, that the earliest Christian movement originated in a simple rural atmosphere" (1992a:47). He is absolutely correct that Jesus, the kingdom-of-God movement, and earliest Christianity all arose in the urban-rural interchange of Lower Galilee. But urban-rural interchange is already and always contained in the term *peasant* itself. There can be rural without urban but not urban without rural. Even the Romans could not eat marble. And there cannot be peasants without urban-rural interaction (to use a benign expression). Nothing that Galilean archeology has discovered about the urbanization of Lower Galilee in the early Roman period militates against its basically peasant society—unless, of course, one mistakenly presumes that *peasantry* means isolated farmers in a rural backwater.

That same misunderstanding of the term *peasant* reappears in a later essay, where Strange asks about archeology's ability "to tell us anything about the social realities of first century Galilee" (1994:88). His reply seems once again to presume that the term *peasant* precludes artisans and/or that peasant artisans are some type of better-off entrepreneur. "Archaeological surveys of the Galilee and other regions of ancient Palestine confirm that large farmhouses, presumably of wealthy land owners, dot the landscape. It is premature to make firm estimates of how much of the land was in the hands of wealthy land owners, but it is enough to be formative in the unfolding of social reality in the first century. From archaeological surveys in Galilee it is possible to posit another dimension of social reality. It seems that there are more farmers on small plots of land than those plots will support. This suggests that the small land owner had to work for somebody else at least part of the time, or else develop a specialty on the side which could be marketed. Thus the simple designation 'peasant' for this social stratum is misleading, since these people appear to have also been artisans and small entrepreneurs as well as agricultural laborers. This fact of life appears to have enforced a diversification in social roles that remains largely unrecognized in modern scholarship" (1994:89). But the Lenski-Kautsky model already includes the permanent squeeze that, at best, forces peasant farmers to be *also* peasant artisans or, at worst, forces peasant farmers to become *only* peasant artisans. And it never presumes that new cities turn unhappy peasants into happy entrepreneurs. In all of this I speak about systems and structures rather than about individuals and persons. My point is not that archeology must obey anthropology but that a cross-cultural anthropological model would warn Strange that what he is clearly describing above about large and small plots is the quite predictable result of commercialization through urbanization and that the equally predictable result is heightening tension between peasant and city.

I find, by the way, a similar confusion concerning the peasantry in other Galilean archeologists. Eric Meyers, in his most recent article on Galilean regionalism, says that "the isolation of the Lower Galilee in view of the Roman road system and trading patterns is simply a datum that cannot be sustained. It goes without saying that most of ancient Palestine outside the urban centers reflected the peasant or agricultural life style" (1985:117). But peasants are not simply outside the city. They are the necessary basis for its power. Meyers, at least, recognizes that "during the Roman period the settlements of Sepphoris and Tiberias exacerbated tensions between the peasantry and townspeople" (1985:118).

Similarly with Tom Longstaff. He notes, first, that "Galilee emerges as an area transformed by the presence of Roman cities and influenced by Roman institutions and ideals. Sepphoris . . . provides a particularly good example of how the process of urbanization affected a mixed population, both in the city itself and in its dependent villages. . . . It is no longer possible to think of Jesus as a simple peasant from Nazareth (dare one say 'a good old country boy'?) nor to describe the disciples as 'hillbillies from Galilee'" (14). All of that is as correct as its opposition of peasantry and urbanization is inadequate. But once again, Longstaff at least recognizes that, "while [his] essay argues that the influence of Roman urbanization was all-pervasive, it should not be understood to romanticize urban culture. While urban culture offers many advantages, there are disadvantages as well. Urbanization often brings with it a measure of oppression. The gap between the wealthy and the poor is frequently widened. Those who thrive in the city often do so at the expense of those in the dependent villages who do not" (14). Although words such as *often* and *frequently* mute somewhat the systemic or structural injustice of peasant-city relationships, that at least warns against moving from the rural romanticism of Renan to the urban romanticism of Batey.

Three final comments on peasants and cities. From Robert Redfield: "There were no peasants before the first cities. And those surviving primitive peoples who do not live in terms of the city are not peasants" (31). From George Foster: "The primary criterion for defining peasant society is structural—the relationship between the village and the city (or the state)" (8). From Moses Finley: "The peasant was an integral element in the ancient city" (1977:322). It is necessary, once and for all, to stop confusing *isolated* with *rural* with *peasant* and to start taking the term *peasant* as it is used in cross-cultural anthropology. Otherwise exegetes who use cross-cultural anthropology and archeologists who do not will simply talk past one another forever. *Peasants and cities go hand in hand. They are the necessarily twin sides of an oppressive or exploitative system.*

Sepphoris and Tiberias

All of the more advanced agrarian societies resembled a tree or plant with a system of feeder roots spreading over a vast area, tapping the surplus and moving it, by stages, to the ultimate consumers, the urban population. At the outer limits of this system were thousands, even hundreds of thousands, of small peasant villages, each typically containing a few hundred residents. . . . On the one hand there was a steady flow of goods from the peasant villages to the urban centers. In return, the villages received certain services of a political, cultural, religious, educational, and commercial nature. . . . Thus these relationships which developed between the villages and the urban centers were essentially symbiotic in character, but with definite overtones of parasitism. . . . This relationship was parasitic to the extent that the military superiority of the urban-based elite forced villagers to yield more of their crops or to accept less in return for them than they would have if the two parties had bargained from a position of equal political strength. However, since villager participation was not simply a function of coercion, the relationship cannot be regarded as purely parasitic.

> Gerhard E. Lenski, *Power and Privilege,* pp. 205–206

My second example asks, against the general background of the Lenski-Kautsky model, what one might expect when two cities are built or rebuilt within about twenty miles and twenty years of one another in an agrarian empire. That model warns us against presuming that new cities are good news for the local peasants.

The 470 square miles of Lower Galilee, rich with grain and cereal on valley floor and with vine and olive on hillside slope, consist of four alternating hill-valley lines running in a generally west-east direction. The village of Nazareth, located in a basin at slightly over 1,100 feet on a range that rises in places to 1,600 feet, overlooks the southern approaches to Lower Galilee. The city of Sepphoris, about an hour's walk to Nazareth's northwest, sits on its own 325-foot hillock west of the Tir'an valley and south of the much larger Beth Netofah valley. At the eastern end of that same Tir'an valley is the city of Tiberias. But Sepphoris and Tiberias were two cities, one rebuilt and the other built, within twenty miles and twenty years of one another. What did their *new or renewed presence* mean for the local peasants? Hear in the background these comments from the 1987 consultations mentioned in the preceding section. From Corbier: "The city, wherever it existed, was the basic unit for tax-collection" (231). From Wallace-Hadrill: "Urbanisation is the unmistakable result of Roman control" (249). But especially this introductory summary from the latter: "The empire is seen as a chequerboard of cities, each with its own set of dependent communities; just as the power and wealth of the individual landlord depended on his ability to extract rents and profits from his tenants and workforce, so the power and wealth of each city depended on the extraction of taxes, rents, and dues from its own network of villages and settlements, while Rome herself depended on the extraction of taxes from the provinces and their component cities" (xiv).

Think, for a moment, about the population density of those two new cities, especially in light of studies by Jonathan Reed, and compute a hectare as about two and a half acres (or 10,000 square meters). "In Galilee," says Reed, "the ruins at Sepphoris cover an area of 60 hectares, and the ruins of Tiberias cover almost 80 hectares. The extent of these two Galilean cities' ruins does not compare to the four major cities in this area of the Levant—Tyre, Ptolemais, Caesarea Maritima, and Scythopolis, which are all well above 100 hectares. But the extent of Sepphoris and Tiberias' ruins extend well beyond any other site in Galilee, as well as the Herodian sites on Galilee's periphery: The ruins atop Bethsaïda's tell, the site fashioned into Julias by Herod Philip, cover only 10 hectares; Gaba, built by Herod the Great for his retired cavalry, measures 14 hectares. The size of the larger villages in Galilee is comparably, at most 17 hectares for first century Capernaum, and of the smaller villages, at most 5 hectares for Gath Hepher. Other small sites in the Galilee, such as hamlets or nucleated farms, cover only a single hectare or less" (Reed 1994a:68–69).

But how do you get from hectares to people? You must first know, as accurately as possible, the site circumference. How big was it at the time in question: How many hectares? You must then decide what density of population could be expected at such a site: How many people per hectare? Mistakes or disagreements on either or both points can result in widely divergent conclusions on a large, unwalled, early-first-century Lower Galilean village such as Capernaum, as evidenced by these conclusions from first Reed (1992:15) and then Meyers and Strange (59):

Capernaum: 17 hectares = 100–150 persons per hectare = 1,700–2,550 persons
Capernaum: 30 hectares = 400–500 persons per hectare = 12,000–15,000 persons

In terms of hectares and people, the standard and best-preserved models for Roman cities are Ostia, Rome's densely populated port at the Tiber's mouth, with its three- to five-storied apartments, and Pompeii, on the Bay of Naples, a more normally populated Italian city with one- and two-storied buildings. Here, from Reed, are the most probable populations for those paradigmatic cities (1992:12–14):

Ostia: 69 hectares = 435 persons per hectare = 30,000 persons
Pompeii: 64 hectares = 125–156 persons per hectare = 8,000–10,000 persons

Even with around the same dimensions, those two cities had widely divergent population densities—divergent, in fact, by a factor of around three to one. Like Ostia and Pompeii, as Reed notes, "Sepphoris and Tiberias were walled cities, which drives up the population density. Historical and ethnographic comparisons show that as a rule walled settlements are more densely populated than open settlements. In the former sites, growth is accommodated by either increasing the number of rooms at the expense of their size, and by adding buildings with more than one story. Indeed, at the sites of Sepphoris and Tiberias, most building foundations were massive and supported more than one story, while unwalled sites in the Galilee tend to have crudely made foundations and walls in domestic quarters that could not have supported a second story" (1994a:69–70). Hence his proposed figures:

Tiberias:80 hectares = 300 persons per hectare = 24,000 persons
Sepphoris:60 hectares = 300 persons per hectare = 18,000 persons

Reed later corrected those figures for Sepphoris: "A more recent estimate by J[ames] Strange of the USF [University of South Florida] Excavations at Seppho-ris puts the area enclosed by the walls at just under 50 hectares—but he notes that the ruins beyond the wall to the southeast *may extend up to* another 50 hectares. . . . If we assume a population density of 300 persons per hectare for the walled city of Sepphoris and only 175 for the inhabited area outside the walls, then Sepphoris would [like Tiberias] have also had a population of around 24,000" (1994b:213). In summary, then:

Sepphoris: 50 hectares (inside walls)   = 300 persons per hectare = 15,000 persons
            50 hectares (outside walls) = 175 persons per hectare = 8,750 persons

But even working with his earlier Sepphoris population, Reed had noted that "a population of 18,000 would require the produce of the entire Beth Netofah and Tir'an valleys [to the north and east, respectively], as well as the land along the Nahal Sippori [to the west]" (1994a:71). If that was the "impact on agriculture" of Sepphoris alone, what would have been the impact when two such cities, Sep-phoris and Tiberias, were built within about twenty years and twenty miles of one another? "In terms of food alone," as Reed concludes, "the agricultural prac-tices of Galilee were completely realigned and stretched with the foundation of these two cities. The picture of numerous self-sufficient farms or hamlets in Galilee radically changed. The entire agricultural focus turned to feeding Seppho-ris and Tiberias" (1994a:70). But what would the peasants have thought of those two cities and of what they were doing to their livelihoods and their lives? Would more and closer cities have been good or bad news for the local peasants?

Jonathan Reed asks that question himself but cannot answer it from material remains alone: "How would the indigenous Galilean population react to Sepphoris and Tiberias? The attitudes and sentiments are not discernible in the archaeological record" (1994a:94). But even apart from cross-cultural anthropology, comparative archaeology might warn us against accepting, against that deficit, the normative viewpoint of urban elites. Here is an archeological example of how not to accept such viewpoints uncritically.

In studying "'Romanisation'—the effects that Roman rule had on the economics and societies of the ancient Mediterranean," John Patterson focused on two mountainous regions, Samnium in the central Italian Apennines and Lycia in southeastern Turkey, to test the hypothesis that there is a general structural relationship between "three important facets of town-country relations—public building in the towns, settlement change in the countryside, and the mobility shown by those members of elites who acquired their wealth in the countryside, but spent it principally in the towns" (147, 148). I focus here on the second element, on rural settlement change as small peasant freeholders yielded before "the increasing agglomeration of rural estates" owned by urban elites (155). "The problem then arises of what this change actually meant in practice for the common people who owned or occupied these estates. Various possibilities could exist: that the peasants remained on the land as tenants of the larger proprietors, living in poor and squalid circumstances; or that they left the land to become bandits . . . or departed the land altogether to go to the city" (155). I presume, speaking systemically rather than individually, that none of those three options is a particularly happy one for the peasants involved. Could an archeologist ask, regarding Sepphoris and Tiberias, a question similar to that asked by Patterson regarding Samnium and Lycia? Is any relationship discernible between city growth and rural consolidation? And if smaller rural plots are being unified into larger holdings, can one legitimately infer something about what those cities were doing to the "livelihoods and lives" of the peasants (and thereby to their "attitudes and sentiments" about them)?

We can note, in any case, that Sepphoris is never mentioned in the gospels and Tiberias is mentioned only in John, once directly in 6:23 and twice indirectly in 6:1 and 21:1. Why is that? Andrew Overman asks this obvious question (and answers it as well): "Why do these cities [Tiberias, Magdala, and Sepphoris] not figure more prominently in the gospel tradition? . . . We would posit that the absence of these significant and unavoidable urban centers relates to the issue of power which these centers represent and possess" (1988:167). He repeats that conjunction of *city* and *power* again in a more recent article: "I would suggest that the designation *city* has mostly to do with power, whether economic, political or symbolic. . . . In no way do I suggest that everyone was comfortable with the freight of this symbol. I do say though that most people in the Galilee were familiar with the symbol and its implications, as well as its concrete economic and cultural ramifications. . . . Any hypothetical program for the Jesus movement, or an analysis of parables or aphorisms in the Gospels, should take account of this information from the Galilean material world" (1993:47–48). All of that is absolutely correct, but I would ask whether the phrase "not comfortable with" might not be too benign a formulation for the reaction of those who may have opposed Roman urbanization because it dislocated the traditional peasant way of life and pushed individuals from poverty into destitution, from small landowner into tenant farmer, from tenant farmer into day-laborer, and from day-laborer into beggar or bandit.

Peasants and Artisans

Even at the village level [in agrarian empires] a measure of specialization was not uncommon, since in the agricultural off-season peasants were frequently obliged to turn to handicrafts to make ends meet, and in time certain villages developed a reputation for superior skill in the production of some particular commodity.

Gerhard E. Lenski, *Power and Privilege*, p. 204

This is my third example, and in some ways it is the most important one. The reason for its importance (if I may look ahead) is that Jesus was probably a peasant artisan rather than a peasant farmer. But maybe peasant artisans are better off than peasant farmers? Maybe in villages specializing in this or that craft, urbanization could vastly increase the customer base and therefore be good rather than bad for the peasant artisans' livelihood?

There is one very specific Galilean case that has been used to suggest that the relationship of cities to peasants was relatively beneficial, since peasants could use the city as a major trading partner. My point is, once again, that a prior awareness of cross-cultural anthropological data—for example, from the Lenski-Kautsky model—would temper not the possibility of village-to-city trade but any too-hasty generalizations about city-to-village benignity in agrarian societies and empires.

MATERIAL DESCRIPTION AND SOCIAL CONCLUSION

It is necessary, first of all, to see clearly the material data in its own integrity. Then, and only then, can social conclusions be discussed concerning the implications of that data. The material data in question concerns the ceramics industry of a very specific Galilean village, Kefar Hananya. (I have taken the liberty in what follows to spell that name consistently as *Hananya*.

Clay and Ceramics.

Pottery fragments are practically indestructible, and the clay in those shards can be traced by neutron activation analysis (which I imagine as something like

DNA for pottery) back to the ground or clay-location whence it came. It carries on it, in other words, the traces of ancient local trade routes. David Adan-Bayewitz's 1985 doctoral dissertation at Jerusalem's Hebrew University used that scientifically precise process to trace the source or provenience of common household pottery in Galilee, west of the lake, and Gaulanitis (the modern Golan Heights), east of the lake, from early Roman to early Byzantine times. He found, as summarized in an article jointly authored with Isadore Perlman, that "the bulk of the common household pottery used in Roman Sepphoris [from about 50 B.C.E. to 430 C.E.] belongs to two distinct provenience groups. The first group [Roman Galilee I], including the majority of the common kitchen ware of the city, was made at Kefar Hananya. The second group [Roman Galilee II] includes the common Galilean storage-jars of the period, specialty bowls and jugs . . . [and was] manufactured at the pottery-making centre of Shikhin, adjacent to Sepphoris. Both of these pottery provenience groups, accounting for the majority of the common pottery used in Roman Galilee, were produced in town or village manufacturing centres, and not by the important cities of the Galilee" (170).

This is an extraordinarily important study, both in its general methods and in its specific conclusions with regard to Galilee and especially to Sepphoris. Most of the Galilean pottery came, for half a millennium, from two villages: Kefar Hananya, modern Kafr Inan, due east of Acco-Ptolemais on the precise border between Upper and Lower Galilee (but closer to the Golan Heights than the Mediterranean coast), and (Kefar) Shikhin, identified by James Strange in 1988 with some ruins about a mile northwest of Sepphoris (1992b:351).

There are two conclusions that Adan-Bayewitz draws from his superbly collected and clearly presented ceramic data. The first one is minor and involves an internal contradiction. The second one is major and involves an external contradiction.

Manufacture and Distribution.

The minor conclusion concerns the relationship between manufacture and distribution. What role did Sepphoris and Tiberias play in the distribution process? If, for example, they were important for distribution, was that good or bad for the village-based manufacturers? "There is good reason," says Adan-Bayewitz, "to suspect that the marketing of Kefar Hananya ware by itinerant potters was probably not an important means of distribution. The predominance of Kefar Hananya ware in cities and villages 25 km. from the manufacturing center cannot easily be explained except in terms of central-place marketing. . . . Likely central market places for Kefar Hananya pottery include the Galilean cities of Sepphoris and Tiberias" (1992:233). That conclusion seems to me in flat contradiction with his own clearly described data.

Were Sepphoris and Tiberias central markets for the sale of Kefar Hananya ware? Was the village production brought to those cities because they were distribution centers for its marketing? If they were such centers, village ceramicists and other village artisans might well have considered those cities to be good news for business, meaning that urbanization would have struck them as a predominantly positive phenomenon. In Adan-Bayewitz's view, the sale and distribution of Kefar Hananya ware was concentrated not in and from that manufacturing village itself but from those two new Galilean cities, each about fifteen miles away. But here is a striking objection to that claim based on his own data. If that village pottery was sold from those central city markets, one would expect the diminishing presence of its shards to have radiated outward from them rather than from the main manufacturing village itself. Yet the archeological evidence and Adan-Bayewitz's own insistence indicate that "although Kefar Hananya ware is plentiful throughout the Galilee, a decrease in the relative quantities of Kefar Hananya ware is evident with increasing distance from *the manufacturing centre*" (1990:158, my italics), that "the relative quantity of Kefar Hananya ware recovered at Galilean sites is inversely related to the distance of the site from *the manufacturing center*" (1992:219, my italics; and see graph of percentage found versus distance traveled in 1992:212). In other words, "the pottery was marketed unidirectionally from Kefar Hananya, *the place of its manufacture,* to the site where it was recovered, its place of use" (1992:247, my italics). As I read and understand that data, Kefar Hananya pottery was sold and distributed, be it by pickup or delivery, from the village itself and not from central markets in Sepphoris and Tiberias. My conclusion is that, even if the presence of those cities increased the customer base for ceramics, it did not seem to change the distribution process. That claim must be left to one side as a distraction, one way or the other.

Pottery and Exploitation.

The major conclusion drawn by Adan-Bayewitz is, for my present purpose, much more important. At the end of both the co-authored article and his book, Adan-Bayewitz makes a very specific social comment. It is done almost in passing, but its terminal location gives it a certain climactic importance. The article concludes like this: "The quantitative distribution of Kefar Hananya ware, on the one hand, and the direct marketing to the consumer of pottery at Kefar Hananya and Shikhin . . . , on the other, do not seem consistent with the picture, common among some scholars, of the exploitation of the Galilean peasant by the urban wealthy. Finally, there seems to be a misconception among certain scholars that rural Galilee was exclusively agricultural in the early Roman period. The present evidence contributes toward a more accurate perspective of the Galilean economy" (1990:171–172). The book makes the same point with the same words:

"It may also be noted that the distribution pattern of Kefar Hananya ware does not seem consistent with the picture, common among scholars, of the exploitation in the early Roman period of the Galilean peasant by the urban wealthy" (1992:219).

Maybe, then, the arrival of two cities, rebuilt Sepphoris and newly built Tiberias, was not at all bad news for the Galilean peasants. Was it simply an opportunity for increased trade, for larger markets? Should we imagine not unhappy peasants but happy potters, not oppressed farmers but enhanced traders? Urbanization, in other words, could be good for such artisan villagers. To test that possibility, I look closely at Adan-Bayewitz's material descriptions and social conclusions, not only in themselves but especially from the viewpoint of cross-cultural *ceramic* anthropology.

CERAMIC THEORY AND CULTURAL PROCESS

There is a major disagreement between those just-cited social conclusions and the conclusions reached in Dean Arnold's 1985 cross-cultural anthropological work on *Ceramic Theory and Cultural Process*. This disagreement is all the more striking in view of Adan-Bayewitz's repeated references to Arnold in his own book (1992:235–238). It was, in fact, those references that prompted me to read Arnold for myself. Since this disagreement touches on peasant exploitation under urban domination, it is the one that concerns me most in the present context.

I presume that Kefar Hananya is not simply an exploited artisan village, capitalized, controlled, and overtaxed from outside. It seems much more likely that its mid-Galilean position enabled it to control its own destiny and distribute its products mostly from producer to consumer with minimal interference. But does that change the general picture of peasant exploitation in Galilee? What, in other words, is the relationship between ceramic production and agricultural land? Does the peasant potter deliberately and willingly abandon the life of peasant farmer for the presumably more lucrative possibilities of entrepreneurial activity? That is not exactly what the cross-cultural anthropology of pottery seems to indicate.

Recall, from above, the position of artisans as "dispossessed peasantry" according to the Lenski-Kautsky model. It is against that background that I read Arnold's thesis "that there are certain universal processes involving ceramics that are tied to ecological, cultural or chemical factors. These processes occur in societies around the world and can provide a solid empirical (as opposed to speculative) base for interpreting ancient ceramics. On a more modest scale, the book presents cross-cultural regularities which relate ceramics to environmental and non-ceramic cultural phenomena ... [and answers] the question why does pottery making develop in an area and why does it evolve into a full-time craft" (ix–x). His book presents, in other words, a cross-cultural anthropology of pottery making: "The book will attempt to provide cross-cultural generalizations about the relationship which can be applied to many different societies in the present and the past. . . . By deriving generalizations from modern cultures, it is possible to understand and explain how ceramics articulate with the rest of culture and environment. By applying these generalizations to the past, it is possible to develop a more precise interpretation of how archaeological ceramics relate to an ancient environment and culture" (16). But if you map the material descriptions from Adan-Bayewitz against the ceramic anthropology of Arnold, you arrive at very different *social* conclusions.

The systems of ceramic production move, according to Arnold, from household production, through household industry and workshop industry, into large-scale industry. In reading the following descriptions, notice how population pressure and the concomitant loss of subsistence farming force peasant farmers to become peasant artisans. *They are not drawn to that change by entrepreneurial opportunity but are forced to it by agricultural necessity.* That is the crucial point for me.

Types of Ceramic Production.

The first type of ceramic production is *household production*. "All adult females have learned the craft and have the same potential to make pots" (226). Each home makes its own pottery for itself, and since females are tied to the home by children, they are the potters.

The second type is *household industry*. "Population pressure forces men into the craft and the social position of the potters thus decreases because of their limited access to or ownership of agricultural land . . . [and it] also forces farmers to go further and further away to obtain suitable agricultural land. . . . At a distance of 7–8 kms . . . travel to their fields becomes uneconomic and people may prefer to exploit resources like ceramic raw materials closer to their homes. . . . Pottery making in the household industry mode of production is thus an adaptation of a population to specific kinds of non-agricultural resources; it is an adaptation to land which is limited or poor agriculturally, but which has ceramic resources" (226–227).

The third type is *workshop industry*. "Population pressure has largely, if not completely, eliminated agriculture as a subsistence base for the potters. Subsistence activities do not conflict with pottery making and thus males are potters since they have no alternative means of subsistence. Once direct food production ceases, the potter's family is dependent on the craft for a living, and the risks inherent in making pottery must be reduced in order to have a reliable income. . . . In order for the potter to realize increased control over the process, capital investment in innovations is necessary (such as constructing a shed for forming and drying pottery, building a kiln, and buying or making molds or a wheel). Because potters in the household industry [the second mode of production] are poor and economically marginal, most potters cannot afford the capital investment that these innovations require and are therefore forced to hire themselves out to those who have them. . . . This change removes pottery production from the household and thus totally eliminates women from the pottery making process. . . . Because of the low status of pottery making and the economic marginality of potters in a household industry [the second mode of production], potters do not often choose to develop a more intensive craft, but rather prefer to enhance their status. They may ultimately abandon pottery making for a more prestigious and lucrative occupation as a middleman or the owner of a pottery workshop. Thus, the development of a workshop mode of production with capital investment (needed for obtaining innovations and paying workers on a regular basis) is a pattern initiated by higher status individuals who are either outside of pottery making completely or socially and economically marginal to the craft" (227–229).

The fourth type is *large-scale industry*. It is "characterized by substantial capital investment in production for a maximum output and minimal cost per unit. The regulating effects of weather and climate are totally eliminated[,] . . . innovations have . . . maximized efficiency[,] . . . production is full-time for the entire year[,] . . . women are totally eliminated[,] . . . potters are men[,] . . . [and] full-time production requires extensive distribution of pottery to provide remuneration for the potter to buy food" (231).

Agriculture and Ceramics.

I take it for granted that Kefar Hananya production is not in the first or fourth system. It must, then, be in the second or third system, where for Arnold it is population pressure and the unavailability of agricultural land adequate in quantity and/or quality that forces people to make use of available ceramic resources. It is not that the availability of such clay resources convinces them to give up adequate subsistence farming and take up the daring life of business entrepreneurs.

Here are a few explicit statements from Arnold, over and above the ones just cited on pottery making's evolution from small-scale household to large-scale commercial production. He proposes as a "general principle" that "when a population exceeds the ability of the land to sustain it (and thus exceeds its carrying capacity), there is movement into other occupations like pottery making" (168). Thus, for example, "it is not unusual that pottery making and other crafts are a secondary choice to agriculture and resorted to by people with poor quality, insufficient or no land. While agriculture provides food directly to a family, craft production does not, but requires additional labor and greater risks than agriculture. . . . It is not unusual, then, that pottery making, as an indirect subsistence technique, is the result of population pressure and not a desirable occupation for most farmers. . . . [O]nce there is a better living with agriculture or more secure or steady work, pottery making is abandoned" (193). Again: "Potters who are dependent on their craft for a living make pottery only out of economic necessity [so that] when better economic opportunities exist they abandon the craft" (194). And yet again: "Except for those who make pottery only for their own use, people probably would not choose to become potters if the subsistence (e.g. agricultural) base was adequate" (200).

Everything I have just cited from Arnold (and even certain sections of Adan-Bayewitz's work, where he himself refers to Arnold's book) warn strongly against generalizations from Kefar Hananya's pottery making that deny the general peasant society of Galilee or the general exploitation of that peasantry in the early Roman period. Such inaccurate or even romantic generalizations could have been disciplined by a specific model, such as Arnold's cross-cultural anthropological one for ceramic production. They could also have been disciplined by a more general cross-cultural anthropological model for agrarian empire, such as the Lenski-Kautsky model itself.

Jonathan Reed notes, "I am unsure how to evaluate, from the archaeological sources, the perceived quality of life of such villagers as might have worked at Kefar Hananya. But whether they were content or not with their relationship can not be gauged by the archaeological record" (1994a:81 note 90). Is that really the best we can do? Or have we simply not tried to do better. It is surely possible to bring anthropology *and* archeology to bear on such a question. William Dever articulated the challenge almost two decades ago: "It would be an oversimplification to say that traditional Near Eastern *historical* archaeology was giving way to the more characteristic *anthropological* archaeology of prehistorians and New World archaeologists, but the *rapprochement* between orientations formerly thought antithetical is pertinent. . . . More fundamental still is the question of whether the archaeology of the ancient Near East should be historically or anthropologically oriented—or both. . . . This dichotomy is, of course, in many ways a false one, but at the very least the presuppositions of anthropological archaeology, drawn largely from prehistory, must be examined and applied both critically and selectively to the archaeology of the Near East, which has a *history*, based both on artifactual remains and an abundance of literary sources, going back 5,000 years" (15, 21).

The most adequate answers come from an interdisciplinary conjunction of all three factors—from anthropology, history, and archeology together. Anthropology tells us what to expect from peasants under rural commercialization. Archeology tells us about rural commercialization through Antipas's urbanization processes in Lower Galilee in the early first century. History tells us something like this, from Keith Hopkins, introducing a book of essays specifically on trade in the ancient economy: "In the first two centuries AD, proportionally fewer food-producers were growing more food than ever before for more non-agricultural producers. . . . Agricultural productivity increased, above all because of the increased pressure of exploitation. Two types of exploitation need to be distinguished. First, agricultural slaves were forced to work longer than free men and were given, on average, more land to work than many free peasants could afford to own. Secondly, free peasants and owners of slaves were forced to work harder in order to produce taxes for the state, and in a significant minority of cases to produce rent for the legal owners of land which they worked. . . . [T]he total amount and the proportion of total production extracted from primary producers in taxes and in rent increased. In other words, the screws of exploitation tightened" (1983:xvi, xvi–xvii, xix). But history also tells us that the Jewish people believed in a covenantal God of justice and righteousness, in equity and equality in a land that belonged to God. When that anthropology, that history, and that archeology come together, we have the situation of Lower Galilee in the 20s of the first common-era century—as sharply as it can be defined.

Peasants and Scribes

The *Gospel of Thomas* and Q share the following social features: literacy and a scribal mentality, a probable setting in village or town life, a group organization that did not entirely withdraw from the larger world of which it constituted a part, and a group mentality characterized more than anything else by the adoption of a particular understanding of the world and a corresponding ethic. Moreover, both documents were composed in a context in which increased exploitation of the countryside and peasantry by the urban elites contributed to considerable social disintegration and economic distress (such as debt, dispossession, tenancy, impoverishment, and hunger). Both groups respond to this crisis by adopting a highly critical stance towards ordinary social conventions and political structures, a critique of wealth, an inversion of normal values, and a rejection or critique of urban-based religious institutions.

William E. Arnal, "The Rhetoric of Marginality," pp. 491–492

Christopher Seeman has raised a terribly obvious but seldom-asked question: Why was it that the Jesus movement emerged in Lower Galilee during the reign of Herod Antipas, rather than at some other time and place? Why in Galilee rather than in Judaea, and why in Lower rather than in Upper Galilee? Why under Antipas rather than under his father, Herod the Great, who ruled from 37 to 4 B.C.E., or under his half-nephew, Agrippa I, who ruled from 40 to 44 C.E.? And, since Antipas ruled between 4 B.C.E. and 39 C.E., why in the late 20s rather than in any other period of that long reign? Why precisely there; why exactly then? Or, broadening Seeman's question: Why did *two* movements arise in the late 20s of that first common-era century in the *two* separated regions of Antipas's territory: John's baptism movement in Perea (east of the Jordan) and Jesus' kingdom-of-God movement in Galilee (to its northwest)? Seeman finds the answer in Antipas's urbanization program for Lower Galilee: "The political, economic, and demographic consequences of Antipas' city foundations generated a new social *situation* for the Galilean peasantry. The Jesus faction emerged in *response* to that situation, acquiring influence among the peasants by *representing* their interests" (84). Anthropology, history, and archeology combine to predict some form of peasant resistance in Lower Galilee by the late 20s. It came with John and Jesus. But by the late 60s, the situation was much worse.

Josephus, defending his role in Galilee during 66–67 C.E. at the start of the First Roman-Jewish War, tells how the Galilean peasants attacked (or tried to attack) both Sepphoris and Tiberias. Notice this text's doubled mention of *hatred, detestation,* and *extermination* (my italics):

> I marched with such troops as I had against Sepphoris and took the city by assault. The Galilaeans, seizing this opportunity, too good to be missed, of venting their *hatred* on one of the cities which they *detested,* rushed forward, with the intention of *exterminating* the population, aliens and all. Plunging into the town they set fire to the houses, which they found to be deserted, the terrified inhabitants having fled in a body to the citadel. They looted everything, sparing their countrymen no conceivable form of devastation. . . . As, however, they refused to listen to either remonstration or command, my exhortations being overborne by their *hatred,* I instructed some of my friends to circulate a report that the Romans had made their way into another quarter of the city with a large force . . . that . . . I might check the fury of the Galilaeans and so save Sepphoris. . . . Tiberias, likewise, had a narrow escape from being sacked by the Galilaeans . . . [who] loudly denounced the Tiberians as traitors and friendly to the king [Agrippa II], and [requested] permission to go down and *exterminate* their city. For they had the same *detestation* for the Tiberians as for the inhabitants of Sepphoris." (*Life* 374–384)

Those renewed or new city elites in Sepphoris and Tiberias needed land in the surrounding countryside, and that meant the possibility of force and violence as well as the actuality of loans and debts, mortgages and foreclosures. Between peasants and cities in agrarian empires stands (however cloaked in reciprocity or masked in mutuality) the presence of raw power and military force. But were only peasants involved in such resistance at the time of John or Jesus? The discussion of that question serves as both a conclusion to Parts IV and V and an introduction to Parts VI and VII.

It is clear that Antipas's urbanization would create peasant dislocation and dispossession resulting, most likely, in various forms of resistance. But my interest in this final section is not on resistance just among the peasant class but also on resistance among Lenski's so-called Retainer Class (discussed in Chapter 11). It involves, therefore, that very dangerous combination of peasant discontent and retainer leadership. What, in other words, about the scribes in all of this? It is, of course, always possible for individuals to resist injustice even when their own particular class interests are not threatened. It is especially possible (if not inevitable) in the Jewish tradition of a God of justice. But, apart from that, what effect did Antipas's policies have on scribal retainers—that is, on those who could read and write, record and file, manage and administer his government even at the lowest levels of the bureaucracy?

Think, for a moment, of exactly what Antipas's policy is against the general background of Roman domination and Herodian collaboration. His father, Herod the Great, had ruled the entire country for over thirty years with the official title "King of the Jews." He was from Idumea, just south of Judea, a territory annexed and converted to Judaism a scant century earlier. But he married a Hasmonean princess named Mariamme and thereby linked himself publicly with more original Jewish tradition and more authentic Jewish royalty. It was an association too close, however, for his paranoia: he executed Mariamme in 29 B.C.E. and their two sons, Alexander and Aristobulus, in 7 B.C.E. Two building projects, among the vast number he carried out, stand out; both were going on simultaneously in the teens B.C.E. On the one hand, for pagans he built a large city at Straton's Tower on his country's mid-Mediterranean coast, gave it a magnificent protected harbor, placed a temple to Rome and Augustus on a centrally located hill, and called it all Caesarea. On the other hand, for Jews he began an equally magnificent reconstruction of Jerusalem's Temple, which was barely finished before it was destroyed in 70 C.E. In the very last days before his death, Herod altered his will to name Archelaus and not Antipas as his heir. When he died in 4 B.C.E., there were armed uprisings in all areas of his country, and it took the Syrian legate and his legions to restore Roman control. Augustus accepted Herod's will only in part. He gave the middle and southern sections of the country—Idumean, Judaea, and Samaria—with their annual income of 600 talents, to Archelaus, but with the title *ethnarch* (people ruler) not *king* (royal ruler). Antipas got Galilee to the north and Perea east of the Jordan, with their income of 200 talents, but received only the title *tetrarch* (section ruler). Philip, a third son, got territories still farther north and east, with income of 100 talents and another tetrarch title. When Archelaus was dismissed in 6 C.E., Augustus appointed not Antipas, as he might have hoped, but a Roman prefect as governor of the country's central and southern regions.

To be Antipas was to be sorely disappointed. But also to be carefully cautious. He restored his capital of Sepphoris, devastated in the rebellions at the death of Herod the Great. And he waited for the death of Augustus, which came in 14 C.E. Then he began immediately to build an entirely new capital on the western shore of the Sea of Galilee, completing it by 18 or 19 C.E. It facilitated access to the twin halves of his disconnected territories, no doubt, but if that were the only benefit, it should not have taken him around twenty-five years to imagine it. Augustus is gone, Tiberius is emperor, and the new capital, with Antipas's first minted coins, is called Tiberias. Herod the Great had Caesarea as his new capital on the coast; Antipas would have Tiberias as his new capital on the lake. Both were named for the ruling Roman emperors. The logic of his policy is clear. Maybe under Tiberias he could become king of the whole country, just as his father had been under Augustus. But he himself was the son of Herod and the Samaritan, Malthace, so a Hasmonean connection was needed. Sometime in the late 20s C.E. he rejected his Nabatean wife and married Herodias, wife of his half-brother Philip. She was a granddaughter of the executed Hasmonean Mariamme and daughter of the executed Hasmonean Aristobulus. It was all too late, however, and Antipas, even though he ruled a decade longer than his father, never obtained the kingship. He died in exile about as far west as Caligula could send him.

Back, however, to Tiberias. The existence of Sepphoris and Tiberias, two cities rebuilt or built within about twenty miles and twenty years of one another in the almost five hundred square miles of Lower Galilee would, as seen above, put serious strains on peasant life and create serious changes in agricultural distribution. But what, precisely, about that change of capital from Sepphoris to Tiberias? How would that affect the scribal class involved in the city itself and in its surrounding villages? This is Josephus's description of the founding of Tiberias:

The new settlers were a promiscuous rabble, no small contingent being Galilean, with such as were drafted from territory subject to him and brought forcibly to the new foundation. Some of these were magistrates. Herod accepted as participants even poor men who were brought in to join the others from any and all places of origin. It was a question whether some were even free without cavil. These latter he often and in large bodies liberated and benefited (imposing the condition that they should not quit the city), by equipping houses at his own expense and adding new gifts of land.

For he knew that his settlement was contrary to the law and tradition of the Jews because Tiberias was built on the site of tombs that had been obliterated, of which there were many there. And our law declares that such settlers are unclean for seven days. (*Jewish Antiquities* 18.38)

That makes Tiberias sound like a very strange city. It is founded in permanent, not just seven-day-long, impurity. It is force-filled with ex-peasants ("Galileans") and ex-slaves. Even some of the administrators had to be brought there forcibly. Allowance must be made, of course, for the problems Josephus had with the lower classes in Tiberias during his short tenure as Jerusalem's military representative there in 66–67 C.E. In reading the above description, we must also remember what happened to Josephus himself in Tiberias:

The second faction (*stasis*) composed of most insignificant people, was bent on war [against Rome]. . . . Jesus, son of Sapphias, [was] the ringleader . . . of the party (*stasis*) of the sailors and destitute class. . . . The principal instigator of the mob was Jesus, son of Sapphias, at that time chief magistrate of Tiberias, a knave with an instinct for introducing disorder into grave matters, and unrivalled in fomenting sedition and revolution. With a copy of the laws of Moses in his hands, he now stepped forward and said: "If you cannot, for your own sakes, citizens, detest Josephus, fix your eyes on your country's laws, which your commander-in-chief intended to betray, and for their sakes hate the crime and punish the audacious criminal." (*Life* 34, 66, 134–135)

You can hardly expect a fair description of a city from which Josephus barely escaped with his life. Still, even allowing for all of that, Antipas's new Tiberias must have dislocated not just peasant farmers but also scribal retainers.

Peasants, almost by definition, are illiterate. William Harris estimated that "the likely overall illiteracy level of the Roman Empire under the principate is almost certain to have been above 90%" (22). Meir Bar-Ilan noted the "data for illiteracy gathered from different societies in the first half of the 20th century: Turkey in 1927: 91.8%; Egypt in 1927: 85.7%; South Africa in 1921: 90.3%; India in 1921: 90.5%; Afghanistan, Iran, Iraq, Saudi Arabia before 1950: above 90%" (47). He asked, rhetorically (but in agreement with Harris's figures), "Can't a tentative conclusion be drawn that in ancient 'traditional' societies the rate of literacy was less than 10%?" (47). He then focused the question down to the first centuries C.E. in the Jewish homeland, concluding that "comparative data show that under Roman rule the Jewish literacy rate improved in the Land of Israel. However, rabbinic sources support evidence that the literacy rate was less than 3%. This literacy rate, a small fraction of the society, though low by modern standards, was not low at all if one takes into account the needs of a traditional society in the past" (56). Jesus was a peasant from a peasant village. Therefore, for me, Jesus was illiterate until the opposite is proven. And it is not proven but simply presumed by Luke, when he has Jesus read from the prophet Isaiah in the synagogue at Nazareth in 4:16–20. But those early gospel texts mentioned in Arnal's epigraph (and central to the next two parts of this book) are, of course, written texts. So even if Jesus was a peasant talking to peasants, others besides peasants were listening. It was not peasants who *wrote* those two gospels, the *Q Gospel* and the *Gospel of Thomas*.

John Kloppenborg drew attention to this some time ago with regard to the *Q Gospel*. Speaking of its earliest layer, he notes two clues to its social location: "The first clue is the perhaps surprising fact that neither the Temple nor the priesthood nor purifications nor *kashruth* [purity rules] nor Israel's epic history nor the Torah figures importantly as a redemptive medium for this layer of Q. . . . [W]e encounter only sheer confidence in the immediacy of divine presence in the ordinary and the availability of God's benefaction without the need of other mediators. . . . A second clue is the frequency of sayings that idealize poverty and the simple life and that warn against the acquisition or service of wealth" (1991:84). He does not think that the "audience of the formative stratum consisted of peasant-farmers, agricultural laborers, and itinerant hand-workers" since "the visible and overt social radicalism of Q seems atypical of peasant protests. A much more likely setting for this stage of Q is among those who might anachronistically be termed the 'petit bourgeois' in the lower administrative sector of the cities and villages" (1991:85). William Arnal concurs with that judgment for both the *Q Gospel* and the *Gospel of Thomas* in the epigraph to this section. He describes such scribal radicalism as a "countercultural position in response to the increasing exploitation of the countryside by the urban wealthy, an intensification of the market reflected in and necessitated by Antipas' recent establishment of Tiberias and Sepphoris as administrative centers" (491).

Since Jesus did not—and, in my opinion, could not—write, and since the *Q Gospel* and the *Gospel of Thomas* are written texts, I formulate the hinge between Parts IV–V and VI–VII of this book as follows: *Jesus' kingdom-of-God movement began as a movement of peasant resistance but broke out from localism and regionalism under scribal leadership.*

PART VI
Kingdom and Eschatology

The heart of the issue is that rigorous asceticism was deviant, and deviance was dangerous. Strident, and often obstreperous, practitioners of physical asceticism were deemed suspect by the political, social, and cultural authorities of the age, and such apprehension put the practice of physical asceticism under a cloud of suspicion generally. This mistrust of ascetics stemmed from their being perceived as radicals expressing discontent with the status quo, advocating norms and values antithetical to the accepted social and political order, and claiming a personal authority independent of the traditional controls of their society and culture. Put simply, they were seen as a threat to the continued and peaceful existence of the Roman Empire. The conflict between asceticism and authority hinged on social and cultural issues. . . . Popular reputation translates into personal power. In the same way ascetics, on the basis of their austere and self-disciplined lives, could challenge the authority of political leaders, social norms, and cultural traditions, and set themselves up as authorities in their own right. . . .

Conservative men of culture within the Church found radical Christian ascetics objectionable in the same way as their counterparts outside the Church. Within Christianity, the ascetics, with their claims to charismatic authority, posed the same sort of threat to hierarchical authority as they did to the institutional authority of the state. Faced with a similar conflict, Christianity effected a similar resolution. Conservative Christian missionaries developed a way of sidestepping the "hard sayings" of the gospels—the proof texts of the radical ascetics—by spiritualizing the ideals of poverty, chastity, and equality. In this they borrowed the concepts of *apatheia* and *ataraxia* [imperturbability] from the Stoics, making virtue more an internal question of attitude than an external matter of physical practice. These ideals were thus stripped of their radical social character and their threat to the social order. This also allowed Christianity to appeal to many more people of higher rank and property than if it had attacked their riches and status in plain material terms. It showed that [as Clement of Alexandria named his book] the "rich man could, indeed, be saved."

James A. Francis, *Subversive Virtue*, pp. xiii–xiv, 2, 188

Parts IV and V established the immediate *context* for Jesus and his companions as clearly and sharply as possible. It is time, finally, to see the *text* that must be put in *conjunction* with that very specific *context*. That takes up the rest of the book.

Part VI looks at two of the earliest extracanonical gospels that we have available: the *Q Gospel* and the *Gospel of Thomas*. Each of them was described separately in Chapter 8, and they will now be considered together across the three chapters of this Part VI. Neither gospel is dependent on any of our intracanonical foursome (although, of course, the *Q Gospel* is now present within Matthew and Luke and is "intracanonical" in that sense). They are also independent of one another, though linked together in several ways.

Chapter 14 begins with an anthropological reminder of the importance of *lists* as orality cedes to literacy, as remembered oral tradition gives way to recorded scribal version. That leads into a comparison of those very list-like gospels, the *Q Gospel* and the *Gospel of Thomas,* in terms of their formal structure, their constitutive genre, their parallel content, and their proposed stratification. These gospels are clearly not biographical narratives like the canonical gospels, so how are they constructed and organized? Is there any overall genre or type of writing into which they both fit? How does it happen that both gospels have about one-third of their content in common (a high percentage for two documents not copying from one another), and what is the nature of the material special to each? The chapter concludes with a correlated stratification of the two gospels, emphasizing how they have divergently redacted their common content.

Chapter 15 establishes the meaning of *eschatology* and continues into a very precise description of the twin types of eschatology present in the *Q Gospel* and the *Gospel of Thomas.* Those divergent eschatologies are described as *apocalypticism* and *asceticism* in Chapter 15. In other words, the common material found in those twin gospels—that shared one-third—is redacted by each gospel variously—in either, both, or neither of those two eschatological directions. But that common material itself—the thirty-seven units that constitute what I call the Common Sayings Tradition—does not favor either of the two eschatologies.

Chapter 16 is a preliminary discussion of a third type of eschatology, the one present in the Common Sayings Tradition itself. It proposes and explains the term *ethical eschatology* for that third type, which is neither *apocalyptic* eschatology as in the *Q Gospel* nor *ascetical* eschatology as in the *Gospel of Thomas.* That chapter prepares for Part VII, which is a detailed study of the Common Sayings Tradition in terms of that proposed eschatology.

Go back, for a moment, to the epigraph, which was carefully chosen to be surprising. Biblical scholars are used to terms like *apocalyptic eschatology* as a way of proclaiming God's impending judgment on an unjust world. But what about forms of socially critical asceticism, first pagan and then Christian, as described in that epigraph? Is that another type of eschatology? How do apocalypticism and asceticism relate to one another? That epigraph is there to start us thinking about that question from this point on.

Finally, this Part VI is in dialogue with foundational research from Helmut Koester to Stephen Patterson on the *Gospel of Thomas* and from James Robinson to John Kloppenborg on the *Q Gospel.* I write with gratitude and appreciation for their seminal work.

CHAPTER 14

A COMPARISON OF
TWO EARLY GOSPELS

As a whole the sapiential speeches of Q are not concerned with the question of law and tradition. . . . Such a situation can be assumed to have existed during the first years after the death of Jesus anywhere . . . the question of the law, triggered by the Pauline mission, was not yet a concern. A Greek-speaking environment is more likely than an area of towns and villages in which the predominant language was Aramaic. . . . It is . . . tempting to assume that the redaction of Q took place somewhere in Galilee and that the document as a whole reflects the experience of a Galilean community of followers of Jesus. . . . The entire development of Q, from the first collection of the sayings of Jesus and their assembly into sapiential discourses to the apocalyptic redaction and, finally, the pre-Matthean redaction, must be dated within the first three decades after the death of Jesus.

Helmut Koester, Ancient Christian Gospels, pp. 162, 164, 170

The text [of the *Gospel of Thomas*] dates to a period in which authority was still *personal*, or dependent upon a leader's personal charisma and powers of persuasion, and not yet *apostolic* properly speaking. . . . All of this would suggest a date close to Paul . . . or to Mark. . . . [T]he basic Thomas collection was already in existence when the Prologue, Thom 13, and Thom 114 were added, presumably still in that early period of jostling personal claims to authority. Precisely when this Thomas layer was added, or how extensive it was, may never be known. One might perhaps speculate that it coincided, more or less, with the martyrdom of James in 62 C.E.

Stephen J. Patterson, The Gospel of Thomas and Jesus, pp. 116–117

You will recall from the discussion of the gospel traditions in Chapter 8 that I accept, as scholarly presuppositions, both the canonical independence of the *Gospel of Thomas* and the written existence of the *Q Gospel*. If those positions are basically invalid—if the *Q Gospel* does not exist or the *Gospel of Thomas* is canonically dependent—then so is this section completely invalid. (Likewise, of course, for the opposing positions.) But if my positions are correct, what follows? I now extend those presuppositions following proposals by scholars such as Koester and Patterson on the *Gospel of Thomas* and Robinson and Kloppenborg on the *Q Gospel*. The paired epigraphs above give approximate dates for the two gospels and indicate what I mean by "early" in my chapter title.

In the Beginning Was the List

[T]he most characteristic form [in the early phases of written cultures] is something that rarely occurs in oral discourse at all (although it sometimes appears in ritual), namely the list.

> Jack Goody, *The Domestication of the Savage Mind*, p. 80

Orality knows no lists. . . . Indeed, writing was in a sense invented largely to make something like lists. . . . Lists begin with writing.

> Walter J. Ong, *Orality and Literacy*, pp. 98, 99, 123

The list is, perhaps, the most archaic and pervasive of genres. It has received surprisingly little scholarly attention.

> Jonathan Z. Smith, *Imagining Religion*, p. 44

This anthropological section on lists prepares for a consideration of two fundamentally important early Christian *list-like* texts, the *Gospel of Thomas* and the *Q Gospel*. But to begin, think, for a moment, about lists and listing. If a group of biblical students were to say, "Jesus spoke in parables, for example, . . ." and then named ten parables, that ten would be, in content and sequence, different for all of us (and even different for each of us on different occasions). We could, I suppose, describe all such ad hoc sets as *oral lists,* but we would have to be very careful about the meaning of that expression. What we have in our heads is a coded mess (or matrix, if you prefer) of stuff that we can process into a list of whatever type is needed for whatever purpose. We have, as it were, a heap in the head but a list on the lips. If we always cited a fixed sequence of parables, it would mean that we were thinking *scribally* rather than *orally,* and it might be better to describe such fixed sets as *scribal lists given orally.* Such a fixed oral operation, apart from magic, ritual, or other short and tightly controlled formulations, would not and could not occur before the conception of a fixed and written format or sequence had been created—that is, before the arrival of literacy on a given scene. In one sense, therefore, and even allowing for the loose usage just mentioned, the term *oral list* is somewhat ambiguous and might better be avoided. In strictest usage, an oral list is something of a contradiction in terms, as Jack Goody emphasized in the book from which I took my first epigraph for this section. He noted that initial literacy may contain "lists of individuals, objects or words in a form that may have no oral equivalent at all" (1977:86).

There is a chapter in his book entitled "What's in a List?" from which I take the following comments: "Particularly in the early phases of written cultures in the first fifteen hundred years of man's documented history, [bureaucratic] materials are often presented in a form which is very different from that of ordinary speech, indeed of almost any speech. And the most characteristic form is something that rarely occurs in oral discourse at all (although it sometimes appears in ritual), namely the list. . . . Lists are seen to be characteristic of the early uses of writing, being promoted partly by the demands of complex economic and state organization, partly by the nature of scribal training, and partly by the 'play' element, which attempts to explore the potentialities of this new medium. They represent an activity which is difficult in oral cultures and one which encourages the activities of historians and the observational sciences, as well as on a more general level favouring the exploration and definition of classificatory schemes. . . . The list . . . increases the visibility and definiteness of classes, makes it easier for the individual to engage in chunking, and more particularly in the hierarchical ordering of information which is critical to much recall" (80, 108, 111). When, therefore, we are dealing with the interface between the oral and the written—especially the initial transition from oral to written in earliest Christianity—we should pay close attention to lists in all their various permutations and combinations.

I turn, then, to two gospels that contain some of the earliest Christian writings outside the authentic Pauline letters. Those documents are the *Gospel of Thomas* and the *Q Gospel,* and they read like lists—or, if you prefer, lists of lists, or lists of sayings centered around Jesus.

Format and Structure

The use of catchwords is itself an organizing principle, with its own internal logic. . . . At any rate, catchword association is the principle upon which the sayings in the Gospel of Thomas were originally collected.

Stephen J. Patterson, *The Gospel of Thomas and Jesus*, p. 102

What types of literary organization does Q exhibit? Perhaps the most obvious form is *topical*. Sayings are not simply strung together but gathered into coherent groupings. . . . It is clear that the Q sayings have been organized thoughtfully into topical groupings.

John S. Kloppenborg, *The Formation of Q*, pp. 90, 92

The first comparison we will consider between the two gospels is in the formal structure of both documents. How are they organized and unified? While the four intracanonical gospels have narrative and biographical frameworks, these two extracanonical gospels lack that type of overall organization. What type of structure *do* they have?

Gospel of Thomas

The *Gospel of Thomas* contains 114 units in the now-standard scholarly numbering, and that external numbering follows certain internal indices. The 114 numbered units are easily distinguished, in that each begins with either a statement *by* Jesus or a comment *to* Jesus. But the artificiality of that construction is evident from the fact that many of those now-numbered units contain several independent sayings within them. If you count multiple versions of the same saying separately, that brings the count to 146 sayings in all. Here, for example, is the *Gospel of Thomas* 111:1–3:

> Jesus said, "The heavens and the earth will roll up in your presence, and whoever is living from the living one will not see death." Does not Jesus say, "Those who have found themselves, of them the world is not worthy"?

That unit contains both a direct ("Jesus said") and an indirect ("Does not Jesus say") combination of two sayings.

The overall collection of the *Gospel of Thomas* has the minimal possible organization—namely, connection by word links or catchword associations. Those verbal links have been noted repeatedly, from Garitte in 1957 (63–64) to Patterson in 1993a (100–102). Garitte cited thirty-five instances, while Patterson gave sixty-four involving links between two sayings (fifty-two examples), three sayings (ten examples), or even four sayings (two examples). But verbal links sometimes develop into formal and even topical ones.

Verbal Links.

Here is an example of word linkage between two, three, and four units, in the *Gospel of Thomas* 25–26, 20–22, and 96–99, respectively, links bolded:

1. Jesus said, "Love your **brother** like your soul, protect that one like the pupil of your **eye**."
2. Jesus said, "You see the speck that is in your **brother's eye**, but you do not see the beam that is in your own **eye**. When you take the beam out of your own **eye**, then you will see clearly to take the speck out of your **brother's eye**."

1. The disciples said to Jesus, "Tell us what the kingdom of heaven is **like**." He said to them, "It is **like** a mustard seed . . ."
2. Mary said to Jesus, "What are your disciples **like**?" He said, "They are **like** little children . . ."

3. Jesus saw some babies nursing. He said to his disciples, "These nursing babies are **like** those who enter the kingdom . . ."

1. Jesus [said], "The **kingdom** of the Father is like [a] woman . . ."
2. Jesus said, "The **kingdom** of the [Father] is like a woman . . ."
3. Jesus said, "The **kingdom** of the Father is like a person . . ."
4. The disciples said to him, "Your brothers and your mother are standing outside." He said to them, "Those here who do what my Father wants are my brothers and my mother. They are the ones who will enter my Father's **kingdom**."

Verbal linkage, therefore, can extend across two, three, or even four of our present numbered units.

Formal Links.

The first three units in that last complex show not only verbal but also formal linkage. Verses 96–98 of the *Gospel of Thomas* are connected, in other words, not only by common words but by their common form as parables. There is a similar set of three parables in the *Gospel of Thomas* 63–65; these have verbal, formal, and probably even topical linkage:

1. Jesus said, "There was a rich **person** . . . [parable of the rich farmer].
   Whoever has ears should hear." (63)
2. Jesus said, "A **person** was receiving guests . . . [parable of the feast].
   Buyers and merchants [will] not enter the places of my Father." (64)
3. He said, "A . . . **person** owned a vineyard . . . [parable of the tenants].
   Whoever has ears should hear." (65)

The linkage is verbal ("person"), formal (parables), and topical (wealth). All three warn against wealth—that is, against a preoccupation with normal worldly activities. That topical unity is underlined by having all three parables conclude with an extraparabolic comment of which the first and last are the same. But such topical or even formal complexes are very unusual in the *Gospel of Thomas*. Verbal complexes or catchword associations are much more usual.

It may be significant that word linkage or association by catchword occurs both internally within and externally between units. It may also be significant that it does not occur every time. Maybe internal linkage indicates oral transmission and external linkage indicates written transmission? It should be emphasized how very difficult it is to find examples of such combinations in independent texts. Yet such independent attestations are the only way we can be sure that combinations go back to either oral transmission or written tradition. It could well be that those combinations were created ad hoc as memory prompted either oral speaker or scribal author to compose clusters of those sayings for discussion. "In this case," as Steve Patterson comments, "the catchwords will not have been part of any conscious design on the part of the editor, but simply the result of his or her own process of remembering" (1993a:102).

Q Gospel

The *Q Gospel* is much more organized than the *Gospel of Thomas* in its general structure, and it is not so much verbal or formal associations as topical connections that dominate the composition. As John Kloppenborg has noted, "Not only are the sayings grouped into several topically coherent clusters, there is also a measure of unity and coherence among the several clusters as well as logical and thematic development throughout the course of the entire collection." If one compares its structure with that of the narrative gospels, of course, it still seems very episodic and almost random, but in terms of its own genre (on which more below), "it ranks with the most sophisticated literary products of its class" (1987a:89). Kloppenborg, who insists "that the Q sayings have been organized thoughtfully into topical groupings," proposes fourteen such groupings (1987a:92):

John's preaching of the Coming One	=	Q 3:7–9, 16–17
The temptation of Jesus	=	Q 4:1–13
Jesus' inaugural sermon	=	Q 6:20b–49
John, Jesus, and "this generation"	=	Q 7:1–10, 18–28; (16:16); 7:31–35
Discipleship and mission	=	Q 9:57–62; 10:2–4
On prayer	=	Q 11:2–4, 9–13
Controversies with Israel	=	Q 11:14–52
On fearless preaching	=	Q 12:2–12
On anxiety over material needs	=	Q 12:(13–14, 16–21), 22–31, 33–34
Preparedness for the end	=	Q 12:39–59
Two parables of growth	=	Q 13:18–19, 20–21
The two ways	=	Q 13:24–30, 34–35; 14:16–24, 26–27; 17:33; 14:33–34
Various parables and sayings	=	Q 15:3–7; 16:13, 17–18; 17:1–6
The eschatological discourse	=	Q 17:23–37; 19:12–27; 22:28–30

Note that it is now customary to designate a unit in the *Q Gospel*—say, Luke 3:7–9, 16–17 = Matthew 3:7–12—simply as Q 3:7–9, 16–17. But in every case, the exact content must be reconstructed by comparing both Luke and Matthew. That, for example, is what the International Q Project under James Robinson and his colleagues is all about.

The general unity and even organization *within* each of those groupings is fairly clear, but the overall sequence *between* them is much less evident. For example, the first four topical units and the final one are in fairly obvious juxtaposition. Not only are those segments unified internally by topical content, they are also unified externally by chronological constraints: John comes before Jesus at the start, and the apocalypse comes at the end. You might almost think from that beginning that a biographical framework was about to appear. But when you look at the central segments in Kloppenborg's list, there is no compelling reason for overall sequence. Those segments could be moved around among themselves without any change of importance. If the *Gospel of Thomas* is a *list* with mostly verbal connections, a few formal ones, fewer topical ones, and no overall structure at all, the *Q Gospel* is a *list of lists* with mostly topical connections in each list but with some overall structure as well. Do not presume, by the way, that a lack of structure is a sign of compositional incompetence. It may instead be an imperative of theological vision. Maybe it is not for humans to overorganize divine wisdom?

Genre and Destiny

It is difficult to find a single suitable translation for λόγος *[logos]* and its plural λόγοι *[logoi]*, for the term covers a wide spectrum of meanings. The English term *word* comes nearest in providing a comparable breadth. It not only designates an individual vocable, whose plural then designates a word-by-word sequence of vocables, . . . it can also designate a whole statement, in such expressions as "a word for today," or "a word to the wise is sufficient." This usage corresponds to the use of the term *word* to designate the self in re-sponsible commitment, in such expressions as "to give one's word"; "to be as good as one's word."

James M. Robinson, "LOGOI SOPHON," pp. 73–74 note 9

The second comparison between the two gospels is their common genre. This was recognized over thirty years ago by James Robinson in a seminal article on the common generic identity of the *Gospel of Thomas* and the *Q Gospel* (1971).

Robinson called the genre "Words of the Wise" or "Sayings of the Sages." He pointed to the genre's origins in scribal traditions from Mesopotamia and Egypt that had flowed into Jewish collections, such as those in the biblical book of Proverbs. The smaller collections in Proverbs 30 and 31, for example, begin respectively with "the words of Agur son of Jakeh" and "the words of King Lemuel." The genre's trajectory continued thence into both Judaism and Christianity. Once into Christianity, it split into Catholic and Gnostic streams. The *Q Gospel*, for instance, continued into the synoptic tradition, adopting the narrative, biographical format of Catholic Christianity's classic gospel format. The *Gospel of Thomas,* on the other hand, ended up within the Thomas tradition, adopting the dialogue-and-discourse format of Gnostic Christianity's classic gospel format. There are, however, two important qualifications to Robinson's very persuasive proposal on the genre of the *Q Gospel* and the *Gospel of Thomas.*

First, there is nothing intrinsically either Jewish as against Christian, or Catholic Christian as against Gnostic Christian, about the genre termed Sayings of the Sages. "It has been pointed out repeatedly," notes John Kloppenborg, "that apart from *Gos. Thom.* none of the other examples of the genre shows any gnosticizing tendency" (1987a:13). The formal openness of a sayings collection makes it easily pulled in diverse directions, but those external pulls are not internal drives. What eventually happens to them derives from social usage and not from inevitable generic proclivity. Seen after the fact, of course, history always looks like destiny.

Second, Sayings of the Sages, the generic title proposed by Robinson, places these gospels in the sapiential traditions of the ancient Near East in general and of Judaism in particular. But that requires careful specification. Wisdom or sapiential (from *sapientia,* Latin for wisdom) traditions are the special ideology of teachers, scribes, and bureaucrats within aristocratic states or agrarian empires. As such they are often assumed to be necessarily and conventionally pro-establishment. They are taken to be inevitably supportive of those elite institutions that employ scribal talents with their educated ability to read and write, count and record, manage and administer. Under the extreme pressures of Hellenistic internationalism and Roman imperialism, all aspects of tradition in the Jewish homeland underwent a certain radicalization in the centuries immediately before and after the common era. The legal traditions were radicalized first by the Pharisees and then by the rabbis in declaring a dual Torah or double Law, one written and one oral, both stemming alike from Moses at Sinai. The prophetic traditions were radicalized by apocalyptic seers and authors declaring a double era of history, the present evil era soon to be destroyed and the imminent era of justice and righteousness soon to be established by God. The sapiential traditions were radicalized by declaring a double wisdom—not just the ordinary everyday wisdom of normal human life but also a radical wisdom whereby one lived divine justice in an evil world. I return to that last point below in discussing the eschatology of the twin gospels. It cannot be presumed, in other words, that sapiential scribes or even sapiential traditions are always conservative and never radical. Members of the genre Sayings of the Sages *need* not end up in Gnosticism, on the one hand, and they *can* end up in radicalism, on the other.

Content and Stratification

Among the sayings of the Gospel of Thomas that have parallels in the synoptic gospels, by far the largest number are sayings that Matthew and/or Luke has drawn from the Synoptic Sayings Source [Q]. There are at least thirty-six sayings that belong in this category, possibly as many as forty-five, if one includes the Q-Mark overlaps and those sayings that Luke may have drawn from Q, although there are no Matthean parallels. On the other hand, there are only fourteen sayings that the Gospel of Thomas shares with Mark (seventeen if the Q-Mark overlaps are counted), thirteen that it shares with Matthew only, and six that have parallels only in Luke. . . . Q contains the largest number of parallels to the Gospel of Thomas by any count . . . [yet] it is obvious that the Gospel of Thomas cannot simply pass as a variant or as an early form of the Synoptic Sayings Source [Q], nor is it possible to consider Q as the source of any of the sayings of the Gospel of Thomas. Nevertheless, the consideration of Q parallels in the Gospel of Thomas is as instructive as it is puzzling if [this question is] asked: To which layer of the development of Q do the parallels in the Gospel of Thomas belong?

Helmut Koester, "Q and Its Relatives," pp. 55–56

The third comparison between the two gospels—and the most important—concerns the stratification of content in each one and especially in the connection between that process for both of them. Stratification refers to evidence of successive layering of content within a text. The study of stratification involves discerning where later material has been added to earlier material. The question here is whether there are direct connections between discernible stratification processes in the *Q Gospel* and in the *Gospel of Thomas*.

The numbers given in the section epigraph above will be refined as I proceed, but their gross-level differences will hold valid: far more of the content of the *Gospel of Thomas* is paralleled in the *Q Gospel* than in any other early Christian document that we now know. That high parallelism in content is a first indication of some relationship closer than similar structure and common genre. Questions of stratification will both increase indications of close relationship and fill out its details. But that epigraph succinctly outlines the problems of this section. First, the greatest number of parallels in content is between the *Q Gospel* and the *Gospel of Thomas*. Second, neither of those gospels is derived from the other. Third, it is "puzzling" when one tries to correlate the stratification of the *Q Gospel* with the parallel in the *Gospel of Thomas*. That is precisely where the problem lies. What is the relationship between earlier stages of those twin gospels? Koester states the difficulty elsewhere like this: "The materials which the *Gospel of Thomas* and Q share must belong to a very early stage of the transmission of

Jesus' sayings. . . . Thus, the *Gospel of Thomas* is either dependent upon the earliest version of Q or, more likely, shares with the author of Q one or several very early collections of Jesus' sayings. . . . The close relationships of the *Gospel of Thomas* to Q cannot be accidental. . . . The *Gospel of Thomas* is either dependent upon Q's earlier version or upon clusters of sayings employed in its composition" (1990a:95, 150). This section, then, attempts to solve that "puzzling" question of the *correlated* stratigraphy of those two gospels.

PARALLEL CONTENT

My first step is to look at that common content in the *Q Gospel* and the *Gospel of Thomas* and to emphasize how striking is the amount of parallel material involved. I use three sets of parallels to build up the case.

A first set of parallels is between the *Gospel of Thomas* and the *Q Gospel*. This set is the most significant for my purpose in this book (see Appendix 1A):

28% (37 out of 132 units) of the *Gospel of Thomas* has parallels in the *Q Gospel*.

37% (37 out of 101 units) of the *Q Gospel* has parallels in the *Gospel of Thomas*.

That first set of comparisons also means that 72 percent (95 out of 132 units) of the *Gospel of Thomas* does not have any parallels in the *Q Gospel* (see Appendix 2A) and that 63 percent (64 out of 101 units) of the *Q Gospel* does not have parallels in the *Gospel of Thomas* (see Appendix 2B). But, for my immediate purposes, about one-third of each gospel has parallels in the other, and that high ratio should be compared with the next two sets of parallels.

A second set of parallels is between the *Gospel of Thomas*, the *Q Gospel*, and Mark's gospel, but watching that difference between what the *Gospel of Thomas* and the *Q Gospel* themselves have in common—namely, 37 units (Appendix 3A)—and what each has in particular—namely, 95 units (Appendix 3B) and 64 units (Appendix 3C), respectively:

30% (11 out of 37 units) of what is common to the *Gospel of Thomas* and the *Q Gospel* has parallels in Mark.

17% (16 of 95 units) of what is particular to the *Gospel of Thomas* has parallels in Mark.

19% (12 out of 64 units) of what is particular to the *Q Gospel* has parallels in Mark.

Those are also very interesting statistics. In terms of the common material, we again see about one-third of it having parallels in Mark (although, to be sure, that is a very small part of Mark's overall gospel). But even what is particular to the *Gospel of Thomas* and to the *Q Gospel* has, in each case, about one-fifth of that separate material paralleled in Mark.

A third set of parallels can be seen between the *Gospel of Thomas* and other sources, such as Special Matthew (Appendix 4A), Special Luke (Appendix 4B), and John (Appendix 4C):

12% (16 out of 132 units) of the *Gospel of Thomas* has parallels in Special Matthew.

7% (9 out of 132 units) of the *Gospel of Thomas* has parallels in Special Luke.

9% (12 out of 132 units) of the *Gospel of Thomas* has parallels in John.

The much lower statistics in that third set of parallels help to emphasize the higher ratios in the earlier sets, especially the first. The large amount of common material in the *Gospel of Thomas* and the *Q Gospel* is more striking in contrast to these lower statistics. That commonality, of course, continues to press the close relationship between these two gospels already seen in terms of formal structure and constitutive genre.

One question before proceeding. Could there be some documentary or written source common to both these gospels that might explain the large amount of parallel data? That seems most unlikely, largely because of the absolute lack of any common order or parallel sequence in the way the common material is presented in the two gospels. Recall, for contrast, that one argument for the existence of the *Q Gospel* as a documentary source is the amount of common sequence for its contents as used by Matthew and Luke. In this present case, however, if you compare those common sayings within their sequential positions in the *Q Gospel* and the *Gospel of Thomas,* there is no common pattern. Neither is there any reason why two gospels so loosely organized would have needed to revise an original common pattern were it present. But all that parallel content or common material, especially in the absence of a documentary source, forces the issue of correlative stratification. When and how did these twin gospels interact with one another?

CORRELATIVE STRATIFICATION

I look here at three proposals concerning stratification in the two gospels. The first proposal is that of John Kloppenborg for the *Q Gospel*. The second proposal is that of William Arnal for the *Gospel of Thomas*. The third is that of Stephen Patterson for both the *Q Gospel* and the *Gospel of Thomas* together. Patterson's suggestion, the first fully correlated stratification for both gospels together, will be basic for my argument in this book. I consider the first two proposals to be correct, but they will have to be integrated into Patterson's analysis rather than the reverse. I am, in any case, deeply grateful and profoundly indebted to those three scholars for their detailed studies.

There are actually divergent modes of stratification involved in the three proposals. There is, first, *compositional stratification,* the sequence in which two or more layers of materials are inserted into a finished composition. Layer A was completed, and later Layer B was added to it. But that tells you nothing one way or the other about the comparative dates of those layers. It tells you only about the successive moments when an author brought them together. There is, second, *traditional stratification,* the sequence in which a tradition was created. Layer A existed, and later Layer B was developed. John Kloppenborg has emphasized that his own stratification of the *Q Gospel* is compositional and not traditional. "To say that the wisdom components were formative for Q and that the prophetic judgment oracles and apophthegms describing Jesus' conflict with 'this generation' are secondary is not to imply anything about the ultimate tradition-historical provenance of any of the sayings. It is indeed possible, indeed probable, that some of the materials from the secondary compositional phase are dominical or at least every old, and that some of the formative elements are, from the standpoint of authenticity or tradition-history, relatively young. Tradition-history is not convertible with *literary history,* and it is the latter which we are treating here" (1987a:244–245). In other words, some of the materials that an author used as the first layer of a composition could be created at that very moment, and some of the ones inserted as a second layer could have been there from long before. *The stratification of a writing's composition is not the same as the stratification of a tradition's history.*

In what follows, both Kloppenborg and Arnal are speaking primarily about compositional stratification. Patterson, however, is concerned with the more fundamental question of traditional stratification, and so am I. Neither of us thinks you can automatically convert one into the other. On that point, Kloppenborg is absolutely correct. But the major significance of Patterson's stratification, in distinction from that of Kloppenborg or Arnal, is that it allows the question of the tradition's trajectory to be raised as forcibly as possible.

Q Gospel

A powerful and persuasive stratigraphy of the *Q Gospel* text has been offered by John Kloppenborg (1987a). Building on earlier studies by Dieter Lührmann in

1969 and Arnold Jacobsen in 1978, he proposed three main strata in the gospel: a sapiential layer (Q¹), an apocalyptic layer (Q²), and a biographical layer (Q³), combined in that sequence. Here is his summary: "The formative component of Q consisted of a group of six 'wisdom speeches' which were hortatory in nature and sapiential in their mode of argumentation. This stratum was subsequently expanded by the addition of groups of sayings, many framed as chriae [short, pithy sayings that are given a brief introduction or setting], which adopted a critical and polemical stance with regard to Israel. The most recent addition to Q seems to have been the temptation story, added in order to provide an aetiology and legitimation for Q's radical ethic, but introducing at the same time a biographical dimension into the collection" (1987a:317). A sapiential saying appeals to common reason or wisdom, to that which is at least theoretically available to all. It says, Look before you leap; or, Whoever fears God will be happy. An apocalyptic saying appeals to special information or revelation. It says, Repent, for the end is near; or, Watch, for you know not the day nor the hour.

The first or formative stratum is sapiential, composed of six wisdom speeches. These are directed inward to those who have already accepted the kingdom of God; they are characterized by persuasion rather than recrimination, preaching rather than polemics; and they have "important similarities in implied audience, constituent forms, motifs and themes and even structure and argumentation" (1987a:243). A typical example is Jesus' inaugural sermon, announcing "an ethic which responds to the radical character of the kingdom" (1987a:190). This now appears as the Sermon *off* the Mount in Luke 6:20b–49 and, in greatly expanded form, as the Sermon *on* the Mount in Matthew 5–7.

The second stratum is apocalyptic, composed of five judgment speeches. These are directed outward to those who have refused the kingdom of God; they are characterized by recrimination rather than persuasion, polemics rather than preaching; and, once again, "the presence of common forms (especially prophetic sayings and chriae), shared motifs and agreement in projected audience unite these five complexes" (1987a:170). A typical example is Jesus' final sermon, announcing "the prophetic proclamation of coming judgment . . . to the unconverted, warning them to repent before the catastrophe overtakes them" (1987a:166). This now appears as the apocalyptic discourse in Luke 17:23–37 and, combined with Mark 13, in Matthew 24:26–41.

The third stratum is introductory and biographical, composed of the story of Jesus' three temptations in the desert located immediately after the account of John the Baptist in the original *Q Gospel* and now present in Luke 4 and Matthew 4. Its purpose, most likely, was "to illustrate and legitimate the mode of behavior and the ethos of the Q group. As hero and leader of the Q community, Jesus provided an example of the absolutely dependent, non-defensive and apolitical stance of his followers" (1987a:256). That term *apolitical* means, of course, not operating by the politics of a world whose power is evil and whose dominion is demonic.

It is important to note that Kloppenborg's analysis is not simply circular, as if he had decided that sapiential materials came first and apocalyptic second, and arranged things accordingly. What he did was first note the distinction in terms of form, content, and audience between those two sets of sermons, one sapiential and the other apocalyptic, and then note that it was the latter that broke into the former's finished products, and not the reverse. One example will suffice. Compare the form and content of the four beatitudes that start Jesus' inaugural sermon in the Q Gospel as now visible in Luke 6:20b–23 = Matthew 5:3–4, 6, 11–12. The first three beatitudes concerning the poor, hungry, and sad are very similar to one another. But while the fourth, concerning the rejected, fits *in general* with the preceding three, it is *in detail* totally different from them. Notice the different format and content used in the fourth: "Blessed are you when . . . on account of [Jesus] . . . reward in heaven . . . so done to the prophets before you." That last phrase, and maybe even some of the preceding ones, read like "an insertion into an originally sapiential collection" of beatitudes (1987a:243).

Gospel of Thomas

Leaving aside, for here and now, that brief, initial, biographical introduction (Q³), the two major layers in Kloppenborg's stratification of the Q Gospel are the sapiential (Q¹) and the apocalyptic materials (Q²). William Arnal has suggested a somewhat similar two-step process for the *Gospel of Thomas,* but in his approach the successive layers are not sapiential and apocalyptic but sapiential and Gnostic. (I let that designation *Gnostic* go for the moment but return to it for more detailed discussion below.)

It is, Arnal argues, "the formal and thematic inconsistency of each of these two main strands [the sapiential and the Gnostic] that suggests a stratification rather than a unitary or aggregation model for the document's composition. It is evidence of an effort to impose redactional consistency on the document as a whole that allows us to discern the hand of the redactor and distinguish it from the remains of the earlier collection which he modified" (476). Each strand, in other words, is a consistent whole, and it is the Gnostic that has been imposed on the sapiential rather than vice versa.

The first of those two main strands or strata "may be characterized, like the materials in Q, as wisdom sayings, both in form and content" (476). This strand includes parables, beatitudes, and aphorisms as well as imperatives with or without motive clauses. It uses "argumentative comparisons, explicit or implicit . . . and observations about and appeals to nature, ordinary experiences, and common sense" (476). But just as Kloppenborg's sapiential layer in the Q *Gospel* contains not regular but radical wisdom—contains, as it were, a counterwisdom to common sense and ordinary attitude—so also here. "All, or nearly all, of the observations made in this vein are inversionary (without being esoteric) while they also appeal to common sense and wise observation" (476). Arnal calls this "inversionary wisdom" (479) and cites these 32 units as the clearest examples of this stratum: the *Gospel of Thomas* 3, 5, 6, 9, 14, 16, 20, 26, 31, 34–36, 42, 45, 47, 54, 55, 57, 63–65, 74, 76, 86, 89, 95–98, 107, 109, 110 (478 note 17). Here is an example:

Jesus said, "Let one who has found the world, and has become wealthy, renounce the world." (*Gospel of Thomas* 110)

The second of the two main strands is imposed on that former stratum. "In contradistinction to the sapiential layer, another body of sayings in the *Gospel of Thomas* is characterized by a gnostic orientation, manifested most trenchantly in their invocation of gnostic mythological motifs" (478). Inversionary or radical wisdom has now become esoteric or Gnostic wisdom. Arnal places 20 units most securely in this stratum: the *Gospel of Thomas* 11, 13, 15, 18, 21–22, 27–28, 49–50, 51, 60, 61, 83, 84, 101, 105, 108, 111, 114 (479 note 32). Here is an example:

Jesus said, "Blessed are those who are alone and chosen, for you will find the kingdom. For you have come from it, and you will return there again." Jesus said, "If they say to you, 'Where have you come from?' say to them, 'We have come from the light, from the place where the light came into being by itself, established [itself], and appeared in their image.' If they say to you, 'Is it you?' say, 'We are its children, and we are the chosen of the living Father.' If they ask you, 'What is the evidence of your Father in you?' say to them, 'It is motion and rest.'" (*Gospel of Thomas* 49–50)

That is the strongest indication of Gnosticism in the *Gospel of Thomas*. Those questions derive, presumably, from the *archons,* those hostile powers guarding the successive spheres of the heavenly cosmos and seeking to prevent the soul's return to the Living Father whence it came. The Gnostic is told how to answer their questions and so pass safely on its way home. I return to the question of this gospel's Gnosticism in Chapter 15.

Common Sayings Tradition
Each of those stratifications is very persuasive, and if those two gospels were quite independent texts, there would be no problem. But how are those stratifications correlated with one another? My answer accepts, with gratitude and appreciation, the seminal work of Stephen Patterson on the comparative stratigraphy

of the *Q Gospel* and the *Gospel of Thomas* (1993b). I have gone over his suggestions in great detail and will indicate differences I see as I proceed. But, let me emphasize once again, the basic and very important idea is his.

The first step establishes the *existence* of that common corpus of materials noted earlier. Patterson begins with what he calls the Common Tradition and I adapt slightly to call the Common Sayings Tradition. It is that corpus of materials common to the *Q Gospel* and the *Gospel of Thomas*. I count those units more conservatively than Patterson, ignoring ones that *could* be in the *Q Gospel* but are not securely present there (Appendix 1: Preliminary Note). This is, therefore, for me that Common Sayings Tradition (Appendix 1A):

28% (37 out of 132 units) of the *Gospel of Thomas* has parallels in the *Q Gospel*.

37% (37 of 101 units) of the *Q Gospel* has parallels in the *Gospel of Thomas*.

We do not italicize that phrase, the Common (Sayings) Tradition, because, unlike the situation with the *Q Gospel* or the *Gospel of Thomas*, we are not presuming a documentary source or a written text.

The second step establishes the *redaction* of that common corpus of materials. Patterson noticed that those 37 units show very interesting differences in how each gospel accepts, uses, and adapts them. They are, in other words, redacted quite divergently by each gospel according to its own particular theology. For Patterson, those theologies are apocalypticism for the *Q Gospel* and Gnosticism for the *Gospel of Thomas*.

There are three ways in which a traditional unit can be redacted in line with the basic theology of a document such as the *Gospel of Thomas* or the *Q Gospel*. First, in broadest focus, the *general direction* or overall context of each gospel changes everything within it. That general context directs the interpretation of every single unit according to the major thrust of the entire document. You read isolated parts in the light of the whole. Second, in narrower focus, the *immediate context*—the units just before or after that traditional unit—serve to bring it into line with their own understanding. The juxtaposition alone may do this even without direct or specific connection. Third, in closest focus, there may be specific or *internal change* within the very wording of the traditional unit itself. Patterson focuses especially on internal change as the best index for redactional change of common materials in each document. Those comparisons help us to see how the 37 units of the Common Sayings Tradition are moved or not moved in different directions in each gospel.

The third step establishes the *typology* of that common corpus of materials as it is or is not redacted internally toward Gnosticism in the *Gospel of Thomas* or toward apocalypticism in the *Q Gospel*. There are four different "types" involved. The statistics regarding redaction of these types, summarized below, are striking—especially the final one (Appendix 1B):

Type 1:   24% (9 out of 37 units) is redacted in the *Gospel of Thomas* but not in the *Q Gospel*.

Type 2:   8% (3 out of 37 units) is redacted in the *Q Gospel* but not in the *Gospel of Thomas*.

Type 3:   19% (7 out of 37 units) is redacted in both the *Gospel of Thomas* and in the *Q Gospel*.

Type 4:   49% (18 out of 37 units) is redacted in neither the *Gospel of Thomas* nor the *Q Gospel*.

Two elements, by the way, are particularly helpful in assessing redactional developments from the Common Sayings Tradition into the *Q Gospel* and/or the *Gospel of Thomas*. First, there are often independent parallels in other early Christian texts, especially in Mark's gospel (Appendix 3A). That is an external help in assessing what is redactionally specific to either the *Q Gospel* or the *Gospel of Thomas*. Furthermore, there are often multiple versions of the same unit in the *Gospel of Thomas* itself (Appendix 5). In those cases one version is much closer to that in the *Q Gospel* and the other (or others) move away from it toward a specifically Thomistic theology. That is an internal help in assessing the trajectory of change within the gospel.

These conclusions, I repeat, are based on a detailed analysis of all 37 items. I agree completely with Patterson on the inevitable conclusion: *the original Common Sayings Tradition contained neither Gnosticism nor apocalypticism but required redactional adaptation toward either or both of those eschatologies.* As Patterson concluded, "In Q and *Thomas* we have the remnants of an early Christian tradition in which emphasis was placed on Jesus' words; this tradition is thus in the broadest sense sapiential. In its later manifestations—in *Thomas* and Kloppenborg's Q²— this early sapiential orientation gave way to theological paradigms better known from later Christian generations: Gnosticism and apocalypticism, respectively. But questions linger. If Q and *Thomas* lie on diverging trajectories each grounded in, yet moving away from, an early sapiential tradition, what can be said about this early tradition itself?" (1993b:194).

That last question will be the burden of Part VII, because that "early tradi-tion" in the unredacted Common Sayings Tradition is the first *text* I intend to put in *conjunction* with the *context* already established in Parts IV and V of this book. But before that, I want to look more closely at those terms, *apocalypticism* and *Gnosticism*, to make them as precise as possible in terms of the *Q Gospel* and the *Gospel of Thomas*, and then to ask what other type of theology—something nei-ther apocalyptic nor Gnostic—is found in that Common Sayings Tradition.

CHAPTER 15

APOCALYPTIC AND ASCETICAL
ESCHATOLOGY

"Eschatology" and "apocalyptic" . . . were initially used in Jesus studies to refer to the end of the world of ordinary history. But subsequent scholarship in this century has given the terms many different senses. "Eschatological" can be used metaphorically in a non-end-of-the-world sense: as a nuanced synonym for "decisive," or as "world-shattering," or to point to the *telos* of history entering history but not in such a way as to end history. Even "apocalyptic," we are discovering, need not refer to the end of the world; some apocalyptic literature describes experiences of another world (visions or other-worldly journeys) and does not refer to the imminent end of the world of ordinary history. Thus, there is considerable terminological confusion in the discipline. For example, I have heard one scholar argue that Jesus' message was eschatological but not apocalyptic, that is, concerned with a decisive change in history, but not with the end of the world. I have heard another scholar argue that Jesus' message was apocalyptic but not eschatological; that is, grounded in the experience of another world, but not concerned with the end of this world.

Marcus J. Borg, *Jesus in Contemporary Scholarship*, pp. 8–9

This chapter is something of an interlude between the preceding and succeeding chapters. My focus is still on those twin texts, the *Q Gospel* and the *Gospel of Thomas,* and especially on that Common Sayings Tradition that they both share. But I pause here to establish terms and types within eschatology. The above epigraph warns us, quite accurately, about "terminological confusion" surrounding that topic in historical Jesus research. My attempt here is to discern the root of that confusion and, whether successful there or not, to clarify very precisely my own usage in what follows. Of crucial importance for me is the sharpest possible delineation of the divergent eschatologies present in the *Q Gospel,* the *Gospel of Thomas,* and the Common Sayings Tradition.

From the very beginning of my own research, I have insisted that the historical Jesus was eschatological but not apocalyptic, although it has always been difficult for me to put a more positive name on that nonapocalyptic eschatology. My first book about Jesus, *In Parables* (1973), distinguished prophetic from apocalyptic eschatology in terms of "ending a world" as against "destroying the globe"

(25–27). Throughout the last twenty-five years I have continued to hold that Jesus was both eschatological and nonapocalyptic and have searched for the best way to articulate positively his nonapocalyptic mode of world-negation. This present discussion is but one more attempt at defining my own terminology as clearly as I can before proceeding. My purpose is not to force others into my own terminology but to clarify my own and to invite others to do likewise.

Eschatology as Genus

When they used what we might call cosmic imagery to describe the coming new age, such language cannot be read in a crassly literalistic way without doing it great violence. . . . Far more important to the first-century Jew than questions of space, time and literal cosmology were the key issues of Temple, Land, and Torah, of race, economy and justice. When Israel's God acted, Jews would be restored to their ancestral rights and would practice their ancestral religion, with the rest of the world looking on in awe, and/or making pilgrimages to Zion, and/or being ground to powder under Jewish feet. . . . Within the mainline Jewish writings of this period, covering a wide range of styles, genres, political persuasions and theological perspectives, *there is virtually no evidence that Jews were expecting the end of the space-time universe.* There is abundant evidence that they . . . knew a good metaphor when they saw one, and used cosmic imagery to bring out the full theological significance of cataclysmic socio-political events. . . . They believed that *the present world order* would come to an end—the world order in which pagans held power, and Jews, the covenant people of the creator god, did not.

N. Thomas Wright, *The New Testament and the People of God*, pp. 284, 285, 333

The word *eschatology* refers, literally, to discussion about the *eschata*, the Greek term for the "last things." But is it the last things of the physical earth or of the human world? Is it an ending of space and time or of power and domination? Is the result earth up in heaven or heaven down on earth? In the above epigraph Wright insists that, in that distant Jewish and Christian past, such language referred to cataclysmic events such as the fall of great nations or the end of imperial powers and the subsequent triumph and ascendancy of God's people. That interpretation is in keeping with the usual view of eschatology, which includes the idea that such an ending comes through divine or transcendental causality, be it from angels or ancestors, spirits or demons, gods or God.

At first glance, then, *eschatology* means the same thing as *apocalypse*. That latter word refers, literally, to an *apokalypsis*, the Greek term for a special divine revelation (particularly about an imminent ending of world), and it usually includes the idea of goodness vindicated and evil eliminated. Contemporary scholarship, therefore, regularly uses the adjectives *eschatological* and *apocalyptic* to designate exactly the same phenomenon. But, on the other hand, that same contemporary scholarship speaks also of *realized eschatology* and of *present eschatology*, which it must be differentiating from some other type of eschatology— usually *apocalyptic eschatology* (even when the adjective *apocalyptic* is not appended). That confusion shows up as well in the use of the term *apocalyptic* as both noun and adjective. When using it as a noun, we speak simply of *apocalyptic* rather than of *apocalypticism*. When using it as an adjective, we speak of an *apocalyptic scenario* or an *apocalyptic sect*. As a noun, *apocalyptic* can stay equal to *eschatology*, but as an adjective it must be subordinate to it (or at least to something else that it qualifies).

The only way I can resolve that confusion is to take *eschatology* as a genus-level term and place *future, apocalyptic, present, realized,* or any other *type* of eschatology as a species-level distinction under that umbrella. I do not use *genus* and *species* here in any profoundly theoretical, taxonomically exact, or even grammatically precise way. I simply intend an upper-level term and its lower-level subterms. And I insist that, in such a case, one lower-level term should not be privileged above all the rest by being implicitly or explicitly equated with the upper-level one. I use those terms in the following very general sense: There are birds (genus) and there are crows and swallows (species). You should not get into an argument where one says, "That's a bird," and the other responds, "No, that's a crow." Upper-level terms should not be confused with lower-level terms.

Taking eschatology as a genus or upper-level term accords, actually, with scholarly practice in using phrases such as *realized eschatology, thorough-going eschatology, imminent eschatology, present eschatology, future eschatology,* and even (sometimes but not consistently) *apocalyptic eschatology*. It also helps us see how easily one might mix and match different types of eschatology, how easily one might slip or slide from one to the other, how readily a visionary might propose one type and an audience hear a different one. But to take *eschatology* openly and explicitly as a genus means that one must define it as such apart from and before any species are mentioned. So here goes.

Eschatology is one of the great and fundamental options of the human spirit. It is a profoundly explicit *no* to the profoundly implicit *yes* by which we usually accept life's normalcies, culture's presuppositions, and civilization's discontents. It is a basic and unusual world-negation or rejection as opposed to an equally basic but more usual world-affirmation or acceptance. For myself, left to myself, I would prefer to bury the term *eschatological* and use instead a term such as *world-negation*. But I presume that *eschatological* is here to stay, so I continue to use it.

In my own usage, the concept and term *eschatological* has three necessary components. First, it indicates a vision and/or program that is radical, counter-cultural, utopian, or this-world-negating. It presumes that there is something fundamentally wrong with the way of the world—not something that could easily be fixed, changed, or improved, but something so profoundly and radically wrong that only something profoundly and radically opposite could remedy it. Second, the mandate of that vision and/or program is taken to be divine, transcendental, supernatural; that is, it does not simply derive from natural or human forces or ideas. Eschatology is, as it were, a divinely mandated utopia, a divine radicality. Third, depending on *why* one announces that radical and cosmic *no* and *how* one intends to live out that *no* in a fundamentally negated world, there are various types and modes of the eschatological challenge. Those types are species of the genus-level term *eschatology*, or world-negation. Three such species will become important as I proceed. Let me state again that my intention is not to force others to use these expressions but rather to clarify the *concepts* I am using and the *terms* I accept for them. If others disagree with my concepts and/or terms, I ask only that they clarify their own positions as fully as I attempt to do here. It is important, however, that we distinguish the significant *concepts* involved and not just argue over different *words* for the same concepts.

Against that general background, I look next at the theologies of the *Q Gospel* and the *Gospel of Thomas* to specify as precisely and accurately as possible the types of eschatology they contain. That will take up the rest of this chapter. Then, in the next chapter, I will suggest the type of eschatology present in the Common Sayings Tradition. We already know, from our brief look at Patterson's fourfold redactional typology in the previous chapter, that the Common Sayings Tradition's eschatology is not that of the *Q Gospel* or the *Gospel of Thomas;* it is a third type of eschatology. But first, then, what about the eschatologies of our two sayings gospels?

Apocalyptic Eschatology

[In Q¹] *discipleship* is conceived in the most radical social and personal terms. It is rigorous in the extreme . . . involving separation from family and rejection of the norms of macro-society . . . and preparedness for poverty, homelessness and martyrdom. . . . More positively, it is understood as imitation of the merciful and generous God . . . and as "following" or "listening to" or "coming to" Jesus.

John S. Kloppenborg, *The Formation of Q*, p. 241

In any accounting of Q, sapiential elements play a major role. It is difficult to miss the pervasive eschatological tenor of those wisdom elements. But it is

another question whether the term apocalyptic is an accurate characterization for the redeployment of these wisdom materials.

John S. Kloppenborg, "Symbolic Eschatology and the
Apocalypticism of Q," p. 291

I begin with a short discussion on apocalypticism in general as a way to reiterate a description from my earlier book on *The Historical Jesus* (103–106). This
brief section is based on two recent articles, each giving a definition of apocalypticism—one too narrow and the other too broad. They will serve, therefore, as
an introduction to apocalypticism in the *Q Gospel*.

Unemployed Wisdom.

About twenty years ago, Jonathan Z. Smith deliberately moved back from
Jewish and Christian apocalyptic materials to look at earlier Babylonian and
Egyptian models, including especially "a variety of full blown apocalypses from
Egypt, spanning a period of almost two millennia." He proposed the following
definition, based on those materials: "Apocalypticism [is] *wisdom lacking a royal
patron*. (A definition which will serve at least to question both the 'lachrymose
theory' of apocalypticism as growing out of a situation of general persecution
and the popular recent theory that it reflects lower-class interests.) . . . Apocalypticism is Wisdom lacking a royal court and patron and therefore it surfaces during the period of Late Antiquity not as a response to religious persecution but as
an expression of the trauma of the cessation of native kingship. Apocalypticism is
a learned rather than a popular religious phenomenon. It is widely distributed
throughout the Mediterranean world and is best understood as part of the inner
history of the tradition within which it occurs rather than as a syncretism with
foreign (most usually held to be Iranian) influences" (1975:141, 149, 154–155).

A few qualifications, especially about that parenthetical remark concerning
lower-class interests and situations of persecution. Our written texts display, by
definition, the scribal interests of learned retainers or priests. It is another question what popular rather than scribal apocalypticism would have looked like.
There is no reason to presume that the Great Tradition (that is, the tradition of
the tiny elite minority) did not have an equivalent in the Little Tradition (that is,
the tradition of the vast peasant majority) concerning apocalypticism. In any
case, when Smith constructs what he calls "a model Egyptian apocalypse," he
emphasizes that the withdrawal of royal patronage is linked with the fact that
"foreigners have appeared and are acting as if they were Egyptian" and notes
that the ideal future involves the hope that "the foreigners shall be driven out"
(1975:142–143). I would consider foreign domination to be a form of persecution
and even concede that those so oppressed might weep as well as write. Smith's
definition is much too narrow.

Perceived Deprivation.

Adela Yarbro Collins wrote more recently that "apocalyptic faith often correlates with marginality, cognitive dissonance, and relative deprivation. 'Marginality' is a sociological term referring to the social status of an individual or group as anomalous, peripheral, or alien. 'Cognitive dissonance' refers to a state of mind that arises when there is significant disparity between expectations and reality. 'Relative deprivation' is a closely related social-scientific term. Simple or absolute 'deprivation' describes the plight of those affected by unmistakable catastrophes and disasters, of 'the poorest of the poor.' 'Relative deprivation' identifies the self-understanding of those whose expectations or perceived needs are not being satisfied" (1992:306). I would want, however, even before proceeding, to distinguish medically between perceived deprivation and patent paranoia and to balance morally the experience of personal or communal desperation and the imagination of cosmic catastrophe as its solution.

Collins also notes that apocalyptic scenarios can be invoked not only to subvert but also to support the status quo. "Those partial to the view of apocalypticism as socially revolutionary might ask whether the rhetoric supporting the social order has as good a claim to be called apocalyptic as that opposing the current order" (1992:307). Such pro-establishment usage often happens, as in medieval Christian apocalypticism, when counter-apocalypticism turns offensive scenarios into defensive ones. It can, of course, be used in both directions, and that too has a long history. Jewish prophecies in Daniel 2 and 7, written around 165 B.C.E., looked to a Fifth Empire, after that of the Babylonian, Medean, Persian, and Greek dominations. In that ideal future God would give power to his own persecuted people under their angelic protectors. But Caius Velleius Paterculus, writing his *Compendium of Roman History* in the early decades of the first century C.E., cited Aemilius Sura, writing in the early decades of the second century B.C.E., as explaining how the four empires of the Assyrians, Medes, Persians, and Macedonians ceded place to a Fifth Empire as "world power passed to the Roman people" (1.6; Shipley 14–15). Such usage by those in power should not lead to Collins's conclusion that "the function of apocalyptic literature and rhetoric may be described as the attempt to interpret the times in the universal framework of the true meaning of reality and history and to move its audience to adopt that interpretation and to live in accordance with it" (1992:306, 307, 308). That is, of course, a description of religion in general and not of apocalypticism in particular. If Smith's definition is too narrow, Collins's is now too broad.

Apocalypticism is the counterattack of those who perceive themselves to be marginalized religiously and/or theologically, spiritually and/or materially, politically and/or economically, at a level too profound for any less radical solution. The disease is fatal; only transcendental intervention can effect a cure. It is against such an understanding that I consider apocalypticism in the *Q Gospel*.

Radical Wisdom.

John Kloppenborg describes the eschatological message of Q[1] within the *Q Gospel* in terms of the social radicality of the kingdom of God. About the beatitudes, he notes, "They pronounce blessing upon a group defined by social and economic circumstances: poverty, hunger, sorrow and persecution. . . . The beatitudes are 'anti-beatitudes': they stand in contrast to the views of the conventional wisdom that those who dwell in affluence and safety are blessed. . . . Seen in this light, the Q beatitudes, while not typically sapiential in content, could well be characterized as the 'radical wisdom of the kingdom'. . . . Both the beatitudes and the admonitions [in Jesus' inaugural sermon in Q] are sapiential forms infused with eschatological content; both evince the presence of the kingdom, its radical nature and its radical demands" (1987a:189). Later that same phrase is extended to describe the entire sapiential stratum of Q[1] within the *Q Gospel*: "With some justification this stratum of Q could be termed 'the radical wisdom of the kingdom of God.' The dawning kingdom motivates the radical ethic of Q, and in turn the community members, by their mode of symbolic action (voluntary poverty, nonviolence, love of enemies, etc.), point to the presence of the reign of God among them" (1987a:242). This means, as mentioned earlier with regard to Robinson's generic title, Sayings of the Sages, that "in contrast to the generally conservative comportment of the [wisdom] instruction, Q presents an ethic of radical discipleship which reverses many of the conventions which allow a society to operate, such as principles of retaliation, the orderly borrowing and lending of capital, appropriate treatment of the dead, responsible self-provision, self-defense and honor of parents" (1987a:318). Again: "The sapiential speeches in Q, by means of their radical comportment, serve a properly kerygmatic function and point to the radical nature of the kingdom which is in the process of manifesting itself. Correspondingly, the imperatives specify the type of radical ethic which is the characteristic of those who have responded appropriately to this new reality" (1987a:320–321). Notice, once again for future reference, that Kloppenborg's "radical wisdom," like Arnal's "inversionary wisdom" seen earlier, is not just a matter of Jesus' words or even faith in Jesus' words; rather, it is a matter of accepting Jesus' lifestyle, following Jesus' program, and thereby living within the radicality of God's kingdom here and now. But what happens to this radical wisdom or sapiential eschatology of Q[1] when Q[2] is added onto it? Put another way, is the apocalypticism of Q[2] the same as that of Paul before it or Mark after it?

Primary or Secondary.

Even when Q² is added to Q¹ and the entire *Q Gospel* is proposing an apocalyptic eschatology, it is more additive than constitutive, more corrective than determinative, more secondary than primary. It is, in other words, a rather different brand of apocalyptic eschatology from that of Paul or Mark. I use the terms *primary* and *secondary* to distinguish the two types of apocalypticism, but what is at stake in this distinction? Is the apocalypticism essential or peripheral? Does it say, The end is imminent and therefore you must do this; if it were not imminent, you would not have to do it. Or, You must do this, whether the end is imminent or not; but you had better do it because it is coming soon. The former says not to buy a mortgage because the end is coming soon. The latter says not to rob a bank because the end is coming soon. Apocalypticism, in the second understanding, is added on as a coercive and cosmic threat to obtain obedience to what one should be doing in any case.

Kloppenborg calls this second or Q²-type apocalypticism *symbolic eschatology* (1987b). Notice, once again, that confusion of terminology, but now (from the passage used as an epigraph to this section) with *eschatology* and *apocalyptic* as opposing concepts: "In any accounting of Q, sapiential elements play a major role. It is difficult to miss the pervasive eschatological tenor of these wisdom elements. But it is another question whether the term apocalyptic is an accurate characterization for the redeployment of these wisdom materials. . . . [I]t is important to ask whether the presence of an eschatological horizon justifies the label 'apocalyptic'" (1987b:291–292). Kloppenborg argues that "Q uses threats of judgment and unsettling apocalyptic metaphors, not because it speaks from an 'apocalyptic situation' of anomie but because the symbolic character of apocalyptic language could be turned to Q's particular aims" (1987b:304). The basic message of the *Q Gospel* is still that of Q¹, but now Q¹ is buttressed by the threatening sanctions of Q². "Perhaps the most surprising of all is Q's restraint when describing the 'positive' outcome of eschatological intervention. While there is a virtual avalanche of images concerning the judgment and destruction of the impenitent, there is no mention at all of the resurrection and only passing references to the motifs of cosmic transformation, re-creation, restoration, and the like" (1987:299).

David Seeley has recently made a very similar point. In the *Q Gospel*, "futuristic eschatology never appears in those passages where the ethics and values on which a community might be based are set forth. Instead, with two exceptions [Q12:54–56 and Q 17:40–41,] it appears only in those situations where the ethics and values have already been set forth, but have encountered some sort of resistance. . . . Even in the two exceptions, there continues to be no link between futuristic eschatology and social formation." Furthermore, "when one seeks out

Q passages which do contain ethics and values, they are resistant to being read in futuristic, eschatological terms." His conclusion, like Kloppenborg's, is that "futuristic eschatology was a late development in the Q community, which was built up without it. . . . Later on, after the community encountered resistance by outsiders and doubts by insiders, it employed futuristic, eschatological threats" (144–145, 152–153).

The *Q Gospel* apocalypticism is certainly different from Pauline or even Markan apocalypticism, but I do not find *symbolic eschatology* a very useful term to underline that distinction. I prefer *apocalyptic eschatology* for all three authors, distinguishing *primary* apocalyptic eschatology for Paul and Mark from *secondary* apocalyptic eschatology for Q². I insist, of course, that those terms are not judgments but descriptions. I have no presumption that primary is somehow better than secondary. It is just different. Secondary apocalypticism is like a cosmic sanction—believed in, of course, but added on as one's primary and essential message is refused and rejected. You had better listen, it says, or else you will be punished at any moment and without warning. My term, therefore, for the completed *Q Gospel* is *secondary apocalyptic eschatology*, but by that I mean exactly the same concept as is described by Kloppenborg's phrase *symbolic eschatology*. It is the presence or absence of that theology that will determine in what follows when texts of the Common Sayings Tradition have or have not been redacted within the *Q Gospel*.

Ascetical Eschatology

The Christology, or Jesusology, of Thomas . . . derives from a naive application of manifold [Jewish] Wisdom speculation to Jesus. . . . Thomas' sophiological Christology [i.e., based on Jewish wisdom speculation] existed prior to or in ignorance of what many call gnosticism. . . . [I]t can be considered gnostic in no meaningful sense.
        Stevan L. Davies, *The Gospel of Thomas and Christian Wisdom*, pp. 146–147

Gnosticism seems to provide the most likely theological framework within which to understand the esotericizing trend one finds throughout Thomas. It may be seen in a number of sayings unique to Thomas, whose meaning has become almost entirely opaque. But more importantly, it can be seen in the manner in which Thomas treats a number of sayings known also from the synoptic tradition.
        Stephen J. Patterson, *The Gospel of Thomas and Jesus*, p. 227

What exactly is the theology of the *Gospel of Thomas*? This is a much more difficult question than the preceding one concerning the theology of the *Q Gospel*.

The views given in those epigraphs are diametrically opposed to one another: it is *not* Gnostic for Davies; it *is* Gnostic for Patterson. Yet those two books are the best, clearest, and most thorough English-language interpretations of this gospel. There are actually two separate aspects to that disagreement—the second one, to my mind, even more important than the first. The first question is whether the theology of the *Gospel of Thomas* is Gnostic or non-Gnostic. The second question is whether that theology, be it Gnostic or non-Gnostic, is theoretical or practical.

It may be helpful, before I begin that discussion, to repeat Kurt Rudolph's definition of Gnosticism, given as the epigraph to this book's Prologue: "This 'religion of knowledge' or of 'insight', as the Greek word *gnosis* may be translated, is . . . a dualistic religion, consisting of several schools and movements, which took up a definitely negative attitude towards the world and the society of the time, and proclaimed a deliverance ('redemption') of man precisely from the constraints of earthly existence through 'insight' into his essential relationship, whether as 'soul' or 'spirit',—a relationship temporarily obscured—with a supramundane realm of freedom and of rest. [It] spread through time and space, from the beginning of our era onwards, from the western part of the Near East (Syria, Palestine, Egypt, Asia Minor) to central and eastern Asia and Mediaeval Europe (14th cent.). . . . One can almost say that Gnosis followed the Church like a shadow; the Church could never overcome it, its influence had gone too deep. By reason of their common history they remain two—hostile—sisters" (1983:2, 368). Presuming some such definition of *Gnosis*, should the *Gospel of Thomas* be considered as gnostic, as a text of gnostic Christianity? I now continue the discussion under three rubrics.

Future or Past.

If your experience of the present world finds it radically amiss, you can only go, in terms of time, either to future or to past to find that ideal or utopian world whose existence profoundly subverts present normalcies and fundamentally criticizes present actualities. Negation of the present world goes either backward or forward in time to locate that perfect otherworld alternative. The *Q Gospel,* for example, could look forward to the end and imagine its perfect world through apocalyptic eschatology. But the *Gospel of Thomas* chose the opposite path: it went backward to a perfect beginning rather than forward to a perfect ending.

Begin with Jewish speculation about divine Wisdom and remember that, in Hebrew, Aramaic, Greek, and Latin, *wisdom* is a feminine noun:

The Lord created me [Wisdom] at the beginning of his work, the first of his acts of long ago. Ages ago I was set up, at the first, before the beginning of the earth. (Proverbs 8:22–23)

Before the ages, in the beginning, he created me [Wisdom], and for all the ages I shall not cease to be. (Sirach 24:9)

For she [Wisdom] is a reflection of eternal light, a spotless mirror of the working of God, and an image of his goodness. (Wisdom 7:26)

Hold together *creation, wisdom, light,* and *image,* reread the creation account in Genesis 1:1–2:2 against that background, and apply those readings to Jesus and to Christians.

God begins, in Genesis 1:3, by saying, "'Let there be light'; and there was light." So Jesus says in the *Gospel of Thomas* 77:1, "I am the light that is over all things. I am all: from me all came forth, and to me all attained." God ends his creative proclamations, in Genesis 1:26–27, by saying, "Let us make humankind in our image, according to our likeness," and the story concludes, in Genesis 2:2, with these words: "[O]n the seventh day God finished the work that he had done, and he rested on the seventh day from all the work that he had done." So the *Gospel of Thomas* 50 can present a small catechetical summary of Christian existence derived from God, light, image, and rest:

Jesus said, "If they say to you, 'Where have you come from?' say to them, 'We have come from the light, from the place where the light came into being by itself, established [itself], and appeared in their image.' If they say to you, 'Is it you?' say, 'We are its children, and we are the chosen of the living Father.' If they ask you, 'What is the evidence of your Father in you?' say to them, 'It is motion and rest.'" (*Gospel of Thomas* 50:1–3)

But what about Genesis 2–3? What about the story of the first sin, the fall, and the expulsion from Eden? To get back to that inaugural moment of creation, of wisdom and light, of motion and rest, you would have to get back before the story of the fall. It would be necessary to get back before sin—better still even earlier, before that androgynous being called Adam-the-Earthling was split into Adam-the-male and Eve-the-female. It was that primal and as-yet-undivided being who was made in God's image. It was those split beings, Adam and Eve, who sinned, fell, and were expelled from paradise. The ideal state imagined by the *Gospel of Thomas* is that of the primordial human being, Adam as one, as single and unsplit, as neither male nor female, as asexual. First came split, thence came the sexes, thence came sin. The *Gospel of Thomas* is about returning to that inaugural moment at the dawn of creation, before sin, before serpent, before split. It is about paradise regained from the past, not about parousia awaited in the future.

Sapiential or Gnostic.

All of the preceding discussion is absolutely within the realm of Jewish wisdom speculation focused on cosmic origins as told in Genesis 1–3 and now applied to Jesus and Christians. Stevan Davies is perfectly right to emphasize that background, and nobody has done it better than he has. He is also technically correct to call it, not an eschatology about *eschata*, or last things, but a protology about *prōta*, or first things. Both eschatology and protology, however, involve radical world-negation, and the term *eschatology* can be used for both as long as one recognizes that present time can be negated equally by looking to past beginnings or to future endings. But there is still the basic question of whether the eschatology (or protology) of the *Gospel of Thomas* is sapiential or Gnostic.

Here is the evidence. First, the *Gospel of Thomas* was discovered within a Gnostic library at Nag Hammadi. That fact proves, however, not how it was written but how it was read. Other non-Gnostic collections of sayings, such as the *Teachings of Sylvanus* and the *Sentences of Sextus,* were also found among those codices, not to speak of a section from Plato's *Republic.* Second, its trajectory continued into the *Book of Thomas the Contender* and the *Acts of Thomas.* That fact proves where it was going but not where it came from. Third, the *Gospel of Thomas* certainly lacks the full theology of later Gnosticism. It has, as Davies says, "the lack of Manichean or Marcionite dualism, the absence of any mythology of Sophia's fall or of Christ's ascent or descent through hostile realms populated by inimical Archons" or spirit-rulers (1983:146). Patterson, of course, agrees with that assessment: "Thomas is not a full-blown gnostic gospel" (1993a:227). His final and rather careful description is this: "What we have in Thomas is a book which stands between the wisdom collection on the one hand, and the gnostic revelation dialogue, in which the redeemer reveals to his followers secret words of knowledge (gnosis) on the other. It therefore helps to document that very important, though murky point of modulation between Jewish wisdom (and other Near Eastern traditions which make use of the descending/ascending redeemer mythos) and Gnosticism" (1993a:227).

What we need to do is not continue an unproductive debate between Gnostic versus non-Gnostic but see if it is possible to describe the theology of the *Gospel of Thomas* in such a way that it could later go in either direction. And here a second and more serious disagreement about theory or praxis arises between Davies and Patterson. Its consideration may help to settle this first disagreement about the text's being Gnostic or non-Gnostic.

Theoretical or Practical.

The question is whether the *Gospel of Thomas* advocated a purely internal renunciation of material goods and worldly interests but allowed or presumed their full external usage (accompanied, of course, by spiritual detachment), or whether it demanded specific social actions, such as asceticism and celibacy. Was the return to a pre-split stage at the dawn of creation effected precisely by celibate asceticism?

Davies thinks that "the degree to which this renunciation is to govern social behavior is debatable. 'If you do not fast as regards the world, you will not find the kingdom' (saying 27) probably advocates avoiding the ordinary perspective on the world in favor of the preferred perspective. If fasting is of this intellectual variety, it means that one cannot hold two contradictory perspectives simultaneously. In other words, the world cannot be understood to be the kingdom and, at the same time, not to be the kingdom. Since fasting from food is disapproved twice (sayings 14, 104) and no ascetic praxis is otherwise recommended, fasting from the world must *not* be considered asceticism" (1992:673). I disagree. The reason temporary fasting on this day or that is negated in the *Gospel of Thomas*, along with all other ordinary piety, is that it is not nearly radical enough. One does not temporarily fast from bread; one permanently fasts from the world. My own working hypothesis, therefore, is that worldly renunciation in the *Gospel of Thomas* involved very specific praxis—namely, celibate asceticism. It may be left open whether all Thomas Christians *observed* such rigor or whether there was, as is common in such world-negating religions, a differentiation between the minority of the perfect and the elect (the spiritual elite who accepted full external renunciation) and the majority of ordinary believers (who accepted, at best, an internal detachment). In any case, on this point, Patterson is much more persuasive than Davies.

Patterson proposes at the start of his book that "the dominant ethos among Thomas Christians was a kind of social radicalism . . . including (though not primarily) homelessness, willful poverty, begging, the rejection of family and local piety, and a critique of the political powers that be" (1993a:4). He repeats that thesis at the book's conclusion: "[In the *Gospel of Thomas*] the rejection of apocalyptic eschatology in favor of the notion that the kingdom might be actualized here and now coordinates well with the social radicalism of this movement. Social radicalism is the attempt to live out of an alternative reality, an alternative dominion. As such, it is the praxis of a theological vision" (1993a:214). It is practical not just theoretical, physical not just mental, material not just intellectual. It is of the body and not just of the mind. It touches society not just as an idea but as an action.

Furthermore, for Patterson "this is not realized eschatology, it is *actualized* eschatology. If the kingdom is to exist at all, it is up to Thomas Christianity to make it exist, to be the leaven (Thom 96), to shine in the world (Thom 24), to enable people to see the kingdom in its full potential 'spread out upon the earth' (Thom 113). In this way the kingdom is present, it is real. It must be tended, lest it slip away (Thom 97); it must be kept in shape, well practiced (Thom 98)" (1993a:210). In that sense the better term might be *realizable* or *actualizable* eschatology rather than either *realized* or *actualized*. It is something potential and possible, not just actual and accomplished. Terms such as Patterson's "social radicalism" for the *Gospel of Thomas* and Kloppenborg's "radical wisdom" for the *Q Gospel* help flesh out what Koester termed the "realized eschatology" of those twin texts. Even more important, though, they indicate that eschatology was realized or realizable not just in the *words* but in the *deeds* of Jesus and his companions. It was actualized or actualizable not just in the *ideas* but in the *lives* of Jesus and his companions. It was an eschatology present in the wisdom of social radicalism. I agree strongly with Patterson against Davies that the theology of the *Gospel of Thomas* had public social consequences.

Next, the social radicalism of the *Gospel of Thomas* involved celibate asceticism. "If eschatology," as Patterson continues, "is a mythological challenge to the world as it exists, the mythological expression of hope for something better, asceticism offers a real, present challenge to the world. It calls into question the ways of the world, its standards, its goals, its notion of what is meaningful in life. Thomas Christianity's social radicalism, as a form of asceticism, has precisely this effect" (1993a:211).

Finally, it is quite possible to derive celibate asceticism from the type of Jewish speculations about wisdom's role in Genesis 1–3 that was seen above. You could even claim that celibate asceticism was an imperative hidden within those texts and that esoteric or secret wisdom was involved. But the *Gospel of Thomas* seeks to find such hidden wisdom not only in Genesis 1–3 but in the words of Jesus, so that they become themselves a source of hidden wisdom. In other words, for the *Gospel of Thomas*, ascetic world-negation is also esoteric, secret, hidden. The text demands, in its opening words, that one understands "the secret sayings that the living Jesus spoke and Didymos Judas Thomas recorded," for, as Jesus said, "Whoever discovers the interpretation of these sayings will not taste death." It is necessary at this point to distinguish such *esoteric* ascetical eschatology from *ordinary* ascetical eschatology. In that latter theology one abandons the world because it is too tempting or distracting. Such an ascetical eschatology might appeal to common sense or even to rational-choice theory. It might argue that it is obviously more reasonable to spend this short life in total and exclusive preparation for an eternal next one. In such a theology no hidden or esoteric interpretation is required. But the *Gospel of Thomas* is esoteric ascetical eschatology, a world-negation based on secret wisdom demanding celibacy as return to the unsplit state of the Primal Androgynous Being.

Some thoughts in summary. The debate over Gnostic versus non-Gnostic status for the *Gospel of Thomas* is not productive. As Davies has demonstrated

quite adequately, that gospel can be totally understood within Jewish speculation about creation, wisdom, and Genesis 1–3—and could have been so understood even if Gnosticism had never existed. On the other hand, since Gnosticism
did exist, it is hard not to see in the *Gospel of Thomas* what Patterson has called
"rudimentary Gnosticism," even while admitting that "the extent of [its] gnosticizing character is not yet fully charted" and that it "is not a full blown gnostic
gospel" (1993a:218, 133, 226). It is, in fact, precisely a borderline text that could
have been pulled either toward or away from gnosticism. It was, as history
unfolded, pulled more in the former direction. I find, however, that it is much
more helpful to define it in terms that specify more closely than *Gnostic* or *non-
Gnostic* its precise form of world-negation. It is, as I have noted, *esoteric ascetical
eschatology,* and it is the presence or absence of that theology that will determine
in what follows when texts of the Common Sayings Tradition have been redacted (or not) within the *Gospel of Thomas.*

CHAPTER 16

ETHICAL ESCHATOLOGY

He comes to us as One unknown, without a name, as of old, by the lake-side, He came to those men who knew Him not. He speaks to us the same word: "Follow thou me!" and sets us to the tasks which He has to fulfil for our time. He commands. And to those who obey Him, whether they be wise or simple, He will reveal Himself in the toils, the conflicts, the sufferings which they shall pass through in His fellowship, and, as an ineffable mystery, they shall learn in their own experience Who He is.

Albert Schweitzer, The Quest of the Historical Jesus, p. 402

To recall where we are, connect Patterson's fourfold typology for the redaction of the Common Sayings Tradition (discussed in Chapter 14) with the two eschatological theologies of the *Q Gospel* and the *Gospel of Thomas*. The statistics would now read like this:

Type 1: 24% (9 out of 37 units) is redacted toward esoteric ascetical eschatology in the *Gospel of Thomas* but not toward secondary apocalyptic eschatology in the *Q Gospel*.

Type 2: 8% (3 out of 37 units) is redacted toward secondary apocalyptic eschatology in the *Q Gospel* but not toward esoteric ascetical eschatology in the *Gospel of Thomas*.

Type 3: 19% (7 out of 37 units) is redacted both toward esoteric ascetical eschatology in the *Gospel of Thomas* and also toward secondary apocalyptic eschatology in the *Q Gospel*.

Type 4: 49% (18 out of 37 units) is redacted neither toward esoteric ascetical eschatology in the *Gospel of Thomas* nor toward secondary apocalyptic eschatology in the *Q Gospel*.

That data presses the question already asked by Patterson: "If Q and *Thomas* lie on diverging trajectories each grounded in, yet moving away from, an early sapiential tradition, what can be said about this early tradition itself?" (1993b:194).

Negatively, we already know what that "early tradition" is *not*. It is neither esoteric ascetical eschatology nor secondary apocalyptic eschatology. Positively, then, what *is* it? That is my primary question in this chapter: What ideology or theology or eschatology is present in the Common Sayings Tradition? In answer I identify what I term *ethical eschatology*, a doctrine whose presence in the Common Sayings Tradition I will demonstrate in Part VII. But first, here in the concluding chapter to Part VI, I want to introduce and think about this third type of eschatology.

I very deliberately chose both the epigraph above and the next one below from Albert Schweitzer, who lived from 1875 to 1965. In 1906 he published a review of preceding historical Jesus research (reissued in 1969) and pronounced it flawed to the core because it refused to face the eschatological vision of Jesus. I begin with Schweitzer because he points forcibly to the twin difficulties in understanding that eschatology. First, he himself equates the terms *apocalyptic* and *eschatology*, and he does so without any explicit discussion. (He generally uses the term *eschatology*, but in such a way that it means *apocalyptic*.) Indeed, the terminological and even logical confusion seen in Chapter 15—confusion that has pervaded contemporary discussion of eschatology and apocalypticism—stems in no small measure from Schweitzer himself. Second, while he describes Jesus as a misguided apocalyptic eschatologist, he still thinks it quite possible to follow Jesus; indeed, he finds it mandatory for the Christian to do so. The epigraph above cites the closing lines of his powerful 1906 classic. But are his words just climactic gush, romantic peroration, Renan in German? For this is the question they invoke: What type of eschatology is both inaccurate and imperative, both misguided and mandatory, both wrong and right at the same time?

Out of Europe

Men feared that to admit the claims of *eschatology* would abolish the significance of His words for our time; and hence there was a feverish eagerness to discover in them any elements that might be considered not *eschatologically* conditioned. . . . But in reality that which is eternal in the words of Jesus is due to the very fact that they are based on an *eschatological* worldview, and contain the expression of a mind for which the contemporary world with its historical and social circumstances no longer had any existence. . . . Because it is thus preoccupied with the general, the universal, modern theology is determined to find its *world-accepting* ethic in the teaching of Jesus. Therein lies its weakness. The world *affirms* itself automatically; the modern spirit cannot but *affirm* it. But why on that account abolish the conflict between modern life, with the *world-affirming* spirit which inspires it as a whole, and the *world-negating* spirit of Jesus? Why spare the spirit of the individual man its appointed task of fighting its way through the *world-negation* of Jesus, of contending with Him at every step over the value of material and intellectual goods—a conflict in which it may never rest? . . . This general *affirmation* of the world, however, if it is to be Christian, must in the individual spirit be Christianized and transfigured by the personal *rejection* of the world which is preached in the sayings of Jesus.

Albert Schweitzer, *The Quest of the Historical Jesus,* p. 402

The words I italicized in that epigraph are basic to my argument. In the first paragraph Schweitzer sets up a dichotomy between Jesus' eschatological message and those moderns who refuse to accept it as such. But the next paragraph switches the dichotomy to one between the world-negating message of Jesus and the world-affirming interpretation of modern researchers. Schweitzer reiterates that disjunction a few times within that same paragraph. On the one hand, there is the "world-accepting ethic . . . world-affirming spirit . . . general affirmation of the world" from moderns. On the other, there is the "world-negating spirit . . . world-negation . . . personal rejection of the world" from Jesus. For Schweitzer, then, *eschatology* and *world-negation* are synonyms.

Schweitzer, however, also interjects the term *apocalyptic* into this debate. On the one hand, he uses *eschatology* and *apocalyptic* to mean the same thing, referring on subsequent pages to, first, "the eschatology of the time of Jesus" (1969:368) and, then, "the apocalyptic movement at the time of Jesus" (1969:370). On the other hand, in between, he distinguishes between "two eschatologies"— one prophetic, with Elijah as hero, and one apocalyptic, with Daniel as hero. He distinguishes them by claiming that apocalyptic eschatology is created by "external events," while prophetic eschatology is created by "great personalities" (1969:369–370), a distinction whose romanticism would probably not hold up well to close scrutiny. But, leaving that explanation aside, we now have (1) *eschatology* used as a genus with at least two species *(apocalyptic* and *prophetic)* and (2) *eschatology* used as a synonym for one of those species. That, I think, is the root of our definitional problem. You cannot have it both ways; you cannot, under any definitions, have *apocalyptic* equal to *apocalyptic eschatology* equal to *eschatology.* When you attempt to do so, you privilege one species as equal to its genus.

Schweitzer reconstructed a Jesus who was quite wrong about the imminent end of the world and was quite mistaken in his attempt to force the hand of God by going deliberately toward martyrdom in Jerusalem. This is his justly famous description of that delusion: "There is silence all around. The Baptist appears, and cries: 'Repent, for the Kingdom of Heaven is at hand.' Soon after that comes Jesus, and in the knowledge that He is the coming Son of Man lays hold of the wheel of the world to set it moving on that last revolution which is to bring all ordinary history to a close. It refuses to turn, and He throws Himself upon it. Then it does turn; and crushes Him. Instead of bringing in the eschatological conditions, He has destroyed them. The wheel rolls onward, and the mangled body of the one immeasurably great Man, who was strong enough to think of Himself as the spiritual ruler of mankind and to bend history to His purpose, is hanging upon it still. That is His victory and His reign" (1969:370–371).

All of that is clear enough, but, having interpreted Jesus as flatly wrong in his mission and message, Schweitzer did not respond by leaving the Christian church. He responded by leaving imperial Europe. And this, in his own words, was how his friends reacted: "What seemed to my friends the most irrational thing in my plan was that I wanted to go to Africa, not as a missionary, but as a doctor, and thus when already thirty years of age burdened myself as a beginning with a long period of laborious study. . . . I wanted to be a doctor that I might be able to work without having to talk. For years I had been giving myself out in words, and it was with joy that I had followed the calling of theological teacher and of preacher. But this new form of activity I could not represent to myself as being talking about the religion of love, but only as an actual putting it into practice" (1933:114–115).

The irony is, of course, that he would not have been accepted as a *missionary*. He was barely accepted, because of his historical criticism of the New Testament, even as a *doctor*. The Paris Missionary Society's Committee had recently turned down a missionary "because his scientific conviction did not allow him to answer with an unqualified *Yes* the question whether he regarded the Fourth Gospel as the work of the Apostle John." When Schweitzer was invited to appear before that same committee to be examined on his orthodoxy, he declined. Jesus, he said, had conducted no such examination on his first disciples. He had only asked them "to follow Him." As a compromise, Schweitzer agreed to visit the committee members individually and allow theological questions on that basis. He was eventually accepted, but with two conditions. He was not to confuse the missionaries with his learning or the natives with his preaching (1933:138–139).

That was Schweitzer in 1913. Now let me back up to an earlier point in his autobiography. The idea of going to Africa had been in his mind for a long time. It was "conceived so long ago as my student days. It struck me as incomprehensible that I should be allowed to lead such a happy life, while I saw so many people around me wrestling with care and suffering. Even at school I had felt stirred whenever I got a glimpse of the miserable home surroundings of some of my schoolfellows and compared them with the absolutely ideal conditions in which we children of the parsonage at Günsbach lived. . . . I could not help thinking continually of others who were denied that happiness by their material circumstances or their health. Then one brilliant summer morning at Günsbach, during the Whitsuntide holidays—it was in 1896—there came to me, as I awoke, the thought that I must not accept this happiness as a matter of course, but must give something in return for it. . . . I would consider myself justified in living till I was thirty for science and art, in order to devote myself from that time forward to the direct service of humanity. Many a time already had I tried to settle what meaning lay hidden for me in the saying of Jesus! 'Whosoever would save his life shall lose it, and whosoever shall lose his life for My sake and the Gospels shall save it.' Now the answer was found. In addition to the outward, I now had inward happiness" (1933:102–103). His first thought was "some activity in Europe," and he worked there for a time, educating "abandoned or neglected children" and helping "tramps and discharged prisoners" (1933:103–104). This social work, which he did in conjunction with scholarly research, did not surprise anyone. What his friends found somewhat scandalous, as he admitted above, was giving up theological investigation for medical study and Europe for Africa.

Schweitzer's own life warns us that his apocalyptic eschatology may not be as simple as we think. He summarized Jesus' message, in one of the quotations above, as announcing the arrival of the kingdom of God, "that last revolution which is to bring all ordinary history to a close" (1969:370). I take that to mean the end of the space-time universe. After that consummation, only some sort of heaven or hell could be imagined. No life on this earth, however ideal or utopian, could be proclaimed by such a vision. We have, if I understand Schweitzer's Jesus correctly, not heaven on earth but earth in heaven. But Schweitzer, having described Jesus' vision as flatly wrong, offered us the first epigraph above, that famous closure to his book on the search for the historical Jesus.

Those words, however, are *only* words—powerful and beautiful words, to be sure, but still just magnificent crescendo to a magnificent book. But we also know what Schweitzer had intended to do for a full decade before he ever wrote those words—what he ultimately *did* do. He did not leave Christianity because Jesus was wrong; he left Europe because Jesus was right. And, in case we might miss the point, he reminds us in his autobiography that he left home "on Good Friday 1913" (1933:210). He went to Lambaréné, inland from the Atlantic coast and just south of the equator on the River Ogowe, in what was then the French colony of Gaboon. He and Helen Bresslau, whom he married in 1912, went at their own expense to spare the Paris Missionary Society any financial burden. But they had to obtain subsidies somewhere, and that meant "a round of begging visits among my acquaintances," during which "the tone of my reception became markedly different when it came out that I was there, not a visitor but as a beggar" (1933:136).

Judging by Schweitzer's commitment to service, Jesus' challenging "world-negation" was profoundly right, even though its apocalyptic or eschatological expression was misguided and even deluded. That world-negation demanded of Schweitzer a very precise response. When his friends asked why he had not chosen to be a *missionary* in Africa or a doctor in *Europe*—in other words, why, specifically, a *doctor* in *Africa*—he explained that it was all very personal and individual. It was not political or social. Nevertheless, it had, at base, to do with ethics and injustice, with the intuition that human inequality cannot simply be ignored or accepted.

I am being very careful not to make Schweitzer a liberation theologian ahead of his time. He did not say that European greed had created African misery. He did not raise economic, political, and social issues. He did not act in radical protest against European imperialism (which, when he left for Africa, had about six more months to live before it brought down on itself horrors as insufferable as any it had earlier inflicted on its colonies). He did not say that he was withdrawing from the colonial evils created by his country and his continent and that, in protest against them, he was heading off to heal what they had hurt. It was not apocalyptic eschatology that sent the Schweitzers to Africa, although in 1913 the European world was staggering toward Armageddon. It was not ascetical eschatology that sent them there, although their lives in Africa were probably harder than those in many monasteries. I need another term for what it was, and *ethical eschatology* is the best I can discover. I repeat that this eschatology is, as it were, a personal and individual ending-of-one's-world, but its logic, whether Schweitzer knew it or not, pointed beyond itself. He knew that it pointed back to Jesus, but he did not say that it pointed toward resisting systemic evil in political and economic (not just in personal and individual) ways.

Jesus, Schweitzer might have said, was completely right and completely wrong about eschatology. Schweitzer, I would say, was completely right and completely wrong about Jesus. But, in both cases, it is the right that was determinative, the wrong that was irrelevant. Schweitzer called his autobiography *Out of My Life and Thought,* and that order is significant. Did Schweitzer get the historical Jesus right or wrong? In his thought he got him wrong, but in his life he got him right. And so, most appropriately, he received the Nobel Prize not for literature but for peace.

Itinerant Radicalism

Their *ethical radicalism* makes Jesus' sayings absolutely impracticable as a regulative for every-day behavior. So we are faced all the more inescapably with the question: Who passed on sayings like these by word of mouth over a period of thirty years and more? Who took them seriously? . . . The sayings tradition is characterized by an *ethical radicalism* that is shown most noticeably in the renunciation of a home, family, and possessions. From the precepts that have to do with these things, we can arrive analytically at some conclusions about the life-style that was characteristic of the people who passed on the texts. . . . We can now formulate our thesis: the *ethical radicalism* of the sayings transmitted to us is the radicalism of itinerants. . . . It is only in this context that the ethical precepts which match the way of life can be passed on without being unconvincing. . . . And that was possible only for homeless charismatics.

Gerd Theissen, *Social Reality and the Early Christians*, pp. 36, 37, 40

The words I italicized in that epigraph indicate why I chose the term *ethical eschatology* for the perspective found in the Common Sayings Tradition. That new label combines, as it were, the "eschatology" of "world-negation" from Schweitzer with "ethical radicalism" from Theissen. Lest you imagine, by the way, that I am inventing some unique theology for a unique Jesus, let me assure you that I find ethical eschatology in the nonviolent resistance to structural evil put forward by such diverse people as the Jain Mahatma Gandhi, the Catholic Dorothy Day, and the Protestant Martin Luther King, Jr. If enough people lived like *they* did—lived in nonviolent protest against systemic evil, against the normalcies of this world's discrimination, exploitation, and oppression—the result would be a new world we could hardly imagine. That is eschatology—possibly the only real type available to us.

But, in any case, back to Theissen. Although I am adapting his language, my *ethical eschatology* is somewhat different from his *ethical radicalism*. I emphasize initially, however, my great respect for his foundational work on this subject and my profound gratitude for his contribution.

When Theissen introduced this subject almost twenty-five years ago, he discussed earliest Christianity in the Jewish homeland using words translated as "itinerant radicalism," "ethical radicalism," "wandering charismatics," and "charismatic begging." Later he also drew attention to the similarities between those itinerant preachers and the Cynic missionaries of the first two centuries (1992:33–59). But he also emphasized the local communities who supported those itinerants, devoting one chapter in his *Sociology of Early Palestinian Christianity* to the "wandering charismatics" and a second one to "the sympathizers in the local communities." In that book, he noted that "there was a complementary relationship between the wandering charismatics and the local communities: wandering charismatics were the decisive spiritual authorities in the local communities and local communities were the indispensable social and material basis for the wandering charismatics. . . . It is impossible to understand the Jesus movement and the synoptic tradition exclusively in terms of the wandering charismatics. In addition to them there were 'local communities', settled groups of sympathizers" (1978:7, 17).

Richard Horsley criticizes Theissen's analysis on several major points. First, he finds his sociological basis too conservative to handle adequately the radical critique of society stemming from Jesus' program. "What appears in the Gospel traditions to pose a sharp challenge to the ruling groups of the society is transformed, by means of functionalist sociology, into a movement supposedly striving to control conflict and maintain the social system" (1989:39). A sociology emphasizing conflict and resistance would have been more useful for Theissen than one emphasizing functional harmony and structural balance.

Second, despite using the word *complementarity* to describe the relationship between itinerants and householders, between wandering charismatics and local supporters, Theissen seems regularly to privilege those itinerant charismatics as somehow more important, more significant, and even more Christian. And yet, as Horsley notes, there are key sayings that "give regulations for the way in which traveling preachers and healers are to obtain support from local communities. They thus provide for a sort of elementary division of labor within the nascent Jesus movement. There is simply no justification in the sources for Theissen's writing . . . as if the Jesus movement consisted primarily of wandering charismatics. Similarly, Theissen's contention that the wandering charismatics are the key to understanding the Jesus movement is simply not borne out by the evidence" (1989:50). That is surely correct. When Jesus tells people to do the same he is doing in crucial sayings to be seen below—for example, the Q *Gospel* in Luke 10:4–11 or Mark 6:7–13—there is an interaction of eating and healing, of itinerants and householders, of the destitute and the poor.

Third, concerning those last-mentioned sayings, Horsley contends that "the 'mission' would thus appear to have more to do with the revitalization of local community life than with a new, itinerant 'way of life' as an object in itself. The key seems to be the purpose and pattern of the itinerancy as focused on social renewal, not an individual life-style of self-sufficiency and independence" (1989:117). That is, once again, quite correct, and I consider below how precisely that "revitalization of local community life" actually operates within the dialectic of itinerant and householder.

Finally, in terms of Theissen's parallels between the kingdom-of-God movement and the Cynic movement, Horsley states that "whereas the Cynics lived without home and possessions as an intentional 'way of life,' the delegates of Jesus left home, possessions, and family behind *temporarily* as an unavoidable but more incidental matter necessitated by their mission" (1989:117, my italics). That, I think, is but half right. There is, as we shall see below, a clear difference between the symbolic attire of the Cynic itinerants and that of the kingdom itinerants. For the former, taking a knapsack and staff indicated personal self-sufficiency. For the latter, *not* taking a knapsack and staff indicated communal dependency. So far so good. But did all those fierce and terrible sayings about home, family, and possessions mean only *temporary* departures and *transient* abandonments? That brings up a much more telling critique and a much better explanation of what was actually at stake.

About a decade before Horsley, Wolfgang Stegemann criticized Theissen's itinerancy proposal on an even more fundamental issue. Did those itinerants leave home, family, and possessions voluntarily at the call of Jesus, or had they lost them all already? Was Jesus *demanding* dispossession or *presuming* it? "The concept of 'ethical norms' (or 'ethical radicalism') assumes that *voluntary renunciations* are in question here. . . . The 'lack of possessions' means for Theissen a 'renunciation of possessions' and not simply the situation of the poor person who has nothing. The abandonment of family . . . is not the result of some social constraint but an 'ethical' consequence of the call to discipleship. For this reason Theissen justly compares the early Christian wandering charismatics to the wandering Cynic philosophers. These two movements, as Theissen sees them, did not make an ethical virtue out of social necessity (beggary), but took real beggary as the model for their own deviant behavior" (155).

That presses hard on the basic issue. Was this itinerancy voluntary in origin? Did it begin as some form of freely chosen renunciation? Was it, in other words, asceticism? Stegemann suggests an alternative reading, which is better than Theissen's *voluntary* abandonment or Horsley's *temporary* abandonment of normal life. "The first followers of Jesus, like their master, were from the poor and hungry, not as the result of any renunciation of possessions but because in fact they possessed nothing" (166). He suggests that modern well-off exegetes may find that difficult to take, because criticism is then "voiced not by ethically motivated heroes of renunciation but by probably very unattractive characters" (166). To be accurate, however, Theissen himself had mentioned (but not emphasized) that same point, not in his original 1974 essay but in a 1977 article: "It has no doubt by now become clear that most socially uprooted people came from the middle classes. It was the people who had declined into poverty, rather than the people born in poverty, who set out to pass their lives beyond the boundaries of normal life, or even to seek for ways of renewing society" (1992:88). While that term "middle classes" may be inaccurate for first-century realities, the distinction between "declined" or "born" into poverty is crucial for understanding Jesus and his first companions.

I accept, therefore, Theissen's proposal and Stegemann's emphasis that the kingdom-of-God movement began by making "an ethical virtue out of social necessity"—that is, by refusing to accept the injustice they were experiencing as normal and acceptable to God. Those first itinerants were, like Jesus himself, primarily dispossessed peasant freeholders, tenants, or sharecroppers. They were not invited to give up everything but to accept their loss of everything as judging not them but the system that had done it to them. It was ethical to accept the abandonment of such a system and no longer to participate in its exploitative normalcy.

This understanding will be clarified in studying individual units from the Common Sayings Tradition in the next chapter. Before we turn to that, though, I want to look in conclusion at apocalypticism, asceticism, and ethicism as modes of eschatology separate from one another but capable of diverse combinations with one another.

Apocalypticism, Asceticism, Ethicism

The conflict over, and eventual triumph of, asceticism should not be cast in terms of a debate on the holy, or of a reaction against rationalism and a rise in superstition and credulity, but in terms of the nature of power in society. On the one side is structure, institution, authority, and accepted norms, on the other is inspiration, individualism, charismatic leadership, and alternative values. So long as the latter nexus was perceived as antithetical to and destructive of the former, the radical ascetic, who was the locus of these phenomena, would remain suspect and an enemy to the prevailing social order.

James A. Francis, *Subversive Virtue*, p. 185

Eschatology is divine radicality. It is a fundamental negation of the present world's normalcy based on some transcendental mandate. In the tradition with which we are involved, that transcendental mandate was the will or law of the covenantal God of Judaism. That God, as we saw in Chapter 12, was a God of justice and righteousness for all the earth, a God who stood on the side of the oppressed against the oppressor, a God who opposed systemic evil not because it was systemic but because it was evil. In that tradition the kingdom of God was always an eschatological challenge. It stood against the kingdom of injustice and undermined, in vision and program, its seeming inevitability.

The primary indication that the Common Sayings Tradition was eschatological is that it, like the Q *Gospel* and the *Gospel of Thomas* after it, speaks repeatedly of the kingdom of God. This is the evidence in summary statistics (with the details given in Appendix 6):

Gospel of Thomas	17 instances in 132 sayings	13%
Q *Gospel*	10 instances in 101 sayings	10%
Common Sayings Tradition	4 instances in 37 sayings	11%

That is a relatively constant percentage across those three sources. And it shows, above all, that the kingdom—be it of God, of the Father, or of the heavens—was solidly there in the tradition from the earliest evidence we have. (All those qualifications, by the way, indicate the same reality.) Kingdom eschatology did not arise in either the *Q Gospel* or the *Gospel of Thomas*. It was already there in the Common Sayings Tradition. We are, in other words, dealing with three divergent eschatologies of the kingdom of God.

DISTINCTION AND COMBINATION

Apocalyptic eschatology (or apocalypticism) negates this world by announcing that in the future, and usually the imminent future, God will act to restore justice in an unjust world. Whether the result will be earth in heaven or heaven on earth can remain quite vague and open. Whether the space-time universe of ordinary experience will continue or not can also remain vague and open. But two aspects are not negotiable if apocalypticism is intended. One aspect is that the primary event is an interventional act of God. Human actors may certainly be important in *preparation*, by their sufferings, in *initiation*, by their symbolic activities, or even in *cooperation*, by military action under angelic or divine control. All of those human details may be open for discussion, but what is not debatable is that some intervening act of overwhelming divine power is imagined and invoked. In plain language, we are waiting for God.

The other aspect that is not negotiable is the total absence of evil and injustice after the apocalyptic consummation takes place. It will not be just a case of kinder, gentler injustice but of a perfectly just world. There will be no evil or evildoers in this postapocalyptic world. One could imagine an apocalyptic revelation of God such that all humans thereafter would freely and voluntarily live together in perfect justice, peace, and love. Willingly and without constraint. That is, after all, how theology has always explained human free will in an after-this-life heaven. But that is not the standard apocalyptic scenario for the unjust. There is all too often a transition from justice to revenge, a divine vengeance that results in human slaughter. When those two aspects are combined, apocalyptic eschatology almost inevitably presumes a violent God who establishes the justice of nonviolence through the injustice of violence. That may well be understandable in particular human circumstances. That may well be understandable when a genocide of *them* from above is invoked to prevent their genocide of *us* here below. But all too often, be it of pagans by Jews or of Jews by Christians, apocalypticism is perceived as a divine ethnic cleansing whose genocidal heart presumes a violent God of revenge rather than a nonviolent God of justice.

Ascetical eschatology (or asceticism) negates this world by withdrawing from normal human life in terms of food, sex, speech, dress, or occupation. It may be personal, as with hermits or anchorites, or communal, as with nuns and monks. It may be conducted privately so that nobody else knows about it or done publicly so that everyone knows about it. It may be practiced in small caves within the emptiness of the desert or lived behind high walls in the midst of the city. Because it involves celibacy, if enough people accepted the ascetic vision, this human world would quite surely and definitely come to an end. Ascetical eschatology postulates a divine vocation and, indeed, requires constant divine empowerment to be humanly tolerable. I myself was a monk for twenty years in a Roman Catholic medieval order, and it was understood that, during the first-year novitiate, one would not be allowed home for any family funerals. Even a parent's funeral belonged "to the world," and we no longer did. We were "out of this world." That was in 1950, and observance was strict. (In 1951, coming from Ireland to the United States, I was sent on the first berth available. It happened to be second-class on the *Queen Mary*. That too was out of this world.) There are many different explanations for the need for ascetical eschatology. The world could be intrinsically evil as the product of an evil creator. It could have become evil because of human injustice. It could be good but simply inferior to higher realities. The material world and the physical body could be taken as distractions to mind, soul, or spirit. Though reasons and explanations can differ, even fundamentally, the lifestyle of celibate asceticism remains the same. One withdraws from the world's normalcy by abstaining totally from sex and procreation and abstemiously from food or drink and from speech or conversation.

Ethical eschatology (or *ethicism*) negates the world by actively protesting and nonviolently resisting a system judged to be evil, unjust, and violent. It is not a question of this group or that government needing some changes or improvements. Ethical eschatology is directed at the world's *normal* situation of discrimination and violence, exploitation and oppression, injustice and unrighteousness. It looks at the systemic or structural evil that surrounds and envelops us all and, in the name of God, refuses to cooperate or participate any longer in that process. Instead, it sets out to oppose systemic evil without succumbing to its own violence. In ethicism, as distinct from apocalypticism, God is waiting for us to act. And in ethicism, as distinct from apocalypticism, God is not a violent God. Ethicism is present wherever nonviolent resistance to structural evil appears in this world. And the courage for it derives from union with transcendental nonviolence. It was present, for example, in these two cases from before and after the ministry of Jesus:

Unarmed Jews gathered before the prefect Pilate at the Roman headquarters in Caesarea, probably in 26 or 27 C.E., to protest his introduction of imperial images on military standards into Jerusalem. After five days of peaceful demonstration, Pilate called in his troops; however, according to Josephus in the *Jewish War* 2.174, "the Jews, as by concerted action, flung themselves in a body on the ground, and exclaimed that they were ready rather to die than to transgress the law." In a separate incident, unarmed Jews gathered before the governor

Petronius, who planned, with a force of two or three legions, to place a statue of the emperor Caligula in Jerusalem's Temple. Faced with that impending desecration in 40 C.E., a "vast multitude" of men, women, and children confronted Petronius at Tiberias in Lower Galilee. They told him, again according to Josephus in the *Jewish War* 2.197, that to proceed he would first have "to sacrifice the entire Jewish nation; and that they presented themselves, their wives and their children, ready for the slaughter." That is the voice of ethical eschatology.

I draw two corollaries from that understanding of ethical eschatology. One corollary is *never to separate the death of martyrdom from the life of resistance*. Martyrdom is a public witness in which official authority unleashes its full destructive power on an individual conscience. But it is an unfortunate necessity, an unwanted inevitability of conscientious resistance to systemic evil. Otherwise, resistance itself colludes with the violence it opposes. Such collusion may entail, minimally, desiring or provoking martyrdom (but every martyr needs a murderer). It may entail, maximally, the hunger-striker or the suicide attacker. Such collusive actions may or may not be humanly ethical, but they are not eschatologically ethical. Another corollary is to *separate the victim from the martyr*. I say that in deliberate disagreement with Helmut Koester's vision of "Jesus the Victim" from 1992. If Jesus had been killed at random in a punitive sweep by the Syrian legions through Lower Galilee, he would be a victim. There are, in fact, many ways one can be a victim, and they are usually sad and tragic. Jesus, however, was not a victim but a martyr. Pilate got it right: he was subversive, he was dangerous—but he was far more subversive and far more dangerous than Pilate imagined.

Those three types of eschatology—apocalyptic, ascetical, and ethical—are not, of course, the only possible ones. They are simply the ones involved in the present discussion. It was necessary, first of all, to see those three types of eschatology as quite clearly distinct. Now that we have done that, certain possibilities become more evident. First, it is possible to slide easily from one specific type to another within the overarching genus of eschatology. Second, it is possible for a speaker to emphasize one type and for individuals or groups to hear other types. Third, it is possible for speakers and hearers, writers and readers, to make certain combinations across those three types. Here, for example, are certain possible combinations.

Apocalypticism and asceticism could easily be combined. Since God's judgment on this world is imminent, withdrawal from its normalcies might be wise or even necessary. The apostle Paul is an example of that combination:

> I mean, brothers and sisters, the appointed time has grown short; from now
> on, let even those who have wives be as though they had none, and those
> who mourn as though they were not mourning, and those who rejoice as

though they were not rejoicing, and those who buy as though they had no possessions, and those who deal with the world as though they had no dealings with it. For the present form of this world is passing away. (1 Corinthians 7:29–31)

Paul practices a combination of apocalypticism and asceticism, or at least ascetic celibacy, but he commends rather than commands it to others.

Asceticism and ethicism could also be easily combined. At the start of Part VI and again earlier in this chapter, I used epigraphs from James Francis's very insightful study of *Subversive Virtue,* about the conflict in Roman paganism between asceticism and authority, which came to a head in the second century C.E. On the one hand, Christians did not invent apocalypticism; they adopted it from Judaism. On the other, Christians did not invent asceticism; they adopted it from paganism. "It is vital to keep this in mind," as Francis insists, "lest Christian asceticism be portrayed as an utterly new phenomenon to the Roman world, and the important point of its familiarity to pagan observers—and thus the prejudice of suspicion against it—be overlooked" (183 note 1).

At a basic level, of course, asceticism is *inherently* a threat to social normalcy, since it bespeaks another world antithetical to the presumed inevitabilities of this one. But it can, however paradoxically, be co-opted to support this world. A Christian conqueror, for example, could establish a monastery where ascetics prayed for the success of his military campaigns. Such co-option was exactly what pagan societies and Christian communities managed to do with their ascetics by the third century. "The same sort of controversy that took place in broader imperial society between ascetic radicals and authoritarian conservatives occurred within the Church itself," as Francis argued; "and just as pagan society ultimately found a way to incorporate the radicals into its ranks, so did the Church. In both, radical ascetics were shorn of their threat, liminized, heroized, and transformed from rivals to authority (whether of emperor or bishop) into allies of that authority and paragons of its values. Seen in this perspective, Christian monasticism amounts to an institutional domestication and incorporation of radicalism—a theory that would profoundly affect the study of Church history" (188). It would indeed. But it is precisely that combination of asceticism *and* ethicism, rather than just asceticism alone, that makes asceticism socially subversive in practice. If authorities, religious or political, can dissociate asceticism from ethicism, asceticism can easily be co-opted practically (even if not theoretically) into supporting established normalcy no matter how violent that may be. This, then, is the key question: Is asceticism an abandonment of the world's injustice or simply an alternative lifestyle chosen without any such criticism? And if it starts as the former, can it be converted to the latter?

The marriage of apocalypticism and ethicism is a much more difficult and delicate issue. Can they be combined? As long as apocalypticism involves a God who uses force and violence to end force and violence, they cannot be combined; one has to choose between them. This is implicit in my terminology. Ethicism, short for ethical eschatology, is ethical radicalism with a divine mandate based on the character of God. What makes it *radical* or *eschatological* ethics is, above all else, the fact that it is nonviolent resistance to structural violence. It is absolute faith in a nonviolent God and the attempt to live and act in union with such a God. I do *not* hold that apocalypticism and asceticism are not ethical. Of course they are. It may also be ethical to go to war in the name of an avenging God. But all ethics is not eschatological or divinely radical. Ethical eschatology is, by definition as I see it, nonviolent resistance to systemic violence.

An attendant issue here is the difference between divine revenge and divine justice. Revenge and justice lie close together in our human hearts and are projected thence, in equally close conjunction, onto our God. It seems to me, however, that Jesus distinguished the kingdom-of-God movement from the baptism movement on precisely that point. It may well have been the absence of an avenging God before, during, or after John the Baptist's own execution that convinced Jesus of a different type of God—the nonviolent God of a nonviolent kingdom, a God of nonviolent *resistance* to structural as well as individual evil.

VIOLENCE AND NONVIOLENCE

One point must be emphasized. I reject emphatically and absolutely any hint that the God of Judaism was a God of violent force and the God of Christianity was a God of nonviolent love. *Both* religions have taken violence *and* nonviolence from their God into their traditions and onto their streets. But the question of ethical eschatology or ethicism derives ultimately from the nature, character, and identity of the Jewish God as seen in the law codes, prophetic criticisms, and Psalm texts of Chapter 12. Maybe ethical eschatology was not always evident, but it was always there.

That last point bears emphasis because of the ancient libel that the Old Testament and Judaism are about revenge and violence while the New Testament and Christianity are about justice and love. In strictest truth, those disjunctive options cut across Judaism, across Christianity and, for that matter, across Islam as well. It is not enough to say that each religion reveres the same God. The more profound issues are *where,* in each religion, we have a God of violence or a God of nonviolence and *how* that God and/or that God's people respond to the initial presence of imperial violence (whether by miracle, by martyrdom, or by revolt).

Let me illustrate my point with four Jewish documents written against imperial domination, religious persecution, and the Temple's desecration across two hundred years of steadfast resistance in the Jewish homeland. I have chosen these texts somewhat at random. They start, in 1 and 2 *Maccabees*, with resistance to Syrian imperialism under Antiochus IV Epiphanes in the middle 160s B.C.E. and end, in 3 and 4 *Maccabees*, with resistance to Roman imperialism under Gaius Caligula in the early 40s C.E.

The first example is 1 *Maccabees*, written at the end of the second century or start of the first century B.C.E. Here the response to imperial violence is local violence—military *revolt* in the form of guerrilla warfare and pitched battle. The situation is Antiochus IV Epiphanes' attempt to unify the Jewish homeland into his Greco-Syrian empire, the collaboration of some Jewish aristocrats with his design, and the revolt of the Hasmonean family, nicknamed the Maccabees, against their plans. 1 *Maccabees* records the successes of three Maccabean generations from 167 to 134 B.C.E. and does not mention God at all. If divine help is presumed, it is left totally implicit. The revolt was militarily most successful and established a Jewish dynasty in the Jewish homeland for a hundred years—that is, until the relentless eastward expansion of Rome was ready for the next stage in 63 B.C.E.

A second example is 2 *Maccabees*, abbreviating a larger work from the first half of the second century B.C.E. The response depicted here combines all three possible solutions to imperial oppression: divine *miracle*, courageous *martyrdom*, and military *revolt*. The historical situation is the same as above, but it is recorded only from 167 to 161 B.C.E. First, *miracle*. In 2 *Maccabees* 3, one Heliodorus, acting on behalf of the Syrian monarch, attempts to rob the Temple treasury in Jerusalem. He is flogged to the ground by angelic intervention, and only the prayers of the high priest "grant life to one who was lying quite at his last breath." Next, *martyrdom*. In 2 *Maccabees* 6–7, an old man and a mother with seven sons refuse to equate Zeus with Yahweh and suffer martyrdom rather than submit to breaking traditional Jewish food laws. Finally, *revolt*. In 2 *Maccabees* 8–15, God is implored "to hearken to the blood that cries out to him" and then, but only then, do martyred deaths guarantee Maccabean victories. All three paradigmatic responses are present in 2 *Maccabees*, but there is also a certain necessary sequence: from miracle through martyrdom to revolt.

A third example is 3 *Maccabees*, written possibly in the 40s C.E. after Caligula's threat to Egyptian Judaism had been ended by his assassination. This response is *miracle* once again, but of a much more lethal nature than that just seen in 2 *Maccabees* 3. The story records an attempted pogrom of Egyptian Jews under Ptolemy IV Philopator at the end of the third century B.C.E. The drink-crazed elephants that are to massacre the Jews "turned back on the armed forces that followed them and they began to trample them down and destroy them" (6:21). The king immediately repents, frees and feasts the Jews, and even allows them to punish their fellows who had defected from Judaism under the royal persecution. "In that day they put to death more than three hundred men; and they kept the day as a joyful festival, since they had destroyed the profaners" (7:15). In this response by *miracle*, imperial violence is stopped by divine violence and consummated with human violence.

A fourth example is 4 *Maccabees*, written possibly around the same time as 3 *Maccabees*. The response illustrated here is *martyrdom*, so just as all three solutions—miracle, martyrdom, and revolt—were present in 2 *Maccabees*, we now have each given separate emphasis in a text to itself: miracle in 3 *Maccabees*, martyrdom in 4 *Maccabees*, and revolt in 1 *Maccabees*. We are, it would seem, dealing with basic human options of resistance. The author of 4 *Maccabees* sets out to prove that "devout reason is sovereign over the emotions" (1:1), that, for example, "as soon as one adopts a way of life in accordance with the law, even though a lover of money, one is forced to act contrary to natural ways and to lend without interest to the needy and to cancel the debt when the seventh year arrives. If one is greedy, one is ruled by the law through reason so that one neither gleans the harvest nor gathers the last grapes from the vineyard. In all other matters we can recognize that reason rules the emotions" (2:8–9). But, above all other arguments, there is an even more expansive description of those martyrs just seen in 2 *Maccabees* 6–7. Not only have those deaths conquered emotion by reason and pleasure by wisdom, they have conquered torture by suffering and tyranny by endurance. And they have done so in the public arena. Paradoxically, precisely, and publicly, as the tyrant wins, he loses; as the martyr loses, she wins. By martyrdom, tyranny is "conquered" (1:11), "nullified" (8:15), "defeated" (9:30) and "paralyzed" (11:24). In the words of Brent Shaw, the Maccabean martyrs defeated the power of violence by "the conscious production of a rather elaborate conception of passive resistance" or, better, by "active resistance through the patient body" (288, 300).

All three responses to oppression illustrated above came out of the same Jewish tradition and were there by the first century. *Revolt*, from banditry to battlefield, presumes human violence, with or without assistance from divine violence. *Miracle*, from individual intervention to apocalyptic consummation, could presume divine nonviolence (those elephants could have all fallen asleep) but more usually presumes divine violence, with or without assistance from human violence. *Martyrdom*, alone among these responses, accepts human violence and opposes it nonviolently, although of course it too can invoke future divine violence as retribution. When, however, it presumes a nonviolent God, it cannot make such an invocation. Martyrdom, in any case, is the ultimate and public act of nonviolent resistance to violent authority, and by its own individual nonviolence it lays bare the corporate violence it confronts. Martyrdom is, therefore, the final act of ethical eschatology.

PART VII
Healers and Itinerants

[There are] evil rumours and reports concerning shameless men, who, under pretext of the fear of God, have their dwelling with maidens, and so expose themselves to danger, and walk with them along the road and in solitary places alone. . . . Others, too, eat and drink with them at entertainments allowing themselves in loose behavior and much uncleanness—such as ought not to be among believers, and especially among those who have chosen for themselves a life of holiness. Others, again, meet together for vain and trifling conversation and merriment, and that they may speak evil of one another; and they hunt up tales against one another, and are idle: persons with whom we do not allow you even to break bread. Then, others gad about among the houses of virgin brethren or sisters, on pretence of visiting them, or reading the Scriptures to them, or exorcising them. Forasmuch as they are idle and do not work, they pry into those things which ought not to be inquired into, and by means of plausible words make merchandise of the name of Christ. . . .

Now we, if God help us, conduct ourselves thus: with maidens we do not dwell, nor have anything in common with them; with maidens we do not eat, nor drink; and, where a maiden sleeps, we do not sleep; neither do women wash our feet, nor anoint us; and on no account do we sleep where a maiden sleeps who is unmarried or has taken the vow [of celibacy]: even though she be in some other place if she be alone, we do not pass the night there. Moreover, if it chance that the time for rest overtake us in a place, whether in the country, or in a village, or in a town, or in a hamlet, or wheresoever we happen to be, and there are found brethren in that place, we turn in to [them . . . and] they set before us bread and water and that which God provides, and we . . . stay through the night with them . . . But the women and the maidens will wrap their hands in their garments; and we also, with circumspection and with all purity, our eyes looking upwards, shall wrap our right hand in our garments and then they will come and give us the salutation on our right hand wrapped in our garments.

Pseudo-Clement of Rome, *Two Epistles Concerning Virginity* (ANF 8.58, 61)

Part VI established the differences between apocalypticism, asceticism, and ethicism, as eschatological options. You can have one without the other, but you can also combine them in different ways or even slide from one to the other. From now on, though, the emphasis will be on ethical eschatology within the Common Sayings Tradition.

Parts VII and VIII form another tandem set representing a dialectic or interactive relationship between the destitute and the poor, between the itinerants and the householders, between those who bring healing and those who offer eating. That dialectic is present as far back as I can go into the earliest kingdom-of-God movement, and I consider it constitutive for that program.

Part VII focuses on those itinerant healers in the Common Sayings Tradition as we move deeply into the world of *text*. All now stands or falls on detailed readings of specific sayings from that extremely early tradition. I begin this part with a Prologue on healing, because of that subject's importance for this entire section. The kingdom of God is not an idea in the mind but an action on the body. The first question, therefore, is the meaning of healing—especially of physical healing as bodily resistance, the basic nonviolent resistance that places God on the side of those injured by exploitation, malnutrition, and disease.

Chapters 17 and 18 discuss the ethical eschatology of the Common Sayings Tradition. In Chapter 17 the Common Sayings Tradition negates the apocalyptic eschatology in the Baptist tradition, but it does so with respect and appreciation. Nevertheless, the baptism movement of John and the kingdom-of-God movement of Jesus are alternative solutions to the same problem. In Chapter 18 the Common Sayings Tradition affirms the lifestyle of the kingdom movement, whereby God's presence is made clearly manifest on earth. I conclude this Part VI with an Epilogue on the social status of Jesus, because of its implications for the social status of at least some of his companions. My point here is that if Jesus was a day-laboring rural artisan—that is, a marginalized or dispossessed peasant—he is in the same status as those itinerants. He is one of them, but he is also leading them into resistance to the systemic evil of Roman commercialization which is the opposite of the kingdom of God—that is, the will of the Jewish God for all the earth.

PROLOGUE:
THE MEANING OF HEALING

African Americans who must suffer discrimination in silence have higher blood pressure than those who can afford to challenge racist treatment. The finding may explain why blacks as a group have such high rates of stroke, heart disease and kidney failure.

Time magazine, "Health Report: The Bad News," November 4, 1996, p. 20

In Part I of this book, I spoke about history as an interaction between present and past, as a reconstruction of the past that cannot be absolutely stopped but only methodologically disciplined from imposing our present selves on past others or from dominating here-and-now over then-and-there. The present is always at an advantage over the past, because the present knows what did happen to the past but the past could not know what would happen to it. How can the present not feel superior to the past, given that very knowledge alone? How, in other words, can the challenge strike at least as hard from them to us as from us to them? It can do so, of course, because the past's unknown future reminds us that our present's unknown future puts us in exactly the same blind position.

Here is a case where the honesty of that interaction must be openly faced. In the following section I speak of Jesus and his companions as healing others. What exactly did that mean for them, and what does it mean for us in engagement with them? I am not satisfied with explanations that say something like this: those ancient people had strange or even weird ideas, but we must just accept and describe them. Or this: they have a right to their superstitions and we must not disparage them. When explained like that, no ancient ideas can challenge us. They simply confirm our superiority and our more adequate knowledge of how the world works. Indeed, we are especially to be admired in that we refrain from external contempt even where internal condescension may be present. They talked about evil spirits and demonic forces responsible for sickness and death. We speak of sanitation and nutrition, of bacteria and germs, of microbes and viruses. How are they not wrong if we are right, and vice versa?

Healing and Curing

Illnesses are *experiences* of disvalued changes in states of being and in social function; diseases, in the scientific paradigm of modern medicine, are *abnormalities* in the *structure* and *function* of bodily organs and system.

Leon Eisenberg, "Disease and Illness," p. 11

A key axiom in medical anthropology is the dichotomy between two aspects of sickness: disease and illness. *Disease* refers to a malfunctioning of biological and/or psychological processes, while the term *illness* refers to the psychosocial experience and meaning of perceived disease.

Arthur Kleinman, *Patients and Healers in the Context of Culture*, p. 72

Scholars working in medical anthropology, comparative ethnomedicine, and the cross-cultural study of "indigenous" healing have proposed a distinction between *curing disease* and *healing illness*. Those preceding epigraphs are two classical descriptions of that dichotomy. To further distinguish the two components, we could say that the surgeon is better at curing disease while the shaman is better at healing illness. And that might be all right, of course, if those two processes were always totally separate.

In explaining that distinction to undergraduate students at DePaul University as a background for discussion of Jesus as an indigenous healer, I was usually met with obedient disbelief—that is, take it down, give it back, forget it. Until the movie *Philadelphia* came along, and then the classroom silence was palpable. The protagonist, played by Tom Hanks, had AIDS, a disease caused by a virus that attacks the immune system. This disease may someday be curable, either by a vaccine that destroys the virus or by a drug that controls its effects. But the movie was not about the *disease,* which for Hanks could not be *cured,* but about the *illness,* for which *healing* was possible. The illness involved the man's own reaction to his disease, as well as the reactions of his lover, his family, his employer, his lawyer, and of society at large through the justice system. He was fired by his employer not just because he had AIDS but because he had become infected as a homosexual, and he successfully sued his firm for that discrimination in court. In *Philadelphia* the distinction between *curing disease* and *healing illness* was devastatingly obvious. But so also was the interactive loop between the twin processes of disease and illness. The patient's immune system was actually under attack on two fronts. The stress of being fired served, as it always does, to put one's immune system in danger. On the other hand, strong support from lover and family, lawyer and jurors, strengthened that immune system and counteracted the stress. That story made sense of the distinction and showed how one could have successful healing where no successful curing was possible. It also showed how, in other places and times, where curing was not generally possible, healing might still be very important. That opened up serious classroom discussion about the necessity of having both processes equally available in an adequate health-care system. But, as Arthur Kleinman and Lilias H. Sung argue, although "ideally, clinical care should treat both disease and illness . . .

modern professional health care tends to treat disease but not illness; whereas in general, indigenous systems of healing tend to treat illness, not disease" (1979:8).

My contemporary undergraduates had one other major difficulty with this topic, even when the disease/illness distinction became clear and acceptable. They were very willing to speak about mind over matter in connection with that distinction: they seldom spoke of mind over matter as a way to cure disease, but they often used that concept to interpret healing and to understand how healing could help in curing. Much of what was said was quite correct, but the discussion never moved to societal questions dealing with society over mind over matter. What happens when social forces, political situations, or economic conditions cause the unhealth, be it disease and/or illness? How does mind over matter work then?

In the *Philadelphia* case, you can see where society could become involved in the illness subsequent to the disease. If, for example, the legal system supported the patient's employers in his dismissal, and if society at large exercised other discriminations against him, society would be exacerbating the illness and thence, through increased stress, the disease. But society did not cause the disease in the first place. Sometimes, though, it does. What of those cases where society causes or allows disease to happen in the first place, perhaps by fostering conditions that put people at risk? Arthur Kleinman, in a subsequent book, introduces a third term, *sickness,* and defines it as "the understanding of a disorder in its generic sense across a population in relation to macrosocial (economic, political, institutional) forces. Thus, when we talk of the relationship of tuberculosis to poverty and malnutrition that places certain populations at higher risk for the disorder, we are invoking tuberculosis as sickness; similarly, when we discuss the contribution of the tobacco industry and their political supporters to the epidemiological burden of lung cancer in North America, we are describing the sickness cancer. Not just researchers but patients, families, and healers, too, may extrapolate from illness to sickness, adding another wrinkle to the experience of disorder, seeing it as a reflection of political oppression, economic deprivation, and other social sources of human misery" (1988:6). Society (and its systemic structures) can not only exacerbate the *illness* that follows from a *disease,* it can create the *sickness* that leads to *disease.*

The point is not to get lost among those terminological variations on unhealth, but to realize the inevitable interaction between them. Society at large makes *sickness* more likely to attack this rather than that individual or class; and, when the *disease* strikes, the responses from patient, family, friends, employers, and society at large vastly affect how the *illness* progresses. It is possible to have unhealth arising from any one, any two, or all three of those aspects—sickness, disease, illness—by whatever names they are called. Some of health and unhealth can be a case of mind over matter. But much more of it is a case of society over mind over matter. And what can be done about that?

Healing and Faith

The Epidaurian collection [of cures from the fourth century B.C.E.] . . . clearly reflects the Classical, Hippocratic idea that the body itself, if left to its own devices, would naturally tend to a balanced condition of health, providing no environmental (external, i.e. "foreign") factors interfered. . . . It is very interesting to note that it is precisely where such an ideology is least satisfying, in cases of chronic disabilities of generally healthy people (blindness, deafness, infertility, paralysis—the overwhelming majority of [Epidaurian] afflictions), that we see divine intervention.

Lynn R. LiDonnici, The Epidaurian Miracle Inscriptions, p. 3

This, then, is a simple fact of our own modern-day experience: certain people, apparently once ill, are now well; they claim that they were suddenly cured by divine power; and no adequate medical explanation of the cure can be found.

John P. Meier, A Marginal Jew, vol. 2, p. 516

In that preceding example of the AIDS patient in the movie *Philadelphia*, healing of the illness was brought about by the *supportive companionship* of those important to the patient. His stress was alleviated, his immune system was strengthened, and the ravages of the disease were delayed if not destroyed. That is certainly not the best one could wish, but neither is it the worst one could imagine. Thus supportive companionship can be seen as a first level of healing. In the case of Tom Hanks's character, it could only postpone inevitable death. But with *some* forms of chronic or long-term pain—especially psychosomatic ailments, where stress or oppression, strain or exploitation have resulted in somatization or embodiment of the general distress as a specifically localized problem—supportive companionship can slowly but surely eliminate the disease itself. Rodney Stark, speaking of ancient epidemics, gives the following statistic: "Modern medical experts believe that conscientious nursing *without any medications* could cut the mortality rate by two-thirds or even more" (89). I cite that to remind us that supportive companionship could be crucial even for epidemic diseases.

There is, however, another mode of healing that is very effective for certain people, under certain circumstances, with certain diseases, in certain places, and at certain times. I am speaking here of healing and even curing by religious faith.

In the movie *Philadelphia,* as far as I can remember, religious faith was not a factor. There it was simply a case of supportive *human* companionship. But what about *transcendental religious faith?*

Faith heals, and that's a fact. Apart from intentional fakes or tricks, aside from deliberate quacks or charlatans, faith heals or even cures *some* people of *some* illnesses or diseases under *some* circumstances. In 1960 I visited the Roman Catholic healing shrines of the Virgin Mary at Lourdes in France and at Fátima in Portugal. In 1965 I visited the pagan healing shrines of the god Asklepios at Epidaurus in Greece and at Pergamum in Turkey. I remember being struck by the general similarity between the ailments involved in stories of healing at all those shrines (as well as by ailments whose reminders could be seen: there were many crutches at the back of the grotto at Lourdes, for example, but no prosthetic limbs or empty coffins). Similarly, Lynn LiDonnici's list of fourth-century B.C.E. votive offerings at Epidaurus includes this rather laconic one (96–97):

A 16. Nicanor, lame. When he was sitting down, being awake, some boy grabbed his crutch and ran away. Getting up he ran after him and from this he became well.

One can, of course, rationalize or psychologize the seventy or so tales of healing in the Epidaurian inscriptions. My Greek guide at Epidaurus extolled Greek culture and spoke of ancient gods, priests, and miracles. My Turkish guide at Pergamum ignored Greek culture and spoke of ancient doctors, psychiatrists, and patients. One can also, according to one's taste, jeer at ancient credulity or sneer at modern skepticism. Neither response is particularly helpful.

Real people with real ailments—including paralysis, blindness, deafness, dumbness, growths, and wounds—were clearly healed at Epidaurus. The patients, having read the miracle inscriptions of those healed before them, spent the night in a special building called the Abaton. They hoped for a dream through which or in which Asklepios would heal them so that they could awake healthy in the morning. Compare, then, these two testimonials, again from LiDonnici (84–85, 110–111, slightly simplified):

A 1. Kleo was pregnant for five years. After the fifth year of pregnancy, she came as a suppliant to the god and slept in the Abaton. As soon as she had left it and was outside the sacred area, she gave birth to a son who, as soon as he was born, washed himself at the fountain and walked about with his mother. After this success, she inscribed upon an offering: "The wonder is not the size of the plaque, but the act of the god: Kleo bore a burden in her stomach for five years, until she slept here, and he made her well."

B 14. A woman from Troizen, concerning children. This woman, sleeping here, saw a dream. It seemed to her the god said that she would have a family and he asked whether her wish was for a male or a female, and she said she wished for a male. After this, within a year a son was born to her.

In that first case, a miraculous ailment obtains a normal cure. In the second case, a normal ailment obtains a miraculous cure. But, whatever about that second instance, no amount of psychologizing explains the first condition. Five-year pregnancies do not happen, and it is not just post-Enlightenment rationalism to say so. What happens in such cases is simply this: devotional inflation. Real healings and even real cures do take place. Women like Kleo who have lost all hope bear children, for example. After such healings, oral tradition from devotees, shrine propaganda from locals, and scribal enthusiasm from priests regularly escalate the details. All such miracles must get bigger, better, and more startling. That is inevitable from their role as witness to transcendental intervention.

I have three conclusions so far. First, society and individual, disease and illness, healing and curing always intertwine together, be it delicately or brutally. Second, supportive companionship and/or religious faith can heal illness and, by so doing, even cure disease, but only in certain cases. We may not be sure of the present or future limits of such healing, but we all make certain decisions about where they are every day of our lives. Third, healing stories tend to increase and become more extraordinary rather than decrease and become more banal.

And now on to one final issue: What role does healing have, what forms can healing take, in situations where social context *creates* the ailment rather than simply exacerbating its presence after an independent arrival?

Healing and Resistance

If the personal is defined by social categories, can we ever identify matter which does *not* reflect social ideology? This question is thrown into particularly sharp relief when we consider the most private religious documents that survive from antiquity, usually referred to as magical or curse inscriptions. Even these sources, however, are increasingly regarded as reflecting a way of dealing with the personal *strain* resulting from social and ideological pressures.
                    Lynn R. LiDonnici, *The Epidaurian Miracle Inscriptions*, p. 3

Arthur Kleinman records the experience of a twenty-nine-year-old internist, Lenore Light, "who comes from an upper middle class black family and works in an inner-city ghetto clinic." She tells, in her own words, how she was revolutionized by the first encounter with "our black under class; the poorest, the most miserable, the most chaotic, and oppressed and oppressive reminder of where we have all of us come from. It has radicalized me; it is a revolutionary encounter with the social sources of mortality and morbidity and expression. The more I see, the more appalled I am at how ignorant I have been, insensitive to the social, economic, and political causes of disease. We learned about these things in the abstract in med school. Here it is a living reality, a medical hell. What we need is prevention, not the Band-Aids I spend my day putting on deep inner wounds. Today I saw an obese hypertensive mother of six. No husband. No family support. No job. Nothing. A world of brutalizing violence and poverty and drugs and teenage pregnancies and— and just plain mind-numbing crises, one after another after another. What can I do? What good is it to recommend a low-salt diet, to admonish her about control of her pressure? She is under such real outer pressure, what does the inner pressure matter? What is killing her is her world, not her body. In fact, her body is the product of her world. She is a hugely overweight misshapen hulk who is a survivor of circumstances and lack of resources and cruel messages to consume and get ahead impossible for her to hear and not feel rage at the limits of her world. Hey, what she needs is not medicine but a social revolution" (1988:216–217). Reading the epigraph from *Time* magazine at the start of this Prologue in the light of that internist's experience, I emphasize the contrast between those who must suffer racist discrimination "in silence" and those who "can afford to challenge" it. In such situations of *sickness,* is resistance a form of healing?

I leave aside "conventional" healing for a moment, then, to focus on resistance to discrimination, oppression, marginalization, and exploitation. In the mid-seventies Eugene Genovese, speaking of slavery in North America, noted that "accommodation itself breathed a critical spirit and disguised subversive actions and often embraced its apparent opposite—resistance." He went on to distinguish the two ends of that continuum of resistance with open "insurrection" at one pole and "day-to-day resistance to slavery" at the other. But all of that continuum in all its parts "contributed to the cohesion and strength of a social class threatened by disintegration and demoralization" (597–598). That idea of oppressed people resisting along a continuum from the most covert to the most overt action was emphasized as a cross-cultural phenomenon by James C. Scott at around the same time. I take three major points from his work across the last twenty years.

The first point is the antithetical relationship between elite and peasant traditions. The Great (or scribal) Tradition of the elites and the Little (or oral) Tradition of the peasants are not just complex versus simple versions of one another. Moving from Europe to Southeast Asia and noting the Little Tradition's common reaction to such disparate variants of the Great Tradition as Christianity, Buddhism, and Islam, Scott argued very persuasively that peasant culture and religion are actually an anti-culture, qualifying alike both the religious and the political elites that oppress it. It is, in fact, a reflexive and reactive inversion of the pattern of exploitation common to the peasantry as such. This is a powerful insight, and I quote Scott at length: "The popular religion and culture of peasants in a complex society are not only a syncretized, domesticated, and localized variant of larger systems of thought and doctrine. They contain almost inevitably the seeds of an alternative symbolic universe—a universe which in turn makes the social world in which peasants live less than completely inevitable. Much of this radical symbolism can only be explained as a cultural reaction to the situation of the peasantry *as a class*. In fact, this symbolic opposition represents the closest thing to class consciousness in pre-industrial agrarian societies. It is as if those who find themselves at the bottom of the social heap develop cultural forms which promise them dignity, respect, and economic comfort which they lack in the world as it is. A real pattern of exploitation dialectically produces its own symbolic mirror image within folk culture. . . . The radical vision to which I refer is strikingly uniform despite the enormous variations in peasant cultures and the different great traditions of which they partake. . . . At the risk of over-generalizing, it is possible to describe some common features of this reflexive symbolism. It nearly always implies a society of brotherhood in which there will be no rich and poor, in which no distinctions of rank and status (save those between believers and non-believers) will exist. Where religious institutions are experienced as justifying inequities, the abolition of rank and status may well include the elimination of religious hierarchy in favor of communities of equal believers. Property is typically, though not always, to be held in common and shared. All unjust claims to taxes, rents, and tribute are to be nullified. The envisioned utopia may also include a self-yielding and abundant nature as well as a radically transformed human nature in which greed, envy, and hatred will disappear. While the earthly utopia is thus an anticipation of the future, it often harks back to a mythic Eden from which mankind has fallen away" (1977:224–226).

The second point is the distinction, at either end of a continuum, between overt and covert resistance. This is an extremely important distinction, because open resistance by insurrection or revolt is only the tip of the iceberg. It is, however, all that gets into the record kept by the elite, since hidden resistance is, by definition, something those in power are not supposed to recognize. "Most subordinate classes throughout most of history have rarely been afforded the luxury of open, organized, political activity. Or, better stated, such activity was dangerous, if not suicidal. . . . For all their importance when they do occur, peasant rebellions—let alone revolutions—are few and far between. The vast majority are crushed unceremoniously. . . . For these reasons it seemed to me more important to understand what we might call *everyday* forms of peasant resistance—the prosaic but constant struggle between the peasantry and those who seek to extract labor, food, taxes, rents, and interest from them. Most forms of this struggle stop well short of outright collective defiance. Here I have in mind the ordinary weapons of relatively powerless groups: foot dragging, dissimulation, desertion, false compliance, pilfering, feigned ignorance, slander, arson, sabotage, and so on. These . . . forms of class struggle . . . require little or no coordination or planning; they make use of implicit understandings and informal networks; they often represent a form of individual self-help; they typically avoid any direct, symbolic confrontation with authority. . . . When such stratagems are abandoned in favor of more quixotic action, it is usually a sign of great desperation" (1985:xv–xvi). But covert resistance uses the "weapons of the weak . . . the tenacity of self-preservation—in ridicule, in truculence, in irony, in petty acts of noncompliance . . . in resistant mutuality, in the disbelief in elite homilies, in the steady grinding efforts to hold one's own against overwhelming odds—a spirit and practice that prevents the worst and promises something better" (1985:350).

The third and final point distinguishes once more "between the open, declared forms of resistance, which attract most attention, and the disguised low-profile, undeclared resistance that constitutes the domain of infrapolitics." It then goes on to identify three different aspects or strata of that covert resistance. The first stratum is *ideological* resistance through the "development of dissident subcultures" such as millennial religions, myths of social banditry and class heroes, world-upside-down imagery, and myths of the ideal king. The next stratum is *status resistance* through a "hidden transcript of anger, aggression, and disguised discourses of dignity," such as tales of revenge, carnival symbolism, gossip, and rumor. The final stratum is *material resistance* through "everyday forms" such as "poaching, squatting, desertion, evasion, foot-dragging" (1990:198).

My proposal is that there is a close correlation between those three strata of covert resistance and the processes of healing. This is particularly true where unhealth (especially sickness) leading to disease derives from social discrimination, exploitation, and oppression. That brings me back to the epigraph about disease and unresisted discrimination and to that black internist who wanted not just medical diagnosis but social revolution. I think she was on the right track. There is a third process of healing besides the two already mentioned (though it can, of course, intertwine with them): besides *supportive companionship* and *religious faith*, the practice of *covert resistance* can contribute to healing. (As an aside, while such resistance is covert and disguised to the oppression it opposes, it is quite obvious to those who practice it.)

We can understand why people went to Asklepios or Mary for healing, but how did people decide to go to Jesus for healing, and/or how did Jesus know he could heal? Watch, in what follows, how ideological resistance-healing moves from the *ideological* level of the kingdom of God through the *status* level of the companionship of the kingdom to the *material* resistance-level of eating together. Healing involves directly both sickness *before* and illness *after* disease; and thereby, but only thereby, does it touch disease itself.

Healing and Miracles

[One] observation on miracles and the modern mind concerns what might be called the academic sneer factor. If a full debate on the possibility and reality of miracles were to take place on American university campuses today—a highly unlikely event—such a debate would be tolerated in many quarters only with a strained smile that could hardly mask a sneer. Before any positions were articulated or discussed, the solemn creed of many university professors, especially in religion departments, would be recited *sotto voce*: "No modern educated person can accept the possibility of miracles."

John P. Meier, *A Marginal Jew*, vol. 2, p. 520

All of that preceding material may be disappointing to some readers. Did not Jesus confront a diseased or even a dead person and by a word eliminate disease or eradicate death itself? What about miracles? Is all that medical anthropology but a hidden negation of their possibility?

I begin with a brief comparison of my own position in *The Historical Jesus* against that of John Meier in *A Marginal Jew*. We are in substantial agreement on three key conclusions about the historical Jesus. Jesus was both healer and exorcist, and his followers considered those actions miracles. But no single healing or exorcism is securely or fully historical in its present narrative form, although historical kernels may be discernible in a few instances. Furthermore, as Meier notes, "most of the so-called nature miracles seem to stem from the early church, but the story of Jesus feeding the multitudes may reflect a special meal Jesus held during his public ministry" (2.13). But there are also two problems left for discussion.

Here is one problem. Meier criticizes the presumption that moderns cannot believe in miracles, citing a 1989 Gallup poll proving that 82 percent of North Americans do so believe. He is quite right: of course people believe in miracles. Every time I buy groceries I read the covers of various tabloids as I wait at the checkout counter. They are filled, apart from diet, gossip, and scandal, with monsters, prophecies, and miracles. In contemporary North America we are once again as close as we have ever been to the entrepreneurial free-trade market in religious experiences that characterized the Roman Empire. But that means that, now as then, we will have not to deny but to discriminate.

The argument cannot any longer be that of the village atheist who disbelieves miracles for everyone, past, present, and future, including Jesus. The argument cannot any longer be that of the pious pastor who disbelieves miracles for everyone besides Jesus and for all other religions besides Christianity. The argument will have to be about what is at stake in claiming this about Jesus rather than about, say, Elvis Presley. It was easier, even if wrong, to say that miracles do not happen and that therefore Jesus did not perform them. It is more difficult to admit that miracles happen all over the world's religions but that *this* is why Jesus' miracles are peculiarly significant for us Christians. Gallup polls are not enough.

There is another problematic area. Meier puts it like this: "Just as a historian must reject credulity, so a historian must reject an a priori affirmation that miracles do not or cannot happen. That is, strictly speaking, a philosophical or theological proposition, not a historical one" (2.11). But there is, actually, not a twofold but a fivefold problem: theological, literary, epistemological, historical, and ethical. And before proceeding, let me give you my own definition of a miracle. *A miracle is a marvel that someone interprets as a transcendental action or manifestation.* There must be, first, not a trick or a deceit but a marvel or a wonder— something that staggers current explanation. There must be, second, certain individuals or groups who interpret that marvel as an intervention by ancestors, spirits, divinities, or God. But now comes that fivefold problem.

- The *theological* problem is that to claim miracles *can* or *cannot* happen is, I agree, an ideological statement. The negation is as theological as the affirmation, and debates between them should recognize that fact.
- The *literary* problem is to make sure that texts are making claims of miracle rather than using some sort of metaphorical language. Aesop's fables, for example, are not claiming miraculous discourse by animals in ancient Greece.
- The *epistemological* problem may be the most intransigent of all. If one accepts a closed universe in which the current *we* know all that could happen normally or naturally, then miracles would be clearly knowable as whatever *we* cannot explain. That would be abnormal or supernatural. But as long as we live in a confusedly open universe where even our securest knowledge is relativized by its being ours, it is hard to see how to know a omarvel from a miracle. The irony is that only rationalists can really believe absolutely in miracles as objectively evident.
- The *historical* problem is simply whether, in this or that particular case, a miracle, so defined, did or did not happen.
- The *ethical* problem is also very difficult. It reverts to that second reason for historical Jesus research proposed in Chapter 2. It is not ethical for an *historian*

to give special protection and privilege to Christian miracles but not to all others, ancient and modern. How does an ancient historian distinguish the miraculous divine-human conception of Augustus from that of Jesus, and how would that same person assess similar claims if made today?

To claim a miracle is to make an interpretation of faith, not just a statement of fact. The fact open to public discourse is the marvel, something that is assessed as neither trickery nor normalcy. One may, of course, disagree on that historical level. But then there is the theological level, which accepts or rejects that marvel as a miracle. I cannot see how miracle status can ever be proved or disproved, because of the epistemological problem of an open universe and the relativities of our own knowledge about it. But it is very significant which events a faith interprets as miracle and which it does not, because that reveals what manner of God one worships. Finally, even for believers and even within a theological framework, faith in an epiphanic God is not the same as faith in an episodic God. The former is a permanent divine presence periodically observed *by* believers. The latter is an absent presence periodically intervening *for* believers.

I myself, in summary, believe in an epiphanic rather than an episodic God. To say, therefore, that the healings or exorcisms of Jesus are miracles does not mean for me that only Jesus could do such things but that in such events I see God at work in Jesus. God, for me, is one who resists discrimination, exploitation, and oppression; who is, for example, on the side of a doomed people rather than their imperial masters at the Exodus and on the side of a crucified Jesus rather than his imperial executioners at the resurrection. And, in the reciprocity of open eating and free healing to be seen in Chapter 18, I see that same God at work—in the healing and in the eating as nonviolent resistance to systemic evil.

CHAPTER 17

NEGATING APOCALYPTIC ESCHATOLOGY

Wandering radicalism does not proclaim the (future) *coming* of the kingdom,
it brings it directly to the front door. With the knock of the itinerant radical,
the old world has already passed away, and the kingdom of God has arrived.
Stephen J. Patterson, *The Gospel of Thomas and Jesus*, p. 211

This chapter and the next one form a tandem set. They are a pair, two sides
of the one coin, as it were. This chapter is the negative; the next chapter is its
positive complement. In this first or negative section I intend to show that the
Common Sayings Tradition knows about apocalyptic eschatology from the
teaching of John the Baptist and, respectfully but definitely, negates his program
in favor of the kingdom-of-God program. The Common Sayings Tradition is, in
other words, anti-apocalyptic but not anti-eschatological. A first indication of its
eschatological thrust is its emphatic retention of the concept of the kingdom of
God. It opposes one *interpretation* of that visionary program rather than the very
program itself. But, in this first chapter, we do not get much further than that
negative opposition. It is not at all clear what is the positive content of this kingdom until we get to the next and complementary chapter.

There are three sayings to be considered in the Common Sayings Tradition's
negation of apocalyptic eschatology, and their presence in that tradition is
extremely significant. By opposing apocalyptic eschatology, they prove that it
was present at the time they negated it. There is, in other words, counterevi-
dence to any claim that a nonapocalyptic eschatology came first and an apocalyptic one developed only later. The earliest *non*apocalyptic eschatology I can
find is already an *anti*-apocalyptic one. In the beginning was John the Baptist, not
Jesus.

The first saying, *Into the Desert*, is extremely complimentary to John. The *Q*
Gospel retained it as such, but the *Gospel of Thomas* removed John's name entirely
and changed its ending completely. The second saying, *Greater Than John*, displaced the Baptist in favor of the kingdom's least member and was accepted in
that form by both gospels. Those first two units, taken together, serve to establish

the negative contrast between the baptism and the kingdom movements. The third saying, *When and Where,* is the most interesting of the three units, with redactional activity fast and furious all around it. The saying points to an alternative eschatological program—one that is present rather than future—but it does not give much positive content to that alternative.

INTO THE DESERT

The first of the three Common Sayings Tradition units to be considered in this chapter is *Into the Desert* (Appendix 1A: #32). It is a Type 3 saying (Appendix 1B); that is, it has been redacted both toward asceticism in the *Gospel of Thomas* and toward apocalypticism in the *Q Gospel.* It appears in the *Q Gospel* as Q 7:24-27—that is, Luke 7:24-27 = Matthew 11:7-10—and in *Gospel of Thomas* 78:1-3. There are no parallel versions anywhere else to help the analysis. It is the same unit of tradition, but with a striking difference between those two sources. Only the *Q Gospel* applies the saying to John the Baptist; the *Gospel of Thomas* does not. The important question, therefore, is whether that application was present in the Common Sayings Tradition itself.

Q Gospel.

There are slightly different versions in Matthew 11:7-10 and Luke 7:24b-27, but there are no substantive problems. Here is the wording in the *Q Gospel:*

Jesus began to speak to the crowds about John: "What did you go out into the wilderness to look at? A reed shaken by the wind? What then did you go out to see? Someone dressed in soft robes? Look, those who put on fine clothing and live in luxury are in royal palaces. What then did you go out to see? A prophet? Yes, I tell you, and more than a prophet. This is the one about whom it is written, 'See, I am sending my messenger ahead of you, who will prepare your way before you.'" (*Q Gospel* 7:24b–27)

That version has two separate parts. There is, first, a rhetorical climax of three questions and answers: what?/reed (implausible!); what?/aristocrat (impossible!); what?/prophet (inadequate!). The first two answers—and even the third one—are incorrect, because John is not *just* a prophet but *more than* a prophet. There is, next, that concluding citation in 7:27. It combines Exodus 23:20 and Malachi 3:1 so that God's angel-messenger is now interpreted as John preparing the way for Jesus.

There is a very strong consensus that *Q Gospel* 7:27 was added on later to a *Q Gospel* 7:24-26 complete in form and content without it. The citation appears, for example, without that triple rhetorical question in Mark 1:2-3. But, in any case, the presence of 7:27 has made 7:24-26 even more emphatically and explicitly apocalyptic. As Kloppenborg concluded: "Q 7:27 explicitly identifies John as the precursor of Jesus and implicitly identifies him with Elijah *redivivus*. Thus John's role is interpreted eschatologically: as the messenger of Yahweh, and as one with a positive, if subordinate, function in the inauguration of the kingdom" (1987a:109). It would be hard, in any case, not to interpret "more than a prophet" as meaning the final prophet, the end-time prophet, or even, maybe, the Messiah. But, once 7:27 is appended to 7:24b–26, "more than a prophet" means simply "preparer for Jesus."

The *Q Gospel* redacts the saying even more explicitly as apocalyptic eschatology but also places John as subordinate to Jesus.

Gospel of Thomas.

The saying in *Gospel of Thomas* 78 is very different from the *Q Gospel* parallel in both content and form, especially in the lack of any reference to John the Baptist (and, of course, in the absence of any biblical citation):

Jesus said, "Why have you come out to the countryside? To see a reed shaken by the wind? And to see a person dressed in soft clothing, [like your] rulers and your powerful ones? They are dressed in soft clothing, and cannot understand truth." (*Gospel of Thomas* 78:1–3)

The problem is clear. The *Q Gospel* applies the saying to John; the *Gospel of Thomas* does not. What was in the Common Sayings Tradition for that unit? Leaving aside the question of the biblical citation, was John the Baptist there from the beginning or not? Did the *Q Gospel* add in the reference to John the Baptist, or did the *Gospel of Thomas* remove it?

Here are two opposite answers to that question. Helmut Koester thinks that John the Baptist was added in by the *Q Gospel*: "As it appears in the Gospel of Thomas, [the saying] has no explicit relationship to John the Baptist. It could be understood as a general statement about the exclusion of the rich, and Q's use of this saying in the context of sayings about John the Baptist may be secondary" (1990b:58). In summary, Koester believes that the *Q Gospel* added it in; the *Gospel of Thomas* did not remove it but simply reflects the original version. Gerd Theissen, on the other hand, argues that the very mention of "reed" links the saying explicitly with Herod Antipas. His argument is that "the reed appears on Herod Antipas' first coins, which he had minted for the founding of his capital city, Tiberias (ca. 19 C.E.). . . . The first (and oldest) type of coin very probably shows a reed (*Canna communis*) on the obverse" (1992:28–29). The contrast between John and Antipas was present, therefore, in that saying from its earliest existence. In summary, Theissen believes that the *Q Gospel* did not add the John reference in but simply reflects the original version; the *Gospel of Thomas* removed it.

In that debate, I prefer Theissen to Koester. Even if his "reed" argument is too specific, it is hard to imagine this saying except in some conjunction with the conflict between desert and palace, between John and Antipas, and most likely after the former's execution by the latter. If one simply wanted a general rebuke of aristocratic luxury, it is hard to see what *desert* and *reed* have to do as an introduction to that criticism. I conclude, therefore, that John the Baptist was connected to this unit in the Common Sayings Tradition and was retained and intensified by the *Q Gospel*.

The version in *Gospel of Thomas* 78 is best seen as a totally truncated version of the common tradition behind the two gospels, which, however, must have been quite close to that now visible in the *Q Gospel*. The tight three-part rhetorical construction is now destroyed. Only the first element is given completely, with explicit question and explicit answer (what?/reed!); the second one is reduced to implicit question and explicit answer (aristocrat?!); and the third disappears completely behind a criticism of those aristocrats. It is as if the entire preceding part had been swallowed up in an almost separate and independent aphorism: "Your rulers and your powerful ones are dressed in soft clothing, and cannot understand truth." Power and luxury are now opposed to truth and asceticism. In itself, that saying is completely in line with other sayings particular to the *Gospel of Thomas*—sayings that emphasize the true wealth of poverty and the false wealth of power:

Jesus said, "Let one who has become wealthy reign, and let one who has power renounce [it]." (*Gospel of Thomas* 81:1–2)

Jesus said, "Adam came from great power and great wealth, but he was not worthy of you. For had he been worthy, [he would] not [have tasted] death." (*Gospel of Thomas* 85:1–2)

Jesus said, "Let one who has found the world, and has become wealthy, renounce the world." (*Gospel of Thomas* 110)

Conclusion.

The Common Sayings Tradition *knows* the Baptist's apocalyptic eschatology as evidenced by *Into the Desert*. The *Q Gospel* accepts it and redactionally emphasizes it. The *Gospel of Thomas* rejects it and redactionally eliminates it. John is not even mentioned in *Thomas*, and the saying becomes a general but somewhat strained admonition against power and luxury. I emphasized the word *knows* in that opening sentence. The next unit shows that the Common Sayings Tradition both *knows* and *opposes* the Baptist's apocalyptic eschatology.

GREATER THAN JOHN

The second unit in the Common Sayings Tradition that *concerns and negates* apocalyptic eschatology is *Greater Than John* (Appendix 1A: #20). It is a Type 3 saying (Appendix 1B); that is, it has been redacted both toward asceticism in the *Gospel of Thomas* and toward apocalypticism in the *Q Gospel*. It appears in the *Q Gospel* as Q 7:28—that is, Luke 7:28 = Matthew 11:11—and in *Gospel of Thomas* 46:1–2. There are no other extant examples. The preceding complex, *Into the Desert,* and the present one, *Greater Than John,* appear sequentially in the *Q Gospel* but appear separately in *Gospel of Thomas* 78 and 46. In this case, however, the *Gospel of Thomas* has no problem with naming John the Baptist.

Q Gospel.

The twin versions in Matthew 11:11 and Luke 7:28 have no substantive differences between them. Here is the wording in the *Q Gospel*:

> I tell you, among those born of women no one is greater than John; yet the least in the kingdom of God is greater than he. (*Q Gospel* 7:28)

It is, of course, one thing to declare John subordinate to Jesus as his divinely appointed precursor. It is quite another to say that the least in the kingdom is greater than John. Supremely high praise, as just seen in *Q Gospel* 7:24–27, is followed here by supremely high praise in 7:28a and then stern negation in 7:28b. Kloppenborg puts the contradiction like this. On the one hand, in *Q Gospel* 7:24–27, "John . . . belongs alongside Jesus as a precursor, not outside the kingdom as the representative of a bygone epoch"; but, on the other hand, *Q Gospel* 7:28 "emphasizes the greatness of the kingdom by asserting that even the greatest representative of the old order, John, paled in comparison with it. . . . It relativizes John by relegating his function to an era prior to the kingdom and indeed [possibly] to a realm outside the kingdom" (1987a:109–110).

It must be emphasized that this unit is very, very unusual within the *Q Gospel*. It is not simply a matter of exalting Jesus above John within the kingdom, but of exalting the least one explicitly inside the kingdom over John implicitly outside it. But that negation is now framed in the following sequence of units:

1.	*Into the Desert:*	Matt. 11:7–10	= Luke 7:24–27
2.	*Greater Than John:*	Matt. 11:11	= Luke 7:28
3.	*Kingdom and Violence:*	Matt. 11:12–13	= Luke 16:16
4.	*Wisdom Justified:*	Matt. 11:16–19	= Luke 7:31–35

The exact location of *Kingdom and Violence* is somewhat uncertain, but I leave it there for the moment. What is most significant in that sequence of three or four units is its climax in *Wisdom Justified*. That unit places John and Jesus together, beyond any question of difference or superiority, as twin "children of Wisdom" rejected alike by "this generation." That is an understanding of John in scant accord with *Q Gospel* 7:28, and it necessarily casts reflective light back on those preceding units.

In summary, therefore, *Q Gospel* 7:28b within, first, *Q Gospel* 7:28, within, next, *Q Gospel* 7:24–35, and within, finally, the *Q Gospel* itself, could be tolerated because its stern negation was contextually muted. But the presence of *Q Gospel* 7:28 warns us that the *Q Gospel* knew a tradition asserting that the baptism movement of John was incompatible with the kingdom movement of Jesus.

Gospel of Thomas.

The presence of a parallel to *Q Gospel* 7:28 in *Gospel of Thomas* 46:1–2 proves, of course, that John the Baptist was known to the *Gospel of Thomas*, as hypothesized to explain *Gospel of Thomas* 78:1–3 in the preceding unit. But, unlike that case, there is no elimination of the Baptist in this instance:

Jesus said, "From Adam to John the Baptist, among those born of women, no one is so much greater than John the Baptist that his eyes should not be averted [*literally:* be broken]. But I have said that whoever among you becomes a child will know the kingdom and will become greater than John." (*Gospel of Thomas* 46)

The most significant difference from the *Q Gospel* version is that phrase "will know the kingdom" in *Gospel of Thomas* 46:2. First, the saying is quite complete without it. Next, it is not the usual verb that describes one's relationship to the kingdom in the *Gospel of Thomas*. We have, for example, "enter" the kingdom in 22:2, 3, 7; 99:3; 114:3; "find" the kingdom in 27:1; 49:1; and "is far from" the kingdom in 82:1. Finally, the theme of *knowing* is very characteristic of the *Gospel of Thomas*. In other words, the saying is already being moved, but delicately and minimally, along the trajectory particular to that gospel's esoteric and ascetical eschatology.

Conclusion.

There was a tension between John the Baptist and Jesus within the Common Sayings Tradition itself. It does not occur only at the redactional level of either the *Gospel of Thomas* or the *Q Gospel*. At that level, the former emphasizes it while the latter mutes it. It is, moreover, a tension between a Jesus who praises John profoundly in one saying, such as *Into the Desert*, and both praises and diminishes him profoundly in another, such as *Greater Than John*. John is greatest among prophets and more than a prophet. But he is *below the least* in the kingdom. It is not that he *is* least in the kingdom, because then he would clearly be in it. John the Baptist is not in the kingdom at all. That seems to indicate that there was already an anti-apocalyptic theology operative within the Common Sayings Tradition itself. But that puts it negatively. What was it *positively?* All of that serves as overture to the next complex, which mentions the positive alternative but still does not fill it out with much content. That still awaits the next chapter.

WHEN AND WHERE

The third saying in the Common Sayings Tradition that *concerns and replaces* apocalyptic eschatology is *When and Where* (Appendix 1A: #2). It is a Type 3 saying (Appendix 1B); that is, it has been redacted both toward asceticism in the *Gospel of Thomas* and toward apocalypticism in the *Q Gospel*. It is an extremely complex unit involving multiple independent sources. It appears, from the Common Sayings Tradition, in the *Q Gospel* as Q 17:23–24—that is, Luke 17:23–24 = Matthew 24:26–27—and, with three or even four versions, in *Gospel of Thomas* 113:1–4; 3:1–3; 51:1–2; and 18:13. It also appears independently in Mark 13:21–22 = Matthew 24:23–24 and in the special source used in Luke 17:20–22. There are, in other words, four mutually independent sources, not to speak of multiple versions within the *Gospel of Thomas* itself. My focus, of course, is on the Common Sayings Tradition, and I look at other versions only to sharpen that focus. Here are the sources and versions involved (in the order of their discussion below):

Source 1: *(Q Gospel)*   Matt. 24:26–27   = Luke 17:23–24
Source 2: (Mark)   Mark 13:21–23   = Matt. 24:23–25
Source 3: (Special Luke) Luke 17:20–21
Source 4: *(Gos. Thom.)*   Gos. Thom. 113:1–4 = 3:1–3 = 51:1–2 = 18:1–3

What makes this complex so important is, first, the multiple number of independent sources and, second, the fourfold alternative versions in the *Gospel of Thomas*. I look at those multiple sources and versions in five steps to build up the argument as clearly as possible: (1) the *Q Gospel* and Mark; (2) Special Luke and the *Gospel of Thomas* 113:1–4; (3) *Gospel of Thomas* 113:1–4 and 3:1–3; (4) *Gospel of Thomas* 51:1–2 and 18:1–3.

Q Gospel *and Mark.*

The twin versions of the *Q Gospel* in Matthew 24:26–27 and Luke 17:23–24 are quite different. Luke has a general "lo, here" and "lo, there," but Matthew has a specific "lo, in the desert" and "lo, in the secret chambers." There is nothing particularly substantive in those differences. I give the passage in the Lukan format:

They will say to you, "Look there!" or "Look here!" Do not go, do not set off in pursuit. For as the lightning flashes and lights up the sky from one side to the other, so will the Son of Man be in his day. (*Q Gospel* 17:23–24)

The version in Mark 13:21–23 has no corresponding parallel in Luke, but Matthew follows Mark closely in Matthew 24:23–25 before combining it with the *Q Gospel* version in Matthew 24:26–27. Here is the Markan version:

And if anyone says to you at that time, "Look, here is the Messiah!" or "Look, there he is!"—do not believe it. False messiahs and false prophets will appear and produce signs and omens, to lead astray, if possible, the elect. But be alert; I have already told you everything. (Mark 13:21–23)

When that *Q Gospel* text is compared with Mark, three points stand out. First, there is a common structure involving (a) some verb of *saying* with the subject left vague in the singular ("anyone") or plural ("they"); (b) double "lo" or "look" with disjunctive local specifications, such as here/there, there/here, or there/there; (c) single (Mark) or, more likely, double (*Q Gospel*) prohibition: "do not, do not." Second, the advent in the *Q Gospel* is that of the Son of Man, while in Mark it is that of the Christ. Third, the *Q Gospel* forbids such expectations because the arrival of the Son of Man will be sudden and unexpected, like lightning. It is future, but it will happen too fast for watching. Mark says that such statements proclaim "false" Christs, but the only reason is given much later, in 13:32: "About that day or hour no one knows, neither the angels in heaven, nor the Son, but only the Father."

Special Luke and Gospel of Thomas.

The next two units for comparison are the special material in Luke 17:20–21 and *Gospel of Thomas* 113:1–4. It is possible that what I have termed Special Luke 17:20–21 is actually from the *Q Gospel,* retained by Luke but omitted by Matthew. Since I am emphasizing what is most securely common to both the *Q Gospel* and the *Gospel of Thomas* I prefer to consider it as Special Luke while acknowledging that it *could* be from the *Q Gospel.* Here are the two texts:

Once Jesus was asked by the Pharisees when the kingdom of God was coming, and he answered, "The kingdom of God is not coming with things that can be observed; nor will they say, 'Look, here it is!' or 'There it is!' For, in fact, the kingdom of God is among you." (Luke 17:20–21)

His disciples said to him, "When will the kingdom come?" "It will not come by watching [=looking] for it. It will not be said [or: They will not say], 'Behold, here!' or 'Behold, there!' Rather, the kingdom of the Father is spread out upon the earth, and people do not see it." (*Gospel of Thomas* 113:1–4)

Those two units are very similar in content. They have the same question-and-answer format, and the reply corrects a "when come?" with an "already here." The former questioners are "the Pharisees"; the latter are "the disciples." The answer has three parts: the kingdom cannot be awaited or expected; there will therefore be no "look here or look there"; because the kingdom is already present. It is implicit from the very question that at least the questioners do not recognize the kingdom's presence among them, but that point is made explicit in *Gospel of Thomas* 113.

I have looked at four sources so far: the *Q Gospel*, Mark, Special Luke, and *Gospel of Thomas* 113. All agree that when people say look/look, they are wrong. But while in the *Q Gospel* and Mark it is the advent of the Christ or the Son of Man that is awaited, in Special Luke and *Gospel of Thomas* 113 it is the advent of the kingdom that is expected.

Gospel of Thomas 3 *and* 113.

The saying in *Gospel of Thomas* 3 has both Coptic and Greek versions. The latter is in P. Oxy. 654, lines 9–16 (Attridge 1989:114, 126). Since there is no substantive difference between them, I give only the former version. *Gospel of Thomas* 113 is extant only in Coptic. Here are the passages:

> Jesus said, "If your leaders say to you, 'Behold, the kingdom is in heaven,' then the birds of heaven will precede you. If they say to you, 'It is in the sea,' then the fish will precede you. Rather, the kingdom is within you and it is outside you. When you know yourselves, then you will be known, and you will understand that you are children of the living Father. But if you do not know yourselves, then you dwell in poverty, and you are the poverty. (*Gospel of Thomas* 3:1–5)

> His disciples said to him, "When will the kingdom come?" "It will not come by watching [=looking] for it. It will not be said [or: They will not say], 'Behold, here!' or 'Behold, there!' Rather, the kingdom of the Father is spread out upon the earth, and people do not see it." (*Gospel of Thomas* 113:1–4)

Even apart from the addition of 3:4–5's "when you know," the similarities and differences between 3:1–3 and 113:1–4 are very significant.

First, with regard to form. That first unit is an implicit dialogue but an explicit antagonism. Jesus and his unspecified hearers are on one side, and "your leaders" are on the other side. Those hearers can hear from their leaders incorrectly but from Jesus correctly. The second unit is an explicit dialogue but an implicit antagonism. Presumably those who "do not see" the kingdom's presence fail because they are "watching/looking" for its advent. But 113:1–4 taken even by itself implies that "the disciples" are among those "people" who cannot see the kingdom's presence; otherwise, they would not have asked that question. In addition, because of the terminal position of 113:1–4, one gets to it only after reading a lot of other dialogues in which the disciples are clearly on the wrong side.

Second, with regard to structure. In 113:1–4 there is a double "behold/here" and "behold/ there," followed by a contrasting alternative "rather [or: but]." In 3:1–3 that structure appears as a single but unbalanced "behold/heaven" and "–/sea" followed by "rather [or: but]." Is that common construction just coincidence, or are both those sayings diversified versions of the same basic unit? I answer tentatively in the affirmative because of the delicate parallels in form and structure just mentioned. Furthermore, the move seems to be from 113:1–4 toward 3:1–4—that is, from criticism of "people" to criticism of "leaders" and from the somewhat clearer "the kingdom of the Father is spread out upon the earth" to the somewhat more enigmatic "the kingdom is within you and it is outside you."

Third, with regard to rhetoric. The text in 113:1–4 is flat and factual. The kingdom is not to be expected because it is here already. The problem is not to await its future arrival but to recognize its actual presence. But clearly there are "people" who do not acknowledge that presence but still await its advent. There is also an implication in the very question itself ("When will the kingdom come?") that the disciples do not realize it is already present before them. But that point is certainly not emphasized. In 3:1–3, on the other hand, the rhetoric is polemically derisive, especially when compared with other usages of heaven/land/sea searches to emphasize impossibility, futility, or lack of necessity. The closest structural parallel is this one concerning the covenant commandment of God in Deuteronomy:

Surely, this commandment that I am commanding you today is not too hard for you, nor is it too far away. It is not in heaven, that you should say, "Who will go up to heaven for us, and get it for us so that we may hear it and observe it?" Neither is it beyond the sea, that you should say, "Who will cross to the other side of the sea for us, and get it for us so that we may hear it and observe it?" No, the word is very near to you; it is in your mouth and in your heart for you to observe. (Deuteronomy 30:11–14)

That is a very close parallel: covenant/kingdom is not distant (heaven/sea) but close, not there but here. The derisive tone, of course, appears much more evident (birds/fish) in 113:1–4. Needless to say, that derision is cheap polemics and no more. But it is interesting that once opposing "leaders" are mentioned, the level of the argument becomes nastier and shallower.

In terms of content, it is possible that 3:1–3 and 113:1–4 are two totally separate sayings making, each in its own way, a similar point. But I think it more probable that they are two versions of the same structural unit: the kingdom of God is not here or there in the future but here and now in the present. But some, be they "people" or "leaders," do not accept that position.

Gospel of Thomas 18 and 51.

I turn now to another set of two sayings. Read these with the former set still in mind.

His disciples said to him, "When will the rest for the dead take place, and when will the new world come?" He said to them, "What you look for has come, but you do not know it." (*Gospel of Thomas* 51:1–2)

The disciples said to Jesus, "Tell us how our end will be." Jesus said, "Have you discovered the beginning, then, that you are seeking after the end? For where the beginning is, the end will be. Blessed is one who stands at the beginning: that one will know the end and will not taste death." (*Gospel of Thomas* 18:1–3)

In terms of form both sayings are explicit dialogues, but there is little structural parallelism. In terms of rhetoric both responses are corrective—the former mockingly so, the latter emphatically so. In terms of content the twin dialogues are quite different: one asks about "our end" and the other about "the rest of the dead" and "the new world." They agree only on that verb "know."

Matrix and Development.

I see those seven texts as the varied developments of a single matrix. To make that clearly visible, I emphasize the common elements in them. Here are the texts, with development to the left and right of that common matrix in the middle:

Q Gospel (Reconstructed)	**Mark** (Mark 13:21)	**—Common Matrix—** (Luke 17:20–21)	(GT 113:1–4)	—*Gospel of Thomas*— (3:1–5)	(51:1–2)	(18:1–3)
		when	when		when	
Son of Man	Christ(s!)	Kingdom	Kingdom	Kingdom		
		come	come		come	
		observing	looking		look	
	say	say	said [say]	say		
behold	behold	behold	behold	behold		
twin places	twin places	twin places	twin places	twin places		
not/not	not/not					
rather		rather	rather	rather		
		among	spread	within/out		
			not see	know	not know	know

That matrix saying can be seen most clearly in Special Luke 17:20–21 and *Gospel of Thomas* 113:1–4. The only difference worth noting is the latter's concluding phrase "and people do not see it." But that only makes explicit what is already implicit in the very question itself ("when"). From that common matrix, the unit develops in three different directions. The first two are rather similar. Mark applies the saying to the advent of false Christs, the *Q Gospel* to the advent of the Son of Man. But the development in the *Gospel of Thomas* is most intense and instructive.

There are both verbal, formal, and structural links as well as very striking differences across those *Gospel of Thomas* texts. I place the four sayings in that left-to-right sequence because I propose that as their basic development. The core saying is 113:1–4. Its structure (say/behold/rather) reappears in 3:1–3, but its form (dialogue) reappears in 51:1–2. Those verbal changes, however, reflect profound theological changes. First, the sequence starts with looking for a future kingdom (wrong) as against recognizing a present kingdom (right) but concludes with seeking the end (wrong) as against discovering the beginning (right). Second, the sequence moves from the impersonal to the personal: 113:1–4 is about "them," but all the others are about "you." Third, and most significant, we begin with outsiders or "people" (*literally:* men) not "seeing" what they look for as already present before them but end with insiders or "disciples" not "knowing" what they look for as already present before them. Finally, separate sayings about "knowledge" (hence "know" above) are added on as *Gospel of Thomas* 3:4–5 to 3:1–3 and as 18:3 to 18:1–2. There is hardly a more obvious case of a pre-*Thomas* saying still visible terminally in 113 but also developed within *Thomas* to mean esoteric wisdom and hidden knowledge—externally by the addition of 3:4–5 to 3:1–3, internally by changes within 51:1–2, and both internally and externally in 18:1–2, 3.

Conclusion.

I interpret *When and Where* along with *Into the Desert* and *Greater Than John* within the Common Sayings Tradition. It opposes the sort of apocalyptic eschatology represented by John the Baptist. It is accepted and redacted in the *Q Gospel* so that it does not negate apocalyptic eschatology but rather confirms it. The event will be too sudden even for anticipatory signs. It is accepted in the *Gospel of Thomas* and then slowly but surely redacted into its own esoteric ascetical eschatology. That means, however, that neither of those gospels represents its original meaning. Each had to redact it in different directions. Put negatively, and in conjunction with those two other common sayings, it denies the validity of apocalyptic eschatology. Put positively, it indicates that the kingdom of God is present upon the earth already. But *how* is it present? The answer is in the units studied in the next chapter.

CHAPTER 18

AFFIRMING ETHICAL ESCHATOLOGY

The body is a model which can stand for any bounded system. Its boundaries can represent any boundaries which are threatened or precarious. The body is a complex structure. The functions of its different parts and their relations afford a source of symbols for other complex structures. We cannot possibly interpret rituals concerning excreta, breast milk, saliva, and the rest unless we are prepared to see in the body a symbol of society, and to see the powers and dangers credited to social structure reproduced in small on the human body.

Mary Douglas, Purity and Danger, p. 115

In all societies, both simple and complex, eating is the primary way of initiating and maintaining human relationships. . . . [O]nce the anthropologist finds out where, when, and with whom the food is eaten, just about everything else can be inferred about the relations among the society's members. . . . [T]o know what, where, how, when, and with whom people eat is to know the character of their society.

Peter Farb and George Armelagos, Consuming Passions, pp. 4, 211

In traditional societies, for instance, health care systems may be *the major* mechanism for social control.

Arthur Kleinman, Patients and Healers in the Context of Culture, p. 41

This chapter must be read as the positive complement of the preceding negative one. What *is* the kingdom of God if it is neither apocalyptically nor ascetically eschatological? It is marked by what I have termed *ethical eschatology,* a divinely mandated and nonviolent resistance to the normalcy of discrimination, exploitation, oppression, and persecution.

The three epigraphs above are the cross-cultural anthropological bases for this chapter, and their relevance will become clearer as I proceed. The foundational principle is the symbolic interaction of body-as-microcosm and society-as-macrocosm proposed by Mary Douglas. Yet what does that interaction mean?

How, for example, does a society's understanding of itself become mapped onto its regulations for the bodies within it? You can work with this other body but not eat with it, or you can eat with this other body but not marry it. Within that inter-action, two phenomena will be particularly important on the mesocosmic (or in-between) level. Eating and healing involve bodily interaction. They are not just about individual bodies as separated microcosms. Neither, though, are they about society as a larger macrocosm. They are perfect examples of that mesocosmic level where bodies come together and where society is symbolized by that interaction.

I used three units in the last chapter to establish the anti-apocalypticism of the Common Sayings Tradition: *Into the Desert, Greater Than John,* and *When and Where.* I use three different units here to establish its replacement: *Blessed the Poor, Hating One's Family,* and *Mission and Message.* Just as *When and Where* was of primary importance in the previous chapter, so is *Mission and Message* here.

BLESSED THE POOR

The first of the three Common Sayings Tradition units to be considered in this section is *Blessed the Poor* (Appendix 1A: #22). It is a Type 4 saying (Appendix 1B); that is, it has been redacted neither toward asceticism in the *Gospel of Thomas* nor toward apocalypticism in the *Q Gospel.* It must be seen in conjunction with two other beatitudes (Appendix 1A: #28, #29):

Blessed the Poor:	*Gos. Thom.* 54	Q: Luke 6:20	= Matt. 5:3
Blessed the Persecuted:	*Gos. Thom.* 68 = 69:1	Q: Luke 6:22–23	= Matt. 5:11–12
Blessed the Hungry:	*Gos. Thom.* 69:2	Q: Luke 6:21a	= Matt. 5:6

This chapter looks only at that first beatitude. But all three refer to the same reality: the poor are the hungry are the persecuted or oppressed. But first a few preliminary words about beatitudes.

Beatitudes.

A *beatitude* is a declaration not just of secular or humanly accredited happi-ness but of religious or divinely approved happiness. It is a declaration that someone or something is blessed by God. The classic translation "blessed" makes that transcendental source more evident than modern ones such as "happy" or "to-be-congratulated." In any case, that generic designation creates certain expectations against its cultural background. Two main points are impor-tant for the present example.

The first point concerns internal structure. Beatitudes often have a two-part structure involving, in the first part, a *declaration* of who or what is blessed and, in the second, the *reason* that they or it is blessed, as in Psalm 128:1–2:

> Declaration: Happy is everyone who fears the Lord,
> who walks in his ways.
>> Reason: You shall eat the fruit of the labor of your hands;
> you shall be happy,
> and it shall go well with you.

The second point concerns external structure. Beatitudes are often found in pairs, and that external poetic parallelism is often mirrored by an internal one within each blessing, as in Psalm 32:1–2:

> Happy are those whose transgression is forgiven,
>> whose sin is covered.
> Happy are those to whom the Lord imputes no iniquity,
>> and in whose spirit there is no deceit.

But beatitudes can also appear in a series, with from three to as many as nine cases. For example, among the 15,000 fragments of about 550 manuscripts found in Cave 4 at Qumran near the Dead Sea, there is one catalogued as 4Q525 (*DSST* 395). It has five beatitudes on the pursuit of divine wisdom still extant, and there may have been several more lost at the beginning of the fragment. That compares with the three beatitudes in the Common Sayings Tradition and the four originally present in the *Q Gospel*—the latter now retained as four in Luke 6:20b–23 but expanded to nine in Matthew 5:3–12.

Q Gospel.

This version of the beatitude is neutral with regard to the *declaration* ("blessed the poor") in both Luke 6:20b and Matthew 5:3, but the former gives the *reason* in the second-person plural with "you," while the latter gives it in the third-person plural with "they." One must, therefore, decide which was in the *Q Gospel* text. I myself prefer the second-person-plural format, because that is found for both *declaration* and *reason* in the fourth *Q Gospel* beatitude, *Blessed the Persecuted*, in Luke 6:2–23 = Matthew 5:11–12.

> Blessed are you who are poor, for yours is the kingdom of God. (*Q Gospel* 6:20b)

Could that variation of "you" and "they" in these beatitudes have developed from an initial first-person formulation: "Blessed [are we] poor, for ours is the kingdom of God"?

Gospel of Thomas.

The beatitude *Blessed the Poor* in *Gospel of Thomas* 54 has the characteristic two-part structure involving a *declaration* of who or what is blessed and the *reason* that they or it is blessed:

> Jesus said, "Blessed are the poor, for yours is the kingdom of heaven."
> (*Gospel of Thomas* 54)

The *declaration* is neutral ("blessed the poor"); only the *reason* is explicitly formulated in the second-person plural with "you."

The Poor or the Destitute?

We have one very serious impediment to a contemporary understanding of that ancient beatitude. How should we translate and understand the Greek word in the phrase "blessed are the *ptōchoi*"? (I am not, by the way, presuming that Jesus spoke Greek, only that those who recorded or interpreted him knew the appropriate words to use.) Here is the problem, as analyzed in the extremely helpful doctoral dissertation of Gildas Hamel. First, the most common words for the needy in the Hebrew Bible are *ani* and *ebyon*. "The difference . . . was in the immediacy of need. Whereas the *ani* was pressed by debts and dependent upon the good grace of an employer or creditor, the *ebyon* needed to be helped at once if he was to survive" (5). Those terms, however, often appear as a tandem set— as they do, for example, in these representative cases:

> You shall not withhold the wages of poor [*ani*] and needy [*ebyon*] laborers, whether other Israelites or aliens who reside in your land in one of your towns. (Deuteronomy 24:14)

> Hear this, you that trample on the needy [*ebyon*], and bring to ruin the poor [*ani*] of the land. (Amos 8:4)

> The murderer rises at dusk to kill the poor [*ani*] and needy [*ebyon*], and in the night is like a thief. (Job 24:14)

Classical Greek usage had also two words for the needy: *penēs* (whence our term penury) and *ptōchos*. Once again, "the latter referred to a more severe, and the former to a less severe, form of poverty" (1983:6). The term *penēs* was applied to "all those people who need to work in shops or in the fields and were consequently without the leisure characteristic of the *plousioi* [rich], who were free to give their time to politics, *paideia* [learning], and war"; but the "*ptōchos* was on the margins, and recognized by everyone as such. . . . Poor and rich belonged to the same world and placed themselves on a common, ever sliding scale, but beggars could not. The *ptōchos* was someone who had lost many or all of his family and social ties. He often was a wanderer, therefore a foreigner for others, unable to tax for any length of time the resources of a group to which he could contribute very little or nothing at all" (1983:8). A representative example of that distinction appears in a comedy of Aristophanes first staged in the spring of 388 B.C.E. One character, Chremulos, asserts that the poor person *(penēs)* and the beggar *(ptōchos)* are but the same thing. A personified Poverty emphatically defends herself from that calumny in *The Plutus*, lines 552–554 (Rogers 1924: 3.414–415):

> 'Tis a *beggar* alone who has nought of his own,
>   nor even an obol possesses.
> My *poor* man, 'tis true, has to scrape and to screw
>   and his work he must never be slack in;
> There'll be no superfluity found in his cot;
>   but then there will nothing be lacking.

We are dealing, quite obviously, with slippery, sliding terms often relative to speaker and class, but the general conclusion of Hamel is clear and correct: "There were two broad categories for which our words 'poverty' and 'indigence' are approximations. The wider category included all those with some income, but without the means, especially leisure, necessary for such social activities as entertaining, education, political and religious service.... The narrower category included all those who had lost this minimal degree of security and were dependent for their food, clothing and lodging on organized charity and the evocation of feelings of pity" (1983:344).

That distinction between poverty and destitution was much more absolute in rural than in urban situations. There the great divide between the poor and the destitute coincided generally with that between the landed peasant and the landless peasant, and especially between the landed peasant and the dispossessed peasant. On one side were the family farmers, however small their plots might be. On the other were the tenant farmers, sharecroppers, day-laborers, and beggars. Whenever, in the New Testament, you read the term *poor* in English, it is *destitute* in Greek. The term *poor* denoted the vast majority of the world, and one might boast of belonging to the hard-working poor as distinct from the idle rich. Nobody, in that world or in any ever since, boasted of beggary. This, then, is the proper translation: "Blessed are the destitute." And that is what requires explanation on, simultaneously, the religious and economic levels.

We tend to think of "poor" or "destitute" as *either* spiritual and religious *or* social and economic. But, as we saw earlier with *justice* and *righteousness*, biblical usage favors words that are emphatically and absolutely *both* at the same time. This is a similar situation. Terms such as *poor* and *destitute* must be taken *both* socially *and* spiritually, *both* religiously *and* economically. And that combined focus raises questions that are structural and systemic, not just individual and personal. There is no biblical delusion that the poor and the destitute are personally better and holier than the rich and the powerful. But since the biblical God is a God of justice and righteousness who prefers slaves to oppressors, to be poor or destitute gets you special protection and concern. You cannot take those terms as *only* economically indicative, but neither can you take them as *only* religiously indicative. Thus, for example, when *we* read that qualification "poor in spirit" in Matthew 5:3, *we* tend to take it as exclusively spiritual. The poor in spirit are the humble, those who recognize their spiritual poverty before God. There is, of, course, no such qualification in Luke 6:20b or *Gospel of Thomas* 54, which means that "in spirit" is best taken as Matthean redaction. If "the poor" are understood only spiritually, it makes no difference whether the text is phrased as "the poor" or "the destitute"; for humans standing spiritually before God, both terms mean the same thing. But it makes a world of difference which term you use when you are speaking *both* economically and socially *as well as* spiritually and religiously—and especially when you are speaking of spirit and religion *because of* society and economics.

Conclusion.

I focused here on the beatitude for the destitute, but *destitute* equals *hungry* equals *persecuted* (in the sense of oppressed, exploited, and rejected). All three beatitudes speak to the same situation. This is an instance where hearing Jesus in personal and individual rather than in structural and systemic terms begets serious misunderstanding. Does Jesus think that the destitute are all good people and that the aristocrats are all evil ones? Does he have some delusion about the romantic charms of homelessness? God is for the destitute and powerless not because they are individually good but because their situation is structurally unjust. God is against the rich and powerful not because they are individually evil but because they are systemically evil. The Jewish God has no preferential option for the poor; rather, the Jewish God has a preferential option for justice.

HATING ONE'S FAMILY

The second of the three Common Sayings Tradition units to be considered in this section is *Hating One's Family* (Appendix 1A: #23). It is a Type 1 saying (Appendix 1B); that is, it has been redacted toward asceticism in the *Gospel of Thomas* but not toward apocalypticism in the *Q Gospel*. It appears in the *Q Gospel* as Q 14:25–26—that is, Luke 14:25–26 = Matthew 10:37—and as twin versions in *Gospel of Thomas* 55:1–2a and 101.

There are several sayings of Jesus about the family whose virulence is striking even in the context of a full canonical gospel, where they might get lost in a larger text. Apart from ones such as *Blessed the Womb* and *Jesus' True Family* (Appendix 2A: #71, #86), which are in the *Gospel of Thomas* but not in the *Q Gospel,* there are two such sayings in the Common Sayings Tradition (Appendix 1A: #6, #23):

Peace or Sword:	Gos. Thom. 16	Q: Luke 12:51–53	= Matt. 10:34–36
Hating One's Family:	Gos. Thom. 55:1–2a and 101	Q: Luke 14:25–26	= Matt. 10:37

Both of those are Type 1 sayings. For now, though, I look only at the latter one.
Q Gospel.
There are differences between the Lukan and Matthean versions of this beatitude, but nothing substantive is at stake. This is my proposal for the original *Q Gospel* version:

> If anyone does not hate his own father and mother, he cannot be my disciple; and if anyone does not hate his brother and sisters, he cannot be my disciple. (*Q Gospel* 14:26)

The *Q Gospel*'s redacted versions cite different family members. Matthew has two sets of kinfolk: "father and mother, son and daughter." Luke has three sets of kinfolk: "father and mother, wife and children, brothers and sisters." What did the original *Q Gospel* have?

The first set of kinfolk—"father and mother"—is quite secure. The second set may be redactional in both cases, but in different ways, as Stephen Patterson suggests (1993a:45). Matthew, on the one hand, placed *Hating One's Family* in 10:37 immediately after *Peace or Sword* in 10:34–36, so that the combination of "father, mother, son, daughter" may have infiltrated from the latter into the former text. Luke, on the other, may have added in "wife and children" to his *Q Gospel* source just as Luke 18:29b added in "wife" to his Markan source (Mark 10:29). The third set of kinfolk—"brothers and sisters"—omitted by Matthew but retained by Luke, was most likely what alone followed "father and mother" in the original *Q Gospel.*
Gospel of Thomas.
There are two separate versions, one very close to the *Q Gospel* account and one moving clearly along its own quite separate redactional trajectory:

> Jesus said, "Whoever does not hate father and mother cannot be a disciple of me, and whoever does not hate brothers and sisters, and bear the cross as I do, will not be worthy of me. (*Gospel of Thomas* 55:1–2)

Whoever does not hate [father] and mother as I do cannot be a [disciple] of me, and whoever does [not] love [father and] mother as I do cannot be a [disciple] of me. For my mother [. . .], but my true [mother] gave me life. (*Gospel of Thomas* 101:1–3)

You can easily see in that second version how *Gospel of Thomas* 52:1–2 is first summarized in 101:1 and then adapted to a new interpretation in 101:2–3. Instead of an earthly (false) mother who brings one into the realm of death and darkness stands a heavenly (true) mother who brings one into the realm of life and light. The earthly family is little better than a house of prostitution:

Jesus said, "Whoever knows the father and the mother will be called the child of a whore." (*Gospel of Thomas* 105)

On the other hand, in the *Gospel of Thomas* Jesus' true male parent is God the Father. He speaks of "the things of *my* Father" in 61:3, of "the places of *my* Father" in 64:12, of "the will of *my* Father" in 99:3, and of "the kingdom of *my* Father" in 99:4. And Jesus' true female parent is Wisdom the Mother, as above in 101:3. Similarly, for example, the *Acts of Thomas*, a text of Edessa in Syria dated to the third century and continuing the traditions found in the *Gospel of Thomas*, has the apostle Thomas pray to Jesus and conclude with these words (*NTA* 2.356):

We glorify and praise thee and thine invisible Father and thy Holy Spirit and the Mother of all creation. (*Acts of Thomas* 39)

For the Common Sayings Tradition, therefore, I look only at *Q Gospel* 14:26 and *Gospel of Thomas* 55:1–2 and 101:1, ignoring 101:2–3 entirely. How is that rather savage attack on the family to be explained? It is, of course, even more surprising against the background of traditional peasant society, where family farm and family cooperation were morally and physically, socially and economically fundamental.

The ordinary answer is that faith is even more fundamental than family, that Jesus is forcing people to believe in him over against even their own family, or that he is criticizing the hierarchical inequalities of society microcosmically present in the family itself. But is there something else at work here as well? Rural commercialization dislocates peasant life and greatly weakens the peasant family itself so that it can no longer protect its members as it breaks into isolated individuals each seeking their own survival. Jesus is not speaking to the well-off, advising them to give up their possessions—advocating asceticism, in effect. He is speaking especially to dispossessed peasants seeking to restore their dignity and security in the name of God. In the same way, he is not speaking primarily to strong peasant families and trying to break them apart for or against himself. He is speaking especially to those whom family has failed and is substituting for that lost grouping an alternative one, the companionship of the kingdom of God. My proposal, therefore, is that Jesus and his first companions were not destroying families who were viable but replacing families who were not.

One final point. There is no mention of husband versus wife in the Common Sayings Tradition, the *Q Gospel*, or the *Gospel of Thomas*, but only in the Lukan redaction of *Hating One's Family*. Only opposition to parents and to siblings is specified elsewhere. Neither is there any husband-versus-wife wording in the *Peace or Sword* saying mentioned earlier. Only opposition between the generations is specified there. That agrees with another very strongly attested saying of Jesus: *Against Divorce* (Appendix 2B: #54). If one wished to break up families, setting husband against wife and wife against husband would be the fastest route. But Antipas's urbanization struck hardest at the responsibility of parents for children and of siblings for one another. It is the debris of totally or partially dispossessed peasant families that are invited into the fictive kinship or new family of the kingdom under a Father who can withstand even Roman commercialization.

Conclusion.

Hating One's Family, along with *Peace or Sword,* confirms my proposal that Jesus' primary focus was on peasants dispossessed by Roman commercialization and Herodian urbanization in the late 20s in Lower Galilee. The itinerants as the just-recently-dispossessed destitute and the householders as the possibly-soon-dispossessed poor are brought together into a new family, a companionship of empowerment that is the kingdom of God. It does not break families apart but regroups those families torn apart already (or soon to be torn apart across the generations).

MISSION AND MESSAGE

The last of the three Common Sayings Tradition units to be considered in this section is *Mission and Message* (Appendix 1A: #5). It is a Type 3 saying (Appendix 1B); that is, it has been redacted both toward asceticism in the *Gospel of Thomas* and toward apocalypticism in the *Q Gospel*. I gave it pride of place in my earlier work *The Historical Jesus,* saying that it indicated "the heart of Jesus' program" and adding, "If that is incorrect, this book will have to be redone" (304). It is still, for me, the most important unit for understanding the historical Jesus, the Common Sayings Tradition, and the continuity from one to the other. It is where I see the continuation from the historical Jesus to his first companions most clearly and even physically. I interpret many ambiguous sayings and open aphorisms from the Common Sayings Tradition in the light of this complex. It is also, for me, the clearest evidence that Jesus and his earliest companions had not just a vision but a program, not just an idea but a plan. Here, clearly, the kingdom of God is not about me but about us, not about individuality but about society, not about heaven but about earth. It is about divine justice here below.

But even apart from all that, the unit demands special emphasis for several independent reasons. First, it is about words and deeds *together*. It is, in fact, about deeds mandated in words. It is therefore a good place to bypass the dreary debate about the ascendancy of words over deeds or deeds over words in historical Jesus research. Two examples, one each way. My Jesus Seminar colleague Burton Mack emphasizes words or teachings. The first two pages of his book on the *Q Gospel* mention "teachings" eight times, as in this example: "It makes a difference whether the founder of a movement is remembered for his teachings, or for his deeds and destiny. For the first followers of Jesus, the importance of Jesus as the founder of their movement was directly related to the significance they attached to his teachings" (1–2). E. P. Sanders emphasizes deeds or "facts." His work, seeking "the securest evidence[,] . . . is based primarily on facts about Jesus and only secondarily on a study of some of the sayings material" (1985:3, 5). The securest evidence, surely, is neither words *without* deeds nor deeds *without* words, but words *and* deeds coming together most profoundly. That combination indicates that Jesus did not have just a powerful vision but also a practical program, not just a personal or individual lifestyle but a communal and social plan.

Second, this unit is present not only in the Common Sayings Tradition. It is also found directly in Mark and indirectly in Paul. Furthermore, it is also important for the *Didache,* a document whose reactions to this program will receive much fuller study in the next chapter. This unit is, as I understand it, the heart of the Common Sayings Tradition. Its presence makes that corpus coherent and helps all the other units fall into place.

Third, this is the unit where *text* moves into closest *conjunction* with *context,* and therefore where my method succeeds or fails most fully and absolutely. But this third point depends on that second one. If this unit is but peripheral to the Common Sayings Tradition and not, as it were, its heart, then any conjunction with the context would not be significant in any case. So, in what follows, watch this unit as central and watch also the conjunction of it and the other Common Sayings Tradition units with the proposed anthropological, historical, and archeological context proposed earlier.

I begin by looking separately at the three versions of this saying in the *Gospel of Thomas,* the *Q Gospel,* and Mark. Next, I consider the common elements in all three (or at least two) of those independent accounts. Finally, I draw some general conclusions from those comparisons.

The Three Versions

Gospel of Thomas.

The version in *Gospel of Thomas* 14:4 is about as brief as possible, and it is probably there not so much for itself as for what follows and interprets it in 14:5. That makes it, however, all the more significant. It is only there residually, as it were, hanging on by its fingertips. It must, therefore, be earlier tradition.

> Jesus said to them, "If you fast, you will bring sin upon yourselves, and if you pray, you will be condemned, and if you give alms, you will harm your spirits. When you go into any country and walk from place to place, when the people receive you, eat what they serve you and heal the sick among them. For what goes into your mouth will not defile you; rather, it is what comes out of your mouth that will defile you." (*Gospel of Thomas* 14:1–5)

The *Gospel of Thomas* repeatedly denies validity to the most basic aspects of traditional Jewish piety and purity. But in each case notice the positive that accompanies the negative judgment:

> If you do not fast from the world, you will not find the kingdom. If you do not keep the sabbath as sabbath you will not see the Father. (*Gospel of Thomas* 27:1–2)

> His disciples said to him, "Is circumcision useful or not?" He said to them, "If it were useful, their father would produce children already circumcised from their mother. Rather, the true circumcision in spirit has become profitable in every respect." (*Gospel of Thomas* 53:1–3)

So also here. There is a negation of fasting, praying, almsgiving, and food-purity codes. All of that normal spiritual discipline is inadequate against the radical demand of celibate asceticism.

What is fascinating, however, is how, even against a totally divergent theological background, the basic elements of the unit are still present: itinerancy, eating with those who receive you, and healing their sick. There are even slight but significant indications that this is a regular rather than an unusual and a rural rather than an urban phenomenon. Focus on that phrase "when you go into any country and walk from place to place." That word "when" indicates a regular situation or a normal occurrence. And that phrase "walk from place to place" uses a specific Greek loan-word meaning the countryside as distinct from the city, so that a more literal translation would be, with Layton, "travel in the (country) places" (1987:383), with Meyer, "walk through the countryside" (1992:29), or, with Patterson, "walk about in the countryside" (1993a:131). That radical itinerancy was, in other words, more normal than special and more rural than urban. But, despite my title for this complex, *Mission and Message,* I underline Patterson's comment that "originally the ideal of radical itinerancy was not necessarily linked with early Christian 'mission' at all but rather had more the quality of a permanent manner of living, a life-style advocated by the Jesus movement" (1993a:132). That point will reappear with the *Q Gospel.*

Q Gospel.

This is a classic instance of a unit that is found in both the *Q Gospel* and in Mark and that therefore posed a problem to Matthew and Luke, who used those twin sources. Their obvious options were duplication, elimination, or conflation; they could, in other words, keep both, choose one and omit the other, or combine both into a single coherent unity. In the present instance Matthew chose conflation in Matthew 9:37–10:14, while Luke, fortunately for us, chose duplication in Luke 9:1–6 and 10:4–11. These are the parallel versions:

Q Gospel:	Luke 10:4–11 =	Matt. 10:7, 10b, 12–14
Mark:	Mark 6:7–13 = Luke 9:1–6 =	Matt. 10:1, 8–10a, 11

What that means, however, is that we must depend very heavily on the *Mission and Message* version in Luke 10:4–11 to recreate the *Q Gospel* original. I give it here along with the immediately subsequent verses in *Q Gospel* 10:12–15, which will be important as we proceed.

Carry no purse, no bag, no sandals; and greet no one on the road. Whatever house you enter, first say, "Peace to this house!" And if anyone is there who shares in peace, your peace will rest on that person; but if not, it will return to you. Remain in the same house, eating and drinking whatever they provide, for the laborer deserves to be paid. Do not move about from house to house. Whenever you enter a town and its people welcome you, eat what is set before you; cure the sick who are there, and say to them, "The kingdom of God has come near to you." But whenever you enter a town and they do not welcome you, go out into its streets and say, "Even the dust of your town that clings to our feet, we wipe off in protest against you. Yet know this: the kingdom of God has come near." (*Q Gospel* 10:4–11)

"I tell you, on that day it will be more tolerable for Sodom than for that town. 'Woe to you, Chorazin! Woe to you, Bethsaida!' For if the deeds of power done in you had been done in Tyre and Sidon, they would have repented long ago, sitting in sackcloth and ashes. But at the judgment it will be more tolera ble for Tyre and Sidon than for you. And you, Capernaum, will you be exalted to heaven? No, you will be brought down to Hades." (*Q Gospel* 10:12–15)

That is, of course, a much more developed text than the one just seen in *Gospel of Thomas* 14:4, but the same three key elements of itinerancy, eating with those who receive you, and healing their sick are all clearly present once again. There are also entirely new elements, such as the dress and equipment commands, the difference between house and city, and especially the mention of the kingdom of God as present.

Mark.

As mentioned earlier, Mark's version was conflated with that of the *Q Gospel* in Matthew but kept as a separate incident in Luke 9:1–6. It is not all in direct discourse, as in *Gospel of Thomas* 14:4 and *Q Gospel* 10:4–12. Instead, two sections of indirect discourse frame a smaller central one in direct address:

He called the twelve and began to send them out two by two, and gave them authority over the unclean spirits. He ordered them to take nothing for their journey except a staff; no bread, no bag, no money in their belts; but to wear sandals and not to put on two tunics. He said to them, "Wherever you enter a house, stay there until you leave the place [*literally:* thence]. If any place will not welcome you and they refuse to hear you, as you leave, shake off the dust that is on your feet as a testimony against them." So they went out and proclaimed that all should repent. They cast out many demons, and anointed with oil many who were sick and cured them. (Mark 6:7–13)

Three small items of Markan redaction are immediately evident. One is an emphasis on both exorcisms and healings, as earlier for Jesus so now for the Twelve:

He cured many who were sick with various diseases, and cast out many demons; and he would not permit the demons to speak, because they knew him. (Mark 1:34)

He had cured many, so that all who had diseases pressed upon him to touch him. Whenever the unclean spirits saw him, they fell down before him and shouted, "You are the Son of God!" (Mark 3:10–11)

Another item is the demand for repentance as a prerequisite for accepting the kingdom of God. Since, for Mark, it came first in humility and hiddenness, it demands a radical change, a repentance (*metanoia* in Greek), in order to accept it as such. Hence, that inaugural summary:

Jesus came to Galilee, proclaiming the good news of God, and saying, "The time is fulfilled, and the kingdom of God has come near; repent, and believe in the good news." (Mark 1:14b–15)

The final small change is the allowance of staff and sandals, two items so normally expected that their permission certifies an earlier negation. And, of course, we already saw that negation of sandals in *Q Gospel* 10:4. Such permissions guarantee that those prescriptions were not idealistic rhetoric. Jesus said sandals or staff were forbidden, and his companions actually tried but found it too difficult; Jesus then had to "say" sandals or staff were permitted. Luke, faced with "no sandals" from *Q Gospel* 10:4 and "sandals" from Mark 6:9, simply omitted any mention of them in his parallel Luke 9:3. Those small Lukan changes are reassuring because, apart from smoothing out such contradictions, Luke's strategy was to stay relatively close to his Markan source in Luke 9:1–6 and to his *Q Gospel* source in Luke 10:4–11.

The Common Elements

Itinerants and Householders.

Itinerants and householders are the official terms I use for *those who arrive* and *those who receive* them in the three texts. They are also, to underline their importance, used in the titles of Parts VII and VIII. Recall the *context* for a moment. Anthropology, history, and archeology came together to form a picture of rural commercialization and Roman urbanization against Jewish tradition and peasant resistance in Lower Galilee during the 20s of the first common-era century. What that process meant was not just taxation or even *heavy* taxation. Taxation was nothing new and may not have been any worse then than at any other time during hundreds of years of imperial control. What that process meant was a complete dislocation of peasant life, family support, and village security. Some peasants, of course, did quite well at the expense of others. But, for those others, it meant certain indebtedness, possible enslavement, and probable dispossession. It meant a move from subsistence on a small family farm to the status of tenant farmer, landless laborer, beggar, or bandit. That commercialization process set against one another those *poor* peasants who might be dispossessed tomorrow and those *destitute* peasants who had been dispossessed yesterday. It is those *destitute landless ones* and *poor landed ones* that the kingdom-of-God movement brings together as *itinerants* and *householders*.

Eating and Healing.

Two points are of importance here. First, the program Jesus outlines is not about almsgiving. It is not about food handed out to beggars at the door. Jesus *could* have inaugurated a kingdom of beggars, but that is not what all three texts agree in emphasizing. Second, given that the program is to be a reciprocal experience rather than almsgiving, what is the logic of that reciprocity? Itinerants need food, of course, but would not a handout suffice? Everyone needs healing, of course, but why do householders need it in particular?

The itinerants look at the householders, which is what they were yesterday or the day before, with envy and even hatred. The householders look at the itinerants, which is what they may be tomorrow or the day after, with fear and contempt. The kingdom program forces those two groups into conjunction with one another and starts to rebuild peasant community ripped apart by commercialization and urbanization. But just as that eating is both symbolic and actual, so also is that healing both symbolic and actual. I understand that process, of course, against the earlier background on the meaning of healing. What the itinerants bring is ideological, symbolic, and material resistance to oppression and exploitation, and that—precisely that—is healing. Such resistance cannot directly cure disease, as vaccines can destroy viruses or drugs can destroy bacteria, but resistance can heal both sickness and illness and thus sometimes indirectly cure disease.

Acceptance and Rejection.

I correlate here two disjunctions: acceptance/rejection and house/city. What is significant about these disjunctions is how they mesh with one another. As you move from house to city, the rhetoric about rejection escalates quite brutally.

All three texts agree on the possibility of rejection. But it is at very best implicit in *Gospel of Thomas* 14:4 with the phrase "when the people receive you." That *implies* that they might not, but nothing more is said about it.

In Mark both possibilities are more explicitly present. There can be acceptance, "wherever you enter a house" in 6:19, and rejection, "if any place will not welcome you" in 6:11. Listeners are told not to respond aggressively but with a gesture almost comic in its dismissive reaction.

In the *Q Gospel*, however, the theme of acceptance or rejection meshes closely with that of house and city. But the situation at the house in *Q Gospel* 10:6 ("And if anyone is there who shares in peace, your peace will rest on that person; but if not, it will return to you") seems much milder and less violent than that in the city in *Q Gospel* 10:12 ("I tell you, on that day, it will be more tolerable for Sodom than for that town"). And the rhetoric continues to escalate against specific places, such as Chorazin, Bethsaida, and Capernaum in the immediately succeeding *Q Gospel* 10:13–15. That is a very striking duplication of acceptance and rejection, first for the *house* in *Q Gospel* 10:5–7 and then for the *city* in *Q Gospel* 10:8–12. Notice, for contrast, that Mark mentions only a "house" in 6:10 for acceptance and a vaguer "place" in 6:11 for rejection. What does that dichotomy of house and city and the escalating rhetoric of acceptance and rejection indicate in the *Q Gospel*?

My proposal is that the *Q Gospel* text tells us not only about what was planned but also about what was experienced. It records not only the program of Jesus but also the effects of that program. And, above all, it recounts what happened in the move from houses and hamlets to towns and cities. A program originally directed at *houses*—that is, at the courtyards in the narrow alleys of small hamlets—moved on to *cities* and met there with a much more aggressive rejection. Things got nastier all around. There are, in other words, two successive historical stages represented in that *Q Gospel* text, one to houses and one to cities. That is why, for example, there are two mentions of eating, in *Q Gospel* 10:7 (house) and *Q Gospel* 10:8 (city).

Power and Authority.

In a 1992 doctoral dissertation at Emory University, Werner Kahl undertook a detailed comparative analysis of about 150 stories of "miraculous restoration to health or to life" in Jewish, pagan Greco-Roman, and Christian traditions up to the year 100 C.E. I focus here on just one point from that very comprehensive study. He distinguished three types of miracle workers, depending on whether they appeared as bearer (BNP), petitioner (PNP), or mediators (MNP) of numinous power. He looked, in other words, at whether miracle workers effected healing by their own inherent authority or by praying to or invoking the power of some other divine being. In appraising Jesus as healer and miracle-worker, Kahl identified him as a BNP rather than a PNP or a MNP. On the one hand, "Moses, Elijah, Elisha, Hanina, Peter, and Paul are usually depicted as men who are able to activate their god by means of *prayer*. . . . This distinction is even more pronounced in comparison with the apostles in Acts. Peter and Paul have to invoke the ascended Jesus or refer to his name in *every* case of a healing miracle" (90, 101). On the other hand, "Yahweh, Jesus, Asclepios, and Apollonios *incorporate* a divine power in themselves. . . . Jesus incorporates the healing power personally, functioning as the *means* of God's healing activity. . . . Jesus generally appears as a BNP in the gospels. Unlike the OT prophets, the rabbis, and the apostles in Acts, he does not need to come before his god as a suppliant, or refer to a BNP mightier than himself whenever he wants to effect healing. . . . As with Asclepios and Apollonios, Jesus' superhuman ability is due to divine descent . . ." (90, 95, 102).

Yahweh, God of Israel, and Asklepios, god of healing, are transcendent figures, so that puts Jesus of Nazareth and the contemporary Apollonios of Tyana in a very special light. "Jesus was generally conceived of as an *immanent* bearer of numinous power, and . . . in this regard he could best be compared with Apollonios of Tyana; to both figures were also attributed a great number of healing miracle stories. In fact, the two characteristics (being an *immanent bearer* of numinous power and having *more than one* healing miracle story attributed to it) are shared only by Jesus in the gospels and Apollonios in Philostratus' *Vita*. Since Philostratus' *Vita Apollonii* dates from around 220 C.E., it is evident that the description of Jesus in the gospels is distinct from the other extant contemporary traditions of the first century C.E. insofar as the BNPs of those stories are *transcendent* figures" (326–327).

It is noteworthy that Jesus does not tell his departing companions to heal by praying to God for help or to heal by invoking Jesus' own name. You could argue, of course, that all of that is implicit, that they operate, as it were, with borrowed power and temporary authority. My point is simply that this expected emphasis is not explicitly present. Jesus heals, and they are told to go do the same.

Those preceding four points—itinerants and householders, eating and healing, rejection and acceptance, power and authority—arise in the Common Sayings Tradition and in Mark as well. There is an additional point on dress and equipment that is found only in the *Q Gospel* and Mark. I mention it in conclusion since it was *possibly* present in the Common Sayings Tradition but omitted by the *Gospel of Thomas*. I do not put any weight on it, however, citing it here only for completion. It simply confirms something already evident—namely, that reciprocity of eating and healing and the difference between generous almsgiving and open commensality. But before turning to a discussion of dress and equipment, I need an aside on the ancient philosophy called Cynicism

An Aside on Cynicism.

Diogenes of Sinope lived from 404 to 323 B.C.E., and his longevity might be considered an argument for his lifestyle. He was a student of Antisthenes, who was a student of Socrates. The term *cynic*, from the Greek word for *dog*, reflects the deliberate disdain with which Cynics provocatively flouted the normal conventions of human life. Their philosophy was above all else populist and practical rather than elitist and theoretical. They not only practiced what they preached, their practice was their preaching and their preaching was their practice. They were to be found more in marketplace and temple courtyard than in study hall and classroom. "The Cynics sought happiness through freedom," as Farrand Sayre summed them up. "The Cynic conception of freedom included freedom from desires, from fear, anger, grief and other emotions, from religious or moral control, from the authority of the city or state or public officials, from regard for public opinion and freedom also from the care of property, from confinement to any locality and from the care and support of wives and children. . . . The Cynics scoffed at the customs and conventionalities of others, but were rigid in observance of their own. The Cynic would not appear anywhere without his wallet, staff and cloak, which must invariably be worn, dirty and ragged and worn so as to leave the right shoulder bare. He never wore shoes and his hair and beard were long and unkempt" (7, 18). Notice the symbolic catechesis of that garb for later discussion.

There has been much discussion recently on the relationship between the historical Jesus (or the Q *Gospel* or early Christianity) and practical Cynicism. Two recent articles that agree quite correctly on many of the problems and excesses of those comparisons come up, nevertheless, with greatly divergent conclusions in their final sentences. On the one hand, from Hans Dieter Betz: "In conclusion, are further investigations of the hypothesis worth doing? In the light of the criticism above, the reply to this question can only be a conditional but resounding yes. Even if in the final analysis the slogan of 'Jesus the Cynic' should turn out to be a contradiction in terms, many of Jesus' sayings would appear in a different light, as would those of Cynics, and historians and exegetes would learn an immense amount in the process" (474–475). On the other hand, from Paul Rhodes Eddy: "The evidence that can be marshaled against the Cynic thesis warrants the conclusion that, with regard to the ongoing search for a viable model for the reconstruction of the historical Jesus, one must look elsewhere" (469).

I make six points to clarify my own position. First, if Cynicism had never existed, nothing would change in my reconstruction of Jesus as a Mediterranean Jewish peasant. I use the doctrine of Cynicism comparatively but do not need it constitutively. I have never considered a *Cynic* Jesus as some sort of replacement for a *Jewish* Jesus; indeed, I find that idea little short of absurd. My reply to the Cynic hypothesis was and is: if you want to imagine a Cynic Jesus, go ahead, but you better imagine a Jewish peasant Cynic (1991:421–422). Some, to my chagrin, took that as postulating an ancient social type rather than a modern scholarly construct, took it as a literal description rather than as a paradoxical challenge. Second, whether Galilean urbanization brought Cynicism to Sepphoris and/or whether Jesus actually knew about Cynicism are questions beyond proof or disproof. Not only has no direct or genetic link between Cynicism and Jesus been either proved or disproved, I am not sure how it could be verified or negated without new evidence. Third, it is on the level of *our understanding*—on the level, that is, of *comparative religion*—that I find Cynicism very illuminating for the historical Jesus. Fourth, I find the general comparison of Cynicism's and Jesus' anti-materialist and anti-imperialist criticism to be helpful. I would use the term *ethical eschatology* to describe *both* those programs and that comparison helps me to distinguish them from *ascetical* or *apocalyptic eschatology*. I am utterly aware that each arises from different traditions about very different gods and that, if they did not, equation rather than comparison would be demanded. Fifth, it is especially in the symbolic catecheses of their dress codes that comparison is

most instructive. I find this very illuminating, even if Jesus knew nothing whatsoever about Cynicism, and I return to it immediately below. Finally, granted
that a listening Jewish peasant would have considered Jesus some sort of a
prophet, what would a listening pagan peasant have considered him to be? "He's
a prophet, like our Elijah!" "He's a cynic, like our Diogenes!" Who's
Elijah?" "Who's Diogenes?" If, in other words, *pagans* heard Jesus speaking about
the kingdom of God, how would they have understood his program? Some sort
of Cynicism, surely.

Dress and Equipment.

Recall Sayre's description of the typical Cynic dress and equipment given
just above: "wallet, staff and cloak, which must invariably be worn, dirty and
ragged and worn so as to leave the right shoulder bare." What is there translated
as "wallet" is the Greek term *pēra*, which we might call a knapsack but which, in
any case, was functionally a begging pouch. It was where itinerants kept whatever they were given. It declared and symbolized their self-sufficiency. They had
all they needed on their hip. They did not need house or shelter, family or kinfolk. But that is precisely what Jesus' companions do *not* carry. They are no-*pēra*
people, however that term is translated in our English texts. It has been suggested that Jesus is distinguishing his group from the Cynics, as if onlookers
would catch that subtle difference. Maybe Jesus had never heard of Cynicism. Or
maybe he knew all about it and was adapting its dress code to his own quite different program. In any case, the no-knapsack dress code is symbolically correct
for his program, in which itinerants are not self-sufficient but interdependent
with the householders. In other words, the interdependency of itinerants and
householders established by that eating and healing conjunction is symbolically
dramatized by the commands about dress and equipment. The no-sandals mandate emphasizes their poverty. The no-knapsack mandate emphasizes their interdependency. The no-staff mandate emphasizes their vulnerability, their defense-
lessness, their nonviolence.

Conclusion.

I consider this unit central for an understanding of the Common Sayings Tradition. It is also the place where *that* text locks hardest in *conjunction* with my *context*.
The peasant dislocation resulting from Antipas's urbanization in Lower Galilee is
reflected directly in those itinerants. They are not general or perennial beggars,
although there may be some beggars included among them. They are not freeholders and probably not tenants either. They are dispossessed and now landless laborers, close to but not yet beggars. They are the expendables. They are the other side
of commercialization in a land that belongs to God. I take, therefore, the following
disjunctive pairs as a series of correlative terms all pointing to the same situation:

landless laborers	and	landed peasants
itinerants	and	householders
eating	and	healing
destitute	and	poor
enough bread for today	and	no debt for tomorrow

This is the great and terrible divide in peasant life. The kingdom movement focuses not just on the permanent existence of that great divide but on its increasing and widening presence in Antipas's Galilee during the 20s C.E. Never forget that context of rural commercialization pushing peasants from landed to landless status—in other words, from poverty to destitution. Think of those itinerants not as beggars born and bred to destitution, surviving and dying in destitution. Think of them as increasingly dispossessed peasants forced off their lost farms into survival on the roads of the countryside or in the streets of the cities. It is, I will argue, on that precise and contemporary divide that Jesus took his stand, and it is against that divide that he proclaimed the kingdom of God. Like all the prophets before him, he spoke of justice and righteousness in a very specific situation of injustice and unrighteousness. Situation always focuses but does not exhaust such challenges.

One final point. I have no presumption that what is primary is always better than what is secondary, or that what is original is better than what is derivative. The historical Jesus or earliest Christianity, as constructed by our best endeavors, could well be realities to be opposed from our contemporary viewpoint. It is vision and program that are determinative for that judgment. And what must be asked most specifically is whether the kingdom of God denotes a realm of domination or one of empowerment. But Jesus' companions can do exactly what Jesus himself was doing. The kingdom is not his monopoly; it is for anyone with courage enough to accept it. Jesus announces its presence, its abiding, permanent possibility. He does not initiate its existence. He does not control its access. It is the kingdom, not of Jesus, but of God. It is the will of God for Israel and therefore for earth. It is not a new idea from God. It is not a change in divine plan. It is not a new strategy in transcendental justice for this world.

Imagine, as an alternative example, that Jesus had settled down with his family at Nazareth or with Peter at Capernaum and had sent out *disciples* to bring or send back to him those in need of healing or teaching. That would have symbolized a God of domination and a kingdom of control and mastery. If that were the historical Jesus I had discovered, he would be promoting domination—kinder and gentler, to be sure, than Caesar's, but still domination and not empowerment. Even the term *disciples* is probably not the proper term for that inaugural community. It presumes a master and students, a teacher and pupils. And even though teaching can be empowerment rather than domination, it can also be the opposite. I prefer, therefore, in the light of those three seminal texts, to describe the kingdom of God not as a *discipleship of equals,* with Elisabeth Schüssler Fiorenza (189), but as a *companionship of empowerment.* Disciples (or students) can all be equal with one another and still subordinate to a teacher. The root question is whether God, and hence the kingdom of God, and thence Jesus as the announcer of its permanent availability, are to be seen within a model of domination or empowerment.

THE COMPANIONSHIP OF THE KINGDOM

I term the group around Jesus the *Companionship of the Kingdom.* The term *companions* is deliberately chosen in preference to *disciples,* which is simply the Greek word for *students.* When a teacher sends out students on their own and tells them to speak exactly, act exactly, and live exactly as their teacher does, they have graduated from students to companions. Those companions are not told to bring everyone back to Jesus, as if he alone had the kingdom of God. They are told to live in a certain way and thereby enter or live that kingdom's presence just as Jesus himself is doing. They are also told to invite others to do likewise.

I have, by the way, no fixed number in my mind for that companionship. Mark 6:7 has twelve, which recalls the twelve tribes of Israel descended from Jacob in Genesis 49:28 and the twelve elders chosen by Moses in Deuteronomy 1:23. No number from the *Q Gospel* is recoverable behind Luke 10:1, which has seventy or seventy-two. Even Luke's original number is textually uncertain, but a change from seventy-two to seventy is more easily explained than the opposite. The number seventy recalls the full progeny of Jacob's sons in Exodus 1:5 or Deuteronomy 12:22 and also the seventy elders chosen by Moses in Exodus 24:1 or Numbers 11:16. Neither do I presume a single sending; I imagine, rather, a permanent process, with Jesus as the moving center of a changing group. The mention of "by pairs" in *both* Mark 6:7 and *Q Gospel* 10:1 is very significant, by the way, because it means that women could also participate, traveling either in twos or singly with a man; both custom and safety concerns kept women from traveling on their own.

My own understanding of those around Jesus, of that companionship in the kingdom of God, is in serious disagreement on two major issues with the recent work of E. P. Sanders on Judaism and on Jesus.

Tax Collectors and Sinners

The first problem is Sanders's failure to distinguish between invective and portrayal, between calling somebody names and describing somebody's program.

Jesus is often imagined as gathering around him the rejected or marginalized of society, those ostracized for moral, physical, or occupational reasons. This image is often interwoven with hints or assertions that his contemporary Judaism was somehow reluctant to offer forgiveness, mercy, or understanding to such outcasts. On that issue, I have two important agreements and one equally important disagreement with Sanders.

I agree with Sanders's understanding of the phrase "tax collectors and sinners." He says that the term we translate as *sinners* is "virtually a technical term. It is best translated 'the wicked', and it refers to those who sinned willfully and heinously and who did not repent. . . . Tax collectors, more precisely, were quislings, collaborating with Rome. The wicked equally betrayed the God who redeemed Israel and gave them his law. There was no neat distinction between 'religious' and 'political' betrayal in first-century Judaism" (1985:177, 178). Later he changed his understanding of tax collectors (that is, toll or customs collectors), saying that they were condemned not as "collaborators" but as "charging too much, and thus of preying on the populace as a matter of course" (1993:229). The phrase "sinners and tax (toll) collectors" indicated those who were "systematically or flagrantly . . . living outside the law in a blatant manner," those who "systematically and routinely transgressed the law" (1993:227, 236). They were, for example, "the wicked" who were oppressing "the weak, the orphan, the lowly, the destitute, and the needy" in Psalm 82 (cited in Chapter 12) as God deposed the gods from cosmic government for malpractice in office. With that I am in complete agreement.

I also agree with the way he has cauterized, I hope forever, assertions that Jesus' contemporary Judaism did not and would not accept repentance from and offer forgiveness to such people. He asks rhetorically, "Is it a serious proposal that tax collectors and the wicked longed for forgiveness, but could not find it within ordinary Judaism?" And he responds correctly, "There was a universal view that forgiveness is *always* available to those who return to the way of the Lord," so that "if Jesus, by eating with tax collectors, led them to repent, repay those whom they had robbed, and leave off practicing their profession, he would have been a national hero. . . . It is simply inconceivable that Jewish leaders would have been offended if people repented, and this is a cliché which should be dropped from Christian scholarship" (1985:202–203, 272–273). That statement, long overdue, is absolutely true and deserves frequent quotation. Early-first-century Judaism, and any other Judaism before or after it, did not need lessons from Jesus on the elimination of impurities, the forgiveness of sins, or the mercy of God. It had had all of that firmly in place for a very long time. *But what, then, was left for Jesus to do that caused trouble?* Sanders makes three claims about Jesus in response to that question that are as "inconceivable" as those anti-Jewish claims he has rightly and justly condemned.

First, he understands Jesus as a prophet of Jewish restoration. Despite that understanding, however, he repeatedly (varying the wording across several pages) makes this assertion: "There is very little evidence which connects Jesus directly with the motif of collective, national repentance in view of the eschaton. . . . [T]here is not a significant body of reliable sayings material which *explicitly* attributes to Jesus a call for *national* repentance. . . . [T]here is no firm tradition which shows that he issued a call for national repentance in view of the coming end, as did John the Baptist. . . . [I]t seems that he did not make thematic that Israel should repent and mend their ways so as to escape punishment at the judgment" (1985:108, 111, 112, 115). This is the fullest statement of that thesis: "The great themes of national repentance and God's forgiveness, shown in restoring his repentant people, are prominent in all the literature that looks towards Jewish restoration. Jesus fits *somehow* into that view of God, the world and his people; but his message curiously lacks emphasis on one of the most important themes in the overall scheme" (1985:113). That "*somehow*" is never explained, except by saying that "the teaching attributed to Jesus is markedly *individualistic,* as we have seen in discussing repentance" (1985:117). I agree with that data but not with its explanation. *If* you believed that imperial oppression was divine punishment for Jewish sin, you would have to call for Jewish repentance prior to God's deliverance. If you did *not,* you would *not.* The data supports the interpretation that Jesus did *not* think imperial oppression was a divine punishment. It was simply an injustice that the Jews and God would have to resist as best they could. Jesus, and probably most peasants, knew exactly where the fault lay, and they did not blame on Jewish sin what came rather from Roman greed. But that first misunderstanding about Jesus' silence on repentance prepares for this second misunderstanding.

Second, Sanders interprets that saying about tax collectors and sinners in this way: "It is quite possible (in fact . . . quite likely) that Jesus admitted the wicked into *his* community without making the normal demand of restitution and commitment to the law. . . . Jesus offered the truly wicked—those beyond the pale and outside the common religion by virtue of their implicit or explicit rejection of the commandments of the God of Israel—admission to *his* group (and, he claimed, the kingdom) if they accepted him" (1985:203). That is not just a passing idea or fleeting thought. It gets an entire chapter to itself (1985:174–211) and is repeated programmatically throughout the rest of the book. It is described as "the one distinctive note which we may be certain marked Jesus' teaching," as "the undeniably distinctive characteristic of Jesus' message," as "a central aspect of Jesus' message," as "the most distinctive aspect of Jesus' message" (1985:174, 271, 323).

Sanders sees that "aspect of Jesus message" as parallel to the Temple in importance: "Jesus offended many of his contemporaries at two points: his attack on the temple and his message concerning the sinners" (1985:293). It is likewise parallel to the kingdom in importance: "We can know the main themes of his particular message with assurance. They are summarized by the words 'kingdom' and 'the wicked'" (1985:322). None of that is withdrawn in his later book, although he notes that "this suggestion has been unpopular" and "is not what most readers will expect" (1993:230, 235). "Jesus thought and said that the wicked who followed him, though they had not technically 'repented,' and though they had not become righteous in the way required by the law, would be in the kingdom, and in fact would be 'ahead' of those who were righteous by the law. . . . [I]f they accepted him and his message, God would include them in the kingdom—even though they had not repented and reformed in the way the law requires" (1993:235–236).

Third, if that was actually Jesus' position, he repudiated thereby not only the Law of God and Judaism but the moral basis of almost all religious life, secular law, and human decency. It would seem, thereafter, quite irrelevant to deny "that there were any substantial points of opposition between Jesus and the Pharisees (that is, with the Pharisees in particular, as distinct from the rest of Jewish Palestine)" or "that there was no substantial conflict between Jesus and the Pharisees with regard to Sabbath, food, and purity laws" (1985:264, 265). That may well be true, but a God, a kingdom, a Jesus, or a community that welcomes sinners without restitution, repentance, or purpose of amendment has so fundamentally repudiated the Law of Judaism that all else is not worth discussing. It is almost like praising a serial killer for paying his traffic fines. What Sanders has done is simply replace one libel with another. He replaces the claim that Judaism had *no acceptance for repentant sinners* with the idea that Jesus *had acceptance for unrepentant sinners*. How did he come up with an idea like that?

Sanders is acutely aware of how Christians have both trivialized and brutalized Judaism in descriptions down through the centuries. He is correct in his comments on that point, and, late as it is, that Christian practice must be stopped for the future and repented for the past. That process of libel had already begun in the New Testament, with Christian Jews attacking every sort of non-Christian Jew who opposed or rejected them. Their attacks and accusations had all the accuracy of political rhetoric in a contemporary election campaign and must be taken precisely as such. But there were also counterattacks against them, and those were just as unfair and inaccurate. It was just as possible, for example, to attack John the Baptist or Jesus, label them derisively, and accuse them of all sorts of appropriately libelous misconduct. *Both sides are, in other words, not describing programs but calling names.* For name-calling to work, of course, it must be based on some connection with reality. Names and accusations, therefore, tell us *something* about what the individual is doing, but only within the protocols of rhetorical abuse. In America, in the 1950s, one could be accused of consorting with commies and traitors simply for advocating civil liberties and human rights.

Jesus was accused of being insane in Mark 3:21 and of being possessed in Mark 3:22. Those accusations are polemical name-calling, not neutral character description. But they tell us something nonetheless; they suggest that perhaps Jesus healed in ecstatic trance. Here is another example. In the *Q Gospel* both John and Jesus are attacked, but in opposite ways:

> For John the Baptist has come eating no bread and drinking no wine, and you say, "He has a demon"; the Son of Man has come eating and drinking, and you say, "Look, a glutton and a drunkard, a friend of tax collectors and sinners!" (*Q Gospel* 7:33–34)

That text contains precious information and serious misinformation, and it is the latter that seduced Sanders into his strange conclusion about Jesus. The first half of each verse tells us something factual and historical about John, Jesus, and their contrasting programs. The second half of each verse is vituperative name-calling. There should, therefore, be no more serious historical discussion about John the Baptist as possessed than about Jesus as glutton and drunkard, friend of tax collectors and sinners. Similarly with the accusation against Jesus in John 8:48 that "you are a Samaritan and have a demon." There need be no serious discussion about the ethnic identity or possessed state of Jesus. Finally, there is a text where Jesus speaks of John the Baptist in terms of tax collectors and prostitutes:

> Jesus said to them, "Truly I tell you, the tax collectors and the prostitutes are going into the kingdom of God ahead of you. For John came to you in the way of righteousness and you did not believe him, but the tax collectors and the prostitutes believed him; and even after you saw it, you did not change your minds and believe him." (Matthew 21:31b–32)

That passage, strictly speaking, has nothing to do with the present discussion, although it is often cited as if it did. Those named individuals could be seen as coming to John in repentance, which would not be a case of name-calling at all. Similarly, Mark 2:13–17 has Jesus say that "he came not to call the righteous, but sinners." Sinners are "called," of course, to repentance and not to continued or increased sinning. In case there is any misunderstanding, Luke expands his Markan source by saying that Jesus "came not to call the righteous, but sinners *to repentance*," in his parallel 5:32. Later on (19:1–10) Luke gives a clear example of such repentance in the case of Zacchaeus, identified as tax collector and sinner.

What has happened here is a confusion between what Bruce Malina and Jerome Neyrey describe as "calling Jesus names" and what Sanders describes as Jesus' programmatic actions. Think of this example. If you were a white racist looking at a black man and a white woman sitting together at a whites-only lunch-counter in the American early sixties, what would you call him and what would you call her? And would that be calling names and slandering people or describing individuals and defining programs?

In conclusion, therefore, the idea of Jesus consorting with *repentant* sinners because his contemporary Judaism would not accept them in the name of God is profoundly wrong about Judaism. But the idea of Jesus consorting with *unrepentant* sinners because he himself would accept them in the name of God is just as profoundly wrong about Jesus. There should never be serious historical debate on Jesus accepting unrepentant tax collectors, sinners, or prostitutes unless there is also serious historical debate on Jesus as a lunatic, a demoniac, a glutton, a drunkard, and a Samaritan.

Individual Evil and Systemic Evil

The second major issue on which I take strong exception is Sanders's failure to distinguish between individual or personal evil and systemic or structural evil, a distinction emphasized frequently in this book.

First, Sanders argues that "the Sadducees were on average upright Jews; and, against the general opinion, I think that this is true of the aristocracy as well." His principle is that "individual immorality, such as greed or sexual promiscuity, does not necessarily make a person a bad leader. . . . We may even have, in the person of Ananias, an example of personal immorality and reasonable diligence when in office" (1992:337). He exemplifies this by referring to Roosevelt and Kennedy as unfaithful husbands but not thereby bad presidents. That is all quite true, but Sanders has the problem turned completely around. We are not talking about personal or private evil and public or systemic good but about personal or private good and public or systemic evil. The question is not whether the poor are individually good and the rich are individually bad but whether and to what degree their relationship is systemically evil. Remember Naboth's vineyard. The question is not whether Ahab or Naboth was *personally* just but whether dispossession of ancestral land was *structurally* just.

Sanders continues: "Today, many of us—not just bishops—have spare bedrooms in our houses, while others are homeless. Those of us with spare bedrooms should do more. I am still unwilling to say, however, that people who have big houses are necessarily wicked" (1992:338). Agreed, once again, on the level of personal or individual wickedness. But that vast Jewish tradition, from prophets and priests to sages and rabbis, was not just about personal piety but about structural justice. Personal justice asks, Should you beat, rape, or brutalize your slave? Systemic justice asks, Should slavery exist? But, as far as I can see, Sanders does not even glimpse that difference. The closest he gets to it is to claim that one could be a bad person but a good administrator. He never asks whether one could be a good person but an evil administrator. He never distinguishes between personal or individual evil and structural or systemic evil.

Read the following judgments: "I rather like the chief priests. . . . I even find things about Herod to like. . . . I rather like the Pharisees. . . . Mostly, I like the ordinary people . . ." (1992:493–494). What is wrong with those comments, apart from a somewhat grating condescension, is that they are irrelevant to the situation. All involved may have been "likable" as individuals or groups, but that does not explain the *systemic* problem that made some of them hate or kill the others. Now read the following judgments: On Herod the Great, King of the Jews: "Herod was, on balance, a good king. . . . Herod was a good king, on balance" (1993:19, 21). On Herod Antipas, tetrarch of Galilee and Perea: "Antipas was a good tetrarch. . . . Antipas was on the whole a good ruler" (1993:21, 93). On Caiaphas, high priest of Jerusalem's Temple: "Joseph Caiaphas was a success. . . . Caiaphas was pretty decent" (1993:27, 265). The point, once again, is not whether those judgments are valid or invalid. The point is that systems are reduced to personalities and structures are equated with individuals. Pilate may have been a saint, but God could still stand against him, for some Jews, as the embodiment of systemic Roman injustice.

Second, the roots of that problem go deep into Sanders's misunderstanding of religion in general and Judaism in particular. It is that same misunderstanding that allowed him, in the preceding case of the tax collectors and sinners, to argue that Jesus faithfully observed God' Law on issues of the sabbath, food, and purity but negated it on acceptance of flagrant evildoers without demanding repentance, restitution, or conversion. Here are the two key statements. In a chapter on "The Common People," he says that "detailed investigation of economic conditions lies beyond the scope of this book" (1992:120); and in a chapter titled "Tithes and Taxes," he says that "the general assessment of economic conditions lies outside the range of this book" (1992:159). My point is not that Sanders is complete on religious thought and practice but inadequate on economic affairs. And neither do I expect him to be an ancient economic historian. But how, within Jewish tradition, can you separate religion from politics, ethics from economics, commercialization from conscience? How, for example, could you discuss the Holiness Code's repossession of property, even as theoretical ideal or utopian dream, without raising economic questions? There is nothing as un-Jewish as a separation of land from covenant, economics from religion, and ritual from justice.

In conclusion, Jesus' kingdom movement was not, on the one hand, about practicing asceticism. That is a luxury for those who have food and shelter, marriage and children to abandon. Nor, on the other hand, was it about gathering general outcasts, marginalized morally by sin, physically by impurity, or socially by occupation. The kingdom movement was precisely focused on the destitute and the dispossessed—that is, on those groups who proliferate in any peasant society under rural commercialization. That was, in this case, Lower Galilee under Antipas's urbanization of Sepphoris and Tiberias in the first twenty years of that first common-era century. In so focusing, the kingdom movement was acting absolutely out of the heart of Judaism, absolutely in obedience to the covenantal God of justice and righteousness. That was signaled explicitly by the name under which Jesus acted: the kingdom of God—in other words, the will of God for this earth here and now. I remind you, finally, of Gerhard Lenski's term for those who dropped below peasant farmers or rural artisans, and of his estimate for their incidence: "The best estimate . . . is that in normal times from 5 to 10 per cent of the population found itself in [the Expendable Class], with the figure rising as high as 15 per cent on some occasions and falling almost to zero on others" (283).

EPILOGUE:
THE SOCIAL STATUS OF JESUS

> We anticipated that the existence of the state, of which peasants are by defi-
> nition a part, would exert an influence on the form of family life by virtue of
> the fact that the state limits the local uses of power and freedom to expand.
> We thought, however, that the influence of the state would essentially be
> constant: i.e., that state organization as such, and not the form, character or
> political policies of the particular state, would be the determinative influ-
> ence. Our data [from forty-six peasant communities] suggest otherwise.
> They suggest that the family structure is influenced directly or indirectly by
> the character of the dominant outside forces. . . . Our analysis demonstrates
> that while the family structure relates to the character of land use and pro-
> ductive activity of the peasant farmer, it is to a very great degree manipu-
> lated by the external influences of the more powerful urban sectors of the
> state of which, by definition, the peasant is a part.
>
> Walter Goldschmidt and Evalyn Jacobson Kunkel, "The Structure of the
> Peasant Family," p. 1070

Here is one extreme for life as an artisan. It is the proud epitaph of a freed
imperial slave, now a Roman citizen, and possibly still operating with patronal
capital. The translator calls it the "onerously honorific epitaph of a Roman carpenter" (Dessau 3.750, #7237; Burford 18–19):

> (Memorial) to Tiberius Flavius Hilarion, freedman of Tiberius, *decurion* of
> the *collegium* of carpenters in the 15th *lustrum,* inspector of the ballot-box for
> the elections in the 16th *lustrum,* quinquennial officer of the *collegium* of
> woodworkers in the 17th *lustrum,* honoured in the 18th, twice censor for
> appointing officials in the 19th and 20th, and judge among the chosen twelve
> from his rank (?) in the 22nd. This monument was put up by Claudia Prisca
> to the best of husbands.

Those dates are given in terms of numbered *lustra*. A *lustrum* was the five-
year term for the two censors, the most senior Roman magistrates. These officials regulated membership in the Senatorial and Equestrian Orders as well as
citizenship in Italy and the provinces. Tiberius Favius Hilarion obviously did all
right as a carpenter, an urban artisan. But what was it like to be a *rural* artisan?
What does it mean to call Jesus a "carpenter"?

A Peasant Artisan

In most agrarian societies, the artisan class was originally recruited from the ranks of the dispossessed peasantry and their noninheriting sons and was continually replenished from these sources. Furthermore, despite the substantial overlap between the wealth and income of the peasant and artisan, the median income of artisans apparently was not so great as that of the peasants.

Gerhard E. Lenski, *Power and Privilege*, p. 278

In that epigraph, which takes us back to the cross-cultural foundations of *context* in this book's method, Gerhard Lenski is thinking primarily of urban rather than rural artisans. He estimates that if "urban populations numbered only 5 to 10 per cent of the total population, then the artisan class could not have numbered more than 3 to 7 per cent." Furthermore, "many were so poor that they were unable to marry, with the result that the sex ratio in agrarian cities was sometimes badly out of balance" (278). Urban artisans, in general, were not better off than peasants; in other words, Tiberius Flavius Hilarion was an anomaly. And that hardly bodes well for rural artisans.

This small unit is almost a miniature of my book's method. I begin with *context* in cross-cultural anthropology and end with *text* in the New Testament. What anthropological guidelines, then, do we have for imagining a peasant artisan? I cite evidence from several different authors.

Teodor Shanin connects peasants and rural artisans. He delineates peasant society through four characteristics: "(1) the peasant family-farm as the basic unit of multi-dimensional social organization; (2) land husbandry as the main means of livelihood directly providing the major part of the consumption needs; (3) specific traditional culture related to the way of life of small communities; (4) the 'underdog' position. The domination of peasantry by outsiders. . . . The political economy of peasant society has been, generally speaking, based on expropriation of its 'surpluses' by powerful outsiders, through corvee [forced labor], tax, rent, interest, and terms of trade" (1971b:294–296). In other words, a peasant is simply an oppressed and exploited farmer. But Shanin also lists "major marginal groups" connected to the peasantry. The first is "agricultural labourers who lack a family farm" and work on a large estate. The second is "rural inhabitants who draw their main means of livelihood from *crafts and trades,* but who live in peasant environments and often work some land, e.g., *rural craftsmen*" (1971b:297). You could talk, then—across a peasantry—of peasant farmers, peasant laborers, and peasant artisans. Remember that category of the *marginal peasant* for future reference.

George Foster also connects peasants, rural artisans, and even fishers within the same definition. He answers the question "What is a peasant?" (while introducing readers to peasant society) by including in that term not only agriculturalists but "other small-scale producers, such as fishermen and rural craftsmen" (4). The reason is his insistence that "like most anthropologists, we agree that peasants are primarily agriculturalists, but we also believe that the criteria of definition must be structural and relational rather than occupational. For in most peasant societies, significant numbers of people earn their livings from nonagricultural occupations. It is not *what* peasants produce that is significant; it is *how* and *to whom* they dispose of what they produce that counts" (6). And that structural relationship is not a very benign one. "Peasants are not only poor, as has often been pointed out, but they are relatively powerless. . . . Peasants know that control over them is held in some mysterious fashion by superior powers, usually residing in cities. . . . It is noteworthy, too, that whatever the form of control held by the elite, they usually drain off most of the economic surplus a peasant creates, beyond the necessity for a bare subsistence living and for local religious expenditures" (9).

Henry Landsberger does not speak about peasant artisans as distinct from peasant farmers. He is, in fact, reluctant even to use the term *peasant*, because its "formal definition . . . is so thoroughly confused" (6). He focuses, however, "on those 'rural cultivators' (for on *that*, everyone is agreed) who occupy relatively low positions on various critical dimensions . . . especially . . . economic and political ones . . . having to do with the control of [1] the relevant economic and political 'inputs' . . . [2] the 'transformation process' within the economy and the polity . . . and [3] the degree of benefit derived from the 'output' of each of these sectors of society" (10–11). Whether that is definition or not, it is exactly the same understanding of the peasantry used elsewhere in this book, be it from Lenski or Kautsky, Scott or Wolf, Shanin or Foster. But its formulation gives Landsberger the ability not only to delimit the peasantry externally from other social groups but also to stratify it internally within itself. Thus he emphasizes the "vertical stratification within the peasantry—the relation of those better-off to the worse-off [which] has often been a central issue for those concerned themselves with peasant movements and uprisings" (15). Hence differentiations of "'higher' versus 'lower', or 'more' versus 'less'" within the peasantry are crucially important for his analysis, which is specifically focused on "peasant unrest" (13). The distinction, for example, between "sharecropper" and "landless labourer" is highly significant for him, because "in our scheme landless labourers (who, incidentally, may differ greatly among themselves) are simply groups at zero point in the control of the key resources of land and capital (though not necessarily at that point either in human skills or managerial capacity)" (13–14). A peasant artisan, if not exactly at that same zero point, is dangerously close to it and may be only politely or semantically different from a landless laborer.

Such internal differentiation, no doubt facilitated and exacerbated by external exploitation, is emphasized by many other recent scholars. Frank Cancian, for example, argues that peasant homogeneity from an external viewpoint must be matched with heterogeneity from an internal one: "The internal heterogeneity of peasant communities is an important key to understanding the economic behavior of the people who live in them—even when there are at the same time local customs that seem to promote socioeconomic homogeneity" (152). And William Roseberry brings that heterogeneity inside the family itself: "Peasantries are generally characterized by marked social differentiation," which may occur even within the same household, especially as "the mix of farm work and off-farm work is unevenly distributed within the household," so that parents may stay on the family farm while siblings have to work elsewhere" (123). That would, of course, have serious implications for the integrity of the peasant family itself, especially if its younger members became, in effect, absent urban laborers. And there would always be an interaction between increasing commercialization from outside and increasing differentiation from inside peasant communities and families.

I append one specific example of that cross-cultural generality, lest all of this get too abstract. Kazimiertz Dobrowolski described traditional, oral, peasant culture in southern Poland before its emancipation in the middle of the last century by noting that "the village population . . . was divided into several landowning classes as well as into different types of landless peasantry." *Landed* and *landless*, the basic distinctions, were broken down as follows: "Among the landed peasantry there were owners of full fields, half fields, half a *rola* (another type of field), quarter-rola, owners of forest-recovered fields, and finally owners of quite small plots. The landless population were differentiated into craftsmen, village labourers who either had a household of their own, or a room and food provided by a rich peasant for whom they had to work" (293–294 note 1, with Polish items omitted). In that description the sequence of the groups indicates the general hierarchy within a traditional peasantry.

It is equally necessary, therefore, to emphasize, *externally,* what distinguishes peasants from other classes in terms of power, and, *internally,* what distinguishes peasants among themselves in terms of status. "The old peasant culture in Southern Poland at the close of the feudal era . . . was a highly differentiated culture, both socially and economically; its social contrasts were often considerable, especially those which existed between rich peasants and the village poor. Thus there were great differences in the sizes of farms and the number of cattle, in the interior of peasant cottages, furniture, implements, food, dress etc. . . . In addition, there was a strong pressure exerted by the rich peasants on the poorer section of the community (the landless and village labourers) which aimed at debarring them from using such elements of culture which the rich claimed as their sole prerogative. Yet it was the poor who played a very conspicuous part in the creation of cultural values. . . . It was they who provided the great majority of craftsmen-carpenters, coopers, wheelwrights, weavers, blacksmiths, potters. The village proletariat produced a large number of folk-artists, sculptors, painters, ornament makers, tailors, singers and players, saga-tellers and folk-writers" (290–291).

I now turn from that general *context* to a specific *text* about Jesus. Though it is not from the Common Sayings Tradition, I introduce it here because it will, in any case, haunt the background to the following discussion of units from that corpus.

The Greek text of Mark 6:3 records that Jesus' contemporaries asked incredulously about him, "Is not this the *tekton?*" We usually translate that term as *carpenter*, which creates a problem for our contemporary imagination. The question is not what that term means for us but what it meant within a peasant economy in the early-first-century Jewish homeland. Mark locates the scene in the synagogue at Nazareth, and he is followed in that detail by both Matthew and Luke. John, who locates it in the synagogue at Capernaum, is probably giving an independent version of that local reaction to Jesus. I give all four texts here, but I am especially interested in how Matthew and Luke rephrase their Markan source:

Is not this the carpenter, the son of Mary and brother of James and Joses and Judas and Simon, and are not his sisters here with us? (Mark 6:3)

Is not this the carpenter's son? Is not his mother called Mary? And are not his brothers James and Joseph and Simon and Judas? And are not all his sisters with us? Where then did this man get all this? (Matthew 13:55–56)

Is not this Joseph's son? (Luke 4:22)

Is not this Jesus, the son of Joseph, whose father and mother we know? (John 6:40)

That is a very interesting change in Matthew 13:55 and Luke 4:22. Each in its own way avoids saying that *Jesus was a carpenter*. Matthew shifts the term to Joseph, and Luke avoids it entirely. This is my question: Do they find Jesus-as-carpenter somewhat offensive, and is that the reason for those changes? The following parallel case prompts an affirmative answer.

Mark 10:35 has "James and John, the sons of Zebedee," ask, with ineffable obtuseness, for first seats in the kingdom immediately after Jesus has described his impending passion in terrible detail. It is hard to miss the awful inappropriateness of that reaction. What do Matthew and Luke do with it? Matthew 20:20 saves their dignity by changing the passage to a request from "the mother of the sons of Zebedee." It is now not the sons themselves but their mother who pleads for first seats on their behalf. And Luke simply omits the entire unit. He follows Mark 10:32–34 (the unit just preceding the first-seats request) in his own 18:31–34, ignores Mark 10:35–45, and then follows Mark 10:46–52 (just after the request) in his own 18:35–43. As earlier with Jesus as carpenter, so here with John and James as dumb and dumber, Matthew and Luke use exactly the same procedure to solve a Markan embarrassment. In both cases, Matthew transfers the problem from son(s) to parent while Luke omits either the problematic word or the entire problematic unit. I conclude that neither of them deemed *carpenter* an appropriate designation for Jesus. The reason, by a *conjunction* of *context* and *text,* is that a *tekton* or peasant artisan is but a euphemism for a dispossessed peasant, for a landless laborer.

A Marginal Jew

Unless "the peasants" can be understood in terms of their internal differentiation along economic and other lines, it may appear that they consist entirely of the prey; in fact, some are commonly among the predators. . . . while peasants are, from one point of view, the underside of a society, from another they include both exploiters and exploited, and cannot be fully understood, if we take for granted that they are economically (and culturally) homogeneous.

     Sidney W. Mintz, "A Note on the Definition of Peasantries," pp. 94, 96

John Meier's ongoing multivolume study of the historical Jesus calls him "a marginal Jew" in its title, and that phrase is explained quite clearly in the first volume (1991:1.6–9). Meier was implausibly attacked for it by Martin Goodman, whose review found that "the six ways in which Jesus was marginal in the society of His day," as proposed by Meier, are all "specious" (1991:3). He was implausibly defended for it by Raymond Brown, who said that "on the implicit point that Jesus was not identifiably an adherent of any of Josephus' three sects of the Jews (Pharisees, Sadducees, Essenes)" that term "is surely right" (1994:353 note 54). That criterion would make the overwhelming majority of all first-century Jews marginal. What is needed, as so often in such disputes, is some discipline from the social sciences. What, there, does *marginal* mean?

Seventy years ago Robert Park argued that "one of the consequences of migration is to create situations in which the same individual—who may or may not be of mixed blood—finds himself striving to live in two diverse cultural groups. . . . This is the 'marginal man'. . . . It is in the mind of the marginal man that the moral turmoil which new cultural contacts occasion manifests itself in the most obvious forms. It is in the mind of the marginal man—where the changes and fusions of culture are going on—that we can best study the processes of civilization and of progress" (1928:881, 893). Park repeated that term a few years later, referring to this "cultural hybrid" as "the so-called marginal man, i.e., the individual who finds himself on the margins of two cultures and not fully or permanently accommodated to either" (1931:109).

About a decade after that original article, Everett Stonequist used the term "marginal man" in the title of a book both dedicated to Park and introduced by him. In his introduction, Park defined "the marginal man" as "one whom fate has condemned to live in two societies and in two, not merely different but antagonistic cultures. . . . He is . . . an effect of imperialism, economic, political and cultural" (1937:xv, xviii). But Park also noted that Stonequist's book was, despite its subtitle (A Study in Personality and Culture Conflict), less concerned with "a personality type, than with a social process, the process of acculturation" (xviii). Stonequist's own definition of the "marginal man" is "the individual who through migration, education, marriage or some other influence leaves one social group or culture without making a satisfactory adjustment to another [and] finds himself on the margin of each but a member of neither . . . one who is poised in psychological uncertainty between two (or more) social worlds; reflecting in his soul the discords and harmonies, repulsions and attractions of these worlds, one of which is often 'dominant' over the other; within which membership is implicitly if not explicitly based upon birth or ancestry (race or nationality); and where exclusion removes the individual from a system of group relations" (2–3, 8). The examples cited involve both racial and cultural hybrids arising from the interaction of Europeans with Africans, Indians, and Asians. But there is still great emphasis on personality type rather than social process, as is indicated by the very term "marginal man."

A more recent study speaks not of "the marginal man" but of "marginality," and that definition is now much, much better. Gino Germani distinguishes explicitly, first of all, "between marginality as a phenomenon at the level of personality (marginal personalities), and marginality as a social situation, the former being a psychological and cultural problem while the latter was usually considered the result of historic and structural conditions." That eliminates a large amount of the individualism, psychologism, and romanticism of the original "marginal man" emphasis. Next, he defines marginality as "the lack of participation in those spheres which are considered to be within the radius of action and/or access of the individual or group. Marginality is imputed through a comparison between a de facto situation and a certain model: the role set which the

individual or group should play according to given *a priori* principles" (9). Or
again: "We may define marginality as the lack of participation of individuals and
groups in those spheres in which, according to determined criteria, they might be
expected to participate. By participation we mean the exercise of roles conceived
of in the broadest sense" (49). In other words, marginality (or marginalization) is
the lack of an expected social participation. Theoretically and quite correctly, therefore, one could imagine a marginalized king among kings just as well as a
marginalized peasant among peasants or even beggar among beggars. Finally,
Germani emphasizes that "many authors differentiate the phenomenon of
poverty from that of marginality. They argue that though they are usually associated, they should be analytically differentiated since marginality can exist without poverty, or with less poverty than in participating sectors. This distinction is
related to the distinction between two sectors of the popular or lower social
strata: those which are established (have a relatively stable occupation or job,
live in normal working class or peasant houses, even if it is a slum and living
standards are quite low), and the population socially located outside of the stratification system, as sort of outcasts, on the margin of the global society and its
class system including its lowest strata" (7).

In Germani's general understanding, and especially in that last specific quotation, a dispossessed peasant—one forced off the farm by debt, for example—is
marginalized. The point is not that he was or is poor but that he can no longer
participate as expected among his fellow peasants. If Jesus was a dispossessed
peasant trying to survive as a rural artisan or landless laborer, he was a marginalized peasant. (By the way, I prefer the term *marginalized* to *marginal* not to be
politically correct but to be politically accurate.)

PART VIII
Teachers and Householders

The transmission of Jesus sayings in the early Christian community is a sociological problem particularly because Jesus gave no fixed, written form to what he said. A written tradition can survive for a time even when it has no bearing on the behavior of men and women, or even if the tradition's intention runs counter to that behavior. But oral tradition is at the mercy of the interest and concerns of the people who pass it on and to whom it is addressed. Its survival is dependent on specific social conditions. To mention only one of these: the people who pass the tradition on must in some way or other identify with that tradition. . . . We can now formulate our thesis: the ethical radicalism of the sayings is the radicalism of the itinerants. . . . The radicalism of their wandering life goes back to Jesus himself. It is authentic. Probably more of the sayings must be "suspected" of being genuine than many a modern skeptic would like to think. But the Jesus tradition is authentic in a different, transferred sense as well. It is *existentially* authentic. It was practiced.

So the wandering charismatics were a widespread phenomenon in early Christianity. As far as numbers go, the local congregations were certainly much stronger. . . . Most socially uprooted people came from the middle classes. It was the people who had declined into poverty, rather than the people born in poverty, who set out to pass their lives beyond the boundaries of normal life or even to seek ways of renewing society.

> Gerd Theissen, *Social Reality and the Early Christians,* pp. 35, 40, 45; pp. 64, 88 (from
> essays originally published in 1973 and 1977)

Part VII showed that there was, from the earliest evidence I can find, a dialectic of itinerants and householders going back to the time of the historical Jesus. The kingdom of God was made present not just in the itinerants but in the interaction of itinerants and householders, in a new community of healing and eating, of shared material and spiritual resources. The itinerants expected and received *external* opposition and even persecution. But did they also encounter *internal* opposition—dissent and criticism from those who had already accepted them? Was there resistance not only by non-Christians from outside but by Christians from within the kingdom-of-God movement? And did that internal negation give a far greater sense of failure to the itinerants than any external one ever could?

Part VII gave the voice of the itinerants; Part VIII gives the voice of the householders. In Part VII the itinerants spoke out; in Part VIII the householders talk back. For the itinerants we have the *Q Gospel* document, for the householders we have the *Didache* document. Both of those texts are much later than the Common Sayings Tradition, with which I am primarily interested, but I use their later interaction to find in that earlier tradition evidence that such tensile dialectic was there from the very beginning. In a way such tension was surely inevitable. What happens when itinerants tell householders to abandon everything, as they have done? It is easy to imagine what those who *oppose* them will do. But what will those who *receive* them do? In what follows, I am reading the *Didache* to imagine some of its developed responses as inchoately present when the very first itinerant was greeted by the very first householder in peace.

What validates that act of imagination is one of most radical sayings of Jesus, *Give Without Return*. It is found in the Common Sayings Tradition at *Q Gospel* 6:30—that is, Luke 6:30 = Matthew 5:42—and at *Gospel of Thomas* 95. But it is also found in a climactic position and with a careful commentary in *Didache* 1:5a (Appendix 1A: #35 = Appendix 7: #4).

Chapter 19 shows that in the *Q Gospel,* as early as Jesus' inaugural sermon in Q[1], the itinerants are criticizing the householders as those who confess the Lord but do not obey him, who hear him but do not do what he asks. They are not speaking against outsiders who do not hear but against insiders who hear but do not act accordingly. That is clear enough, but then we wade into murkier waters. Some of those insider-critical sayings in the *Q Gospel* are found already in the Common Sayings Tradition, but, of course, without the *Q Gospel* context which determines their meaning. Do they have the same insider-critical focus even at that earlier stage?

Chapter 20 shows the *Didache's* householders moving carefully and delicately both to accept and to contain itinerant radicalism. They do so by establishing their own communally approved teaching, but also by making clear rules for itinerant prophets who visit the community. That is a first and fundamental move of containment.

Chapter 21 addresses the second and even more important move of containment. The most radical sayings involving imitation of God's nonviolent character on earth are carefully integrated into the *Didache's* basic catechism, and one is told to "do what you can" about them. But, above all, radical despoliation, as in that *Give Without Return* saying, becomes transmuted into salvific almsgiving, so that having nothing is translated into sharing everything.

Chapter 22 is a connective pivot between the tradition of Jesus' life in these Parts VII and VIII and the tradition of Jesus' death in the succeeding Parts IX and X. It is presented primarily in dialogue with past and present work by Helmut Koester.

CHAPTER 19

CRITICIZING THE
HOUSEHOLDERS

The group as a whole may enter into an antagonistic relation with a power
outside of it, and it is because of this that the tightening of the relations
among its members and the intensifications of its unity, in consciousness and
in action, occur.

Georg Simmel, "Conflict, " p. 191

Such "searching for the outside enemy" (or exaggeration of the danger
which an actual enemy represents) serves not only to maintain the structure
of the group, but also to strengthen its cohesion when threatened by a relaxation of energies or by internal dissension. Sharpness of outside conflict
revives the alertness of the membership, and either reconciles divergent tendencies or leads to concerted group action against the dissenter.

Lewis A. Coser, The Functions of Social Conflict, p. 106

Those epigraphs are from classic sociological works on the dynamic interaction between external threat and internal cohesion in small struggle-groups. The
presence, exaggeration, or even creation of an external threat assists in establishing internal unity and controlling internal dissent within the group itself. "There
are," as Coser concludes, "shifting gradations between the exaggeration of a real
danger, the attraction of a real enemy, and the complete invention of a threatening agent" (110). But, of course, a siege mentality may also generate besiegers. To
call outsiders enemies may often turn strangers into foes or force them from
contempt to oppression, from discrimination to persecution.

When you read through the *Q Gospel* you find reiterated attacks on "this generation." Kloppenborg, for example, makes those units the defining characteristic
of the gospel's second, apocalyptic, or Q² layer (1987a: 102–170). Is "this generation"
actually reading those descriptions of itself? Of course not. Or again, recall those
woes uttered in *Q Gospel* 10:13–15 against Chorazin, Bethsaida, and Capernaum,
three towns in a small triangle around the northern shores of the Sea of Galilee.
Were those towns hearing those attacks on themselves? Of course not, once again.
But the above proposals from Simmel and Coser help to understand the *internal*

purpose of such *external* diatribes. Think of its situation within a peasant culture undergoing the severe disruption of rural commercialization. "Traditional [i.e., oral] culture manifested a tendency towards uniformity," as Kazimiertz Dobrowolski concluded. "It was expressed in the social pressure towards a common, unchanging pattern of social institutions and ideological contents within particular classes or village groups. The individuals who deviated from the commonly accepted pattern of behaviour obtaining within their respective classes or groups, met with such repressive measures as ridicule, reproach, moral censure, ostracism or even the application of official legal sanctions" (291). The *Q Gospel* might sometimes exaggerate that external opposition, but it did not need to invent it.

Strong opposition from outsiders and to outsiders is very clear in the Common Sayings Tradition. It warns about strong external opposition, for example, in such sayings as *Carrying One's Cross* and *Blessed the Persecuted* (Appendix 1A: #24, #28). It also asserts a rather general opposition against the Pharisees in *On Hindering Others* (Appendix 1A: #16). But I now ask a more precise question: Is there evidence in the Common Sayings Tradition itself that there was already internal dissent within the communities involved? Apart from extra-Christian resistance, was there intra-Christian resistance as well? I rephrase the question in the light of those sociological epigraphs: Is outside opposition emphasized to control internal opposition? What evidence is there, in other words, that those itinerants seen in Part VII were meeting with dissent from Christian householders?

Internal Dissent in the *Q Gospel*

> Conflict with outsiders, as Lewis Coser has shown, actually serves a positive and constructive purpose as a means to define more clearly group boundaries, to enhance internal cohesion and to reinforce group identity. . . . Thus, while ostensibly directed at the "out-group," these polemical and threatening materials function in fact to strengthen the identity of the "in-group" and to interpret for them the experience of persecution, rejection, and even the failure of their preaching of the kingdom.
>
> John S. Kloppenborg, *The Formation of Q*, pp. 167–168

Kloppenborg describes the beatitudes that open Jesus' inaugural sermon in *Q Gospel* 6:20b–23 as "'anti-beatitudes' [that] stand in contrast to the views of the conventional wisdom that those who dwell in affluence and safety are blessed." They are a "programmatic statement" of "the 'radical wisdom of the kingdom.'" But, he continues, "other examples of such radical wisdom are to be found in the immediate context: in 6:27–35, 36–38, 39–45" (1987a:188–189). That is not exactly accurate. This *Q Gospel* sermon breaks down into two rather clear halves. The first half in *Q Gospel* 6:23–35 is the manifesto of the kingdom's radicality. Kloppenborg is perfectly correct on that point. And the tone there is almost rhapsodic or even ecstatic. But the second half, in *Q Gospel* 6:36–45, is ordinary, everyday, non-radical wisdom. And the tone there is critical and censorious. Here are the units involved in that second half:

As Your Father	Q 6:36		(Appendix 2B: #8)
Judgment for Judgment	Q 6:37a		(Appendix 2B: #9)
Measure for Measure	Q 6:38bc		(Appendix 2B: #10)
The Blind Guide	Q 6:39	= *Gos. Thom.* 34	(Appendix 1A: #13)
Disciple and Servant	Q 6:40		(Appendix 2B: #11)
Speck and Log	Q 6:41–42	= *Gos. Thom.* 26	(Appendix 1A: #10)
Trees and Hearts	Q 6:43–45	= *Gos. Thom.* 45	(Appendix 1A: #19)
Invocation Without Obedience	Q 6:46		(Appendix 2B: #12)
Rock or Sand	Q 6:47–49		(Appendix 2B: #13)

As you move through those sayings from beginning to end, three details become steadily clearer. The first is that the sayings are directed against dissent from inside rather than outside the community. The second is that the dissent involves leaders or at least ideals for the community. The third is that the dissent involves hearing and *doing* as against hearing and *not doing*. Behind *Q Gospel* 6:36–49 you must hear the criticisms made against the itinerants by the householders even as you read the itinerants countercriticizing the householders in defense of themselves.

The saying in *Q Gospel* 6:36 about the Father as model of mercy is a programmatic overture to the entire second half of the sermon. It leads into a warning against judging others in *Q Gospel* 6:37–38 (that is, do not *you* judge us). That is the first warning of internal dissent, but it becomes explicitly internal as we proceed. *The Blind Guide* saying in *Q Gospel* 6:39 focuses that somewhat general criticism into a warning against blind leaders and blind followers (that is, *you* are blind). That is then specified in *Q Gospel* 6:40 by asserting that disciples cannot improve on their teacher (that is, *you* should not try); it is enough to be like him. That countercriticism then continues into *Speck and Log* as well as *Trees and Hearts* in *Q Gospel* 6:41–45 (judge *yourselves* first; *you* are bad people). Those countercriticisms in *Q Gospel* 6:36–45 may read like rather banal and proverbial wisdom, but they are used here in an internal debate over following or not following the radical wisdom just proclaimed in *Q Gospel* 6:20b–35.

Finally, then, the last two aphorisms, in *Q Gospel* 6:46–49, make the precise point of criticism and countercriticism extremely clear. Kloppenborg comments that "many sapiential instructions end (or sometimes begin) with descriptions of the rewards which await those who attend to the instructions, and the consequences for those who do not" (1987a:186). He gives several examples. I cite two of them, one from a biblical book and the other from a popular philosophical treatise of that time (1987a:186–187):

> Therefore walk in the way of the good, and keep to the paths of the just. For the upright will abide in the land, and the innocent will remain in it; but the wicked will be cut off from the land, and the treacherous will be rooted out of it. (Proverbs 2:20–22)

> If you pay attention and understand what is said, you will be wise and happy. If, on the other hand, you do not, you will become foolish, unhappy, sullen and stupid and you will fare badly in life. (*Cebes' Tablet* 3.1)

There is, then, nothing surprising about a sapiential sermon such as *Q Gospel* 6:20b–49 ending with disjunctive sanctions, with sayings that promise reward and benefit or threaten punishment and damage. In this case, though, those disjunctive sanctions are made extremely precise:

> Why do you call me "Lord, Lord," and do not do what I tell you? I will show you what someone is like who comes to me, hears my words, and acts on them. That one is like a man building a house, who dug deeply and laid the foundation on rock; when a flood arose, the river burst against that house but could not shake it, because it had been well built. But the one who hears and does not act is like a man who built a house on the ground without a foundation. When the river burst against it, immediately it fell, and great was the ruin of that house. (*Q Gospel* 6:46–49)

That conclusion is as clear as one could want. It is not about outsiders warned and insiders praised. It is not about outsiders refusing Jesus' words while insiders accept them. It is about insiders—that is, about those who confess Jesus as Lord within the kingdom community. Within that very community there are those who *hear and do* while others *hear and do not*. That is, *all hear* but only *some do*. Furthermore, those who *hear and do not* criticize those who *hear and do*. And *Q Gospel* 6:46–49 concludes the countercriticism of those who hear and do against their intracommunity opponents. In other words, the second half of the sermon in *Q Gospel* 6:36–49 concerns dissent within the kingdom community over the radical kingdom wisdom announced in the first half, in *Q Gospel* 6:20b–35.

That is all fairly clear and certain, but only three of those sayings, *The Blind Guide, Speck and Log,* and *Trees and Hearts* have *Gospel of Thomas* parallels. Only those three, therefore, are certainly present in the Common Sayings Tradition. Because of that I offer here only a tentative hypothesis—namely, that those three sayings are evidence for internal dissent even at the stage of the Common Sayings Tradition.

Internal Dissent in the Common Sayings Tradition

Q 6:39–45, of course, takes particular aim at teachers (actual or imagined) who do not follow Jesus in his radical lifestyle and ethic. But there is no compelling reason to suppose that 6:39–42 is formulated with outsiders and opponents in mind.

John S. Kloppenborg, The Formation of Q, p. 185

The Blind Guide.

The first of the three sayings in this set is *The Blind Guide* (Appendix 1A: #13). It is a Type 4 saying (Appendix 1B); that is, it has been redacted neither toward asceticism in the *Gospel of Thomas* nor toward apocalypticism in the *Q Gospel*. It appears in the *Q Gospel* as Q 6:39b—that is, Luke 6:39b = Matthew 15:14b—and in *Gospel of Thomas* 34. These are the twin texts:

Can a blind person lead a blind person? Will not both fall into the pit? (*Q Gospel* 6:39)

Jesus said, "If a blind person leads a blind person, both of them will fall into a hole." (*Gospel of Thomas* 34)

The self-contradictory image of the *blind guide* "was a commonplace in the ancient world," as Kloppenborg notes with examples (1987a:184), so the significant issue is not just whether Jesus cited this proverb but what the context might have been. Was it, for example, internally or externally directed? Was it warning for insiders or invective for outsiders?

The context in Matthew 15:12–14 directs the saying specifically against the Pharisees. But the *Q Gospel* context, as in Luke 6:39b, directs it internally against teachers within the community "who do not emulate their master . . . who try to outstrip their master by judging others," as Kloppenborg summarizes its meaning (1987a:184). *Gospel of Thomas* 34 could be read either internally or externally, but lack of context makes it impossible to decide. There is not, however, any explicit link to the Pharisees as there is, for example, in *Gospel of Thomas* 39:1–2 and 102. All in all, therefore, the saying's meaning in the Common Sayings Tradition is more likely to be internal admonition than external accusation. But it also seems to bespeak a situation of debate about how one follows, teaches, or imitates Jesus rather than a situation within the life of Jesus himself.

Speck and Log.

The second of the three sayings in this set is *Speck and Log* (Appendix 1A: #10). It is a Type 4 saying (Appendix 1B); that is, it has been redacted neither toward asceticism in the *Gospel of Thomas* nor toward apocalypticism in the *Q Gospel*. It appears in the *Q Gospel* as Q 6:41–42—that is, Luke 6:41–42 = Matthew 7:3–5—and in the *Gospel of Thomas*, with both Coptic and Greek versions, as *Gospel of Thomas* 26 and P. Oxy. 1, lines 1–4. But only the very end of this saying's Greek version is extant, since the fragmented P. Oxy. 1 begins at that point. Here are the three texts:

Why do you see the speck in your neighbor's eye, but do not notice the log in your own eye? Or how can you say to your neighbor, "Friend, let me take out the speck in your eye," when you yourself do not see the log in your own eye? You hypocrite, first take the log out of your own eye, and then you will see clearly to take the speck out of your neighbor's eye. (*Q Gospel* 6:41–42)

[. . .] and then you will see clearly to take out the speck that is in your brother's eye. (*Gospel of Thomas* 26:2b [Greek])

Jesus said, "You see the speck that is in your brother's eye, but you do not see the beam that is in your own eye. When you take the beam out of your own eye, then you will see clearly to take the speck out of your brother's eye." (*Gospel of Thomas* 26:1–2 [Coptic])

That central sentence from "how" to "hypocrite!" in *Q Gospel* 6:42a has no parallel in *Gospel of Thomas* 26, which parallels only the first and third sentences. I read that saying as countercriticism from the *Q Gospel*'s radical proponents against those who oppose them from within the Christian community.

Trees and Hearts.

The last of the three sayings in this set is *Trees and Hearts* (Appendix 1A: #19). It is a Type 4 saying (Appendix 1B); that is, it has been redacted neither toward asceticism in the *Gospel of Thomas* nor toward apocalypticism in the *Q Gospel*. It appears in the *Q Gospel* as Q 6:43–45—that is, Luke 6:43–45 = Matthew 7:16–20 and Matthew 12:33–35—and in *Gospel of Thomas* 45. These are the twin texts:

No good tree bears bad fruit, nor again does a bad tree bear good fruit; for each tree is known by its own fruit. Figs are not gathered from thorns, nor are grapes picked from a bramble bush. The good person out of the good treasure of the heart produces good, and the evil person out of evil treasure produces evil; for it is out of the abundance of the heart that the mouth speaks. (*Q Gospel* 6:43–45)

Jesus said, "Grapes are not harvested from thorn trees, nor are figs gathered from thistles, for they yield no fruit. A good person brings forth good from the storehouse; a bad person brings forth evil things from the corrupt storehouse in the heart, and says evil things. For from the abundance of the heart this person brings forth evil things." (*Gospel of Thomas* 45:1–4)

I am, once more, reading that saying against internal or intra-Christian dissent within the Common Sayings Tradition. Like the two preceding sayings, it is still internal dissent that is at stake in their *Q Gospel* usage. Its secondary usage in Matthew 12:33–35, however, directs it externally against those accusing Jesus of demonic possession.

CHAPTER 20

CONTROLLING THE ITINERANTS

The silent majority of those who awaited the coming of the kingdom were careworn and decent householders, long used to the punctilious rhythms of Jewish life. Secure in their moral horizons, they were in no position to allow the painfully assembled fabric of their social person—their wives, their children, their kinfolk, and the few ancestral fields that they would inherit when they buried their father—to evaporate at the call of the wandering few. Christian communities where such men came to the fore would look at the world around them in a very different manner from those who imagined that, on the open road, they already breathed the heady air of the kingdom.

Peter Brown, *The Body and Society*, p. 44

So far the discussion has mostly involved two texts, the *Q Gospel* and the *Gospel of Thomas*, as well as the Common Sayings Tradition, out of which they both developed in very different ways. I now add a third and equally important text, the *Didache*. I place this new text in tensive dialogue with the *Q Gospel*, but at an earlier stage than the finished document we now have in Matthew and Luke. For example, both the *Didache* and the *Q Gospel* contain secondary apocalyptic eschatology, but, while the latter expects the advent of the Son of Man, the former awaits the arrival of the Lord God (with no mention of the Son of Man or the Lord Jesus). It is as if the *Didache* knows the *Q Gospel* at a stage somewhere in between the Common Sayings Tradition and the final *Q Gospel* itself.

Recall that in the preceding chapter the *Q Gospel* criticized some Christians in 6:46 for *calling* Jesus "Lord, Lord" but not *doing* what Jesus wanted and warned them in 6:47–49 about *hearing* but not *doing*. That is the voice of the radical itinerants reproaching the settled householders. But in the *Didache*, the conservative householders get to answer back, both respecting and containing the radicalism of those itinerants.

Those three texts—the *Q Gospel*, the *Gospel of Thomas*, and the *Didache*—were hidden from sight for centuries in very different ways. The *Q Gospel* was hidden in the gospels of Matthew and Luke. The *Gospel of Thomas* was hidden in a sealed jar near the Nile-side cliffs. The *Didache* was hidden in a manuscript codex, along with six other early Christian texts, in an ancient library.

Over one hundred years ago, about a decade after the *Didache*'s discovery and almost immediately after its publication, Philip Schaff gave this description of its location: "The Jerusalem Monastery of the Most Holy Sepulchre is an irregular mass of buildings in the Greek quarter of Constantinople. . . . It belongs to the Patriarch of Jerusalem. . . . The Jerusalem Monastery possesses, like most convents, a library. It is preserved in a small stone chamber, erected for the purpose and detached from the other buildings. It receives scanty light through two strongly barred windows. Its entrance is adorned with holy pictures, it contains about a thousand bound volumes and 'from four hundred to six hundred manuscripts,' as the present superior, the archimandrite Polycarp, informed a recent visitor 'with characteristic indefiniteness.' Among the books of this library was one of the rarest treasures of ancient Christian literature. It is a collection of [seven] manuscripts bound in one volume, covered with black leather, carefully written on well preserved parchment by the same hand, in small, neat, distinct letters, and numbering in all 120 leaves or 240 pages of small octavo (nearly 8 inches long by 6 wide)" (1–2).

The scribe who copied those seven texts signed the last leaf as "Leon, notary and sinner," and dated that completion to June 11, 1056. The first of the seven was *A Synopsis of the Old and New Testaments,* attributed to St. John Chrysostom. That single title was how the library's catalogue listed this, its most ancient holding—not a title calculated to excite much interest. After going unnoticed by scholars who checked the library in the 1840s and 1850s, the codex was finally discovered in 1873 and published in 1883 by Archbishop Philotheos Bryennios, then Metropolitan of Sérrai in Macedonia. Philip Schaff described Bryennios as "next in rank to the Patriarch of Constantinople, and the Bishop of Ephesus, and usually residing in Constantinople, in a narrow, unpainted, wooden house of four stories, opposite the entrance of the patriarchal church and a few steps from the Jerusalem Monastery. He is probably the most learned prelate of the Greek Church at the present day" (8). The *Didache,* then, was a small text, fifth among others mostly much larger than itself, lost in a small library in the Fener section of Istanbul, halfway up the west side of the Golden Horn. Now known as Codex Hierosolymitanus 54, that volume was removed to the Patriarchate at Jerusalem in 1887, where it remains.

Earlier Coptic and Ethiopic versions also exist for a few chapters of this text. Especially important are two Greek fragments, Papyrus Oxyrhynchus 1782, dated to the "late fourth century" and published by Grenfell and Hunt in 1922 (12–15). These tiny scraps, about two inches by two inches apiece, contain verses 1:3c–4a and 2:7–3:2. Despite small differences, the wording on those scraps is very close to Bryennios's text. That is very important confirmation for the basic accuracy of Codex Hierosolymitanus 54, given the gulf of centuries between it and the earlier fragments.

Training Pagans

The Greek word *didache* makes reference to the training which a master-trainer *(didaskalos)* imparts to apprentices or disciples. In classical Greek, basket weaving, hunting with a bow, and pottery making represent typical skills transmitted under the term *didache*. . . . [I]t is significant to note that the verb *didaskein*—customarily translated as "to teach"—was not used when the mere transmission of information was implied. . . . In our contemporary society, "teaching" is associated with classroom instruction, and, in the popular mind, this often evokes the passing on of information from professor to student. The word "training," on the contrary, has the advantage of suggesting the dynamics of an apprenticeship wherein novices gradually and progressively enlarge their skills by submitting themselves to a master-trainer *(didaskalos)*.

Aaron Milavec, "The Pastoral Genius of the Didache," p. 107

The only full manuscript of the *Didache* bears two titles. The first one, in the usual translation, is "The Teaching of the Twelve Apostles," written with four dots in a diamond pattern before and after. On the next line is a longer title: "The Teaching of the Lord Through the Twelve Apostles to the Nations [i.e, Pagans]." That is the last we ever hear of those Twelve Apostles; whenever apostles are mentioned in the text, they simply designate those *sent* *(apostellein* in Greek) from one community to found another one elsewhere. Those titles, in other words, were added to this originally anonymous document from such places as Acts 2:42 ("the apostles' teaching") and Matthew 28:19 ("make disciples of all nations"). They do not help us at all in determining the purpose of the *Didache*. An abbreviated title such as "The Teaching" does, however, especially when translated with Milavec as "The Training."

TRAINING AND COMMUNAL SPLIT

The *Didache* is neither epistle nor gospel but community rule—manual of discipline or church order. That is the first and most important factor in determining the work's purpose. That is also its very special importance. It lets us see, probably as best we ever will, how an early Christian community regulated its life. But there is also another factor, the specific occasion that necessitated the establishment of this discipline in written format at precisely this time. Why was this specific training program required now rather than earlier or later?

The four major divisions of the *Didache* are noted by most commentators, but Aaron Milavec, whose work on the text is extremely sensitive and whose translation (and bracketed interpolations) I am using, has also noted the different percentages involved (1989:101):

I	(1:1–6:2):	The training program for new members, or the Two Ways (44%)
II	(6:3–10:7):	Norms for eating, baptizing, fasting, praying, eucharistizing (24%)
III	(11:1–15:4):	Regulations for testing various classes of visitors (22%)
IV	(16:1–8):	Closing apocalyptic appeals (10%)

That second section has several clues about the social situation that produced this written text. First, there are three major subjects flagged by similar-
style openings:

Concerning food, take . . . (6:3)
Concerning baptism, baptize thus . . . (7:1–4)
Concerning eucharist, eucharistize thus . . . (9:1–10:7)

Each subject gets an increasing length of attention, from one to four to twelve
verses. But that first subject, with a format less similar than the other two, is somewhat surprising in such a prominent location. It reads in full (Milavec 1989:96):

Concerning food, take what [kinds of food which] you are able [to bear], but
absolutely abstain from the meat offered to idols for this is servitude to gods
of the dead. (*Didache* 6:3)

Why is the food question so important that it is put in first place? I hold that
question, for a moment, to consider another point that may help answer it. That
baptismal section in 7:1–4 ends with a command about fasting, which is then
word-linked (*fasting*) with the next two also-word-linked commands (*hypocrites*)
as follows (Milavec 1989:96–97):

Prior [to baptism], let the one baptizing, then one being baptized and all
who are able [to do so] **fast** for one or two days beforehand. Do not let your
fast take place in the manner of the **hypocrites**. For they fast on the second
and fifth [day] of the sabbath. You, on the other hand, fast during the fourth
[day] and the [day] of preparation [for the sabbath]. Likewise, do not pray
like the **hypocrites** but like the Lord commanded in his good news. Pray
thus: [The Our Father]. Pray *thus* three times per day. (*Didache* 7:4–8:3)

Another question now joins that former one concerning food. Who are the
hypocrites? *They* fast on Mondays and Thursdays, but *we* fast on Wednesdays
and Fridays. We pray the Our Father thrice daily, and they presumably do not.
What is at stake in all of this?

That mention of "hypocrites" and that intransigent separation over details
of fasting and praying seem primarily intended to establish firm boundaries between

an *us* and a *them*. But who are *they?* We are not dealing with Christian Jews against non-Christian Jews or with Christian pagans against Christian Jews. The *Didache*, in fact, is a very clear example of a text that is both totally and profoundly Jewish *and* totally and profoundly Christian. We are dealing, more likely, with a fairly recent split within the *Didache* group itself. Perhaps in correlating those preceding items— the emphatic position and relative freedom of the food regulation in 6:3, the double mention of hypocrites in 8:1–3, and the quantitative emphasis on training in 1:1–6:2 (in the so-called Part I)—we can learn more about the *Didache* split.

Milavec brings those three points together by focusing them around the inclusion of pagan converts in the *Didache* community. This is the social situation or communal crisis that generated the document itself. Jews who became Christian would already know the basics of Jewish ethics and piety, but what about Gentile converts? If Christian pagans were not living up to the ethical standards of Christian Jewish converts, could the latter continue to associate with them? And, in any case, how would food regulations be maintained in common meals of Christian pagans and Christian Jews? "Judging from the basics covered in the initiation program, however, one can surmise that Gentiles were being accused of practicing the pagan ways that they were supposed to have left behind. The pastoral genius of the Didache is that it proposed to put into place two novel programs which would attack the very source of these outbursts of righteous anger. This was effected in two ways: (1) by demanding of all future Gentiles a systematic training in the basic standards of conduct which the Lord requires of them [1:1–6:2], and (2) by requiring a weekly confession of faults against these basic standards prior to the community Eucharist [14:1–2]" (1989:123). That training program would establish a common level of ethical accountability for all converts, but it was needed especially for pagan ones— those who, unlike their Jewish counterparts, had to be reminded (for example, in *Didache* 5:2) that "not being merciful to the poor, not working for him who is oppressed with toil" or "turning away the needy, oppressing the distressed" or being "advocates of the rich, unjust judges of the poor" was "altogether sinful." That preliminary training program and its subsequent weekly confession of faults should have sufficed so that Christian pagans and Christian Jews could live together. And, as we see in more detail below, the *Didache*'s discipline is basically a Christian Jewish training program for Christian-pagan converts.

But even that program was not enough to reassure some members of the community that eating together in open commensality was now appropriate. They must have demanded stricter food regulations than those given in 6:3. As Milavec notes, "Minimally, however, one can judge that the Didache does give evidence of an inter-Jewish schism that has already taken place. The actual historical causes and terms of this in-house disagreement are not given or discussed. It is suspicious, however, that the ruling respecting foods forms the first order of community business. Might this indicate that the 'hypocrites' are those Jewish-Christians who have been unwilling to relax the traditional food regulations imposed upon Gentiles?" (112). This is very similar to the situation concerning food regulations for the mixed Christian community of converted Jews and pagans at Antioch as described in Galatians 2:11–13 and Acts 15:28–31. Luke describes it as an amicable agreement, but Paul says the compromise was "hypocrisy." That is the more radical calling the more moderate position hypocrisy. A similar case arose in the *Didache,* but now it is the moderate calling the more conservative position hypocrisy. There are, of course, important issues at stake in all those cases, but calling one's opponents hypocrites probably did not help to do anything but confirm separation and solidify boundaries.

SERENITY AND COMMUNAL CONTROL

Those twin instances of name-calling in *Didache* 8:1–3 are all the more striking amidst this document's prevailing serenity. That serenity is evident, for example, in the regulation about foods just seen in *Didache* 6:3. Only one thing is absolutely forbidden—namely, participation in pagan banquets where one's food is shared with pagan gods. With regard to anything else, "[T]ake what [kinds of food which] you are able [to bear]." That is an example of the "Do what you can" principle, which is abrogated only when something absolutely indispensable is at stake. Take, for another example, something as important as baptismal initiation into full community membership when the training program is complete. This is *Didache* 7:1–3, in the system of analytical lineation used by Milavec (1989:96):

[A] Baptize in the name of the Father and the Son and the Holy Spirit,
    [1] in running water. But if you do not have running water, baptize in other [than running] water.
    [2] And if you are not able to do so in cold water, [then do so] in warm water.
    [3] But if you do not have either, pour water on the head three times,
[B] in the name of [the] Father and of [the] Son and of [the] Holy Spirit.

The external frames of Father, Son, and Holy Spirit tell us what is not negotiable. The internal distinctions of running or still water, cold or warm water, immersion or aspersion processes are quite negotiable. *Whatever,* says the *Didache.* This community will not split up into running-baptizers against still-baptizers, warm-baptizers against cold-baptizers, immersers against aspersers. That confirms, of course, that the split with the "hypocrites" was not over thisday or that-day fasting, this-time or that-time praying, but over things much more profound whose divisiveness was simply manifested in those distinctions.

That prevailing sense of peaceful consensus was recently underlined by Ian Henderson. He spoke of "the coolness of normative tone in *Didache,* its sapiential imperatives notwithstanding." He saw "its argumentative goal as more eirenic than polemic or even didactic," and he summarized it as "a deliberately low-key eirenicon." He concluded that, historically, "it indicates a much less conflictual response to substantially the same range of symbolic stresses attested in canonical sources, a normative calmness that is probably underrepresented in early Christian literature (and its interpretation)" (292, 294). Given that the Greek word for peace is *eirenē,* *eirenic* and *eirenicon* are good words to describe the peaceful rhetoric that pervades the *Didache.* Henderson is quite correct that this peaceful aspect is all the more striking against our earliest Christian letters, and he exemplifies that "normative calmness" especially with regard to orality and literacy. This text, he says, "remains a book essentially about the normativity of various kinds of speech, a text which, though written and dependent on written sources, takes in itself no cognizance of writing. . . . *Didache* argues for the complementarity of diverse authorities by receiving them conversationally and pragmatically rather than ideologically. . . . [T]he symbols chosen for this task are therefore preferentially and not only accidentally or subliminally those of speech and action rather than those of a more literary logic. Thus from a point of view of literary purism, *Didache* must always seem enigmatic if not inarticulate. . . . *Didache's* overall poetic effect, characteristic also of oral sensibility in general, is a simultaneity of impressions leading not to critical, ideological clarity but to decent, pragmatic accommodation. . . . *Didache* suggests the possibility of creating or re-creating an atmosphere in which the variety of normative language may be simultaneously and cumulatively, not hierarchically, maintained" (293, 304–305). It is not at all that the *Didache* considers nothing worthy of stern disagreement. But, on the other hand, only those items receive it that deserve it. The *Didache* accepts the primacy of living and doing over speaking and writing, the ascendancy of life and action over voice and text. It is about how to live in Christian community, and it is always tolerant except where intolerance is absolutely demanded and articulated. It is that consensus on lived reality that keeps the oral sensibility so evident even in a written text. It bespeaks matters worked out in face-to-face encounter and then summarized in a written text rather than imposed by a written text from outside or above. It is the serenity of achieved consensus.

GENDER AND COMMUNAL EQUALITY

During the session on "Women and the (Search for the) Historical Jesus" at the Society of Biblical Literature's 1996 annual meeting in New Orleans, Deborah Rose-Gaier presented a paper on "The Didache: A Community of

Equals." She began with a small but significant item. The training component of the *Didache*—the so-called Two Ways (1:1–6:2)—addresses the Way of Life with gendered neutrality to "my child" (Greek *teknon*) in 3:1, 3, 4, 5, 6, and 4:1. In the book of Proverbs, by contrast, the student is consistently addressed as "my son." When the advice given applies equally to females as well as to males, the New Revised Standard Version reads "my child" instead of the older and more literal "my son." That is rather like our changing "He who hesitates is lost" to "Anyone who hesitates is lost." There is a significant difference, though: in the case of Proverbs, "my son" is not so much inaccurately subsuming both sexes chauvinistically under the male title as accurately reflecting the engendered priority of male over female education in the writer's world. That is rather obvious in Proverbs 5, which forms an interesting contrast with *Didache* 1–6. The context is a slightly paranoid warning against the Strange-Woman as distinct from the Wife-Woman, so that the gendered "my son" (not the ungendered "my child") is necessary in 5:1, 7, and 20. Here, for example, is Proverbs 5:20:

Why should you be intoxicated, my son, by another woman and embrace the bosom of an adulteress?

This verse, where a married man is warned away from "an adulteress" rather than being warned against becoming an adulterer himself, highlights the contrast with the *Didache;* the latter, in offering training for both females and males, reveals not a hint of misogyny.

Furthermore, when the *Didache* speaks about household relationships there is a striking lack of anything about wives and husbands. It forbids, on the one hand, infanticide (specifying "murderers of children") and pederasty (specifying "corrupters of the creatures of God") in 5:1. It commands, on the other hand, these intrahousehold relations (Milavec 1989:95):

You will not relax control over your son or your daughter, but you will train them to reverence the Lord from their youth. You will not angrily command your male slave or your female slave who trust in the same God [as you] lest they fear not the God who is over you all. For he [God] does not come to call [someone] in recognition [of status], but [he calls] those on whom he placed his Spirit. But you slaves, you will be submissive to your masters as if [you were being submissive] to the image of God, [both] in respect and in fear. (*Didache* 4:9–11)

The ethical codes of household relations in other early Christian documents usually mention husbands and wives, parents and children, owners and slaves.

This is an example from a treatise written around 100 C.E. as if it were a letter of Paul to the Ephesian community:

> Wives, be subject to your husbands as you are to the Lord. . . . Children, obey your parents in the Lord, for this is right. . . . And, fathers, do not provoke your children to anger, but bring them up in the discipline and instruction of the Lord. Slaves, obey your earthly masters with fear and trembling, in single-ness of heart, as you obey Christ. . . . And, masters, do the same to them. Stop threatening them, for you know that both of you have the same Master in heaven, and with him there is no partiality. (Ephesians 5:22; 6:1, 4, 5, 9)

The basic direction in that passage is obedience of inferiors to superiors accompanied by kindness of superiors to inferiors. Implicit in that direction is the absolute assumption that wives, children, and slaves *are* the inferiors. The *Didache,* on the other hand, mentions only children and slaves. "The remarkable aspect regarding the household in the *Didache* remains," in Rose-Gaier's words, "the extent to which it does not concern itself with rendering a household code whereby wives are subordinated to their husbands" (9).

Finally, the *Didache* has no injunctions against women in any of the roles it mentions. One could, of course, argue that men were exclusively in charge of all those activities in the *Didache* tradition, so nothing further had to be said about it. But the Pauline and post-Pauline tradition had to command against women teaching and, in fact, against them teaching men:

> Women should be silent in the churches. For they are not permitted to speak, but should be subordinate, as the law also says. If there is anything they desire to know, let them ask their husbands at home. For it is shameful for a woman to speak in church. (1 Corinthians 14:34–35)

> Let a woman learn in silence with full submission. I permit no woman to teach or to have authority over a man; she is to keep silent. . . . Yet she will be saved through childbearing, provided they continue in faith and love and holiness, with modesty. (1 Timothy 2:11–12, 15a)

In the light of that situation, the *Didache's* total silence about submission of wives to husbands and about their nonparticipation in leadership roles points more likely to Rose-Gaier's conclusion that "there are no prohibitions recorded against women as trainers, baptizers, eucharistizers, apostles, prophets, or teach-ers so it must be assumed that these functioning roles within the community were open to women" (12).

THE FIRST RURAL CHRISTIANS?

When you consider Henderson's "normative calmness" or Rose-Gaier's "radical equality" in the *Didache*—especially in contrast with so many other early Christian texts—the question presses: Why is it so different?

You cannot reply that it indicates "Christian" equality over "Jewish" inequality. The *Didache,* while admitting pagans into its Christian community, is profoundly Jewish. In many instances, from eucharistic celebration in *Didache* 8–9 to apocalyptic consummation in *Didache* 16, it is still far closer to its Jewish roots than Paul is, for example, in 1 Corinthians 11 and 15. Nor will it do to presume that the *Didache's* community is somehow more particularly virtuous than other Christian communities. What, then, makes it so different?

First, we sometimes talk about the public spaces belonging to men and the private ones to women in the ancient world. And, of course, public is much more important than private! Rose-Gaier quotes this comment by the Jewish philosopher Philo of Alexandria (citing Yonge 611):

> There are two kinds of states, the greater and the smaller. And the larger ones are called really cities; but the smaller ones are called houses. And the superintendence and management of these is allotted to the two sexes separately; the men having the government of the greater, which government is called a polity; and the women that of the smaller, which is called oeconomy. (*Special Laws* 3.170)

That puts men in charge of "politics" and running the government and women in charge of "economics" and running the household. But earliest Christianity was far more involved with the household than with the government. Whether it liked it or not, therefore, women were extremely important in its organizational basis in house-based communities and house-based churches. It was a question of authority and power. At later stages, as Christianity moved more and more into the public and governmental sphere, men had actively to retake such control from women. Women, as Luke 10:38–42 put it, should passively *listen* like Mary rather than actively *administer* like Martha.

Second, the *Didache* may derive from a rural rather than an urban situation. It may stem from the consensus of rural households rather than the authority of urban patrons. Willy Rordorf and André Tuilier, writing in a major French series, located the *Didache* in northern Palestine or western Syria, but not in the capital city of Antioch. They noted that the text is addressed to "rural communities of converted pagans" (98). It "reveals a Christianity established in rural communities who have broken with the radicalism of earlier converts" (100). It "speaks principally to rural milieus converted early on in Syria and Palestine and no doubt furnishing the first Christian communities outside of cities" (128). Kurt Nieder-wimmer, however, writing in a major German series, considered it still possible that "the Didache could derive from an urban milieu," but he agreed that it was not from the great metropolis of Antioch (80). It is not enough, in any case, simply to note the mention of "firstfruits" in *Didache* 13:3–7, since that could indicate urban-based landowners. My own preference for a rural over an urban setting comes not from those few verses but from the *Didache*'s rhetorical serenity, ungendered equality, and striking difference from so many other early Christian texts.

Controlling Prophets

The prophets are not actually the leaders of the community since the *Didache* continually invites the Christian assembly to make collective decisions and, because of that communal address, it deliberately uses "you" in the plural.

       Willy Rordorf and André Tuilier, *La doctrine des douze apôtres (Didachè)*, p. 64

At this point it would seem that the *Didache* community has matters under full communal control. It has in place a complete training program for new and especially pagan converts. That is clearly outlined in the Two Ways of *Didache* 1:1–6:2. And that moral catechesis forms the basis for examination of conscience and confession of faults. The Way of Life concludes like this (Milavec 1989:95):

Within the congregation [*ecclesia*], you will confess your transgressions, and you will not go to your prayer with a bad conscience. (*Didache* 4:14a)

In a later text that confession is located before the Sunday eucharist, on, literally, "the Lord's day of the Lord" (Milavec 1989:100):

On the [day] belonging to the Lord, gather together and break bread and eucharistize, first confessing your faults. (*Didache* 14:1)

The community has established its basic moral code and has established a way to keep all accountable to it before the group. But there is still one major problem. What about itinerants who come from outside the community? How are they to be contained and controlled?

It is necessary to be quite clear about the problem. It is not simply one of Christian visitors who receive periodic hospitality but who have no particular claims to power or authority over the community. The problem is not about travelers and hospitality but about itinerants and authority. Thus the *Didache* makes an explicit distinction between "travellers" and "prophets," the latter being its term for my "itinerants." It is very clear on how to handle "travellers." Here is *Didache* 12:1–5. Notice its carefully divided cases as translated and delineated by Milavec (1989:99):

Let everyone who comes in the name of the Lord be received [hospitably].

[A] Then, when you have tested him (or her), you will know [whether he or she is good or evil],

[B] for you will have the understanding of the right and of the left [i.e., of good and of evil]:

    [1a] If, on the one hand, the one coming is a traveler passing through, help him (or her) as much as you are able.

    [1b] But he (or she) will not remain with you for more than two or three days, if there is [some] necessity.

    [2a] On the other hand, if [the one coming] wants to settle among you and knows a trade, let him (or her) work and eat.

    [2b] If someone does not know a trade, use your own judgment to determine how he (or she) should live with you as a Christian without being idle.

[C] If someone does not wish to cooperate, he (or she) is a Christ-peddler. Be on guard against such ones.

What a startlingly exact term: a "Christ-peddler." In Greek it is *Christemporos*, combining the roots from which we get *Christ* and *emporium*. The community knows already about the distinction between a *Christianos* and a *Christemporos*, between a Christ-person and a Christ-hustler. It knows about the possibility of such hustling, guards prudently against it, but does not solve it with a "No Solicitors" sign outside the household. "Travellers" and even "Christ-hustlers" are under control. They are taken care of in five verses. *They* are not the problem.

The itinerants who receive extensive and repeated attention are those who come with divine authority, who come in the name of God. *And the problem is not just those itinerant authorities but, much more profoundly, the authority of itinerancy itself.* One aspect of that itinerancy must always be kept in mind for what follows. Just as *didache* means practical training for Christian life and not just abstract learning for Christian belief, so will itinerant authorities be judged not primarily on what they say but on what they do. If we think, for example, of prophets only as those who *talk* in the name of God, we may miss the *Didache's* understanding of prophets as those who *act* in the name of God.

Itinerant authorities come, for the *Didache,* in three types: apostles, prophets, and teachers (trainers). And you could almost describe the *Didache* as the slow and careful ascendancy of teacher (trainer) over prophet and apostle. But it is more accurate to describe it as the ascendancy of the *didachē,* the teaching or training itself, over teacher, prophet, or apostle. But it is all done very slowly and very carefully. In the end, however, the community will prevail and communal consent will control even the pyrotechnics of itinerancy.

ITINERANT TEACHERS

With the moral program detailed in *Didache* 1–6 and the ritual program detailed in *Didache* 7–10, itinerant teachers or trainers are easily controlled in *Didache* 11:1–2 (Milavec 1989:98):

Whoever comes and trains you in all these previously said things, receive him:
[A] But if the one training, turning [aside], should train [you] in another tradition
   (didachēn) for the purpose of undermining [the above], do not listen to him.
[B] But if his training fosters righteousness and understanding of the Lord receive him as the Lord.

(An aside. Do not take the male pronouns in this and other *Didache* quotes as contradiction of the text's gender neutrality. Such pronouns generally tell us about the gender of the Greek nouns involved—*apostle, prophet,* or *trainer,* for example—rather than indicating the sex of the individuals involved.)

This passage is very clear. The community has its own *didachē,* its own moral and ritual training program clearly articulated in *Didache* 1–10, so that the itinerant trainers mentioned next, in *Didache* 11:1–2, must submit to it or be indicted by their divergent *didachē* as undermining the official one.

Furthermore, on that secure basis the community is ready and willing to let itinerant trainers settle down and be supported by the community's firstfruit dona-tions in *Didache* 13:2. So too with prophets, in *Didache* 13:1, 3–7 (Milavec 1989:99):

[A] Every true prophet who wishes to settle among you deserves his food.
[B] Similarly, a master-trainer also deserves, like the laborer, his food.

Didache 13:2 is actually imbedded in 13:1–7, which concerns itinerant prophets who settle down permanently in the community. I return to that section when considering the prophets, below.

ITINERANT APOSTLES

Itinerant apostles are also relatively easy to prevent from disturbing the community. Apostles, as mentioned above, are simply prophets on their way to found new Christian households or communities elsewhere, and they are sup-ported by already established ones while on their journey. Since their designa-tion means *ones sent,* they are, by definition, on their way through to elsewhere.

They can, according to *Didache* 11:4–6, stay only one or two days and take only bread until the next night's lodging (Milavec 1989:98):

Let every apostle who comes to you be received as the Lord:
[A1] But he will not remain more than one day, and, if there is some necessity, the following [day] as well.
[A2] But if [he should remain] for three, he is a false prophet.
[B1] But when the apostle departs, he should take nothing except the bread [which he needs to tide him over] until he finds lodging.
[B2] But if he requests money, he is a false prophet.

With apostles, unlike prophets and trainers, there is no discussion about settling down in the community. A settled-down apostle is an ex-apostle.

ITINERANT PROPHETS

Third, finally and most importantly, there are the itinerant prophets. Because this issue is much more difficult, the text returns to focus on itinerant prophets four separate times: in *Didache* 10:7, in 11:7–12, in 13:1, 3–7, and in 15:1–2.

Didache 10:7.

The first time the prophets appear is in *Didache* 10:7. At the end of two detailed chapters on the proper prayers for the eucharistic celebration in *Didache* 9:1–10:6 comes this final injunction (Milavec 1989:98):

Turn to the prophets [in order to permit them] to eucharistize as much as they wish. (*Didache* 10:7)

The minimal interpretation of that phrase is given by Milavec: "The text implies that the community completed its eucharistic prayers and then turned towards the prophets allowing them to offer the prayers unique to themselves *as often* and *as much* as they wished.... This points in the direction of indicating what must have been unique about prophetic prayer, namely, that their prayer spontaneously flowed from the Spirit which inspired them on the occasion and not from a pre-arranged formula which they memorized in advance" (1994:121). The maximal alternative is suggested by Kurt Niederwimmer. "The prophets (as liturgists) had the right to formulate the eucharistic prayers quite freely so that they were not limited to those fixed models" (205).

Didache 11:7–12.

The next mention of prophets is in *Didache* 11:7–12, which is a marvelously delicate and intricate dance of containment. The basic principle concerning itinerant prophets is very clear, but notice its emphasis on behavior (*tropoi* or "characteristics"), a term that should not be taken just as ethically good behavior but as continuity with Jesus' own ethically radical behavior. Here is the core principle, in *Didache* 11:7–8a (Milavec 1989:98):

And do not either test nor pass judgment on every prophet who speaks in the spirit:

[A] For every sin will be forgiven, but this sin will not be forgiven;

[B] [Furthermore,] not everyone who speaks in the spirit is a [true] prophet, but only if he has the characteristics *[tropoi]* of the Lord.

That is a rather startling and somewhat contradictory principle. Do not judge prophetic utterance *unless* the prophet lacks the lifestyle of the Lord. The Greek word *tropos* (plural *tropoi*) is translated, in a standard lexicon, as "manner, way, kind, guise, way of life, turn of mind, conduct, character." We could restate that principle, then, as follows: the lifestyle of the Lord is determinative.

The *Didache* has a calculatedly ambiguous use of *Lord* to mean "the Lord God" and/or "the Lord Jesus." Ian Henderson termed *Lord* "the *Didache*'s ambiguous theo-/christological symbol" (296). But in this case the emphasis is on the Lord Jesus. What is fascinating, however, is the text's presumption that the *Didache* community members know the lifestyle of the Lord Jesus and can use it to judge the validity of itinerant prophets. It is not just a matter of knowing this or that saying of the historical Jesus but of knowing the basic way of life that he lived while on earth. Itinerancy is modeled and must stay modeled on Jesus.

Examples 1 and 2. Next follow four examples, in *Didache* 11:8b–12. The first two examples give criteria by which one can judge a prophet to be false, in 11:8b–10 (Milavec 1989:98–99):

[C] From his characteristics *[tropoi]*, then, will the false and the true prophet be known:

    [1] And every prophet designating, in the spirit, a table [fellowship to be convened] shall not eat therefrom. If he does, he is a false prophet.

    [2] Every prophet training [you] in the truth, if he does not do the things he trains [you to do], is a false prophet.

The first case is more interesting than the second one, which involves simple hypocrisy. It presumes the normal situation of the eucharistic ceremony as communal meal. The eucharist is, in other words, both liturgical celebration and actual meal. It celebrates, as Jesus did, the God of justice who gave the earth and its food equally to all. But while the better-off members of the *Didache* community would have eaten adequately at home in any case, the eucharist meant a decent meal for the poor or even destitute members of the community. It was, therefore, the community that established the times and places for such eucharistic rituals. By the time of *Didache* 14:1, the set time was once a week on Sunday, the Lord's day. But what if itinerant prophets called a eucharist for the benefit of the communal poor? Simple: if you call it, you do not participate in it. The possibility of self-interest is thereby precluded. Notice, as ever, the delicacy of the *Didache*'s discrimination. It does not say, There will be no such meal. It says instead, The prophet will not eat from it.

Example 3. The third example is very hard to understand, but it helps us see the difference between prophet and teacher. With a prophet we are looking primarily at performance, at lifestyle, at symbolic catechesis, and not just at teaching, word, or saying, even when utterances are backed by divine revelation. Here is *Didache* 11:11 (Milavec 1989:99):

[3]   Every tested and true prophet who acts in view of the cosmic mystery of the church but does not train others to do what he himself is doing, he shall not be judged before you,
[a]   for he has his judgment before God,
[b]   for, in such a way, the ancient prophets also acted.

This is the exact opposite of the preceding example. That directly forbids the prophets training others to do what they themselves do not do. This indirectly forbids them training others to do what they themselves do. But the meaning is also much more complicated, enigmatic, and even deliberately cryptic. What does it mean to act "in view of the cosmic mystery of the church" so that others should neither judge nor imitate? It is obviously something both surprising and also shocking for the ordinary Christian.

Gerd Theissen suggests that "this is probably an allusion to women who accompanied the wandering prophets, and whose relations with them were not unequivocal. Sexual abstinence was no doubt an official requirement. However, the passage is still a *mysterion* for us too" (1992:41). Other commentators agree with this general idea: Willy Rordorf and André Tuilier describe this earthly reflection of heavenly reality as "a 'spiritual marriage' between a prophet and a sister" (187); Kurt Niederwimmer also describes "a spiritual marriage or betrothal between a prophet and his female companion" (221). The celibate "marriage" of a female and a male prophet is an earthly symbol of the heavenly marriage between God (Christ) and the Church.

I think that proposal is quite correct, but I wonder a little about such terms as "sister" and "companion." In such a "spiritual marriage" are not both individuals equally prophets? The only way a woman could have been involved in the earliest Jesus movement as an itinerant prophet, given the cultural situation of the day, was if she traveled with a male as his "wife" (or in some other acceptable female role). As long as she was with a male, nobody would have really cared about the relationship or bothered to ask about it. Such companionship did not threaten patriarchal domination in any way; a woman accompanying a man could be servant or slave, sister, mistress, or wife without male chauvinism caring enough even to ask for definition. That is how we should also understand Paul's mention of a "sister wife" in 1 Corinthians 9:5, the "two by two" behind Mark 6:7 and Luke 10:1, and Cleopas's unnamed companion on the road to Emmaus in Luke 24:13, 18. It is fascinating to watch the *Didache* handle the problem: do not dare to judge them, but do not learn to imitate them either. Gently, delicately, carefully lines are being drawn between itinerant and householder, between the symbolic catechesis of the former and the settled *didache* of the latter. It is hard not to wonder, across two thousand years of Christian history, where else that principle of *do not judge but do not imitate* might have been usefully invoked. It is, in any case, one of the supreme examples of the *Didache*'s irenic tone of "normative calmness," as Ian Henderson so accurately put it.

There is one interesting footnote to that mysterious text. A Coptic papyrus containing *Didache* 10:3b–12:2a, dated to the end of the fourth or start of the fifth century, was bought in 1923 for what was then the British Museum and catalogued as British Library Oriental Manuscript 9271. F. Stanley Jones and Paul A. Mirecki offer a photographic reproduction along with an excellent transcription, translation, and commentary on this document. They conclude that "this sheet was originally cut from a roll of papyrus in order to serve as a double-leaf in a codex," but instead it was used "as a space for scribal exercises" (87). It was, in other words, a rather casual copying of that section of the *Didache* for purposes of writing practice. Stephen Patterson, on the contrary, considers it the end of an earlier edition of the *Didache*, which concluded precisely at 12:2 (1995:319–324). In any case, although the document is a translation, it is centuries older than our only full text of the Greek *Didache* and is therefore very important. And the Greek text it translated could go back even into the third century. If that is correct, British Library Oriental Manuscript 9271 would be the earliest piece of the *Didache* now extant.

Here is *Didache* 11:11 as translated by Jones and Mirecki (55, 57), but I have taken the liberty of delineating it as above to make comparison easier:

[3] Every true prophet, having been approved, having taught and testified to
an orderly tradition in the church, those among you should not judge him,
[a] but his judgment is with God.
[b] Thus did the prophets of the (old) times.

You will notice that "the cosmic mystery of the church" is now "an orderly tradition in the church." That erases anything suspiciously improper about those prophetic actions but creates another problem in its place. Why, now, would anyone want to judge such persons, why is their judgment left up to God, and what do the ancient prophets have to do with them? "Perhaps," suggest Jones and Mirecki, "the easier reading of 'having taught and testified to an orderly tradition in the church' (as supported by the Coptic text) is to be preferred over the enigmatic and classically problematic Greek phrase 'though he enact a worldly mystery of the church'" (68). I would presume the exact opposite. The Coptic translation either does not like or does not understand that "cosmic mystery" and replaces it with something both known and liked—namely, "orderly tradition." The more difficult text, whatever it meant, is the earlier one. That would also render doubtful Patterson's proposal that the Coptic fragment represented an earlier and shorter edition of the *Didache*.

Example 4. Finally, there is the fourth example. Relatively straightforward, it links backward with the opening preamble in 11:7 on speaking "in the spirit," with the first example in 11:9 on asking for others only, and with that last example in 11:11 on not judging. It brings fitting closure to the series (Milavec 1989:99):

[4]   Whoever says in the spirit, "Give me money or any other thing," you will not listen to him. But if he says to give to others who are in need, let no one judge him.

The prophets can ask for a eucharistic meal in 11:9 and money or anything else in 11:12, but only for others, never for themselves. It is delicately unclear at the end of 11:12 whether one should give whatever the prophets demand even for others. The *Didache* leaves it open and would probably answer, if directly asked, *Do what you can*, as in 6:1 on teaching, 6:2 on food, and 12:2 on hospitality.

Didache 13:1, 3–7.

This is the third time the text comes back to the prophets. It is clearly a new situation not envisaged in that earlier series in *Didache* 11:7–12. What if a prophet wants to settle down and stay in the community *as a prophet?* This is quite acceptable (Milavec 1989:99–100):

[A]   Every true prophet who wishes to settle among you deserves his food.

[B]   Similarly, a true master-trainer also deserves, like the laborer, his food.

[C]   As a consequence:

[1]   taking every first fruit of the produce of [your] wine press and threshing floor and of [your] cattle and sheep,

[a] you will give this first fruit to the prophets for they are your
     high-priests.

[b] But if you do have a prophet, give it to the poor.

[2] If you make a batch of dough, take the first fruit [of your baking] and
     give it according to the rule [governing first fruits].

[3] Similarly when you open a jug of wine or of oil, take the first fruit
     and give it to the prophets.

[4] Similarly with money, clothing, and every possession, take whatever first
     fruit which seems appropriate to you and give in accord with the rule.

Firstfruits are not exactly the same as alms. They belong to those who
receive them. The recipients have a designated share in the produce itself. The
text in *Didache* 13:1, 3–7 originally spoke only about settled-down prophets.
Didache 13:2 was added to apply the same principles to settled-down teachers, as
seen earlier.

Didache 15:1–2.

The fourth passage concerning prophets links them again with teachers, but
in these verses both were there from the beginning. It is, once again, classic
Didache in its delicacy (Milavec 1989:100):

Elect for yourselves, then, bishops and deacons who are worthy of the Lord:

[A] [Let these be] men who are unassuming, not greedy, honest, and have
     been tested, for they also are performing for you the official service of the
     prophets and the master-trainers.

[B] Do not hold them in contempt, then, for they are honored by you in
     company with the prophets and master-trainers.

In the *Didache*'s experience, itinerant prophets and teachers have ceded to
settled prophets and teachers, but now newer leadership from bishops and deacons is envisaged. These leaders are not fully accepted as yet; everything about
those verses breathes transition and change. The obvious advantage of the new
system is permanent actuality over charismatic possibility, and it seems linked
especially with the eucharistic celebration on Sundays by the "therefore" of
Didache 15:1 after the preceding 14:1–3. Once again, of course, the *Didache* proceeds gently and delicately.

Even after all of that, however, the community is not secure against the radicalism of itinerant prophets, whom it is quite willing to accept and revere but
also wishes to contain and control. Those preceding passages gave the *Didache*'s
community control over prophetic actions. The spiritual power and authority of

itinerant prophets were not negated; prophets were accepted and respected still, but they were also contained and controlled. They would not be allowed to wreck the community and then move on to repeat the damage elsewhere. But what if itinerant prophets insisted that it was the Lord Jesus who demanded this or that action? Think, for a moment, about the insistence on "Jesus said" in both the *Q Gospel* and the *Gospel of Thomas.* For whom was that significant? If followers of Jesus said that to strangers, the listeners would simply ask, "Who is Jesus?" or "Why should we care what *he* said?" But said to those already Christian, the phrase would have a profoundly challenging effect. Those who had *said,* "Lord, Lord," responding in faith, would be disturbed if told that they had disobeyed that same Lord by what they *did.* How, in other words, could the *Didache* community contain and control the most radical *sayings* attributed to Jesus by his itinerant followers? That is the next chapter.

CHAPTER 21

INTERPRETING THE COMMANDS

In the Synoptics we are told the rules given to the first Christian missionaries. The *Didache* gives the rules for dealing with these people.

Gerd Theissen, *Social Reality and the Early Christians,* p. 41
(from essay originally published in 1973)

There are three linked questions that arise as we consider the *Didache* as part of a larger body of early Christian writings. First, what, in general, is the relationship of the *Didache* to the three synoptic gospels? Is it dependent on them or independent of them? Second, what, in particular, is the relationship of *Didache* 1:3b–2:1, sometimes termed the text's "evangelical section," to Matthew, Luke, the *Q Gospel,* and any earlier source of those documents? Third, how does the *Didache* connect with that other earliest tradition in Paul's letters? Of those three problems, the first two are addressed in this chapter, and the final one will reappear later in Chapter 23.

The Independence of the *Didache*

There is only one instance in which sayings quoted in the *Didache* are certainly drawn from written gospels: *Didache* 1:3–5. This passage is a compilation of sayings from the Sermon on the Mount, but with distinct features of harmonization of the texts of Matthew and Luke. It is an interpolation that must have been made after the middle of the 2nd century and cannot, therefore, be used as evidence for the original compiler's familiarity with written gospels.

Helmut Koester, *Ancient Christian Gospels,* p. 17

The *Didache* shows no evidence of knowing either the Pauline or the Johannine tradition. But does it know the synoptic tradition? Is it dependent on one or more of the gospels of Matthew, Mark, and Luke? Or is it completely independent of them all? Two different sets of scholars have studied the *Didache* and, with quite divergent focuses, have arrived at equally divergent conclusions concerning its relationship with one or more of the synoptic gospels.

One set of researchers has been primarily interested in whether *Didache* sayings were or were not dependent on the gospels of Matthew, Mark, or Luke, and their studies have led to an almost total impasse. We now have on the table four major options.

A first opinion holds that the *Didache* is totally independent of the synoptic gospels. Richard Glover concluded forty years ago that "the *Didache* does not bear witness to our gospels, but quotes directly from sources used by Luke and Matthew"—that is to say, "from their common source," the *Q Gospel* (12, 25, 29).

A second opinion holds that the *Didache* is totally dependent on the synoptic gospels. Christopher Tuckett's address to the thirty-sixth Biblical Colloquium at the University of Louvain, given in 1986 and published in 1989, concluded that the synoptic parallels in the *Didache* "can be best explained if the Didache presupposes the finished gospels of Matthew and Luke. . . . [It] . . . is primarily a witness to the post-redactional history of the synoptic tradition. It is not a witness to any pre-redactional developments" (230).

A third opinion also goes back forty years to an early work of Helmut Koester (1957), which was further developed a decade later by Bentley Layton (1968). They held, as in the above epigraph, that the *Didache* is totally independent of the synoptic gospels except for *Didache* 1:3b–2:1, which is a later insertion into the completed text. That later insertion derived from harmonizing together the different versions of certain sayings in Matthew and Luke.

A fourth opinion is more complicated than the others. Clayton Jefford, for example, concluded that the *Didache* knew both "a tradition of sayings materials that were similar in nature to those materials which were collected in the Sayings Gospel Q and in the Marcan Gospel" but also "the Synoptic Gospels in some final literary form (or some harmony of those Gospels)" (142).

Such divergent results are not derived from disagreements over methodology. Tuckett states the basic principle most clearly: "If material which owes its origin to the redactional activity of a synoptic evangelist reappears in another work, then the latter presupposes the finished work of that evangelist" (199). That is the crucial principle for determining dependency, as discussed earlier in Chapter 8. But that principle works best when we have Matthew and Luke using Mark as a source, since we ourselves still have all three texts in front of us. We can then determine, by comparison with Mark, what exactly is redactional in their texts. We can see with relative clarity how each edits its Markan source. The principle works worst, however, when we have Matthew and Luke using the *Q Gospel* as a source. We know the *Q Gospel* itself for sure only when Matthew and Luke agree exactly in their separate presentations of it—when, in other words, they fail to redact it at all. If one but not the other redacts it, or if both redact it differently, we lose any secure base text for comparison and cannot be sure what was in the *Q Gospel* and what was done to that gospel by either or both evangelists. Although we can, in some cases, be quite certain that a saying was in the *Q Gospel* because we have redacted versions of it in both Matthew and Luke, we may be unable to determine the exact wording of it in the *Q Gospel*. That less-than-certain result may be quite adequate for general purposes, but it is quite inadequate if one needs to compare a precise word or phrase from the *Q Gospel* with some other text. And that is exactly the situation we are in with *Didache* 1:3b–2:1. The parallels from that section of the *Didache* appear in the *Q Gospel* as Matthew 5:39b–42, 44b–48 = Luke 6:27–30, 32–36; however, those verses are so different that it is notoriously difficult to decide for sure the sequence and content of that *Q Gospel* section. Judging, therefore, by two such careful analyses as Koester's and Tuckett's, it may be almost a lost cause to approach the *Didache* along that narrow focus. There is, however, a different possible approach.

Another set of researchers has been primarily interested in the *Didache* itself—and as a *whole,* so that relations with the synoptic gospels arise only within that wider and more complete framework. In general, many of those scholars have concluded that the *Didache* is totally independent of synoptic tradition and should be studied in its own right and in its own entirety and integrity. Here are a few representative examples of that scholarship.

Jean-Paul Audet, in his 1958 commentary for the Études Bibliques series, found three successive stages in the text, dating them all to the years between 50 and 70 C.E. The first level in *Didache* 1:1–3a; 2:2–5:2; 7:1; 8:1–11 was composed before any written gospel. The second level in *Didache* 11:3–13:2; 14:1–16:8, written by the same author under later and different circumstances, knew only some written proto-gospel of pre-Matthean tradition. But even the third level in *Didache* 1:3b–2:1; 6:2–3; 7:2–4; 13:3, 5–7 (with 1:4a and 13:4 added even later) knew none of our present canonical gospels (104–120). Two more recent French scholars, Willy Rordorf and André Tuilier, in a 1978 commentary, agreed with Audet on the *Didache*'s independence from our canonical gospels but opted for only two redactional layers, *Didache* 1–13 and *Didache* 14–16. Then, in a 1981 article, Rordorf concluded, against Audet, that *Didache* 1:3b–2:1, while clearly an interpolation, was not so much a late and additional as an early and constitutive insertion. Hence, for example, when he asked in the title of a 1992 article, "Does the Didache Contain Jesus Tradition Independently of the Synoptic Gospels?" he answered himself affirmatively, but based on those earlier studies. Jonathan Draper came to a similar conclusion of independence, but his 1985 article on "The Jesus Tradition in the Didache" was derived, once again, from a commentary situation—from his 1983 doctoral dissertation at Cambridge University entitled "A Commentary on the Didache in the Light of the Dead Sea Scrolls and Related Documents." Finally, two recent North American scholars have also agreed on the *Didache*'s independence, but once again from holistic considerations of the text's own compositional rhetoric. Aaron Milavec insists that the *Didache* is not just a quarry for synoptic parallels but that it has "its own agenda, its own logic, its own passionate concerns" (1989:90), and he considers 15:1–2 (on bishops and deacons) to be the only later interpolation. Ian Henderson emphasizes "the independence and priority of composition-critical (i.e., poetic and rhetorical) questions over against historical and sociological judgments—however legitimate the latter may be" (285) and concludes that "the unity of poetic sensibility and rhetorical function does tend to favor a relatively simple redactional history, despite the text's diversity" (305–306).

That survey does not indicate a closed case on the *Didache*'s synoptic dependence. Kurt Niederwimmer's 1989 commentary is rather agnostic on the whole subject. He concludes that the *Didache*'s final version, in general, knows some written gospel, but he adds that "the jury is still out" on whether it is canonical Matthew or an unknown extracanonical text (77). *Didache* 1:3b–2:1 he describes as a redactional interpolation "of uncertain origins" (115).

In my own earlier work, *The Historical Jesus,* I accepted the arguments of Koester and Layton that only *Didache* 1:3b–2:1 was dependent on synoptic tradition and that it was a much later insertion derived from harmonizing Matthean and Lukan versions of the sayings involved. I thought, at that time, that it was the best solution. Layton's explanation was that "the concern of the author, or rather, compositor, of the *Didache* passage—his choice of material once having been made—seems to have been primarily stylistic, to the exclusion of any overriding theological or scholarly interests—a fact which perhaps sets him apart from his colleagues. It is such concern for style and form that appear to control the relationship between the *Didache* verses and their postulated sources" (351). That insertion was made "after A.D. 150 *ca.* into a form of the *Didache already published* some fifty or a hundred years earlier," he concluded, because "within the circles in which the first edition of the *Didache* circulated, only by the time of the interpolation had Christianity felt itself to be clearly differentiated from the matrix of Jewish teaching within which it arose" (1968:381–382).

Layton's article showed, and showed rather brilliantly, *how* such a harmonization of the Matthean and Lukan versions of the sayings in *Didache* 1:3b–2:1 *could* have been done. But *if* it was done and *why* it was done are even more preliminary problems. I now see four basic objections to his interpretation. First, it is necessary to postulate a Christian-Jewish community's written constitution operating for fifty to a hundred years without any such Jesus tradition in its official training program. That might be feasible: one could respond that it was the "ways" *(tropoi)* and not the "words" *(logoi)* of the Lord Jesus that were normative for this community. (You will recall an emphasis on the "ways" of the Lord from my earlier discussion of *Didache* 11.8.) But then, second, somebody who knew

Matthew and Luke changed the *Didache* only by adding in the few sayings in 1:3b–2:1. Nothing was added to change its eucharistic ritual or its apocalyptic expectation to agree with those gospels. Next, by the time of that postulated insertion, those gospels were taking on normative status, yet the inserter harmonized them rather freely. The result, in effect, is a third version rather than a simple harmonization, and, as Layton notes, style seemed to be foremost in the inserter's mind. Finally, there is no indication that those inserted sayings came from Jesus or from the gospel of Jesus. They are never cited as such.

It was not, however, primarily those objections that changed my mind. It was focusing on the wider question of the *Didache*'s overall purpose and integrity, and not just focusing on the narrower question of its synoptic dependence or independence, that changed my own position. It was especially the works by Milavec and Henderson that revolutionized my own understanding of the *Didache,* and I recommend them as the best introduction to a new and more profitable way of studying that document. My present working hypothesis, then, is that the *Didache,* and especially 1:3b–2:1, is totally independent of any of the synoptic gospels (see Appendix 7). But that position only intensifies the problem of the relationship between that section of the *Didache* and the synoptic texts.

A Radical Mini-Catechism

Passive resistance is actually a specifically peasant contribution to politics with a long history. . . . The existence of a relationship between the basic features of peasant society and passive resistance seems evident.
Teodor Shanin, "Peasantry as a Political Factor," pp. 258–259

If *Didache* 1:3b–2:1 was simply a much later insertion from sayings in Matthew and Luke (Koester 1990a:17), especially as harmonized by some rather pedantic stylist (Layton 1968), that section would be of very minimal interest. If, however, it is independent from those canonical texts, it becomes extremely important. Layton himself indicated one aspect of that importance: "If written sources *cannot* be postulated, the way is open to label 1:3b–2:1 as the recording of a branch of oral tradition independent of Matthew's or Luke's casting of the Sermon on the Mount. Thus a fragment of a potentially 'pre-Matthean' Christian tradition and, indeed, one of a somewhat different theological viewpoint from that of the NT parallels would have been recovered and could be used as a source for study of the earliest Christian community, especially if one dates the *Didache* itself to the first century" (1968:345). But there is another importance as well. If *Didache* 1:3b–2:1 is independent, say, of the Q *Gospel*, it can then be compared with it. That comparison is what interests me here.

CONTENT

There are several sayings within *Didache* 1:3b–2:1 which not only have parallels in Matthew and Luke but whose sixfold linkage parallels a sixfold linkage from the inaugural sermon of Jesus in the *Q Gospel*. I follow here the reconstruction of the International Q Project accepting the *Q Gospel* sequence as Luke 6:27–36 rather than Matthew (Robinson et al. 1994:496–497). The closest comparison, in other words, is between the sequences in *Didache* 1:2b–5a and *Q Gospel* 6:27–36. Here are the sayings in the *Didache* sequence:

	Didache	Luke	Matthew	*Gos. Thom.*
(1) *The Golden Rule:*	1:2b	6:31	7:12	6:3a
(2) *Love Your Enemies:*	1:3b	6:27–28, 35a	5:43–44	
(3) *Better Than Sinners:*	1:3b	6:32–35	5:45–47	
(4) *The Other Cheek:*	1:4b	6:29	5:38–41	
(5) *Give Without Return:*	1:5a	6:30	5:42	95
(6) *As Your Father:*	1:5a	6:36	5:48	

That comparison indicates *some* form of very close relationship between the *linked series* of six sayings in *Didache* 1:2b–5a and the *linked set* of six sayings in *Q Gospel* 6:27–36.

There is, first of all, no common sequence. If the *Didache* sequence is given as numbers 1, 2, 3, 4, 5, 6, then the *Q Gospel* sequence is, as reconstructed, numbers 2, 4, 5, 1, 3, 6. I intend, of course, no presumption that either sequence is normative over the other but consider the common material across four points.

The first point is *The Golden Rule* itself. In *Didache* 1:2b it is in negative formulation and second-person singular, but in *Q Gospel* 6:31 it is in positive formulation and second-person plural (Milavec 1989:92):

Didache 1:2b	**Q Gospel 6:31**
All those things which you do not want done to you, do not do to another.	Do to others as *you* would have them do to *you*.

The second point is *Love Your Enemies* and *Better Than Sinners*. Here are the texts with their plural "you" italicized (Milavec 1989:92):

Didache 1:3b	**Q Gospel 6:27–28, 32–35**
(1) Bless those who curse *you;*	(1) Love *your* enemies,
(2) pray for *your* enemies;	(2) do good to those who hate *you,*
(3) fast for those who persecute *you.*	(3) bless those who curse *you,*

(4) What merit [is there] for loving those who love *you*? Don't the Gentiles do this?

(4) pray for those who abuse *you*. If *you* love those who love *you*, what credit is that to *you*? For even sinners love those who love them. If *you* do good to those who do good to *you*, what credit is that to *you*? For even sinners do the same. But [*you*] love your enemies, do good . . .

You, on the other hand, must love those who hate *you*, and *you* will not have a [single] enemy.

Both *Love Your Enemies* sayings have a basic fourfold structure. It is *bless, pray, fast,* and *love* in the *Didache*, but *love, do good, bless,* and *pray* in the *Q Gospel*. And both those sayings connect to *Better Than Sinners* sayings, that is, to a comparison with outsiders—either pagans or sinners—as motivation. They are challenged, as Christian *Jews* or as Christian *ex-pagans,* to do better than pagans: if the latter love their friends, they must love their enemies.

The third point, *The Other Cheek* and *Give Without Return,* is actually another single and fourfold saying. Here are the texts, with "you" now always singular and with the masculine to be taken inclusively (Milavec 1989:92):

Didache 1:4–5a

(1) If someone gives you a slap on your right cheek, turn the other [cheek] to him also, and you will be perfect.

(2) if someone presses you to go one mile, go with him for two [miles];

(3) if someone takes your coat, give him also your tunic;

(4a) if someone takes from you your goods, do not reclaim them, for you are not able [to do so];

(4b) give to every person who asks anything of you and do not make any counter-demands.

Q Gospel 6:29–30 (Matthew 5:39b–42)

(1) If anyone strikes you on the [right] cheek, offer the other also;

(2) and from anyone who takes away your coat do not withhold even your tunic.

(3) [and if anyone forces you to go one mile, go also the second mile]

(4b) Give to everyone who begs from you;

(4a) and if anyone takes away your goods, do not ask for them again.

The square-bracketed materials under *Q Gospel* 6:29–30 are found only in Matthew and so are not securely from the *Q Gospel*. "Whether the verse belongs in Q or not could not be decided with a grade higher than D," according to the International Q Project (Robinson et al. 1994:497). I think that it probably *was* in *Q Gospel* 6:29–30 and that Luke omitted it, but its presence or absence does not change the overall meaning.

In this case the fourfold sequence is much closer in both sayings. It is *cheek, mile, coat,* and *goods* in the *Didache* and *cheek, coat, (mile?),* and *goods* in the *Q Gospel.* Only the central two are reversed. The fourth and final injunction is doubled, but the meaning is not the same in each half. One involves not refusing those who ask (4b); the other involves not resisting those who take (4a).

The fourth point, the saying *As Your Father,* is the most problematic but also the most important. The first difficulty is reconstructing the original *Q Gospel* text. Here are its twin versions:

Luke 6:36:   "Be merciful, just as your Father is merciful."
Matthew 5:48:   "Be perfect, therefore, as your heavenly Father is perfect."

Luke never uses "merciful" again, but Matthew uses "perfect" once more in 19:21, where the rich man is told to give all his possessions to the destitute "if you wish to be perfect." That usage is redactionally Matthean over his source in Mark 10:21. The International Q Project prefers "merciful" as the original *Q Gospel* adjective (Robinson et al. 1994:497). We do have, however, the following parallels, following Matthew rather than Luke:

Didache 1:4b and 5a2	*Q Gospel* 6:36 (from Matthew 5:48?)
. . . and you will be perfect.	Be perfect, therefore,
. . . for the Father wishes that his goods be shared with everyone.	as your heavenly Father is perfect.

If the *Didache* is independent, I think that is too much for coincidence. But, in any case, God—be it as "merciful" or as "perfect"—is the model for human action in both *Q Gospel* 6:36 and *Didache* 1:5a².

INTERPRETATION

Common to *Didache* 1:2b–5a and *Q Gospel* 6:27–36 is a mini-series of linked sayings involving four basic points, as we have just seen. Now that we have read and compared those points, here is a more detailed appraisal.

The first point encountered in this portion of the *Didache, The Golden Rule,* requires some special attention. The saying appears in negative format in *Didache* 1:2b and *Gospel of Thomas* 6:3 ("Do not do unto others"), and in positive format in *Q Gospel* 6:31 ("Do unto others"). It appears with the singular "you" in *Didache* 1:2b and the plural "you" in *Gospel of Thomas* 6:3 and *Q Gospel* 6:31.

The saying appears not only in those Christian texts, of course, but also in purely Jewish texts from before and after them. In the book of Tobit, for example, dated to the fourth or third century B.C.E., Tobit advised his son Tobias in 4:15, "What you hate, do not do to anyone." Another example is attributed to Hillel, an older contemporary of Jesus, in *Shabbath* 31a of the *Babylonian Talmud,* completed by the seventh century C.E.: "What is hateful to you, do not do to your neighbor; that is the whole Torah, while the rest is the commentary thereof: go and learn it."

The most important question, however, is not plural or singular, positive or negative, which all amount to the same thing in any case. *It is whether the aphorism is taken as forbidding offense only or as also forbidding defense.* Does it mean, Since you do not want others to attack you, do not attack others yourself? Or, Since you do not want others to attack you, do not attack them back, even in self-defense? Is it about nonaggression or about nonviolence? Is it against offense or also against defense? In many cases, it may not be clear how radically the injunction is intended or taken. But in the present case and context of *Didache* 1:2b–5a and *Q Gospel* 6:27–36, I can only interpret it as commanding absolute nonviolence. In fact, the whole point of this mini-catechism is to interpret *The Golden Rule* as radically as possible.

The second basic point is a fourfold saying in plural-you format that specifies quite explicitly the nonviolence enjoined by the general aphorism. Four aggressive actions of attack must receive four counteractions not only, negatively, of nonattack but, positively, of loving, blessing, praying, fasting or doing good for the attackers.

The third point, another fourfold saying (this time in singular-you format), illustrates or exemplifies the preceding saying. That change from plural to singular is found in both *Didache* 1:3b–4 and *Q Gospel* 6:27–29, as is the sequence of the two fourfold sayings. They could, of course, be separated and their sequence reversed, as in Matthew 5:38–42 and 5:43–48, but that presumes the quite different climactic structure of those six antitheses in Matthew 5:21–48. In the original mini-series, the second foursome were concrete examples of the first foursome in practice.

The fourth point involves some insecurity in reconstructing the *Q Gospel* text of Luke 6:36 ("merciful") = Matthew 5:48 ("perfect"). Whatever the original *Q Gospel* adjective, all forms reflect the admonition of Leviticus 19:2b: "You shall be holy, for I the Lord your God am holy." That makes the character, nature, or being of God the normative model for human action. When *Didache* 1:4 speaks of being "perfect" and 1:5a speaks of what "the Father wishes," is that just two different ways of formulating the model? I consider the independent presence of "perfect" and "Father"-as-norm in both *Didache* and the *Q Gospel* (Matthew) too strong for coincidence and therefore indicative of an original emphasis.

We have, then, behind *Didache* 1:2b–5a and *Q Gospel* 6:27–36 a radical mini-catechism built around an absolutely nonviolent interpretation of *The Golden Rule* derived from God the Father as model of that perfection. Its content involved those four points, but they could be arranged in diverse sequences depending on rhetorical presentation. One could, for example, start with *The Golden Rule* as first principle or end with it as final climax. Whether that mini-catechism represents oral or scribal tradition is impossible to say for sure. That is another way of saying that neither can be ruled out for sure.

ORIGIN

My proposal is that the radical mini-catechism in *Didache* 1:2b–5a comes from the itinerant prophets and represents their manifesto, as it were. Perhaps accompanied by an accusatory "Jesus said," it may well have represented a bill of particulars against those who said "Lord, Lord" or "heard and did not do," as mentioned in *Q Gospel* 6:46–49. I offer two arguments for that position, one here and another in the next section.

In 1989 Ronald Piper published a very persuasive analysis of smaller sayings-clusters in the earlier, sapiential, or Q¹ layer of the *Q Gospel*. He proposed six relatively clear examples with the following fourfold structure: "(1) Each collection begins with a rather general aphoristic saying. . . . (2) The opening saying is then usually followed by a general maxim in statement form which provides ostensible support for whatever is being encouraged. . . . (3) The third stage of the aphoristic sayings-collections is frequently marked by a complete change of imagery and the presentation of two sayings which are similar in theme but different in illustration. The hallmark of this section is the rhetorical question formulation. . . . (4) The final unit of the aphoristic collection always provides the key for interpreting the meaning" (61–63). He also concluded, quite correctly, that *"these are not haphazard collections of aphoristic sayings; they display a design and argument unique in the synoptic tradition"* (64).

Piper's sixth and most tentative example is *Q Gospel* 6:27–36. It is, of course, his most difficult case, because, as seen above, the differences between Matthew and Luke result in no "consensus as to what the original sequence might have been" (78). It seems to me, however, that the aphoristic collection or radical mini-catechism behind *Didache* 1:2b–5a and *Q Gospel* 6:27–36 fits quite well into Piper's fourfold structural sequence if one accepts all those four elements I suggested above. Here is how I would apply his words to that collection. First, there is the "general aphoristic saying," *The Golden Rule*. Next, there is a "general maxim" but in imperative form, *Love Your Enemies*. Following that is a "complete change of imagery," *The Other Cheek* and *Give Without Return,* which contain, in the *Q Gospel* but not in the *Didache* version, "the hallmark . . . rhetorical question formulation" about the Gentiles or sinners. Finally, God as model is the conclusion that "provides the key for interpreting the meaning" of the whole complex.

What would the householders of the *Didache* have done if itinerant prophets had used such a radical mini-catechism? They might have cited it as the "words" *(logoi)* of Jesus, or, more likely, seen it as summarizing the "ways" *(tropoi)* of Jesus, that is, the lifestyle they had accepted in imitation of his own. What *did* the householders do? They first glossed it with *Didache* 1:5b–6 and then embedded the whole within the Two Ways—the training program in *Didache* 1:1–6:2. The next two sections give the details of that containment.

Redemptive Almsgiving

Redemptive almsgiving as a doctrine functions for the theological benefit of the rich but for the material benefit of the poor. It was the rich who struggled to gain entry into the kingdom. . . . A tradition that once ridiculed the idea that a wealthy man could enter the kingdom of God actually came to regard wealth as a blessing, a potential means of redemption. . . . Almsgiving provides a ransom for sin.

Roman Garrison, *Redemptive Almsgiving in Early Christianity,* pp. 10–11, 15

The first step in containing the radical abnegation of *Didache* 1:2b–5a is to interpret it with *Didache* 1:5b–6. The four injunctions in *Didache* 1:4 are prefaced with the command to "keep away from fleshly and bodily attachments," but the fourth is surely the hardest of all. Indeed, the command to *give without return* incorporates the three preceding ones. If one were able to do that, then turning the other cheek, giving the other garment, or going the other mile would hardly be too difficult. That final injunction is also the only one of the four that is securely present in the Common Sayings Tradition, as evidenced by both the *Q Gospel* and the *Gospel of Thomas:*

[Jesus said], "If you have money, do not lend it at interest. Rather, give [it] to someone from whom you will not get it back." (*Gospel of Thomas* 95:1–2)

Notice how the second half of that aphorism is much more radical than the first one. That same duality of more and less radical reappears in *Q Gospel* 6:30 as given by Luke but not by Matthew:

Give to everyone who begs from you; and if anyone takes away your goods, do not ask for them again. (Luke 6:30)

Give to everyone who begs from you, and do not refuse anyone who wants to borrow from you. (Matthew 5:42)

In Matthew both halves say the same thing, but in *Thomas* and Luke the second half is much more radical than the first. In *Didache* 1:4b–5a it is the reverse: the first half is the more radical one. And it is precisely this second or less radical part that receives a detailed gloss in *Didache* 1:5b–6. That move from 1:4b through 1:5a to 1:5b–6 indicates how the *Didache*'s community understood and practiced this hard commandment of total self-desfoliation.

I give the text of *Didache* 1:5–6 (Milavec 1989:92, slightly adapted) in parallel with another early Christian version of that "rule" *(entolē)* and commentary, from Mandate 2 of the *Shepherd of Hermas*, dated from Rome around the year 100 C.E (Lake 2.73):

Didache 1:5a–6	*Shepherd of Hermas*, Mandate 2:4–7
[A] *Give to every person who asks anything of you* and do not make any counter-demands, *for the Father wishes that his goods be shared with everyone.*	[A] Do good, and of all your toil which God gives you, give in simplicity to all who need, not doubting to whom you shall give and to whom not: *give to all, for to all God wishes gifts to be made of his own bounties.*
[B] Blessed is the one who gives according to this rule *(entolē),* for that one is blameless.	[C] He therefore who gives is innocent; for as he received from the Lord the fulfillment of this ministry, he fulfilled it in simplicity, not doubting to whom he should give or not give. Therefore this ministry fulfilled in simplicity was honourable before God. He therefore who serves in simplicity shall live to God.
[C] Woe to the one who receives: for, on the one hand, if someone who is in [real] need receives, he is blameless; but, on the other hand, someone who is not in [real] need will be called to account as to why that one received and with what results. Placed in prison [by God, one] will be examined [as to why such	[B] Those then who receive shall render an account to God why they received it and for what. For those who accepted through distress shall not be punished, but those who accepted in hypocrisy shall pay the penalty.

things were done] and will not
leave from there until one has paid
the last penny [of illegitimately
received alms].

[D] Concerning this [giving], it has
been said: "May your alms
[i.e., the metal coin] sweat in
your hands until you know to
whom you are giving it."

[D] Keep therefore this commandment
(*entolē*) as I have told you, that your
repentance and that of your family
may be found to be in simplicity.

That is another mini-catechism involving aphorism plus commentary, but
the parallelism between those versions is much too close for coincidence. Each
of them mentions "the rule" (*entolē* in Greek), and the citation is very similar in
each instance (see my italics in A above). The command is not cited from Jesus
but from God, and the reason for the command is that all good things come
from God and are given to some for sharing with all. Each commentary focuses
on the receiver and the giver, with that order in one (BC) and the reverse in the
other (CB). The conclusion is quite different in each case (D).

In other words, a very similar and set-format combination of rule plus commentary is found in two documents, one from rural Syria and the other from
urban Rome. There might be some direct connection, as there is between *Didache*
1:2b–5a and *Q Gospel* 6:27–36. That direct connection is not just dependent on those
texts, however, but derives from the general dialectic of itinerants and householders throughout the *Didache*. I am not, therefore, as sure of a direct connection in
this second case. But what is much more certain is that this mini-catechism derives
from deep in the earliest interface between Judaism and Christianity as Christian
Judaism. It shows a dialectic between itinerants and householders in which the
radical desfoliation of the farmer is muted and delicately transformed into fervent
almsgiving by the latter.

The Two Ways

The Teaching of the Apostles . . . is totally lacking in art or genius, and seems to
attempt to foist the essence of the old legalism upon the new religion, reducing its living faith to the keeping of a set of rules.

Edgar J. Goodspeed, *The Apostolic Fathers*, p. 1

The Two Ways is too often put forward as a prime exhibit of the "degener-
acy" of the Christian movement in the postapostolic era. Supposedly it is an
example of the repressive moralizing of the spontaneous faith of the earliest

church. . . . It may rather be a legitimate extension of a form which is the product of primitive Christianity's pronounced ethical concern.

M. Jack Suggs, "The Christian Two Ways Tradition," p. 73

A pronounced ethical concern derived, be it noted, from its Jewish roots, and often endangered as it got too far away from them. This is the second of those two above-mentioned steps through which the *Didache* contained the radical sayings of itinerant prophets. It embedded all of *Didache* 1:2b–6 within a very traditional form of moral catechesis known as the Two Ways—the ethical way of life *versus* the unethical way of death. This tradition usually has a four-part structure, as summarized by Margaret McKenna: Introduction, Way of Life (or positive deeds), Way of Death (or negative deeds), and Conclusion (189–190). The format is intensely dualistic and antithetical, but that antagonism can range from cosmic ontology to human morality.

The Two Ways teaching is found in both Jewish and Christian texts and comes, as emphasized above, from the former into the latter tradition. I give two Jewish examples from the immediate pre-Christian centuries, citing only their opening lines. The first comes from the *Rule of the Community* (or *Serek ha-Yaḥad*, in Hebrew), found among the Dead Sea Scrolls in the first cave discovered at Qumran (hence the abbreviation by which it is known, 1QS [*DSST* 6]). The second, from *The Testament of Asher* in *The Testaments of the Twelve Patriarchs,* is a set of fictionalized farewell speeches from Jacob's twelve sons modeled on his own departing speech in Genesis 49 (*OTP* 1.816–817):

> God . . . created man to rule the world and placed within him two spirits so that he would walk with them until the moment of his visitation: they are the spirits of truth and of deceit. In the hand of the Prince of Lights is dominion over all the sons of justice; they walk on paths of light. And in the hands of the Angel of Darkness is total dominion over the sons of deceit; they walk on paths of darkness. (*Rule of the Community* 3:17–21)

> God has granted two ways to the sons of men, two mind-sets, two lines of action, two models, and two goals. Accordingly, everything is in pairs, the one over against the other. The two ways are good and evil; concerning them are two dispositions within our breasts that choose between them. (*Testament of Asher* 1:3–5)

That general Jewish tradition is then taken over into Christian Jewish texts in the first common-era century. Here are two Christian examples, again citing only their opening lines. The first is from the Greek *Epistle of Barnabas* (Lake

1.401); the second is from the Latin *Teaching of the Apostles* or *De Doctrina Apostolorum* (Goodspeed 5).

> There are two Ways of teaching and power, one of Light and one of Darkness. And there is a great difference between the two Ways. For over the one are set light-bringing angels of God, but over the other angels of Satan. And the one is Lord from eternity and to eternity, and the other is the ruler of the present time of antiquity. (*Epistle of Barnabas* 18:1b–2)

> There are two ways in the world, that of life and that of death, of light and of darkness. Over them are set two angels, one of right *(aequitatis)*, the other of wrong *(iniquitatis)*. Moreover there is a great difference between the two ways. (*Teaching of the Apostles* 1.1)

When you put those two Christian texts alongside the two preceding Jewish ones, you can see how cosmic and angelic dualism can be present or absent, in a spectrum from *Rule of the Community* 3:17–21 and *Epistle of Barnabas* 18:1b–12, through *Teaching of the Apostles* 1.1, into *Testament of Asher* 1:3–5.

The *Teaching of the Apostles* will be of great importance as I proceed. The Two Ways traditions depicted in the *Teaching of the Apostles,* the *Epistle of Barnabas,* and the *Didache* all go back to a common source. But the *Teaching of the Apostles* is much closer to that lost original than are the other two texts. Remember that for future discussion, because it is against that general background and especially that final text that I consider the Two Ways in the *Didache.*

Didache 1–6 is a classic example of the Two Ways tradition. Applying Margaret McKenna's four-part structure, cited earlier, we can break that passage down into its components: Introduction in 1:1, Way of Life in 1:2–4:14, Way of Death in 5:1–2, and Conclusion in 6:1–2. But it is also quite clear that *Didache* 1:2b–6, those two mini-catechisms discussed above, has been inserted into a preset formulation of that Two Ways tradition. This can be shown by a comparison of the opening of the *Teaching of the Apostles* with that of the *Didache:*

Teaching of the Apostles 1:1–2:2	*Didache* 1:1–2:2
[A] There are two ways in the world, that of life and that of death, of light and of darkness. Over them are set two angels, one of right, the other of wrong. Moreover there is a great difference between the two ways.	[A] There are two way, one of life and one of death, but there is a great difference between the two ways.

[B] The way of life is this: first, you shall love the eternal God who made you, second, your neighbor as yourself. Moreover, anything that you would not have done to you, you shall not do to anyone else.

[C] Now the meaning of those words is this:

[D] You shall not commit adultery, you shall not commit murder, you shall not bear false witness, you shall not corrupt a boy, you shall not commit fornication, you shall not practice magic, you shall not use enchanted potions, you shall not murder a child by abortion, nor kill one when it is born, you shall not desire any of your neighbor's goods, [etc.].

[B] The way of life is this: first, you will love the God who made you; second, your neighbor as yourself; all things which you do not want done to you, do not you do to another.

[C] The teaching of these words is this:

[Insertion of Didache 1:3b–2:1]

[D] You will not murder, you will not commit adultery, you will not commit pederasty, you will not fornicate, you will not steal, you will not use magic, you will not use sorcery, you will not commit abortion nor infanticide, you will not covet the goods of your neighbor, [etc.].

Neither of those versions is directly dependent on the other. Both, as Rordorf and Tuilier argue (27–28), are dependent on a common source. But while *Teaching of the Apostles* 1:1–2:2 follows closely the opening of that source, *Didache* 1:1–2:2 adds in those twin mini-catechisms discussed above. Why did it do that?

One explanation seen already is that of Bentley Layton. Originally "no sharp difference was yet felt between a special Christian exegesis (that of the Sermon on the Mount) of the command to love God and one's neighbor (*Didache* 1.2) and that of the Hellenistic synagogue." But the insertion of *Didache* 1:3b–2:1 was intended to differentiate "Christianity . . . from the matrix of Jewish teaching within which it arose" (1968:382). Two objections, one minor, one major.

The minor objection is that the insertion is not attributed to Jesus or even to "the Lord," the *Didache*'s usually ambiguous term for Jesus and/or God. The "rule" in *Didache* 1:5a is that of "the Father." There is nothing particularly Christian about that. But the major objection is much more significant. The *contents* of that insertion is, to a large extent, already present in the Two Ways passage even before the insertion of *Didache* 1:3b–2:1. The following section, for example, appears in the Way of Life at *Didache* 4:5–8, and we can be sure it was originally there since it is also in *Teaching of the Apostles* 4:5–8 (Goodspeed 6). I give it, as usual, in Milavec's translation and delineation (1989:94):

Do not extend your hand [when it comes time] to receive and then withdraw it [when it comes time] to give:

[A] if you possess something due to the work of your hands, you will give it [to the community] *for the atonement of your sins.*

[B] You will not hesitate to give,
and you will give without murmuring,
for you will know who is the good paymaster of the wages [on the last day].

[C] You will not turn yourself away from the needy,
but you will share everything with your brother,
and you will not claim anything for your exclusive use,
for, if you are sharers in the immortal [things], how much more in the mortal.

Those commands are as strong as the ones in the insertion. Stronger, in fact, if you consider that phrase I italicized (about which more below). And those positive commands in the Way of Life are repeated as negatives in the Way of Death in *Didache* 5:2a (Milavec 1989:96):

not being merciful to the poor
not working for him who is oppressed with toil
turning away the needy
oppressing the distressed
advocates of the rich
unjust judges of the poor
altogether sinful

In the light of those passages, to claim that the insertion of *Didache* 1:3b–2:1 completed an inadequate source or "Christianized" a "Jewish" source is not very plausible.

My alternative proposal is that the insertion was intended primarily to absorb within the community's training program the most radical sayings of the itinerant prophets, their most challenging defense of lifestyle differences from the householders. The *Didache*'s Two Ways tradition already contained a version of *The Golden Rule* in 1:2b and its detailed interpretation in 2:2–4:14 (using, by the way, the singular "you"). From those itinerant prophets it took their radical mini-catechism with *The Golden Rule* and their interpretation (using the plural "you"). Their conjunction explains the intrusive plural "you" in *Didache* 1:3b. But how exactly did that insertion contain the radical content of those sayings?

First, it included them under communal control as part of their consensual training program for new converts. Second, it interpreted the desfoliation of possessions (easier, no doubt, for those who had none) *as heavy and repeated almsgiving.* Third, it did not cite them as "words" of Jesus. I do not presume any deceit in that process. The itinerant prophets validated themselves primarily in their lifestyle imitation of Jesus' "ways," and the householders formally accepted that norm, as we saw above, in *Didache* 11:8. I do not know to what extent they and their hearers considered *any* saying, whether attributed to Jesus or not, as simple verbal articulation of actual practice. Jesus "said" this by "doing" that. But, in any case, it comes from "the Father" in *Didache* 1:5, and that is what counts. But there is a fourth detail that is the heart of the matter.

Any Two Ways tradition is inherently disjunctive and antagonistic. It presents you with a Way of Life *versus* a Way of Death. No in-between or half-and-half positions are proposed. It is an absolute either/or split, and it can reach from human ethics to cosmic spirits to divine beings. Compare, then, the following two endings of the Two Ways traditions as given in the *Didache* and the *Teaching of the Apostles* (which is as close as we can get to the former's unredacted source):

Teaching of the Apostles 5:2–6:1, 4	*Didache* 5:2–6:2
[A] Abstain, my son, from all these things.	[A] May you be delivered, my children, from all these things.
[B] And see that no one leads you astray from this Teaching; otherwise, you will be taught outside the true instruction.	[B] Watch, lest anyone turn you away from this way of teaching, since such a person teaches you without regard for God;
	[C²] for, on the one hand, if you are able to carry the [entire] yoke of the Lord, you will be perfect; but, on the other, if you are not able, undertake that which you are able [to bear].
[C¹] If you do these things daily with reflection, you will be near the Living God but if you do not do them, you will be far from the truth.	

Notice in passing (but recalling Rose-Gaier's earlier point about the gendered equality of the *Didache*), that difference in address between "my children" and "my son."

My main point, however, concerns a comparison of those twin conclusions. First, both agree in [A] on concluding the Way of Death with a general injunction against "all these things." Next, both agree in [B] on a warning against anyone teaching apart from the Two Ways discipline just detailed. Finally, however, comes a very striking difference. The *Teaching of the Apostles* ends in good, disjunctive Two Ways style in C¹. It is an either/or with God and the truth on only one side of that choice. There are no in-betweens, no other options, no alternative selections. But, in C², *Didache* 6:2 omits any mention of that dichotomy and ends, instead, with a choice not between absolute Life and Death but between relative "being perfect" and "doing what you can." Those latter options must certainly not refer to such deeds as magic or sorcery, abortion or infanticide, fornication or adultery, theft or murder. Those, surely, are not "Do what you can" situations. That distinction between "being perfect" and "doing what you can" refers, I suggest, to that earlier insertion at the start of the *Didache*'s Two Ways teaching. That initial redactional insertion in 1:3b–2:1 corresponds to this final redactional insertion in 6:2, and the opening "You will be perfect" in 1:4 corresponds with the closing "You will be perfect" in 6:2. It is those radical commands from the itinerant prophets that are accepted but contained, cited but controlled by that serene distinction between *perfection* and *adequacy*.

When compared with an earlier Christian version of the Two Ways tradition, such as the *Teaching of the Apostles,* the *Didache*'s somewhat permissive conclusion is extremely surprising. And that surprise is confirmed by a later Christian version of the Two Ways given in a document that uses the *Didache* as a source. The *Apostolic Constitutions* is a church-order document from the late fourth century that quotes the *Didache* as the basis for Book 7:1–32 (Funk 1.386–423). It cites, paraphrases, omits, and expands on its *Didache* source, but here is all it gives from *Didache* 6:2 (Funk 1.404):

> *See that no one leads you astray* from piety. Do not turn, it says, to the right or to the left from it, that in all things you may know what to do. Where you turn from the *way* of piety, you will be impious. (*Apostolic Constitutions* 7:19)

That paraphrased version picks up only seven Greek words from *Didache* 6:2 (italicized above) and omits any mention of perfection versus adequacy. We are back again with a proper Two Ways disjunction between piety and impiety.

Here, however, a cautionary note is necessary. The *Didache* is willing to be gentle and delicate in demanding full perfection of everyone. It is willing to take a "Do what you can" stance on these most difficult challenges. But it is not willing to create two classes of Christians, the "perfect" ones and the "ordinary" ones. All alike are called to perfection and should get as close to it as possible.

One must take very seriously, therefore, this final warning in the apocalyptic section that concludes the *Didache* (Milavec 1989:100):

> The whole time of your faith will not be of any use to you if, in that last
> moment, you are not perfected. (*Didache* 6:2)

Because that "you" is plural, the saying presses a little harder on the community as a whole than on isolated individuals. Still, the *Didache,* even while
containing those radical sayings within its own protective teaching, does not
consider "perfection" something only for charismatic elites. It is something for
all to strive after by doing "what you can."

Let us return for a moment to the subject of redemptive almsgiving, to address
one final and very difficult question that this section has raised. Recall that recent
phrase from *Didache* 4:5 about almsgiving as "atonement for one's sins," which I
italicized above. The very idea of almsgiving comes not from Greco-Roman paganism but from Judaism. And so does the idea that almsgiving can be atonement for
one's sins, can gain remission from sins before God. It is from Judaism that early
Christianity obtained both those ideas. But belief in redemptive almsgiving fits
there in some tension with belief in the redemptive death and resurrection of Jesus.
The retention and emphasis on redemptive almsgiving in early Christianity requires
explanation beyond the obvious one of Jewish tradition. There were also all those
hard sayings about poverty and possessions in the gospels. They could not be
exactly ignored, but neither could they be exactly followed. Luke 6:20b says,
"Blessed are you who are poor," and 6:24 says, "Woe to you who are rich." But the
Shepherd of Hermas, in Similitude 2:10, has this: "Blessed are they who are wealthy
and understand that their riches are from the Lord, for he who understands this will
also be able to do some service" (Lake 2.147). And 2 *Clement* 16:2 agrees with this:
"Blessed is every man who is found full of these things; for almsgiving lightens sin"
(Lake 1.155). We have, as it were, mediated Luke's dichotomy with a new beatitude:
Blessed are you rich who give alms to you poor.

Judaism, however, knew not just about redemptive almsgiving but also
about divine justice. Those texts seen earlier in Chapter 12 did not speak just of
alms but also of rights. They did not simply demand alms for the indebted,
enslaved, and the dispossessed. They also demanded that those statuses be abrogated at least every so-many years. Here, then, is the problem. Is almsgiving on
the side of justice or injustice? But how could one dare to criticize almsgiving
when people are in desperate need and demand instant or immediate relief? And
how could one dare to criticize almsgiving when almsgivers may then desist all
too readily or eagerly from any generosity at all? Yet it must be said that almsgiving can cover over chasms of systemic injustice and structural inequity. That, in

fact, may be the only logic that makes redemptive almsgiving religiously valid in the sight of God. It is actually restitution, as it were, of stolen goods. Alms may be necessary, but it is equally necessary not to confuse them with justice.

Words and Ways of the Lord

The Oral phase of the Jesus tradition is now forever lost. The *spoken word* is transitory by nature and exists for but a moment. It lives on only in the memory of the audience and its recovery is entirely dependent upon the accuracy of that memory to bring it back into being. . . . Even the written tradition continues to be edited and improved. This warns us against assuming that the Gospels offer a directly transcribed orality: the tradition may have been thoroughly textualized and altered in the transmission process, a process that did not end with the synoptic evangelists! . . . It has not been possible to establish even one instance where a chain of *oral sayings* has reached two literary authors independently. . . . The unconscious—and uncritical—evolutionary model of sequential tradition (oral then written) must give way to a more sophisticated acknowledgement that these two "phases" of tradition are far more interrelated than is often acknowledged.

Barry W. Henaut, *Oral Tradition and the Gospels,*
pp. 295, 296–297, 299, 303 (my italics)

I conclude with two final thoughts on the *Q Gospel* and the *Didache*—one concerning sayings and oral tradition, the other concerning sayings and community formation.

The first point, then: sayings and oral tradition. The problem just mentioned in the epigraph links all the way back to earlier parts of this book. By the end of Part II, you knew that I had very little confidence in peasant memory or oral transmission as it is usually invoked to explain the early decades of the Jesus tradition. If there were *only* oral memory at work, then the historical Jesus would probably be lost to us forever. By the end of Part III, you knew that I considered certain early sources, such as the gospels of Q, *Thomas,* and Mark, to be independent of one another. But even *if* those sources had pointed back before themselves to orality rather than textuality, or at least to some delicate interface between orality and textuality, such oral memory had already been rendered questionable in Part II.

This epigraph from Barry Henaut seems, therefore, an epitaph for historical Jesus research. It is taken, in fact, from a concluding chapter entitled "Oral Tradition: The Irrecoverable Barrier to Jesus," which upgrades to imperative Rudolf Bultmann's proposal to place "the name 'Jesus' always in quotation marks and let it stand as an abbreviation for the historical phenomenon with which we are concerned" (295, 305). I consider, as mentioned earlier, that suggestions to put the name of Jesus in quotation marks or to surround Jesus with a cloud of unknowing are attempts to protect him, alone in all the world, from publicly argued evidence and historically conditioned reconstruction. Historical Jesus agnosticism is simply epistemological uniqueness, the negative historical side of a positive theological issue. Why is Jesus more unknowable or less reconstructable than any other ancient person about whom data has survived?

Leaving that aside, however, I agree absolutely that the invocation of an oral tradition about Jesus that is fortunately beyond disproof but unfortunately beyond proof is not a very good strategy of reconstruction. But notice those two phrases that I italicized in the epigraph: "spoken word" and "oral sayings." It is this emphasis on *words* and *sayings* that I want to discuss here. I ask whether *remembering his sayings* or *imitating his life* is the primary mode of continuity from the historical Jesus to those who walked around with him and remained around after him. The *Didache,* as we have just seen, did not even cite his sayings *as his.* But it used as a criterion of authenticity the ways *(tropoi)* rather than the words *(logoi)* of the Lord. Continuity was in mimetics rather than in mnemonics, in imitating life rather than in remembering words.

Let me take a concrete example. I think it is as likely as anything historical ever is that Jesus said, "Blessed are the destitute." But even if that were a direct quotation, its meaning could have changed as the saying was cited and transmitted. It could, for example, have moved from ethical into ascetical or apocalyptic eschatology. My confidence in reconstructing the historical Jesus does not derive from accuracy of memory or even validity of interpretation among his first companions. It comes from them and Jesus living a common lifestyle that incarnated the kingdom of God on earth. Within the continuity of that lifestyle, such a saying could have been remembered because it would have been regularly used. But even if the saying was created after Jesus' death—or even if all thirty-seven sayings of the Common Sayings Tradition were so created—they would still be adequate summaries of attitude because of that lifestyle continuity. If, however, nobody else had lived like the historical Jesus and continued to do so after his execution, then, indeed, the way back would be closed forever.

The second point concerns sayings and community formation. Earlier, in Chapter 15, I quoted from both Koester and Kloppenborg on the divergent eschatologies of the sayings tradition and the Pauline tradition. Although, in the past, the Pauline tradition was often taken as uniquely normative in earliest Christianity, it is not now useful to react by elevating the Common Sayings Tradition into a new ascendancy. The present challenge is to hold on equally to them both, to see their connections as well as their separations, to explain both of them as present within the same earliest Christianity, and to reconstruct the historical Jesus using both those vectors.

Koester proposed that, instead of historical Jesus research, "the primary focus would have to be the investigation of Christian beginnings itself" and that "such investigation would have to start with the earliest available evidence, that is, with the genuine letters of Paul and with the Synoptic Sayings Source [the Q Gospel], or even its earliest layer of composition [Q¹]. It must be admitted at once that these two oldest sources present the scholar with a conundrum. . . . There is no agreement among the oldest witnesses about the significance and value of Jesus' words, deeds, and fate for the message that his followers proclaim" (1994b:540, 541). I note, in passing, that I myself do not find that divergence such an "conundrum" as Koester does. Both traditions are eschatological. Both are ultimate challenges from the Jewish God to human injustice, currently exemplified by its Roman embodiment but not exhausted, of course, by that or any other incarnation. One tradition finds that eschatology incarnated in Jesus' life of nonviolent resistance to Roman exploitation, thereby making the kingdom of God available for anyone with the courage to emulate his program. The other finds that eschatology incarnated in Jesus' death by official Roman execution, which is negated by a God who raised him from that death. There is no need to set Jesus' life and Jesus' death against one another or even over one another. It is a life so lived that led to a death so accepted. Be that as it may, however, Koester has pointed to a very important dichotomy as far back as we can get in the Jesus tradition.

When, however, we think of the Pauline letters, we can see immediately how they are instrumental in community creation and conservation. But when we speak of the Q Gospel, what type of community are we imagining? A written text indicates, no doubt, some form of organization, but what type is it? "The Q community," writes Koester, "stood in a demonstrably direct continuity to Jesus' own ministry—indeed the members of this community seem to have emulated Jesus' behavior." But what type or mode of "community" does that indicate? "The most plausible explanation," responds Koester, "seems to be that 'community' for these disciples was identical with the relationship of wandering ascetics to each other. Moreover, sayings assigned to the Sayings Gospel Q, especially in its earliest stage, tend to emphasize the self-denial of the wandering missionary and the ascetic prescriptions for an elite group. It may therefore be doubted whether this religious 'movement' was able to establish viable community structures that could function in conformity or in opposition to the existing organization of the society" (1994a:543, 545).

Karen King and Stephen Patterson have raised a similar question with regard to the Gospel of Thomas. King argues that "the term 'kingdom' is a code word for community" (1987:95), but Patterson replies that "there is little in Thomas that provides for community organization or structure: there is no Thomas community per se, but rather a loosely structured movement of wanderers." He concedes, however, that "a Thomas movement" so described "would not be incompatible with King's thesis" (1993a:151 and note 123). It depends, actually, on what one means by *community*. I agree with Koester and Patterson that the *Q Gospel* and the *Gospel of Thomas* do not derive from settled and located communities similar to those in the Pauline tradition. We are dealing, I agree, with connections rather than communities. Radicals do not organize easily any more than anarchists institutionalize readily. But, of course, written texts indicate some minimal form of cooperation and some minimal type of organization.

Actually, however, even the situation with just the "words" or "sayings" of Jesus is somewhat more complicated. Across twenty-five years of publications Koester has emphasized, concerning such texts as the *Q Gospel* and the *Gospel of Thomas,* that, for example, "faith is understood as belief in Jesus' *words,* a belief which makes what Jesus proclaimed present and real for the believer" (1971:186), and again, most recently, that "the presence of Jesus was tangible in the *words* he had spoken" or that "wandering preachers ... were proclaiming salvation through the *words* of Jesus" (1994a:543, 544). I italicize that repetition of *words* because, even if we had only those *words,* we would know, from the Common Sayings Tradition studied in Chapter 18, that they involved a reciprocal program of eating and healing, of householders and itinerants, of destitution and poverty. We do *not* have just the sayings of Jesus, but even if that *was* all we had, those words themselves are not just *words about words* but *words about deeds;* those sayings are not just about vision but about action. *Faith is not just in words but in the God who through words demands deeds.* Whether each group likes it or not, itinerants and householders are locked together in dialectic by Jesus himself. The kingdom of God is not in either group alone but in their interaction. But for interaction to occur, both groups must continue to exist. To look at the *Q Gospel* or the *Gospel of Thomas* alone is to look at a half-picture or a half-community. It is the *Didache* that gives us our best glimpse of the other half of that picture and that community.

CHAPTER 22

A DIVIDED TRADITION

There are only few traces, if any, of the kerygma (as understood by Paul and Mark) in some of the earlier collections [of Jesus' sayings]. But this does not imply that they had no particular theological purpose; no doubt, this purpose was somehow related to the earthly Jesus, who was the speaker and/or actor in a large part of this tradition. . . . Such collections were made according to principles and patterns which have no relation to the pattern of the classic passion-resurrection creed and the "gospel" produced by it. . . . If the kerygma of the passion and resurrection played no role, how much do such different (and perhaps more primitive) documents relate to the "historical Jesus" as content or origin of the tradition?

Helmut Koester, "One Jesus and Four Primitive Gospels," pp. 165–166

This chapter is a very important connective between the preceding tandem Parts VII and VIII and the succeeding tandem Parts IX and X. Those former parts followed one very early tradition, that of the sayings of Jesus and the lifestyle they demanded. I traced the sayings from the historical Jesus, through the Common Sayings Tradition, and into, on the one hand, the *Q Gospel* and, on the other, the *Gospel of Thomas*. I also looked at the *Didache*, which crosses the *Q Gospel*'s trajectory at a very early stage—certainly closer to its Common Sayings Tradition roots than to its finished apocalyptic consummation emphasizing the Son of Man. My primary focus was not so much the full trajectory of that tradition but the earliest continuation from the historical Jesus to his first companions. That dialectic of itinerants and householders, still visible in those later written texts, goes back as early into the tradition as I can trace the evidence. It goes back into the life of the historical Jesus; it is, in fact, the program of the kingdom of God itself. Parts IX and X look at another tradition, one based not in rural Galilee but in urban Jerusalem. In studying that tradition I will be in constant dialogue with the work of Helmut Koester. The purpose of this pivotal chapter is to look at his position on those two traditions.

From Koester's epigraph above I take only its distinction between "collections of Jesus' sayings" and "the kerygma of the passion and resurrection." That is what I mean by a divided tradition. Whether the former is "perhaps more primitive" than the latter is possibly insoluble and probably irrelevant. More or less primitive, earlier or later—that is not the point. That epigraph is from thirty years ago, but Koester has repeated its key point in later work. With regard to the *Gospel of Thomas*: "The basis of the *Gospel of Thomas* is a sayings collection which is more primitive than the canonical gospels, even though its basic principle is not related to the creed of the passion and resurrection. Its principle is nonetheless theological. Faith is understood as belief in Jesus' words, a belief which makes what Jesus proclaimed present and real for the believer" (1971:186). With regard to both the *Q Gospel* and the *Gospel of Thomas*: "One of the most striking features of the *Gospel of Thomas* is its silence on the matter of Jesus' death and resurrection—the keystone of Paul's missionary proclamation. But Thomas is not alone in this silence. The Synoptic Sayings Source (Q), used by Matthew and Luke, also does not consider Jesus' death a part of the Christian message. And it likewise is not interested in stories and reports about the resurrection and subsequent appearances of the risen Lord. The *Gospel of Thomas* and Q challenge the assumption that the early church was unanimous in making Jesus' death and resurrection the fulcrum of Christian faith. Both documents presuppose that Jesus' significance lay in his words, and in his words alone" (1990a:86).

John Kloppenborg has also emphasized that earliest Christianity involved what I have just called a divided tradition, and he agrees with Koester's description of that division as between Jesus sayings and passion-resurrection kerygma. He insists, moreover, and quite correctly, that whatever term is used for the passion-resurrection faith type in earliest Christianity—be it kerygma or proclamation, soteriology or salvation, theology or eschatology—that same term must likewise be used for the very different message of the *Q Gospel* faith type in earliest Christianity. The Pauline message should not be privileged in any way above the *Q Gospel* message. Nor, of course, vice versa. They both represent very early but divergent visions of Christian salvation. In Kloppenborg's words: "If [the *Q Gospel*] is not merely parenesis [catechetical supplement] but preaching of the eschatological event itself, we must either posit two somewhat asymmetrical 'kerygmas' [preachings of the eschatological event] existing side by side in the same churches, or alternatively presume that Q's 'kerygma' derives from circles different from those which created the 'Crucified and Risen Lord' kerygma. . . . Q had an understanding of soteriology which was at variance with the passion kerygma, the alleged centre of Christian theology. . . . Q [is] an independent kerygma reflecting a 'second sphere' of Christian theology" (1987a:22). In my own understanding, I rephrase those twin traditions of the sayings and of the passion-resurrection as the twin traditions of Jesus' life and of Jesus' death. They are, for me, two sides of a single coin.

The Tradition of Jesus' Life

In the understanding of Jesus' words of wisdom as a revelation providing life and freedom—this seems to be the case in the earliest compositional strata of Q—an eschatological dimension of these words seems to be hardly detectable. That is open to question. Good arguments can be brought forward for the eschatological implications of these wisdom sayings.

Helmut Koester, "The Historical Jesus and the Historical Situation of the Quest," pp. 540–541

That divided tradition has never meant for Koester that the sayings tradition is not theological or, indeed, eschatological. Both traditions *are* eschatological, and Koester's long insistence on the validity and value of the sayings tradition is remedial rather than hierarchical. He does not exalt it over the passion-resurrection eschatology but, in the presence of the latter's eventual theological normativity, pleads for the sayings tradition's historical existence and importance. He speaks of a form of *realized eschatology* in the various sayings gospels. He finds that eschatology in Q¹ (the earliest stratum of the *Q Gospel*), for example: "It cannot be argued that Q originally presented Jesus simply as a teacher of wisdom without an eschatological message," although, following Kloppenborg's stratification, "the *eschatological orientation* of the original composition of Q [Q¹] is distinctly different from the *apocalyptic perspective* of the redactor" [Q²] (1990a:150, my italics). He also finds realized eschatology in the sayings collections behind both the *Gospel of Thomas* and the *Q Gospel*, which do not "reflect a purely proverbial wisdom orientation: rather, prophetic sayings are included which incorporate the wisdom material into the perspective of a realized eschatology, centered upon the presence of revelation in the words of Jesus" (1990a:95).

There is, in that quotation, some of the terminological confusion between *eschatological* and *apocalyptic* noted at the start of Chapter 15. What is the relationship between an "eschatological orientation" and an "apocalyptic perspective"? Although Koester repeatedly uses those terms—especially the former one—he never explains their meaning or their relationship. Furthermore, Koester repeatedly speaks of "the "words of Jesus" in the realized eschatology of the sayings tradition. That is the term used in most of the preceding quotations, for example. It is almost as if the *content* of those words was irrelevant. Jesus is present, as it were, in their very utterance. But should that emphasis be on the *words* of Jesus or the *life* of Jesus? Is it remembering (or even repeating) his words or imitating and replicating his life that is eschatological?

Other scholars who work on the sayings tradition with similar historical pre-suppositions to Koester's have agreed with his basic point—namely, that there is a profoundly divided tradition in earliest Christianity. They do not, however, explain the eschatology of the sayings tradition as being about *words;* they focus, rather, on *lifestyles.* Two examples will suffice, both of them touched upon in Chapter 15.

John Kloppenborg insists, as just noted, that there were originally two primitive kerygmas, two early proclamations of salvation, two separate spheres of Christian theology. But he also holds that this *other* kerygma is eschatological but not apocalyptic: "In any accounting of Q, sapiential elements play a major role. It is difficult to miss the pervasive eschatological tenor of those wisdom elements. But it is another question whether the term apocalyptic is an accurate characterization for the redeployment of these wisdom materials" (1987b:291). He repeatedly identifies that sapiential eschatology as "the radical wisdom of the Kingdom of God" (1987a:189, 242, 318) and explains it by saying, for example, that "the sapiential speeches in Q, by means of their radical comportment, serve a properly kerygmatic function and point to the radical nature of the kingdom which is in the process of manifesting itself. Correspondingly, the imperatives specify the type of radical ethic which is the characteristic of those who have responded appropriately to this new reality" (1987a:320–321). Sapiential eschatology or radical wisdom is a matter not just of words but of lives, not just of sayings but of lifestyles. And the model is not just the historical Jesus but God. *"Discipleship . . . is understood as imitation of the merciful and generous God . . . and as 'following' or 'listening to' or 'coming to' Jesus"* (1987a:241).

The case is similar with Stephen Patterson. He does not speak of a divided tradition or of two kerygmatic proclamations, one based on the life, the other on the death of Jesus. His emphasis is rather on the common basis of those twin traditions, and he finds that commonality in "social radicalism." That is where the Pauline tradition and the Jesus tradition intersect for Patterson. "One may see the continuity between Paul and the sayings tradition precisely in terms of the tradition of social radicalism that both share. . . . Paul shared with the Jesus movement its social radicalism; he simply could not arrive there by the same route. For them, the reign of God was present in the spoken word; for Paul it became real only when one could accept the cross as one's own death to the world" (1991:35, 39–40). That same term "social radicalism" reappears repeatedly in Patterson's book on the *Gospel of Thomas* (1993a:4, 241). It is also quite clear that more than "the spoken word" is involved in such radicalism, in Patterson's view. It is word acted out in life that counts. "This is not realized eschatology, it is *actualized* eschatology. If the kingdom is to exist at all, it is up to Thomas Christianity to make it exist," and Thomas Christians do this by lives of celibate asceticism—an asceticism that "offers a real, present challenge to the world. It calls into question the ways of the world, its standards, its goals, its notion of what is meaningful in life. Thomas Christianity's social radicalism, as a form of asceticism, has precisely this effect" (1993a:210, 211).

Those two visions of the eschatology of the sayings tradition as Kloppenborg's "radical wisdom of the Kingdom of God" or as Patterson's "social radicalism" are necessary correctives to Koester's almost contentless emphasis on "the words of Jesus" in that tradition. Instead of the words of Jesus, we must speak of the radical life of Jesus. And instead of the death of Jesus, we must speak of the imperial crucifixion of Jesus. Then, in both Jesus' imitated lifestyle and in Jesus' resurrected deathstyle, the Jewish God of justice and righteousness stands radically— that is, eschatologically—against injustice and exploitation. But, since Koester himself did not follow that route, the sayings tradition and the cross-resurrection tradition seem to have come into intolerable tension for him in his recent articles. He now exalts the passion-resurrection tradition over and even against the sayings tradition.

The Tradition of Jesus' Death

The history of Christian beginnings demonstrates that it was most effective to establish and to nurture the community of the new age without any recourse to the life and work of Jesus of Nazareth. All that was needed was a ritual (the eucharist) and a story, namely the story of Jesus' suffering and death and, of course, hymns of mythic poetry.

Helmut Koester, "The Historical Jesus and the Historical Situation of the Quest," pp. 535–536

As I understand his earlier work, Koester's point about two separate, very early Christian traditions did not intend to exalt one over the other. His heavy emphasis on the sayings tradition was simply an attempt to restore balance against the almost exclusive emphasis on the death and resurrection tradition. But now there is a deliberate denigration of the former tradition in favor of the latter in Koester's recent work.

On the one hand, his views on the sayings tradition seem exactly the same as always. In the *Q Gospel*, "the presence of Jesus was tangible in the words he had spoken," and in the *Gospel of Thomas*, "wandering preachers . . . were proclaiming salvation though the words of Jesus" (1994a:543, 544). Then, however, comes a profound criticism: "While the essential elements, which are constitutive for the establishment of a community, are missing in the tradition of sayings and in the writings it produced, witnesses for the understanding of groups of believers as community are abundant in the Pauline Corpus and in the canonical gospels in their final form" (1994a:546). To that claim of a lack of community in the sayings tradition, I offer a single-word reply: Didache—that is, the community behind the document studied earlier. It was, by the way, a community with far greater serenity than anything we find in the Pauline churches. Even if the itinerants in the Q Gospel could not or did not want to establish their own settled communities, could and did householders do so in tensive dialectic with the radicalism of itinerant prophets in the Didache? That is, in any case, the point I have been arguing throughout the Part VIII.

There is, however, another factor operating in Koester's recent hesitancy about "the tradition of Jesus' sayings"—something besides that tradition's supposed inability to create communities. First, in connection with the wisdom traditions behind both the Q Gospel and the Gospel of Thomas, he notes that "some scholars see a close affinity of this wisdom tradition to the secular preaching of Cynic philosophers" (1994a:542). He footnotes, among others, to Burton Mack. Second, "Mack's work epitomizes also the general tendency that denies any eschatological elements in Jesus' message" (1995:14). Finally, "We have to ask ourselves, whether our search for the historical Jesus is not actually predetermined by the conditions of the cultural paradigm that dominates the second half of our century in the Western world. . . . That is most clearly evident in the aversion to eschatology. Perfection and success of the self, whether in political, industrial, moral, or religious terms, cannot conceive of a genuinely eschatological message—except for the syndrome of 'reward and punishment,' that miserable residue of an eschatological tradition. While nobody wants to take political eschatology seriously today—it is in fact perceived as a threat—very few people, on the other hand, are willing to eliminate social concern" (1994b:539). (I should note that Mack's work strongly validates the sayings tradition over the passion-resurrection tradition. In his view they are not just two separate but equally valid traditions.)

A few comments. To equate "secular" and "Cynic" in the ancient world or to use "secular" in describing Jesus is profoundly wrong—and that applies to anyone who uses the term "secular" in those contexts. The religious dimension of ancient life was too utterly embedded in its economic, political, and social dimensions to allow for the distinction of "secular" and "sacred" that some today take for granted as normal. On June 3, 17 B.C.E., a choir of fifty-four girls and boys sang a hymn composed by Horace in celebration of Augustus's new world order as the golden age come round at last. In Latin the word age is seculum, so the hymn was called "Carmen Seculare"; now, however, "Secular Hymn" would ring rather false to us, and "New Age Hymn" would not sound much better. A fair translation might be "Eschatological Hymn," a song in praise of Augustan peace, cosmic fertility, and imperial eschatology. Furthermore, the Cynics were not secular but religious and eschatological, but in the exact opposite sense to Augustus's triumphalism. They subscribed, in fact, to a pagan style of ethical eschatology. You are free to dislike them if you wish, or even to dislike all of Greco-Roman paganism. You are not free, however, to say that Cynicism was secular. It was simply a pagan eschatology with an anti-imperialist and anti-materialist drive based on totally different divine principles from similar Jewish and Christian eschatologies. *If* Burton Mack or others argue that either Cynicism or Jesus is secular rather than eschatological, the best response is to argue that they are quite wrong—but without negating either the Cynic philosophy or the Jesus tradition in the process. Finally, there is that last statement setting political eschatology against social concern. Those terms are equivalent, in my understanding, for the historical Jesus and for the Jewish God whose kingdom he proclaimed. Social justice as divine mandate necessarily involves political, social, and economic eschatology. (And to my ear, by the way, "social concern" is a rather feeble way of expressing divine justice for earth.)

It is almost as if, in the light of those three concerns in general and Burton Mack in particular, Koester is seeking to distance himself not only from Mack but from his own earlier analysis of the tradition of Jesus' sayings (and even from that very tradition itself). That is, of course, fiercely ironic, since nobody has done more to establish that tradition than Koester himself. It is now much too late to dismiss or even denigrate it. What is needed, however, is to give *both* those traditions *equal* consideration, not to exalt one over the other, not to set one against the other, and not to separate one from the other more than we should. In any case, I now leave that aside to focus on Koester's more positive analysis of that second tradition.

He builds a powerful picture of earliest Christianity as a deliberate counterempire to Roman imperialism. "There are two things that Julius Caesar and Jesus of Nazareth have in common. Both were murdered, and both received divine worship after their death. There is another interesting parallel. Neither Augustus nor Virgil wrote a life of Caesar, nor did Paul write a life of Jesus" (1994b:535). That is not, of course, just a series of accidental coincidences. Both sides are claiming the arrival of the eschatological or golden age. That fundamental parallelism is, therefore, a profound antagonism: two eschatological programs clashing with one another. Christianity knew that from the beginning and clearly. Rome knew it from the beginning but unclearly. Koester develops that basic antagonistic parallelism over four inaugural aspects: ritual, myth, story, and community.

In the Roman case, cultic ritual began in 42 B.C.E. when the assassinated Julius was declared divine and Octavius, his adopted son, became "divi filius," son of a god. In 27 B.C.E. Octavius was declared "Augustus," not quite divine but close enough for now. In 14 C.E., within a month of his death, Augustus was declared "divus" in his own right, son of a god and a god as well. A mythological hymn was mentioned by Koester above. Augustus had it: in 17 B.C.E., as I mentioned, Horace's "Carmen Seculare" acclaimed Augustus as descended, across more than a thousand years, from the Trojan Anchises and the goddess Aphrodite or Venus. Virgil, who died two years earlier, had told the epic story behind that mythical acclaim in his *Aeneid*. Reversing Homer's sequence of heroic wars and homeward wanderings, he brought Aeneas, son of Anchises, and Aphrodite-Venus, from Troy to Italy as ancestor of the Julian clan. "The eschatological story of the Augustan age was told by Virgil in his *Aeneid*, which anchored the new age in the distant past; it became the Roman national epic. The followers of Jesus in the churches of Paul told the story of Jesus' suffering and death; this story also reached back to the past of Israel as it cast the narrative in the words of the singers of Psalms and of the prophets" (1994b:535). The cult, myth, and story of Augustan eschatology can be seen today in Rome at the *Ara Pacis Augustae*, the Altar of Augustan Peace, reconstructed from original and copied fragments and now relocated between the Tiber and the Julio-Claudian Mausoleum. It is all there in marble, from fertile Earth Goddess, to Aeneas sacrificing, to Augustus and his family. Finally, as Koester concludes, Augustus used power and authority while Paul used letter and persuasion to build two quite different types of community.

Koester is completely correct that myth, ritual, and story are constitutive of community, but there is no need to give them to only one of those twin traditions, to the passion-resurrection tradition but not to the sayings tradition. In any case, as we shall see, they have both common elements and divergent developments that indicate that *both* traditions could generate and support community life. In what follows, therefore, I seek, negatively, not to privilege one of those twin traditions over the other and, positively, to emphasize connections and similarities where those are present. I am not, in other words, imagining two ideologically opposed traditions.

Rural and Urban Christianity

If Paul and his followers seem to have avoided the empire's villages and countryside, Jesus himself seems to have avoided the towns. . . . But instead of the Palestinian countryside, [the *Acts of the Apostles*] actually follow the mission in the cities of the Graeco-Roman world and end up with Paul a prisoner at Rome. The Palestinian countryside where Jesus had travelled and taught in fact disappears completely from all New Testament sources. . . . It must be stressed, however, that although urban and rural Christianity represent two different types of the new religion—the former more conservative and tending to compromise with secular power, the latter more subversive and with social reformist tendencies—their conflict but rarely came out into the open.

Dimitris J. Kyrtatas, *The Social Structure of the Early Christian Communities*, pp. 92, 95

It is necessary, then, to distinguish two traditions in earliest Christianity, one emphasizing the sayings of Jesus and the other emphasizing the death and resurrection of Jesus. We should not privilege one over the other, as I have said—not the death and resurrection over the sayings, as in past theology, nor the sayings over the death and resurrection, as in present reaction. There should be no overt ascendancy of *either* over the other. Furthermore, whatever descriptive term is used for one, be it proclamation or kerygma, tradition or gospel, the same term should be used for the other. In other words, there should be no *covert* ascendancy of *either* over the other. Finally, my own preferred terminology is the Life Tradition and the Death Tradition. That former phrase presumes that Jesus' sayings were a question not of memory but of imitation, not of aphorisms to be recited but of lives to be lived. The latter phrase presumes that Jesus' death was always dyadic, was always a dialectic of persecution *and* vindication, execution *and* resurrection.

The Life Tradition and the Death Tradition could be distinguished as northern and southern traditions. That works well in the former case, where the *Q Gospel,* the *Gospel of Thomas,* and the *Didache* can all be plotted on geographical trajectories from Galilee into Syria. It does not work so well for the southern traditions, which move from Jerusalem to Damascus and Antioch at a very, very early date. They could also be distinguished as rural and urban traditions. That works better for both as long as *rural* is not taken to mean isolated illiteracy, on the one hand, or bucolic delusion, on the other. In any case, and however one names or distinguishes those twin traditions, it is important—I cannot stress this enough—not to privilege one over the other too heavily, set one against the other too readily, or separate one from the other too absolutely. The future of Catholic Christianity belonged to neither of them alone but to both of them together.

Dimitris Kyrtatas's work, cited as epigraph above, has the signal advantage of taking that distinction of rural and urban Christianity seriously and trying at least to imagine *both* forms. The birth of Christianity took place precisely on that fault line and involved both rural Galilee and urban Jerusalem as early as the evidence lets us see what actually happened. Kyrtatas associates the distinction of rural and urban with that of revolutionary and conservative: "Few questions about early Christianity have caused greater disagreement than the question of its social standing. Practicing Christians historians and theologians have always been divided as to whether early Christianity was a revolutionary or a conservative movement. Today, much more easily than in the past, it is coming to be accepted that Christianity was both revolutionary and conservative. To accept this, however, is to reject the traditional view that there ever existed such a thing as a single early Christian Movement or Church" (89). But it is not just a standard case of rural-revolutionary becoming urban-conservative. There is, instead, a more complicated development. "In the early second century, when Christianity emerges again into history after New Testament times, it was already an urban religion. Culturally, socially, theologically, Christianity became adapted to needs and systems of thought of the cities.... It would therefore seem reasonable to conclude that when Christianity reached the countryside of the Roman world in its new form, it was socially, culturally and theologically marked by urban predispositions. We find, however, that this was not so. As soon as Christianity came into contact with the world of peasants and villagers, much of its original nature was revived. We have no idea in what way and to what extent this happened, but there are reasons to believe that the original message developed in the countryside of Palestine, and though allegorized by church leaders was once again understood by people living under similar conditions of material existence and exploitation by city dwellers" (93–94).

The tradition of Jesus' life and example filled Parts VII and VIII of this present book. That of Jesus' death and vindication will fill Parts IX and X. But there is a leap involved in the move from one of those tandem sets to the other. It is a leap that I wish to acknowledge but not to overemphasize to the point of mystification. Christianity was possibly present in Rome itself by the late 40s and was certainly present by the mid-50s. The *possibility* stems from the emperor Claudius's decree expelling Jews from Rome in 49 because of disturbances "at the instigation of Chrestus [= Christus? = Jesus?]," as Suetonius recorded in *The Lives of the Caesars: The Deified Claudius* 25.4 (Rolfe 2.53). The *certainty* stems from Paul's letter to the Roman community, written from Corinth around 55. If you move, as in that epigraph above, from Jesus in the tiny hamlets of Jewish Lower Galilee to Paul in the great metropolises of the pagan Roman Empire, the leap seems unimaginably great and miraculously inexplicable. But there were stages in between, stages that were not successive evolutionary moves but simultaneous options and overlapping developments.

Look, for a moment, at the range of hamlets, villages, towns, cities, and metropolises involved. Think also of the differences in class of leadership as you move up that locational hierarchy, from peasants to scribes to scholars. Recall what was seen in Chapter 13 about calculating site dimensions and population densities in antiquity. Even when, as in walled cities, that first variable is firmly established, that second may vary widely among scholars. I warn you, for example, that calculations of the total population of the Jewish homeland in the first century have ranged from one to six million, and calculations of its Jewish component have ranged from one-half to five million (Byatt 51–52). I am using these population statistics as rough indicators of increasing locational power, prestige, and importance:

I. Hamlet/Village Level
    Jesus is from Nazareth, "a hamlet of little more than a hundred" people (Malina and Rohrbaugh 295).
II. Village/Town Level
    The *Q Gospel* curses (in Q 10:13–15) places such as Capernaum, with 1,700 people (Reed 1992:15).
III. City Level
    Pre-Pauline situation involving Damascus (45,000), Jerusalem (80,000), and Antioch (150,000).
IV. Metropolis Level
    Pauline situation involving Corinth (100,000), Ephesus (200,000), and Rome (650,000).

The numbers for those first two levels are relatively secure. The population of Jerusalem at 180 hectares and 444 people per hectare (Broshi 14) makes it denser even than Ostia, and that figure is probably twice too large. The numbers in the last two levels are simply cited as given (Stark 131–132). My point is simply to emphasize that the "first urban Christians" were certainly not in the Pauline churches. Christians were in Damascus before Paul was converted; we know that because he persecuted them there. They were in Jerusalem even before that. And from Jerusalem some moved to Antioch, capital of the Roman province of Syria.

It is one of the major strengths of Kyrtatas's study, cited in the epigraph above, that he attempts to pay equal attention to countryside and city, to rural as well as urban Christianity, to the Little Tradition and to the Great Tradition. My move from Parts VII and VIII to Parts IX and X is a move from rural to urban situation, from the villages of Galilee to the city of Jerusalem. Without that move, a move outward to the great pagan cities would be inexplicable. It is on Jerusalem, therefore, that these final parts will concentrate.

PART IX
Meal and Community

We have [in the ancient Mediterranean] a society marked by two features. The first has been exhaustively studied and evoked with tones of understandable disapproval: there is a direct and unveiled link between wealth and the power to draw to oneself, with varying degrees of unabashed brutality, a share of the limited goods of others. In the eastern Mediterranean, the fight for the control of what little agrarian surplus there was was usually at its most remorseless within range of the great towns. The victims were almost inevitably the peasantry; and the result was a chronic condition of shortage and malnutrition, always ready to tip over into famine and epidemics. If abundance existed, it could only be found among the rich and their clients in the towns. The second aspect is less well-known: the pervasive linking of status and diet. Power was the power to eat. The divisions of society coincided transparently with gradations of access to foodstuffs: more food, more varied and better-prepared at the top; less food and less varied towards the bottom. . . . This is an age where thought about eating was, inevitably, a form of second thought about society and its blatant divisions. How to break the iron grip of shortage? Inevitably, the best and most stunning miracles refer, not to the millennial hope of restoring the lost generosity of the earth, but to the far more difficult feat of persuading the harder hearts of men to open up. . . . In this process of persuasion, apocalyptic topics played a discreet role in molding the expectations and sensibilities of contemporaries. . . .

It may be that one of the deepest changes of mentality associated with the rise of Christianity in the Mediterranean world is the rise to prominence of one single meal (the Eucharist), which, though heavy with associations of interpersonal bonding in a single *human* society, was carefully shorn, from an early time, of any overtones of organic, non-human abundance. Previously, a widespread frame of mind had tended to take for granted the solidarity of any settled community around the rare commodities of food and relaxation, and had intended, through moments of high and leisurely eating, to shame the dull world of Nature out of its accustomed stinginess. Everything that we know about the festivals of the Christian Church in Late Antiquity shows the resilience of the old mentality. . . . Only a shrill elite of clerics opposed the Mediterranean urge for the banquet. . . . Indeed, in the straitened world of the Mediterranean, the kingdom of Heaven had to have something to do with food and drink.

Peter Brown, "Response," pp. 18–20, 22–23

Throughout Parts IX and X I am in debate with recent articles by Helmut Koester. Our disagreements here are not so much about what we have discovered

as about the meaning of it. The heart of this disagreement is my refusal to privilege one of those two very early traditions, the Life Tradition and the Death Tradition, over the other or, indeed, even to separate them too absolutely apart. It is
very tempting to do so, but future research demands that we refuse that temptation. Furthermore, if their separations and connections cause us unease or refuse
intransigently to come together in unity, we had better not solve that dilemma too
easily or too soon.

Part IX has two chapters. Both of those chapters—Chapter 23 on ritual meal
and Chapter 24 on community life—focus on the earliest Jerusalem community.
In Chapter 23 I look at the ritual meal in two separate traditions, as Eucharist and
as Lord's Supper. The former derives from the *Q Gospel* tradition, as seen in
Didache 9–10. The latter derives from Jerusalem tradition, as seen in Paul's first
letter to the Corinthians. Similarities between those twin traditions point to a
basic but developing meal tradition, one that I term the Common Meal Tradition. There is a parallel here with the Common Sayings Tradition, but there are
also two major differences, despite the similarity in title. First, the Common
Meal Tradition is basic to both the Life Tradition (focused on the sayings and life
of Jesus) and the Death Tradition (centered on the passion and resurrection of
Jesus). It has, therefore, a far more profound presence than that of the Common
Sayings Tradition, which is basic primarily to the *Q Gospel* and the *Gospel of
Thomas*. Furthermore, those gospel redactions change the Common Sayings Tradition in diametrically opposed directions: the *Q Gospel* is apocalyptic, while the
Gospel of Thomas is anti-apocalyptic. The Common Meal Tradition as seen, on
the one hand in *Didache* 9–10 and on the other in 1 Corinthians 10–11, does not
receive such antithetical development. It is more, indeed, like a single process,
from *Didache* 10 (food and drink) to *Didache* 9 (cup and bread) to 1 Corinthians 10
(cup/bread) to 1 Corinthians 11 (bread/body and cup/blood). It would be hard,
however, to imagine the opposite direction taking place—that is, 1 Corinthians
10–11 developing through *Didache* 9 into *Didache* 10. In using the term Common
Meal Tradition in what follows, I intend both to parallel it and to differentiate it
from my earlier term, the Common Sayings Tradition.

What is of prime importance for me in the Common Meal Tradition is the
full and *normal* meal that, as *communal share-meal,* symbolized the presence of a
sharing God in both the life and death of Jesus. I use that term *share-meal* in distinction from regular *family-meals* or rotating *host-meals.* I will, as we proceed,
distinguish three types: patronal, communal, and societal share-meals. My primary focus will be on *communal share-meals* as the earliest location of the Christian meal tradition. All of that content of Chapter 23 will be presumed when I
turn to community life in Chapter 24. A meal ritualizes a certain type of community. I do not imply, as one more dreary attempt at denominational triumphal-

ism, that Christian Jewish community in Jerusalem was uniquely unique. I compare, therefore, Essene Jews and Christian Jews, not to claim any direct genetic connection but to consider forms of radical commonality and communal resistance to imperial commercialization in first-century Jewish communities.

I append an autobiographical footnote to the epigraph above. I have never been unwillingly hungry in all my life. I was five when the Second World War broke out in Europe, but politically neutral and minimally rationed Ireland had enough food so that hunger was not a wartime reality. At boarding school, between 1945 and 1950, food was never a problem in quantity, though it certainly was in monotony. I can still smell Friday's fish and the inevitable tapioca pudding that we called frogspawn and seldom ate. After an Irish boarding school, an American monastery was no problem at all. I said "unwillingly hungry" in my opening sentence. As a monk I fasted on Fridays, in Advent, and in Lent. That was done willingly, and, in any case, temporary hunger from what is there is never the same as permanent hunger from what is not there. In my life's experience, therefore, food has always been available if I wanted it, when I wanted it, and in as great a quantity as I wanted. If I think at all about food, it is more in terms of diet and fitness than in terms of hunger and want.

As I wrote that paragraph, I decided on an experiment. In an earlier chapter I mentioned *Angela's Ashes,* Frank McCourt's memoir of his Irish childhood, a book that relocates Yeats's line "a terrible beauty is born" from the national to the individual level. McCourt, who grew up in destitution, writes about difficult circumstances in language that soars the spirit and sears the conscience. I opened the book at random seven times in a row, and somewhere on those facing pages there was always something about food. I stopped after seven checks, but you can try it for yourself to see how well it works. If I had written a childhood memoir, food would not have been a theme of such recurring inevitability. If it were there at all, it would probably be about getting too much special stuff this or that time rather than about not getting enough basic stuff all the time. But then I did not grow up hungry.

Meal as actuality or meal as metaphor cannot resonate the same for two such disparate life experiences. The *eucharist-as-meal* or *heaven-as-banquet* falls a little flat for those who have always been well fed. What does *messianic banquet* mean for us, not as *messianic* but as *banquet?* If you surveyed North American images of heaven, how many would emphasize food and drink—enough or more than enough of it—as a primary metaphor? If I think about a meal, I do not think, Good, there will be enough for me to eat. If I think about a banquet, I do not think, Good, there will be *more* than enough for me to eat. In the latter case—banquet rather than meal—I probably think not of food but of dress. Is a business suit acceptable, or is a tuxedo required? Is it ordinary tie or black tie?

In Chapters 23 and 24, therefore, those of us who have always been well nourished must walk carefully. We must, first of all, take that epigraph very seriously. We must, second, keep together flesh and spirit, body and soul, religion and politics, theology and economics. God's Law always embraces those dichotomies together; for example, food is about justice and justice is about God. The kingdom of God is about food and drink—that is, about divine justice for material bodies here on material earth. We do not live by bread alone. But bread is never alone.

CHAPTER 23

THE COMMON MEAL TRADITION

Paul's calling must be dated in the year 35 C.E., perhaps even two or three years earlier. There are compelling reasons to give a very early date to the Christianity that Paul knew, when he was called as a missionary, and whose traditions and rites he accepted and faithfully continued. These traditions are the primary evidence for the earliest churches, while many features derived from the canonical gospels that one is accustomed to ascribe to the early Palestinian Christianity probably had not even come into existence at the time of Paul's call. . . . As far as the churches of Judea and Jerusalem are concerned, the traditions preserved in the Pauline Corpus are probably a better witness for their praxis than any sayings and narratives preserved in the Synoptic tradition.

Helmut Koester, "Jesus' Presence in the Early Church," pp. 547–548, 550

Koester did not explain his choice of the word *presence* in that article's title, but I take it as a deliberately wider and more inclusive term than, say, *resurrection*. The reason for my interpretation is found in the headings of the article's first two sections. The first section is called "The Tradition of Jesus' Sayings," which refers to the fact that within the *Q Gospel*, for example, "the presence of Jesus was tangible in the words he had spoken" (1994a:541, 543). But in discussing the *Q Gospel* or the *Gospel of Thomas,* Koester could not have replaced *presence* with *resurrection* in that sentence, since *resurrection* is not basic to those texts' understanding of Jesus. The second section is entitled "Jesus' Presence in the Churches of Jerusalem and Antioch. The Pauline Evidence" (1994a:541, 546). In that case, to the contrary, *presence* could be replaced with *resurrection.*

That second heading could be taken to mean: first, the churches of Jerusalem and Antioch; next, the churches of Paul. Koester, however, uses it to mean: the Pauline evidence for the churches of Jerusalem and Antioch. That represents a crucially important principle for me. I have not extended this book into Pauline theology or the Pauline churches, as I have noted, but I do include the Jerusalem community within its focus on the companions of Jesus and the birth of Christianity. I accept the use of what Koester calls "the Pauline evidence"— that is, *the evidence of received tradition that Paul proclaims*—as a window onto the earliest Jerusalem community. When, for example, Paul speaks against Corinthian meal practice, I read him not for Corinthian meal practice but for

Jerusalem meal practice; not for the present Corinth customs he criticizes but for the past Jerusalem customs that he opposes to them.

A Typology of Share-Meals

The purely symbolic meal of modern Christianity, restricted to a bite of bread and a sip of wine or juice, is tacitly presupposed for the early church, an assumption so preposterous that it is never articulated or acknowledged.

Robert Jewett, "Tenement Churches and Pauline Love Feasts," p. 44

That epigraph adds another dimension to our distance from the Common Meal Tradition, be it in Jerusalem, Antioch, or anywhere else. It is another facet rendering understanding almost impossible. It is not just that some Christians get too *much* normal food; it is that all Christians get too *little* eucharistic food. The Christian Eucharist is today a morsel and a sip. It is not a real meal. You may reply, of course, that such is sufficient to symbolize the presence of Jesus and God in the community of faith. But why symbolize divinity through a medium of food that is non-food? Maybe non-food symbolizes a non-Jesus and a non-God? Notice, therefore, the ambiguity in Jewett's phrase "symbolic meal." Of *course* the Eucharist is a symbolic meal. But does that mean it should be *a morsel and a sip symbolic of a real meal* or *a real meal symbolic of God's presence*? And what makes *that* real meal so symbolic? What makes *that* real meal any different from a real meal in any grateful Christian home? That question is at the heart of this Chapter 23, and its answer connects to Chapter 24's discussion of both Essene and Christian communities.

My proposal is that those meals were *real meals as share-meals*. The community *shared* together whatever food it had available, which both symbolized and ritualized but also actualized and materialized the equal justice of the Jewish God. I am, as that epigraph indicates, especially indebted to recent work by Robert Jewett for the distinction to be explored below between the Common Meal Tradition as either *patronal* or *communal* share-meal. And, just to give a third example, I also look at a *societal* share-meal in Greco-Roman paganism. That triad establishes a typology within which the Common Meal Tradition can be located.

PATRONAL SHARE-MEALS

In one of the very few places where Paul cites a saying of Jesus, he disobeys it and then defends his decision to do so. He is, in context, absolutely correct in that decision. But we have, as usual, to read Paul's response and imagine what it is he is responding to. Writing from Ephesus to the community at Corinth between late 52 and early 55, he says, in 1 Corinthians 9:3, that "this is my defense to those who would examine me." Their accusation is that he is working to support himself rather than depending entirely upon their generosity. And that, as they probably said to him, is despite the fact that, according to 1 Corinthians 9:14, "the Lord commanded that those who proclaim the gospel should get their living by the gospel." That is, of course, exactly the situation we saw from the historical Jesus and the itinerant prophets of the *Q Gospel* and the *Didache*. Paul has been accused of not following that model and maybe even of not having enough trust to let himself be so dependent.

Gerd Theissen wrote a very insightful commentary on that situation over twenty years ago (1982:27–67). He notes, first, that we are dealing with *dependency-as-command* from the Lord in 1 Corinthians 9:14. But before Paul cites dependency there, he mounts up multiple examples of *dependency-as-privilege* in 1 Corinthians 9:5–13. He uses particular Christian examples from the other apostles, the brothers of the Lord, and Cephas. He uses general human examples from the army, the vineyard, and the flock. He uses specific legal examples from the ox, the temple, and the altar. Since, therefore, command has been reinterpreted as privilege and duty as right, Paul can decline that privilege and right as follows:

> We have not made use of this right, but we endure anything rather than put an obstacle in the way of the gospel of Christ. . . . I have made no use of any of these rights . . . that in my proclamation I may make the gospel free of charge, so as not to make full use of my rights in the gospel. (1 Corinthians 9:12b, 15, 18)

That is rhetorically very clever, but what justifies it ethically? Theissen argues that there were "two types of primitive Christian itinerant preachers, to be distinguished as itinerant charismatics on the one hand and community organizers on the other. The most important difference between them is that each adopts a distinctive attitude to the question of subsistence. The first type arose in the social circumstances of the Palestinian region. The second, represented by Paul and Barnabas, arose in the movement of the mission into Hellenistic territory. Both types work side by side but come into conflict at Corinth" (1982:28).

I do not underestimate the differences between the tiny hamlets of the eastern Mediterranean and the great cities around the Aegean Sea, but there are two major problems with that analysis. First, both types of preachers appear together at Corinth, so it may not be useful to distinguish them as Theissen does. It is precisely the presence and acceptance of the "Palestinian" type in "Hellenistic" territory that puts Paul on the defensive in his own community. Second, Paul himself is quite ready to accept subsidies for his mission—for example, from the Philippians in northern Greece.

I rejoice in the Lord greatly that now at last you have revived your concern for me; indeed, you were concerned for me, but had no opportunity to show it. Not that I am referring to being in need; for I have learned to be content with whatever I have. . . . You Philippians indeed know that in the early days of the gospel, when I left Macedonia, no church shared with me in the matter of giving and receiving, except you alone. For even when I was in Thessalonica, you sent me help for my needs more than once. (Philippians 4:10–11, 15–16)

That first instance of Philippian support was around the year 50; the second was around 55. Paul mentions that support to the Corinthians in a letter written around the same time as that to the Philippians:

I robbed other churches by accepting support from them in order to serve you. And when I was with you and was in need, I did not burden anyone, for my needs were supplied by the friends who came from Macedonia. So I refrained and will continue to refrain from burdening you in any way. (2 Corinthians 11:8–9)

We have, therefore, to presume that Paul refused support because of some specific problem *at Corinth* rather than because of general principles separating community organizers from itinerant charismatics. What was that problem? Theissen, in fact, points to an alternative solution:

Consider your own call, brothers and sisters *[adelphoi]*: not many of you were wise by human standards, not many were powerful, not many were of noble birth. (1 Corinthians 1:26)

But to say "not many" is to say "some." There were, in other words, *some* relatively or comparatively well-to-do members in the Corinthian community. Paul also mentions, in 1:14–16, that he himself baptized only Crispus, Gaius, and the household of Stephanas at Corinth. But in Acts 18:8–9 Crispus is "the official of the synagogue," in Romans 16:23 Gaius is "host to me and to the whole church," and in 1 Corinthians 16:15–17 the household of Stephanas "devoted themselves to the service of the saints" and Stephanas himself visited Paul at Ephesus. "It thus appears," as Theissen notes, "that Paul confined his baptizing to a few influential and important members of the community" (1982:55). On the other hand, "Chloe's people" in 1 Corinthians 1:11 "are likely to have been slaves, since members of a family would have used their father's name, even if he were deceased" (1982:57). A major problem at Corinth, therefore, was the "struggle for position within the congregation, carried on primarily by those of high social status" (1982:56). What faced Paul at Corinth was something probably new—namely, competing patronal possibilities, *not many* but therefore *some* well-to-do members vying with one another for positions of authority based on patronage. Paul refused to submit himself to such patronage and was attacked in turn for his refusal. He was, they said, disobeying the command of the Lord.

If that analysis is correct, there had to be a concomitant problem at Corinth's eucharistic meals. Paul brings up this subject with a flat accusation: "When you come together, it is not really to eat the Lord's supper." He develops this over four steps in 1 Corinthians 11.

1. *Criticism* (11:17–22): "For when the time comes to eat, each of you goes ahead with your own supper, and one goes hungry and another becomes drunk. What! Do you not have homes to eat and drink in?"
2. *Tradition* (11:23–26): Institution of the Lord's Supper "on the night he was handed over."
3. *Commentary* (11:27–32): Unworthy participation in the Lord's Supper is why "many of you are weak and ill, and some have died."
4. *Criticism* (11:33–34a): "When you come together to eat, wait for one another. If you are hungry, eat at home, so that when you come together, it will not be for your condemnation."

Those double frames with their very specific *criticism* of "not waiting" make it possible to see rather clearly what was the problem. We are talking about a *patronal share-meal* in which one of the wealthier members hosts the entire community. This is the typical situation of the *house church*. On the one hand, Paul clearly presumes that there are those who have food to eat at home and need not come to the Lord's Supper for sustenance. They are the *haves*. On the other hand, those *haves* "show contempt for the church of God and humiliate those who have nothing." Those latter are the *have-nots*. The Lord's Supper is supposed to be a *patronal share-meal* in which *haves* and *have-nots* can eat food together in common, but, of course, all or most of the food and drink must come from the *haves*. What happens, however, is that the nonworking *haves* can arrive before the working *have-nots* and eat together whatever they bring or their host prepares for them. When the *have-nots* arrive, there is nothing left for them, hence "one goes hungry [the *have-nots*] and another becomes drunk [the *haves*]," as Paul put it. I return below to consider the logic of Paul's reply in the sections named *tradition* and *commentary* within those frames of *criticism*.

COMMUNAL SHARE-MEALS

James Packer's fascinating studies of Ostia, Rome's port at the Tiber's mouth, can serve as an introduction to this section (1967; 1971). Ostia's population "probably did not exceed 27,000" at the time of Paul. Its upper-end aristocracy was about five hundred people housed in only "22 mansions scattered throughout the site," and its lower-end aristocracy was about two thousand people housed in apartment buildings looking into a central garden. Everyone else—the other 90 percent—lived in upper-level tenements, with either shops or factories on the ground floor. Shops averaged 1.7 rooms and were actually themselves shop-apartments (1971:70). Those tenements or *insulae* (literally: islands) were usually four or five stories high, and "the higher one went in a Roman building, the worse conditions became" (70 note 30). The reason was that the higher the floor, the greater the subdivision for its renters.

We should not think of individual apartments as dwelling places in our sense of the word. People did not eat or live in them; they did not cook or defecate in them; they simply slept and stored in them. "The majority of Ostian flats were not homes in the modern sense of the world. They were not equipped to take care of all the physical needs of their inhabitants, and, save for [garden apartments], they were probably not used to entertain friends. They would have served merely for household life and for the storage of family property. The pattern of Ostian streets suggests that the real life of the community was lived outside individual dwellings. Shops bordered almost every street, and the apparent lack of kitchens in most Ostian houses may indicate that many shops supplied the inhabitants of the surrounding buildings with partially or completely prepared food and drink" (1971:73). Shop-apartments, in other words, were a major public-private location. Furthermore, lest we think of Ostia's apartments as inhumanly crowded, we must remember that "in ancient Ostia almost all the requirements of the vast majority of citizens were taken care of outside the home. Thus, in some sense, the whole city constituted a single, complex habitation of which the individual residence was perhaps the least important part. Ancient Ostia represents communal living on a massive scale, which by its very intensity and public nature is entirely foreign to the modern Western conception of privacy" (1971:74). Ostia is fairly indicative of normal Roman city life, with *some* shining marble and *much* stinking slum. But in what follows, remember those shop-apartments on the ground floor of *insulae*.

Robert Jewett has recently suggested another form of the Lord's Supper: communal share-meals in tenement churches. I think that this is a powerfully persuasive proposal. We should now take those two models—patronal share-meals in house churches and communal share-meals in tenement churches—as ends of a spectrum that has all sorts of combinations and permutations in between. "It is likely that the majority of early Christian converts lived in the *insulae* of the inner cities rather than in private villas. . . . 90% of the free population and an even higher percentage of the slave population in the cities of the empire lived in apartment blocks called *insulae*. The upper floors of the four- and five-story apartment blocks typically contained cubicles of about 10 square meters, representing the space for one family. . . . [There was] a population density of 300 per acre for the residential areas of the city of Rome, almost 2.5 times higher than twentieth century Calcutta and 3 times higher than Manhattan" (1993:26). Jewett's proposal is that Christian cells met together within those *insulae* with mutual rather than patronal support. Each brought what he or she could to the common meal, and thus all were assured, no matter what happened, of at least one Eucharist—one thanksworthy meal, say—per week.

Jewett points to a section in Paul's second epistle to the Thessalonians as the primary direct evidence for that proposal. That letter is probably not an authentic letter of Paul's, but, in that case, its later situation makes the verse even more striking.

Now we command you, beloved, in the name of our Lord Jesus Christ, to keep away from believers who are *living in idleness* and not according to the tradition that they received from us. For you yourselves know how you ought to imitate us; we were not idle when we were with you, and we did not eat anyone's bread without paying for it; but with toil and labor we worked night and day, so that we might not burden any of you. This was not because we do not have that right, but in order to give you an example to imitate. For even when we were with you, we gave you this command: *Anyone unwilling to work should not eat.* For we hear that some of you are *living in idleness,* mere busybodies, not doing any work. Now such persons we command and exhort in the Lord Jesus Christ to do their work quietly and to earn their own living. (2 Thessalonians 3:6–12)

I have italicized the frames about "living in idleness" in 3:6 and 3:11. But what is wrong with living in idleness if you can afford to do so? The answer is evident in that other phrase I italicized between those frames: *Anyone unwilling to work should not eat.* Jewett emphasizes that, in terms of form, the statement is a sentence of casuistic law and that, in terms of content, *"the creation of the regulation required a community that was eating its meals together, for whom the willingness or unwillingness to work was a factor of sufficient importance to require regulation, and in which the power to deprive members of food was in fact present. . . . A kind of Christian* commune or cooperative is required, in which meals were being shared on a regular basis, and for which the refusal to work posed a significant threat" (1993:38, italicized phrase was underlined in original). Notice, of course, that the problem is the "unwillingness" to work and not the inability to find work or the incapacity to do work. If food was supplied patronally, it would be irrelevant whether clients worked or not. But if food was supplied mutually, anyone unwilling to work (and thereby unable to contribute something to share) was, as the *Didache* said, a Christ-hustler. Theissen suggests the term "love-patriarchalism" for *patronal* share-meals in house or villa settings (1982:37). Jewett proposes the term "love-communalism" for those *communal* share-meals in tenement or apartment settings (1993:33). But since the term "love" tends to be trivialized by overuse, I emphasize that the word had a very precise and specific material meaning for Paul: it meant *share* with one another. And the ability so to share was evidence that they were, in the word Paul coined for 1 Thessalonians 4:9, "God-taught" people. God is a god who shares. Furthermore, when Paul describes Christians with the Greek root *adelf-*, we should translate not just as *sisters and brothers* but as *sharers*. That is what the term *meant* for him and them.

SOCIETAL SHARE-MEALS

I append this third type—societal share-meals—as an example of how things could have been done but were not done in Essene or Christian Jewish share-meals. The societal share-meal is exemplified by the meal protocol of an ancient burial society. Even more horrible than the experience of isolation and loneliness in ancient (and any?) life was the possibility of abandonment and nonburial in death. *If* you had a family and *if* they could afford it and *if* they survived you, they would, no doubt, perform the proper pieties and obsequies at your death. But how long could such care and memory last? Because the answer, all too often, was "not long enough," there stood, between close family and distant society, the funerary association, with titular deity, wealthy patronage, and members, eating and drinking together when alive and guaranteeing one another's proper burial, adequate mourning, and continued remembrance when dead.

The bylaws of one such funerary society were discovered in 1816 at Lanuvium, modern Lanuvio, outside Rome on the southwestern reaches of the Alban Hills. The Latin text is in Dessau (3.737–739, #7212), with an English translation in Lewis and Reinhold (2.273–275). The details are precise and fascinating.

The group was founded on January 1 of 133 C.E. under the patronage of a local magistrate named Lucius Caesennius Rufus. It was dedicated to the goddess Diana and to the deified Antinoüs, the emperor Hadrian's catamite, drowned in the Nile three years before. That gave them divine, divinized, and human patronage. On May 28 of 136 C.E. the group was endowed by its magistrate-patron with fifteen thousand sesterces, which was to supply interest of four hundred sesterces payable twice a year, once on August 13, birthday of Diana, and again on November 27, birthday of Antinoüs. (For that and what follows, calculate monetary values at one denarius = four sesterces = sixteen asses [coins, not donkeys]; and think of seventy sesterces as a month's subsistence allowance for an adult male.) At that same time, the group's bylaws were inscribed forever on the inner portico of the local temple dedicated to Antinoüs.

Such groups were officially licensed by the Roman senate, and that decree was recorded at the start of that temple inscription:

These are permitted to assemble, convene, and maintain a society; those who desire to make monthly contributions for funerals may assemble in such a society, but they may not assemble in the name of such a society except once a month for the sake of making contributions to provide burial for the dead.

The Lanuvium Benevolent Society met once a month for a business session, and members were enjoined to bring up "any complaint" at those meetings so that "we may banquet in peace and good cheer on festive days." Those days were six in all: the birthdays of Diana, Antinoüs, Lucius Caesennius Rufus, and Rufus's brother, mother, and father. Fines were set at four sesterces for a "disturbance," twelve sesterces for "speaking abusively or causing an uproar," and twenty sesterces for "using abusive or insolent language to a *quinquennalis* at a banquet." (The *quinquennalis* was the chief officer with a five-year term.)

The bylaws begin with "It was voted unanimously" and continue through twelve more "It was voted further . . ." rules. They are almost evenly divided between prescriptions for burials and prescriptions for meals. This is the opening set:

It was voted unanimously that whoever desires to enter this society shall pay an initiation fee of 100 sesterces and an amphora of good wine, and shall pay monthly dues of 5 *asses*. It was voted further that if anyone has not paid his dues for six consecutive months and the common lot of mankind befalls him, his claim to burial shall not be considered, even if he has provided for it [the arrears] in his will. It was voted further that upon the decease of a paid-up member of our body there will be due him from the treasury 300 sesterces, from which sum will be deducted a funeral fee of 50 sesterces to be distributed at the pyre [among those attending]; the obsequies, furthermore, will be performed on foot.

Only those in arrears and suicides were precluded from that guaranteed funeral service. One of the most interesting aspects of this society is that it included slaves, freed slaves, and freeborn members. Here are two specific rules for the enslaved and the freed:

It was voted further that if a slave member of this society dies, and his master or mistress unreasonably refuses to relinquish his body for burial, and he has not left written instructions, a token funeral ceremony will be held. . . .

It was voted further that if any slave member of this society becomes free, he is required to donate an amphora of good wine.

So much for funeral rites. What about those festive meals? Members had to take turns supplying a meal for the society:

Masters of the dinners in the order of the membership list, appointed four at a time in turn, shall be required to provide an amphora of good wine each, and for as many members as the society has a bread costing 2 *asses*, sardines to the number of four, a setting, and warm water with service. . . .

It was voted further that if any master, in the year when it is his turn in the membership list to provide dinner, fails to comply and provide a dinner, he shall pay 30 sesterces into the treasury; the man following him on the list shall be required to give the dinner, and he [the delinquent] shall be required to reciprocate when it is the latter's turn.

Privilege within the society came from service rather than status. The *quinquennalis* did not have to be master of the dinner and received a double share of it during the five-year term. The current "secretary and the messenger" were likewise exempt and got a share and a half, as did past *quinquennales*. That, however, was sanction as well as honor. The privilege presumed that those officials had "administered the office . . . honestly" and was given in the expectation that others would "also hope for the same by properly discharging their duties." The current *quinquennalis*, on the other hand, had "on the festive days of his term in office . . . to conduct worship with incense and wine . . . clothed in white, and . . . on the birthdays of Diana and Antinoüs he is to provide oil for the society in the public bath before they banquet."

The Lanuvium Benevolent Society's dinner was not a *patronal* meal—as if, for example, Lucius Caesennius Rufus had invited the membership to villa or temple for a free feast. Neither was it a *communal* meal in which everyone shared equally whatever they had. It was a *societal* meal in which paid dues guaranteed certain collegial rights and duties, and its fairness was protected by decency and humanity carved in stone. And it included, without any particular fuss, the enslaved, the freed, and the freeborn together in one group. The question, however, is this: Did communal meals implicitly or explicitly criticize society in a way that patronal or societal meals did not? Was it precisely the *communal sharing* of Essene or Christian meals that made ordinary food and drink sacred, that made an ordinary meal into the presence of the Jewish God?

The Communal Share-Meal

There is good evidence that Jesus celebrated common meals with his disciples and friends. . . . Jesus' common meals resulted in two different cultic meal traditions which were developed independently of each other: (1) the tradition of the *Didache,* in which the eucharistic prayers express the eschatological consciousness of the congregation; (2) the tradition that is preserved in 1 Corinthians 10 and 11 and in Mark 14, in which the religious significance of the meal is expressed in the words of institution. In both traditions, the eschatological orientation is evident. It must be assumed that this eschatological component derives directly from Jesus himself.

Helmut Koester, "The Historical Jesus and the Cult of the *Kyrios Christos,*" p.15

I am once more in debate with Helmut Koester. Recall, first of all, the epigraph to this chapter, which expressed his principle that "as far as the churches of Judea and Jerusalem are concerned, the traditions preserved in the Pauline Corpus are probably a better witness for their praxis than any sayings and narratives preserved in the Synoptic tradition" (1994a:550). That is why in looking at Paul's *received* tradition I am still primarily concerned with the Jerusalem community and not with Pauline communities. Next, connect that epigraph with the one just above, which states that there are two separate meal traditions, one in *Didache* 9–10 and another in 1 Corinthians 10–11. You would conclude at that point, putting both epigraphs together, that Paul received his own meal tradition in 1 Corinthians 10–11 from Jerusalem. But then there is this following statement: "It is quite possible that the Jerusalem celebration of the common meal had more the character of a messianic banquet and was primarily oriented toward the expectation of the coming of Jesus as the Messiah. The meal prayers and liturgy of a Jewish-Christian church, which are preserved in Didache 9–10, may mirror the practice of the Jerusalem church. . . . The messianic banquet of Jerusalem (and of the Didache) may not have included the words of institution, as they are known from Paul and from the Synoptic Gospels" (1994a:550–551). That connects *Didache* 10–11 with the Jerusalem tradition and 1 Corinthians 10–11 with an Antioch tradition, thus providing "evidence for the close relationship of the eucharist celebration of Jerusalem and Antioch" (1994a:551). But would it not be more likely, on Koester's own principles, that *Didache* 9–10 is the eucharistic meal of the rural sayings tradition and 1 Corinthians 10–11 is the eucharistic meal of the urban passion-resurrection tradition? That is, actually, what he himself suggested in a more recent essay: "The community of Q did not directly contemplate the significance of the death of Jesus, and certainly not in terms of expiation for sins. Bread, however, and the feeding of all who are hungry . . . are undeniably emphasized in Q. The eucharistic prayers of the *Didache,* which also do not imply an interpretation of Jesus' death, could well be assigned to the heirs of the community of Q" (1996:349). That, in any case, is the position I intend to follow. The Common Meal Tradition appears in twin but separate developments as *Didache* 9–10 (from the *Q Gospel* tradition) and as 1 Corinthians 10–11 (from the Jerusalem tradition).

Those two separate eucharistic traditions are as old as we can trace the evidence. The core difference between them is this. One tradition, that in Paul and Mark, involves a ritual meal institutionalized by Jesus himself and connected with his own execution. The bread and wine are separated from one another to symbolize the separation of Jesus' own body and blood by execution. The other tradition, that in *Didache* 9–10, has none of those connections, and its prayers are extremely similar to standard Jewish prayers. Furthermore, both traditions show stages of development even within themselves. Paul and Mark agree that it was a Last Supper, but Paul, unlike Mark, commands repetition for remembrance, and Mark, unlike Paul, explicitly describes it as the Passover meal. The earlier *Didache* 10:3 speaks only about "food and drink" together, but the later *Didache* 9:2–3 separates, in this sequence, "the cup" and "the bread." The full sequential stages of those traditions have been worked out by Willi Marxsen (1970; 1992) and John Riggs (1984; 1995). I presume the basic validity of their research, but it is not my present concern.

Neither is my present concern to compare those two traditions and assert one over the other, as if, somehow, the *Didache* were preferable to Paul or vice versa. I consider them, historically and theologically, to be equally valid ritualizations of the historical Jesus' meal tradition. Indeed, there seems an inevitable move from *Didache* to Pauline tradition. If you *actively* insist that open commensality is the kingdom of God, that food and drink, the material bases of human life, must be equally available to all by God's command, you should be ready for some form of social elimination. Because open commensality and official execution are concomitants, the Lord's Supper is both about God's justice and the price for attempting that justice here below. All of that is presumed as valid, but my present concern is with the Common Meal Tradition itself. Its careful consideration will indicate that those twin developments in *Didache* 9–10 and 1 Corinthians 10–11 are actually quite close to one another.

I now look at five elements of the Common Meal Tradition: actual meal, shared meal, biblical Jesus, symbolic unity, and apocalyptic sanction. These elements are common to *Didache* 9–10 and 1 Corinthians 10–11; indeed, they predate both those versions, indicating the earliest ritualization of the historical Jesus' own meal tradition after his death. I am especially interested in the Common Meal Tradition as involving a *communal share-meal*. But that focus raises a couple of questions. First, was the Eucharist originally a full supper or a token meal;

and, if full, when did it change to token and what was lost in that change? Is there a difference between a real meal ritualized as symbolic of divine realities and an unreal meal, morsel and sip, symbolic of a real meal symbolic of divine realities? Second, whether full or token, was it symbolic of communal sharing as divine command? Is that what makes the meal holy and sacred? Is that what makes it a Eucharist—that we are thankful for a God whose justice demands a shared earth? Is that what makes it the Lord's Supper and not just *our* supper?

With those questions in mind, I turn now to the five elements.

ACTUAL MEAL

The first element in the Common Meal Tradition undergoes a similar change in both the *Didache* and 1 Corinthians, and that change is important because it points to what was originally there beforehand. The change can be seen most clearly in the difference, first, between Pauline tradition and Corinthian practice in that community and, second, between *Didache* 10 and *Didache* 9 in that document.

Corinth.

The first example of this change takes us back to Paul's Corinth and to his criticism of its eucharistic practice seen above. You will recall that Corinthian practice, especially as interpreted by Theissen, had created the sequence of meal and ritual, which allowed the Corinthian Christians to separate the share-meal from the ritual-meal. They probably argued that they were faithful in the later ritual to the bread/body and wine/blood symbolization taught them by Paul and that the prior meal was not part of the Lord's Supper anyway. As nonworkers *(haves)* they could therefore come early and eat a full meal before workers *(have-nots)* arrived late and found only symbolic bread and wine. Corinthian practice was, as early as the 50s, the first clear signs of separation between full meal and ritual action. This is Paul's response. Notice the sequence of italicized words:

> For I received from the Lord what I also handed on to you, that the Lord Jesus on the night when he was betrayed [*literally:* handed over] took a loaf of *bread,* and when he had given thanks, he broke it and said, "This is my *body* that is for you. Do this in remembrance of me." In the same way he took the cup also, *after supper,* saying, "This *cup* is the new covenant in my *blood.* Do this, as often as you drink it, in remembrance of me." (1 Corinthians 11:23–25)

What exactly is the logic of Paul's response in that citation of tradition *already given* to them but now repeated for the present problem? Notice how the ritualization of bread and the parallel ritualization of wine take place before and after the meal. Paul insists that the sequence is not, as in Corinthian practice, meal + ritual of bread/body and cup/blood but, as in the pre-Pauline tradition, ritual of bread/body + meal + ritual of cup/blood. There is, in other words, no way to separate meal from ritual. The Lord's Supper is both fully meal and fully ritual. And, says Paul, Jesus himself instituted that process and commanded that it be done that way "in remembrance of him." You will understand that, even though I do not accept the historicity of such a Last Supper, I accept completely Paul's understanding of the initial ritualization of the meal tradition and his accusation that the Corinthian *haves* betrayed its intention. Paul was absolutely correct to insist that symbolism *and* reality should go together, that the Eucharist should involve a *full* but communal share-meal, and that anything else was not the Lord's Supper but business as usual. A very similar transition within the eucharistic share-meal from symbolic full meal to symbolic token meal can be discerned in the *Didache,* although it is not as crudely evident as at Corinth.

Didache.

The point here is a delicate comparison between the earlier Eucharist depicted in *Didache* 10 and the later one in *Didache* 9. First, though, a preliminary case as introduction. We already caught glimpses of the *Didache's* Eucharist as a communal share-meal in discussions above concerning the prophets and the destitute. Recall this example (Milavec 1989:99, my emphasis):

If [the one coming] wants to settle among you and knows a trade, let him (or her) *work and eat.* If someone does not know a trade, use your own judgment to determine how he (or she) should live with you as a Christian without being idle. (*Didache* 12:3–4)

The context, in *Didache* 12:1–5, is the distinction between a *Christianos* and a *Christemporos,* between a Christ-ian and a Christ-hustler. But the logic I find behind those verses is exactly the same logic Jewett found behind 2 Thessalonians 3:10b. The former says, If you work, you eat. The latter says, If you don't work, you don't eat. *Both stipulations must presume a communal share-meal or they make no sense.* And notice, of course, that the problem for both texts concerns one who is "not willing" to work, with the same Greek verb in 2 Thessalonians 3:10b and *Didache* 12:5. That logic of work-share-eat draws attention to certain differences between the eucharistic prayers in *Didache* 9 and 10.

Those differences are emphasized by the similar fourfold structure and similar dividing refrains in both the earlier *Didache* 10 and the later *Didache* 9. In what follows, watch those similarities and differences within common structures and refrains, because the latter makes the former even more palpable. To assist comparison, I italicize those common words and refrains. Compare, first, the twin introductions (Milavec 1989:97):

Didache 10:1 (earlier version)	*Didache* 9:1 (later version)
And after having been filled [by the eucharistic banquet], *eucharistize thus: . . .*	Concerning the Eucharist, *eucharistize thus: . . .*

The word "filled" in 10:1 is the ordinary, everyday verb for a true meal. The sequence is clearly meal + ritual, but the meal is a real one at which satiety was possible. That crucial phrase is missing from 9:1. Can we presume a full meal before those ritual prayers, and, if so, why that change?

Next, compare these linked and doubled thanksgivings, which I read in the light of those divergent opening phrases, because, of course, "to give thanks" is "to eucharistize" in Greek (Milavec 1989:97):

Didache 10:2–4 (earlier version)	*Didache* 9:2–3 (later version)
(1) *We give you thanks,* holy *Father,* for your *holy* name which you have made to dwell in our hearts. And for the faith and under-standing and immortality *which you have revealed to us through Jesus, your servant. Glory to you forever.* [Amen!]	(1) First concerning the cup: *We give you thanks,* our *Father,* For the *holy* vine of David, your servant, *which you have revealed to us through Jesus, your servant. Glory to you forever.* [Amen!]
(2) You, Almighty Monarch, have created all things for the sake of your name. You have given food and drink to people for their pleasure, so that they might give you thanks. And, to us, you have graciously given spiritual food and drink and eternal life *through Jesus, your servant.* For all [these] things, we give you thanks, because you are powerful [on our behalf]. *Glory to you forever.* [Amen!]	(2) Next, concerning the breaking [of the loaf]: We give you thanks, our Father, For the life and the understanding which you have revealed to us *through Jesus, your servant.* *Glory to you forever.* [Amen!]

Didache 10:2–4 is about physical "food and drink" given by God "to people for their pleasure." But it is also symbolic of spiritual food and drink giving faith, understanding, and immortality to Christians. The basis for that symbolism is still a full share-meal, and, of course, it is "through Jesus" who is identified as the "servant" *(pais)* of God. *Didache* 9:2–3, however, mentions and separates, in this sequence, the cup to be passed and shared, the bread to be broken and shared. Maybe there is still a full meal involved, but if so, it is far less explicit. My suspicion is that just as the eucharistic prayers get shorter as you move from *Didache* 10 to *Didache* 9, so does the eucharistic menu.

I have looked only at the first two parts of those twin fourfold structures in *Didache* 9–10 to make a single point. The Common Meal Tradition involved originally a full meal ritualized precisely as such. The specific bread/wine or body/blood ritualizations were not intended to remove that reality and should not have done so. That did not happen for Paul, but it did happen for the Corinthian *haves*, and it also seems to have happened in the move from *Didache* 10 to *Didache* 9. The point in all of this is not whether ritualizations are done before, during, or after the meal but whether the meal itself is an intrinsic part of the eucharistic symbolism. Bread and wine should summarize, not substitute for, the Eucharist; otherwise, it is no longer the Lord's Supper.

SHARED MEAL

The second element in the Common Meal Tradition is equally important. It is both an actual meal and a shared meal. There is an emphasis not just on bread but on *breaking* the bread, and that is symbolic of sharing by passing it around. The bread is not, as it were, just there on the table. It is broken and passed around. There is also an emphasis not just on the wine but rather on the *cup*. I take that also as symbolic of sharing, since the cup can be passed around. The wine is not just there. It must be taken from a common cup.

In *Didache* 9:2–3, cited just above, what is actually mentioned is a ritual: "First concerning the *cup*," and "Next, concerning the *breaking* [of the loaf]." Strictly speaking, wine and bread are not even mentioned. What is noted is cup(-passing) and (bread-)breaking. There is a similar situation in Paul, but now, of course, there is a conjunction of meal and death. In this first text, the order is cup and bread, as in *Didache* 9:2–3, but in the second one, as seen already, it is bread and cup.

The *cup* of blessing that we bless, is it not a sharing in the blood of Christ? The bread that we *break,* is it not a sharing in the body of Christ? (1 Corinthians 10:16)

The Lord Jesus . . . took a loaf of bread, and when he had given thanks, he *broke* it and said, "This is my body that is for you. Do this in remembrance of me." In the same way he took the *cup* also, after supper, saying, "This *cup* is the new covenant in my blood. Do this, as often as you drink it, in remembrance of me." (1 Corinthians 11:23–25)

I do not presume, of course, that everything at the share-meal operated like that. It is simply a case that passed cup and broken bread ritualized the entire meal as a communal share-meal. But they symbolized a reality whose material manifestations were on the table before them.

BIBLICAL JESUS

The third element in the Common Meal Tradition is deliberately designated by that rather strange title "biblical Jesus." Both developments connect the meal to Jesus himself, but it is to a Jesus embedded in the same specific scriptural background. Both 1 Corinthians 11 and *Didache* 9–10 refer to Jesus in connection with Isaiah 53.

There are two key words involved in that connection. The first one is in Paul's opening to the received and transmitted tradition in 1 Corinthians 11:23 above. It concerns "the Lord Jesus on the night when *paredideto.*" That Greek verb, *paredideto,* should not—emphatically *not*—be translated as "betrayed." It means, literally, "handed over," and, since it is in the passive voice with no agent mentioned, it means "handed over by God." The second key word is in *Didache* 9–10. In both the earlier and later eucharistic prayers of the *Didache,* God is called "the Father" and Jesus is that Father's *"pais"* in *Didache* 9:2 and 10:2, 3. Those are reiterated refrains: "through Jesus, your *pais.*" That Greek noun means both *servant* and *child,* with context usually determining which is being emphasized. The significant point is that both *paredideto* and *pais* point back to the so-called Suffering Servant in Isaiah 53. But first some background.

The book of Isaiah contains three originally independent prophetic collections. The first part, in chapters 1–39, comes from Isaiah of Jerusalem between 740 and 700 B.C.E. The second part, in chapters 40–55, is called Deutero-Isaiah. It comes from an anonymous prophet toward the end of the Babylonian Exile between 550 and 540 B.C.E. The final part, in chapters 56–66, called Trito-Isaiah, is by another anonymous prophet at the beginning of the Persian Restoration between 540 and 500 B.C.E. It is with Deutero-Isaiah that I am presently concerned.

When the Babylonian Empire destroyed Jerusalem and its Temple in 587 B.C.E., the Jewish aristocracy was taken into exile around Babylon, and to judge from the stories in Daniel 1–6, some of them became Babylonian bureaucrats while remaining loyal Jews. Deutero-Isaiah is located in those dangerous final years of the Babylonian Empire's death throes. It asserts that the Jewish exiles should not support the Babylonians but should conspire with the Persians against them. Four poems, called the Songs of the Suffering Servant, appear in

Isaiah 42:1–6; 49:1–6; 50:4–9; and 52:23–53:12. The Servant is Israel *and* the prophet, insofar as *both* are persecuted by Babylonian power, betrayed by Jewish collaboration, and then liberated through Persian intervention. This is Norman Gottwald's summary of that situation: "A strong odor of political conflict surrounds the acclamation of Cyrus [Isaiah 44:28; 45:1, 13] and the hostile treatment of the servant. Given the individual thanksgiving form of chap. 53, there is good reason to hypothesize that the actual imprisonment, persecution, and deliverance of a historical contemporary, most likely the prophet himself, has been employed as a microcosm of the macrocosm of Israel's fate insofar as the people's suffering has exceeded its deserved punishment. And that some of this suffering was inflicted on Jews by fellow Jews is not at all surprising in context. . . . That some Jews were profiting from supporting Babylonian hegemony while other Jews were active in a pro-Persian underground preparing for Cyrus's seizure of Babylon would be one more instance of the structurally embedded conflicts of interest in which prophets and other leaders had been involved from the very origins of prophecy" (1985:500). All of that is quite likely except for one point. The Servant-as-author may not have escaped death except insofar as his hopes were realized in the Servant-as-Israel. But, in any case, Christians much, much later, whether they knew that historical background or not, could easily see close parallels between the fate of the Servant and of Jesus.

The first of those parallels is the use of the word *pais* ("servant") in the Greek Septuagint translation of the following Hebrew texts, with God as speaker in all three cases:

> Here is my *servant,* whom I uphold, my chosen, in whom my soul delights; I have put my spirit upon him; he will bring forth justice to the nations. . . . He says, "It is too light a thing that you should be my *servant* to raise up the tribes of Jacob and to restore the survivors of Israel; I will give you as a light to the nations, that my salvation may reach to the end of the earth." . . . See, my *servant* shall prosper; he shall be exalted and lifted up, and shall be very high. (Isaiah 42:1; 49:6; 52:13)

Similar allusions to the Suffering Servant lie behind Jesus as God's servant *(pais)* in Acts 3:13 and 16 and 4:27 and 30, where the context is his death and resurrection.

The second parallel is the use of the same verb as in *paredideto* ("handed over") in the Greek Septuagint translation of the following Hebrew texts, with God as agent in both cases:

> All we like sheep have gone astray; we have all turned to our own way, and the Lord *handed him over* for our sins. . . . Therefore I will allot him a portion with the great, and he shall divide the spoil with the strong; because his soul was *handed over* to death, and was numbered with the transgressors; yet he

bore the sins of many, and was *handed over* for their iniquities. (Isaiah 53:6, 12)

Similar allusions to the Suffering Servant make "hand over" the chosen verb for Mark's prophecies about Jesus' passion in 9:31 and 10:33, for Judas's action in 3:19 and 14:10–44, for the high-priestly action in 15:1 and 10, and for Pilate's action in 15:15. To be "handed over" was an expression not just for Jesus, but for John before him in 1:14 and for Christians after him in 13:9, 11, 12.

The third element in the Common Meal Tradition was that connection to Deutero-Isaiah's Suffering Servant through "servant/child" in the *Didache* and through "handed over" (by God) in the pre-Pauline tradition. But that common element means that Jesus' death, while explicitly present in 1 Corinthians 10–11, is implicitly present even in *Didache* 9–10.

SYMBOLIC UNITY

The fourth element in the Common Meal Tradition was noted by Koester: "Paul shares with the meal prayers of the Didache . . . that the bread symbolizes the unity of the church" (1994a:551), that "the bread [is] a symbol of the gathering of the community into one" (1996:349). That symbolism appears in the later *Didache* 9 and not the earlier *Didache* 10, as you can see in this third section of those twin eucharistic prayers (Milavec 1989:98):

Didache 10:5 (earlier version)	*Didache* 9:4 (later version)
Remember, Lord, your church, [remember] to deliver it from all evil and to perfect it in your love, [and, in the end] *Gather* this sanctified [church] *from* the four winds,	Just as this broken [loaf] was scattered [as grain] on the hills, and, having come together again, it becomes one, So may your church be *gathered* [on the last day] *from* the ends of the earth
into your kingdom which you have prepared for her. *For the power and the glory are yours forever.* [Amen!]	*into your kingdom.* *For the glory and the power are yours forever . . .* [Amen!]

Both texts refer to an apocalyptic ingathering of the church now scattered across the world, but only *Didache* 9:4 uses the bread as symbol. As the grain comes together into one loaf, so may the church be gathered apocalyptically into one.

What is interesting, however, is that Paul emphasizes the bread not just as symbolic of future but also of present unity:

Because there is one bread, we who are many are one body, for we all partake of the one bread. (1 Corinthians 10:17)

Many grapes become one cup of wine. Many grains become one loaf of bread. The symbolism of many becoming one is in the very ingredients of the meal itself. But they serve to underline the unification of the shared meal. If there is no sharing on earth, why should there be sharing in heaven?

APOCALYPTIC SANCTION

The fifth and final element in the Common Meal Tradition was also noted by Koester. In an earlier article, he wrote of an agreement between the eucharistic traditions of the Jerusalem community as reflected in Didache 9–10 and those of the Antioch community as reflected in Paul. "The meal prayers and liturgy . . . preserved in *Didache* 9–10, may mirror the practice of the Jerusalem church. However, the eschatological orientation is equally strong in the Lord's Supper formulary of Paul that he inherited from the church of Antioch" (1994a:551). But in a more recent article he says, more correctly I think, that the Q *Gospel* and *Didache* traditions, on the one hand, and "the Pauline words of institution," on the other, "share outlook into the future" (1996:349). It is, actually, a specifically apocalyptic rather than a generally eschatological outlook, but the basic point is quite correct.

We have already seen the first three parts of the parallel fourfold structure still evident in both *Didache* 9 and 10. Here, then, is the final part (Milavec 1989:98):

Didache 10:6 (earlier version)	*Didache* 9:5 (later version)
(a) Let the gift [of the kingdom] come and let this world pass away!	
(b) Hosanna to the God of David!	
(c) If anyone is holy, let him (or her) enter!	(c) Let no one eat or drink from your Eucharist except those who are baptized in the name of the Lord,
(d) If anyone is not, let him (or her) repent!	(d) for the Lord has said concerning this: "Do not give dogs what is holy."
(e) *Maranatha* (=Come Lord!). Amen.	

There are three sentences present in *Didache* 10:6 (abe) but absent from *Didache* 9:5. There are also striking differences between the Greek text in Codex Hierosolymitanus 54 and the Coptic version in British Library Oriental Manuscript 9271 (Jones and Mirecki 53).

The first sentence reads "Let the gift come and let this world pass away!" in the Greek but "Let the Lord come and let this cosmos pass away" in the Coptic (Jones and Mirecki 53). The former could easily be "a scribal error," reading *charis* (gift) for *kyrios* (Lord), so that, as Riggs suggests, the Coptic "is to be preferred" (1984:90).

The second sentence reads "Hosanna to the God of David!" in Greek but "Osanna to the House of David!" in Coptic. Riggs prefers "God" rather than "House" as more original (1984:90). If you read "God of David," however, that "Lord" before and after it refers to God as well. If you read "House of David," those titles·could refer more precisely to Jesus. A change from a theocentric to a christocentric apocalyptic understanding could best explain that transition, in other words, and "God of David" would therefore be the more likely original reading.

The final sentence is *"Maranatha. Amen"* in Greek but "The Lord came! Amen" in Coptic. That Aramaic phrase can be read as *"Marana tha,"* meaning "Our Lord, come!" or as *"Maran atha,"* meaning "Our Lord *has* come." Riggs suggests that both translations catch different facets of the Aramaic: "Jesus is present in the community (actual present-Sacrament) between the moments of his life (historical perfect-Incarnation) and his imminent return-Parousia" (1984:97 note 46).

What is fascinating, however, is that the same Aramaic expression is also found in Paul's conclusion to his first Corinthian epistle. Furthermore, there too the prayer is accompanied by an exclusionary clause:

Let anyone be accursed who has no love for the Lord. *Marana tha* [Our Lord, come]! (1 Corinthians 16:22)

In both usages the Aramaic prayer terminates the unit. Finally, although *Didache* 9:5 has no such terminal apocalyptic comment, it does have the balance of inclusion and exclusion common to 1 Corinthians 16:22 and *Didache* 10:6. Why is that condemnatory clause in three places, and why is it immediately associated with *maranatha* in two locations?

The conjunction between eucharistic meal and apocalyptic consummation was already explicitly present in Paul:

For as often as you eat this bread and drink the cup, you proclaim the Lord's death until he comes. (1 Corinthians 11:26)

It was also explicitly present in *Didache* 9:4 and 10:5, which pray for the apocalyptic ingathering of the single church now scattered across the world. Why, then, this special conjunction of apocalyptic prayer and inclusion/exclusion from the meal? Remember that the conjunction must stem from the Common Meal Tradition and not just from either Paul or the *Didache* alone. It must come, in other words, from the early Jerusalem community. Why?

We are back, I suggest, with the "Christ-hustlers" of *Didache* 12:3–5, with those who do not work and therefore should not eat from the common eucharistic share-meal. That is, as we saw, the same problem behind 2 Thessalonians 3:6–12. That inclusion/exclusion clause applies specifically to those who are abusing the sacred share-meal. It is holy food because participants commit themselves to sharing together as the Father taught them through his servant Jesus. Apocalyptic consummation stands as sanction against those who abuse the holy share-meal either from below (with the *Didache*'s freeloaders) or from above (with the Corinthian patrons).

As sociologist Rodney Stark put it, "free-rider problems are the Achilles' heel of collective activities. . . . This perverse dynamic threatens all groups engaged in the production of collective goods, and it pertains to social and psychic benefits such as enthusiasm and solidarity no less than material resources" (174, 176). What the *Didache* calls "Christ-hustlers" Stark calls "free-riders." But what Paul discovered at Corinth was that, even if *have-nots* could hustle Christ for food and drink, *haves* could also do so for power and prestige. Paul found that latter possibility more serious.

The Common Meal Tradition may look to a Last Supper in the past, to a communal meal in the present, or to a messianic banquet in the future—or, quite validly, to all of those at the same time. But it can never get away from this: *it is in food and drink offered equally to everyone that the presence of God and Jesus is found.* But food and drink are the material bases of life, so the Lord's Supper is political criticism and economic challenge as well as sacred rite and liturgical worship. It may be all right to reduce it from a full eat-and-drink meal to a token nibble-and-sip meal as long as it still symbolizes that same reality—namely: Christians claim that God and Jesus are peculiarly and especially present when food and drink are shared equally among all.

CHAPTER 24

COMMUNITIES OF RESISTANCE

Because of their anxious desire for an immortal and blessed existence, thinking that their mortal life had already come to an end, [the Therapeutics]
leave their possessions to their sons and daughters . . . to other relatives . . .
[or] to their companions or friends. . . . No one of them may take any food
or drink before the setting of the sun . . . and some . . . can endure . . . for
three days without even tasting it . . . and some . . . will scarcely at the end of
six days taste even necessary food. . . . The possession of servants or slaves
[they hold] to be a thing absolutely and wholly contrary to nature. . . . Explanations of the sacred scriptures are delivered by mystic expressions in alle-
gories. . . . [In an annual ritual, possibly at Pentecost] they all stand up
together, and . . . when each chorus of the men and each chorus of the
women has celebrated separately by itself . . . they join together, and the
two become one chorus.

Philo, *On the Contemplative Life*, 13, 34, 70, 78, 85 (Yonge 698–706)

By *communities of resistance* I mean groups whose style of communal life was
a calculated rejection and replacement of the entrepreneurial greed of Roman
commercialization.

My primary concern in this section is with the Essene communities in the
Jewish homeland. But that epigraph concerns an early-first-century Jewish community near Lake Mareotis outside Alexandria. The description was written by
the Jewish philosopher Philo, who lived between about 25 B.C.E. and 50 C.E., and
belonged to a rich and powerful Alexandrian family. He adapted Platonic dualism, in which material objects (the body, for example) are but pale and rather
feeble reflections of spiritual realities (the soul, for example), so that the Hebrew
scriptures could be read allegorically. That community, called Therapeutics
(from a Greek verb meaning both *to heal* and *to worship*) was composed of both
female Therapeutrides and male Therapeutae. The group had a daily ritual practiced in isolation, a weekly ritual practiced in segregated togetherness, and an
annual ritual practiced in full community. The above epigraph is given as a
warning for us to be very careful in reading Hellenized and specially Platonized
descriptions of the Essenes in the Jewish homeland. Philo has interpreted the
community in terms wholly understandable to a Greek audience and, indeed,
wholly understandable to his own mind, where Greek has won out over Jew at

very profound levels of sensibility. When Philo, or Josephus for that matter, describes the Essenes, we should compare their explanations very critically with any self-descriptions now available from Qumran.

The Essene Communities

Unless they are careful to act in accordance with the exact interpretation of the law for the age of wickedness: to separate themselves from the sons of the pit; to abstain from wicked wealth which defiles, either by promise or by vow, and from the wealth of the temple and from stealing from the poor of the people, from making their widows their spoils and from murdering orphans; to separate unclean from clean and differentiate between the holy and the common; to keep the sabbath day according to the exact interpretation, and the festivals and the day of fasting, according to what they had discovered, those who entered the new covenant in the land of Damascus; to set apart holy portions according to their exact interpretation; for each to love his brother like himself; to strengthen the hand of the poor, the needy and the foreigner; for each to seek the peace of his brother and not commit sin against his blood relation; to refrain from fornication in accordance with the regulation; for each to reprove his brother in accordance with the precept, and not to bear resentment from one day to the next; to keep apart from every uncleanness according to their regulations, without anyone defiling his holy spirit, according to what God kept apart for them.

Damascus Document (A) 6:14–7:4. (*DSST* 37)

When we compare the group in that epigraph with the one in the immediately preceding epigraph, we seem to be in different worlds. Yet it would not be at all difficult to connect the concerns of those "who entered the new covenant in the land of Damascus" with the Jewish traditions seen much earlier in Chapter 12. When we read Philo or Josephus describing the Essenes below, then, we must be very careful with their Hellenistic interpretations of Jewish actions, especially when those actions were designed specifically to oppose the Hellenization of Jewish traditions. Was celibate asceticism, if present, primary for Essenes or only for Philo and Josephus? And is earlier Jewish celibacy, if present, the same as later Christian celibacy? Is time or place more significant for the former and endurance or permanence more significant for the latter?

ESSENES IN PHILO

In *Every Good Man Is Free* 75–91 (Yonge 689–690), Philo describes the Essenes in the Jewish homeland, "in number something more than four thousand in my opinion," as living "in villages, avoiding all cities on account of the habitual law-lessness of those who inhabit them" (75). They have nothing to do with war, commerce, or slavery, that last evil being against "the ordinances of nature" for the Essenes, as it was for the Therapeutics (78–79). How do those communities work? Like this (Yonge 690):

> In the first place, then, there is no one who has a house so absolutely his own private property, that it does not in some sense also belong to every one: for besides that they all dwell together in companies, the house is open to all those of the same notions, who come to them from other quarters; then there is one magazine among them all; their expenses are all in common; their garments belong to them all in common; their food is common, since they all eat in messes; for there is no other people among which you can find a common use of the same house, a common adoption of one mode of living, and a common use of the same table more thoroughly established in fact than among this tribe: and is not this very natural? For whatever they, after having been working during the day, receive for their wages, that they do not retain as their own, but bring it into the common stock, and give any advantage that is to be derived from it to all who desire to avail themselves of it. (*Every Good Man Is Free* 85–86)

There is also, Philo continues, special care given to the sick and the aged (87). Above all, they "devote all their attention to the moral part of philosophy, using as instructors the laws of their country which it would have been impossible for the human mind to devise without divine inspiration" (80). They also practice "a continued and uninterrupted purity throughout the whole of life" (84). That last point is made more explicit in another essay.

This text is entitled *Hypothetica: Apology for the Jews,* now extant only as quotations in Eusebius's work *The Preparation for the Gospel* 11:1–18, an apologetical treatise composed between 314 and 318 C.E. (Yonge 742–746). The description of Essene life is very similar to that in the first essay, although the Essenes now "dwell in many cities of Judaea, and in many villages, and in great and populous communities" and are "all full-grown men, such as are no longer carried away by the impetuosity of the passions" (11:1, 3). But while everything else in the two essays is quite similar and even parallel, there is now this new information (Yonge 746):

> They repudiate marriage; and at the same time they practice continence in an eminent degree; for no one of the Essenes ever marries a wife. (*Hypothetica* 11:14)

Philo continues with a virulently misogynistic diatribe against women, reaching the somewhat illogical conclusion that to be bound by marriage—that is, by "the necessary ties of nature . . . [is to] become a slave instead of a free man" (11:14–17). But, leaving such invective aside, Philo's Essenes are, unlike his Therapeutics, an exclusively male order of ascetic celibates who work in the world at peaceful occupations, pool their incomes to live a very frugal common life, and study their sacred writings not in solitary isolation but in communal gathering each sabbath.

ESSENES IN PLINY

Pliny the Elder concludes his description of the Jewish homeland by working southward along the western shore of the Dead Sea. He mentions first the Essene settlement, then south of it *(infra)* Engedi, and further south *(inde)* the rocky fortress of Masada. His description of the Essenes manages, in a single sentence, to agree and also to disagree with those preceding accounts in Philo. I cite Pliny's text from the very useful collection of Essene-related classical references by Vermes and Goodman (33):

> To the west [of the Dead Sea] the Essenes have put the necessary distance between themselves and the insalubrious shore. They are a people *[gens]* unique of its kind and admirable beyond all others in the whole world, without women and renouncing love entirely, without money, and having for company only the palm trees. (*Natural History* 5.73)

Despite this celibacy, continues Pliny, their numbers have remained constant for "thousands of centuries" because "a throng of newcomers" is always ready to repent of "their past lives." Leaving exaggerations aside, that agrees with Philo about ascetical celibacy but locates only a single group of Essenes in one specific but unnamed location. A similar assertion, however, is recorded indirectly from another first-century source.

Dio Cocceianus, nicknamed Chrysostomos for his golden-mouthed oratory, lived between about 40 and 112. He was born at Prusa in Bithynia and was prosecuted there in 111 by that same Pliny the Younger whom we saw prosecuting Christians in Chapter 1. Although he was another first-century author, the following comment is now extant only in a biography by Synesius of Cyrene, composed around 400, as given in Vermes and Goodman (59):

> Also somewhere he praises the Essenes, who form an entire and prosperous city near the Dead Sea, in the centre of Palestine, not far from Sodom. (*Dio* 3.2)

The location of the Essenes was not named by Pliny the Elder, and neither was their "prosperous city" named by Dio in Synesius's account. Once again, however, you would presume that the Essenes were congregated in just one place near the Dead Sea.

ESSENES IN JOSEPHUS

Josephus mentions the name *Essenes* fourteen times across three of his writings. There are strong similarities between his comments and all the preceding descriptions, but also two rather striking differences.

His longest and most detailed description is in *Jewish War* 2.119–161, but there is also an important shorter one in *Jewish Antiquities* 18.18–22. Except for one point to be mentioned later, he agrees basically with Philo, even on the detail that "there are more than 4,000 who behave in this way" (*Jewish Antiquities* 18.20). He agrees with Philo that the Essenes "occupy no one city, but settle in large numbers in every town" (*Jewish War* 2.124) and that they live a common life in which "each gives what he has to any in need and receives from him in exchange something useful to himself" (*Jewish War* 2.127), or, in other words, that "they put their property into a common stock" (*Jewish Antiquities* 18.20). He agrees with Philo that "marriage they disdain to protect themselves from women's wantonness" (*Jewish War* 2.121); they "neither bring wives into the community nor do they own slaves, since they believe that the latter practice contributes to injustice and that the former opens the way to a source of dissension" (*Jewish Antiquities* 18.21). But he also adds very many details not given by Philo—for example, that "they carry nothing whatever with them on their journeys, except arms as a protection against brigands" (*Jewish War* 2.125). No provisions are necessary because they are guaranteed local hospitality by other Essenes. Josephus also adds precise descriptions of their daily life, hierarchical order, and restrained speech, as well as their cultic prayers, meals, and purifications. The two daily meals are sacred repasts taken in special garments and begun and ended with prayers from a "priest" (*Jewish War* 2.128–136): there are "priests to prepare bread and other food" (*Jewish Antiquities* 18.22). That priestly presence, by the way, is a very significant new detail. Josephus also adds specific details about how new members become Essenes, how communal discipline is maintained, and how purity and sabbath restriction are very strictly observed among them (*Jewish War* 2.143–149).

But there are also two elements contradictory to those earlier reports in Philo and Pliny. First of all, there is a set of references to individual Essenes, and none of those individuals is leading a village life, let alone an isolated life. They may be ascetical celibates, but they are also deeply involved with power and government, whether as prophets, dream-interpreters, or military commanders. As described by Josephus, the Essenes are city phenomena. The four references to individuals span about 170 years. In 105 or 104 B.C.E. there is "Judas of the

Essene group [genos], who had never been known to speak falsely in his prophecies" (Jewish Antiquities 13.311). In the middle of the first century B.C.E. there is "a certain Essene named Menahem, whose virtue was attested in his whole conduct of life and especially in his having from God a foreknowledge of the future" (Jewish Antiquities 15.373). In 106 C.E., there is "a certain Simon, of the sect [genos] of the Essenes," who interpreted the dream of Archelaus (Jewish War 2.113 = Jewish Antiquities 17.346). Finally, in late 66 C.E., "John the Essene," commanding northwestern Judaea in the revolt against Rome, died in an assault on the coastal city of Ascalon (Jewish War 2.567; 3.11, 19).

The second difference is even more interesting. Philo, Pliny, and Josephus (in Jewish War 2.120–121 and Jewish Antiquities 18.21) agree on frugality, communality, and ascetical celibacy for the Essenes. But then comes this surprising comment from Josephus:

> There is yet another order of Essenes, which while at one with the rest in its mode of life, customs, and regulations, differs from them in its view on marriage. They think that those who decline to marry cut off the chief function of life, the propagation of the race, and, what is more, that, were all to adopt the same view, the whole race would very quickly die out. (Jewish War 2.160)

But, Josephus continues, since they marry not for pleasure but for children, they marry only women who are already certainly menstruating, and they do not have intercourse during pregnancy, "thus showing that their motive in marrying is not self-indulgence but the procreation of children" (2.161). That raises this major question. Does the term Essenes refer to male ascetics living in communal isolation only, or also to those who marry, raise families, and are associated with towns, cities, and spheres of government?

ESSENES INSIDE QUMRAN

For almost two hundred years before its destruction by the Roman legions in 68 C.E., a Jewish community lived in caves, huts, or tents around a central complex of communal buildings later called Khirbet Qumran on the Dead Sea's northwestern shore. That community is almost certainly the Essene group mentioned by Dio and Pliny. (Engedi, for example—one of the landmarks used by Pliny—is twenty miles south of Qumran, and Masada is thirty-one miles south.) Between 1946 and 1956, not only was their communal center excavated, their hidden library was recovered from eleven nearby caves. That literary treasure ranges from relatively full manuscripts to tattered fragments. There are, for example, the first seven manuscripts from Cave 1 and the Temple Scroll from Cave 11. But there are also six hundred fragments of seventy different manuscripts from Cave 1 and fifteen thousand fragments of 550 different manuscripts from Cave 4. How does this new information, from excavated complex to recovered library, compare with those first-century descriptions given above?

On the one hand, as Todd Beall has shown quite clearly, it is possible to write a detailed commentary on the longer Josephan texts about the Essenes using those newly discovered Qumran texts. Here are two comparisons between Josephus and the *Rule of the Community*, discovered in Cave 1 at Qumran (1QS). A minor example concerns spitting: "They are careful not to spit into the midst of the company or to the right," in *Jewish War* 2.147. "The person who spits in the course of a meeting of the Many [the full community] shall be punished thirty days," in *Rule of the Community* 7.15 (DSST 11). A major example concerns eating: "Before the meal the priest says a prayer, and none may partake until after the prayer," in *Jewish War* 2.131. "And when they prepare the table to dine or the new wine for drinking, the priest shall stretch out his hand as the first to bless the first fruits of the bread and of the new wine," in *Rule of the Community* 6:4–6 (DSST 9). Furthermore, as Beall notes, "there is archaeological evidence for the common meal at Qumran as well. De Vaux [its excavator] has identified the largest room in the ruins of Qumran as a refectory. This identification is supported by the existence of a pantry for crockery adjoining the large room, containing more than one thousand vessels needed for eating" (57).

The *Rule of the Community* was found among a set of texts stored in a sealed jar whose security indicated their very precious status (DSSP 1.1–107). But besides that full copy from Cave 1 (1QS), ten fragmentary copies were recovered from Cave 4 (4Q255–264), and a final possible but very fragmentary copy was found in Cave 5 (5Q11). That community order presumes a congregation of male, celibate ascetics, presumably at Qumran itself. There is nothing about marriage, procreation, or children in it. That agrees with preliminary excavations in the main cemetery located between the communal complex and the shoreline. All its graves were in rows on a north-south axis, and a random sample of twenty-six graves yielded only adult male skeletons. But one grave separated from the others held a female skeleton. Excavations in smaller cemeteries to the east, north, and south of the main one turned up graves with one male, four children, and six females. However those women and children are to be explained, the ordered ranks of parallel graves in the central cemetery indicate, most likely, a male, celibate community at Qumran. They led a totally communal life with all possessions and decisions, all prayers and meals held in communal but hierarchical mutuality.

It is most likely, in other words, that all Qumranites were Essenes, but were all Essenes Qumranites? What about Philo and Josephus agreeing that Essene communities existed in many different locations? At Qumran the main cemetery's eleven hundred graves indicate a community between a hundred and fifty and two hundred at any given time. What about Philo and Josephus agreeing that they numbered over four thousand?

ESSENES OUTSIDE QUMRAN

In the Qumran library there were also multiple copies of another community-order document or rulebook, the so-called *Damascus Document* (DSSP 2.4–79). It exists in eight fragmentary copies from Cave 4 (4Q266–273), one from Cave 5 (5Q12), one from Cave 6 (6Q15), and two copies, one quite long (CD-A) and the other much shorter (CD-B), from outside Qumran. Those last two copies are not from ancient but from medieval manuscripts, the former from the tenth, the latter from the twelfth century. They were discovered by Solomon Schechter in 1896 among 100,000 other fragments in the *genizah* (or old-book repository) of Cairo's Ezra Synagogue—hence its coding as CD, the Cairo *Damascus Document*. Those multiplied copies indicate the importance of *both* rulebooks within the Qumran library, yet the two documents indicate rather different situations, one inside and one outside the Qumran settlement. As Geza Vermes puts it, "The Community Rule legislates for a kind of monastic society, the statutes of the Damascus Rule for an ordinary lay existence. . . . There can be only one logical conclusion: this was a single religious movement with two branches" (1985:87, 106).

The *Damascus Document* is remarkably different from the *Rule of the Community,* although, of course, it demands the same strict observance of God's Law. Todd Beall notes two words, for example, that are significant in the *Damascus Document* but are never mentioned in the *Rule of the Community:* the word "camp(s)" appears fifteen times, the word "city" three times, and those places "seem to point to groups of the sectarians living in areas outside of Qumran" (49). Those places are called "camps" from the inaugurally holy and nostalgically ideal desert encampments of the Israelites en route to the Promised Land. In addition, the *Damascus Document* imagines an overseer for each camp, as well as one responsible for all the camps. That official has a special Hebrew title variously translated as the *guardian, examiner,* or *inspector.* There is, for example, an assembly "of the camps" but also "of all the camps" (CD 12:23, 14:3), and there is "the Inspector of the camp" but also "the Inspector who is over all the camps" (CD 12:7, 14:9). We can conclude, in other words, that there were many more Essene communities than that isolated one at Qumran, and those others lived as communities within towns or cities. They could have been, on the one hand, among Gentiles, for "no-one should stay in a place close to gentiles on the sabbath" (CD 11:14–15). They could have been, on the other hand, in Jerusalem itself, for "no man should sleep with his wife in the city of the temple, defiling the city of the temple with their impurity" (CD 12:1–2). But how did their communal life work in those "encampments" far from Qumran?

What about common property, that "placing of his possessions in common," legislated in *Rule of the Community* 6:22? There is nothing about full communal life in the *Damascus Document*. But there are many rules for entering and staying in the community as well as for being accused, judged, and sentenced within it. There must, therefore, have been far more communal living than is indicated at first glance, although common property or pooled wages are not presumed (*DSST* 44):

This is the rule of the Many, to provide for all their needs: the salary of two days each month at least. They shall place it in the hands of the Inspector and the judges. From it they shall give to the orphans and with it they shall strengthen the hand of the needy and the poor, and to the elder who [is dy]ing, and to the vagabond, and to the prisoner of a foreign people, and to the girl who has no protector, and to the unma[rried woman] who has no suitor; and for all the works of the company. (*Damascus Document* 14:12–17)

That is, in effect, a tithe of one's salary as alms to be administered by the community's leaders. Otherwise, private property was the normal situation.

What about celibate asceticism? The *Damascus Document* explicitly imagines marriage and children (*DSST* 37, 45):

And if they reside in the camps in accordance with the rule of the land, and take women and beget children, they shall walk in accordance with the law and according to the regulation of the teachings. (*Damascus Document* 7:6–8[A] and 19:2–4[B])

The two preceding quotations indicate that those Essene communities included orphans and prisoners, poor and needy, children and adults, wives and husbands, celibates who did not wish to remain so, and possibly, of course, celibates who did. They were, in other words, ordinary people trying to lead extraordinary lives in an ordinary world.

A similar presumption of marriage appears in the *Rule of the Congregation* (*DSSP* 2.108–117), extant in only one fragmentary copy but included in the same manuscript as the main version of the *Rule of the Community*. This third rule is for "the congregation of Israel in the final days" (1QSa = 1Q28a 1:1), but it involves children, women, and men. It also legislates specifically about marriage for one who has grown up in the community (*DSST* 126):

When they come, they shall assemble all those who come, including children and women, and they shall read into their ea[rs], all the regulations of the covenant, and shall instruct them in all its precepts, so that they may not stray in their [errors]. . . . He shall not [approach] a woman to know her through carnal intercourse until he is full twenty years old, when he knows [good and] evil. Then she shall be received to give witness against him (about) the precepts of the law and to take his place in the proclamation of the precepts. (*Rule of the Congregation* 1:4–5, 9–11)

What could a wife witness against her husband? She could witness whether "he lay with her who sees the blood of her menstrual flow" (CD 5:7), for example, and, if Josephus was right about married Essenes, whether they had intercourse during pregnancy.

What about ritual meals? There is nothing in the extant *Damascus Document* similar to that summary statement in the *Rule of the Community* that "they shall eat together, together they shall bless, and together they shall take counsel" (1QS 6:2–3). But the following comparison between those two rules persuades me that the encampment Essenes had sacred meals just as did the Qumran Essenes.

The Qumran *Rule of the Community* has decrees about the progressive two-year initiation into the full community known as the Many. During that first year of testing, "he must not touch the pure food of the Many" (1QS 6:16), and during that second year, "he must not touch the drink of the Many" (1QS 6:20). Thereafter, and by communal vote, he enters into full membership "for the law, for the judgment, for purity and for the placing of his possessions in common" (1QS 6:22). The same Hebrew word is translated as "pure food" and "purity" in those sentences, and it seems clear, from the contexts, that they indicate the ritual meal of the community. Furthermore, there are these two sanctions mentioned later (*DSST* 10, 11):

If one is found among them who has lied knowingly concerning goods, he shall be excluded from the pure food of the Many for a year and shall be sentenced to a quarter of his bread. . . . And if he has spoken angrily against one of the priests enrolled in the book, he will be punished for a year and shall be excluded, under sentence of death, from the pure food of the Many. (*Rule of the Community* 6:24–25; 7:2–3)

It is that same Hebrew word once again—the "purity" or the "pure food" of the ritual meal. A question in passing: Does that first decree indicate that *not all* Qumran meals were sacred ones but that the offender was excluded from the periodic ritual meals and limited even at the regular meals? Or does it mean that *all* Qumran meals were sacred ones but that the offender got only a quarter of what would have been considered a regular meal for outsiders?

There is nothing specific about the communal or sacred meal in extant copies of the *Damascus Document*. But similar sanctions are mentioned that presume its existence (*DSST* 41):

If they are two, one and one, who testify about a different matter [in which a man sins against the law], the man is only to be excluded from the pure food on condition that they are trustworthy, and that on the same day on which he saw him, he denounces him to the Inspector. And concerning riches, they shall accept two trustworthy witnesses. And one, to exclude from the holy food. (*Damascus Document* 9:21–23)

The same Hebrew word is used for the "purity" of pure, holy, or sacred food as previously in the *Rule of the Community*. Furthermore, another same Hebrew word is used for "goods" (1QS 6:25) and for "riches" (CD 9:22) in both texts, so that the subject is lying about what one owns, be it property or salary, in relationship to communal obligations. All in all, therefore, I presume that the communal, ritual, or sacred meal was practiced not only at Qumran—where, despite Josephus, it *may* not have been every meal—but also in the local Essene communities as well.

ESSENES IN JERUSALEM

Josephus interrupts his description of Titus's troop dispositions around Jerusalem in May of 70 C.E. in order to explain the city's fortifications. He starts with the first wall, "most ancient" and "well-nigh impregnable," at its northwest corner and runs it first due east to the Temple and then due south to the Hinnom Valley. He describes that southward leg as descending "past the place called Bethso to the gate of the Essenes" (*Jewish War* 5.145). At that point the wall moved eastward across the Tyropeon Valley and eventually northward along the slope of the Kidron Valley to the Temple. The Gate of the Essenes, in other words, was at the southwestern corner of Jerusalem's old first wall.

For over a decade, beginning in 1977, archeologist Bargil Pixner supervised excavations at and around what he judges to be that Gate of the Essenes. It is located in the Protestant Cemetery on the southern slope of Mount Zion, with the Benedictine Abbey and Church of the Dormition to the north and then, even farther north, the present southern wall of the Old City. Three different gates have stood on that same site, their superimposed bottom sills still clearly visible. The topmost sill is from the fifth to seventh centuries C.E., the cruder middle sill is from the third to fourth centuries C.E., and the bottom sill is from before Jerusalem's destruction in 70 C.E. "We did manage, however, to extract some ceramic sherds from beneath the lowest, and therefore earliest, of the three sills. Coming from a sealed-off, undisturbed location, the sherds provided a reliable indication of the date of the first gate at the site. All our experts agreed that the pottery beneath the lowest threshold predated 70 C.E., the year of the destruction of Jerusalem by the troops of the Roman general Titus, son of Emperor Vespasian. We had little doubt that this was the gate Josephus called the gate of the Essenes. . . . The socket, in which the wings of the gate turned, remains *in situ,* perfectly round and smooth, suggesting that the bottom of the hinge was made of metal. The Gate of the Essenes was destroyed in 70 C.E. when Titus' Roman legionnaires razed Jerusalem" (27, 29). That gate "must have been inserted into an already existing wall" (27), and there are indications that the work was done by Roman engineers working for Herod the Great, possibly as early as 30 B.C.E. "To construct the gate, builders made a breach in the existing wall. Then they dug a sewage channel (discovered by Bliss [in the 1890s]) that ran along a street leading from the interior of the city and emptied into the Hinnom Valley, south of Mount Zion. Limestone slabs of fine workmanship cover the channel as it passes beneath the gateway. When the doyen of Israeli archaeologists, the late Benjamin Mazar, visited us, he remarked that only the workmen of Herod the Great [37 B.C.E. to 4 C.E.] were likely to have achieved such stonecutting perfection" (28).

There is one final fascinating point. Pixner asks the obvious topographical question: "Who would have built a gate at this unlikely location, on the shoulder of a ravine descending into the Hinnom Valley, atop a hill so steep that the gate could only be reached on foot?" (31). Why was a gate added precisely there? Recall that, as Josephus described the southern leg of that old first wall, it went "past the place called Bethso to the gate of the Essenes" (*Jewish War* 5.145). Where or what is Bethso? "Since the 19th century," says Pixner, "most scholars have agreed that the term 'Bethso' derives from the Hebrew *beth-soa,* or latrines" (84). At this point some background is necessary, to help us place this new information. It is very significant background, because it warns those of us thinking from viewpoints in Hellenistic asceticism or Christian monasticism that Jewish Essenism is not exactly either of those phenomena.

There was this traditional law for the desert encampments as Israel journeyed from Egypt to the Promised Land:

> You shall have a designated area outside the camp to which you shall go. With your utensils you shall have a trowel; when you relieve yourself outside, you shall dig a hole with it and then cover up your excrement. Because the Lord your God travels along with your camp, to save you and to hand over your enemies to you, therefore your camp must be holy, so that he may not see anything indecent among you and turn away from you. (Deuteronomy 23:12–14)

The Essenes applied that law to their camp communities, to Qumran as substitute Jerusalem, and, of course, to Jerusalem itself as the Temple's urban extension. Josephus mentions defecatory purity explicitly:

A candidate anxious to join their sect . . . [is presented] with a small hatchet . . . [On the sabbath they do not even] go to stool. On other days they dig a trench a foot deep with a mattock—such is the nature of the hatchet which they present to the neophytes—and wrapping their mantle about them, that they may not offend the rays of the deity, sit above it. They then replace the excavated soil in the trench. For this purpose they select the more retired spots. And though the discharge of the excrements is a natural function, they make it a rule to wash themselves after it, as if defiled. (*Jewish War* 2.137, 148–149)

There is nothing explicit about such defecatory purity in either the *Rule of the Community* or the *Damascus Document,* but it does appear in two other very important Qumran documents.

The first one is the *War Scroll*—in Hebrew *Milḥamah*—discovered in Cave 1 at Qumran, hence its coding as 1QM (DSSP 2.80–203). There are also six related fragments and one similar fragment from Cave 4 (4Q491–497). This is a pre-Qumran text imagining the great apocalyptic battle between the Sons of Darkness under Belial and the Sons of Light under God. Here the term *community* designates Israel as a whole and not just the Essenes as a sect (*DSST* 100):

And no young boy or any woman at all shall enter the camps when they leave Jerusalem to go to war, until they return. And no lame, blind, paralyzed person nor any man who has an indelible blemish on his flesh, nor any man suffering from uncleanness in his flesh, none of these will go out to war with them. . . . And there will be a space between all their camps and the 'place of the hand' of about two thousand cubits. (*War Scroll* 7:3–7)

What is at stake in those decrees, of course, is not battle discipline or military hygiene but ritual purity. They are to go into battle like priests into the Temple. Latrines, therefore, must be about one thousand yards from their encampments.

The second document is the *Temple Scroll* from Cave 11. The main copy, coded as 11QT^a or 11Q19, is the longest of all the scrolls, but there is also a fragmentary copy, coded as 11QT^b or 11Q20. It gives, with God speaking in the first person, a definitive Law for Jerusalem, its Temple, and its king, according to presumably Essene ideals (*DSST* 138):

They shall make my temple holy and respect it, for I dwell among them. You shall make latrines for them outside the city, where they are obliged to go, outside, to the North-east of the city: houses with beams and wells within them into which the excrement shall drop; they shall not be visible from a total distance from the city of three thousand cubits. (*Temple Scroll* 46:11–13)

It is, once again, a question not of urban hygiene but of Temple-city purity. Defecation is forbidden anywhere in Jerusalem, as is sexual intercourse: "Anyone who lies with his wife and has an ejaculation, for three days shall not enter anywhere in the city of the temple in which I shall install my name" (1QTª 45:11–12).

Locations, directions, and measurements in the *Temple Scroll* should not be pressed too far, as if one could correlate its details with actual Jerusalem topography. The point is not that the *Temple Scroll's* ideal latrines need to be equated with actual Bethso any more than that its ideal city gates (which were twenty-one feet wide [11QTª 41:14]) need to be equated with the actual Essene Gate (which was nine feet wide). The point is this: the presence of the Essene Gate at that rather difficult topographical location and of latrines outside the walls and to the northwest is best explained by postulating an Essene Quarter immediately inside the northwestern corner of the city's old first wall. That Herodian-style Essene Gate may even have been constructed specially for them so that they could observe the Law as faithfully as they desired.

ESSENES IN HISTORY

You will recall from the beginning of Chapter 12 that for 372 years the Jewish homeland had been not a king-state but a Temple-state. It was ruled externally by first the Persian Empire and then, after Alexander, by its Greco-local replacements in Egypt or Syria. It was ruled internally by Jewish high priests legitimated by traditional dynastic descent from Aaron at the time of Moses through Zadok at the time of Solomon. After Alexander had Hellenized their world, the Jewish homeland was caught between those warring Hellenistic empires to its south and north, but it was also threatened even more insidiously by Hellenistic mono-culturalism and international commercialism. That placed increasing external and internal strain on the very existence of the Jewish people in covenant with a God of justice and purity in a land of justice and purity. And it placed the high priesthood itself in the very eye of the Hellenistic storm.

In the early decades of the second century B.C.E., the Jewish homeland was under Syrian control. But the Syrian Empire was under military pressure from Rome, steadily expanding on Syria's western front, and from Egypt, always threatening on Syria's southern front. The Jewish homeland was vital to Syria, both for tribute to pay off Rome and for security to ward off Egypt. But attempts to integrate it economically and politically into the Syrian Empire kept foundering on religious and theological obstacles. In the 170s the legitimate high priest was Onias III, but rivals—first Jason from within his own family and then Menelaus from outside it—promised Antiochus IV Epiphanes of Syria greater tax revenues if they were appointed high priest and allowed to turn Jerusalem into a full Greek city (Antioch South, as it were). What follows is a rather terse summary of the situation, but there is a fuller account in 2 *Maccabees* 4.

> In those days certain renegades came out from Israel and misled many, saying, "Let us go and make a covenant with the Gentiles around us, for since we separated from them many disasters have come upon us." This proposal pleased them, and some of the people eagerly went to the king, who authorized them to observe the ordinances of the Gentiles. So they built a gymnasium in Jerusalem, according to Gentile custom, and removed the marks of circumcision, and abandoned the holy covenant. They joined with the Gentiles and sold themselves to do evil. (1 *Maccabees* 1:11–15)

Finally, the Syrian monarch decided to solve Jewish disagreements on that program of political amalgamation by enforcing religious integration. If Jewish religion stood in the way, then Jewish religion itself would have to go. Profanation of the Temple by Syrian paganism and destruction of the faithful by Syrian persecution began in 167 B.C.E. The Hasmonean family of Jewish priests, nicknamed the Maccabees, led the Jewish counterattack, and within three years they defeated the Syrians, retook Jerusalem, and purified the Temple. Then, for one hundred years—until the Roman general Pompey took Jerusalem in 63 B.C.E.— an indigenous Jewish monarchy ruled the Jewish homeland. But they also declared themselves to be high priests. Instead of restoring the traditional and nonroyal high priesthood, the Hasmoneans themselves became a new and royal high priesthood, first with Jonathan in 160–142 and then with Simon in 142–134 B.C.E. That was, for some Jews, worse than the Syrian persecution itself. If the high priest was illegitimate, how could the Temple service be valid, the covenant between people and God be maintained, and the linkage between earth and heaven be certified?

The Essenes arose within that general background in the first half of the second century B.C.E., and the Qumran community is particularly connected to that situation of high-priestly illegitimacy. Their revered early leader, the Teacher of Righteousness (that is, the true, proper, or right teacher) was opposed both externally by the Wicked Priest (that is, those illegitimate Hasmonean high priests in turn) and internally by the Man of the Lie (that is, another leader who turned many possible followers away from the Teacher of Righteousness). That very specific background is crucially important for understanding the Essenes, and it leads into the next and final point concerning them.

ESSENE ESCHATOLOGY

Recall those different types of eschatology mentioned in Chapters 15 and 16. Think, first, about ascetical eschatology. When Philo and Josephus explain the Essenes, they emphasize celibate asceticism or ascetical eschatology, and they base it, mildly in Josephus but virulently in Philo, on misogyny. That emphasis on celibate asceticism is, however, much more their Hellenism than their Judaism speaking. When you read, for example, the *Rule of the Community*, the *Damascus Document,* or the *Rule of the Congregation,* celibate asceticism does not seem the most important concern. Arguments about whether the Qumranites were fully celibate for the whole of life, temporarily celibate for a part of life, or terminally celibate for the end of life seem also a little beside the point. Take, for example, the preamble to the *Rule of the Community*. It has a whole series of "in order to" phrases that outline the purpose of their community. Here are the opening ones in 1QS 1:1–7 (*DSST* 3, my italics):

in order to	seek God [with all (one's) heart and with all (one's) soul;
in order] to	do what is good and just in his presence as commanded by means of the hand of Moses and his servants the Prophets;
in order to	love everything which he selects and to hate everything that he rejects;
in order to	keep oneself at a distance from all evil, and to become attached to all good works; to bring about truth, justice and uprightness on earth and not to walk in the stubbornness of a guilty heart and of lecherous eyes performing every evil.

There is nothing anywhere about "in order to practice asceticism" or "in order to observe celibacy." The Qumranites were, first of all and above all, seeking to live faithfully the purity and holiness of God in a world peculiarly impure and unholy. It was justice and righteousness, not celibacy and asceticism, that was on their minds and in their hearts. Furthermore, since their own high priesthood and those priests who supported it were no longer pure and holy according to God's Law for priests, all Essenes would live that purity and holiness for them and instead of them. All else followed from those intentions.

Think, next, about apocalyptic eschatology and remember that distinction between primary and secondary apocalypticism. In the former case, the end-time is the only reason you do something—say, abandon home, family, and possessions. If the end were not imminent, you would not do those things. In the latter case, the end-time is simply a sanction to enforce what you should be doing in any case—say, observe justice, holiness, and purity. If the end were not imminent, you would still be required to do those things. Reading the Qumran *War Scroll*, for example—with its climactic battle between good and evil, light and darkness, God and Belial at the end of days—you can easily see the Essenes in general and Qumran in particular as apocalyptic eschatologists. But turn, once again, to the *Rule of the Community* or the *Damascus Document*. Are those rules in effect only because it is the end-time? Or should everyone be following them in any case, be it end-time or not? The *Rule of the Community*, for example, describes the ordinary meal of the Qumran community in 6:4–6 (*DSST* 9). The *Rule of the Congregation* "in the final days" describes the end-time meal with the Messiahs present in 2:17–20 (*DSST* 127). The only difference between the eschatological and the regular meal at Qumran is that the Messiahs (apparently) bless the food and drink first. A footnote. Just as Christian Jews interpreted the general messianic expectation as one Messiah but two comings, so the Essene Jews interpreted it as two Messiahs but one coming. Their twin Messiahs were a priestly one and a lay one, separated in that authoritative order, an obvious rebuke of Hasmonean king-priests, combined in that authoritative order.

Think, finally, about ethical eschatology. What is emphasized for the Essenes is a life radically submissive to the Law of God. Shared possessions, be they total or partial, and common meals, be they regular or special, are indicative of that life. So, of course, is priestlike purity as fully as one can practice it. It seems to me that the term *ethical eschatology* is more accurate than either *ascetical* or *apocalyptic eschatology* for the basic ideology of the Essene lifestyle. But in that ideology it is impossible to separate ritual and morality, justice and purity. Here is one example of that impossibility.

The *Halakhic Letter* is another very important Qumran document detailing differences in legal interpretation between the writer and some unidentified recipient. It begins by saying that "these are some of our regulations [concerning the law of G]od" (1:3–4) and ends by repeating that "we have written to you some of the works of the Torah which we think are good for you and for your people, for in you [we saw] intellect and knowledge of the Torah." It has been given a Hebrew title, *Miqsat Maaseh ha-Torah* (or *Some Works of the Law*), hence coded as 4QMMT but derived from combining 4Q394–399 into a single composite text (*DSST* 77–85). The first item, however, even before those itemized legal rulings, concerns the solar calendar: "The year is complete, three hundred and sixty-four days" (1:2)—that is, twelve months of thirty days plus four extra days after each trimester. But why is that so important? Is it simply quibbling to establish difference, to create an *us* against *them*? What is at stake in the calendar? What has calendrics to do with ethics?

People live in coordinates of space and time, of here and now, and God is the Lord of time and space. But for the Jews of that day, it had become progressively more difficult to see God as Lord of space with Mediterranean Sea, homeland, city, and Temple under pagan or impure control. God as Lord of time became, then, proportionately more and more important. The Temple authorities used a lunar calendar similar to the surrounding pagans. The Essenes counterused a solar-lunar calendar based on the fact that God created the sun, moon, and stars on the fourth day of creation—that is, on our Wednesday. The first day of the New Year therefore had to be on a Wednesday (and *always* on a Wednesday). Both Qumranites and other Essenes, as we know from *Damascus Document* 6:18–19 (*DSST* 37), observed a quite different calendar from the rest of their fellow Jews. That is why, for example, the Wicked Priest could attack the Teacher of Righteousness "during the rest of the Day of Atonement . . . the day of fasting, the sabbath of their rest" (1QpHab11:6–8; *DSST* 201–202). It was the Teacher's but not the Priest's Day of Atonement.

In conclusion, what? It is still not clear what relationship the other Essene communities had to Qumran or it to them. Was Qumran just one among many, first among equals, or some sort of ideal or even jurisdictional mother-community? Why were there so many *copies* of key texts found in the caves, especially in Cave 4, which seems to have been the principal library? If Qumran was a copying center—the Essene Publishing Company, as it were—why are there hundreds of different scribal hands evident in the scrolls? Or was Qumran always the central community so that other Essenes fled there with their own documents before Vespasian's legions?

My point in all of this is not to narrow Essene identity to one monolithic option but to open it up fully across the widest possible spectrum. The Essene communities were radical attempts to live faithfully and fully the Law of God, in justice and righteousness, in purity and holiness, when *everyone* around them, from their own high priests to their own people, was failing to do so. One could disagree with that judgment and still honor its integrity.

It is against that background that I now look at another early-first-century community, the Christian Jews around James the Just in Jerusalem.

James the Just

The outcome of the conflict between teachers and bishops had important social consequences. If the school had prevailed, the Christian communities would have assumed an intellectual character, with little place for the uneducated. The circles of Clement and Origen, as they appear from their writings and the scanty prosopographic evidence given by Eusebius, consisted of people who already had Greek learning and who were sometimes students of philosophical schools. The monarchical episcopate, on the other hand, was much more effective in bringing together members from all social classes, learned or illiterate, and uniting them under the authority of a strict hierarchy. The episcopate asked not for wisdom or education but for discipline. The subordination of the school to the bishop, as at Alexandria, preserved much of the intellectual character of the Christian communities and hence favoured the participation of educated and wealthy people—without, however, excluding the poor and underprivileged.

Dimitris J. Kyrtatas, *The Social Structure of the Early Christian Communities*, p. 145

If you read only Paul's letters you would know—from Galatians 1:18–19 or 2:11–12, for example—that both Simon "the Rock" (Peter in Greek, Cephas in Aramaic) and James "the Lord's brother" were important figures in early Christianity. If you read only the canonical gospels you would know that Peter was very important but you would know James only as one among the siblings of Jesus named in passing in Mark 6:3. If you read a non-Christian source such as Josephus, however, you would know only two individuals in earliest Christianity: one is Jesus himself and the other is his brother James. You would not know, for example, that Peter or Paul had ever existed. James the brother of the Lord, James the Just, James of Jerusalem, James by whatever name requires very special attention.

The preceding epigraph concerns institutional tensions between bishop-leader and scholar-teacher when Demetrius and his successors were rulers of the Alexandrian church and Clement or Origen headed its catechetical school between the mid-second and mid-third centuries. My intention in quoting it is not to retroject the monarchical episcopate back to the early first century with James of Jerusalem. I use it, rather, to introduce this question: What mode of power and authority did James have, and what were the sociopolitical advantages and disadvantages of that mode?

JAMES IN JOSEPHUS

We saw in Chapter 1 what Josephus says about Jesus. But what he says about James, the brother of Jesus, is much, much longer. If we knew nothing save these two texts, James would probably seem the far more important person. His execution was enough to topple a high priest:

Upon learning of the death of Festus, Caesar sent Albinus to Judaea as procurator. The king [Agrippa II] removed Joseph from the high priesthood, and bestowed the succession to this office upon the son of Ananus, who was likewise called Ananus. . . . The younger Ananus . . . was rash in his temper and unusually daring. He followed the school of the Sadducees, who are indeed more heartless than any of the other Jews . . . when they sit in judgement. Possessed of such a character, Ananus thought that he had a favourable opportunity because Festus was dead and Albinus was still on the way. And so he convened the judges of the Sanhedrin and brought before them a man named James, the brother of Jesus who was called the Christ, and certain others. He accused them of having transgressed the law and delivered them up to be stoned. Those of the inhabitants of the city who were considered the most fair-minded and who were strict in observance of the law were offended at this. They therefore secretly sent to King Agrippa urging him, for Ananus had not even been correct in his first step [in convening the Sanhedrin], to order him to desist from any further such actions. Certain of them even went to meet Albinus, who was on his way from Alexandria, and informed him that Ananus had no authority to convene the Sanhedrin without his consent. Convinced by these words, Albinus angrily wrote to Ananus threatening to take vengeance upon him. King Agrippa, because of Ananus' action, deposed him from the high priesthood which he had held for three months and replaced him with Jesus the son of Damascus. (*Jewish Antiquities* 20.197–203)

There are three important points to make regarding this text. First, Ananus was not just the high priest. He was from a most important high-priestly family. His father, Ananus the Elder, was high priest from 6 to 15 C.E., and is known to us from the gospels as Annas. The elder Ananus was father-in-law of Joseph Caiaphas, high priest from 18 to 36 C.E., a figure also known to us from the gospels. He was furthermore the father of five other high priests, Eleazar, Jonathan, Theophilus, Matthias, and Ananus the Younger (above), and the grandfather of Matthias, high priest in 65 C.E. Ananus the Younger, in other words, came from a family that dominated the high priesthood for most of that pre–66 first century, with eight high priests in sixty years. Second, because (in the interregnum between Roman governors in 62 C.E.) he convened a Sanhedrin for a capital case and had James and some others put to death, Ananus the Younger brought down on himself the wrath of the Herodian ruler Agrippa II and the Roman governor Albinus. Finally, Josephus names Ananus a "Sadduccee" and those who opposed him as ones "strict in observance of the law," which probably means Pharisees. The execution of James and the others was assumed into that rivalry, and it was sufficient to have Ananus deposed after only three months in office. James, however, must have had some public standing or his name would hardly have been recorded; in fact, he is identified as "the brother of Jesus who was called the Christ." Why was James so significant a figure that Pharisees, presumably, could unseat a high priest on his account? What else do we know about James before his execution in the early 60s?

JAMES IN PAUL

Paul became a Christian three to five years after the crucifixion of Jesus, and he visited Jerusalem three times thereafter—once in the late 30s, again in the late

40s, and finally in the late 50s. In writing to the Galatians, he insists that he is a full apostle sent by a revelation of God and Jesus rather than a subapostle sent by a commission of the Jerusalem church and its leaders. He did not go to ask their permission for what he was doing, and when he eventually went to see them it was just for a visit with the leaders:

> Then after three years I did go up to Jerusalem to visit Cephas and stayed with him fifteen days; but I did not see any other apostle except James the Lord's brother. (Galatians 1:18–19)

If you date the execution of Jesus to 30 and the conversion of Paul to 35, then the first Jerusalem visit took place in 38. You would think from that formulation that Peter (Cephas) was more important than James at that time, at least from Paul's point of view.

The second visit is much more significant and took place, if Paul is dating both events from his conversion, in 49:

> Then after fourteen years I went up again to Jerusalem with Barnabas, taking Titus along with me. . . . But even Titus, who was with me, was not compelled to be circumcised, though he was a Greek . . . and when James and Cephas and John, who were acknowledged pillars, recognized the grace that had been given to me, they gave to Barnabas and me the right hand of fellowship, agreeing that we should go to the Gentiles and they to the circumcised. They asked only one thing, that we remember the poor [ptōchōn], which was actually what I was eager to do. (Galatians 2:1, 3, 9, 10)

At issue was whether male Christian pagans had to be circumcised at conversion, and Titus was a visual aid for the negative viewpoint. There were Christian Jews, termed "false brethren" by Paul in Galatians 2:4, with an affirmative viewpoint, but they were not supported by the leaders, now named with James in first place. Since God's Law was not a menu from which one could pick and choose, how could that have been justified? Only in a context of apocalyptic consummation, as Paula Fredriksen has shown: "What place, if any, do Gentiles have in such a kingdom? We can cluster the material around two poles. At the negative extreme, the nations are destroyed, defeated, or in some way subjected to Israel. . . . At the positive extreme, the nations participate in Israel's redemption. The nations will stream to Jerusalem and worship the God of Jacob together with Israel" (1991:544–545). Gentiles will no longer be pagans, but neither will they have to become Jews. "When God establishes his Kingdom, then, these two groups will together constitute 'his people'; Israel, redeemed from exile, and the Gentiles, redeemed from idolatry. Gentiles are saved as Gentiles:

they do not, eschatologically, become Jews" (1991:547). You can, however, sense a tension even within that more benign program for spiritual conversion rather than physical extermination. Gentiles do not become Jews, but neither do they remain pagans. What is a nonpagan Gentile? What minimally or maximally must those pagans do? And who decides?

At the Jerusalem Council, in any case, the immediate question of male Gentile circumcision was resolved. But a far greater one was created, because there was now a double mission, one to Jews led by Peter and one to pagans led by Barnabas and Paul. That would have worked well if Jews and pagans had lived in completely isolated enclaves. And if only Christian Jews preached to Jews and Christian pagans to pagans. It was magnificent as apocalyptic idealism. But how would it work as practical program? Apocalypse, after all, is easier to imagine as a divine instant than a human process. In a great city like Antioch, for example, would there be two separated communities, one of Christian pagans and another of Christian Jews? And, apart from that case, how would Jews such as Barnabas and Paul treat their own Jewishness in contact with pagans?

Those unresolved issues soon erupted at Antioch, where a combined community of Christian Jews and Christian pagans were eating together without observing the kosher commandments in the Law of God.

> But when Cephas came to Antioch, I opposed him to his face, because he stood self-condemned; for until certain people came from James, he used to eat with the Gentiles. But after they came, he drew back and kept himself separate for fear of the circumcision faction. And the other Jews joined him in this hypocrisy, so that even Barnabas was led astray by their hypocrisy. But when I saw that they were not acting consistently with the truth of the gospel, I said to Cephas before them all, "If you, though a Jew, live like a Gentile and not like a Jew, how can you compel the Gentiles to live like Jews?" (Galatians 2:11–14)

James presumed that Christian Jews would observe the Law while Christian pagans would not. But in a combined community, such as that at Antioch, Christian Judaism had to prevail over Christian paganism. Peter and Barnabas presumed that kosher regulations were no longer important, *one way or the other*. It was not important to follow them, but neither was it important to not follow them. Hence, before James's intervention, they ate with pagans like pagans. After it, they wanted everyone, including pagans, to eat like Jews. Paul called that hypocrisy; they probably considered it courtesy. Paul, in any case, refused to give in, found himself isolated, and, in my view, went westward, never to return to Antioch.

All of that emphasizes two major points concerning James. He was the authoritative leader of the Jerusalem mother-church, which was operating two major missions, one to the Jews and one to the pagans. He was a Christian Jew who believed that Jesus was the Messiah but also followed the full Jewish Law. That explains, negatively, why, unlike Stephen in the early 30s or James, son of Zebedee, in the early 40s, James was not attacked, persecuted, or executed until the early 60s. It does not fully explain, positively, why he was so strongly defended by non-Christian Jews after his execution. He was clearly important for Christian Jews. But why was he important for *non*-Christian Jews? He observed the Law? He did, of course, but so he *should* have, with all other Jews. What is special about that?

JAMES IN EUSEBIUS

Eusebius, bishop of Caesarea, lived between 263 and 339 and saw Christianity pass from persecuted cult to imperial religion. His *History of the Church,* published in successively longer versions during the first quarter of the fourth century, is hampered, as Timothy Barnes puts it, "by his inability to contemplate theological development"; as a result, "his account of the internal history of the Church and of Christian literature is less a coherent narrative than a series of disconnected notes" (132). One of Eusebius's sources is Hegesippus's five-book *Memoirs,* dated around 150, and from its last book he cites the following about James (Williamson 99–100):

Control of the Church passed to the apostles, together with the Lord's brother James, whom everyone from the Lord's time till our own has called the Righteous, for there were many Jameses, but this one was holy from his birth; he drank no wine or intoxicating liquor and ate no animal food; no razor came near his head; he did not smear himself with oil, and took no baths. He alone was permitted to enter the Holy Place, for his garments were not of wool but of linen. He used to enter the Sanctuary alone, and was often found on his knees beseeching forgiveness for the people, so that his knees grew hard like a camel's from his continually bending them in worship of God and beseeching forgiveness for the people. Because of his unsurpassable righteousness he was called the Righteous and *Oblias*—in our own language 'Bulwark of the People, and Righteousness'—fulfilling the declarations of the prophets regarding him. (*History of the Church* 2.23)

Hegesippus describes James as under a lifelong nazarite vow. The temporary version of this vow is described in Numbers 6:1–21, but lifelong versions are described for Samson in Judges 13:5 and 14 and 16:17 and for Samuel in 1 Samuel 1:11 and 22. The nazarite, like the high priest in Leviticus 21:11, is forbidden to

become impure by touching a corpse, even to bury his own parents. Furthermore, James, as a nazarite, is treated like a priest and allowed to enter the Holy
Place—maybe even, although the Temple's topography seems confused, to
enter the Holy of Holies itself, as the high priest would on the Day of Atonement.

From all of that I take only one element as probably historical: James was
famous for his asceticism. A second element is possible: James was a nazarite. I
label that second element *possible* rather than *probable* because Hegesippus could
have inferred it from Acts 18:18 and 21:24, where, in a context I return to below,
James tells Paul to join four others undergoing purification at the end of their
temporary nazarite vows. A third element, James as priest-privileged or even
high-priest-privileged, I leave aside as overenthusiastic. There is, I recognize, a
strong inclination to discard that entire story because of its imaginative expan-
sions, but I retain its core for one reason: the combination of historical fact *and*
apologetical expansion that occurs here with regard to James's life also occurs
with regard to James's death. For that execution Eusebius cites from the eighth
book of the lost *Outlines* by Clement of Alexandria, who lived between about 150
and 215 (Williamson 72, 99):

> [James] the Righteous . . . was thrown down from the parapet and beaten to
> death with a fuller's club." . . . So they killed him, seizing the opportunity for
> getting their own way provided by the absence of the government, for at
> that very time Festus had died in Judaea, leaving the province without gov-
> ernor or procurator. How James died has already been shown by the words
> quoted from Clement, who tells us that he was thrown from the parapet [of
> the Temple] and clubbed to death. (*History of the Church* 1.1, 2.23)

Eusebius knows, presumably from Josephus (whom he cites on other matters), about the interregnum at the death of Festus, and he knows about the execution of James. The death is factual, the details apologetical. So also with his
life. The asceticism is factual, the details are apologetical. I am presuming, therefore, that James was an ascetic, be it nazarite-style or not. In such a context, of
course, kosher observance would not have been too difficult. Asceticism would
be, as it were, ultra-kosher observance.

Paul and Eusebius, together, indicate why James was so important to both
Christian and non-Christian Jews. But what about those "certain others" who
died with him? Was there any corporate dimension to that execution? What
about the Jerusalem community in connection with James?

The Jerusalem Community

The rule which I dare to enact and declare,
Is that all shall be equal, and equally share
All wealth and enjoyments, nor longer endure
That one should be rich, and another be poor,
That one should have acres, far-stretching and wide,
And another not even enough to provide
Himself with a grave: that this at his call
Should have hundreds of servants, and that none at all.
All this I intend to correct and amend:
Now all of all blessings shall freely partake,
One life and one system for all I will make.

Arisotphanes, *The Ecclesiazusae*, 590–594

At the start of 393 B.C.E. Aristophanes' comedy *The Ecclesiazusae*, or *Women in Charge*, was enacted for the first time at Athens. Its plot imagines women instead of men as the new rulers of the city, and communal ownership instead of private property as the new economics of the city. The great comedian takes the communalism of Plato's ideal *Republic*, limited there to certain aspects of leadership, and lampoons it by applying it to everything and everyone as in those lines cited above (Rogers 1924:246, 300–301, last line slightly adapted). Blepyros, for example, asks his wife Praxagora about sex, love, and marriage, wondering if "all women and men will be common and free." How can preferences for the most attractive or choices of the most desirable be precluded even if "no marriage or other restraint there will be"? Praxagora explains that before individuals can choose the most attractive, they must first accept the least desirable as well. She judges this "a nice democratic device" and "a popular system as ever was tried" (lines 611–630). The idea of absolute communalism of money, land, and sex was easily imagined and easily mocked. It is interesting, however, that male control and private property, or female control and communal ownership, should stand or fall together for Aristophanes and his audience.

I cite that text as epigraph to indicate how easy it is to mock and deride attempts at human equality through common property and shared possessions. Maybe derision is appropriate, but it is also appropriate to ask who gains by such derision. In any case, I leave Aristophanes' words there as a warning.

AN EGALITARIAN COMMUNITY?

The second half of Luke's two-volume gospel is now called the Acts of the Apostles, and its theological intention is clearly proclaimed in Acts 1:8. The book is about the Holy Spirit's movement from Jerusalem through Judaea and Samaria and thence out to the ends of the earth, or at least to Rome as the world's center. It is about the change in the Holy Spirit's headquarters from Jerusalem to Rome. Against that background Luke describes the Jerusalem community as follows:

> All who believed were together and had all things in common; they would sell their possessions and goods and distribute the proceeds to all, as any had need. (Acts 2:44–45)

That is a rather swift and passing description for something so radical, but Luke repeats it later on, giving more details. There are three sections in this later account. The first one more or less repeats the earlier claim. The second and third sections give positive and negative examples of the process at work.

[1] Now the whole group of those who believed were of one heart and soul, and no one claimed private ownership of any possessions, but everything they owned was held in common. With great power the apostles gave their testimony to the resurrection of the Lord Jesus, and great grace was upon them all. There was not a needy person among them, for as many as owned lands or houses sold them and brought the proceeds of what was sold. They laid it at the apostles' feet, and it was distributed to each as any had need.

[2] There was a Levite, a native of Cyprus, Joseph, to whom the apostles gave the name Barnabas (which means "son of encouragement"). He sold a field that belonged to him, then brought the money, and laid it at the apostles' feet.

[3] But a man named Ananias, with the consent of his wife Sapphira, sold a piece of property; with his wife's knowledge, he kept back some of the proceeds, and brought only a part and laid it at the apostles' feet. "Ananias," Peter asked, "why has Satan filled your heart to lie to the Holy Spirit and to keep back part of the proceeds of the land? While it remained unsold, did it not remain your own? And after it was sold, were not the proceeds at your disposal? How is it that you have contrived this deed in your heart? You did not lie to us but to God!" Now when Ananias heard these words, he fell down and died. And great fear seized all who heard of it. The young men came and wrapped up his body, then carried him out and buried him. After an interval of about three hours his wife came in, not knowing what had happened. Peter said to her, "Tell me whether you and your husband sold the land for such

and such a price." And she said, "Yes, that was the price." Then Peter said to her, "How is it that you have agreed together to put the Spirit of the Lord to the test? Look, the feet of those who have buried your husband are at the door, and they will carry you out." Immediately she fell down at his feet and died. When the young men came in they found her dead, so they carried her out and buried her beside her husband. And great fear seized the whole church and all who heard of these things. (Acts 4:32–5:11)

How is that claim to be assessed? Is that an imaginary community that never existed as such? Is it unhistorical and dreamy idealism? Is it just Luke's insistence on the peaceful and serene life of the earliest Jerusalem community? They had, he says, not only a common purpose and intention; they had common possessions as well. Does that description, however idealized, point to some serious attempt at radical commonality in the earliest Jerusalem Christian community?

You could, on the one hand, point to that sanction in Qumran's *Rule of the Community* seen above: "If one is found among them who has lied knowingly concerning goods, he shall be excluded from the pure food of the Many for a year and shall be sentenced to a quarter of his bread" (1QS 6:24–25). So maybe Ananias and Sapphira are fact? You could, on the other hand, point to Aristophanes' comedy, also seen above. Praxagora intends to apply her new program by creating a common fund of "silver and land" into which all must contribute everything they own and out of which all will receive whatever they need. But what, her husband Blepyros asks, if somebody holds back not land, which would be difficult to hide, but "talents of silver and Darics of gold," which would be much easier to conceal? Why do that, she responds, when all have whatever they want in any case? (lines 596–607). In any account of common-property initiation, that seems an obvious question: What if somebody cheats? So maybe Ananias and Sapphira are fiction?

In a recent essay, S. Scott Bartchy argues for the basic historicity of Luke's account against the background of honor and shame, patronage and clientage, real kin and fictive kin in the Mediterranean world. On the one hand, "Joseph Barnabas is regarded first of all as one of the significant patrons in the Jewish Christian communities in Jerusalem" (315). On the other, "Ananias and Sapphira not only dishonored and shamed themselves as patrons but also revealed themselves to be outsiders, non-kin" (316). That is true enough. Those are respectively positive and negative examples of patronal sharing. It is also very true that, in both his volumes, Luke pushes hard for increased almsgiving, greater patronal support, and the responsibility of Christian *haves* for Christian *have-nots*. Whether, therefore, as fact or fiction, Ananias and Sapphira are the negative patronal foils for Joseph Barnabas's positive image. But is *patronal* sharing the only type possible, and was it the only type available to that Jerusalem community? "Those disciples of Jesus who had come to Jerusalem from Galilee would most likely have had to resort to working as day laborers to earn their own living," as Bartchy notes (315). Could there not have been another type of sharing, not *patronal* but *communal,* a sharing of whatever one had with others in a like position? Just as we saw in Chapter 23 that there were *patronal* and *communal* share-meals, were there also *patronal* and *communal* share-possessions? In any case, I hold on to that distinction and do not equate all sharing with patronal sharing. Communal sharing is a far more radical criticism of commercialized community than patronal sharing, because the more individual almsgiving is increased, the more systemic injustice is ignored. Patronal sharing (alms) is an act of power. Communal sharing is an act of resistance.

Recall from above that Essene communalism could range from donating one's entire property at Qumran to donating a minimum of two days' salary per month in the other communities. I think of that communalism as a spectrum from maximum to minimum, but, whatever its specific details, it indicates that a holy Law for an unholy time demands modes of communal sharing. I emphasize, however, that sharing means both giving and taking. If, for example, one depends absolutely on the community, one must give absolutely to the community. Similarly, with Jerusalem. I leave open whether "all things in common" should be taken absolutely or relatively. I propose that there was a serious attempt to establish what we could call *share-community* to which one gave, at maximum, all one had or, at minimum, all one could. Against that background, the fault of (fictional?) Ananias and Sapphira was lying to the community, claiming to have given all when some was withheld. But that was a practical not just a theoretical lie. They were now taking from the community *as if* they no longer had any resources of their own. The story admits, in fact, that they did not have to sell their property and that, even after selling it, they did not have to hand it over to the community. But claiming an absolute gift was also claiming an absolute right, an absolute right to receive what one needed, an absolute right to share in the eucharistic share-meal of the community. All the Christ-hustlers were not in Galilee and Syria. In Jerusalem, then, as in Qumran: no deliberate lies about goods, no spurious claims to sustenance. What I see in both cases, with the Essene Jews and the Christian Jews, is a thrust toward establishing *sharing community* in reaction against *commercializing community*—an effort made, of course, to live in covenant with God. It is, in any case, the collection for the poor that convinces me to take Luke's "all things in common" not as imaginary idealism or even patronal sharing but as communal sharing.

THE COLLECTION FOR THE POOR

The important question is not whether everyone in the Jerusalem community gave up everything but whether there was a serious attempt to live communally together. The question, in other words, is whether this was the urban and Jerusalem equivalent to that rural dialectic of eating and healing seen in Parts VII and VIII of this book. What convinces me to take that communalism seriously is something we learn about from Paul quite directly and from Luke quite obliquely.

Some background is necessary to understand this argument, and in presenting it I critically integrate data from both the Lukan Acts and the Pauline epistles. Some Jews had long imagined an apocalyptic scenario in which pagans were saved and justified without becoming Jews, as I cited earlier from Paula Fredriksen: "Eschatological Gentiles ... those who would gain admission to the Kingdom once it was established, would enter as Gentiles. They would worship and eat together with Israel, in Jerusalem, at the Temple. The God they worship, the God of Israel, will have redeemed them from the error of idolatry: he will have saved them—to phrase this in slightly different idiom—graciously, apart from the works of the Law" (1991:548). But how exactly would that work itself out down here on earth? If God and God's Law were not to be trivialized, Gentiles would have to cease being Gentiles before any such common meal could occur. Even if they did not have to become Jews, they would certainly have to become ex-pagans—that is, ex-Gentiles. And what was, minimally or maximally, involved in being an ex-pagan? What would be required? If they were excused "from works of the Law," who would define such "works"? For example, was not belief in the one true God, the first commandment, the very first work of the Law? It was certainly possible to debate intensely this or that *interpretation* of God's Law, but how could it be possible to choose between this or that *part* of God's Law?

All of those questions came to a head in two incidents recorded by Paul in Galatians 1–2, with all original animosities fully displayed, and by Luke in Acts 15, with any original animosities firmly removed. We saw the details of those incidents above—details that are now background for my present concern. The last item from the Jerusalem Council recorded by Paul is this agreement:

They asked only one thing, that we remember the poor (*ptōchōn*), which was actually what I was eager to do. (Galatians 2:10)

If we had only that single sentence, it would be hard to know exactly what it meant. But it is clear from other texts that money from Christian pagan communities was to be collected for the benefit of the Christian Jewish community of Jerusalem. That is the easy part. The difficult part is whether this was simple poor-relief—monies intended to relieve destitution among Jerusalem's Christian Jews and, beyond them, non-Christian Jews—or whether it was intended to support the Jerusalem community itself under the theologically charged name of the Poor Ones. If we are speaking only of poor-relief, why should the poor of Jerusalem take precedence over the poor of Antioch, Ephesus, Philippi, Corinth, or any other Christian pagan community? Why would the Christian poor of Jerusalem be in any worse straits than the Christian poor of any other city? I am inclined, therefore, to consider that the collection was primarily for the Jerusalem community itself and that they called themselves the Poor Ones. It seems to me, however, that such a title required some form of commonality, some type of communal lifestyle, some degree of difference between the Jerusalem community and other Christian communities.

Think, for a moment, of the annual Jewish collection for the Temple at Jerusalem. The money involved was the annual half-shekel or *didrachmon* "tax levied on all Jews over the age of twenty, including freedmen and proselytes" (*GLAJJ* 1.198) for the Temple in Jerusalem. That annual subvention was for the public cult of the Temple. It was not a collection for the poor of Jerusalem, and, if such had been proposed, the same obvious question would probably have been asked: Were there not Jewish poor in every city, and should not each city take care of its own? Similarly, I would argue, the collection for the Poor Ones was in support of something quite public: the Jerusalem community as eschatological ideal, with its paradigmatic lifestyle of communal sharing. Only something as important as that can account for the amount of space given to the collection. The references in Paul's letters are explicit and extensive. Those found in the Acts of the Apostles are once again problematic, however. Luke certainly knows traditions about the collection, but he either does not know what he has or he does not want to admit what he knows. He does not have a single explicit word about the collection, but he has several crucial references that can apply only to it. Here are the major texts (but notice that Luke makes sense only if you know what is happening from Paul):

Promise:	Gal. 2:10	
Collection:	1 Cor. 16:1–4; 2 Cor. 8–9	Acts 11:27–30
Delivery:	Rom. 15:30–31	Acts 20:4
Disaster:		Acts 21:17–26

The *promise* was made at the Jerusalem Council in Galatians 2:10. The *collection* was taken up in four Roman provinces: Galatia, Asia, Macedonia, and Achaia. Paul's plans for the collection involved two steps. First, each community would collect what it could every Sunday. Second, two accredited representatives would eventually accompany Paul to Jerusalem with each province's donation. Paul's fears for the outcome of the collection's delivery are poignantly clear as he writes to the Romans from Corinth in the winter of 55 to 56:

I appeal to you, brothers and sisters, by our Lord Jesus Christ and by the love of the Spirit, to join me in earnest prayer to God on my behalf, that I may be rescued from the unbelievers in Judea, and that my ministry to Jerusalem may be acceptable to the saints. (Romans 15:30–31)

There is a double danger in Jerusalem. Non-Christian Jews could consider Paul a traitor who had defamed God's Law by claiming that *neither* Jews *nor* pagans should observe it. Christian Jews could consider him at least a danger and possibly even a traitor as well. They could refuse to accept the collection as collusion with a position they did not accept. Luke, not Paul, tells us what happened:

James and all the elders . . . said to him, "You see, brother, how many thousands of believers there are among the Jews, and they are all zealous for the law. They have been told about you that you teach all the Jews living among the Gentiles to forsake Moses, and that you tell them not to circumcise their children or observe the customs. What then is to be done? They will certainly hear that you have come. So do what we tell you. We have four men who are under a vow. Join these men, go through the rite of purification with them, and pay for the shaving of their heads. Thus all will know that there is nothing in what they have been told about you, but that you yourself observe and guard the law." (Acts 21:17b–24)

Paul was told, I presume, that the collection would not be accepted unless he used some of it as James and the elders demanded. I am not sure how they formulated those conditions. According to the speech made by Luke, Paul would have been a hypocrite to have accepted the collection since he himself did not "observe and guard the law." But, as Luke tells the story, Diaspora Jews attacked Paul in the Temple for having brought a pagan inside the forbidden area; he was arrested, and executed four years later in Rome. No wonder Luke, if he knew about the collection, did not want to describe too clearly what had happened. Paul hoped it would hold together Christian Jews and pagan Jews on the level of charity rather than of theology. It did not do so, and it cost him his life.

My purpose in discussing the collection is to see if it casts any light on the Jerusalem community. It is certainly another indication that James and the Christian Jews in the Jerusalem community were Law-observant. God's Law was still binding on them as Christian Jews. But my point is that the Jerusalem community could not have expected such administrative "service for the saints" unless their lifestyle was somehow special, unless they could justify their title of the Poor Ones by a communal existence similar to that of an Essene encampment. Such communities lived God's Law fully and faithfully through sharing goods, possessions, and salaries according to whatever rules they adopted. And a common meal was both the powerful symbol and actual heart of that commonality.

The Jerusalem church was a share-community with a communal share-meal as its cultic center. It was also an apocalyptic community, and that explains why it was where it was—in Jerusalem and not, for example, still in Galilee. The imminent apocalyptic consummation would take place in Jerusalem; it would be there that Jesus would return. Finally, that commonality was mirrored in the ecstatic experience recorded in Acts 2:

> When the day of Pentecost had come, they were all together in one place. And suddenly from heaven there came a sound like the rush of a violent wind, and it filled the entire house where they were sitting. Divided tongues, as of fire, appeared among them, and a tongue rested on each of them. All of them were filled with the Holy Spirit and began to speak in other languages, as the Spirit gave them ability. (Acts 2:1–4)

Luke once again interprets against his data. That was not instant Berlitz, in which all began to speak unlearned foreign languages. It was "speaking in tongues," tongue-speaking rather than word-speaking—that is, prolonged and ecstatic utterances involving meaningless words. Participants, numbered at 120, were identified as both men and women in Acts 1:14–15. But notice that the Spirit came down on all alike—divided itself up, as it were, to fill all members equally so that they all responded in the same way, with a single voice of ecstatic non-speech. It was a Spirit that shared itself equally for a community supposed to do likewise.

PART X
Story and Tradition

[One] assumes that there was once an older historical report which was later supplemented with materials drawn from scriptural prophecy.... There are, however, serious objections to this hypothesis. Form, structure, and life situation of such a historical passion report and its transmission have never been clarified. The alternative is more convincing: In the beginning there was only the belief that Jesus' suffering, death, and burial, as well as his resurrection, happened "according to the Scriptures" (1 Cor 15:3–4). The very first narratives about Jesus' suffering and death would not have made the attempt to remember what actually happened. Rather, they would have found both the rationale and the content of Jesus' suffering and death in the memory of those passages in the Psalms and the Prophets which spoke about the suffering of the righteous.... [In] the teaching and preaching of the earliest Christian communities ... the passion of Jesus from the very beginning was probably never told without the framework of such scriptural reference.

Helmut Koester, "Apocryphal and Canonical Gospels," pp. 127–128

It is inconceivable that they [the Twelve] showed no concern about what happened to Jesus after the arrest. True, there is no Christian claim that they were present during the legal proceedings against him, Jewish or Roman; but it is absurd to think that some information was not available to them about why Jesus was hanged on a cross.... Thus from the earliest days available historical raw material could have been developed into a PN [passion narrative] extending from the arrest to the burial, no matter what form it might receive in the course of evangelistic use and how it might have been embellished and added to by Christian imagination. Some scholars, however, insist that the evangelistic enterprise means that Christians had no interest in historical raw material whether or not it was available.... The first followers of Jesus would have known many things about crucifixion in general and almost surely some of the details about Jesus' crucifixion, e.g., what kind of cross was employed. Nevertheless, what is preserved in the narrative is mostly what echoes Scripture (division of garments, offering of vinegary wine, final words of Jesus).

Raymond E. Brown, *The Death of the Messiah*, pp. 14–15

In Parts VII and VIII of this book the life and program of the historical Jesus was traced through the Common Sayings Tradition and into its separate redactions in the *Q Gospel* and the *Gospel of Thomas*. Those texts reflected primarily the voice of the itinerants, the prophetic radicals who cited Jesus' ways and words in

justification of their own lives. Their necessary correlatives were the householders, such as those in the *Didache,* who accepted the prophetic challenge but also
controlled its disruptive radicality. What is most striking throughout that entire
trajectory is its complete silence about the death and resurrection of Jesus. The
tradition studied in Parts IX and X, while emphatically interested in Jesus' death
and resurrection, is equally silent about his life and program. In Chapter 23 I
noted that the Common Meal Tradition links both those trajectories at a very
profound level, possibly even the most profound level. In Chapters 25 and 26 I
look at another profound linkage between those twin trajectories, now not with
regard to *meal* but with regard to *story.* It is not a story of Jesus' *individual* persecution and vindication, since that is present only in the passion-resurrection tradition. It is a story, in mythic hymn and biographical narrative, of *collective* persecution and *collective* vindication.

In this final Part X, the focus is on the *story* about the death and resurrection
of Jesus. There are always two aspects under discussion; separate but connected,
they must be studied in this order: *sources* and *origins.* The first question: What
dependent and independent *sources* do we have for this story of Jesus' death and
resurrection? The second question: What *origins* must be postulated to explain
the source relationships revealed? Those questions must be approached in that
order, because any conclusion on origins will be based on the answer on sources.
If, for example, Matthew, Mark, Luke, John, and the *Gospel of Peter* were identified as five independent sources for that story, origins would be interpreted in
one way. If, however, those five versions were all traced to a single line of
dependent and copied tradition, very different origins would have to be proposed. Furthermore, just as the *Gospel of Thomas* was crucial for an understanding of the tradition of Jesus' life, so the *Gospel of Peter* is crucial for the tradition of
Jesus' death. One is the fifth gospel for the Life Tradition; the other is the fifth
gospel for the Death Tradition.

Chapter 25 asks two questions. First, is there a *consecutively narrated* and
canonically independent account of the death and resurrection of Jesus now
embedded in the *Gospel of Peter?* That first italicized phrase—*consecutively narrated*—excludes random and disconnected units of tradition. It asks about a
sequential story with a beginning, middle, and end, with integrity as a text, identity as a genre, and depth as a theology. That second italicized phrase—*canonically independent*—excludes dependence on our present four canonical gospels.
(There is no presumption that such an account would thereby be historically
more accurate or theologically more profound than one or all of the canonicals.)
The second question is a far wider one: Where does such a story come from? Is
it, in my terms, *history remembered*—that is, a record, however adapted and developed, of what happened to Jesus such as a camera might have recorded were

such available at the time? Or is it, again in my terms, *prophecy historicized*—that is, the brute facts of execution made into story from a tissue of biblical texts, types, patterns, and models on all levels of the narrative?

Chapter 26 depends directly on the answers given to those two questions in the preceding chapter. If all is basically history remembered, then of course it inevitably appears as story. Not all story is history, but all history is story. One would *not* ask, in that understanding, Why is the passion-resurrection account a story? What else *could* it be? But if you understand it as prophecy historicized, then a new question presses hard on that interpretation: Why or how did it ever become such a story? What or who turned exegesis into narrative?

A few words about the two-part epigraph above. First, there are three contemporary North American scholars involved in those paragraphs: Brown, Koester, and myself. I intend here, as mentioned earlier, to continue the debate between those three authors throughout this Part X. I will underline where we disagree, especially where such disagreement is profound and intractable. But I want to see also whether there are any glimmers of agreement or any possibilities of understanding between our opposing opinions.

Second, beware the rhetoric of that second epigraph. The opening phrase of Raymond Brown's quotation—"showed no *concern*"—confuses the issue, which is not *concern* but *knowledge*. What did Jesus' companions *know* about the passion events? The issue is further confused when Brown (in text not included above) interweaves *concern* and *knowledge,* first denying that "the earliest followers of Jesus *knew or cared* nothing about what happened" (16) and then refusing to descend "into the nihilism of assuming that no writer *knew or cared* about anything that happened in Jesus' passion" (1361 note 20, my italics). It is not a question of care or of concern. It is a question of what Jesus' companions *knew* and, more important, what they needed to *express* in the passion-resurrection story. Furthermore, going back to the epigraph, the debate is not over *could* but over *did,* not over what *could* have happened but what, in one's best historical reconstruction, *did* happen.

Finally, in Chapters 25 and 26 my focus is always on the story of the passion and resurrection. By *story* I mean a consecutive narrative and not just a confessional statement. By passion *and* resurrection I mean a story that always includes both accusation *and* justification, danger *and* deliverance, persecution *and* vindication, defeat *and* triumph. Even if there were earlier stages when the emphasis was not on a crucified person resurrected by God, the story was always about an innocent one vindicated by God. It was never, never, never simply a passion story. Whenever, therefore, in these final chapters, I speak of the *story*, it is always an abbreviation for the passion-vindication story.

CHAPTER 25

THE OTHER PASSION-RESURRECTION STORY

[1] *GPet* . . . had a source besides Matt, namely, a more developed account of the guard at the tomb. (That point is also supported by the consecutiveness of the story in *GPet*.) The supplying of the centurion's name, the seven seals, the stone rolling off by itself, the account of the resurrection with the gigantic figures, the talking cross, the confession of Jesus as God's Son by the Jewish authorities, and their fear of their own people—all those elements could plausibly have been in the more developed form of the story known to the author of *GPet* and absent from the form known to Matt.

[2] *GPet* had [no] written Gospel before him, although he was familiar with Matt because he had read it carefully in the past and/or had heard it read several times in community worship on the Lord's Day, so that it gave the dominant shaping to his thought. Most likely he had heard people speak who were familiar with the Gospels of Luke and John—perhaps traveling preachers who rephrased salient stories—so that he knew some of their contents but had little idea of their structure. . . . I see no compelling reason to think that the author of *GPet* was directly influenced by Mark.
Raymond E. Brown, *The Death of the Messiah*, pp. 1307, 1334–1335

Raymond Brown is extremely clear on his source presuppositions for the passion-resurrection story. First, with regard to the three synoptic gospels: "Mark is the oldest of the Synoptic Gospels and . . . Matt and Luke drew the outline, substance, and much of the wording of their PNs [passion narratives] from Mark's" (1994:40). Second, with regard to the synoptics and John: "I shall work with the thesis that John wrote his PN [passion narrative] independently of Mark's" (1994:82). There are, in other words, two independent and consecutive written sources for the story, one in Mark and the other in John.

I agree with Brown on the synoptic gospels. That position, as he said, is "clearly the majority view among scholars" (1994:40). I explained that view in Chapter 8 as the first of my six major source presuppositions in this book. I disagree with him on his second position, however. There is now a split in scholarship about John's dependence on or independence from the synoptic gospels, and Brown and I come down on opposite sides of that debate. As I explained in that same Chapter 8, John's dependence on the synoptics for its passion-resurrection story is my third major source presupposition in this book. But the final source decision on the passion-resurrection story is the relationship of the extra-canonical *Gospel of Peter* to the intracanonical gospels. That will be my sixth major source presupposition in this book.

I focus, in this chapter, on the points where Brown and I come closest together on that relationship. I show Brown's position in the epigraph just above, numerically emphasizing its main components. We actually agree on two basic points. First, the *Gospel of Peter* is a late and composite document—that is, a second-century composition that includes both intracanonical and extracanonical sources. Second, the *Gospel of Peter* contains a consecutive and canonically independent source that constitutes about half its content. Once again, as always, and for everyone: wrong on sources, wrong on reconstructions.

Composite Document

[In the *Gospel of Peter*] old statements are suppressed, or wilfully perverted and displaced: new statements are introduced which bear their condemnation on their faces. Nothing is left as it was before. Here is "History as it should be": "Lines left out" of the old familiar records. And no one who will take the pains to compare sentence by sentence, word by word, the new "Lines left out" with the old "Line upon Line," will fail to return to the Four Gospels with a sense of relief at his escape from the stifling prison of prejudice into the transparent and the bracing atmosphere of pure simplicity and undesigning candour. . . . And so the new facts are just what they should be, if the Church's universal tradition as to the supreme and unique position of the Four Canonical Gospels is still to be sustained by historical criticism.

J. Armitage Robinson, "The Gospel According to Peter," pp. 31–32

One hundred years after that somewhat strident assessment of the *Gospel of Peter,* Brown gives a much more balanced summary: "*GPet* is a gospel reflecting popular Christianity, i.e., the Christianity of the ordinary people not in the major center of Antioch, where public reading and preaching would have exercised greater control, but in the smaller towns of Syria. . . . *GPet* was not heterodox, but it incorporated many imaginative elements that went beyond the canonical gospels. . . . [It] belatedly supplied us with a fascinating insight into how dramatically some ordinary Christians of the early 2nd cent. were portraying the death of the Messiah. Beneath the drama, in its own way *GPet* proclaimed that Jesus was the divine Lord, victor over all that his enemies could do to him by crucifixion" (1345–1348). What, in between those opposite reactions, is the *Gospel of Peter*?

It is not a necessary hypothesis, like the *Q Gospel*, but an extant text, like the *Gospel of Thomas*. It exists in the Codex Panopolitanus or Codex Cairensis 10759, a large fragment of sixty verses copied onto a parchment codex dated between the seventh and ninth centuries, which was discovered at ancient Panopolis in Egypt, and published separately in 1892 by Urbain Bouriant and Adolfe Lods. It also exists as Papyrus Oxyrhynchus 2949, two tiny scroll fragments of three verses dated to the late second or early third centuries, discovered at ancient Oxyrhynchus in Egypt, and published by R. A. Coles in 1972. Careful comparisons of both texts have been made by Dieter Lührmann (1981) and Jay Treat (1990). It is clear that there are differences in the common material between those two versions, but fewer than, for instance, in the common material between the Greek and Coptic versions of the *Gospel of Thomas* or the Greek and Coptic versions of the *Didache*. In all cases, we have to work, however tentatively and hypothetically, with what we have available.

The larger text was already fragmentary even when copied along with other texts into a pocket-book for eternity buried in the grave of a Christian monk. It begins in the middle of Jesus' trial and ends at the start of what might be a risen apparition at the Sea of Galilee. Since that broken-off ending mentions "I, Simon Peter," the document has been equated by scholars with that against which Bishop Serapion of Antioch wrote his treatise on *The So-Called Gospel of Peter* in the last decade of the second century. Eusebius of Caesarea says that Serapion "wrote to refute the lies in that document, which had induced some members of the Christian community at Rhossus to go astray into heterodox teachings." But he then cites a long paragraph from Serapion that indicates a somewhat more ambiguous judgment (Williamson 252):

> I have been able to go through the book and draw the conclusion that while most of it accorded with the authentic teaching of the Saviour, some passages were spurious additions. (*History of the Church* 6.12)

Ambiguity, one could say, was destined to stalk this text from its first notation, and Serapion's ambivalence still hangs over it like a cloud. Scholars even have a distinctive way of citing it: by chapter and verse, yes—but, unlike canonical citations, the verses continue across chapters. We have, for example, *Gospel of Peter* 8:28–33 followed by 9:34–37 followed by 10:38–42, and so on.

Since its publication in 1892, the first and narrower scholarly question has been the relationship between the *Gospel of Peter* and the canonical gospels. But there is also a second and wider question. What was the redactional purpose of the author? No matter how one answers the first question, the second must also be addressed. If, for example, it was a later condensed version of the canonical versions, what is the logic of its conflation: why was this omitted, this changed, and this added; what is the compositional intention of the final product?

How have scholars answered that first question across the last one hundred years? Individuals have advocated each one of the three logically possible positions. First, the *Gospel of Peter* is canonically dependent. Second, the *Gospel of Peter* is both canonically dependent and canonically independent—that is, it contains both intracanonical and extracanonical traditions. Third, the *Gospel of Peter* is canonically independent. I underline that triple response because it is often summarized as only a double one of dependence or independence. Actually, those first two options were there right from the start. The third option arrived much later.

First, the *Gospel of Peter* is canonically dependent. That is the position of the Cambridge scholar J. Armitage Robinson, quoted in the epigraph above. His "lecture on the 'Gospel according to Peter' was given in the Hall of Christ's College on the 20th of November, three days after the text was first seen in Cambridge," and the Preface of its published version was dated December 1—all in 1892, the very same year that Bouriant and Lods published the preliminary transcription of the newly discovered text (7–8). Robinson decided on "the unmistakable acquaintance of the author with our Four Evangelists. . . . He uses and misuses each in turn. . . . He uses our Greek Gospels; there is no proof (though the possibility of course is always open) that he knew of any Gospel record other than these" (32–33).

Second, the *Gospel of Peter* is both canonically dependent and canonically independent. It conflates both intracanonical and extracanonical traditions. I entitled this section "Composite Document" to emphasize that second option. The position was staked out (almost as speedily as the first) by the Berlin professor Adolf von Harnack. His addresses on the *Gospel of Peter* to the Prussian Academy of Sciences were given on November 3 and 10, and his book's Preface has a publication date of December 15—again in 1892. First, von Harnack concludes that the *Gospel of Peter* contains data from the intracanonical gospels, but it is unclear from his comments whether such data were obtained by direct literary borrowing, by indirect oral knowledge, or simply by the use of common traditions. He concludes, second, that the relationship with Mark is most probable, that with Matthew is less probable, and the order of declining probability continues with Luke and then John or even John and then Luke. Third, he claims that the text also contains independent traditions that "should not be collectively dismissed even over against their intracanonical counterparts" (47). It was Robinson who divided the document into fourteen mini-chapters and Harnack who divided it into sixty verses. Every time we cite the text we combine their separate divisions and recall that inaugural division of opinion about it.

Third, the *Gospel of Peter* is canonically independent. Over thirty years after

THE OTHER PASSION-RESURRECTION STORY ✛ 485

Robinson's trenchant dismissal of the gospel's value, Percival Gardner-Smith's comments were just as biting. "A book so absurd and fantastic seems unworthy of serious attention" (1925–1926a:255). The author of that gospel, noted Gardner-Smith, "had many faults, he was credulous, muddle-headed, incompetent, and possibly heretical" (1925–1926b:407). Nevertheless, despite those criticisms, Gardner-Smith's two articles argued that "the strength of the evidence for the dependence of 'Peter' upon the canonical gospels has been greatly overestimated, and on the other hand, not enough has been made of the independent features of the Petrine narrative which are very difficult to explain on the hypothesis of literary dependence" (1925–1926a:270). He concluded that the *Gospel of Peter* "did not know the work of Matthew, Mark, Luke, and John" but that Peter and they worked from "the floating traditions with which they were familiar and made of them the best narratives they could" (1925–1926a:270). With that contention, all three possible positions are in place. And I emphasize, once again, that there are *three* such positions, not just the usually highlighted first and third.

There are *three* positions, to be sure, but the first position has always been the dominant or majority viewpoint. The *first* option, dependence, appears in older commentaries (from Swete in 1893 through Vaganay in 1930 to Mara in 1973) and in more recent review articles (from Green in 1987 and Neirynck in 1991 through Charlesworth and Evans in 1994 to Kirk in 1994 and Van Voorst in 1995). The *third* option, independence, is clearly a minority opinion. It appears especially from Denker in 1975 through Koester in 1980a and 1990a (and his students, Johnson in 1965 and Hutton in 1970) to Dewey in 1989, 1990, and 1995. The *second* option, conflation of dependence and independence, is a minority amid a minority opinion. Why, then, do I even bother arguing it against such a strong opposing majority? Put another way, what would persuade me that the first, majority option is correct? What would falsify the second or third options for me?

My answer is simple. This would persuade me: any adequate explanation of how an author got from one or more of the canonical gospels to the *Gospel of Peter* as now extant. Why and how was it actually composed? You will recall from Chapter 8 that genetic relationship and redactional confirmation are the criteria normally used for arguing a source. First, do you find canonical DNA present in the *Gospel of Peter*? I myself answer yes to that question, but I see genetic evidence in only certain parts of it. Second, what about all the *rest*? What is the redactional purpose or editorial intention of the *whole*?

Two possible redactional explanations are, for example, the vagaries of memory and/or the needs of theology. The former solution, redaction by memory (discussed earlier in Chapters 2 and 8), is Brown's answer. My objection is still the same. Even bad memory has its logic, so why does the *Gospel of Peter* come out the way it does? Why, especially, does it remember so much material that was never canonically present in the first place? The latter solution, redaction by theology, has two main possibilities. One is Docetism, the desire to diminish the reality of Jesus' bodily existence, a problem you will recall from Chapter 2. But, if that was the plan, it was, as Jerry McCant has shown, a rather dismal failure. Another and much more plausible intention is anti-Judaism. In other words, the *Gospel of Peter* may omit, conflate, and expand the canonical gospels to increase the attack on some other Jews or even on all other Jews except those for whom it was written. I leave that possible intention aside for now but will return to it in detail below.

In books published in 1988 and 1995, I argued three connected but separable points about the *Gospel of Peter*. I give them in what I consider the ascending order of historical and theological importance. First, the *Gospel of Peter* is a careful combination of two passion-resurrection stories, an extracanonical one (where Jesus was buried by his *enemies,* to whom he later appeared) and an intracanonical one (where he was buried by his *friends,* to whom he later appeared). Second, that extracanonical or enemies-version is consistently older than the intracanonical or friends-version and was used as its source. Third, that basic passion-resurrection story was not history remembered but prophecy historicized, a distinction to be explained further below. I called that extracanonical or enemies-version the *Cross Gospel,* to emphasize that it was an earlier source and not equivalent to the fuller and later *Gospel of Peter* itself. The name is unimportant; call it anything you want for purposes of discussion or even dismissal.

That theory was greeted, I think it fair to say, with almost universal rejection. I have read all the counterarguments but, at the end, the *Gospel of Peter* is still there and still not adequately explained. It is similar to the problem with the *Didache*. Parts have been argued very plausibly in either direction: this or that unit is dependent or independent of the canonical gospels. But at the end the question of the *whole* still presses. What is the overall redactional purpose of the document as a complete entity with its own integrity?

I do not withdraw any of those three major points, nor will I do so unless somebody comes up with a better interpretation of the *Gospel of Peter*'s redactional intention, compositional logic, and authorial purpose. But those three points can clearly be separated, and that is what I want to do here. Looking *only* at that first point, and presuming the arguments given in those 1988 and 1995 books, I seek to extend rather than repeat them. I ask, therefore, a single question: Granted intracanonical sources in the *Gospel of Peter,* is there also a consecutive, independent, extracanonical source there as well? I am not talking about random oral traditions or scattered written fragments, but a consecutive, narrative source. That is the rock-bottom first step in my overall proposal, and I want to discover if any consensus is possible on just that point alone. I leave aside for now any overall theory, to ask only that single, preliminary question. Does the *Cross Gospel,* by whatever name, exist within the present *Gospel of Peter*? I have at the moment, therefore, a very limited object. I begin with how Brown and I agree and disagree on that single question.

Independent Source

Brown . . . comes close to Crossan's *Cross Gospel* in his approach to the guard-at-the-sepulcher story [in *Gospel of Peter* 8:28–11:49]: the author knew an independent form of this long story, and a less developed pre-Matthean form of the same story is preserved in the Gospel of Matthew.

Frans Neirynck, "The Historical Jesus: Reflections on an Inventory," p. 229

Regarding Brown's hypothesis [about that independent form of the guard-at-the-sepulcher story], Crossan's reply makes sense: "there could never have been such an independent story without some preceding account of condemnation and crucifixion."

Frans Neirynck, review of *Who Killed Jesus?* p. 456

Neirynck disagrees completely with my theory on the *Gospel of Peter* (1989), but he concedes the two points mentioned in those epigraphs (1994a; 1995b). Those two points form the core of the following discussion. But since the term "guard-at-the-sepulcher story" may be a somewhat minimal title, here is that full narrative. It involves two of the three acts in my proposed *Cross Gospel* and twenty-two out of the sixty verses in the extant *Gospel of Peter.* We are not, in other words, talking about a tiny segment but a large section with a very awkward opening sentence (*NTA* 1.224–225, slightly modified and italics added):

8:28But the scribes and pharisees and elders, being assembled together and hearing that all the people were murmuring and beating their breasts, saying, "If at his death these exceeding great signs have come to pass, behold how righteous he was!", 8:29The elders were afraid and came to Pilate, entreating him and saying, 8:30"Give us soldiers that we may watch his sepulchre for three days, lest his disciples come and steal him away and the people suppose that he is risen from the dead, and do us harm." 8:31And Pilate gave them Petronius the centurion with soldiers to watch the sepulchre. And with them there came elders and scribes to the sepulchre. 8:32And all who were there, together with the centurion and the soldiers, rolled thither a great stone and laid it against the entrance to the sepulchre and 8:33put on it seven seals, pitched a tent and kept watch.

9:34Early in the morning, when the sabbath dawned, there came a crowd from Jerusalem and the country round about to see the sepulchre that had been sealed. 9:35Now in the night in which the Lord's day dawned, when the soldiers, two by two in every watch, were keeping guard, there rang out a loud voice in heaven, 9:36and they saw the heavens opened and two men come down from there in a great brightness and draw nigh to the sepulchre. 9:37That stone which had been laid against the entrance to the sepulchre started of itself to roll and give way to the side, and the sepulchre was opened, and both the young men entered in.

10:38When now those soldiers saw this, they awakened the centurion and the elders—for they also were there to assist at the watch. 10:39And while they were relating what they had seen, they saw again three men come out from the sepulchre, and two of them sustaining the other and a cross following them, 10:40and the heads of the two reaching to heaven, but that of him who was led of them by the hand overpassing the heavens. 10:41And they heard a voice out of the heavens crying, "Have you preached to them that sleep?" 10:42and from the cross there was heard the answer, "Yea."

11:43Those men therefore took counsel with one another to go and report this to Pilate. 11:44*And while they were still deliberating, the heavens were again seen to open, and a man descended and entered the sepulchre.* 11:45When those who were of the centurion's company saw this, they hastened by night to Pilate, abandoning the sepulchre which they were guarding, and reported everything they had seen, being full of disquietude and saying, "In truth he was the Son of God." 11:46Pilate answered and said, "I am clean from the blood of the Son of God, upon such a thing have you decided." 11:47Then all came to him, beseeching him and urgently calling upon him to command the centurion and the soldiers to tell no one what they had seen. 11:48"For it is better for us," they said, "to make ourselves guilty of the greatest sin before God than to fall into the hands of the people of the Jews and be stoned." 11:49Pilate therefore commanded the centurion and the soldiers to say nothing. (*Gospel of Peter* 8:28–11:49)

A few words of explanation before continuing. That story describes the actual resurrection itself and not just consequent apparitions. First of all, those "sustaining" angels are not simply helping an incapacitated Jesus, as I thought before Kathleen Corley drew my attention to a discussion by Josef Jungmann (131). They are, as in the protocols of Eastern court ceremonials, attending him on either side, his hands resting on their extended arms. "Sustaining" is what Naaman the Syrian did for his king as that monarch entered the Temple of Rimmon to worship "leaning on [Naaman's] arm" in 2 Kings 5:18. And, after Constantine, that privilege was extended to bishops and popes during High Mass. The two angels, then, are described as "sustaining him." Jesus is an imperial king entering into his kingdom. And since it is resurrection-ascension that is being described, his stature reaches from earth to heaven. Second, what about that "talking" cross? This is not an individual but a communal resurrection-ascension. As in 1 Corinthians 15:20, Jesus is "the first fruits of those who have died (*literally:* them that sleep)." Jesus died to invade Hades and free "those who sleep" from the power of death. Those are the holy ones who died before him, and they must rise with him. Since they too have suffered for their faith, they are imagined as a great cruciform procession coming out behind him. God asks Jesus whether he has "preached" to them, and they reply that he has indeed done so. That translation "preached" is very misleading. It makes you wonder, Preached *what?* The Greek verb means "announce" or "proclaim," and what Jesus announced or proclaimed was liberation from death. *It was a proclamation that effected what it announced.* That scene is, of course, serenely mythological. It is also theologically profound and communally beautiful. It was created by *Christian Jews* who cared about the past of their people and who could not imagine or celebrate a resurrection that left their past behind in the dust. That belief would hang on by its fingernails in the Christian creed ("He descended into hell"), but our lack of enthusiasm for it merits an examination of conscience. The problem is not that it is mythological. Of course it is. The problem is that we do not like its meaning. With all that as background, I now pursue the debate across five propositions, each one building on the preceding one.

The first proposition is that Brown and I agree on a consecutive and canonically independent source in *Gospel of Peter* 8:28–11:49. Neirynck is both perceptive and correct on that point. Here, in confirmation, are several assertions of that position from Brown's *The Death of the Messiah*, each a little more detailed than the preceding one. Notice the keys terms, "consecutive" and "independent," in these citations. "The author of *GPet* drew not only on Matt but on an independent form of the guard-at-the-sepulcher story" (1287). Again: "The author of *GPet* may well have known Matt's account of the guard (a judgment based on his use of Matthean vocabulary), but a plausible scenario is that he also knew a consecutive form of the story and gave preference to that" (1301 note 35). And again: "Matt broke up a consecutive guard-at-the-sepulcher story to interweave it with the women-at-the-tomb story [from Mark], while *GPet* preserved the original consecutive form of the guard story" (1305–1306). Finally, and most completely: "*GPet* . . . had a source besides Matt, namely, a more developed account of the guard at the tomb. (That point is also supported by the consecutiveness of the story in *GPet*.) The supplying of the centurion's name, the seven seals, the stone rolling off by itself, the account of the resurrection with the gigantic figures, the talking cross, the confession of Jesus as God's Son by the Jewish authorities, and their fear of their own people—all those elements could plausibly have been in the more developed form of the story known to the author of *GPet* and absent from the form known to Matt" (1307). We are not, I emphasize, dealing with random nuggets of tradition but with a sequential story involving about a third of the extant *Gospel of Peter*.

The second proposition is that Brown and I also agree on the redactional function of *Gospel of Peter* 11:44. We agree, as just seen, that all of 8:28–11:49—the whole guard-at-the-sepulcher story, twenty-two out of sixty verses in the *Gospel of Peter*—is derived from a consecutive and canonically independent source. But we also agree on 12:50–13:57, the women-at-the-sepulcher story that follows immediately after the guard-at-the-sepulcher story. We agree that it is derived from the canonical gospels. I think, more specifically, that it is from Mark and John, because the *redactional* "young man" from Mark 16:5 is in *Gospel of Peter* 13:55 and the redactional "fear of the Jews" from John 20:19 is in *Gospel of Peter* 12:50, 52, 54. Brown thinks, more generally, that it "has many similarities to the canonical forms and could represent simply an imaginative retelling of memories from them" (1994:1306 note 47). But that minor divergence can be left aside for here and now.

But we also agree, as stated in my second proposition, about *Gospel of Peter* 11:44, which I italicized above. (I would include 11:43 as well, but that is not important here.) That "man" plays no part in the rest of the guard-at-the-sepulcher story in 8:28–11:49. What, then, is the function of that verse? Brown's answer is that "in order to join it [the guard-at-the-sepulcher story] to the women-at-the-tomb story, the author of *GPet* had to make one adaptation: the awkward second angelic descent from heaven in 11:44. The two angelic males of the first descent (9:36) belonged to the guard story, but they left the tomb supporting Jesus. As we know from all the canonical gospels, the women story that the *GPet* author was about to tell required angelic presence at the empty tomb when the women arrived (see *GPet* 13:55); and so he had to have another angelic man come down" (1994:1301 note 35). I had noted earlier that the "Arrival of Youth in 11:43–44 as preparation for Women and Youth in 12:50–13:57" was a style of redactional preparation that the author used whenever extracanonical and intracanonical materials were being integrated together (1988:21). We are, then, in agreement on at least this one case.

The third proposition is that *Gospel of Peter* 8:28–11:49 could never have existed without some prior unit about the death of Jesus. It tells about burial and resurrection, but such a story could never have existed without some explanation of why and how the buried person got to that fate. I make that proposition minimally. Trial or trials, mockery or scourging, specific condemnation or detailed execution are maximal. But *something* about the death had to precede that burial in any imaginable consecutive passion-resurrection source.

The fourth proposition is that the necessary account of Jesus' death preceding 8:28–11:49 must also have contained some explanation of why his tomb needed guarding by *both* Roman and Jewish authorities. The guarding of the tomb is essential to the story in *Gospel of Peter* 8:28–11:49. If you were to take it out, there would be no story or, to put it another way, there would have to be a completely different story. Without those guards, there would be nobody to witness the actual resurrection, hear about the descent into Hades, see the resurrected dead, or report to Pilate; there would be no Roman authorities to confess Jesus or Jewish authorities to deny him. Why, then, did a condemned criminal's tomb *need* such careful guarding? The answer must have been present in the prior account of the crucifixion.

The fifth proposition is that such a death story detailing why the tomb needed guarding is now present in the preceding *Gospel of Peter* 1:1–6:22. You *could* concede the third and fourth propositions but deny this fifth one. Maybe that unit explaining how Jesus died and why his tomb needed guarding was once in the source but is now lost forever. That is possible, but I find the alternative much more probable. That account of why Jesus died and why the tomb was guarded is still right there in the *Gospel of Peter* itself. Here is that preceding section (*NTA* 1:223–224, slightly modified and italics added):

1:1But of the Jews none washed their hands, neither Herod nor any one of his judges. And as they would not wash, Pilate arose. 1:2And then Herod the king commanded that the Lord should be marched off, saying to them, "What I have commanded you to do to him, do you."

2:3*Now there stood there Joseph, the friend of Pilate and of the Lord, and knowing that they were about to crucify him he came to Pilate and begged the body of the Lord for burial.* 2:4*And Pilate sent to Herod and begged his body.* 2:5a*And Herod said, "Brother Pilate, even if no one had begged him, we should bury him, since the Sabbath is drawing on. For it stands written in the law: the sun should not set on one that has been put to death."* 2:5bAnd he delivered him to the people on the day before the unleavened bread, their feast.

3:6So they took the Lord and pushed him in great haste and said, "Let us hale the Son of God now that we have gotten power over him." 3:7And they put upon him a purple robe and set him on the judgment seat and said, "Judge righteously, O King of Israel!" 3:8And one of them brought a crown of thorns and put it on the Lord's head. 3:9And others who stood by spat on his face, and others buffeted him on the cheeks, others nudged him with a reed, and some scourged him, saying, "With such honour let us honour the Son of God."

4:10And they brought two malefactors and crucified the Lord in the midst between them. But he held his peace, as if he felt no pain. 4:11And when they had set up the cross, they wrote upon it: This is the King of Israel. 4:12And they laid down his garments before him and divided them among themselves

and cast the lot upon them. 4:13But one of the malefactors rebuked them, saying, "We have landed in suffering for the deeds of wickedness which we have
committed, but this man, who has become the saviour of men, what wrong
has he done you?" 4:14And they were wroth with him and commanded that
his legs should not be broken, so that he might die in torments.

5:15Now it was midday and a darkness covered all Judaea. And they
became anxious and uneasy lest the sun had already set, since he was still
alive. [For] it stands written for them: the sun should not set on one that has
been put to death. 5:16And one of them said, "Give him to drink gall with
vinegar." And they mixed it and gave him to drink. 5:17And they fulfilled all
things and completed the measure of their sins on their head. 5:18And many
went about with lamps, since they supposed that it was night, [and] they
stumbled. 5:19And the Lord called out and cried, "My power, O power, you
have forsaken me!" And having said this he was taken up. 5:20And at the
same hour the veil of the temple in Jerusalem was rent in two.

6:21And then they drew the nails from the hands of the Lord and laid him
on the earth. And the whole earth shook and there came a great fear.
6:22Then the sun shone (again), and it was found to be the ninth hour. (*Gospel
of Peter* 1:1–6:22)

Two comments on that unit. First, it is exactly the story needed to explain
how Jesus died and why his tomb needed guarding. The Romans have nothing at
all to do with the condemnation or crucifixion. It is done under Herod's command
in 1:2 but by "the people" in 2:5b. After the miraculous death signs, however, there
is a breach between "all the people" and the Jewish authorities in 8:28. That results
in the latter's fear that, if the disciples manage to revive Jesus' body, people might
"suppose that he is risen from the dead and do us harm" in 8:30. So the tomb is
guarded, Roman and Jewish authorities see the actual resurrection, and the latter
plead for a cover-up lest "they fall into the hands of the people of the Jews and be
stoned" in 11:48. There may be, I repeat, another and now completely lost first part
of that consecutive and independent source in *Gospel of Peter* 8:28–11:49, but the
most economical solution is that it is *Gospel of Peter* 1:1–6:22.

My second comment concerns that section in 2:3–5a italicized above. It is
exactly the same redactional device seen earlier in 11:44 about whose function
Brown and I agreed. There it served as an authorial preparation for joining the
extracanonical guards-at-the-tomb story with the intracanonical women-at-the-
tomb story. Here it serves as an authorial preparation for joining the extracanonical
Herod-in-charge and burial-by-enemies story with the intracanonical Pilate-in-
charge and burial-by-friends story. That extracanonical source in 1:1–2 and 2:5b–6:22
had the Jewish authorities burying Jesus out of obedience to Deuteronomy
21:22–23, which forbids crucified bodies on crosses overnight. That intracanonical

source follows immediately after 1:1–6:22 in 6:23–24 as the account of Jesus' burial by Joseph of Arimathea, which is canonically derivative (because the "linen" from Mark 15:46 = Matthew 27:59 = Luke 23:53 is in *Gospel of Peter* 6:24a and the "garden" from John 20:41 is in *Gospel of Peter* 6:24b). Here are the parallel redactional devices:

Consecutive extracanonical source:	1–2 and 2:5b–6:22	8:28–11:42 and 11:45–49
Preparatory redactional linkage:	2:2–5a	11:43–44
Consecutive intracanonical source:	6:23–24	12:50–13:5

I argue, therefore, for the same redactional hand and same authorial purpose behind both those complexes.

My own proposed *Cross Gospel* source (by whatever name) involved a three-act drama: The first act is the Crucifixion and Deposition in 1:1–2 and 2:5b–6:22. The second act is the Tomb and Guards in 7:25 and 8:28–9:34. The third act is the Resurrection and Confession in 9:35–10:42 and 11:45–49. Brown has accepted the last two of those acts, and must presume some initial first act (which I claim is most economically present right there in the *Gospel of Peter* itself).

Anti-Jewish Text

The people as a whole *[pas ho laos]* answered, "His blood be on us and on our children!"

Matthew 27:25

When the centurion saw what had taken place, he praised God and said, "Certainly this man was innocent *[dikaios]*." And when all the crowds who had gathered there for this spectacle saw what had taken place, they returned home, beating their breasts *[ta stēthē hypestrephon]*.

Luke 23:47–48

All the people *[ho laos hapas]* were murmuring and beating their breasts *[koptetai ta stēthē]*, saying, "If at his death these exceeding great signs have come to pass, behold how righteous *[dikaios]* he was!"

Gospel of Peter 8:28

I return now to a point mentioned above but postponed until now. Is that proposed source within the *Gospel of Peter* (which I call the *Cross Gospel* for easy reference) intensely anti-Jewish? That is asserted repeatedly in the scholarly literature, although it is seldom clear whether "anti-Jewish" means Christian pagans who are against Jews or Christian Jews who are against all other Jews except themselves. I think myself that "anti-Jewish" should be used only when speaking of pagans or ex-Jews who attack or oppose Judaism. I will use the term "anti-Jewish" here, however, because others do so and I have to discuss their claims. But what exactly *is* the proper term for a statement such as this from Paul to his Thessalonian converts?

> For you, brothers and sisters, became imitators of the churches of God in Christ Jesus that are in Judea, for you suffered the same things from your own compatriots as they did from the Jews, who killed both the Lord Jesus and the prophets, and drove us out; they displease God and oppose everyone by hindering us from speaking to the Gentiles so that they may be saved. Thus they have constantly been filling up the measure of their sins; but God's wrath has overtaken them at last. (1 Thessalonians 2:14–16)

Both persecutors *and* persecuted in Thessalonica are Thessalonians. Both persecutors and persecuted in Judaea were Jews. Paul is surely not "anti-Jewish" or even "anti-Judean"; but, even though "the churches of God in Christ Jesus that are in Judea" included Judaean Jews, Paul uses the term "Jews" in a sweeping and indiscriminate manner. "Jews" comes to mean all those other bad Jews except us (few?) good ones. Be that as it may, I return to the claim that the *Gospel of Peter* is intensely more anti-Jewish than the canonical gospels, especially where that claim is an explanation for its redactional content and authorial intention. Three examples will suffice.

SADISTS AND HYPOCRITES

The first example is from an article by Alan Kirk. He proposes that the *Gospel of Peter reads* rather than *remembers* the canonical gospels and changes, adds, or omits from them for "special religious concerns" that "have coerced the narrative in its own distinctive directions" (574). Or again: "The author was driven by special concerns and tendencies which guided the production of the narrative and led to the reshaping of the Lukan (and Matthean, Markan, and Johannine) material" (577). Those concerns, directions, and tendencies were to increase the anti-Jewishness of the story. Thus, in the story of the good thief, the author is "driven by an anti-Jewish *Tendenz*. . . . [T]he intention was to focus on the evil actions of the Jews . . . to focus the narrative upon the 'villainous Jews'" (578 and note 23); it is "sadistic, hard-hearted Jews who inhabit the narrative" (582). And, in the story of the non-breaking of Jesus' legs, the author "is interested in putting the Jews in as bad a light as possible" so that "the Jews are depicted as the cruel torturers and murderers of Jesus and as dour legalists" (582). That, if it works, is a complete redactional explanation of the *Gospel of Peter*. The author reads "the texts of the New Testament gospels" (574) and conflates them selectively for greater anti-Jewishness.

The second example is from *The Death of the Messiah* once again. For Brown, the *Gospel of Peter* is more anti-Jewish than any of the canonical gospels, a feature that indicates that it is later than they are, is popular rather than official, and is also heterodox rather than orthodox. Here are a few representative examples: "In the later *GPet*, where one finds a popularization freer from the controls of the standardized preaching and teaching discernible in much of Matt, the antiJewish feeling is even more unnuanced" (63). Again: "This work . . . is sharply more antiJewish than the canonical Gospels" (834). And again: "The antiJewish sentiment . . . is much more prominent in *GPet* than in the canonical Gospels" (1065). Finally: "I would hope that today Christians would recognize another heterodox tendency in *GPet*: its intensified antiJewish depictions" (1347 note 62).

The third example is from a doctoral dissertation by Susan Schaeffer. She finds the anti-Jewish tone even more virulent than does Brown. This is very important, because that tone determines for her the document's function and setting in the second century. Here are a few examples. (Notice especially the final one.) "The Jews are revealed as cruel, murderous, hypocritical, and stupid" (1991a:226). Again: "[T]he *GosPet*'s portrait of the Jews is scathing. They are depicted as being sadistic, foolish, and hypocritical" (244). Finally: "The *GosPet* also implies that the Jewish leaders themselves might have believed in the resurrection but that they are afraid of being stoned by the Jews (11:49), that is by those who have not become apostates [Christians]. . . . In their last official act in the gospel (as far as we know it), the Jewish leaders seem weak and almost pitiable. In the background, behind their actions, stands a murderous, faceless force of apostate-hating Jews. If actual persecution is in the background, the *GosPet* could have come from the post-Bar Cochba period, ca. 135–140 C.E." (254–255).

JEWISH AUTHORITY AGAINST JEWISH PEOPLE

I have two basic arguments against those assertions of increased anti-Jewishness in the *Gospel of Peter*. My first argument is that they are flatly wrong. Focus, for example, on the three acts in that consecutive source I call the *Cross Gospel* in the text given above:

Act 1:	Crucifixion and Deposition	=	*Gos. Pet.* 1:1–2 and 2:5b–6:22
Act 2:	Tomb and Guards	=	*Gos. Pet.* 7:25 and 8:28–9:34
Act 3:	Resurrection and Confession	=	*Gos. Pet.* 9:35–10:42 and 11:45–49

In Act 1 it is "the Jews" and not the Romans who condemn Jesus, it is Herod not Pilate who is in charge of the crucifixion, and it is "the (Jewish) people" not the Roman soldiers who abuse and execute him. Only here is Pilate fully innocent and capable of true hand-washing, a gesture somewhat hypocritical in

Matthew's account, where he supplies the executioners. So far claims of increased anti-Jewishness *and* increased pro-Romanism seem absolutely correct. And if the story stopped at that point, the *Gospel of Peter* would certainly be the most anti-Jewish of the five passion accounts. It is the Jewish "people," after all, who directly crucify Jesus!

But then, at the start of Act 2, something very strange happens—something that must be read within the unfolding narrative development. Without that "popular" crucifixion, this second step would not have happened. The marvelous signs at the death of Jesus result in this reaction:

> Then the Jews and the elders and the priests, perceiving what great evil they had done to themselves, began to lament and to say, "Woe on our sins, the judgment and the end of Jerusalem is drawn nigh." (*Gospel of Peter* 7:25)

At this point *all participants* recognize that they have done something evil. But, as Act 2 continues, that acknowledgment begets a split between Jewish *authorities* and Jewish *people*. The *authorities* know they have done wrong, know that they will be punished; but, far from being repentant, they seek guards from Pilate for Jesus' tomb lest the *people* harm them (in, as noted, a very awkward sentence):

> But the scribes and Pharisees and elders, being assembled together and hearing that all the people were murmuring and beating their breasts, saying, "If at his death these exceeding great signs have come to pass, behold how righteous he was!"—The elders were afraid and came to Pilate, entreating him and saying, "Give us soldiers that we may watch his sepulchre for three days, lest his disciples come and steal him away and the people suppose that he is risen from the dead, and do us harm." (*Gospel of Peter* 8:28–30)

Notice, by the way, the logic of their position. Why "for three days"? I agree with Brown's interpretation: "In the *GPet* storyline the wish to safeguard the burial place 'for three days' (8:30) need imply only that after such a period the imposter would surely be dead" (1994:1309 note 55). Recall this different version:

> The chief priests and the Pharisees gathered before Pilate and said, "Sir, we remember what that impostor said while he was still alive, 'After three days I will rise again.' Therefore command the tomb to be made secure until the third day; otherwise his disciples may go and steal him away, and tell the people, 'He has been raised from the dead,' and the last deception would be worse than the first." (Matthew 27:62b–64)

Only in Matthean redaction at Matthew 12:38–40 have the authorities heard Jesus' three-day resurrection prophecy—a development that allows a quite different logic. There a three-day watch is necessary lest the disciples steal the corpse and "tell the people" a lie about resurrection. In *Gospel of Peter* 8:30 the problem is quite different. Only after three days—that is, on the fourth day, as with Lazarus in John 11:17—is someone surely and certainly dead. Guards are needed until that point of possible resuscitation is securely past. If the disciples were to resuscitate Jesus (or so it goes in the minds of the authorities), the people, in their present state of mind, might assume resurrection. They would not even need to be told by the disciples! Because of the repenting people, then, the Jewish authorities enlist Roman help in guarding the tomb.

A crucial distinction is now established between Jewish *authorities* and Jewish *people,* and this distinction reaches a climax in Act 3. Both Roman and Jewish authorities are actually at the tomb and witness the resurrection of Jesus. The Roman authorities confess Jesus, but the Jewish *authorities* conspire with Pilate to deceive their own *people:*

> Then all came to him, beseeching him [Pilate] and urgently calling upon him to command the centurion and the soldiers to tell no one what they had seen. "For it is better for us," they said, "to make ourselves guilty of the greatest sin before God than to fall into the hands of the people of the Jews and be stoned." Pilate therefore commanded the centurion and the soldiers to say nothing. (*Gospel of Peter* 11:47–49)

A story must be read in its narrative entirety, from "the people" in 2:5b through "all the people" in 8:28 and into "the people of the Jews" in 11:48. The result of this *consecutive* account is, first, to make "the people" extremely guilty; next, to make them extremely repentant; and, last, to make them extremely dangerous to their own authorities. I reject categorically Schaeffer's interpretation of that last cited unit. She claims that the Jewish authorities are afraid to acknowledge the resurrection lest their own people stone them for becoming, as it were, Christian apostates. That is profoundly wrong and reads the text against its own narrative logic. The *Jewish authorities* actually believe in the resurrection, because they witness it. But they decide to commit the terrible sin (which they admit is such) of not announcing that triumph lest the *Jewish people* stone their own authorities for leading them astray over Jesus' crucifixion.

My reading of the *Gospel of Peter,* therefore, is that it is more anti-Jewish with regard to the *authorities* than any of the canonical gospels but also more pro-Jewish with regard to the *people* than any of them. I do not, of course, take that as straightforward history. It is religious polemics and theological apologetics.

Still, it confirms that anti-Jewishness is not an adequate explanation of the *Gospel of Peter's* redactional purpose.

Let me repeat the narrative core of that account, which sets Jewish people and Jewish authorities in opposition to one another. It is not simply a matter of onlookers repenting, as in my epigraph from Luke 23:47. *It is a story about the Jewish authorities knowing the truth of Jesus' resurrection and lying to protect themselves from their own people, who are dangerously ready to believe such an event.* Narrative logic holds closely to that basic theme. The authorities lead the people into crucifying Jesus. All see the death miracles and recognize what they have done. The people repent and strike their breasts. Seeing that, the authorities obtain Roman soldiers and guard the tomb. Because of that, they are there to witness the resurrection-ascension of Jesus leading out from Hades those other holy Jews who died before him. Knowing the full truth, and afraid lest those they led astray—that is, "the people of the Jews"—might stone them, they obtain a cover-up from the Roman authorities. That is the story, and it is almost impossible to break up its consecutive cohesion. But there is nothing whatsoever like that in the canonical gospels.

I turn next to a scriptural pattern or biblical model through which that story could have been developed. This generic paradigm was proposed to explain Mark's passion-resurrection account. My point is that it explains the *Cross Gospel* just as well (or even better).

Biblical Model

The protagonist is a wise man in a royal court. Maliciously accused of violating the law of the land, he is condemned to death. But he is rescued at the brink of death, vindicated of the charges against him, and exalted to a high position (sometimes vizier, sometimes judge or executioner of his enemies), while his enemies are punished. . . . In the Wisdom of Solomon and the earlier stages of the tradition that can be extrapolated from it, three important changes occur. 1) The exaltation scene is greatly expanded through the use of materials from Isaiah 13, 14, and 52–53. 2) The protagonist is, in fact, put to death. 3) He is exalted to the heavenly court, where he serves as a vice-regent of the heavenly king. The roots of those latter two developments are inherent in the servant theology of Second Isaiah.

George Nickelsburg, *Resurrection, Immortality, and Eternal Life in Intertestamental Judaism*, p. 170

In his 1967 Harvard dissertation, published in 1972, Nickelsburg drew attention to a generic pattern in Jewish texts involving the persecution and vindication of righteous or innocent people. The archetypal model was, however, the pagan *Story of Ahiqar,* "one of the best known and most widely disseminated tales in the ancient Mediterranean world," with manuscript evidence dating back to the fifth century B.C.E. (*OTP* 2.479). Ahiqar was a scholarly minister under Sennacherib and Esarhaddon, seventh-century monarchs of the Assyrian Empire. When his nephew Nadin falsely accused him of treason, he escaped death only because the executioner owed him a favor. He was later vindicated and restored to power, and the evil Nadin was punished. It is a story of innocence vindicated, in a court situation where the king eventually restores the innocent one and punishes the guilty one.

TWO VARIATIONS ON VINDICATION

Pagan model and Jewish imagination combined to create two different variations on that archetype. The key distinction is whether vindication happens in the *present* or in the *future, before* or *after* death.

The first variation is present in these seven cases: Joseph accused by Potiphar's wife in Genesis 39–41; Tobit accused by "one of the men of Nineveh" in Tobit 1:18–22; Shadrach, Meshach, and Abednego accused by "certain Chaldeans" in Daniel 3; Daniel himself accused by "the presidents and the satraps" in Daniel 6; "all Jews" accused by Haman in Esther 3; Susanna accused by the elders in *Susanna;* and Egyptian Jews accused by the king himself in *3 Maccabees* 3. In all those wisdom tales, those falsely accused are saved *before death* by divine assistance or miraculous intervention.

The second variation is present in three cases. One is the Suffering Servant of Isaiah 52–53, seen already in Chapter 23. Another is the martyrdom of the mother and her seven sons in *2 Maccabees* 7. Deliverance from death in that case is deliverance not *before* but *after* death. It is vindication not as earthly life restored but as eternal life promised. Because they died innocently in obedience to divine law, "the King of the universe will raise us up to an everlasting renewal of life" in 7:9, or "the Creator of the world . . . will in his mercy give life and breath back to you again" in 7:23. A final case is in *Wisdom* 2–5, which uses Isaiah 52–53 to criticize that classical deliverance from death *before* death, replacing it with deliverance from death *after* death. "Wisdom 2:4–5 differs from the wisdom tale and agrees with Isaiah 52–53," as Nickelsburg says. "In the wisdom tales the rescue of the hero *prevents* his death. In Wisdom of Solomon, he is rescued *after* his death" (1972:66). Here is the voice of the ungodly persecutors in that last case:

Let us see if his words are true, and let us test what will happen at the end of his life; for if the righteous man is God's child, he will help him, and will deliver him from the hand of his adversaries. Let us test him with insult and torture, so that we may find out how gentle he is, and make trial of his forbearance. Let us condemn him to a shameful death, for, according to what he says, he will be protected. (*Wisdom* 2:17–20)

They propose, as it were, a test case on the validity of court tales of divine protection for those unjustly accused. But that is not how God works; those are not "the secret purposes of God." This is God's approach:

But the souls of the righteous are in the hand of God, and no torment will ever touch them. In the eyes of the foolish they seemed to have died, and their departure was thought to be a disaster, and their going from us to be their destruction; but they are at peace. For though in the sight of others they were punished, their hope is full of immortality. (*Wisdom* 3:1–4)

Persecutors will have to admit, not in this world but in the next, that the righteous one has "been numbered among the children of God" and that they themselves have "strayed from the way of truth," according to *Wisdom* 5:5–6's conclusion. It is probably fair to conclude that *before-death* vindication is older and more pervasive than *after-death* exaltation.

In a 1980 article Nickelsburg applied all of that to the passion story in Mark 14–15. He worked with a very complete profile for the genre to which he assigned it, involving twenty-one motifs and concluded "that almost all the components of our genre [the vindicated-innocence wisdom tale] are present in the Markan passion narrative" (165). The most problematic motifs, however, are those that involve deliverance: rescue, vindication, exaltation, and acclamation. Nickelsburg finds those motifs realized by Mark in four places. The first is in 15:17–18, where Roman soldiers mock Jesus as king of the Jews. The second is in 15:26, where the charge attached to the cross announces the king of the Jews. The third is in 15:38–39, where the Temple veil is torn and the Roman centurion confesses Jesus. But the fourth place is most emphasized, and it has to contain three different motifs within its single verse (rescue, vindication, exaltation).

You will see the Son of Man seated at the right hand of the Power, and coming with the clouds of heaven. (Mark 14:62)

Spoken in response to the high priest, these words announce both the final exaltation of Jesus and the final punishment of those who persecute him.

Nickelsburg's analysis of Mark 14–15 is very persuasive: that is exactly how Mark sees Jesus' public vindication. At the imminent apocalyptic consummation, all will see his exaltation, but for now only believers can see it by faith. For Mark, Jesus' vindication is very close to that in *Wisdom* 2–5, the second of the twin variations of the suffering-righteous model. Jesus is saved not *before* but *after* death, and persecutors will realize that fact only in the future. Since Jesus did in fact die, the story cannot, strictly speaking, be told on the model of that first variation (where the righteous one is saved *before* death). Still, the *Cross Gospel* source in the *Gospel of Peter* does the best it can to realize that first variation. Jesus dies, enters Hades to liberate "them that sleep," and exits at their head in the very presence of his enemies. The Jewish authorities then "sin" by covering up the resurrection while the Roman authorities "convert" by admitting that Jesus is the Son of God. In terms of generic constraints we have, therefore, two investments:

Suffering-righteous model (variation 1, present vindication):   *Cross Gospel*
Suffering-righteous model (variation 2, future vindication):   Mark 14–15

I do not argue that one of those variations is better than the other, but I do want to stress their basic difference. In addition, I want to raise the issue of relationship. Are those texts simply two independent variations of the basic model? They are *at least* that, but are they more? Is Mark a criticism of the *Cross Gospel* variation just as *Wisdom* 2–5 is a criticism of the court-tale variation? I leave that question aside until the next chapter, to raise a different one here.

There is, as we saw, a Common Meal Tradition that developed separately in the Life Tradition in *Didache* 9–10 and in the Death Tradition in 1 Corinthians 10–11, serving as a profound linkage between those twin traditions. I ask now why there is no comparable passion-resurrection linkage. There is certainly a passion-resurrection story in the Death Tradition—the *Cross Gospel*, for example. Why is there nothing similar in the Life Tradition—the *Q Gospel*, for example?

COMMUNAL PERSECUTION, COMMUNAL VINDICATION

John Kloppenborg accepts the presence of those two great early Christian traditions, the Life Tradition and the Death Tradition, as we saw in Chapter 22. But he has also raised the question of their relationship on precisely this point of passion-resurrection faith. "The Q document," he says, "reflects in some important way the theology of a 'second sphere' of primitive Christianity uninfluenced by the kerygmatic assertion of the saving significance of Jesus' death and resurrection," but, of course, that "'second sphere' of Christian tradition . . . was chronologically in fact the first" (1990:71, 73). To avoid any hint of ascendancy, I rephrase his terms *first sphere* and *second sphere*, referring instead to the *double sphere* of earliest Christian faith and tradition. But his point stands, raising the question of the relationship between those double spheres (or those twin traditions) with regard to the passion-resurrection of Jesus. Is the passion-resurrection component simply present in one and absent in the other?

This is his answer: "It is not simply a matter, then, of Q's *silence* in regard to the pre-Markan passion account (if there ever was one), but of the use of a quite *different explanation* of suffering and the conceptualization of suffering and vindication in corporate terms. In Q we seem to be at a very primitive stage of theologizing the experience of persecution. Jesus' fate evidently was not yet an issue which required special comment. Parenthetically, it might be observed that Q's communal/corporate theologizing is comparable to that posited by Crossan for his 'Cross Gospel,' although there is no evidence of Q's dependence on the 'Cross Gospel' either. Indeed it might be argued that Q's corporate interpretation of suffering is a factor in the 'Cross Gospel's' deployment of motifs from the wisdom tale in an inclusive, communal way" (1990:81–82). The *Q Gospel* and the *Cross Gospel* share a communal rather than a personal and a corporate rather than a private understanding of persecution and/or vindication. They share, but differently, the pattern of the wisdom story as established by Nickelsburg.

Q Gospel.

I begin with the *Q Gospel*. In the preceding section I described Nickelsburg's genre of the vindicated-innocence wisdom tale. Kloppenborg showed that "while Q has many of the elements of the wisdom tale, it consistently deploys these elements in relation to the *collective* experience of the community, which evidently sees itself as continuing the work of the prophets" (1990:79). There is no presumption, of course, that the *Q Gospel* does not know about Jesus' death, but it is not theologically interested in any "privatistic interpretation of persecution, ordeal and vindication," since it considers that "persecution and death are the 'occupational hazards' of the envoys of God or Sophia" (1990:79, 80). The heart of the *Q Gospel*'s theology is that divine Wisdom, personified as Sophia, has repeatedly sent prophets to recall her people to God's Law:

> The Wisdom of God said, "I will send them prophets and apostles, some of whom they will kill and persecute," so that this generation may be charged with the blood of all the prophets shed since the foundation of the world, from the blood of Abel to the blood of Zechariah, who perished between the altar and the sanctuary. Yes, I tell you, it will be charged against this generation. (*Q Gospel* 11:49–51)

In particular, to "this generation" she sent both John and Jesus, and, despite their rejection, "Wisdom is vindicated by her children," as *Q Gospel* 7:35 puts it. She is vindicated by them because, despite their persecution or even execution, they remain faithful to her command. Such a theology does not mean that John and Jesus are just two more among many before and after them. Neither does it mean that John is just as important as Jesus, especially since "Q 10:21–22 makes Jesus functionally equivalent to Sophia" (1990:88). But it does mean that Jesus can never be considered alone—not in persecution and not in vindication. In fact, the more he is equated with Wisdom herself, the more he must send out prophets to do the same as s/he does. Patrick Hartin has also emphasized that corporate rather than private understanding of persecution-vindication in the *Q Gospel*. "The traditions related to Divine Sophia in the Sayings Gospel Q are understood predominantly in a collective sense (and not an individualistic sense). . . . [W]here one would have expected to find references to or reflections of a passion theology, nothing occurs. Q has a totally different conception of suffering and vindication. It is far more a communitarian, rather than individualistic, experience" (161).

We are so accustomed to the Markan passion-resurrection account that it is almost impossible for us to imagine an alternative mode of describing or theologizing about the Death Tradition. But the *Q Gospel* forces us to imagine such an alternative theology, one in which Jesus, however exalted, is never isolated. We have to imagine a *communal* persecution and a *communal* vindication, as Kloppenborg reiterated in a more recent article: "While Q used elements of the 'wisdom tale' to rationalize persecution and rejection, it neither used the psalms of lament [Psalms 22, 42, 69, 109] nor did it privatize the interpretation of Jesus' death as an expiatory death. . . . Q shows that the development of a passion narrative was *not* inevitable and encourages one to look for multiple origins of early Christian attempts to render plausible and meaningful the facts of persecution and death" (1996:332).

Cross Gospel.

I now turn to the *Cross Gospel* as a passion-resurrection story preserved within the *Gospel of Peter*. In *The Cross That Spoke* I noted that "almost every single verse describing the Passion of Jesus in the *Cross Gospel* contains an implicit allusion to texts of the Hebrew scriptures describing the suffering of Israel's persecuted righteous ones" (386–387). These are the major examples:

1. The authorities at the trial in *Gos. Pet.* 1:1 from Psalm 2:1
2. The abuse and torture in *Gos. Pet.* 3:9 from Isaiah 50:6–7 and Zechariah 12:10
3. The death among thieves in *Gos. Pet.* 4:10a from Isaiah 53:12
4. The silence in *Gos. Pet.* 4: 10b from Isaiah 50:7 and 53:7
5. The garments and lots in *Gos. Pet.* 4:12 from Psalm 22:18
6. The darkness at noon in *Gos. Pet.* 5:15 from Amos 8:9
7. The gall and vinegar drink in *Gos. Pet.* 5:16 from Psalm 69:21
8. The death cry in *Gos. Pet.* 5:19 from Psalm 22:1

My conclusion was that "in the *Cross Gospel* the Passion is not just exclusive, personal, and individual with Jesus but inclusive, communal, and collective for both Jesus and the holy ones of Israel. This means, however, that the resurrection must also be communal and collective or else the ancient promises of vindication and exaltation for those earlier martyrs remain unfulfilled and what use then are further promises for the future?" (387). That is what makes the extraordinary scene in *Gospel of Peter* 10:39–42 so important. That text, given above in full (p. 488), describes Jesus arising at the head of "them that sleep," leading out the holy ones who are released from Hades in his triumphant train. They form a great cruciform procession behind him—hence my *Cross Gospel* title—and respond to God's question about their deliverance with a choral *yes*. My 1988 conclusion still stands: "Jesus did not die alone and neither did he rise alone. The holy and righteous ones of Israel were always present in that process. He died in their passion, they rose in his Resurrection. . . . He died in their pain, they rose in his glory" (388).

It is inadequate to state that the Life Tradition has no story *plot* about Jesus' passion-resurrection. While that is true, it is much more significant that both the Life Tradition and the Death Tradition *share* a story *pattern*—the general persecution-vindication theme, with its emphasis on communal rather than individual persecution and on corporate rather than personal vindication. Jesus, of course, was steadily exalted over others within that pattern, but he was not originally isolated from others within it. Furthermore, that story pattern shared by the great inaugural traditions underlies the historical plot in the *Cross Gospel*, the corporate destiny in the *Q Gospel*, and the mythical hymn in Philippians 2:6–11.

The next point is to seek an historical setting for that *Cross Gospel* composition. My conclusion will involve a response similar to the one I made to Nickelsburg in this present section. He argued for the narrative genre of vindicated innocence behind the composition of Mark's passion-resurrection account. I found that his proposal worked as well or better for the *Cross Gospel*. In the next section Gerd Theissen proposes an historical setting in the early 40s for a hypothetical source in Mark's passion-resurrection narrative. I find that his proposal works as well or better for the hypothetical *Cross Gospel*.

Historical Setting

Taking for granted that narratives are marked by the conditions under which their narrating community lives, we wish to develop the hypothesis that the choice, shaping, and stylizing of traditions into a connected Passion account was especially feasible in the 40s. . . . Under Agrippa I the conditions could have existed in which accounts of the Passion of Jesus could exaggerate the role of the Jewish court beyond historical reality [at the time of Jesus]. . . . Probably we can limit the phase in which this Passion tradition underwent its critical shaping still more: it could well have been composed in light of the persecutions that occurred during Agrippa I's reign (41–44 C.E.).

Gerd Theissen, *The Gospels in Context*, pp. 189, 193, 198

In the view of most scholars Mark gives the earliest extant account of the passion story. Many commentators go on to seek and propose a pre-Markan version, however, believing that Mark did not create that entire story in the early 70s. According to prevailing opinion, he must have worked from some earlier version.

In Appendix IX of *The Death of the Messiah,* Brown adapted from Marion Soards a list of authors who distinguished pre-Markan passion sources from their present Markan redaction, and he presented thirty-four of them in tabular and parallel-column format. Brown concluded that "the sharp differences among them suggest that the project is self-defeating, for no theory will ever get wide or enduring acceptance" (1994:23). Neirynck (1994b:408) criticized the list's alphabetical rather than chronological order, pointing out that it made it more difficult to assess influences and add new suggestions, such as that of Adela Yarbro Collins. It does seem, however, that thirty-four examples are more than enough to establish Brown's point: proposals for a pre-Markan passion source derived from the Markan text itself have been mutually self-defeating.

That is not very consoling for someone like myself, who is proposing a pre-Petrine source, the *Cross Gospel,* in the *Gospel of Peter!* What chance does an extra-canonical source have if an intracanonical one has never achieved a glimmer of consensus? Maybe, however, the *Cross Gospel* is the very pre-Markan source that scholars keep postulating. When I first read Nickelsburg's analysis of the genre of the wisdom tale applied to Mark, it struck me immediately, as stated above, that it made even better sense applied to the *Cross Gospel.* Jesus, there, is vindicated in the sight of his enemies, who are forced to concede the truth before a neutral ruler. And Pilate confesses in *Gospel of Peter* 11:46 just as, for example, Darius does in Daniel 6:26–27. Exactly the same point applies to Theissen's analysis as summed up in the epigraph above. It is from a chapter entitled "A Major Narrative Unit (the Passion Story) and the Jerusalem Community in the Years 40–50 C.E." (1991:166–199). He is proposing "a precanonical Passion story" (1991:168), but his argument works quite accurately for the *Cross Gospel* itself as derived from the Jerusalem community in the very dangerous period under Agrippa I.

AGRIPPA I AND THE JEWISH TEMPLE

The only way to date and locate a source such as the *Cross Gospel* is to extrapolate from rhetorical content to social setting. What do we learn from that process in this case? First, in the *Cross Gospel's* passion-resurrection account, the Roman authorities are completely innocent. They have no participation whatsoever in condemnation or crucifixion; apart from some cooperative cover-up after the resurrection, they are totally free of both responsibility and guilt. Here, at least, Pilate can wash his hands and declare his innocence without hypocrisy. Second, the Jewish authorities are not just totally responsible, they are totally guilty. They know the truth and hide it deliberately from their own people. Third, "all the people," led by their authorities to crucify Jesus, are so repentant after his death miracles that they would have believed the resurrection and stoned their leaders were it not for that cover-up. That is not, of course, the historical situation of Easter Sunday. Nor is it the historical situation at any other time. But at what time and in what place would that have been a *credible* scenario? When and where would it have so cohered with communal experience that a group would have accepted it as a believable story? I do not ask about just one of those factors but about all three of them together, at the same time and place. The Roman authorities are totally guiltless. The Jewish authorities are totally guilty. The Jewish people would all be Christians if only their leaders had not lied. Where do *all three* come together simultaneously? At the time I wrote *The Historical Jesus* I thought pro-Roman Sepphoris in Herodian Galilee was the most likely location for the creation of such a story (1991:387). I now find the time and place that Theissen proposed for *his* pre-Markan passion source the more likely location for *my* proposed *Cross Gospel* source: in the Jerusalem community at the time of Agrippa I in 41–44 C.E.

Agrippa I was the grandson of Herod the Great and the Hasmonean princess Mariamme, but he lived almost exclusively in the imperial household at Rome from age five to age fifty, under the emperors Augustus and Tiberius and alongside the emperors-to-be Caligula and Claudius. In the last years of Tiberius he was imprisoned for an indiscreet remark desiring the emperor's speedy replacement by Gaius Caligula. Six months later, with Tiberius dead and Caligula enthroned, Agrippa was released, given the northern territories of Philip in 37 and the central territories of Antipas in 39. Finally, in 41, after Caligula's assassination and the enthronement of Claudius, the rest of the Jewish homeland was added to his kingdom. He was now king of the Jews, like his grandfather Herod the Great; and, if all went well, he might someday be Agrippa the Great. He was, to be sure, already fifty years of age. But Tiberius had become emperor at fifty-six and ruled for another twenty-three years. Caligula, on the other hand, had become emperor at twenty-nine and lasted only four years. The future was open and, in any case, he was now Jewish king of the entire Jewish homeland.

Daniel Schwartz's carefully critical and magnificently detailed study concludes that Agrippa was not involved in any subversive activity but that he wanted to be "Rome's most important man in the East." For that he needed to cultivate the Roman emperor Claudius far more than he would and to placate the Syrian governor Marsus far more than he could (143–144). Agrippa was the last hope of averting disaster between Roman power, the Jewish homeland, and even the Jewish Diaspora. And it does not seem that the brevity of his reign was what made that hope hopeless. This is Schwartz's very perceptive judgment: "Agrippa's short reign seems to be most notable due to two interrelated ironies. On the one hand, under Agrippa all of Palestine was re-united under a Jewish monarch—only to allow all of it, rather than a third as formerly, to return to direct Roman rule after his death. In other words, while it briefly appeared that through Agrippa Judaea could avert the steamroller of Roman history, it turned out that he helped smooth its path. And, on the other hand, a man who knew better than anyone that the fate of Judaea, and of the Jews of the Mediterranean world, was dependent upon Rome, was stubbornly viewed by too many people as harbinger of the type of anti-Roman Jewish nationalism embodied by some of his ancestors. The hopes which were raised by his enthronement, and which refused to die with him, contributed to the faith which led to the great rebellion of 66–73 C.E., and to catastrophe" (175).

That is certainly correct as the long-term retrospective view. But imagine how things looked to Jerusalem's Christian Jewish community in the first years of the 40s. How did that present look to those who did not know its future? They would have known about Agrippa from events at Jerusalem, which, in Schwartz's rereading of Josephus, should be kept to separate dates in 38 and 41 (11–14).

In 38, Agrippa returned from Rome to the Jewish homeland. Josephus records and rather clearly distinguishes three separate actions. The first action had to do with his *piety:*

> On entering Jerusalem, he offered sacrifices of thanksgiving, omitting none of the ritual enjoined by our law. Accordingly he also arranged for a very considerable number of Nazirites to be shorn [paying, that is, for the ritual at the completion of their vows of ascetic self-negation]. Moreover, he hung up, within the sacred precincts, over the treasure-chamber, the golden chain which had been presented to him by Gaius, equal in weight to the one of iron with which his royal hands had been bound [by Tiberius], as a reminder of his bitter fortune and as a witness to his reversal for the better, in order that it might serve as a proof both that greatness may sometime crash and that God uplifts fallen fortunes. (*Jewish Antiquities* 19.293–294)

The second action had to do with his *authority,* and I return to this point below. The third had to do with his *popularity:*

> The king recompensed the inhabitants of Jerusalem for their goodwill to him by remitting to them the tax on every house, holding it right to repay the affection of his subjects with a corresponding fatherly love. (*Jewish Antiquities* 19.299)

Be that fatherly love or practical politics, Agrippa was preparing for a far grander role than royal heir to Philip's tetrarchy, which was all he had obtained at that time.

I return now to that question of *authority*. Josephus records Agrippa's second action as the removal of the high priest Theophilus and his replacement by Simon Cantheras. That, however, was a change not just of individuals but of families. Herod the Great had chosen high priests from the family of Boethus, who was both a father-in-law to Herod and a high priest from 23 to 5 B.C.E. Once the Romans took over direct control of the Jewish homeland's southern half in 6 C.E., the governors chose high priests almost exclusively from the family of Ananus (or Annas), as we saw earlier. There was Ananus himself in 6–15, Eleazar in 16–17, Caiaphas in 18–36, Jonathan in 36–37, and Theophilus in 37–38. But in 38, Agrippa removed the family of Ananus and replaced it with that of Boethus. The point was symbolically quite clear: direct Roman rule is on the way out and another Herod the Great is on the way in.

All of that may have looked like good news for the Christian community in Jerusalem. Schwartz maintains that "there was no Roman governor in Judaea under Gaius, but that the province was instead attached to Syria" (65). That would have given the high priest very great local power, and it may well have been under the Ananides Jonathan or Theophilus that Stephen was killed. Schwartz thinks, however, that he was executed under their Agrippa-appointed replacement, the Boethian Simon Cantheras. He is correct to note "the glaring absence of the Roman governor" (72) in Stephen's death, but that also applies to Jonathan and Theophilus in 36–38 as well as to Simon Catheras in 38–41. After what certainly happened to Jesus under Caiaphas, an Ananide son-in-law, and probably happened to Stephen under Jonathan, an Ananide son, Agrippa's ascendancy may well have seemed relatively good news to Jerusalem's Christian community in 38, especially when he departed once more for Rome in 39. But all that changed in the summer of 41.

AGRIPPA I AND THE CHRISTIAN COMMUNITY

In 41, when Agrippa again returned to Jerusalem, everything had changed. In the fall of 39 Caligula ordered his statue erected in Jerusalem's Temple, and only the procrastination of the Syrian legate Petronius, the intervention of Agrippa himself, and the assassination of Caligula prevented the war of fall 66 starting in spring 40. But by the early summer of 41, Caligula was dead, Claudius was emperor, and Agrippa was back in Jerusalem as king of the Jews. We know of two events consequent upon his arrival there.

First, according to Josephus, he deposed Simon Cantheras, from the Boethian dynasty, and gave the office back to the Ananide dynasty. He offered it first to Jonathan once again, but when Jonathan proposed his brother Matthias instead, Agrippa accepted his recommendation (*Jewish Antiquities* 19.313–316). Why did Agrippa go back to the Ananide dynasty? There was now a new emperor, Claudius, whose financial secretary was M. Antonius Pallas, freedman of Claudius's mother, Antonia, younger daughter of Marc Antony. Agrippa still had very powerful friends in Rome but so now had Jonathan. As Schwartz concluded, "It is reasonable, moreover, to suppose that Jonathan had links with Pallas, Felix's brother, who was a very influential advisor of Claudius" (71). Agrippa was wise to accept a draw: the house of Herod had the kingdom once again; the house of Ananus had the high priesthood once again. A decade later, with Agrippa I dead, Jonathan was still very powerful. At the start of the 50s he was important enough to have one governor, Cumanus, banished (*Jewish War* 2.245) and another governor, Felix, appointed (*Jewish Antiquities* 20.162). At the end of the 50s he was still powerful enough to be the first one assassinated by the Jerusalem *sicarii*, whose hidden daggers used urban terrorism against imperial collaboration (*Jewish War* 2.256 = *Jewish Antiquities* 20.164). In any event, the return of the Ananides was not good news for Jerusalem's Christians.

Second, according to the Acts of the Apostles, Agrippa moved not against James, brother of Jesus, but against two members of the Twelve, first James, brother of John, and then Peter:

> About that time King Herod laid violent hands upon some who belonged to the church. He had James, the brother of John, killed with the sword. After he saw that it pleased the Jews, he proceeded to arrest Peter also. (This was during the festival of Unleavened Bread.) When he had seized him, he put him in prison and handed him over to four squads of soldiers to guard him, intending to bring him out to the people after the Passover. (Acts 12:1–4)

Luke uses very broad terms in 12:1, 4, and 11: "the Jews . . . the people . . . the Jewish people," but, as Schwartz comments, "if Agrippa meant to find favor in the eyes of 'the Jews' (Acts 12:3), it would have been with the Sadducees that he would have succeeded most" (124 note 70). I would be even more specific. All early Christian executions, from Jesus himself in 30, through Stephen in 37–38, to James, brother of John, in 41 and James, brother of Jesus, in 62, were carried out under Ananide high priests, under Caiaphas, Jonathan or Theophilus, Matthias, and the younger Ananus, respectively. In 41, from the viewpoint of the Jerusalem Christian community, the Ananides were back in power and Agrippa was on their side. I do not presume that all of Jerusalem's Jews agreed with the execution of James (or even that all of those with scribal or sacerdotal power did so). Peter, arrested just after that execution, escaped from prison by angelic intervention, but one might well wonder what human intervention was hidden behind that story.

That is the precise background I propose for the creation of the *Cross Gospel*. It laminates the situation of the Jerusalem community under (Herod) Agrippa I in 41 back onto the situation of Jesus under Herod Antipas in 30. The friends and enemies of 41 are retrojected to 30. Recall the three characteristic claims I identified earlier in the passion-resurrection account of the *Cross Gospel*:

1. The Romans, including Pilate, are completely innocent.
2. The villains are Herod and the religious authorities.
3. The "people of the Jews" would all be Christians if only their own authorities had told them the truth.

All three of those factors—the absolute innocence of the Roman authorities, the absolute responsibility of the Jewish civil and religious authorities, and the absolute readiness of "the people" to become Christians—indicate a date in the early 40s for the creation of the *Cross Gospel*. It is the Jerusalem community's response to the crisis created by the combination of Agrippa as king, Matthias as high priest, and both as concerned with the Temple in Jerusalem.

There is one other point that supports that position. It is a tentative one, but it may serve to confirm that linkage between Agrippa I's ascendancy and the *Cross Gospel*'s creation.

This point brings us back to that biblical persecution-vindication pattern seen earlier. As I indicated above, that pattern (and especially its wisdom-tale format) underlies the narrative logic of the *Cross Gospel*. But Schwartz has shown that exactly the same pattern underlies the major source that Josephus used in his *Jewish Antiquities* account of Agrippa I: "Two aspects of [that source], namely, the way it emphasizes extreme turnabouts of fortune and the way it avoids bringing God into the picture, recall two biblical models: the stories of Joseph and Esther . . . two biblical stories (which are similar to one another as well) which also describe the successful adventures of Jews in imperial courts" (34–35). Both those stories, seen earlier as examples of the biblical persecution-vindication pattern, involve individual Jews whose deliverance also involves the deliverance of their people. There is, as it were, a dialectic of the personal and the collective in both those tales. So also with Agrippa and his people. He no longer "figured only as an individual, playing no significant public role"; as Schwartz sees it, he had become "an advocate of the Jews of the Empire—who encountered one difficulty after another during the latter years of Gaius' tenure" (77). And the persecution-vindication pattern was very obvious. Agrippa was endangered by the emperor Tiberius and within half a year Tiberius was dead.

Egyptian Jews were endangered by the governor Flaccus and within a few months he was removed. Palestinian Jews were endangered by the emperor Caligula and within a year he was assassinated.

Was that biblical interpretation of Agrippa I's fate current during his life? Was it his self-portrayal for propaganda purposes in the Jewish homeland? Since Josephus does not have this view of Agrippa I in his *Jewish War* but only in his *Jewish Antiquities*, Schwartz thinks it first appeared between those texts—that is, "thirty or forty years, or more, after Agrippa died" (36). Be that as it may, two texts of Egyptian Judaism using the persecution-vindication pattern, *3 Maccabees* and *Wisdom*, both seen above, derive from that same lethally dangerous period of Caligula's four-year reign. I think it likely, therefore, that the biblical pattern of persecution and vindication was applied to both Agrippa I and eastern Judaism in the period between 37 and 41. In rebuttal, the Jerusalem Christians used the same pattern for Jesus upon the death of Agrippa in 43 or 44.

If, then, the *Cross Gospel* was created by the Jerusalem community in the early 40s, is there evidence of it anywhere else, especially in connection with that same community? My affirmative reply comprises the next section.

Continuing Tradition

One form of second-century Jewish Christianity [*Recognitions* 1.33–71] does indeed have a strong connection with the primitive church.
Robert E. Van Voorst, The Ascents of James, p. 180

The author [of *Recognitions* 1.27–71] stood in some sort of direct genetic relationship to earliest Jewish Christianity.
F. Stanley Jones, An Ancient Jewish Christian Source on the
History of Christianity, p. 165

This next section requires some background. First, there existed, around the end of the first common-era century, a man called Clement of Rome. In *Vision* 2.4.3 of his *Shepherd*, written in Rome around 100 C.E., Hermas is commanded to give his revelation to "Clement [who will] send it to the cities abroad, for that is his duty" (Lake 2.25). Second, there exists a letter generally attributed to Clement (known for that reason as *1 Clement*) that was written anonymously around 96 or 97 C.E., "from the Church of God which sojourns in Rome to the Church of God which sojourns in Corinth" (Lake 1.9). Finally, there exists a large body of pseudepigraphical Clementine literature—that is, texts attributed fictionally to Clement of Rome. My present interest is in one such text: the *Pseudo-Clementines* (or rather, to be more precise, a specific source within one of its twin versions).

The *Pseudo-Clementines* is a romantic novel built around the imaginary adventures of Clement of Rome. He is portrayed as a religious searcher who, dissatisfied with the various pagan philosophies, hears about the gospel, travels to Caesarea, and is baptized by Peter himself. He then accompanies Peter as his missionary companion. Clement's parents and brothers have become separated from one another by various disasters but are eventually reunited and baptized as well. That story is now extant in two separate versions from the fourth century, the *Recognitions* and the *Homilies*. They are, however, so similar that they presuppose a common source, the *Base Text* (which comes from the third century). But even within that *Base Text* there are several earlier sources. The one that concerns me is a proposed source postulated in *Recognitions* 1.

I am dependent here on two recent doctoral dissertations about that proposed source. In 1989 Robert Van Voorst located it in *Recognitions* 1.33–71 (minus 44–54) and identified it with the *Ascents of James*, attributed to the heretical Ebionites by Epiphanius's *Panarion*, written in 377. Van Voorst located it in a "Greek-speaking Jewish Christian community living probably in Transjordan," dated it "in the second half of the second century," and described it as having "a strong connection with the primitive church" as well as a "strong insistence on universal law-observance" (178, 180). In 1995 F. Stanley Jones delimited it as *Recognitions* 1.27–71 (minus 44–53) and identified it not as the *Ascents of James* but simply as "an ancient Jewish Christian source on the history of Christianity." He located it "in the direction of Judaea. . . . Jerusalem itself . . . is also not out of the question," dated it "circa the year 200 C.E.," and described it as having "some sort of direct genetic relationship to earliest Jewish Christianity," though he found it "highly unlikely that [it] would have demanded circumcision of the gentile believers" (159, 164–166). Both of those scholars gave summaries of previous research at the start of their books, but Jones had already published a far more exhaustive review in 1982. For that review and both their studies, I am deeply grateful, since I need only a very short section of the *Pseudo-Clementines* and am glad to avoid getting lost forever in either its primary texts or its secondary literature.

Recognitions 1.33–71 has three sections. The first section (in 1.33–44) has a history of salvation from Abraham up to the first years of the earliest Jerusalem community. It describes a split between Jewish people and Jewish authorities after the death signs of Jesus—a split that, in this account, continues to widen. The Christian Jews gain so many converts that the priests challenge the Twelve Apostles and James to debates in the Temple. The second section (in 1.55–69) has the Christian Jews so prevail in the seven-day debate that "all the people and the high priest" are ready for baptism in 1.69:8. Then comes disaster. The final section (in 1.70–71) has Paul, appearing anonymously as "a certain hostile man," rush into the Temple, attack the imminent conversion, cause a riotous massacre, and personally kill James himself. Is that history? Of course not. Is that anti-Jewish? Of course not. It is, however, rather viciously anti-Pauline. It combines the persecution by Paul in the early 30s with the death of James in the early 60s. It claims that Paul is to blame for all Jews not becoming Christian Jews. The reason is Paul's theological claim that neither Christian Jews nor Christian pagans should observe the ritual law of Judaism—for example, circumcision for males or kosher practices for all. That theology is here personified in his person; and that person, not just that theology, is blamed for the death of James and the failure of Christian Judaism! That is a counter-theology that came from the earliest Jerusalem church and developed after that community's flight to Pella in Transjordan and the destruction of the Temple itself in 70 C.E. It is possible, in other words, to be early, to be Christian Jewish, and to be very anti-Pauline.

My present focus is on *Recognitions* 1.41–43's account of Jesus' crucifixion. I remind you that it is the connection of this with the *Cross Gospel* in the *Gospel of Peter* and with the earliest Christian Jewish community in Jerusalem that is at stake in all of this. Van Voorst sees that connection with the *Gospel of Peter,* but Jones does not. So, in what follows, I use the former's rather than the latter's translation of *Recognitions* 1.33–71. As introduction, however, a few comments are necessary on the theology of the *Pseudo-Clementines.*

First, Moses promised the Israelites that God would always send them prophets just like himself:

I will raise up for them a prophet like you from among their own people; I will put my words in the mouth of the prophet, who shall speak to them everything that I command. Anyone who does not heed the words that the prophet shall speak in my name, I myself will hold accountable. (Deuteronomy 18:18–19)

That formulation intended regular prophetic guidance, but it could also be read as looking forward to a unique and specific prophet-like-Moses to come at some future time.

Second, in *Recognitions* 1.33–38, Moses led the Israelites out of Egypt but kept them forty years in the Sinai wilderness to purge them of Egyptian paganism. He wanted, for example, to eliminate blood-sacrifice to idols—that is, to eliminate *both* blood-sacrifice *and* idols. In the end, though, he had to compromise and allow them blood-sacrifice, but to the one, true God.

Third, Jesus as prophet-like-Moses came to eliminate that compromise and to replace blood-sacrifice with water-baptism (Van Voorst 1989:55):

But the time began to approach for fulfilling what we have reported to have been lacking in those things instituted by Moses, and for the prophet whom he predicted to appear. From the first he warned them by the mercy of God to put an end to the sacrifices. Lest perhaps they think that at the cessation of sacrifices there would be no forgiveness of sins for them, he established baptism by water for them. In it they would be freed from all sins by the invocation of his name, and for the future after a perfect life might continue in immortality because they had been cleansed not by the blood of animals, but by the purification of the wisdom of God. Finally, this is given as a proof of this great mystery, that everyone who upon believing in this prophet predicted by Moses was baptized in his name, shall be kept uninjured in the destruction of war which hangs over the unbelieving nation and the place itself. But those who do not believe will become exiles from the place and kingdom, so that even against their will they may know and obey God's will. (*Recognitions* 1.39 [Latin])

That terminal allusion is, definitely, to the destruction of Jerusalem in 70 C.E. and, probably, to the tradition that the Christian Jewish community had fled Jerusalem for Pella in Transjordan before the disaster struck. In this theology Jesus is also "the eternal Christ/Messiah" and "the Lord" in *Recognitions* 1:43–44, but it is as prophet-like-Moses that those other titles receive their content. Forgiveness of sins is no longer effected by blood-sacrifice but by water-baptism.

Fourth, there is one very important parallel that serves to confirm that Jesus is the one foretold by Moses: both of them worked miraculous signs and wonders (Van Voorst 1989:56–57):

Recognitions 1.41:1b–2 (Latin)	*Recognitions* 1.41:1b–2 (Syriac)
For Moses indeed worked wonders and healings in Egypt. This prophet like Moses, whose rise he himself predicted, although he healed every weakness and every infirmity in the common people, worked innumerable wonders and preached the good news of eternal life, was driven to the cross by wicked men. This deed, however, was turned into good by his power.	For Moses did signs in Egypt. And that prophet who arose even as he arose did signs among the people, drove out every sickness, and proclaimed eternal life. But by the folly of the evil stupidity of evil persons they brought crucifixion upon him, which very thing was changed by his power into grace and goodness.

Those citations exemplify the differences and similarities between the twin fifth-century translations from the lost Greek of the original *Pseudo-Clementines* into Latin and Syriac. Jones concludes that "while each of the two translations has its own peculiar shortcomings, they were both carried out in a fairly conscientious manner and are of approximately the same accuracy"; he adds, however, that "a proclivity of the Syriac translator reveals itself in R 1.40.2 where the Syriac alone has a very negative statement about the Jewish people" (1995:3, 49). In what follows, therefore, watch carefully for different descriptions of Jewish opponents to see if the Syriac is always the more antagonistic.

Fifth, those just-cited passages bring the text right up to the description of the crucifixion of Jesus; and just as there were signs, wonders, and miracles during his life, so there would be the same at his death. There are actually two crucifixion descriptions interrupted by a section about the Gentiles. This the logic of the section: there were miraculous signs at the death of Jesus; because of that there was a split among the people; because of that loss it was necessary to bring in the Gentiles. This is the general sequence:

(A¹)   Signs at Jesus' crucifixion and split among Jewish people   =   *Recognitions* 1.41:3–4
(B)   Gentiles called in as replacements for unbelievers   =   *Recognitions* 1.42:1–2
(A²)   Signs at Jesus' crucifixion and split among Jewish people   =   *Recognitions* 1.42:3–4

When I give the twin translations of those frames in A¹ and A², watch two aspects very carefully. First, notice the differences between them, especially in descriptions of the split itself. Second, could you understand them if you did not know some story like that in the *Cross Gospel*? Do they, in other words, presume some story rather than some story presuming them? Here is the first account in A¹ (Van Voorst 1989:57):

Recognitions 1.41:3–4 (Latin)

Finally, when he suffered the whole world suffered with him. The sun was darkened and the stars were disturbed; the sea was shaken and the mountains moved, and the graves opened. The veil of the temple was split, as if lamenting the destruction hanging over the place.

Nevertheless, although the whole world was moved, they themselves are still not yet moved to the consideration of such great things.

Recognitions 1.41:3–4 (Syriac)

For when he suffered, this whole world suffered with him. Even the sun grew dark and the stars were moved, the sea was troubled, and the mountains loosened and the tombs were opened. The veil of the temple was torn as if in mourning for the coming desolation of the place.

Because of these things, all the people were afraid and were constrained to question them. But some, although all the people were moved in their minds, did not move themselves to this matter.

The first half of that section about the cosmic signs is very similar in both translations. The second is quite different. The Latin has nothing at all about a split among the people. It is simply a matter of the "world" against "them." The Syriac, however, has a clear opposition between "all the people" and "some" unidentified ones.

The section about the Gentiles in B is an insertion. That is evident from the repetitive opening lines of the framing sections in A¹ and A² about Jesus' sufferings and the Earth's darkness. In A² the text starts like A¹, but it continues with new content, as follows (Van Voorst 1989:58):

Recognitions 1.42:3–4 (Latin)	*Recognitions* 1.42:3–4 (Syriac)
In the meantime, after he had suffered, and darkness had overcome the world from the sixth hour to the night, when the sun returned things came back to normal. Wicked people once more went back to themselves and to their old customs, because their fear had ended.	While he suffered, there was darkness from the sixth hour to the night. But when the sun appeared, and matters returned firmly as they were before, evil ones of the people returned to their ways.
For some of them, after guarding the place with all diligence, called him a magician, whom they could not prevent from rising; others pretended that he was stolen.	For some of them said about him who had suffered, and who was not found although they had guarded him, that he was a magician; thus they were not afraid to dare to lie.

Notice that those texts are intelligible only *if* you know some sort of story presumed behind them. The cosmic sign, darkness, was already included among those in the first account, but now it is given a timespan. In both translations, the split is far less clear than in the Syriac of *Recognitions* 1.41:4 above. The Latin has "wicked people" (all the people?) but then specifies "some." The Syriac is slightly better. It has "evil ones of the people" and then specifies "some." There are, however, three other differences between the Latin and Syriac versions that are more significant.

First, both agree in very general terms about guarding, but, while the Syriac says Jesus was "not found," the Latin says they "could not prevent [him] from rising." Second, the Latin but not the Syriac speaks about stealing the body, introducing the option that Jesus did not rise from the dead. Third, both agree on an alternative response that negates the phrase about stealing: Jesus did rise from the dead because he was a magician. But only the Syriac introduces the theme of deceit or lies. What exactly is the lie? The Syriac says that "they lied that we were fewer than they," in *Recognitions* 1.43:1. Finally, both translations clarify that the priests are those evil "some" ones and that it is "the whole people" who could end up opposing them (Van Voorst 1989:58):

Recognitions 1.43:1–2 (Latin)
Nevertheless, the truth was victorious everywhere. For as a sign that these things were accomplished by divine power, as the days passed we who had been very few became many more than they by the help of God. At last the priests became very much afraid that, to their own embarrassment, the whole people would perhaps, by the providence of God, come into our faith. Sending to us frequently, they used to ask us to discuss with them about Jesus, whether he were the prophet whom Moses predicted, who is the eternal Christ.
For only about this does there seem to be a difference for us who believe in Jesus over against the Jews who do not believe.

Recognitions 1.43:1–2 (Syriac)
But the uprightness of the truth was victorious; for because they lied that we were fewer than they, they were not upright. For by the zeal of God we more and more were steadily increasing more than they. Then even their priests were afraid, lest perhaps by the providence of God the whole people might come over to our faith, to their own confusion. Sending to us frequently, they asked us to speak to them about Jesus, if he were that prophet who was prophesied by Moses, who is the eternal Messiah.
For only on this is there a difference between us, we who believe in Jesus, and those sons of our faith who do not believe.

I do not, of course, take any of that "whole (Jewish) people" against (Jewish) "priests" as historical information. My point is that it presumes some sort of known story that would have made it credible as narrative—a story at least similar to the proposed *Cross Gospel* source in the *Gospel of Peter*. In all of early Christian literature only those suggested sources, the *Cross Gospel* and *Recognitions* 1:33–71, have that same linked combination of the signs at Jesus' death, the guards at Jesus' tomb, and a split between Jewish people and Jewish authorities both before and after the lied-about resurrection.

Van Voorst's commentary first drew my attention to that preceding connection, and his parallel-column translations were extremely helpful in seeing its implications. But I have two important footnotes to his discussion.

First, with regard to Matthew 27:51b–53 and the death signs in *Recognitions* 1.41:3 (A¹ above), he concludes, "As these last two portents are given only in Matthew, *AJ* [*Ascents of James* = *Recognitions* 1.33–71] is dependent on the Matthean account, and is an expansion of it. There seems to be no literary relationship between *AJ* at this point and the second-century *Gospel of Peter*, which makes the rending of the temple veil contemporaneous with Jesus' death (5.20) and places the earthquake after it (6.21)" (1989:106). Matthew, however, far from being the basic text, is an almost perfect example of the unsuccessful redactional combination of two irreconcilable sources. Matthew knows about the cosmic disturbances at the death of Jesus, as in *Recognitions* 1.41:3 and *Gospel of Peter* 5:20–6:21, and also about the resurrection of the holy ones along with Jesus, as in *Gospel of Peter* 10:39–42. The solution is to *double* the shaking of the earth and the opening of the tombs from Friday in Matthew 27:51–52 (the holy ones) to Sunday in 28:2 (Jesus) as well as to *spread* the collective resurrection from Friday (the holy ones arise) to Sunday (the holy ones arise and appear). Nothing can conceal the difficulties in Matthew's solution:

The tombs also were opened, and many bodies of the saints who had fallen asleep were raised. After his resurrection they came out of the tombs and entered the holy city and appeared to many. (Matthew 27:52–53)

That will not work, not for Matthew and not for anyone else. To be *raised* is to *come out* of their tombs, and that cannot happen both before and after the resurrection of Jesus. Neither *Recognitions* 1.41:3, where the tomb-openings happen at the death of Jesus, nor *Gospel of Peter* 10:39–42, where the tomb-openings happen at the resurrection of Jesus, need Matthew's impossible combination. If anything, therefore, Matthew is the dependent tradition.

Second, with regard to the split of Jewish people against Jewish authorities (A² above) Van Voorst was quite clear in 1989: "The *Gospel of Peter* 8:28–30 says that the effect of the portents on the common people continued after Jesus' death, and led them to conclude that he was righteous. This shared motif of the effect of the portents may indicate that the *AJ* is in touch at this point with the traditions behind the *Gospel of Peter*" (107 note 36). But, in a more recent discussion of *Recognitions* 1.41:2–43:4 there is no mention at all about the *Gospel of Peter*, and only the "Latin version (against which the Syriac version varies little)" is given (1995:156). But, as we saw above, the Syriac version is clearest that the split is "all the people" against "some," and "all the people" is, of course, exactly what one finds in *Gospel of Peter* 8:28. I agree, in other words, with that 1989 footnote and not with its 1995 elimination.

Let me summarize my argument so far before starting the final section of this chapter. The first and most basic point is that there is a canonically independent and narratively consecutive source within the present *Gospel of Peter,* which carefully collates that source with canonically dependent ones. The whole is a typically second-century attempt to bring discordant traditions into harmonious unity. That source not only contained an account of guarded tomb and visible resurrection, as Brown argues, but also (and necessarily) some prior account of juridical execution explaining why a *guarded* tomb was necessary. I call that source the *Cross Gospel,* and once again I challenge my colleagues to explain the *Gospel of Peter* without recourse to some such source. If you claim, for example, that the *Gospel of Peter* is based entirely on the canonical gospels, how do you explain that so much of that text is not in them?

The second point is in frontal contradiction with those who claim that such a source—or even the *Gospel of Peter* in general—is anti-Jewish (and is much more so than any of the canonical gospels). That ignores the rhetorical purpose of the narrative *as a whole.* It is because the Jewish people crucify Jesus that the Jewish people repent at his death signs. It is because the Jewish people repent at his death signs that the Jewish authorities guard the tomb. It is because the Jewish and Roman authorities guard the tomb that they see the resurrection itself. It is because they see the resurrection actually happen that the Roman authorities confess Jesus and the Jewish authorities "lie" about Jesus to protect themselves from "the people of the Jews." Is that history? Of course not. Is that anti-Jewish? Of course not.

The third point confirms that second one. There is only one other place in early Christian literature where I have found that same combinations of signs at the death, guards at the tomb, and a split between "all the people" and "the priests" about the execution and resurrection of Jesus. That is in the *Pseudo-Clementines,* in the source delineated generally as *Recognitions* 1.33–71. The account of the death and resurrection in *Recognitions* 1.41–43 presumes some such story as that in the *Cross Gospel.* Those brief references are needed to conclude the preceding signs-and-wonders parallel with Moses and to begin the succeeding split between people and authorities that is crucial for the debates to come. But those passing references are unintelligible without some story at least similar to that in the *Cross Gospel* source of the *Gospel of Peter.*

Finally, recall, from above, that Van Voorst said *Recognitions* 1.33–71 had "a strong connection with the primitive church" (1989:180) and that Jones said its "author stood in some sort of direct genetic relationship to earliest Jewish Christianity" (1995:165). The more that source in *Recognitions* 1.33–71 is connected to the earliest Christian Jewish community in Jerusalem, the more that story in the *Cross Gospel* is pushed back to that same situation.

Scriptural Memory

The issue of scriptural background becomes more debatable in views like those of Koester and J. D. Crossan, who . . . dismiss any rooting of the passion in Christian memory. Koester [1980a:127] states with assurance that in the beginning there was only belief that Jesus' passion and resurrection happened according to the Scriptures so that "the very first narratives of Jesus' suffering and death would not have made any attempt to remember what actually happened." Crossan [1988:405] goes even further: "It seems to me most likely that those closest to Jesus knew almost nothing about the details of the event. They knew only that Jesus had been crucified, outside Jerusalem, at the time of Passover, and probably through some conjunction of imperial and sacerdotal authority." He does not explain why he thinks this "most likely," granted the well-founded tradition that those closest to Jesus had followed him for a long time, day and night. Did they suddenly lose all interest, not even taking the trouble to inquire about what must have been the most traumatic moment of their lives?

Raymond E. Brown, The Death of the Messiah, pp. 15–16

I conclude this chapter by asking about a more basic and important issue than sources: that of origins. The most fundamental debate about the passion-resurrection story is not about the problem of *sources* (or how our versions relate to one another) but about the problem of *origins* (or how that story was first created). The problem is not about the *brute facts* of Jesus' crucifixion outside Jerusalem around Passover but about the *specific details* of that consecutive story, blow by blow and word for word, hour by hour and day by day. There are two major disjunctive options that I summarize as prophecy historicized versus history remembered. Those twin options were given respectively in the epigraphs from Helmut Koester and Raymond Brown at the start of this Part X. They are continued in the epigraph just above. What is at issue in this debate?

RECORDING HISTORY

Brown's position, which I summarize as *history remembered,* seems at first sight both obvious and commonsensical. Jesus' companions knew or found out what happened to him, and such historical information formed the basic passion story from the very beginning. Allusions to biblical precedents were illustrative or probative for that story, but not determinative or constitutive of its content. Maybe, from all the details known to them, they chose those that fitted best with such biblical precedents, but in general it was history and not prophecy that determined narrative sequence and structure. Outsiders looking at that proposal might easily judge it self-evident. We have five versions of that story—four intra-canonical and one extracanonical—and, despite minor discrepancies, they can easily be coordinated into a single passion play. Why would anyone suggest an alternative to history remembered as the basis for the passion-resurrection story?

Koester's position is that, apart from the bare and brutal facts of the crucifixion itself, the narrative was built up from biblical models, precedents, and prophecies. It took its specific details, its larger themes, and its overall structure from such scriptural sources. His general criticism of the history-remembered interpretation is that the "form, structure, and life situation of such a historical passion report and its transmission have never been clarified" (1980a:127). I agree with Koester, as you can tell from the above epigraph, but for the following two reasons.

The first reason is negative, against the position of *history remembered,* and it reverts to the problem of sources. If there were, from the beginning, a detailed passion-resurrection story or even just a passion narrative, I would expect more evidence of it than is currently extant. It is totally absent from the Life Tradition, and it appears in the Death Tradition as follows. On the one hand, outside the gospels, there are no references to those details of the passion narrative. If all Christians knew them, why do no other Christians mention them? On the other hand, within the gospels, everyone else copies directly or indirectly from Mark. If one story was established early as history remembered, why do all not "copy" from it rather than depend on Mark? Why do Matthew and Luke have to rely so completely on Mark? Why does John, despite his profound theological innovation, depend so completely on synoptic information? The negative argument is not that such a history-remembered narrative *could* not have happened. Of course it *could.* The argument is that we lack the evidence for its existence; and, if it existed, we would expect some such evidence to be available.

The second reason is positive, for the position of *prophecy historicized.* The individual units, general sequences, and overall frames of the passion-resurrection stories are so linked to prophetic fulfillment that the removal of such fulfillment leaves nothing but the barest facts, almost as in Josephus, Tacitus, or the Apostles' Creed. By *individual units* I mean such items as these: the lots cast and garments divided from Psalm 22:18; the darkness at noon from Amos 8:9; the gall and vinegar drink from Psalm 69:21. By *general sequences* I mean such items as these: the Mount of Olives situation from 2 Samuel 15–17; the trial collaboration from Psalm 2; the abuse description from the Day of Atonement ritual in Leviticus 16. By *overall frames* I mean the narrative genre of innocence vindicated, righteousness redeemed, and virtue rewarded. In other words, on all three narrative levels—surface, intermediate, and deep—biblical models and scriptural precedents have controlled the story to the point that without them nothing is left but the brutal fact of crucifixion itself.

I need to clarify, however, what I mean by *prophecy* historicized. I do not intend the apologetical or polemical use of biblical texts as prophecies about Jesus, as if such texts were uniquely and exclusively pointing to Jesus the future Messiah. *Prophecy* historicized means that Jesus is embedded within a biblical pattern of corporate persecution and communal vindication. Such texts may point particularly or especially to Jesus, but, at least originally, they did not point privately or exclusively to him. The question, in other words, is whether those passion-resurrection details derive from historical recall or biblical model? I gave the evidence for that latter alternative in *The Cross That Spoke* and *Who Killed Jesus?* and shall not repeat it here. But, lest all of this get too abstract, I give one example of this process, one instance of prophecy historicized, one case in which a text about mutual passion and mutual vindication is actualized during the crucifixion of Jesus. It was just mentioned as the gall and vinegar drink from Psalm 69:21.

RECALLING SCRIPTURE

Psalm 69 itself has a dyadic structure of persecution and vindication. The first and longer part in 69:1–29 is a catalogue of sufferings from one whose "eyes grow dim with waiting for my God." Then, in 69:30–36, there is an abrupt shift from pleading to thanksgiving, a sudden change from lament for persecution to gratitude for vindication. These are the transition verses:

But I am lowly and in pain; let your salvation, O God, protect me. I will praise the name of God with a song; I will magnify him with thanksgiving. (Psalm 69:29–30)

The verse I am interested in occurs in that former section as the catalogue of woes gives way to a series of curses against the persecutors:

They gave me poison for food, and for my thirst they gave me vinegar to drink. (Psalm 69:21)

The sufferer receives poison (gall) and vinegar instead of food and drink. In context it is the climax of derision and oppression suffered at the hand of enemies. That is, of course, a general metaphor for lethal attack, but how can it be applied to Jesus, who is already being crucified?

The *Cross Gospel* in the *Gospel of Peter* makes it cohere quite literally and successfully with the actual situation of execution. In that gospel, as you recall, it is the Jewish people who crucify Jesus and then repent when they see the miracles that accompany his death. But here is what happens before that moment:

Now it was midday and a darkness covered all Judaea. And they became anxious and uneasy lest the sun had already set, since he was still alive. [For] it stands written for them: the sun should not set on one that has been put to death. And one of them said, "Give him to drink gall with vinegar." And they mixed it and gave him to drink. And they fulfilled all things and completed the measure of their sins on their head. (*Gospel of Peter* 5:15–17)

The more ancient Jewish style was crucifixion *after death,* in which an already executed person was impaled for demonstration purposes. Joshua 10:26–27 has five enemy kings "struck down and put to death" then "hung on the trees until evening," but "at sunset Joshua commanded, and they took them down from the trees." That procedure is also codified as law:

> When someone is convicted of a crime punishable by death and is executed, and you hang him on a tree, his corpse must not remain all night upon the tree; you shall bury him that same day, for anyone hung on a tree is under God's curse. You must not defile the land that the Lord your God is giving you for possession. (Deuteronomy 21:22–23)

Since the Roman method was crucifixion *before death,* that Deuteronomic law could be followed only if the executed person was already dead by sunset. Otherwise, he would have to be killed by some other method before removal from the cross. That is exactly the point of *Gospel of Peter* 5:16, where Jesus is given a poisoned drink to finish the crucifixion speedily so that his body can be removed before dark. The food/poison (gall) and vinegar/drink is simply and necessarily collapsed into gall and vinegar—or, in other words, into poisoned vinegar. It is that act which both "fulfilled all things and completed the measure of their sins on their head." That manages to apply the psalm verse quite literally to the death of Jesus. He is poisoned to death on the cross. Biblical parallels and not historical memories are dictating that incident's inclusion. A communal prayer applicable to any sufferer is actualized in Jesus. That is what I mean by prophecy historicized, not history remembered.

REWRITING GOSPEL

I conclude with an autobiographical incident to indicate why the *Cross Gospel* hypothesis is so important for me. In the weeks before Easter of 1995 I was on a book tour to promote *Who Killed Jesus?* On the evening of Wednesday, April 5, I spoke and autographed books at Barnes & Noble in midtown Manhattan, 6th Avenue and 22nd Street. Such events in other stores usually took place in a bay where about thirty chairs could encircle the speaker, meaning that no microphone was necessary. But in this case, my voice was amplified through the entire store at seven-thirty in the evening. I did not like that process, since it forced everyone, regardless of interests, to listen to twenty minutes on the historical Jesus. At the end there were about thirty seated people who had come to hear the talk and another thirty standing people who had arrived during it. I thought that some of the standers, drawn to the talk more by volume than interest, might be annoyed, and the first question seemed to confirm my expectations. It was clearly inimical in tone, but it was also absolutely fair and, in the long run, extremely helpful for my own understanding. It went something like this.

Questioner: "You said that the Barabbas story was created by Mark because, as he saw it, the Jerusalem crowd had picked the wrong saviors, namely the brigand-rebels, in the war against Rome that started in 66 C.E.?" *Myself:* "Yes." *Questioner:* "Mark himself made it up? The choice of Barabbas over Jesus never happened? It's not true?" *Myself:* "Yes." *Questioner:* "Then why can't you just call it what it is: a lie?" I cannot remember what I said in response, but it was probably defensive because I had never thought of the problem that way before. Why did I not call that incident or the many others created, in my view, by the traditions or the evangelists, lies? They were not true, so were they not lies? The question stuck with me over the following weeks, and it was in thinking about the *Cross Gospel* and not about any of the canonical accounts that I first saw the answer.

I knew I was not afraid to call things, even gospel things, by their proper names. If I had thought *lie* was the proper term, I would have used it. So why *not* use it? What had always prevented me from doing so? I had called the claim that the Jews killed Jesus "the longest lie." But did not the gospels say just that?

Recall the number of times in this book that I have emphasized gospel as *updated* good news, rewriting the Jesus of the late 20s as the Jesus of the 70s, 80s, and 90s. I knew, of course, that *words and deeds* of Jesus were updated to speak to new situations and problems, new communities and crises. They were adopted, they were adapted, they were invented, they were created. But then so, of course, were the *friends and enemies* of Jesus. That I had ignored. The community and author behind the *Cross Gospel* described the friends and enemies of Jesus at his execution as their own friends and enemies in the early 40s. The Romans were completely innocent *then* because that was how they appeared *now*. The house of Herod and the Jewish authorities were completely guilty *then* because that was how they appeared *now*. The "people of the Jews" were ready to convert *then* because that was how they appeared *now*. We may not like it, but that is what gospels do in Catholic Christianity. That is their generic destiny and compositional function. They are not straight history, straight biography, straight journalism. The author of the *Cross Gospel,* or of any other gospel, did not say this: I know that the Roman authorities crucified Jesus, but I will blame the Jewish authorities; I will play the Roman card; I will write propaganda that I know is inaccurate. If they *had* done that, the resulting text would have been a lie. No matter how weak the gospel writers were, or how threatened their existence, such a tactic would not have been apologetics and polemics; it would have been libel and lie. That intuition helped me understand how the *Cross Gospel* was composed. But it helped me understand as well the continuing nature of the passion-resurrection tradition. That tradition, in my view, developed from the *Cross Gospel* basis and is a single genetic stream of transmission.

No gospel written after the war of 66–73/74 C.E. is willing to leave the Romans totally guiltless, as did the *Cross Gospel*. No matter what Pilate thinks, he supplies the soldiers for the crucifixion. Mark blames the "crowd" in Jerusalem, Matthew blames "all the people," and John blames "the Jews." As Christian Jewish communities are steadily more alienated from their fellow Jews, so the "enemies" of Jesus expand to fit those new situations. By the time of John in the 90s, those enemies are "the Jews"—that is, all those other Jews except us few right ones. If we had understood gospel, we would have understood that. If we had understood gospel, we would have *expected* that. It is, unfortunately, tragically late to be learning it.

CHAPTER 26

EXEGESIS, LAMENT, AND BIOGRAPHY

Could one suggest that women, whose involvement with the dead body is an intimate one (in most societies it is women who tend the dying, wash the corpse and dress it) need no heightened retelling of the stories of death to comprehend its reality or to quicken their emotional response? They move from experience to art, from tears to ideas. Men, whose experience of death is, in many traditional societies, less physical, in that they do not tend the dying or handle the corpse except when they kill one another (a situation which demands a particular relationship to the dead-as-enemy) must re-read death in art or play in order to experience it. The movement, in this case, might be seen as the obverse of women's lamentation, one that progresses from ideas to tears.

Gail Holst-Warhaft, *Dangerous Voices*, p. 22

Here is the argument so far. There is a consecutive and canonically independent passion-resurrection story, the *Cross Gospel*, within the *Gospel of Peter*. Its present form derives from the Jerusalem community in the early 40s. Its central theme of Jewish authorities versus Jewish people concerning Jesus' passion-resurrection is the story presumed by the heirs of that Jerusalem community about a century later in the *Ascents of James* from *Recognitions* 1.41–43. This final section goes in the opposite direction, not from the *Cross Gospel* to the *Ascents of James*, but from the *Cross Gospel* backward into the Jerusalem community of the 30s. It focuses especially on gender roles within that community, on the interaction of exegesis and lament, and on the relationship between named females and named males in those earliest days after the execution of Jesus.

Biography in Lament

I follow women's cultural response to historical fragmentation as they weave together diverse social practices: dreaming, lament improvisation, care and tending of olive trees, burying and unburying the dead, and the historical inscription of emotions and senses on a landscape of persons, things, and places. These practices compose the empowering poetics of the periphery. . . . For the poetics of the periphery is always concerned with the imaginary

dimension of material worlds, of things and persons made and unmade. . . .
The poetics of the cultural periphery is the poetics of the fragment. One thing
must be made clear about the fragment. It may be marginal, but it is not necessarily dependent, for it is capable of denying recognition to any center. I am
concerned with the global vision that emerges from the particular. To stand in
the margin is to look through it at other margins and at the so-called center
itself.

Constantina-Nadia Seremetakis, The Last Word, p. 1

First, did the female companions of Jesus lament his death and mourn his
execution? Second, did such activities influence the communal tradition? Those
are obvious questions. But they were obvious to me *only* after scholars such as
Marianne Sawicki and Kathleen Corley had raised them persuasively and powerfully in their own writings.

Sawicki raised them in terms of burial, tomb, and apparition within the
gospel texts. "Calvary had been a quarry in antiquity, and after executions the
police dumped the bodies into any convenient hole together with some lime to
cut the stench. But possibly the Sanhedrin took custody of Jesus' corpse according to the procedure recalled in Mishnah *Sanhedrin* 6:5 [that is, burial in a common criminal tomb], since the sentence of the court was not considered satisfied
until the body decomposed [one year later]. . . . In either case—limed pit or confiscation—the interruption of the dying process causes grief. . . . I suggest that
such grief over loss of the body was the starting point of the reflection that cul-
minates in a 'finding' of the empty tomb and a 'seeing' of Jesus as already risen
from the dead" (1994a:257).

Corley raised them against a wider background in the cross-cultural anthropology of female lament tradition. "In many parts of the world, such as Greece,
Ireland, Central America, Finland, China, the Middle East, Africa, New Guinea,
and Spain, women have in past and present times habitually keened and
mourned the dead. Many of these lament traditions in fact sustain a poetic genre
that goes back in some cases hundreds, or in the case of rural Greece, thousands
of years. . . . Such laments contain the details of the story of the death of the
deceased. . . . The Passion narrative itself could have its roots in the formal context of repeated, sung storytelling, which could have preserved basic details of
the tale of Jesus' death. . . . I am suggesting that the Passion narrative had its
origins in a grass-roots liturgical context dominated by women and ordinary
people" (chapter 7, from ms. of forthcoming book).

In what follows I am deeply indebted to both those scholars. I am completely persuaded that there is *some* very basic connection between female
lament tradition and the development of the passion-resurrection story. I have

cited those summaries, however, because I differ with them on how narrative-lament tradition and passion-resurrection story interact with one another. The challenge, in any case, is how best to imagine that interaction. It must pay equal attention to anthropological expectations and to transmissional analyses of the gospel texts and sources.

THE MOTHER AS MARTYR

I talked in Chapter 16 about the martyrdom of the mother and her seven sons in 2 *Maccabees*. That story, from the persecution of the Greco-Syrian monarch Antiochus IV Epiphanes in 167 B.C.E., is also told in 4 *Maccabees*, a text dated to between 19 and 54 C.E. (*OTP* 2.534). George Nickelsburg is even more precise on that date: "*Fourth Maccabees* may well have been written around the year 40 in response to Caligula's attempt to have his statue erected in the Jerusalem Temple" (1981:226). It argues that full observance of the Jewish Law is true wisdom and proves the superiority of religious reason over human emotion. It is in this context that it repeats and develops the story of mother and sons from 2 *Maccabees* 7 into 4 *Maccabees* 8–18. But there is one very special development pointed out by Nickelsburg. "The mother of the seven brothers, whose speeches are integrated into the narrative of 2 *Maccabees* 7, is here treated in a separate section (14:11–17:6). She is the ultimate example of the author's thesis" (1981:225). Religious reason conquers even maternal emotion!

In her 1994 doctoral dissertation Barbara Butler Miller analyzed very closely the male viewpoint of those stories. That viewpoint begins in 2 *Maccabees* 7: "In most of the references to the young men, they are called 'brothers.' In only two references does the narrator refer to them as her sons (2 *Maccabees* 7:20, 41). In one of her speeches, the mother uses 'my son' and 'my child' (2 *Maccabees* 7:27). The sons never speak to their mother despite her intimate speeches to them. When the young men speak of each other, they always use the filial term 'brother.' The dominant use of the 'brother' terminology by the narrator stresses male/male bonding, rather than the mother/son relationship" (147–148). And the male viewpoint continues rather dramatically into 4 *Maccabees*. The author cites a lament the mother *did not make* in 16:6–11 and he frames it fore and aft with that negation in 16:5, 12:

Consider this also: If this woman, though a mother, had been fainthearted, she would have mourned over them and perhaps spoken as follows:

O how wretched am I and many times unhappy! After bearing seven children, I am now the mother of none!

O seven childbirths all in vain, seven profitless pregnancies, fruitless nurturings and wretched nursings!

In vain, my sons, I endured many birth-pangs for you, and the more
grievous anxieties of your upbringing.

Alas for my children, some unmarried, others married and without offspring. I shall not see your children or have the happiness of being
called grandmother.

Alas, I who had so many and beautiful children am a widow and alone,
with many sorrows.

And when I die, I shall have none of my sons to bury me.

Yet that holy and God-fearing mother did not wail with such a lament for
any of them, nor did she dissuade any of them from dying, nor did she
grieve as they were dying.

That is a rather fascinating text. It is a man describing what he thinks
women normally do and applauding the mother for *not* doing it. And it presumes that lament and grief are somehow antithetical to courage and martyrdom. But Miller's comment is very perceptive: "Since the lament is treated with
disdain by the writer, there seems some possibility that it might have been composed by women, or at least, echo the laments of real women of the eastern
Mediterranean area. Second, the literary and sociological analyses of Greek
laments carried out by M. Alexiou and A. Caraveli-Chaves, among others, offer
parallels between this lament and other modern laments from the eastern
Mediterranean area" (288). Here are examples of such parallels from those two
authors.

Margaret Alexiou, in her classical study of the Greek ritual lament across
three thousand years from antiquity to modernity, highlights the *contrast* convention: "In the ancient lament, the commonest formula for this convention was
to contrast one clause, introduced by *before* or *then*, with a second clause, introduced by *now*" (166). She exemplifies from the *Testament of Job*, a text dated to
either the last century B.C.E. or the first century C.E. (*OTP* 1.850). There is a series
of six contrasts in *Testament of Job* 25:1–8 between the rich past life of Sitis, wife of
Job, and her present desperate situation. Each past/present contrast ends with
the same refrain: "Now she sells her hair for bread." There is a similar contrast
convention in *4 Maccabees* 16:6–11: "After bearing seven children, I am now the
mother of none," or, "Alas, I who had so many and beautiful children am a
widow and alone, with many sorrows." Such stylized conventions indicate that
laments are formal, ritual, and traditional poetry.

Anna Caraveli-Chaves studied the "distinct thematic units . . . conventional
to lament poetry in particular" and identified five that appear and reappear
throughout a composition (135–136). They are intention, praise/invocation,

history of the deceased, mourner's plight, and invitation to share mourning. It is especially with that third of the "building blocks with which the singer will develop her song"—with the "history of the deceased"—that I am primarily interested in what follows. Here is one example of such a lament, given to underline that specific aspect but also to note some others every bit as important.

HISTORY OF THE DECEASED

On October 25, 1984, Peter Levi read Eilís Dillon's translation of *The Lament for Arthur O'Leary* in his inaugural lecture as the University of Oxford's Professor of Poetry. "It was composed in Irish at the end of the eighteenth century, and recovered in several different versions from illiterate or scarcely literate countrymen and fishermen in the south of Ireland in the 1890s and later. . . . I think it is the greatest poem written in these islands in the whole eighteenth century. . . . With this poem a world ended: we had not known that it had lived so long" (18–19). It was composed by Eibhlín Dhubh Ní Chonaill, widow of the murdered man. She was "born around 1743, her mother was a poet and her family had been patrons of traditional, wandering Irish poets" (19).

The lament's background is the anti-Catholic laws that Eileen's younger kinsman Daniel O'Connell would eventually destroy—though far too late to save Arthur O'Leary from them. The latter was a captain in the Austrian army, but wearing a sword was illegal for a Catholic in Ireland. He won a horserace against Abraham Morris, high sheriff of Cork, and then refused to sell him the winning horse when asked; that refusal was likewise illegal for a Catholic in Ireland. On the run as an outlaw for these two crimes, O'Connell was betrayed by John Cooney and shot by one of Morris's soldiers. Then a man named Baldwin, married to Eileen's twin sister, Máire, gave O'Leary's horse to Morris. All of those characters are named in Eileen's lament. Morris is wished "bad luck and misfortune." Cooney of the "black heart" is "a piddling lout." Máire O'Connell gets "no bad wish," but "I have no love for her." Baldwin is "the ugly wretch with spindle shanks."

Eileen O'Connell married Arthur O'Leary in 1767, and he was killed in 1773. By that time they had two children, Conor and Farr, and a third "still within me / And not likely I'll bear it." All of those biographical details are mentioned in the lament, as are pertinent geographical locations connected to them: Killnamartyr, Cork, Toames, Macroom, Inchigeela, Carriganima, Geeragh, Caolchnoc, Ballingeary, Grenagh, Derrynane, Capling, and "all Munster." It is lyric poetry edging toward epic in this lament of friend, lover, wife, and mother for friend, lover, husband, and father. These are stanzas VII and VIII (25):

My friend you were forever!
I knew nothing of your murder
Till your horse came to the stable
With the reins beneath her trailing,
And your heart's blood on her shoulders
Staining the tooled saddle
Where you used to sit and stand.
My first leap reached the threshold,
My second reached the gateway,
My third leap reached the saddle.

I struck my hands together
And I made the bay horse gallop
As fast as I was able,
Till I found you dead before me
Beside a little furze-bush.
Without Pope or bishop,
Without priest or cleric
To read the death-psalms for you,
But a spent old woman only
Who spread her cloak to shroud you—
Your heart's blood was still flowing;
I did not stay to wipe it
But filled my hands and drank it.

I am primarily interested here in narrative detail and biographical content in traditional lament poetry, and their relationship to the passion-resurrection tradition. But those stanzas draw attention to another and even more widespread aspect of female ritual mourning. There in stanza VIII and again later in stanza XXVII Eileen laments that Arthur had no official religious ministers to attend his death. But that is all there is to it. Nothing else in the poem speaks of Roman Catholicism or even general Christianity. There is nothing about the resurrection of the dead or about reunion in heaven. Here, in fact, is how the poem ends in stanza XXXVI (35):

All you women out there weeping,
Wait a little longer;
We'll drink to Art son of Connor
And the souls of all the dead,
Before he enters the school—

Not learning wisdom or music
But weighed down by earth and stones.

That is absolutely characteristic of ritual lament from female poets. It is not that they resist or oppose official, male religion. That would be to give that alternative too much attention or relevance. They ignore it; they bypass it; they operate on a level far more physical and primitive and profound.

I have noticed that again and again in reading those traditional lament poems, though I have never heard a *living* lament, even in Ireland. But those who *have* heard them—in Greece, for example, as bodies were being exhumed from grave to charnel house—often interpret them quite differently. Patrick Leigh Fermor takes that dialectic of female lament and male religion as a simple syncretism: "There is, in practice, little belief in a conventional after-life and the rewards and sanctions of Christian dogma. In spite of the orthodox formulae of the priest at the graveside it is not for a Christian eternity, for a paradise above the sky, that the dead are setting out, but the Underworld, the shadowy house of Hades and the dread regions of Charon; and Charon has been promoted from the rank of ferryman of the dead to that of Death himself, a dire equestrian sword-wielder. . . . There is no clash in the Greek mind between these two allegiances, but a harmonious unchallenged syncretism" (54). But there is surely something far more subversive at work in that dialectic. It is far more subversive because, as in the epigraph to this chapter, it is a dialectic between "tears" and "ideas," and somewhere deep down inside us we wonder if the "tears" have it right over the "ideas."

Anna Caraveli sees it not as serene syncretism but as sharp protest: "Implicitly, in terms of subject matter alone, laments comprise a 'protest' against the official church and the Christian doctrine of death. The very notion of death expressed in laments is contrary to the Christian views of a rewarding afterlife for the pious. The Hades of the laments is marked by darkness and despair, and it retains its pagan name. Christian attitudes toward death preach patience, acceptance, and perseverance. Laments express despair, fear, and anger toward death and the deceased" (184). They protest, in fact, not just against the injustice of death over life but the injustice of male over female. That is why Gail Holst-Warhaft calls them "dangerous voices" and why male institutions, from city to state and from nation to church, have tried to restrain and control them. And now that the "traditional women's lament has been almost eliminated from the modern western world," we are left, as she says, "without a language to express not only the grief but the rage of the living in the face of death" (6, 11). Where does that rage go?

Multiforms of Mourning

Like epic songs, another ancient oral tradition, the laments rely upon formulaic verse structure and make use of epithets, patterns of repetition,
metaphoric images, and various other poetic structures, drawn from a common stock. These formal elements serve to enrich the tradition but also function as memory aides and devices to serve in the combining of familiar with
new phrases and melodies that constitutes the process of improvisation.
                          Janice Carole Jarrett, *The Song of Lament,* pp. 139–140

Laments, in the present context, are not inarticulate cries of mourning, no
matter how powerful, magical, or evocative such may be. They are formal, ritual, and traditional compositions that may, of course, be just as powerful, magical, or evocative as that other mode of mourning. They are, in fact, the oral,
female, and lyric poetry whose parallel is the oral, male, epic poetry seen earlier
in this book. Both genres span thousands of years, and they can both be seen
together in Homer's *Iliad.* That epic starts with the anger of Achilles but ends
with the burial of Hector. In the words of Peter Levi, "Andromache wails in
words, briefly, eloquently and personally: Hecuba follows more briefly, then,
Helen, that is first the widow, then the mother, then the sister-in-law. Hektor's
burial follows at once, and the *Iliad* is over. . . . Homer has utterly altered the
narrative of war to a tragic and compassionate poetry on as vast a moral scale as
War and Peace. . . . [T]he final, essential moment, and the climax of this vast
transformation of values, of the whole *Iliad,* is the lamentation of the dead
Hektor. However Homer may have cooled down the ritual laments of women,
which appear in a wilder form a little earlier in the conclusion, it remains true
that it was by adapting women's poetry at the climax, and by accepting women's
views, that he gave the *Iliad* its extraordinary power. The lamentation of Hektor
is not a stray incident, nor a merely formal closure" (13). Female lament questions the morality of male heroism and of many other male characteristics and
institutions as well.

At the moment I look at lament in preparation for some very specific questions. They are the questions to be seen later in Helmut Koester's claim that "the
different versions of the passion narrative in the gospel literature" derive from
"the *oral performances* of the story in the ritual celebrations, ever enriched by new
references to the scriptures of Israel" (1995:18). They were seen already in the quotations from Marianne Sawicki and Kathleen Corley. These, then, are the questions: Are the different versions of the passion-resurrection in our gospels but the
written accounts of oral multiforms? Are they inscribed from divergent traditions

of female lament, especially from the narrative or biographical content of such mourning rituals? How, in other words, do female lament and the passion-resurrection tradition relate to one another? In preparation for answering those questions in the next and final sections, I look here at actual oral multiforms of female laments. It is impossible to prove or disprove claims of oral traditions that are completely lost. But if one has some written records of a tradition, there may be sufficient evidence to prove oral multiforms at base. That was seen for the oral and epic poetry of male performances at the start of this book. It can now be seen for the oral and lyric poetry of female laments in what follows. When we *read* such poetry today in *books,* we recognize another world staring us in the face from behind the written page. This is what oral multiforms look like.

THE LAMENT OF CHRYSA KALLIAKATI FOR HER MOTHER

Anna Caraveli-Chaves studied female lament poetry in "Dzermiathes . . . a large village, situated on the Lassithi plateau of the island of Crete, and the capital of the Lassithi province" where *"moirologia* (laments)—like other forms of ritual poetry—are rapidly becoming extinct. The present generation of lament poets is almost certainly the last." Against them stand male attitudes, "the underlying fear of laments as magic songs, songs which open up perilous channels of communication between the living and the dead," and modern standards and values. Her work is superbly evocative of the social context of those laments for "the women of the 'patriarchal' Greek village society . . . as strategies of survival" (1980:130, 131). In what follows I focus for my own present purpose on one somewhat minor aspect of her study.

Chrysa Kalliakati was an eighty-five-year-old woman whose lament for her mother had become famous. "Both mother and daughter were great poets and story-tellers; both were skilled midwives and medicine women, possessors of a miraculous recipe for a potion which had reputedly cured many women of infertility" (1980:132). Caraveli-Chaves, a woman participating in a woman's network, recorded two versions of the lament. The first and "passionate" one was from Alexandra Pateraki, Chrysa Kalliakati's fifty-nine-year old daughter, in Dzermiathes. The second and "halting" one was from Chrysa Kalliakati herself, at her other daughter's home in Athens (1980:133–136). I code those versions as AP and CK, respectively.

The twin versions are classic examples of an oral multiform even within the close constraints of family and female tradition about the same lament. Exactly the same line opens them both: "Oh slowly, oh mournfully, I will begin lamenting," but AP has thirty-nine lines while CK has forty-four lines. Here are three instances of the similarities and differences that can be expected in such a situation.

The first instance concerns the "history of the deceased" motif. Although very similar in both versions, it is six lines separated into lines 11–12 and lines 20–23 in AP, while it is eight lines joined together as lines 5–12 in CK:

Lines 11–12 and 20–23 (Alexandra Pateraki)	Lines 5–12 (Chrysa Kalliakati)
	because at the prime of your youth, you clothed yourself in black
	and then the darkness of your heart matched that of your dress;
Fate had written that at the prime of youth	because at the prime of your youth fate had written
you should lose our father, you should become a widow. . . .	that you should lose our father, you should become a widow.
You used to come home each night, mother, I say each night;	Ah how many times at midnight, after the roosters had crowed
you walked home from deliveries and made darkness scatter.	wouldn't you be coming down the road— pale and tired out! . . .
How many times wouldn't you come back from work—pale and tired out—	How many times at midnight, on nights steeped in darkness
way past midnight, near dawn, after roosters had crowed!	wouldn't you come home from the road—lips saddened and embittered!

Both versions agree on the mother's biography as that of widow and midwife, but AP has missed those first lines that give "an insight into the mother's 'heart'" and especially into the peculiar plight of a widow in a patriarchal society (1980:138).

Another instance concerns the "praise/invocation" motif. There are four stunningly powerful lines combining and rhyming Chrysa Kalliakati's work as "embroidery" *(xobliástra)* of the "stars" *(ástra)* in the sky. AP puts that superb image at the start in lines 3–6; CK places it at the end in lines 41–44:

Lines 3–6 (Alexandra Pateraki)	Lines 41–44 (Chrysa Kalliakati)
Ah, mother, keeper of the home and mistress of embroidery,	Eh mother, woman from Kritsa, eh keeper of the home,
you knew how to embroider the sky with all its stars.	beloved spinner of the yarn and twister of the cloth.
Ah mother, keeper of the home, mother, weaver and spinner	Eh mother, keeper of the home and mistress of embroidery
even the night sky itself was woven in your loom.	you knew how to embroider the sky with all its stars.

I hope it is not disrespectful to admit that I prefer CK's terminal location but AP's doubled rendition of those passionately accurate lines.

A final instance shows the "mourner's plight" motif. This gets only lines 13–14 in AP but lines 27–34 in CK. The difference, however, is far greater than two against eight lines. There are no parallels to any of lines 27–40 from CK in the AP version. It is a long and stern reproach to the Holy Trinity, all the saints, and the miraculous Virgin Mary of Tinos Island. She vowed offerings; they did nothing. CK will go to church next Sunday (but only?) to remember her mother bringing her to communion long ago—that is, only "to see my mother." Those lines make up one-third of the CK version. Does AP omit them because she is *less* religious or *more* religious than her mother? Less religious and therefore uninterested in them? More religious and therefore embarrassed by them? The omission, in any case, is hardly a vagary of memory. It is part of the standard censorship of oral repetition.

THE LAMENT OF KALLIOPI FOR POULOS

This second example comes from the other aside of the Cretan Sea, where three fingers point southward from the Greek Peloponnese into the Mediterranean. The middle finger is spined by the Taygetos Mountains and flanked by the Ionian Sea's Messenian Gulf to the west and the Aegean Sea's Laconian Gulf to the east. The southernmost part, past Outer Mani and Lower Mani, is Inner Mani. At its tip is Cape Tenaron, traditional entranceway into Hades.

The female dirges of the Inner Mani are, in Fermor's words, "entire poems, long funeral hymns with a strict discipline of metre. Stranger still, the metre exists nowhere else in Greece, The universal fifteen-syllable line of all popular Greek poetry is replaced here by a line of sixteen syllables" (57–58). Constantina-Nadia Seremetakis is interested in "the particular optic of Inner Mani" against the background of "recent anthropological literature that pluralizes the concept and tangible presence of power by identifying strategies of resistance that emerge and subsist in the margins" (1991:12). I have, as in the previous case, a far more limited focus at the moment. It is in oral multiforms, in the three different versions she gives of the lament for "the premature death, in 1932, of a young man [Poulos] who was engaged to be married to Kalliopi, a woman from a high-status clan. The deceased man was a schoolteacher, as was his fiancée. Both had studied in urban centers, and he died of an urban disease, tuberculosis, before the marriage could occur" (130). The lament was antiphonally performed between Kalliopi and Poulos's mother at the graveside. Later Kalliopi married another man, whom she also outlived. The first two versions of the antiphonal lament are recorded from female relatives of her late husband; the third is from Kalliopi herself, "an elderly widow now, who has been living in Athens (earlier in Piraeus) for decades" (130–137):

From a First Relative	From a Second Relative	From Kalliopi herself
Poulos's mother speaks:	*Poulos's mother speaks:*	*Poulos's mother speaks:*
Ah, my sweet, golden crown,	Ah, icon of Christ,	Ah, icon of Christ,
didn't I come up to Dri	how am I to separate from	how am I to separate myself
on Easter Day	you?	from you?
with the big bread rolls	To lose bride and groom	I was proud of you,
and the red eggs,	and all the in-laws?	to come to my household
with a silk dress	Wasn't I coming Easter	as a bride
and the fat goat?	and Easter day	gave me great honor.
How can I part from you icon	to bring the fat lamb?	
of Christ?		
Kalliopi responds:	*Kalliopi responds:*	*Kalliopi responds:*
Listen, my sweet mother,	Stop, my sweet mother,	I will mourn him today,
don't cry for your sweet, little	you melt my heart.	your only cherished son,
crown	Me, what kind of good	I am not mourning a fiancé,
cry for the professor	do I bring you	for I hardly came to know
for you have no other child.	that you are warmly receiving	him
For I will get married,	me?	one month only.
another professor I will find.	Such good [let it go] to the sea	He passed from Dri
For I, on my part,	and to the deepest waters.	as if an itinerant.
have no need of anything,	I, on my part,	Generous Poulo _____,
my father is a teacher,	have no need of anything,	my poor one, won't you
my brother is a doctor,	for I am well in my household,	change your mind,
I am educated myself.	the household of my father,	and not for my sake,
I, on my part,	for my father is a teacher,	I am well in my household,
don't mourn him as my	my brother is a doctor,	queen I am and *kira*
husband	a teacher I am myself.	in the king's palaces,
nor as my fiancé,	I beg your pardon, please,	my father is a teacher,
I only mourn him as a brother	I am not mourning a fiancé,	my brother is a doctor,
for we studied together	but a neighbor and covillager,	I am educated myself.
over there in Areopoli.	an only child.	

Seremetakis comments that "the women of her present affinal clan, in recounting the 1932 event, play down the high status of the dead fiancé's clan and the depth of Kalliopi's mourning" (1991:144). It seems to me that Kalliopi was already doing that in her own lament as she disengaged herself from her dead fiancé and announced her present status and future plans for all to hear. My point, however, is that those three oral versions of the same lament show exactly the similarities and differences one would expect in such oral multiforms.

Anthropology, History, Archeology

Knowledge of the Risen Lord cannot be theoretical, detached, and visual. The eyes do not connect with Jesus, apart from practices addressing hunger and injustice. The tradition of resurrection appearances was not originally intended to stand apart from a community that fed the hungry and observed the laws of justice. . . . The women at the tomb were observing the customs of mourning. They were weeping for Jesus. Their eyes were full of tears when the realization hit them that Jesus was not in the grave. For the poor, for widows, for a colonized nation, the eyes are the organs that register pain. The Marys were using their eyes in that graveyard, but not like Greeks. They "saw" Jesus through tears. . . . Sixty years afterward, the churches had four sanitized little stories about a trip to a garden and a lovely surprise. But it wasn't like that when it happened. Grief may also be a precondition for resurrection, and tears for permitting the eyes to see.

Marianne Sawicki, *Seeing the Lord,* pp. 92–93

In this last chapter I bring together the various strands of Part X, and I do so in a way reflective of this book's overall method: first *context,* then *text* in *conjunction* with it. The *context* is built up from cross-cultural anthropology through Judeo-Roman history into early Roman archeology in the Jewish homeland. Here is that full context.

ANTHROPOLOGY

The cross-cultural anthropological basis of this synthesis is that preceding section on the narrational and biographical component in the traditional oral poetry of female ritual lament. I will not repeat it here even in summary but simply emphasize two of its aspects: women lament; men complain. I have a photo in mind that can serve as symbol of that engendered interaction.

Loring Danforth's book on death rituals in rural Greece is a commentary on the powerful photos of Alexander Tsiaras that conclude it. Plate 30 shows a customary exhumation, in which the bones are taken from their individual grave to a communal charnel house just before the fifth anniversary of burial. In this case, the diggers have worked down through packed earth and broken wood to find, first, the skull. The picture shows fifteen women around the open grave. In their center is Matinio, holding the skull in her hands. She and the skull look straight out of the photo at the photographer and the viewer. This is the caption: "Matinio has just lifted the skull from the grave and turned abruptly toward Alexander Tsiaras. She asked him if he wanted to photograph her holding the skull in her hands. As Tsiaras photographed Matinio, she addressed him directly: 'We'll all look like this in the end. Some day you'll see the remains of your mother and father exhumed this way. Some day you'll get exhumed, then you'll look like this too.'" Who controls that photograph?

Women lament. "What is common to laments for the dead in most 'traditional' cultures is that they are part of more elaborate rituals for the dead, and that they are usually performed by women," as Holst-Warhaft writes. "Men and women may both weep for the dead, but it is women who tend to weep longer, louder, and it is they who are thought to communicate directly with the dead through their wailing songs. . . . [W]hile in early literate texts such as the Bible and the Homeric poems it was proper for men to weep and be wept over, it later became unacceptable. . . . Such a dialogue with the dead places a certain power in the hands of women" (1–2, 3). Any attempt to separate the genders—women in private home and men in public square—breaks down rather totally when it comes to funeral and grave, lament and mourning. It is not the noise of wailing but the power of lamenting that creates tension at this point between women and men.

Men complain. Fermor speaks of male reaction to female lament primarily in terms of mild unease. "The men of the family often appear uncomfortable while all this goes on; changing feet, turning their caps nervously round and round in their fingers, keeping their eyes glued to the ground with all the symptoms of male embarrassment at a purely feminine occasion" (57). Caraveli-Chaves uses stronger language, speaking of "men's ambivalent attitude towards women's lamentation ranging from outright hostility to uneasy mocking of the tradition and, in some cases, to thinly disguised admiration" (130). What exactly is at stake in that male reaction?

This is Danforth's explanation: "Because a woman's identity depends greatly on her relationship to a man, the death of this man deprives her of the crucial component of her identity. . . . It is for this reason that women participate so much more fully than men in the performance of death rituals. They must do so in order to continue to be who they were prior to the deaths of the men who gave their lives definition and meaning" (138). But, if that were true, one would surely expect female laments to emphasize much more the death of fathers, husbands, and sons over that of mothers, sisters, and daughters. That is negated not only by the examples I cited in the previous section but by Danforth's own case studies from a Thessalian village in north-central Greece. He begins his book with Irini's lament for her twenty-year-old daughter Eleni, who was killed in a hit-and-run accident in Thessaloniki a month before she was to begin her career as a teacher. He combines Irini with Maria, whose thirty-year-old son Kostas was killed in a construction-site accident and buried in the grave next to Eleni. As those two mothers share grief and counterpoint lament, there is no hint that a daughter's loss is less than a son's, that identities derived from men and lost with their deaths are what fuel female mourning. Caraveli is surely right to deny Loring's interpretation: "In the villages where I did my fieldwork," she says, "narratives about female 'heroes' (worthy mothers or wives, skilled midwives or healers, talented singers, story-tellers, or craftswomen) constituted a female history of the village, a body of women's expressive gestures, and a female line of transmission" (1986:170).

What is at stake in female lament is an alternative mode of power that protests the general injustice of death over life but also the particular injustice of men over women. That theme appears again and again in the studies cited above, from Alexiou in the 1970s to Caraveli(-Chaves) in the 1980s and Seremetakis in the 1990s. Female lament poetry is not just a case of females temporarily out of male control or temporarily controlling public ritual and performance. Female lament poetry is a direct social protest against oppressive male institutions, whether political and economic or religious and theological. I noted above how female laments totally ignore and bypass institutional religion. The antiphonal collectivity of lament performance is, as Seremetakis puts it, "a political strategy that organizes the relations of women to male-dominated institutions." It is "in critical relation to the male-dominated social order. The deployment of pain to detach the self and body from residual social contexts is but a prelude to the staging of women's reentry (as individuals and as a collectivity) into the social order on their own terms"(1990:482, 508–509). When Andromache laments for Hector at the end of Homer's *Iliad,* she does not say a word about his past fame as a Trojan warrior or his future fame as a fallen hero. She speaks about herself; she protests against him; she laments as a widow with a father-orphaned son, as one bereft of male protection in a male-dominated world. She weeps not for him but for herself and for her child.

HISTORY

The Judeo-Roman history of crucifixion can be summarized over four stages. The first stage is biblical crucifixion—the traditional Jewish method, which is quite different from the later Roman system. Jewish crucifixion was *dead* crucifixion. An executed and already-dead criminal was hung upon a cross. *Crucifying after death* was the public warning in the Jewish tradition. That style of crucifixion is mentioned in the laws of Deuteronomy and the conquest stories in Joshua. As we saw in the previous chapter, the law of Deuteronomy 21:22–23 commands that, when anyone "is convicted of a crime punishable by death and is executed, and you hang him on a tree," the corpse must be removed by sunset. Notice the sequence: executed and hung. Thus, for example, Joshua took the five Amorite kings, "struck them down and put them to death, and he hung them on five trees. And they hung on the trees until evening" (Joshua 10:26).

The second stage is Roman crucifixion. Contrary to the biblical tradition, this was *live* crucifixion. The condemned person was affixed to the cross to die in agony and was usually left thereafter as carrion for birds and dogs. *Death after crucifying* was the public warning in the Roman tradition. Martin Hengel, in his

1977 book, gathered together a vast number of references to Roman crucifixion. I once looked up all those references, and I have not been able to see crucifixion in the same way since. Consider his general conclusion: "Crucifixion was aggravated further by the fact that quite often its victims were never buried. It was a stereotyped picture that the crucified victim served as food for wild beasts and birds of prey. In this way his humiliation was made complete. What it meant for a man in antiquity to be refused burial, and the dishonour which went with it, can hardly be appreciated by modern man" (87–88). In the Roman author Petronius's famous novel *Satyricon* of 61 C.E., for example, some crucified robbers have a "soldier, on guard by the crosses to stop anyone from taking down a body for burial" (111–112). It was actually *nonburial* that made being crucified alive one of the three supreme penalties of Roman punishment (along with being devoured alive or burned alive). It was the typical execution reserved for runaway slaves and for other members of the lower classes who subverted the Roman order. Because of the ignominy and dishonor of this type of execution, it necessarily involved guarded crosses or at least severe sanctions against removal of the body before death and burial of the body after death.

The third stage is Hasmonean crucifixion. The biblical and Roman traditions were clearly contradictory. It was quite possible, in the biblical tradition, to hang the body on the cross until sunset and then remove it before nightfall. But how could that be done in the Roman system, where the person might not be dead by sunset, prolonged death agony was part of the public effect, and nonburial was the consummation of the procedure? Josephus says, in *Jewish War* 1.97 and *Jewish Antiquities* 13.380, that the Jewish king Alexander Jannaeus crucified eight hundred of his Pharisaic enemies in 88 B.C.E. It was live crucifixion, because he "slaughtered their children and wives before the eyes of the still living wretches." There is a coded reference to that massacre in 4Q169, a *pesher* or application of the book of Nahum to the life of the Dead Sea Essenes that was discovered in Cave 4 at Qumran (*DSST* 185–197). In fragments 3–4, column 1, lines 6–8, Alexander Jannaeus is called "the Angry Lion" who "hanged living men *[hole in the manuscript]* in Israel since ancient times." Because of that hole it is not certain whether the text would have read "which was not done" or "which was done." But, in any case, it is live crucifixion that is in view, so it is clear that the Hasmoneans adopted Roman-style live crucifixion rather than traditional Jewish dead crucifixion. There is nothing said about removal of the bodies by sunset, and, in context, that issue does not seem a major concern of Alexander Jannaeus.

The fourth stage is Essene crucifixion. This involves another one of the Dead Sea Scrolls, 11Q19–20, the Temple Scroll from Cave 11, longest of all those found at Qumran (*DSST* 154–184). From within this text, which dates from around the year 100 B.C.E., God legislates in first-person voice. In Lawrence

Schiffman's words, "The author/redactor called for a thoroughgoing revision of the existing Hasmonean order, desiring to replace it with a Temple, sacrificial system, and government which was the embodiment of the legislation of the Torah according to his view. . . . The text is a polemic against the existing order, calling for radical change in the order of the day, putting forward reforms in areas of cultic, religious and political life. So the true *Sitz im Leben* [life-setting] of the scroll is precisely one in which the circumstances of real life are the opposite of those called for by the author" (1994a:50, 51). It is a divine rereading of the Law prescribing how things will be when the Essenes take over Jerusalem and its Temple, the Jewish homeland and its government. It reflects, as Schiffman says, how things are *not* at the moment of its composition. Crucifixion is legislated for two crimes in 11Q19, column 64, lines 7–13. One criminal is a spy who betrays his people to a foreign nation; the other is a condemned person who escapes and curses his people among foreigners. In describing what is to happen to these criminals, there is an intercalation of these phrases in 64:8–11: "You shall hang him from a tree and he will die. . . . [H]e [shall] be executed and they shall hang him on the tree. . . . [H]e also you shall hang on the tree and he will die." That describes Roman-Hasmonean live crucifixion twice as frames around biblical crucifixion as center. And then, in 64:11–13, there follows the command for sunset removal from Deuteronomy 21:22–23. In other words, whether one deals with dead or live crucifixion, removal and burial must take place before nightfall. That tells us, however, what was *not* happening under the Hasmoneans (and presumably under the Romans as well). At the time of Jesus, therefore, live crucifixion made obedience to Deuteronomy 21:22–23 almost impossible, and burial before nightfall was, at best, a hope for future implementation under post-Hasmonean and post-Roman Essene control.

ARCHEOLOGY

Jesus was not the first Jew executed by Roman crucifixion outside the walls of Jerusalem in the first century. Nor was he the last. Josephus mentions three major incidents of *corporate* crucifixion in the decades before and after Jesus. The Roman governor Varus crucified "about two thousand" in 4 B.C.E. (*Jewish War* 2.75 = *Jewish Antiquities* 17.295). The Roman procurator Florus crucified "about three thousand six hundred" in 66 C.E. (*Jewish War* 2.307). The Roman general Titus crucified "five hundred or sometimes more . . . daily" in 70 C.E. (*Jewish War* 5.450). Yet only a single crucified skeleton has been found so far from that terrible first-century in the Jewish homeland.

Typical first-century Jewish tombs were carved into limestone rock with an antechamber opening into a room containing several deep niches into which a body could be placed at right angles to the room. Such niches were used over and over again once the flesh of a given corpse had decomposed. The bones were then buried together in pits dug in the floor or were gathered together into bone-boxes called ossuaries.

In June 1968 a complex of four tombs was excavated at Giv'at ha-Mivtar in northern Jerusalem. Three tombs held fifteen ossuaries containing the bones of thirty-five different individuals: eleven males, twelve females, and twelve children. Professor Haas of the Hebrew University/Hadassah Medical School's Department of Anatomy has observed that "evidence of death by violence was found in five cases: . . . crucifixion . . . conflagration [two cases] . . . arrow wound . . . blow from a mace" and that "there were three cases . . . of children who had died of starvation" (38). There was also one woman who had died in childbirth "because of the lack of a simple intervention by a midwife" (48). Of the two adults who had died from conflagration, one was a female, twenty-four to twenty-six years old, the other a male, sixteen to seventeen years old (44, 46). A picture of his left fibula shows striations indicating that "this individual had been put on a burning rack, and left on the fire long after death" (46). This is the first century in the Jewish homeland even before the horrors of total war in 66–73/74 C.E.

Ossuary 4, in Tomb I, held the bones of one man twenty-four to twenty-eight years old and one child three to four years old. The adult's name, incised on the ossuary, was Jehochanan; at five and a half feet, he was "no taller than the classical mean for Mediterranean peoples" (55). He had a cleft palate, an asymmetrical face, and a plagiocephalous cranium (one side more developed in front, the other side more developed in back), as can be seen in his "restored portrait" (53). The first two linked abnormalities stem from "a critical change in the manner of life of the pregnant woman in the first two or three weeks of pregnancy . . . an unexpected deterioration in the woman's diet, in association with psychical stress . . . produced by some catastrophe in the life of a well-to-do woman" (54). The third abnormality stems from "disturbances in the final period of pregnancy or as a result of difficulties in the act of parturition" (54).

Haas's initial analysis of the crucified skeleton was hurried due to religious reburial priorities, and the skeleton had to be disinterred and restudied later by Zias and Sekeles. Here are the main points of that reappraisal. First, there was a bone from another adult in Ossuary 4 by a first-century ossuary-reburial mistake. Second, the crucified man's arms were not nailed but tied to the crossbar and are pictorially depicted as bent over and behind it at the elbows (27). Third, his legs were not broken to hasten death. Fourth, his feet were affixed separately on either side of the upright by iron nails about four and a half inches long with olive-wood squares between their heads and his heel bones. Finally, there was "no evidence of the left heel bone" (25), but the right one still had the nail embedded in it, offering certain evidence of crucifixion in this case. "The nail was bent near its head and also at its pointed end"; after penetrating the olive wood and the right heel bone, it "may have accidentally struck a knot in the upright, thus bending the nail downwards. Once the body was removed from the cross, albeit with some difficulty in removing the right leg, the condemned man's family would now find it impossible to remove the bent nail without completely destroying the heel bone. This reluctance to inflict further damage to the heel led to the eventual discovery of the crucifixion" (23, 27). That too is the first century in the Jewish homeland even before the horrors of total war in 66–73/74 C.E.

That discovery emphasizes two points. First, however it was managed, be it through patronage or mercy, bribery or indifference, a crucified person could receive honorable burial in the family tomb in the early- or mid-first-century Jewish homeland. That agrees with what we know from Jewish texts of the same period. The Jewish philosopher Philo observed, in his *Flaccus* 83, that decent governors sometimes had crucified criminals "taken down and given up to their relations, in order to receive the honours of sepulture" at the time of the emperor's birthday, since "the sacred character of the festival ought to be regarded" (Yonge 732). The Jewish historian Josephus recorded, in his *Life* 420–421, that he found three of his friends crucified after the sack of Jerusalem in 70 C.E. and implored mercy from Titus. "Two of them died in the physicians' hands; the third survived." Second, with all those thousands of people crucified around Jerusalem in the first century alone, we have so far found only a single crucified skeleton— and that, of course, preserved in an ossuary. This supports the view that burial was the exception rather than the rule, the extraordinary rather than the ordinary case.

The next step is to place text in conjunction with that context. By *text* I do not mean the entire passion-resurrection tradition but three concluding units, all of which concern women: women watch the burial of Jesus, women find the tomb of Jesus, and women see the apparition of Jesus.

Mary and the Other Women

In all four Gospels Mary Magdalene is the first to discover the empty tomb. She provides proof that there is no confusion about having the right tomb where the right body had been buried. In two Gospels she is the first to see the risen Jesus. Yet in many ways we have seen the Gospels soft-pedal these elements. The evangelists seem to erase partially the women's role from the narrative. Their discomfort hints at how firmly entrenched the tradition of women's involvement must have been, since the authors do not feel free to eliminate it.

Claudia Setzer, "Excellent Women: Female Witness to the Resurrection," p. 268

You will recall the principle from Koester that I placed as epigraph to Chapter 23: "As far as the churches of Judea and Jerusalem are concerned, the traditions preserved in the Pauline Corpus are probably a better witness for their praxis than any sayings and narratives preserved in the Synoptic tradition" (1994a:550). The pre-Pauline traditions of the share-meal eucharist in 1 Corinthians 10–11 (discussed earlier), and now the passion-resurrection account in 1 Corinthians 15 point, therefore, to the earliest Jerusalem community.

ACCORDING TO THE SCRIPTURES

I focus on 1 Corinthians 15 not for Pauline theology at Corinth but for pre-Pauline tradition at Jerusalem. This is 1 Corinthians 15:1–11:

> [1]Now I would remind you, brothers and sisters *(adelphoi)*, of the good news that I *proclaimed* to you, which you in turn received, in which also you stand, [2]through which also you are being saved, if you hold firmly to the message that I *proclaimed* to you—unless you have come to *believe* in vain. [3]For I handed on to you as of first importance what I in turn had received:
>
> that Christ died for our sins in accordance with the scriptures,
>
> [4]and that he was buried,
>
> and that he was raised on the third day in accordance with the scriptures,
>
> [5]and that he appeared
>
> [1] to Cephas,
>
> [2] then to the twelve.
>
> [3] [6]Then he appeared to more than five hundred brothers and sisters at one time, most of whom are still alive, though some have died.
>
> [4] [7]Then he appeared to James,
>
> [5] then to all the apostles.
>
> [6] [8]Last of all, as to one untimely born, he appeared also to me. [9]For I am the least of the apostles, unfit to be called an apostle, because I persecuted the church of God. [10]But by the grace of God I am what I am, and his grace toward me has not been in vain. On the contrary, I worked harder than any of them—though it was not I, but the grace of God that is with me.
>
> [11]Whether then it was I or they, so we *proclaim* and so you have come to *believe*.

The whole unit is framed between the terms *proclaim* and *believe* as repeated in 15:1 and 11, but it is obvious that Christ's appearance to Paul himself in 15:8–11 is not part of his *received* tradition. One must also allow for some redactional organization, whereby Paul concludes with "all the apostles" in 15:7b in order to prepare for himself as "least of the apostles" in 15.9. But granted that, 15:3b–7 is certified as tradition *received* by Paul (15:3a) and thence *received* by the Corinthians

(15:1b). Within 15:3b–7 I look first at the parallel phrases about death and resurrection in 15:3b+4b and then at the list of appearance in 15:5–7.

In 15:3b+4b the twin phrases "died for our sins" and "raised on the third day" are cited as "in accordance with the scriptures." The phrase "for our sins" connects, as Koester has noted, with the Suffering Servant of Isaiah 52–53 (1994a:553):

> But he was wounded for our sins, crushed for our iniquities; upon him was the punishment that made us whole, and by his bruises we are healed. All we like sheep have gone astray; we have all turned to our own way, and the Lord handed him over for our sins. (Isaiah 53:5–6)

As you will recall from Chapter 23, the Common Meal Tradition saw Jesus as the Suffering Servant through its use of the noun "child/servant" *(pais)* in *Didache* 9–10 from Isaiah 52:13 and the verb "handed over" in 1 Corinthians 10–11 from Isaiah 53:6, 12. Since the phrase "handed over for our sins" in 1 Corinthians 15:3b also links with Isaiah 53:5–6, Koester is surely correct to link the Common Meal Tradition and the Suffering Servant. But he goes beyond that general conjunction: "There is strong evidence that Paul knew such a *story* of Jesus' suffering and death—not as historical information but as a *story* that was told 'according to the scriptures,' and a *story* that made Jesus present for the participants in the celebration of the eucharist" (1994b:553, my italics). Did Paul know such a *story?*

First, Koester speaks about the Bible's "suffering righteous" and of Jesus' "suffering and death." I insist that it is never an issue of persecution (by whatever name) but a balanced dyad of persecution-vindication (by whatever names). Paul, therefore, certainly knew that narrative *pattern*. It is, in fact, the dyadic structure of 1 Corinthians 15:3b+4b, now articulated as death-resurrection. Further, he certainly knew that narrative pattern in a mythical *hymn*, because that is how it appears in the pre-Pauline text of Philippians 2:6–11. The question is this: Did Paul know it already as a *story?* Koester's argument for *story* is primarily 1 Corinthians 11:23, which locates the institution of the Lord's Supper "on the night when he was handed over." It is almost impossible for us to read that phrase, especially if mistranslated as "on the night he was betrayed," without imagining behind it the entire Markan nighttime scenario from upper chamber to garden arrest. But once the Lord's Supper is told not just as Christian ritual but as Jesus' institution, its location as last-supper-before-death is almost inevitable. Maybe Paul *does* know a story, but that single phrase is not enough to prove it.

Second, Koester adduces "one further piece of evidence for Paul's knowledge of a narrative sequence of the story of Jesus' suffering and death; it appears in the phrase of 1 Cor 5,7, 'Our Passover has been sacrificed, Christ'. . . . This statement may imply that Christ died on the day of the slaughtering of the Passover lambs, thus revealing that Paul followed the same dating of Jesus' death as the Gospel of John" (1994a:553). But that is also the same dating for Jesus' death as in my proposed *Cross Gospel*. The *Gospel of Peter* 2:5b, says that Herod "handed him over to the people on the day before the unleavened bread, their feast." That is to say, both John and the *Cross Gospel* agree, against the three synoptics, that Jesus died on Passover Eve, not Passover Day. I am not convinced from those two phrases in 1 Corinthians 5:7 and 11:23 that Paul does know a death-resurrection *story*, but, if he does, it could well be an antecedent version of the *Cross Gospel*.

There is another major question concerning those parallel phrases in 1 Corinthians 15:3b+4b. Even apart from Isaiah 52–53 there are very many other biblical texts and types, from single verses in Psalms to wider patterns of persecution-vindication, that can be suggested behind "died according to the scriptures." But what about "raised on the third day according to the scriptures"? One specific passage is often suggested:

> Come, let us return to the Lord; for it is he who has torn, and he will heal us;
> he has struck down, and he will bind us up. After two days he will revive us;
> on the third day he will raise us up, that we may live before him. (Hosea 6:1–2)

In itself that is simply a standard biblical parallelism, where the numerical pattern x/x+1 means a few—that is, in context, a few days. It is a promise that God will deliver them *soon*. When you think of the myriad biblical citations backing up "died according to the scriptures," that is surely a very scant background for "raised on the third day according to the scriptures."

It is clear enough that what is actually "according to the scriptures" is that dyad of persecution-vindication. From Joseph to Susannah, from *3 Maccabees* to *2 Maccabees,* from Isaiah 52–53 to *Wisdom* 1–5, from the Law through prophecy to wisdom, the persecuted are vindicated, and their deliverance is either effected *before* death or promised *despite* death. But how are such promises fulfilled, *despite* death? That is what the descent into hell is all about. It is about Jesus at the head of the communal resurrection. It is about "the third day," when the Son of God is dead enough to enter Hades and destroy its power forever. A first or second day might be about individual resuscitation, but the third day is about communal resurrection "according to the scriptures." Recall that Brown and I agreed in Chapter 25 on the purpose for guarding Jesus' tomb "for three days" in *Gospel of Peter* 8:30. By Jewish reckoning, a dead person is surely and securely dead only after three days. That is why, for example, it is important that Lazarus has "already been in the tomb four days" in John 11:17. He is really and truly dead, dead, dead. That is also the logic of *Gospel of Peter* 8:30. If the authorities had simply been afraid of grave robbery, an empty tomb, and claims of resurrection from the disciples, they would have needed to guard the tomb for a much longer time. Such claims could have been made at any time, not just within three days. Three days establishes that the body is really and irrevocably a corpse so that the disciples cannot resuscitate Jesus and remove him. Thereafter, the people, finding an empty tomb and already repentant because of the "exceeding great signs" at Jesus' death, might believe all by themselves (without any apostolic prompting) that Jesus is risen from the dead. The authorities' plan, in other words, is to prevent resuscitation by the disciples from being interpreted as resurrection by the people.

An aside. Such thinking was quite correct until modern death certification became available. Peter Linebaugh has written a fascinating chapter about public hangings at Tyburn Tree in London during the eighteenth century. It addresses, among other things, riots between the condemned's friends and the surgeons who wanted the body for dissection. "At times it was reasonable to regard the surgeons, not the hangman, as the agent causing death. During the first half of the eighteenth century the cause of death at Tyburn was asphyxia, not dislocation of the spine. A broken neck was decisive. Asphyxia, however, could result in temporary unconsciousness if the knot was tied, or the noose placed around the neck, in a particular fashion. . . . Incomplete hangings without fatal strangulation were common enough to sustain the hope that resuscitation ('resurrection' as it was called) would save the condemned. Life after 'death' therefore had a quite practical reality for those sent to Tyburn to hang, and for many of them their time in Newgate before the hanging day was spent in preparation for such 'resurrections'" (102–104). There is, for example, the case of William Duell in 1740, who hung at Tyburn for half an hour and revived as the surgeons were about to dissect him.

The certainty of death is the macabre reality behind guarding a body "for three days." Resuscitation was a possibility—albeit remote—for at least a few days. But, as we also saw above, Jesus had to be truly dead to enter into Hades and release "them that sleep" from their bondage down below. For Jesus to rise on the third day or to rise after three days meant to rise after true death and true descent into Hades. That meant communal resurrection, meant Jesus rising at the head of the holy ones; and, since such vindication-resurrection was biblically promised, it was "according to the scriptures." Notice, by the way, that as Paul continues in 1 Corinthians 15, it never occurs to him that Jesus' resurrection might be an absolutely unique and personal privilege, like Elijah taken up to God long ago. Jesus' resurrection takes place only *within* the general resurrection:

If there is no resurrection of the dead, then Christ has not been raised. . . . [I]f the dead are not raised, then Christ has not been raised. (1 Corinthians 15:13, 16)

In fact, the Greek verb that Paul uses for the communal resurrection in 15:20, "Christ has been raised from the dead, the first fruits of those who have *slept*," is the same as that in *Gospel of Peter* 10:42, "Have you preached to them that *sleep?*" Jesus preaches—better, proclaims like a herald—liberation to those who have died in persecution and now at last are vindicated "according to the scriptures."

BURIAL, TOMB, AND VISION

There was, as seen already, a common basis in the persecution-vindication pattern and the eucharistic meal behind both the Life Tradition and the Death Tradition. But there is no equivalent Common Resurrection Tradition or Common Apparition Tradition distinguishable in both of them. And even when those Life and Death Traditions came together in the canonical gospels, conjunction between the pre-Pauline tradition in 1 Corinthians 15 and the final chapters of the gospels is still very difficult to establish. On the one hand, that basic sequence of death-burial-resurrection-apparition appears with credal brevity in 1 Corinthians 15:3b–7 and with full narrative detail in Mark 15–16, Matthew 27–28, Luke 23–24, and John 19–21. On the other hand, there is not the slightest indication that the sequence or even the list of apparitions in 1 Corinthians 15:5–7 was a tradition behind any of our present gospel conclusions. But the most striking difference is this: While the pre-Pauline tradition speaks of *Peter and the Twelve,* and of *James and the apostles,* the canonical gospel texts emphasize much more the role of *Mary and the women.* We need to take a closer look at what that means.

First, two men, Peter and James, are named in 1 Corinthians 15:5–7, but no women are named. Here are some *maybes* in that regard. *Maybe* Paul knew that Mary and the other women had found Jesus' tomb empty but left that fact implicit between "buried" and "appeared." (But it is certainly not *explicit.*) *Maybe* Paul knew that Mary and the other women had seen the risen Jesus but left them implicit among "all the apostles." (Again, it is certainly not *explicit.*) *Maybe* Paul knew both those items as received tradition but omitted them because of trouble with women prophets at Corinth. (But Paul had far greater trouble with James and Peter-Cephas, according to Galatians 2:11–14, and there was even some trouble concerning Peter-Cephas in 1 Corinthians 1:12, yet Paul does not omit either man from officially received tradition.)

Second, the consecutive and canonically independent source in the *Gospel of Peter* has nothing about women finding the tomb empty or about Jesus appearing to women. Instead, it is the Roman guards and the Jewish authorities who find the tomb empty in that *Cross Gospel*, and it is to them that Jesus appears.

Neither of the two preceding texts mentions the women finding the empty tomb or seeing the risen Jesus. But maybe, as Claudia Setzer suggested in the epigraph to this section, male writers are deliberately reducing the importance of female witnesses. That has happened and still happens so often that it is certainly a possibility. But is it the best reading of the evidence in this case?

Those twin texts just cited are the *earliest* extant accounts of the resurrection. When, for contrast, you look at two of the *latest* ones, the women are firmly present. This is from the longer ending added to Mark's gospel in 16:9–20:

Now after he rose early on the first day of the week, he appeared first to Mary Magdalene, from whom he had cast out seven demons. She went out and told those who had been with him, while they were mourning and weeping. But when they heard that he was alive and had been seen by her, they would not believe it. After this he appeared in another form to two of them, as they were walking into the country. And they went back and told the rest, but they did not believe them. Later he appeared to the eleven themselves as they were sitting at the table; and he upbraided them for their lack of faith and stubbornness, because they had not believed those who saw him after he had risen. (Mark 16:9–14)

The same happens in the final redaction of the *Gospel of Peter*. As the extra-canonical *Cross Gospel* is combined with intracanonical materials, we get this summary:

Early in the morning of the Lord's day Mary Magdalene, a woman disciple of the Lord—for fear of the Jews, since (they) were inflamed with wrath, she had not done at the sepulchre what women are wont to do for those beloved of them who die—took with her women friends and came to the sepulchre where he was laid. (*Gospel of Peter* 11:50–51)

The evidence seems to be moving in the opposite direction. The women are not so much being eliminated or reduced as being introduced and emphasized in the tradition of that story. What exactly is happening to the women who watch the burial, find the empty tomb, and see the risen Jesus? Paul mentions burial and vision, but nothing about finding an empty tomb in between. But above all, he has nothing about the women. Peter, James, and Paul are named, but not Mary. The Twelve and the apostles are mentioned, but not the women (unless implicitly as apostles). How is that to be explained?

Before proceeding, let me offer a graphic summary of the data. I will keep it simple to emphasize the main differences. There are three narrative units: the description of the burial, the finding of the empty tomb, and the vision of the risen Jesus. There are also three groups of narrative protagonists: nondisciples such as the enemies or the guards; women disciples such as Mary Magdalene, the other Mary, and Salome; and men disciples, such as Joseph or Nicodemus, Peter, the Beloved Disciple, and others. Those two axes of units and protagonists interact as follows:

	Nondisciples	Women Disciples	Men Disciples
Burial	(1) *Cross Gospel*	(1) Mark	
		(2) Matthew	(1) Matthew
		(3) Luke	(2) John
Tomb	(1) *Cross Gospel*	(1) Mark	(1) Luke
	(2) Matthew	(2) Matthew	(2) John
		(3) Luke	
		(4) John	
		(5) *Gospel of Peter*	
Vision	(1) *Cross Gospel*	(1) Matthew	(1) Matthew
		(2) John	(2) Luke
			(3) John
			(4?) *Gospel of Peter*

In what follows I look at those three units in that order: burial, tomb, and vision. I have two points to make. First, Mark created both the women's discovery of the empty tomb and the burial story needed in preparation for it. Second, Matthew created the story of the apparition of Jesus to the women to change Mark's negative ending into a more positive one. John copied that vision from Matthew. In both those cases, it was a message-vision (tell the disciples) and not a mandate-vision (change the world). There is, therefore, no anterior tradition, let alone historical information, in any of those three units. That, however, raises an even more fundamental issue. Why were those stories about the women created at all?

The Women and the Burial of Jesus

Both anthropological and historical evidence would lead us to expect that, after the death of Jesus, females would bury him and males would observe. What we find in Mark, however, is exactly the opposite: a man buries Jesus and women watch.

When evening had come, and since it was the day of Preparation, that is, the day before the sabbath, Joseph of Arimathea, a respected member of the council, who was also himself waiting expectantly for the kingdom of God, went boldly to Pilate and asked for the body of Jesus. Then Pilate wondered if he were already dead; and summoning the centurion, he asked him whether he had been dead for some time. When he learned from the centurion that he was dead, he granted the body to Joseph. Then Joseph bought a linen cloth, and taking down the body, wrapped it in the linen cloth, and laid it in a tomb that had been hewn out of the rock. He then rolled a stone against the door of the tomb. Mary Magdalene and Mary the mother of Joses saw where the body was laid. (Mark 15:42–47)

The question is not, as formulated by Gerald O'Collins and Daniel Kendall, "Did Joseph of Arimathea exist?" The question is whether Jesus was buried as described in Mark 15:42–47. I look only at that male burial here and hold the female observation until the next section.

We saw historical evidence above, both textual and archeological, that a crucified person could end up buried by friends or relatives, be it through mercy or humanity, bribery or patronage. Joseph of Arimathea *could* have buried Jesus, perhaps out of personal piety or communal duty.

Personal piety is exemplifed in *Tobit*, a fourth- or third-century B.C.E. novel set in Assyria at the end of the eighth and start of the seventh centuries B.C.E. First, in 1:17, a pious Jew named Tobit says, "I would give my food to the hungry and my clothing to the naked; and if I saw the dead body of any of my people thrown out behind the wall of Nineveh, I would bury it." For this he forfeits all his property and almost loses his life as well. He is saved, however, by Ahiqar (remember him from the previous chapter?), who happens to be his "nephew and so a close relative" (it's a novel!). Next, in 2:2, at the feast of Pentecost, Tobit invites "whatever poor person you may find of our people among the exiles in Nineveh, who is wholeheartedly mindful of God, and he shall eat together with me." Finally, in 2:4, he gets up from that untouched dinner to recover an unburied Jew from the market square, and he "laid it in one of the rooms until sunset when I might bury it." Joseph of Arimathea *could* have been a pious Jew like Tobit in that novel a few centuries before Jesus.

Communal duty is exemplified by Jewish law in the *Mishnah,* a code of Jewish life assembled around the year 200 C.E. The fourth of its six divisions is on *Damages,* and the fourth of the ten *Damages* tractates is on the *Sanhedrin* or Supreme Court. *Sanhedrin* 6:5–6 (mentioned by Sawicki above) notes that "they used not" to bury executed criminals in their ancestral tombs but kept two burial places in readiness, one for those "beheaded and strangled," the other for those "stoned or burnt." After a year in such places, "when the flesh had wasted away," their bones could be taken and reburied honorably by their families but without any public mourning (Danby 391). *If* that was ever operational in real (as distinct from ideal) law, and *if* it was operational in early-Roman Jerusalem, Joseph *could* have been the official whose duty it was to bury condemned bodies.

The problem with Joseph of Arimathea is not on the level of *could* but of *did*. It is not on the level of possibility but of actuality. In one's best historical reconstruction, did such a person do what Mark described? Two points convince me that Mark 15:42–47 is Mark's own creation.

The first point concerns who Joseph was, as Mark tells it and as Matthew and Luke rewrite it. Mark 15:43 describes him as "[1] a respected member of the council *[bouleutēs]*, [2] who was also himself waiting expectantly for the kingdom of God." That is doubly (and I think) deliberately ambiguous. The ambiguity with regard to the first part is this: Was Joseph among those who judged Jesus? In 14:55 and 15:1 Mark calls those who judged Jesus "the whole council *[synedrion]*" or sanhedrin, and he says in 14:64 that "all of them condemned him as deserving death." But Joseph is described not as a member of the *synedrion*-council but as a member of the *boulē*-council, as if there were two councils in charge of Jerusalem, a civil council and a religious council, with Joseph a member of the former body *(bouleutēs)* but not in the latter one at all *(synedrion)*. There was, of course, no such distinction in historical life; there was only one council by whatever name. Convened whenever Pilate and/or Caiaphas had need of it, that body was made up of those citizens they deemed appropriate. Those divergent terms indicating the council—*bouleutēs* and *synedrion*—make it impossible to know whether Joseph was among the judges of Jesus, and that is precisely their Markan purpose. But the text is equally ambiguous with regard to that second half: Was Joseph among those who followed Jesus? We know from as early as 1:14 that the kingdom of God is a crucial term for Mark. But is "looking for it" the same as accepting it, entering it, believing in it? That oblique expression "looking for" makes it impossible to be sure whether Joseph was among the followers of Jesus; again, that is precisely its Markan purpose.

Matthew and Luke, those first and most careful readers of Mark, see that double problem and respond to Mark's calculated ambiguity. Matthew 27:57 eliminates any mention of the council and makes Joseph explicitly a follower of Jesus. He is now "a rich man from Arimathea, named Joseph, who was also a disciple of Jesus." Luke 22:66 picks up the term *synedrion*-council from Mark but solves the problem of Joseph the sanhedrist-disciple in 23:50–51: "[T]here was a good and righteous man named Joseph, who, though a member of the council *[bouleutēs]*, had not agreed to their plan and action. He came from the Jewish

town of Arimathea, and he was waiting expectantly for the kingdom of God."
Notice that Luke does not repeat Mark's comment (14:64) that "all" of the council's judges had condemned Jesus to death.

The second point concerns what Joseph did, as Mark tells it and as Matthew
and Luke rewrite it. Mark 15:46 says that Joseph took Jesus' body and "laid it in a
tomb that had been hewn out of the rock." That is clear enough unless you wonder who Joseph was and why he buried Jesus. If he acted out of either personal
piety or communal duty, would he not have done the same for the two other
criminals crucified with Jesus? And unless one imagines three separate tombs,
they would all have been buried together in a single tomb or even in a communal tomb for criminals. Were that the case, though, how could you continue into
an empty-tomb story? How ghastly to imagine probing among corpses to identify the missing one as that of Jesus.

Once again, Matthew and Luke see the problem and respond to it separately
but emphatically. They both find the obvious solution: Joseph's tomb has to be
one in which nobody is buried before or with Jesus; he must be alone in that
tomb. Matthew 27:60 rephrases Mark this way: Joseph took the body of Jesus
"and laid it in his own new tomb, which he had hewn in the rock." Luke 23:53
rephrases Mark this way: Joseph took the body of Jesus "and laid it in a rock-
hewn tomb where no one had ever been laid."

Mark's story presented the tradition with double dilemmas. First, if Joseph
was in the council, he was against Jesus; if he was for Jesus, he was not in the
council. Second, if Joseph buried Jesus from piety or duty, he would have done
the same for the two other crucified criminals; yet if he did that, there could be
no empty-tomb sequence. None of those points is unanswerable, but together
they persuade me that Mark *created* that burial by Joseph of Arimathea in
15:42–47. It contains no pre-Markan tradition.

As the tradition developed, Jesus' burial moved from enemies to friends and
from an inadequate and hurried entombment to one of regal magnificence. The
Cross Gospel has only the hope that his enemies would have buried him out of
obedience to Deuteronomy 21:22–23. Mark is much more consoling with his
Joseph story, and Matthew and Luke both improve on that. But John's account is
in climactic accord with his theology of passion-as-resurrection, crucifixion-as-
ascension to the Father whence Jesus came. Joseph is a secret disciple; he is
accompanied by another one, Nicodemus, and they bury Jesus with "a mixture
of myrrh and aloes, weighing about a hundred pounds" in 19:39. I find there a
trajectory of hope but not of history. Behind that hope lies, at worst, the horror
of a body left on the cross as carrion or, at best, a body consigned like others to a
"limed pit," as Sawicki put it above. I would hope for a Joseph, but what you
hope for is not always what happens.

The Women and the Tomb of Jesus

All five gospels agree that Mary Magdalene and some other women are the *first* of Jesus' companions to find his tomb empty. Mark 16:1 mentions "Mary Magdalene, and Mary the mother of James, and Salome." Matthew 28:1 has "Mary Magdalene and the other Mary." Luke 24:10 cites "Mary Magdalene, Joanna, Mary the mother of James, and the other women with them." John 20:1 has only "Mary Magdalene," although he uses "we" in 20:2. *Gospel of Peter* 12:50–51 speaks of "Mary Magdalene, a woman disciple of the Lord . . . [who] took with her women friends." That is a very impressive consensus, but it is all dependent on a single source. It is not five *independent* witnesses; it is Mark, with four other writers copying directly or indirectly from him. It does not help to speak of "all four Gospels and . . . even . . . the *Gospel of Peter*" or of "all four Gospels" or of "the triple tradition" of Matthew, Mark, and Luke, as Setzer does (160, 261, 268). That is simply counting versions while ignoring sources. The question is this: Do we have one, two, three, four, or five *independent* sources? And if, as I believe, we have only one independent source in Mark, it all comes down to these two issues: Is there any pre-Markan tradition in Mark 16:1–8, and what is Mark's purpose for that incident? There are three linked texts to be considered:

[*After the death:*] There were also women looking on from a distance; among them were Mary Magdalene, and Mary the mother of James the younger and of Joses, and Salome. These used to follow him and provided for him when he was in Galilee; and there were many other women who had come up with him to Jerusalem. (Mark 15:40–41)

[*After the burial:*] Mary Magdalene and Mary the mother of Joses saw where the body was laid. (Mark 15:47)

[*After the sabbath:*] When the sabbath was over, Mary Magdalene, and Mary the mother of James, and Salome bought spices, so that they might go and anoint him. And very early on the first day of the week, when the sun had risen, they went to the tomb. They had been saying to one another, "Who will roll away the stone for us from the entrance to the tomb?" When they looked up, they saw that the stone, which was very large, had already been rolled back. As they entered the tomb, they saw a young man, dressed in a white robe, sitting on the right side; and they were alarmed. But he said to them, "Do not be alarmed; you are looking for Jesus of Nazareth, who was crucified. He has been raised; he is not here. Look, there is the place they laid him. But go, tell his disciples and Peter that he is going ahead of you to Galilee; there you will see him, just as he told you." So they went out and fled from the tomb, for terror and amazement had seized them; and they said nothing to anyone, for they were afraid. (Mark 16:1–8)

While the reaction in that third passage could be explained as numinous awe, the text offers a rather negative portrayal of the women. It is also self-contradictory. If they told nobody, how did Mark, unless "he" was one of them, know about it? But it all fits quite exactly as a conclusion to Mark's gospel.

Mark is severely and relentlessly critical of the Twelve in general, of Peter, James, and John in particular, and of Peter above all the others. That has been interpreted as Markan criticism of other Christian communities that are less emphatic about the suffering destiny of Jesus, less enthusiastic about the mission to the pagans, and more dependent on traditions about Peter, the Three, and the Twelve, for their theological viewpoints. It has also been interpreted as Markan consolation for those in his own community who have failed Jesus in recent persecutions attendant on the First Roman-Jewish War of 66–73/74 C.E. and who need to be told that, as with Peter, the Three, and the Twelve, failure, flight, and even denial are not hopeless. But, against that background, how could Mark end his gospel with apparitions to Peter, or the Inner Three, or the Twelve? He had to end his gospel very differently. Mark's ending in 16:1–8 must be understood against that general background and within this specific foreground:

(A¹) Failure over crucifixion (named male disciples): Mark 10:32–42 (Gethsemane)

(B²) Success over resurrection (unnamed female disciple): Mark 14:3–9 (anointing)

(A²) Success over crucifixion (unnamed male disciple): Mark 15:39 (centurion)

(B¹) Failure over resurrection (named female disciples): Mark 16:1–8 (empty tomb)

All of that structure is important to understand Mark's purpose. Female and male companions of Jesus are important for Mark, and the inner three from each group are especially important for him. But they are important as models of failure—not of *hopeless* failure, but still of failure. That explains why Mark created the empty-tomb story just as he created the sleeping disciples in Gethsemane. The outer frames of the passion story in 10:32–42 and 16:1–8 have male and female disciples failing Jesus. But each of those twin failures is counterpointed with a twin success. Male disciples flee Jesus because they fear the crucifixion, but the centurion confesses him because he sees the crucifixion. Female disciples fail Jesus because of anointing, but another female succeeds precisely there. That needs some explanation.

In Mark's story Jesus had told the disciple three times, and very clearly, that he would be executed in Jerusalem and that he would rise after three days. That prophecy is repeated in 8:31, 9:31, and 10:33–34. It always concludes with the resurrection "after three days." Bringing burial spices to Jesus' tomb after those prophecies is certainly an act of love but hardly an act of faith. Indeed, for Mark it is a *lack* of faith. That, rather than flight or silence, is what makes 16:1–8 failure for Mark. It is not that the women fly the tomb with fear but that they approach the tomb with ointment. That is why Mark insists that the women "bought spices, so that they might go and anoint him." But before Mark tells of that failure by named women in 16:1–8, he tells this story of stunning faith:

While he was at Bethany in the house of Simon the leper, as he sat at the table, a woman came with an alabaster jar of very costly ointment of nard, and she broke open the jar and poured the ointment on his head. But some were there who said to one another in anger, "Why was the ointment wasted in this way? For this ointment could have been sold for more than three hundred denarii, and the money given to the poor." And they scolded her. But Jesus said, "Let her alone; why do you trouble her? She has performed a good service for me. For you always have the poor with you, and you can show kindness to them whenever you wish; but you will not always have me. She has done what she could; she has anointed my body beforehand for its burial. Truly I tell you, wherever the good news is proclaimed in the whole world, what she has done will be told in remembrance of her." (Mark 14:3–9)

This unnamed woman believes the prophecies of his death and resurrection given by Jesus in Mark 8:31, 9:31, and 10:33–34. She *believes* them and knows, therefore, that if she does not anoint him for burial now, she will never be able to do it later. That is why she gets that astonishing statement of praise, one unparalleled in the entire gospel: "[W]herever the good news is proclaimed in the whole world, what she has done will be told in remembrance of her." That accolade is given because, in Mark's gospel, this is the first complete and unequivocal act of faith in Jesus' suffering and rising destiny. It is the only such full act before that of the equally unnamed centurion beneath the cross in 14: 39b: "Truly this man was God's Son!" For Mark, that unnamed woman is the first Christian.

The empty-tomb story is neither an early historical event nor a late legendary narrative but a deliberate Markan creation. Sleeping male disciples in the garden and anointing women disciples at the tomb are Mark's own redactional frames for the passion-resurrection story. It is not in 16:1–8 but in 14:3–9 that Mark portrays an "excellent woman" as a "female witness to the resurrection," to borrow Setzer's titular terms. But that is surely far more startling than to claim that a woman was (or women were) first to *find* an empty tomb or even first to *see* the risen Jesus. Mark says that a woman was first to *believe* in the resurrection. If you are concerned with firsts, that does seem the more significant one.

Finally, if Mark created both the burial by Joseph and the finding of the empty tomb by women, the function of 15:47 becomes clear. It is the necessary conjunction between those twin units: "Mary Magdalene and Mary the mother of Joses saw where the body was laid." But those women were first introduced near the cross:

> There were also women looking on from a distance; among them were Mary Magdalene, and Mary the mother of James the younger and of Joses, and Salome. These used to follow him and provided for him when he was in Galilee; and there were many other women who had come up with him to Jerusalem. (Mark 15:40–41)

That is the fullest identification given to those three women. In Mark 15:47 neither James nor Salome is mentioned. That verse speaks only of "Mary Magdalene and Mary the mother of Joses." In Mark 16:1 the three women are there, but Joses is not mentioned. That verse speaks of "Mary Magdalene, and Mary the mother of James, and Salome." It is as if Mark dismembered 15:40 to create divergently briefer versions of it in 15:47 and 16:1.

Mark knows about a group of male disciples, among whom are the inner three of Peter, James, and John. He criticizes them repeatedly and cumulatively, as I have noted. But, while that criticism is from Markan redaction, the existence and names of those men are from pre-Markan tradition. Mark also knows a group of female disciples. Just as with the men, so also with the women. Their existence and names in 15:40–41 are pre-Markan tradition, but their criticism in 15:47–16:8 is Markan redaction. In other words, the inclusion of women observing the burial and visiting the tomb is no earlier than Mark, but the inclusion of women watching the crucifixion is received tradition. But is the latter historical fact? My best answer is yes, because the male disciples had fled; if the women had not been watching, we would not know even the brute fact of crucifixion (as distinct, for example, from Jesus being summarily speared or beheaded in prison).

The Women and the Vision of Jesus

A similar situation arises with regard to the women and/or Mary seeing the risen Jesus. Those stories are not pre-Markan tradition or even Markan creation but post-Markan development. They were created not by Mark but, after him, by Matthew and John. Mark ended in 16:8, as we saw above, with the women disobeying the "young man" in the tomb, failing to spread the word of Jesus' resurrection. Here is how Matthew rephrases his Markan source from disobedi-ence to obedience:

Mark 16:8	Matthew 28:8
So they went out and fled from the tomb,	So they left the tomb quickly
for terror and amazement had seized them;	with fear and great joy,
and they said nothing to anyone,	and ran to tell his disciples.
for they were afraid.	

The angelic command just before this passage (in Matthew 28:7) asks the women to "go quickly." Their obedience is underlined by the repeated "left quickly" in 28:8. Next, each of Mark's three comments is changed into its oppo-site: instead of "fled" there is "quickly" leaving to bring the good news; instead of "terror and amazement" there is "fear and great joy"; instead of saying "nothing to anyone" there is, as ordered, running "to tell his disciples."

But even those changes are not enough to offset Mark's terrible negativity. So Matthew adds this unit:

Suddenly Jesus met them and said, "Greetings!" And they came to him, took hold of his feet, and worshiped him. Then Jesus said to them, "Do not be afraid; go and tell my brothers to go to Galilee; there they will see me." (Matthew 28:9–10)

On the one hand, Jesus' message in 28:10, "Go and tell my brothers to go to Galilee; there they will see me," simply summarizes the angelic message in 28:7, "Go quickly and tell his disciples, 'He has been raised from the dead, and indeed he is going ahead of you to Galilee; there you will see him.'" On the other hand, their "worship" prepares for the next unit on a Galilean mountain, when the dis-ciples "worshiped him." In other words, that apparition to the women in 28:9–10 is a pure Matthean composition, created to efface the Markan ending and pre-pare for the apparition of Jesus to the disciples. Furthermore, the women get a message-vision; the disciples get a mandate-vision. As Frans Neirynck concludes, "The account of the empty tomb in Matt. xxviii [1–10] presupposes no other ver-sion than that of Mark" (1982:289).

What about the apparition of the risen Jesus to Mary Magdalene in John 20:14–17 and her report to the disciples in 20:18? Is this independent Johannine tradition or is it derived from Matthew 28:9–10? That latter text, as just seen, is a complete Matthean creation; therefore, if any of its characteristic elements re-appear in John 20:14–17, John's dependence on Matthew would be the likeliest explanation. There are three such Matthean elements present in John 20:14–17.

First, Matthew repeated but contracted the command and promise from the empty tomb in 28:7, "Go . . . and tell his disciples, '. . . he is going ahead of you to Galilee; there you will see him,'" to the risen vision in 28:10, "Go and tell my brothers to go to Galilee; there they will see me." Similarly, John repeated but expanded the question and answer from the empty tomb in 20:13, "They [the angels] said to her, 'Woman, why are you weeping?' She said to them, 'They have taken away my Lord, and I do not know where they have laid him,'" to the risen vision in 20:15, "Jesus said to her, 'Woman, why are you weeping? Whom are you looking for?' Supposing him to be the gardener, she said to him, 'Sir, if you have carried him away, tell me where you have laid him, and I will take him away.'" In both cases the tomb dialogue was adapted to create the vision dialogue.

Second, there is a parallelism between the sequence of the two visions that is especially evident at one particular point. In Matthew 28:9b the women "came to him, took hold of his feet, and worshiped him." But in John 20:17a Jesus tells Mary, "Do not hold on to me." Those texts use different "hold" verbs in Greek, but since there is nothing about Mary grasping Jesus earlier in John 20:14–17, you have to presume something like Matthew 28:9b to understand John 20:17a. They hold Jesus only in Matthew. They are told to let him go only in John.

Third, there is this final and most important point. The tomb message was for "his disciples and Peter" in Mark 16:7. In copying Mark, Matthew 28:7–8 simplified that to "his disciples." Then, in creating his own risen vision in Matthew 29:9–10, he changed that to "my brothers." That last term, in other words, is redactionally Matthean. But this same "my brothers" reappears in John 20:17b. That is the most direct use of a redactional word from Matthew 28:9–10 in John 20:14–17. I agree, once again, with Frans Neirynck's conclusions. John 20:14–17 shows "John's indebtedness to the tradition of the appearance of Jesus to the women as it is found in Mt 28,9–10" (1982:398), and "as a further consequence of our interpretation of Mt 28,9–10 and its parallel in John we can conclude that the so-called protophany of Mary Magdalene has no traditional basis. The third witness, Mk 16,9, is of course not an independent witness" (1991:588).

The women's discovery of the empty tomb was created by Mark to avoid a risen apparition to the disciples, and the women's vision of the risen Jesus was created by Matthew to prepare for a risen apparition to the disciples. There is no evidence of historical tradition about those two details prior to Mark in the 70s. Furthermore, the women, rather than being there early and being steadily removed, are not there early but are steadily included. They are included, of course, to receive only message-visions, never mandate-visions. They are told to go tell the disciples, while the disciples are told to go teach the nations. But is that all there is to be said about Mary Magdalene and the other named and unnamed women with her?

Mark created the *sleep* of the three male disciples in the garden at the start of the passion, but he did not create those three named individuals. Similarly, Mark created the *visit* of the three female disciples to the tomb at the end of the passion, but he did not create those individuals. Mark balanced both sets of disciples against one another and opposed them both, so that just as the three males represented for Mark authority to be criticized, so also the three named females represented for Mark authority to be criticized. But what type of authority or importance?

John has the same situation. In John 20 three named disciples are criticized over against the Beloved Disciple: Peter in 20:3–10, Mary Magdalene in 20:1–2, 11–18, and Thomas in 20:19–29. In the first case, it is said that the Beloved Disciple "saw and believed" at the empty tomb, but nothing is said about Peter believing. In the second case, Mary discovers the empty tomb but misinterprets it three times as corpse-removal. She says to the male disciples in 20:2, "They have taken the Lord out of the tomb, and we do not know where they have laid him." She says to the angels in 20:13, "They have taken away my Lord, and I do not know where they have laid him." She says to Jesus in 20:15, "Sir, if you have carried him away, tell me where you have laid him, and I will take him away." Finding the empty tomb or seeing the risen Jesus is not enough. The former can be interpreted as grave robbery; the latter as the gardener. In the third case, Thomas will believe only after he has seen and touched the risen Jesus. As the chapter begins with the Beloved Disciple believing after seeing only the empty tomb, it ends with the risen Jesus admonishing Thomas, "Blessed are those who have not seen and yet have come to believe." Those scenes are John's creations, but they make the same point as do Mark's creations. Criticism and opposition indicate importance and authority. The Beloved Disciple is contrasted against and exalted over Peter, Mary, and Thomas.

For Mark's gospel, then, Mary Magdalene, Mary, mother of James and Joses, and Salome are important and authoritative figures, just as are Peter, James, and John. For John's gospel, Peter, Mary Magdalene, and Thomas are significant leaders in other communities, just as the Beloved Disciple is in this one. Since, as we have seen, that importance, authority, and leadership do not arise from a first finding of the empty tomb or a first seeing of the risen Jesus, whence *do* they arise?

From Exegesis to Story

Neither was Mark the inventor of the passion narrative, nor was there just one older written document upon which all later passion narratives were directly or indirectly dependent. Rather, three different versions of the same passion narrative are extant, namely, the passion narratives of Mark, John, and the Gospel of Peter which are independent of each other but are all dependent upon the telling of the same story as they all reveal the same basic structure.

Helmut Koester, "Jesus' Presence in the Early Church," p. 556

In the early church, the story of Jesus' suffering and death remained fluid for a long time. Evidence for this are the different versions of the passion narrative in the gospel literature, owing to the *oral performances* of the story in the ritual celebrations, ever enriched by new references to the scriptures of Israel. This process of *oral performances* intended to establish an inclusive statement of truth in the establishment of a new nation—Pan-Christianity.

Helmut Koester, "The Historical Jesus and the
Cult of the *Kyrios Christos*," p. 18 (my italics)

Koester's position on "passion" sources is quite clear and consistent over the last fifteen years, but he has recently added a very important qualification. In older work he presumed a *single written source* behind the three independent accounts in Mark, John, and the *Gospel of Peter*. In 1982, for example, he said that "there was certainly a *written* form of the Passion Narrative at an early date. It was used independently by Mark and John, and it is possible that the apocryphal *Gospel of Peter* employed a very similar source" (1982:2.49, my italics). That claim is repeated later in the same book: "If Peter was the first and most important witness to the resurrection in the oldest tradition of Syrian churches, it is not unlikely that the old tradition about the *passion and resurrection* of Jesus was also written down under his authority" (1982:2.163, my italics).

This, then, is the early Koester hypothesis: not only was there an early written source used later and independently by those three authors, that original source was composed under Petrine authority. In 1990 Koester did not speak about a *written* source but still presumed a single account behind all three later versions. "The account of the passion of Jesus must have developed quite early because it is one and the same account that was used by Mark (and subsequently by Matthew and Luke) and John, and by the *Gospel of Peter*. In this respect, Crossan's reconstruction of one single source for all passion narratives seems justified. However, it is doubtful whether this account was as comprehensive and as fixed a literary document as Crossan assumes" (1990a:220 note 1). Or again: "Studies of the passion narrative have shown that all gospels were dependent upon one and the same basic account of the suffering, crucifixion, death, and burial of Jesus" (1990a:231).

In all those years, however, Koester has never attempted to indicate the content or sequence of that single source that was used independently of one another by Mark, John, and the *Gospel of Peter*. Anyone who proposes a source should spell it out as clearly as possible so that it can be debated as precisely as possible. We can deduce the bare minimum, anyway: the basic source must have had whatever common sequence or content *any two* or *all three* of those written versions presently contain.

ORAL MULTIFORM AND SCRIBAL UNIFORM

More recently Koester has moved from discussion of a *scribal uniform*—that is, a single writing—to what is known as an *oral multiform* (hence that repetition of "oral performances" in the epigraph above). The general background is the cultic recitation of a people's foundational story. The primary model is the Greek creation of a convergent Homeric story to create Pan-Hellenism (from separate cities); other examples are the Exodus story creating Pan-Judaism (from separate tribes) and Virgil's *Aeneid* creating Pan-Romanism (from separate peoples). In all those cases, myth and ritual, epic and history, cultic action and narrative recital were woven interactively together. Koester proposes a similar situation for earliest Christianity. During ritual eucharistic meals, "the telling of the same story" with "the same basic structure" was repeatedly done in diverse "oral performances," as Koester's epigraph suggests. There was not, in other words, any single written or even oral account; there was only "the same basic structure." What we have, therefore, in Mark, John, and the *Gospel of Peter* are later written versions of three independent "oral performances" within that original "same basic structure." That "structure," however, must have contained whatever elements are present in any two or all three of those diverse "oral performances." It must have, for example, contained these major elements: an account of Jesus' trial and crucifixion, an account of Jesus' burial by friends, and an account of the women at the empty tomb.

Koester's theory takes us back to Chapter 5 of this book. The Parry-Lord theory explains the ancient Homeric epics on the analogy of modern illiterate bards who perform thousands of lines working within a fixed *tradition* that gives them, on the one hand, basic stories, subordinate themes, and individual phrases, and, on the other, musical accompaniment, appropriate occasion, and appreciative audience. It is a tradition of oral performance, and any given tale exists as oral multiform. Each tale is the sum total of all its performances; there is no source as normative, scribal uniform. Nevertheless, be it two thousand or ten thousand lines, be it good performance or bad, the Greeks must win and Troy must fall; Hector cannot kill Achilles, and Ulysses cannot get drowned at sea. Even—or especially—in an oral multiform there must be some recognizable narrative structure; otherwise you cannot distinguish the *Iliad* from the *Aeneid*.

In response to Koester's theory, I ask only one very basic question: Are those three extant versions mutually independent? My answer is that they are not, because John is not independent of Mark, and the *Gospel of Peter* is not independent of either Mark or John. (You will note that I am referring not to the *Cross Gospel* source, which is canonically independent, but to the composite *Gospel of Peter* itself, which—as seen earlier—combines both intracanonical and extracanonical material.)

Mark and John

My first problem is that the passion-resurrection stories presented in Mark and John are not independent versions. John is dependent on Mark, which raises a major objection to Brown's theory of two independent versions (Mark and John) as well as to Koester's theory of three independent versions (Mark, John, and *Gospel of Peter*). In Chapter 8 I mentioned that genetic relationship can be proved (beyond a reasonable doubt!) when *redactional* content or sequence from one gospel is found in another. When individual DNA or the personal fingerprint of one author is present in another, we have the best available argument for dependence. It is not, as you will recall, a simple case of similar tradition or common material in both writers but of *redactional* peculiarities of one writer discovered in another. The example I used there was the classic one of Markan intercalation, for which I gave six of the most commonly accepted examples. The last one cited was the intercalation of Peter's denials and Jesus' confession in Mark 14:53–72. By *intercalation* I do not mean the simple *juxtaposition* of two units. A simple juxtaposition of Peter's denials and Jesus' confession could easily happen in two separate texts independent of one another, since both are linked to the same event: the nighttime judgment before Jewish religious authority. But Markan intercalation is not—emphatically *not*—a general juxtaposition. It is, as we saw in Chapter 8, a literary device with a theological purpose, and it is a quite uniquely Markan phenomenon. *But that intercalation is also found in John 18:13–27.* Furthermore, that *genetic relationship* can be corroborated by *redactional confirmation.* You can see very clearly why John accepts it from Mark and then expands it as follows:

> Simon Peter and the other disciple followed Jesus. Since that disciple was known to the high priest, he went with Jesus into the courtyard of the high priest, but Peter was standing outside at the gate. So the other disciple, who was known to the high priest, went out, spoke to the woman who guarded the gate, and brought Peter in. (John 18:15–16)

John increases the Markan contrast between Peter's denials and Jesus' confession by placing one full denial before and two after the confession. His purpose is an implicit comparison between Peter and "the other disciple"; while it is explicitly said that Peter denied thrice, nothing is said about that "other disciple" denying. That is a counterpart to the implicit comparison made in John 20:2–10, where Peter and "the other disciple, the one whom Jesus loved," raced to the tomb on Easter Sunday morning. It is explicitly said that "the other disciple, who reached the tomb first, also went in, and he saw and believed"; nothing is said about Peter believing. Those are typically oblique examples of the exaltation of the Beloved Disciple over Peter in John's gospel. But my present point is that John 18:13–27 is dependent on Mark 14:53–72; therefore, my working hypothesis is that John's passion-resurrection story is not an independent one. That wider dependence is confirmed by studies such as those of Maurits Sabbe (1991:355–388, 467–513; 1994; 1995) and Frans Neirynck (1982:181–488; 1991:571–616). John, in other words, is not a synoptically independent passion-resurrection story.

John and the Gospel of Peter

My second problem is that the *Gospel of Peter* and John are not independent versions. The *Gospel of Peter* is dependent on John for its story of Jesus' burial by friends. That story is extant in Mark 15:42–47, John 19:38–42, and *Gospel of Peter* 6:23–24. As Koester reads the situation, "the story of the burial belongs to the source used by Mark and John and also by the *Gospel of Peter*" (1990a:231 note 5).

John's account of Jesus' passion depicts him in total control of the situation. From the garden, which has no agony, to the death, which has no cry, Jesus judges others; they do not judge him. He is, for John, the king exalted upon the cross. All that is consistent Johannine redaction of the synoptic passion accounts. The burial fits perfectly with that redaction. It is a burial fit for a king—indeed, for a divine king. John 19:39 has Jesus buried along with "a mixture of myrrh and aloes, weighing about a hundred pounds." Brown, equating that with "about seventy-five of our pounds," concludes that it "is still an extraordinary amount. If powdered or fragmented spices are meant, such a weight would fill a consider- able space in the tomb and smother the corpse under a mound" (1994:1260). John 19:41 has Jesus buried in a garden tomb: "[T]here was a garden in the place where he was crucified, and in the garden there was a new tomb in which no one had ever been laid." Abundant spices and garden tombs are regally appropriate. They conclude and consummate the Johannine passion of Jesus the king; therefore, that "garden" is redactionally Johannine. But it is also present in the *Gospel of Peter:*

> And the Jews rejoiced and gave his body to Joseph that he might bury it, since he had seen all the good that he (Jesus) had done. And he took the Lord, washed him, wrapped him in linen and brought him into his own sepulchre, called Joseph's Garden. (*Gospel of Peter* 6:23–24)

Once again, then, and on the same principle (but now of Johannine DNA in the *Gospel of Peter*), that latter author is here dependent on John's gospel.

Mark and the Gospel of Peter

My third problem is that the *Gospel of Peter* and Mark are not independent versions. The *Gospel of Peter* is dependent on Mark for the story of the women at the empty tomb. That story is present in Mark 16:1–8, John 20:1 and 11–18, and the *Gospel of Peter* 12:50–13:57. For Koester, therefore, it must have been in their common basis, whether you call that basis an oral structure, a single source, or a scribal document. In fact, what alone makes that basis a passion-resurrection story and not just a passion story is the presence of the women at the empty tomb as its conclusion. "In the passion narrative which was used by both the Gospel of Mark and the Gospel of John, the story of the discovery of the empty tomb by the women must have followed immediately upon the account of the burial of Jesus" (1980a:128). Again: "Except for the story of the discovery of the empty tomb, the different stories of the appearances of Jesus after his resurrection in the various gospels cannot derive from one single source. . . . The passion narrative that was used by the Gospels of Mark and John and that also formed the basis for the *Gospel of Peter*'s passion narrative . . . ended with the discovery of the empty tomb" (1990a:220, 231). In other words, as noted earlier, Koester's "basic structure" was not just a passion narrative but a passion-resurrection narrative involving Jesus' execution and burial as well as Jesus' resurrection and vindication, as told, however, by the empty tomb story rather than by any risen apparition stories.

When, in Mark 16:1–8, "Mary Magdalene, and Mary the mother of James, and Salome" enter Jesus' tomb on Easter Sunday morning, they see only a "young man" who announces to them that "Jesus of Nazareth, who was crucified . . . has been raised; he is not here. Look, there is the place they laid him." My focus is on that term "young man" (*neaniskos*). Insofar as a single word can be redactionally identified as authorial DNA, that word is a Markan creation. It appeared earlier in Mark 14:51 when "a young man" fled naked from Jesus' captors in the Garden of Gethsemane. Whatever 14:51 may mean, and however one chooses to explain the connection between 14:51 and 16:5, "a young man" is best considered as Markan redaction. Furthermore, all other versions dependent on Mark omit 14:51–52 entirely and change 16:5 to something else. The "young man" becomes an "angel" in Matthew 28:2, 5, "two men" in Luke 24:4 but "angels" in Luke 24:23, and "two angels" in John 20:12. No other canonical dependent accepts Mark's strange "young man." It is too Markan.

But when, in *Gospel of Peter* 12:50–13:57, "Mary Magdalene, a woman disciple of the Lord. . . [and] her women friends" look into Jesus' tomb, it is again "a young man" (*neaniskos*) who gives them the message of Jesus' resurrection. That word's presence in *Gospel of Peter* 13:55, therefore, is best seen as dependent on Mark.

In summary, then, that common story proposed by Koester, be it oral structure or scribal source—that "basic structure" underlying Mark, John, and the *Gospel of Peter*—included not just the passion account but also the burial by friends and the announcement of resurrection given in a tomb empty of Jesus. But those three extant written versions of that basic passion-resurrection story are not independent of one another. Even *if* there once existed multiple oral performances, our four canonical versions now constitute one written version, adapted from Mark into Matthew and Luke and from the synoptics into John. And whether you put the *Cross Gospel* at the start of that genetic process or the *Gospel of Peter* at its end, you are still dealing with a single, linear line of transmission. That, however, only intensifies the question of origins: What is that single written source, and how did it arise? How did the general pattern of persecution-vindication and the biblical modeling of individual incidents coalesce into a narrative structure, a unified plot, a sequential story?

MALE EXEGESIS AND FEMALE LAMENT

One point must be emphasized before continuing. If the passion-resurrection story is history remembered—that is, an account of what actually happened—there is no problem with its being a story. Of course it is a story, since it is a history of what occurred before and after the execution of Jesus. It simply recounts those events. But Koester and I insist that, first, the smaller units, second, the intermediate complexes, and third, the overall structure of the passion-resurrection story were created by developing the bare and brutal facts of crucifixion "according to the scriptures." That detailed story was created from scriptural patterns and not from historical remembrances. And that creates this first and very basic problem: Why did the story ever develop beyond a general sequence of persecution-vindication—beyond, for example, the passion-resurrection schema of the credal statement in 1 Corinthians 15:3–4 or the descent-ascent schema of the mythic hymn in Philippians 2:6–11? Why did it become the biographical scenario that develops, in my view, as a single genetic tradition from the *Cross Gospel,* through the canonical gospels, and into their combination in the final *Gospel of Peter*? Why *biographical* story at all? That is the most fundamental problem of all, and yet it is an almost invisible one. After two thousand years of Christian prayer and piety, art and music, liturgy and theology, it is almost impossible not to see the passion-resurrection story absolutely necessary and totally inevitable precisely as story. We think: they just told what happened—what is so difficult about that? We think: they just decorated it with biblical allusions and references—what is so difficult about that? Nothing, of course, if that is what happened. *But if exegesis came first, why did story ever happen at all?* How did exegesis *become* story? That is the final question for this book, and the answer pulls together the major strands of this Part X.

I summarize where we are at the moment in terms of two problems with a single, common solution. I present the first problem over four steps.

The first step. The passion-resurrection story in the *Cross Gospel* is built from a tissue of biblical references. So, of course, is the passion-resurrection story in Mark. I listed the main references in the *Cross Gospel* earlier in Chapter 25 and exemplified them from smallest unit to largest structure. I now presume all of that, as well as the fuller details in my 1988 and 1995 books on this subject.

The second step. Not a single one of those biblical themes or types, patterns or structures breaks overtly through the surface of the story. If you recognize their hidden presence, well and good. But the text does not openly proclaim them or explicitly cite them. They are not so much proofs from scripture making Jesus individually unique as patterns from scripture making Jesus communally climactic. He does not die alone, and he does not rise alone. He may climax those who die through unjust persecution and lead those who rise through divine vindication, but he is never, never alone.

The third step. As the passion-resurrection tradition continues within the canonical gospels themselves, such biblical references break through the surface of the story as divine validations. What was originally there implicitly is now there explicitly. What was originally there as general biblical pattern is now there as specific scriptural proof. In John 19:28–37, for example, three different incidents at the death of Jesus occur "to fulfill the scriptures." That phrase frames the unit at start (in 19:28) and finish (in 19:36–37). In between, Jesus' thirst receives the vinegar-wine (no mention of gall) from Psalm 69:21, Jesus' legs are not broken from Exodus 12:46 and Numbers 9:12, and Jesus' side is pierced from Zechariah 12:10.

The fourth step. That searching of the scriptures continued after the passion-resurrection schema became a story. It did not stop at that point, as if finished and consummated in the creation of that story. It continued in Christian texts composed after the canonical gospels, and now the argument from typology and proof from prophecy became more and more determinative. It was as if all those psalm texts referred exclusively and prophetically to Jesus alone.

That preceding step requires some emphasis, because it is there that I see how *not necessary* and *not inevitable* that story was, how it might not have happened at all. There was an alternative—namely, the continuing process of exegesis that had preceded it, grounded it, and continued on its own trajectory after it. One example will suffice, but it is a crucial and paradigmatic instance.

The *Epistle of Barnabas* was composed at the end of the first century, probably between 96 and 98 C.E. Despite an interest in finding prophetic foretellings or typological foreshadowings of Jesus' persecution-vindication, it shows no knowledge of the canonical passion-resurrection stories. It is a classic example of *exegesis* instead of *story* on that persecution-vindication theme. This is what exegesis before story, exegesis without story, and exegesis instead of story looks like. But I emphasize once again that in this case exegesis was there *before* story, because the only passion-resurrection story we have (be it the *Cross Gospel* or Mark) already presumes such exegetical activity. I cite this text of prophetic exegesis to underline the *noninevitability* of passion-resurrection as biographical story.

The text from *Barnabas* 7:6–11 takes that standard dyad of persecution-vindication to mean passion-parousia. The twin comings of Jesus, once in suffering and once in triumph, are exemplified in the two goats of the Day of Atonement. As the text proceeds through four questions and answers, my italics indicate the biblical references underlying its argument:

> Note what was commanded: "Take two goats, goodly and alike, and offer them, and let the priest take the one as a burnt offering for sins."
>
> [1] But what are they to do with the other? "The other," he says, "is accursed." Notice how the type of Jesus is manifested: "And do ye all *spit* on it, and goad [*literally:* pierce] it, and bind the scarlet wool about its head, and so let it be cast into the desert." And when it is so done, he who takes the goat into the wilderness drives it forth, and takes away the wool, and puts it upon a [thorny] shrub. . . .
>
> [2] What does this mean? Listen: "the first goat is for the altar, but the other is accursed," and note that the one that is accursed is *crowned* because then "they will *see* him on that day" with the long scarlet *robe* "down to the feet" on his body, and they will say, "Is not this he whom we once crucified and rejected and *pierced* and *spat* upon? Of a truth it was he who then said that he was the Son of God."
>
> [3] But how is he like the goat? For this reason: "the goats shall be alike, beautiful, and a pair," in order that when they *see* him come at that time [i.e., the parousia] they may be astonished at the likeness of the goat. See then the type of Jesus destined to suffer.
>
> [4] But why is it that they put the wool in the middle of the thorns [on that shrub above]? It is a type of Jesus placed in the Church, because whoever wishes to take away the scarlet wool must suffer much because the thorns are terrible and he can gain it only through pain. Thus he says, "those who will see me, and attain to my kingdom must lay hold of me through pain and suffering."

The basic background is the Day of Atonement from Leviticus 15, which is known from actual pre–70 C.E. ritual and not just from that biblical text. The author refers to a popular scapegoat ritual in which the people spit their sins upon the animal and hurry it toward the desert by goading (piercing) it with reeds. The *spitting* recalls Isaiah 50:6, the *piercing* and *seeing* recall Zechariah 12:10, and the *robing* and *crowning* recall Zechariah 3:5. It is almost impossible for us today to read that text and not imagine the abusive mockery of Jesus by the soldiers in the *Cross Gospel* at *Gospel of Peter* 3:6–9 or in Mark 15:17–20. But that presumes that somebody turned prophetic exegesis into biographical story. It is not just that there were two alternative ways, prophetic exegesis and biographical story, separate and distinct and equiprimordial with one another. There is no evidence for a passion-resurrection *story* that does not presume, absorb, embody, and integrate *exegesis* as its hidden substratum and basic content.

I summarize that first problem before moving on to the second one. Exegesis was there first. Exegesis became story. But exegesis was not at first explicitly evident on the surface of that story—for example, in the *Cross Gospel* or Mark 15–16. Exegesis continued on its own trajectory into, for example, the *Epistle of Barnabas* at the end of the first century and Justin Martyr's writings at the middle of the second century. But exegesis also started to become explicitly evident on the surface of that story in, for example, Matthew 27:9–10 and John 19:28–37. I draw one firm conclusion from that data. *The group or process that created exegesis is not the same group or process that created story.* I do not argue that the obverse of that conclusion is absolutely impossible, just that is it extremely unlikely. Those who were involved in creating, continuing, and interjecting exegesis into story were not those who created story in the first place. They may have been involved in continuing or controlling story, but not in creating it. Who then created story? Let me reiterate the precise problem: it is not just who spoke or wrote the hypothetical *Cross Gospel* or the hypothetical source of Mark 15–16; it is who created the very idea of the passion-resurrection schema as a story. Who saw over, under, around, and through exegesis to story?

The second problem goes back to those stories about women watching the crucifixion, observing the burial, visiting the tomb, and seeing a vision of Jesus. They are named most fully in Mark 15:40 as Mary Magdalene, Mary the mother of James and Joses, and Salome. Why are all those texts so negative? Standard male chauvinism simply ignores women or describes them, when necessary, within the roles, positions, and confines presumed as normal. But when, for example, 1 Timothy 2:12 forbids women to teach or control men, we can be sure they are doing just that. What, then, explains all the negative description of women before and after the execution of Jesus? I summarize the examples seen earlier.

Mark 15:40 has Mary Magdalene, another Mary, and Salome at the crucifixion, "looking on from a distance (*makrothen*)." Leaving aside for the moment any questions of historicity, that is not a complimentary description in terms of Markan redaction. Mark 14:54 had Peter following the arrested "at a distance (*makrothen*)" before denying him thrice. Psalm 38:11 may stand behind both texts: there the righteous but afflicted person complains that "my friends and companions stand aloof from my affliction, and my neighbors stand far off (*makrothen*)."

John, to the contrary, changes the three women to Jesus' mother Mary, Mary of Clopas, and Mary Magdalene, adds on the Beloved Disciple, and moves them all to stand "by the cross" in 19:25. The first named Mary and the Beloved Disciple are singled out again as "standing near" in 19:26. But Mary Magdalene is in last place, against all other texts that mention her in first place. Furthermore, that coheres with what happens to Mary Magdalene and the other women as Mark and John continue.

As seen earlier, Mark criticizes the women in 15:47–16:8 because, first, they plan to anoint Jesus despite his having foretold his resurrection and, second, they do not deliver the message that the "disciples and Peter" (note order) are to leave Jerusalem and return to Galilee. The Markan ideal is that woman in 14:3–9 who believed Jesus and knew she had to pre-anoint him before his execution, then and there or never at all. As seen earlier, Mary Magdalene is the first to find the empty tomb in John 20:1–2, but her immediate and continuing interpretation (in 20:2, 13, 15) is grave robbery. She is also the first to see the risen Jesus, but she thinks he is the gardener in 20:15. All of that is as deliberate as it is derogatory. (Of course, Peter and Thomas are put down in comparison with the Beloved Disciple just as firmly in 20:3–10 and 20:24–29.)

Finally, the one positive story is the women's vision of Jesus in Matthew. Matthew 28:9–10 was created to reverse the ending of the empty tomb in 28:1–8, which he copied from Mark 16:1–8, and to prepare for the eleven disciples' vision of Jesus, which he created in 28:16–20. That vision is positive, but, as mentioned before, it is a message-vision rather than a mandate-vision; it is secretarial-level rather than executive-level apparition. All of that, especially in Mark and John, is not a case of ancient tradition being redacted negatively but a case of negative tradition being created before our eyes. Why do it?

I now bring all those preceding problems together and offer a single solution. In the passion-resurrection tradition, women appear more frequently but also more negatively in texts at and after the execution of Jesus. Why is that? In the passion-resurrection tradition, those who created prophetic exegesis are not those who created biographical story. Who are they? In the passion-resurrection tradition, there are no accounts of female lament or ritual mourning for Jesus. Why is that? My simultaneous answer to those three questions is that *ritual lament is what changed prophetic exegesis into biographical story.*

The Life Tradition, the tradition of how Jesus lived, predominated among the hamlets and small towns of Galilee and Syria. The Death Tradition is associated primarily with Jerusalem, a city linked very early, even before Paul, with other cities such as Damascus and Antioch. But from the Common Sayings Tradition, through the *Q Gospel* and the *Gospel of Thomas*, into the *Didache*, the Life Tradition shows no evidence of knowing any passion-resurrection story. The biblical pattern of persecution-vindication is fundamental for the Life Tradition, and that tradition is every bit as mythological, eschatological, and theological as is the Death Tradition. But even more striking than the absence of sayings collections in the Death Tradition is the absence of passion-resurrection narrative in the Life Tradition. The reason for that absence is that the narrative was created at one time in one place. It was composed in Jerusalem, where the female and male companions of Jesus whose names we know stayed from the very beginning. That was where Jesus had been crucified and that was where God would act to vindicate Jesus. They stayed in Jerusalem because that was where they expected the imminent apocalyptic consummation to take place.

I imagine in that Jerusalem community two equiprimordial processes, *exegesis* and *lament*, engendered respectively by male and female members. In the absence of a body and a tomb, female ritual lament wove exegetical fragments into a sequential story. I do not find any evidence that multiple oral performances of such a passion-resurrection story are represented by *any* set of our extant gospels. What we have there in my best reconstruction is but a single line of scribal tradition, from the *Cross Gospel* into and through the canonical gospels. If such oral multiforms existed and were eventually written down in independent gospels, I would expect their similarities and differences to look something like those varied versions of a single lament seen above. What I imagine instead is that in the Jerusalem community the female lament tradition turned the male exegetical tradition into a passion-resurrection story once and for all forever. The closest we can get to that story now is the *Cross Gospel*, whose insistence on communal passion and communal resurrection may be the strongest index of those origins. The gift of the lament tradition is not just that we know the names of Mary Magdalene and the other women, but that their passion-resurrection story moved into the heart of the Christian tradition forever. And once it was there, within a decade of the death of Jesus, others would compose variations on it, but nobody would ever replace it or eliminate it.

EPILOGUE

The Character of Your God

God has taken his place in the divine council; in the midst of the gods he
   holds judgment:
"How long will you judge unjustly and show partiality to the wicked?
Give justice to the weak and the orphan; maintain the right of the lowly and
   the destitute.
Rescue the weak and the needy; deliver them from the hand of the wicked."
They have neither knowledge nor understanding, they walk around in darkness;
   all the foundations of the earth are shaken.
I say, "You are gods, children of the Most High, all of you;
   nevertheless, you shall die like mortals, and fall like any prince."
Rise up, O God, judge the earth; for all the nations belong to you!

Psalm 82

I place Psalm 82 as epigraph to this Epilogue, repeating it from the earlier discussion of Yahweh as the Jewish God of justice and righteousness (Chapter 12). It
is, for me, the single most important text in the entire Christian Bible, and it
comes, of course, from the Jewish Bible. It is, for me, more important than John
1:14, which speaks of the Word of God becoming flesh and living among us. Before
celebrating that incarnation, we must address a prior question about the character
of the divinity involved. And that short psalm best summarizes for me the character of the Jewish God as Lord of all the world. It imagines a mythological scene in
which God sits among the gods and goddesses in divine council. Those pagan gods
and goddesses are dethroned not just because they are *pagan*, nor because they are
other, nor because they are *competition*. They are dethroned for injustice, for divine
malpractice, for transcendental malfeasance in office. They are rejected because
they do not demand and effect justice among the peoples of the earth. And that
justice is spelled out as protecting the poor from the rich, protecting the systemically weak from the systemically powerful. Such injustice creates darkness over
the earth and shakes the very foundations of the world.

Peoples and nations write constitutive texts, record constitutive histories, tell
constitutive stories, and make constitutive laws. Those foundations judge everything they do thereafter. One must, therefore, be very careful about constitutive
proclamations. They may come home to haunt you. So also with a religion and
its God. Psalm 82 tells us how we are to be judged by God but also how God

wants to be judged by us. Everything else that God says or does in Bible or life should be judged by that job description. Is this or that the transcendental justice defined in Psalm 82 at work? Or is this or that just transcendental testosterone?

JUSTICE AND ECONOMICS

> The Mishnah will be seen as attacking the problem of man's livelihood within a system of sanctification of a holy people with a radicalism of which no later utopian religious thinkers were capable. None has ever penetrated deeper into the material organization of man's life under the aspect of God's rule. In effect, they posed, in all its breadth, the question of the critical, indeed definitive, place occupied by the economy in society under God's rule.
>
> Jacob Neusner, *The Economics of the Mishnah*, p. 5

An objection to my initial comments is immediately obvious. It is very simple to declare an individual or group, people or deity to be on the side of justice and righteousness. Who, after all, has ever declared him- or herself to be on the side of injustice and unrighteousness? But as Psalm 82 and the Chapter 12 discussion suggest, divine justice is spelled out in rather precise details within the Jewish biblical tradition, depicted there as enfleshed spirit or enspirited flesh (to recall Boyarin from my Prologue). That tradition seldom goes in for great abstract manifestoes and sweeping intellectual pronouncements. It goes in especially for careful cases, specific laws, and particular instances. I give two examples, a first one summarizing materials already seen, and a second one extending their application.

The first example summarizes what was seen earlier about indebtedness and slavery. I referred in Chapter 24 to the philosopher Philo's description of the Jewish Therapeutics outside Alexandria. This, he says, was their attitude toward slavery (Yonge 704):

> They do not use the ministrations of slaves, looking upon the possession of servants or slaves to be a thing absolutely and wholly contrary to nature, for nature has created all men free, but the injustice and covetousness of some men who prefer inequality, that cause of all evil, having subdued some, has given to the more powerful authority over those who are weaker. (*On the Contemplative Life* 70)

You will also recall that Philo described the Essenes in two texts seen earlier. The first of those claimed that they, like the Therapeutics, considered slavery unnatural (Yonge 689):

There is not a single slave among them, but they are all free, aiding one another with a reciprocal interchange of good offices; and they condemn masters, not only as unjust, inasmuch as they corrupt the very principle of equality, but likewise as impious, because they destroy the ordinances of nature, which generated them all equally, and brought them up like a mother, as if they were all legitimate brethren, not in name only, but in reality and truth. (*Every Good Man Is Free* 79)

Those are clear and ringing generalizations. Slavery is unnatural because all should be equal. That is not, however, the biblical method that uses law rather than philosophy. It does not make a constitutional declaration that all Jews are equal before God and slavery is therefore against the Law. Recall, instead, all that we saw earlier about forbidding interest, defining collateral, remitting debt, controlling slavery, reversing dispossession, and establishing rest. What logic underlies all those procedures? If slavery is just natural, as Aristotle argued, why should slaves be remitted? Marriages, for example, are not divorced every seven years. All those laws make sense only if there is a constitutional presumption that divine justice involves radical equality, involves a covenantal commitment to maintain equality, involves a ceaseless rejection of creeping inequality. Everyone is for justice until it is spelled out as equality, and everyone is for equality until it is spelled out as accepting *this* but rejecting *that*. The Jewish tradition is specifically interested in *this* and *that*.

The second instance concerns farmers and profits. The background here is a combination of Daniel Boyarin and Jacob Neusner on what I call the *sarcophilia* of the rabbinical tradition. Neusner describes the *Mishnah* as "a utopian system expressed in the form of a law code and closed in ca. A.D. 200" (ix)—closed, that is, after the three great Jewish revolts against Rome, under Nero and his successors in 66–74, under Trajan in 115–117, and under Hadrian in 132–135 C.E. Because of those terrible events, the *Mishnah* wisely avoids even verbal confrontation with imperial injustice or pagan evil. Instead, the focus of mishnaic economics is on the Jewish household—that is, "the farm, for the household is always the agricultural unit ... the fundamental, irreducible, and, of course, representative unit of the economy, the means of production, the locus and the unit of production.... Householders were farmers of their own land, proprietors of the smallest viable agricultural unit of production—however modest that might be" (50–51, 64).

That narrow focus is the *Mishnah*'s strength. The text shows exactly how a Jewish peasant farmer, a small-holding householder, lives in holiness on God's holy land. But that is also its limitation. "Time and time again we shall find no economics pertaining to commercial, professional, manufacturing, or trading, let alone laboring persons and classes.... [L]andless workers, teachers, physicians, merchants, shopkeepers, traders, craftsmen, and the like, cannot, by definition, constitute, or even affiliate with, a household: an amazing narrow economics indeed. . . . That is to say that the economics of Judaism omitted reference to most of the Jews, on the one side, and the economic activities and concerns of labor and capital alike, on the other" (52). Neusner is very much aware of that restriction in focus. He repeats it again later, wondering if such a system can even be called an economics: "If we were to list all of the persons and professions who enjoy no role in the system, or who are treated as ancillary to the system, we have to encompass not only workers—the entire landless working class!— but also craftsmen and artisans, teachers and physicians, clerks and officials, traders and merchants, the whole of the commercial establishment, not to mention women as a caste. Such an economics, disengaged from so large a sector of the economy of which it claimed, even if only in theory, to speak, can hardly be called an economics at all" (69). It is, clearly, an economics for Jews rather than Gentiles, for Jewish landowners rather than for other Jews, and for Jews in the Jewish homeland rather than for Diaspora Jews. It is for Jewish landowners in the Jewish homeland who were recovering, carefully, from three terrible wars with the Roman Empire.

The *Mishnah* has no systemic criticism of the fact that rich and poor exist in society. But it presumes the existence of poor relief—indeed, of two very different types of such assistance. One belongs to the poor by right, from biblical law: "the rear corner of the field . . . gleanings . . . the forgotten sheaf . . . the separated grape . . . the defective cluster . . . and poorman's tithe, a tenth of the crop separated in the third and sixth years of the sabbatical cycle and handed over to the poor" (125). The other is theirs by alms, received through "a system of soup kitchens. Through them transient poor are supported" (125). But just as the focus of mishnaic economics is strictly confined to the Jewish landowner in the Jewish homeland, so also is its emphasis on equality restricted to them. But what it means for them is very clear, at least in theory.

It means a static or steady-state situation in which every negotiation or business transaction ends up with the involved parties no better or worse off than they were before. "No party in the end may have more than what he had at the outset, and none may emerge as the victim of a sizable shift in fortune and circumstance" (72). What is forbidden, in other words, is not just usury (an unfair profit) or interest (a fair profit) but *any profit at all*. The model is friends or associates exchanging equal objects in a commonly agreed barter. The end is "to insure equal exchange in all transactions, so that the market formed an arena for transactions of equal value and worth among households possessed of a steady-state worth" (76). Here is a rather graphic example of what that equality entails. It is from the *Mishnah's* fourth division (on *Damages*) in the tractate entitled *The Middle Gate* 5:10 (111):

A. A man [may] say to his fellow, "Weed with me, and I'll weed with you."
B. "Hoe with me, and I'll hoe with you."
C. But he [may] not say to him, "Weed with me, and I'll hoe with you."
D. "Hoe with me, and I'll weed with you."

Those minute details make the underlying principle superbly evident. Because weeding and hoeing are not exactly equal, a trade of weeding for hoeing would not be a fair, just, and equal exchange. Neusner himself judges that case "so lacking in concrete action, let alone potential sanction, as to indicate the end of actualities and the entry of mere morality" (111). But of course morality—or, better, holiness—was there all along from the beginning. One has to choose, in the final analysis, between "God lives in the details" (113) and "the enchantment of sanctification expressed in glorious triviality" (135). But the principle of equality is no detail and no triviality.

Toward the end of his fascinating book, Neusner seems almost to doubt the validity of his title, *The Economics of the Mishnah;* he seems almost to lose his nerve. "The economics of the Mishnah addresses only one sector of the economy, and the distributive economics that prevailed clearly ignores important arenas of economic action, e.g., trade, commerce, manufacturing, as well as labor. So I must wonder, have I then established that the Judaism of the Mishnah has an economics at all? . . . An economics that speaks of one component of the economy and utterly ignores others, that treats value as something inhering in land but not in merchandise, that exacts taxes only from the things it deems of worth and so imputes value to one activity and denigrates all others—such an economics is a theory of politics in society, expressed in economic terms" (139). That seems to me perfectly correct. It is very clear that, just as Aristotle subordinated economics to politics to ethics in his way, so did the *Mishnah* in its. It subordinated market economics to distributive economics and found profit incompatible with holiness. Neusner asks again, "Who ever heard of an economics that pertained only to certain persons living in a certain place? Aristotle could not imagine such an economics; his theory pertained everywhere. The Mishnah's framers' economics, by contrast, explained the rules governing not an economy but a holy society, abstracted from economics, made up only of certain persons, owners of land who were Israelites, located only in a certain place, the land called the land of Israel" (140). That is, once again, absolutely correct. Those framers asked how holiness expressed itself economically, and they answered quite clearly: by refusing to profit from one another and by maintaining the original equality established by God. "But," Neusner concludes, "the economics of the Mishnah is not an economics at all . . . [for] economics can emerge as an autonomous and governing theory only when disembedded from politics and society" (142). Did such a disembedded economics ever exist in the past of the world? Could such a disembedded economics ever exist in the future of the world?

I am interested here in Neusner's analysis for just one reason. The *Mishnah's* vision is not impossible, however ideal, theoretical, or utopian it may seem. Maybe it would not work, but at least it could be tried. And I have no doubt that, if and when tried, it would have been changed and adapted by the sages who proposed it. I presume the same for the Jubilee Year, which we saw much earlier. Prophets, priests, and rabbis were not economic fools, but they deeply believed in commercial markets subservient to a just society and in a just society subservient to a just God. But, as Neusner insists over and over again, the *Mishnah's* regulations about justice are restricted to Jewish landowners in the Jewish homeland. What the *Mishnah* proposed was a radical egalitarianism, but restricted to certain people in a certain place. It was interpreted as holding them all to a rest, a stasis, a steady-state situation in which nobody could become richer or poorer through profit and loss. All financial or economic operations were to come out exactly equal, because that was the will of God. And the *Mishnah* detailed how one could attempt to work that out in practice. But Jewish faith that God was Lord of all the earth could easily expand those prescriptions not only to all other market activities but also to all peoples and all places. It was prudent for the rabbis not to press that logical extension, however, after three terrible revolutions against Rome. It was prudent to focus on what might be possible here and now for Jewish landowners in the Jewish homeland as tenant farmers of God.

What was at stake in all of that was not chauvinism, exclusivism, or hatred of outsiders and foreigners. (The *Mishnah* protected Jews and resident aliens equally.) It was simply this: How do you live with a God of freedom and liberation in a world of injustice and oppression?

JUSTICE AND PURITY

John Dominic Crossan asserts: "It was obviously possible for the first Christian generations to debate whether Jesus was for or against the ritual laws of Judaism. His position must have been, as it were, unclear. I propose . . . that he did not care enough about such ritual laws either to attack or to acknowledge them. He ignored them, but that, of course, was to subvert them at a most fundamental level" [1991:263]. By the same token, neither to attack nor to acknowledge may translate into taking something "for granted," which is to accept it at a most fundamental level.

Amy-Jill Levine, "Second Temple Judaism, Jesus, and Women," p. 17

I accept Levine's criticism in that epigraph and withdraw my earlier statement. I think her interpretation, not mine, is correct. Jesus observed whatever purity codes were customary for Jewish peasants of his time and place. But that simply intensifies, for me at least, the relationship and interaction between moral law and ritual law, between justice and purity, especially when both facets intertwine together within a single Torah or Law of God. I give a single textual example to serve as focus.

Ezekiel was a priest of Jerusalem's Temple deported with other Jewish elites by the Babylonian Empire in 597 B.C.E., in the first of three expatriations known collectively as the Babylonian Exile. The Temple itself was destroyed in 580 B.C.E. and the prophecies of Ezekiel turned from deserved doom to anguished hope. In Ezekiel 18:5–9 he summarizes what it means to be righteous before God:

> If a man is righteous and does what is lawful and right—
> [1] he does not eat upon the mountains or lift up his eyes to the idols of the house of Israel,
> [2] does not defile his neighbor's wife
> [3] *or approach a woman during her menstrual period,*
> [4] does not oppress anyone,
> [5] but restores to the debtor his pledge,
> [6] commits no robbery,
> [7] gives his bread to the hungry
> [8] and covers the naked with a garment,
> [9] does not take advance or accrued interest,
> [10] withholds his hand from iniquity,
> [11] executes true justice between contending parties,
> [12] follows my statutes, and is careful to observe my ordinances, acting faithfully—
> such a one is righteous; he shall surely live, says the Lord God.

As indicated by its external frames, that is a description of one who is "righteous" before God. Within those external frames, there are three interconnected elements, and it is that interconnection that I intend to explore.

The first element is found in the combination of the first and the twelfth criteria: avoidance of idolatry, and *fidelity* to God. Those *internal* frames form the basis for the entire code of righteousness. We are back with divine character, as it were. It is not the gods and goddesses of the Canaanite high places or mountain shrines who command what follows. It is Yahweh who establishes this righteousness. The second element is *justice,* and it is described in very specific detail in the second, and fourth through ninth criteria. Those criteria illustrate how the term *justice* has been used throughout my book: to describe how equity and fairness are established between human beings so that life's dignity and integrity are maintained for all alike. The third element, found in the third criterion, is the focus of our present concern, and I have italicized it for emphasis. That criterion concerns, as we might say, *purity* or defilement rather than justice or sin, but it is embedded among those other items by Ezekiel without any separation or distinction. Why, on the one hand, is it so important to Ezekiel? What, on the other hand, do *we* mean by purity defilements, purity rules, or purity codes?

Paula Fredriksen explains the meaning of Jewish "purity codes" in this summary statement. "Purity concerned not just the priests (though they did have additional rules peculiar to their station), but in principle the entire people of Israel. Some rules prohibit contact with or consumption of certain unclean animals, or eating the fat or blood of permitted ones: willful, deliberate transgression of these rules is sinful. Other purity rules focus primarily on the human body. Discharges from the genital area—menstruation, miscarriage or childbirth; seminal emissions—cause 'impurity,' as does contact (or even proximity to) a corpse. 'Leprosy' (which can afflict houses as well as persons) also conveys impurity. For all these conditions, the Bible prescribes periods of separation, lustrations and offerings, after which, in the language of Leviticus, the person can again 'approach the Tent of Meeting'—that is, enter the zone of holiness surrounding the altar—and make a sacrifice to God. *Purity enables proximity to holiness.* Scripture assumes, in other words, that people will contract impurity as a matter of course. . . . An impure person—a menstruant, a leper or a mourner—is not thereby a sinner, nor is a pure person necessarily righteous" (1995b:22, my italics).

At one end of the defilement spectrum are those impurities that must always be avoided; at the other end are those that inevitably will be contracted. But how is it that some impurities *must be avoided* and some *will be contracted?* That ambiguity mirrors a more profound one. God is total justice, unmixed with any hint or trace of injustice. God is the total separation of justice from injustice. Humans must both approach as close as possible to that divine separation and, in their own inevitable mixed state, be rendered impure by that very proximity. That is why I italicized one phrase in Fredriksen's description, and I repeat it now for emphasis: *purity enables proximity to holiness.* Purity is not holiness or righteousness or justice. It is the appropriate preparation and necessary condition for contact with the God of justice. And purity's emphasis on bodily flesh permanently reminds us that justice is about bodily flesh. When humans come close to the sources of life, be it in menstrual blood or seminal emission, they approach the divine too closely. For Ezekiel, then, life is in the blood, and lifeblood belongs to God. It is not "righteous" either to take innocent blood in murder or to contact menstrual blood in marriage. We may call one case justice and the other purity, if we will, but Ezekiel would probably not appreciate that distinction, and his viewpoint is worth considering. Purity is like the outer ramparts of justice; and, while it is possible to have a purity code without divine justice, the key question is whether it is possible to have divine justice without a purity code.

Recall, in what follows, the fact that the Jewish homeland was a colonial people under imperial control in the early first century. In Galilee, it was a lay aristocracy that had to collaborate with external Roman rule. In Judaea, it was a priestly aristocracy that had to collaborate with internal Roman rule. Caiaphas, be he saint or sinner, had to cooperate with Pilate. But Caiaphas was also high priest, and he it was who had *both* to represent his people in the inmost sanctuary of the Temple on the Day of Atonement *and* to collaborate with the Roman governor every other day of the year. It was possible, therefore, for some Jews to judge that collaboration and even the Temple itself as hopelessly contaminated. They might argue, to use the three terms from above, that high priesthood and Temple now constituted infidelity and/or injustice and/or impurity. It was, in that situation, quite possible to attack the Temple itself in the name of purity itself.

First, then, first-century Jews could disagree with one another on where the lines between fidelity, justice, and purity should be located. Was tolerating an imperial taxation-census so acknowledging the lordship of Caesar that it negated the Lordship of God? And if so, what should be done about it?

Second, such disagreements could range from irenic debate through heated dispute to lethal attack. And disagreements could occur between *sects* or within *factions* of the same sect. In *factional* debates within Christian Judaism, Paul accused Peter of "hypocrisy" at Antioch in Galatians 2:13. I take it for granted that we do not accept that as a fair description of Peter (or of the peripherally accused Barnabas or James, for that matter). But have we seriously considered that Peter rather than Paul might have been right in that dispute? Have we considered how we would have adjudicated such a claim? Invective does not define character. Polemic does not describe program. They simply mark unfinished business. In sectarian debates, Christian Jews attacked Pharisaic Jews. There is only a single, secure criticism in the Common Sayings Tradition, *On Hindering Others* (Appendix 1A: #16). But it escalates to bitter invective and sevenfold woe in the *Q Gospel* at Luke 11:39–52. By Matthew 23, those woes have further escalated with a constant accusation of hypocrisy in 23:13, 15, 23, 25, 27, and 29. That polemical crescendo charts the increasing alienation of Christian Jews over against Pharisaic Jews but tells us nothing, of course, about Pharisaic programs, motives, or intentions. Neither does it help us assess fairly the relative merits of each position within first-century options or twentieth-century traditions. All such name-calling, no matter how bitter, is intra-Jewish strife in the heated atmosphere of imperial divide-and-conquest policy. It is absolutely important, after two thousand years of Christian anti-Judaism and the final obscenity of European anti-Semitism, to emphasize that point as strongly as possible. It is terribly too late to do so, but it must still be done over and over again, not to be polite, ecumenical, or politically correct, but simply, at long last, to be accurate, ethical, and truthful.

Once those first two points—that first-century Jews could disagree with one another on definitions of righteousness, and that such disagreements could range from irenic debate through heated dispute to lethal attack—are firmly established, a third and most important one becomes clear. The Jewish God, and the Christian God insofar as we have not changed gods, is a God of justice by nature and character, not just by will and command. This God could be no other, and that is what Psalm 82 is all about. To be in covenant with such a God, to be the people of such a God, to accept the land of such a God involves, constitutionally and creatively, a commitment to union with transcendental justice. It is not possible, therefore, to drive a wedge between fidelity to God and commitment to justice in this tradition. Justice is how this God is incarnated in human history. It is, of course, absolutely possible for infidelity to create injustice in this God's name, but the question is whether it is possible to establish justice on earth except as the embodiment of that God.

Fourth, is it possible to seek and foster, to celebrate and maintain such divine justice on earth without purity customs, defilement codes, and bodily restrictions? As long as the person is soul or spirit dwelling accidentally and temporarily in irrelevant flesh or indifferent body, that question seems downright silly. What intrinsic value could circumcision of males or kosher practice at meals have if flesh is denied and body is negated? But if you insist on humans as enfleshed spirit or enspirited body, is it possible to maintain divine justice without purity codes of some sort? Divine justice for earth is derived from encountering a God who is transcendental justice itself. Can you abandon all *purity* codes as protocols for such an encounter? If you do, will you eventually lose *justice* as well? And what then is left of *fidelity?*

JUSTICE AND YAHWEH

Under the Egyptian monarch Ptolemy VIII Euergetes II Physcon, ruler from 145 to 116 B.C.E., an Alexandrian Jew composed the fictional *Letter of Aristeas to Philocrates,* a work that insists on the complete homogeneity of Jewish and Greek wisdom. It recounts a serenely mythical story about the reasons and methods whereby the Hebrew scriptures, "the Law of the Jews," were first translated into Greek. This was done, the text claims, under Ptolemy II Philadelphus, ruler from 285 to 247 B.C.E., at the request of Demetrius of Phalerum, curator of the great library at Alexandria. Demetrius tells the king why he wants a copy made (*OTP* 2.13):

The (same) God who appointed them their Law prospers your kingdom, as I have been at pains to show. These people worship God the overseer and creator of all, whom all men worship including ourselves, O King, except that we have a different name. Their name for him is Zeus and Jove. (*Letter of Aristeas* 15–16)

Although speaking fictionally through the lips of a pagan, this Jewish writer is quite willing to consider that Jews and Greeks worship the same God under different names. Yahweh for Jews, Zeus for Greeks, Jove or Jupiter for Romans—these are but different names for the same God.

That quite extraordinary admission from a Jew about paganism is matched in the next century by an equally extraordinary admission from a pagan about Judaism. Marcus Terentius Varro lived between 116 and 27 B.C.E. in very dangerous Roman times. A follower of Pompey, he was pardoned after Caesar's victory and then condemned after Caesar's assassination, but he escaped to become, as Menahem Stern put it, "the greatest scholar of republican Rome and the forerunner of the Augustan religious restoration" (1.207). Most of his prodigious work is no longer extant, but Saint Augustine has preserved this report (1.210):

Yet Varro, one of themselves [i.e., the pagans]—to a more learned man they cannot point—thought the God of the Jews to be the same as Jupiter, thinking that it makes no difference by what name he is called, so long as the same thing is understood. . . . Since the Romans habitually worship nothing superior to Jupiter . . . and they consider him the king of all the gods, and as he perceived that the Jews worship the highest God, he could not but identify him with Jupiter.

That reciprocal agreement is perfectly irenic, beautifully ecumenical, and profoundly wrong. Why wrong? Because gods too carry baggage. We know that individuals and groups, peoples and nations have historical baggage. We know that sects and cults, creeds and religions have historical baggage. We sometimes forget, though, that gods do too. It is at this point that my Epilogue connects directly to my Prologue. We are enfleshed spirit and enspirited flesh, and we meet divinity not just in abstract speculation but in historical deployment.

Zeus, Jupiter, and Yahweh are not simply different names for the same ultimate reality. Zeus is not just another name for Yahweh, because Zeus grounds a Hellenistic internationalism that directly threatens Jewish traditionalism. Jupiter is not just another name for Yahweh, because Jupiter grounds a Roman imperialism that directly threatens Jewish traditionalism. But is this not just the chauvinistic exclusivity of one people against another (or even all others)? Is it not just a Jewish *us* against a pagan *them*? There is, I think, much more at stake than that. What is at stake is the challenge of Psalm 82, quoted above. What is at stake is the character of your God. This is what *our* God is like, says that psalm. What is *your* God like? I have two footnotes to the vision of Psalm 82.

One footnote concerns justice as distinct from revenge and recalls what was said earlier about apocalypticism. Yahweh is a God not of revenge but of justice. I reject absolutely the ancient libel that the God of the Old Testament or of Judaism is a God of anger and vengeance while the God of the New Testament or of Christianity is a God of love and mercy. But I ask emphatically whether apocalypticism, be it in Judaism or in Christianity, is about divine justice or divine revenge. Justice and revenge dwell close together in the human heart. When we examine our conscience, we usually find them happily wedded and bedded together. We find it hard, therefore, not to project their amalgam onto God. When Judaism imagines apocalyptic consummation, what will happen to the pagans; and when Christianity imagines apocalyptic consummation, what will happen to the Jews? If, confronted with the blinding glory of God, all convert freely *not* to Judaism or to Christianity *but* to justice and righteousness, then all is well in our religious imagination. But if we await a divine slaughter of those who are not Jews or those who are not Christians, then we are the killer children of a Killer God. It is a question, once again, of character. Is your God a God of justice or of revenge?

Another footnote concerns justice as distinct from compassion and recalls what was said earlier about almsgiving. Yahweh is a God not only of justice but also of compassion. It is crucial, however, not to confuse those aspects—justice and compassion—in either God's divinity or our humanity. It is impossible (fortunately) to have justice without compassion, but it is possible (unfortunately) to have compassion without justice. That sequence of justice *and* compassion is, therefore, significant. We are back, in fact, with the distinction between, on the one hand, individual good or evil and, on the other, systemic good or evil. Where there is justice without compassion, there will be anger, violence, and murder. A thirst for justice without an instinct for compassion produces killers. Sometimes they are simply believers in a Killer God. Sometimes they are assistant killers of a Killer God. But compassion without justice is equally problematic. In any unjust system, there are people needing immediate assistance. And, even in a perfectly just system, there would still be those who would need compassion. But compassion, no matter how immediately necessary or profoundly human, cannot substitute for justice, for the *right* of all to equal dignity and integrity of life. Those who live by compassion are often canonized. Those who live by justice are often crucified.

Appendix 1

Common Sayings Tradition in the
Gospel of Thomas and the *Q Gospel*

Preliminary Note

I count as *Q Gospel* only units with secure attestation in both Matthew and Luke. I also watch carefully the consensus reconstruction of the *Q Gospel* proposed by the International Q Project (IQP). That reconstruction requires three changes to the list of Common Sayings Tradition units that I included in *The Historical Jesus* (1991: Appendix 1B), bringing my earlier inventory of 102 units down to 101 units here: 102 − 2 + 1 = 101.

First, there are certain units in either Matthew alone or Luke alone that may well have been accepted from the *Q Gospel* by one but omitted by the other author. I did not count such units in my original inventory. Second, there are other units that appear in both Matthew and Luke but in divergent contexts and, since they are also present in Mark, may possibly be from that source rather than from the *Q Gospel*. I counted one such unit, *First and Last,* in my original inventory (1991: Appendix 1B: #31) but omit it here (IQP 1993:506). Third, there is one unit in Matthew whose parallel in Luke is textually uncertain. I counted that unit, *Knowing the Times,* in my original inventory (1991: Appendix 1B: #53) but omit it here (IPQ 1995:481). Fourth, there is one unit, *Strong One's House,* that I did not count as part of the *Q Gospel* in my original inventory (1991: Appendix 1B: #81) but do include here (IQP 1993:504).

A. Inventory of Common Sayings Tradition in the *Gospel of Thomas* and the *Q Gospel*

28% (37 out of 132 units) of the *Gospel of Thomas* has parallels in the *Q Gospel*
37% (37 of 101 units) of the *Q Gospel* has parallels in the *Gospel of Thomas*
59% (22 out of 37 units) of the Common Sayings Tradition has parallels in Q^1
41% (15 out of 37 units) of the Common Sayings Tradition has parallels in Q^2

Primary bold parenthetical numbers are for this appendix. Secondary bold nonparenthetical numbers cross-reference to Crossan 1991: Appendix 1B. Units are given in the order of the *Gospel of Thomas*.

(1) 4. Ask, Seek, Knock: (1a) *Gos. Thom.* 2 = P. Oxy. 654.5–9; (1b) *Gos. Thom.* 92:1; (1c) *Gos. Thom.* 94; (2) *Gos. Heb.* 4ab; (3) Q^1: Luke 11:9–10 = Matt. 7:7–8; (4) Mark 11:24 = Matt. 21:22; (5a) *Dial. Sav.* 9–12; (5b) *Dial. Sav.* 20d; (5c) *Dial. Sav.* 79–80; (6a) John 14:13–14; (6b) John 15:7; (6c) John 15:16; (6d) John 16:23–24; (6e) John 16:26

(2) 8. When and Where: (1a) *Gos. Thom.* 3:1–3 = P. Oxy. 654.3:1–3; (1b) *Gos. Thom.* 51; (1c) *Gos. Thom.* 113; (2) Q^2: Luke 17:23 = Matt. 24:26; (3) Mark 13:21–23 = Matt. 24:23–25; (4?) *Dial. Sav.* 16; (5) Luke 17:20–21

(3) **32. Hidden Made Manifest:** (1a) *Gos. Thom.* 5:2 = P. Oxy. 654.29–30; (1b) *Gos. Thom.* 6:5–6 = P. Oxy. 654.38–40; (2) Q¹: Luke 12:2 = Matt. 10:26; (3) Mark 4:22 = Luke 8:17

(4) **33. The Golden Rule:** (1) *Gos. Thom.* 6:3 = P. Oxy. 654.36–37; (2) Q¹: Luke 6:31 = Matt. 7:12; (3) *Did.* 1:2b

(5) **1. Mission and Message:** (1a) 1 Cor. 9:14; (1b) 1 Cor. 10:27; (2) *Gos. Thom.* 14:4; (3) Q¹: Luke 10:4–11 = Matt. 10:7, 10b, 12–14; (4) Mark 6:7–13 = Matt. 10:1, 8–10a, 11 = Luke 9:1–6; (5) *Dial. Sav.* 53b[139:9–10]; (6) *Did.* 11:(3)4–12; (7) 1 Tim. 5:18b

(6) **74. Peace or Sword:** (1) *Gos. Thom.* 16; (2) Q²: Luke 12:51–53 = Matt. 10:34–36

(7) **14. Eye, Ear, Mind:** (1a) 1 Cor. 2:9a; (1b) 1 *Clem.* 34:8; (2) *Gos. Thom.* 17; (3) Q²: Luke 10:23–24 = Matt. 13:16–17; (4) *Dial. Sav.* 57a

(8) **35. The Mustard Seed:** (1) *Gos. Thom.* 20; (2) Q¹: Luke 13:18–19 = Matt. 13:31–32; (3) Mark 4:30–32 = Matt. 13:31–32

(9) **12. Knowing the Danger:** (1a) 1 Thess. 5:2; (1b) 2 Pet. 3:10; (2a) *Gos. Thom.* 21:5–7; (2b) *Gos. Thom.* 103; (3) Q²: Luke 12:39–40 = Matt. 24:43–44; (4a) Rev. 3:3b; (4b) Rev. 16:15a

(10) **76. Speck and Log:** (1) *Gos. Thom.* 26 = P. Oxy. 1.1–4; (2) Q¹: Luke 6:41–42 = Matt. 7:3–5

(11) **79. Open Proclamation:** (1) *Gos. Thom.* 33:1 = P. Oxy. 1.41–42; (2) Q¹: Luke 12:3 = Matt. 10:27

(12) **36. Lamp and Bushel:** (1) *Gos. Thom.* 33:2–3; (2) Q²: Luke 11:33 = Matt. 5:15; (3) Mark 4:21 = Luke 8:16

(13) **80. The Blind Guide:** (1) *Gos. Thom.* 34; (2) Q¹: Luke 6:39 = Matt. 15:14b

(14) **81. Strong One's House:** (1) *Gos. Thom.* 35; (2) Q²: Luke 11:21–22 (= Matt. 12:29); (3) Mark 3:27 = Matt. 12:29 (= Luke 11:21–22)

(15) **82. Against Anxieties:** (1) *Gos. Thom.* 36 = P. Oxy. 655, col. i.1–17; (2) Q¹: Luke 12:22–31 = Matt. 6:25–33

(16) **84. On Hindering Others:** (1a) *Gos. Thom.* 39:1–2 = P. Oxy. 655, col. ii.11–19; (1b) *Gos. Thom.* 102; (2) Q²: Luke 11:52 = Matt. 23:13

(17) **40. Have and Receive:** (1) *Gos. Thom.* 41; (2) Q²: Luke 19:26 = Matt. 25:29; (3) Mark 4:25 = Matt. 13:12 = Luke 8:18b

(18) **23. All Sins Forgiven:** (1) *Gos. Thom.* 44; (2) Q²: Luke 12:10 = Matt. 12:32; (3) Mark 3:28–30 = Matt. 12:31; (4) *Did.* 11:7

(19) **41. Trees and Hearts:** (1) *Gos. Thom.* 45; (2a) Q¹: Luke 6:43–45 = Matt. 7:16–20; (2b) Matt. 12:33–35; (3) Ign. *Eph.* 14:2b

(20) **85. Greater Than John:** (1) *Gos. Thom.* 46; (2) Q²: Luke 7:28 = Matt. 11:11

(21) **86. Serving Two Masters:** (1) *Gos. Thom.* 47:1–2; (2a) Q¹: Luke 16:13 = Matt. 6:24; (2b) 2 *Clem.* 6:1

(22) **43. Blessed the Poor:** (1) *Gos. Thom.* 54; (2a) Q¹: Luke 6:20 = Matt. 5:3; (2b) Pol. *Phil.* 2:3e; (3) James 2:5

(23) **89. Hating One's Family:** (1a) *Gos. Thom.* 55:1–2a; (1b) *Gos. Thom.* 101; (2) Q¹: Luke 14:25–26 = Matt. 10:37

(24) **44. Carrying One's Cross:** (1) *Gos. Thom.* 55:2b; (2) Q¹: Luke 14:27 = Matt. 10:38; (3) Mark 8:34 = Matt. 16:24 = Luke 9:23

(25) **91. Taken or Left:** (1) *Gos. Thom.* 61:1; (2) Q²: Luke 17:34–35 = Matt. 24:40–41

(26) **45. Father and Son:** (1) *Gos. Thom.* 61:3; (2) Q²: Luke 10:22 = Matt. 11:27; (3a) John 3:35b; (3b) John 13:3a

(27) **95. The Feast:** (1) *Gos. Thom.* 64; (2) Q²: Luke 14:15–24 = Matt. 22:1–13

(28) 48. Blessed the Persecuted: (1a) *Gos. Thom.* 68; (1b) *Gos. Thom.* 69:1; (2a) Q¹: Luke 6:22–23 = Matt. 5:11–12 [except for Q²: 6:22b = 5:11b & 6:23c = 5:12c]; (2b) Matt. 5:10; (2c) Pol. *Phil.* 2:3f; (3a) 1 Pet. 3:14a; (3b) 1 Pet. 4:14

(29) 96. Blessed the Hungry: (1) *Gos. Thom.* 69:2; (2) Q¹: Luke 6:21a = Matt. 5:6

(30) 50. Harvest Is Great: (1) *Gos. Thom.* 73; (2) Q¹: Luke 10:2 = Matt. 9:37–38; (3) John 4:35

(31) 99. Treasure in Heaven: (1) *Gos. Thom.* 76:3; (2) Q¹: Luke 12:33 = Matt. 6:19–20

(32) 51. Into the Desert: (1) *Gos. Thom.* 78; (2) Q²: Luke 7:24–27 = Matt. 11:7–10; (3) Mark 1:2–3 = Matt. 3:3 = Luke 3:4–6 = (?) John 1:19–23

(33) 101. Foxes Have Holes: (1) *Gos. Thom.* 86; (2) Q¹: Luke 9:57–58 = Matt. 8:19–20

(34) 102. Inside and Outside: (1) *Gos. Thom.* 89; (2) Q²: Luke 11:39–40 = Matt. 23:25–26

(35) 103. Give Without Return: (1) *Gos. Thom.* 95; (2) Q¹: Luke 6:30, 34, 35b = Matt. 5:42; (3) *Did.* 1:4c, 5a

(36) 104. The Leaven: (1) *Gos. Thom.* 96:1–2; (2) Q¹: Luke 13:20–21 = Matt. 13:33

(37) 107. The Lost Sheep: (1) *Gos. Thom.* 107; (2) Q¹: Luke 15:3–7 = Matt. 18:12–14.

B. Redaction of Common Sayings Tradition in the *Gospel of Thomas* and the *Q Gospel*

Primary bold parenthetical numbers cross-reference to part A of this appendix. Secondary bold nonparenthetical numbers cross-reference to Crossan 1991: Appendix 1B.

Redaction is toward apocalyptic eschatology in the *Gospel of Thomas* but toward ascetic eschatology in the *Q Gospel*. That gives the following four types:

Type 1: 24% (9 out of 37 units) is redacted in the *Gospel of Thomas* but not in the *Q Gospel*
Type 2: 8% (3 out of 37 units) is redacted in the *Q Gospel* but not in the *Gospel of Thomas*
Type 3: 19% (7 out of 37 units) is redacted in both the *Gospel of Thomas* and the *Q Gospel*
Type 4: 49% (18 out of 37 units) is redacted in neither the *Gospel of Thomas* nor the *Q Gospel*

Type 1: Common Sayings Tradition Redacted in the *Gospel of Thomas* but Not in the *Q Gospel*

(1) 4. Ask, Seek, Knock: (1a) *Gos. Thom.* 2 = P. Oxy. 654.5–9; (1b) *Gos. Thom.* 92:1; (1c) *Gos. Thom.* 94; (2) *Gos. Heb.* 4ab; (3) Q¹: Luke 11:9–10 = Matt. 7:7–8; (4) Mark 11:24 = Matt. 21:22; (5a) *Dial. Sav.* 9–12; (5b) *Dial. Sav.* 20d; (5c) *Dial. Sav.* 79–80; (6a) John 14:13–14; (6b) John 15:7; (6c) John 15:16; (6d) John 16:23–24; (6e) John 16:26

(3) 32. Hidden Made Manifest: (1a) *Gos. Thom.* 5:2 = P. Oxy. 654.29–30; (1b) *Gos. Thom.* 6:5–6 = P. Oxy. 654.38–40; (2) Q¹: Luke 12:2 = Matt. 10:26; (3) Mark 4:22 = Luke 8:17

(6) 74. Peace or Sword: (1) *Gos. Thom.* 16; (2) Q²: Luke 12:51–53 = Matt. 10:34–36

(7) 14. Eye, Ear, Mind: (1) *Gos. Thom.* 17; (2) Q²: Luke 10:23–24 = Matt. 13:16–17

(15) 82. Against Anxieties: (1) *Gos. Thom.* 36 = P. Oxy. 655, col. i.1–17; (2) Q¹: Luke 12:22–31 = Matt. 6:25–33

(23) 89. Hating One's Family: (1a) *Gos. Thom.* 55:1–2a; (1b) *Gos. Thom.* 101; (2) Q¹: Luke 14:25–26 = Matt. 10:37

(27) 95. The Feast: (1) *Gos. Thom.* 64; (2) Q²: Luke 14:15–24 = Matt. 22:1–13

(30) 50. Harvest Is Great: (1) *Gos. Thom.* 73; (2) Q¹: Luke 10:2 = Matt. 9:37–38; (3) John 4:35

(33) 101. Foxes Have Holes: (1) *Gos. Thom.* 86; (2) Q¹: Luke 9:57–58 = Matt. 8:19–20

Type 2: Common Sayings Tradition Redacted in the *Q Gospel* but Not in the *Gospel of Thomas*

(12) 36. Lamp and Bushel: (1) *Gos. Thom.* 33:2–3; (2) Q²: Luke 11:33 = Matt. 5:15; (3) Mark 4:21 = Luke 8:16

(17) 40. Have and Receive: (1) *Gos. Thom.* 41; (2) Q²: Luke 19:26 = Matt. 25:29; (3) Mark 4:25 = Matt. 13:12 = Luke 8:18b

(34) 102. Inside and Outside: (1) *Gos. Thom.* 89; (2) Q²: Luke 11:39–40 = Matt. 23:25–26

Type 3: Common Sayings Tradition Redacted in Both the *Gospel of Thomas* and the *Q Gospel*

(2) 8. When and Where: (1a) *Gos. Thom.* 3:1–3 = P. Oxy. 654.9–16; (1b) *Gos. Thom.* 51; (1c) *Gos. Thom.* 113; (2) Q²: Luke 17:23 = Matt. 24:26; (3) Mark 13:21–23 = Matt. 24:23–25; (4?) *Dial. Sav.* 16; (5) Luke 17:20–21

(9) 12. Knowing the Danger: (1a) 1 Thess. 5:2; (1b) 2 Pet. 3:10; (2a) *Gos. Thom.* 21:5–7; (2b) *Gos. Thom.* 103; (3) Q²: Luke 12:39–40 = Matt. 24:43–44; (4a) Rev. 3:3b; (4b) Rev. 16:15a

(20) 85. Greater Than John: (1) *Gos. Thom.* 46; (2) Q²: Luke 7:28 = Matt. 11:11

(25) 91. Taken or Left: (1) *Gos. Thom.* 61:1; (2) Q²: Luke 17:34–35 = Matt. 24:40–41

(26) 45. Father and Son: (1) *Gos. Thom.* 61:3; (2) Q²: Luke 10:22 = Matt. 11:27; (3a) John 3:35b; (3b) John 13:3a

(28) 48. Blessed the Persecuted: (1a) *Gos. Thom.* 68; (1b) *Gos. Thom.* 69:1; (2a) Q¹: Luke 6:22–23 = Matt. 5:11–12 [except for Q²: 6:22b = 5:11b & 6:23c = 5:12c]; (2b) Matt. 5:10; (2c) Pol. *Phil.* 2:3f; (3a) 1 Pet. 3:14a; (3b) 1 Pet. 4:14

(32) 51. Into the Desert: (1) *Gos. Thom.* 78; (2) Q²: Luke 7:24–27 = Matt. 11:7–10; (3) Mark 1:2–3 = Matt. 3:3 = Luke 3:4–6 =(?) John 1:19–23

Type 4: Common Sayings Tradition Redacted in Neither the *Gospel of Thomas* Nor the *Q Gospel*

(4) 33. The Golden Rule: (1) *Gos. Thom.* 6:3 = P. Oxy. 654.36–37; (2) Q¹: Luke 6:31 = Matt. 7:12

(5) 1. Mission and Message: (1a) 1 Cor. 9:14; (1b) 1 Cor. 10:27; (2) *Gos. Thom.* 14:4; (3) Q¹: Luke 10:(1), 4–11 = Matt. 10:7, 10b, 12–14; (4) Mark 6:7–13 = Matt. 10:1, 8–10a, 11 = Luke 9:1–6; (5) *Dial. Sav.* 53b[139:9–10]; (6) *Did.* 11:(3)4–12; (7) 1 Tim. 5:18b

(8) 35. The Mustard Seed: (1) *Gos. Thom.* 20; (2) Q¹: Luke 13:18–19 = Matt. 13:31–32; (3) Mark 4:30–32 = Matt. 13:31–32

(10) 76. Speck and Log: (1) *Gos. Thom.* 26 = P. Oxy. 1.1–4; (2) Q¹: Luke 6:41–42 = Matt. 7:3–5

(11) 79. Open Proclamation: (1) *Gos. Thom.* 33:1 = P. Oxy. 1.41–42; (2) Q¹: Luke 12:3 = Matt. 10:27

(13) 80. The Blind Guide: (1) *Gos. Thom.* 34; (2) Q¹: Luke 6:39 = Matt. 15:14b

(14) 81. Strong One's House: (1) *Gos. Thom.* 35; (2) Q²: Luke 11:21–22 (= Matt. 12:29); (3) Mark 3:27 = Matt. 12:29 (= Luke 11:21–22)

(16) 84. On Hindering Others: (1a) *Gos. Thom.* 39:1–2 = P. Oxy. 655, col. ii.11–19; (1b) *Gos. Thom.* 102; (2) Q²: Luke 11:52 = Matt. 23:13

(18) 23. All Sins Forgiven: (1) *Gos. Thom.* 44; (2) Q²: Luke 12:10 = Matt. 12:32; (3) Mark 3:28–30 = Matt. 12:31; (4) *Did.* 11:7

(19) 41. Trees and Hearts: (1) *Gos. Thom.* 45; (2a) Q¹: Luke 6:43–45 = Matt. 7:16–20; (2b) Matt. 12:33–35; (3) Ign. *Eph.* 14:2b

(21) 86. Serving Two Masters: (1) *Gos. Thom.* 47:1–2; (2a) Q¹: Luke 16:13 = Matt. 6:24; (2b) 2 *Clem.* 6:1

(22) 43. Blessed the Poor: (1) *Gos. Thom.* 54; (2a) Q¹: Luke 6:20 = Matt. 5:3; (2b) Pol. *Phil.* 2:3e; (3) James 2:5

(24) 44. Carrying One's Cross: (1) *Gos. Thom.* 55:2b; (2) Q¹: Luke 14:27 = Matt. 10:38; (3) Mark 8:34 = Matt. 16:24 = Luke 9:23

(29) 96. Blessed the Hungry: (1) *Gos. Thom.* 69:2; (2) Q¹: Luke 6:21a = Matt. 5:6

(31) 99. Treasure in Heaven: (1) *Gos. Thom.* 76:3; (2) Q¹: Luke 12:33 = Matt. 6:19–20

(35) 103. Give Without Return: (1) *Gos. Thom.* 95; (2a) Q¹: Luke 6:30, 34, 35b = Matt. 5:42; (2b) *Did.* 1:4b, 5a

(36) 104. The Leaven: (1) *Gos. Thom.* 96:1–2; (2) Q¹: Luke 13:20–21 = Matt. 13:33

(37) 107. The Lost Sheep: (1) *Gos. Thom.* 107; (2) Q¹: Luke 15:3–7 = Matt. 18:12–14

Appendix 2

Particular Sayings Tradition in the *Gospel of Thomas* and the *Q Gospel*

This Appendix is based on Crossan 1991: Appendix 1B, but see changes given in the Preliminary Note to Appendix 1 above.

A. Particular Sayings Tradition in the *Gospel of Thomas* but Not in the *Q Gospel*

72% (95 out of 132 units) of the *Gospel of Thomas* does not have any parallels in the *Q Gospel*.

(1) 205. Not Taste Death: (1) *Gos. Thom.* 1 = P. Oxy. 654.3–5; (2) John 8:51–52; **(2) 206. Knowing Oneself:** (1) *Gos. Thom.* 3:2 = P. Oxy. 654.16–21; (2) *Dial. Sav.* 30; **(3) 278. Man and Child:** (1) *Gos. Thom.* 4:1 & P. Oxy. 654.21–25; **(4) 31. First and Last:** (1) *Gos. Thom.* 4:2–3 & P. Oxy. 654.25–27; (2) Mark 10:31 = Matt. 19:30; (3) Matt. 20:16; (4) Luke 13:30; **(5) 279. In Your Sight:** (1) *Gos. Thom.* 5:1 = P. Oxy. 654.27–29; **(6) 207. Buried and Resurrected:** (1) P. Oxy. 654.31; (2) Oxyrhynchus shroud [*NTA*[1] 1.300]; **(7) 280. On Telling Lies:** (1) *Gos. Thom.* 6:2+4 = P. Oxy. 654.36 + 37–38; **(8) 281. Man and Lion:** (1) *Gos. Thom.* 7 = P. Oxy. 654.40–42; **(9) 71. The Fishnet:** (1) *Gos. Thom.* 8:1; (2) Matt. 13:47–48; **(10) 9. Who Has Ears:** (1a) *Gos. Thom.* 8:2; (1b) *Gos. Thom.* 21:5; (1c) *Gos. Thom.* 24:2; (1d) *Gos. Thom.* 63:2; (1e) *Gos. Thom.* 65:2; (1f) *Gos. Thom.* 96:2; (2a) Mark 4:9 = Matt. 13:9 = Luke 8:8b; (2b) Mark 4:23 = Matt. 13:43b; (3) Matt. 11:15; (4) Luke 14:35b; (5) Rev. 2:7, 11, 17, 29; 3:6, 13, 22; 13:9; **(11) 34. The Sower:** (1) *Gos. Thom.* 9; (2) Mark 4:3–8 = Matt. 13:3b–8 = Luke 8:5–8a; (3) *1 Clem.* 24:5; **(12) 72. Fire on Earth:** (1) *Gos. Thom.* 10; (2) Luke 12:49; **(13) 208. Life and Death:** (1a) *Gos. Thom.* 11:1–2a; (1b) *Gos. Thom.* 111:1–2; (2) *Dial. Sav.* 56–57; **(14) 282. Two and One:** (1) *Gos. Thom.* 11:2b; **(15) 30. Revealed to James:** (1) *1 Cor.* 15:7a; (2) *Gos. Thom.* 12; (3) *Gos. Heb.* 7; **(16) 73. Who Is Jesus?** (1) *Gos. Thom.* 13; (2a) Mark 8:27–30 = Matt. 16:13–20 = Luke 9:18–21; (2b) *Gos. Naz.* 14; (2c) John 6:67–69; **(17) 283. Fasting, Praying, Almsgiving:** (1) *Gos. Thom.* 6:1 + 14:1; **(18) 19. What Goes In:** (1) *Gos. Thom.* 14:3; (2) Mark 7:14–15; (3) Matt. 15:10–11; (4a) Acts 10:14b; (4b) Acts 11:8b; **(19) 284. Your Father:** (1) *Gos. Thom.* 15; **(20) 285. Beginning and End:** (1) *Gos. Thom.* 18:1–3; **(21) 86. Before One's Creation:** (1) *Gos. Thom.* 19:1; **(22) 287. Stones and Trees:** (1) *Gos. Thom.* 19:2; **(23) 288. Children in Field:** (1) *Gos. Thom.* 21:1–2; **(24) 75. The Harvest Time:** (1) *Gos. Thom.* 21:4; (2) Mark 4:26–29; **(25) 20. Kingdom and Children:** (1) *Gos. Thom.* 22:1–2; (2) Mark 10:13–16 = Matt. 19:13–15 = Luke 18:15–17; (3) Matt. 18:3; (4) John 3:1–5, 9–10; **(26) 13. Two As One:** (1a) Gal. 3:27–28; (1b) 1 Cor. 12:13; (1c) Col. 3:10–11; (2) *Gos. Thom.* 22:3–4; (3) *Eger. Gos.* 5b; (4) *2 Clem.* 12:1–6; **(27) 289. The Chosen Few:** (1) *Gos. Thom.* 23; **(28) 21. The World's Light:** (1) *Gos. Thom.* 24:1–3 = P. Oxy. 655, fr.d.1–52; (2) Matt. 5:14a; (3a?) *Dial. Sav.* 14; (3b?) *Dial. Sav.* 34; (4a) John 8:12; (4b) John 11:9–10; (4c) John 12:35–36; **(29) 290. Love Your Brother:** (1) *Gos. Thom.* 25; **(30) 291. Fasting and Sabbath:** (1) *Gos. Thom.* 27 = P. Oxy. 1.4–11; **(31) 292. Drunk, Blind, Empty:** (1) *Gos. Thom.* 28; **(32) 293. Flesh As Poverty:** (1) *Gos. Thom.* 29; **(33) 77. Two or Three:** (1) *Gos. Thom.* 30 = P. Oxy. 1.23–27; (2) Matt. 18:20; **(34) 22. Prophet's Own Country:** (1) *Gos. Thom.* 31 = P. Oxy. 1.30–35; (2) Mark 6:1–6a = Matt. 13:53–58; (3) Luke 4:16–24; (4) John 4:44; **(35) 78. The**

Mountain City: (1) *Gos. Thom.* 32 = P. Oxy. 1.36–41; (2) Matt. 5:14b; **(36) 37. New Garments:** (1) *Gos. Thom.* 37 = P. Oxy. 655, col. i.17–col. ii.1.17; (2a) *Dial. Sav.* 49–52; (2b) *Dial. Sav.* 84–85; (3) *Eger. Gos.* 5a; **(37) 294. Desire to Hear:** (1) *Gos. Thom.* 38:1 = P. Oxy. 655, col. ii.2–11; **(38) 83. Seeking Too Late:** (1) *Gos. Thom.* 38:2; (2) John 7:34a, 36b; **(39) 38. Serpents and Doves:** (1) *Gos. Thom.* 39:2 = P. Oxy. 655, col. ii.19–23; (2a) Matt. 10:16b; (2b) *Gos. Naz.* 7; (3) Ign. *Pol.* 2:2; **(40) 39. Plant Rooted Up:** (1) *Gos. Thom.* 40; (2) Matt. 15:12–13; (3a) Ign. *Trall.* 11:1b; (3b) Ign. *Phld.* 3:1b; **(41) 295. Become Passers-By:** (1) *Gos. Thom.* 42; **(42) 296. From My Words:** (1) *Gos. Thom.* 43; **(43) 297. Horses and Bows:** (1) *Gos. Thom.* 47:1; **(44) 87. Drinking Old Wine:** (1) *Gos. Thom.* 47:3; (2) Luke 5:39; **(45) 88. Patches and Wineskins:** (1) *Gos. Thom.* 47:4; (2) Mark 2:21–22 = Matt. 9:16–17 = Luke 5:36–38; **(46) 298. Unity and Mountain:** (1a) *Gos. Thom.* 48; (1b) *Gos. Thom.* 106; **(47) 299. Solitary and Elect:** (1) *Gos. Thom.* 49; **(48) 300. If They Ask:** (1) *Gos. Thom.* 50; **(49) 42. Scriptures and Jesus:** (1) *Gos. Thom.* 52; (2) *Eger. Gos.* 2.1; (3) John 5:39–47; **(50) 301. The True Circumcision:** (1) *Gos. Thom.* 53; **(51) 302. Superior to World:** (1a) *Gos. Thom.* 56; (1b) *Gos. Thom.* 80; **(52) 90. The Planted Weeds:** (1) *Gos. Thom.* 57; (2) Matt. 13:24–30; **(53) 303. Blessed the Sufferer:** (1) *Gos. Thom.* 58; **(54) 304. Take Heed Now:** (1) *Gos. Thom.* 59; **(55) 305. Samaritan and Lamb:** (1) *Gos. Thom.* 60; **(56) 306. Jesus and Salome:** (1) *Gos. Thom.* 61:2–5; **(57) 92. Knowing the Mystery:** (1) *Gos. Thom.* 62:1; (2a) *Secret Mark* f2r10; (2b) Mark 4:10–12 = Matt. 13:10–11, 13–15 = Luke 8:9–10; **(58) 93. On Secrecy:** (1) *Gos. Thom.* 62:2; (2) Matt. 6:3b; **(59) 994. The Rich Farmer:** (1) *Gos. Thom.* 63:1; (2) 1Q?: Luke 12:16–21; **(60) 46. The Tenants:** (1) *Gos. Thom.* 65; (2) Mark 12:1–9, 12 = Matt. 21:33–41, 43–46 = Luke 20:9–16, 19. (3) *Herm. Sim.* 5.2:4–7; **(61) 47. The Rejected Stone:** (1) *Gos. Thom.* 66; (2) Mark 12:10–11 = Matt. 21:42 = Luke 20:17–18; (3) *Barn.* 6:4; **(62) 307. Knowing the All:** (1) *Gos. Thom.* 67; **(63) 308. From Within Yourselves:** (1) *Gos. Thom.* 70; **(64) 49. Temple and Jesus:** (1) *Gos. Thom.* 71; (2a) Mark 14:55–59 = Matt. 26:59–61; (2b) Mark 15:29–32a = Matt. 27:39–43 = (!) Luke 23:35–37; (2c) Acts 6:11–14; (3) John 2:18–22; **(65) 97. The Disputed Inheritance:** (1) *Gos. Thom.* 72:1–3; (2) Luke 12:13–15; **(66) 309. The Cistern:** (1) *Gos. Thom.* 74; **(67) 209. The Bridal Chamber:** (1) *Gos. Thom.* 75; (2) *Dial Sav.* 50b; **(68) 98. The Pearl:** (1) *Gos. Thom.* 76:1; (2) Matt. 13:45–46; **(69) 310. Light and All:** (1) *Gos. Thom.* 77:1; **(70) 311. Stone and Wood:** (1) *Gos. Thom.* 77:2 = P. Oxy. 1.27–30; **(71) 24. Blessed the Womb:** (1) *Gos. Thom.* 79:1–2; (2) 1Q?: Luke 11:27–28; (3?) John 13:17; (4?) James 1:25b; **(72) 100. Jerusalem Mourned:** (1) *Gos. Thom.* 79:3; (2) Luke 23:27–31; **(73) 312. Riches and Power:** (1) *Gos. Thom.* 81; **(74) 313. Near the Fire:** (1) *Gos. Thom.* 82; **(75) 314. The Father's Light:** (1) *Gos. Thom.* 83; **(76) 315. The Primordial Images:** (1) *Gos. Thom.* 84; **(77) 316. Adam's Death:** (1) *Gos. Thom.* 85; **(78) 317. Body and Soul:** (1) *Gos. Thom.* 87; **(79) 318. Angels and Prophets:** (1) *Gos. Thom.* 88; **(80) 52. Yoke and Burden:** (1) *Gos. Thom.* 90; (2) Matt. 11:28–30; (3) *Dial. Sav.* 65–68; **(81) 53. Knowing the Times:** (1) *Gos. Thom.* 91; (2) Luke 12:54–56; (3?) Matt. 16:2–3; (3b?) *Gos. Naz.* 13; (4?) John 6:30; **(82) 319. Then and Now:** (1) *Gos. Thom.* 92:2; **(83) 54. Dogs and Swine:** (1) *Gos. Thom.* 93; (2) Matt. 7:6; (3) *Did.* 9:5; **(84) 320. The Empty Jar:** (1) *Gos. Thom.* 97; **(85) 321. The Assassin:** (1) *Gos. Thom.* 98; **(86) 105. Jesus' True Family:** (1) *Gos. Thom.* 99; (2a) Mark 3:19b–21, 31–35 = Matt. 12:46–50 = Luke 8:19–21; (2b) 2 *Clem.* 9:11; (2c) *Gos. Eb.* 5; **(87) 55. Caesar and God:** (1) *Gos. Thom.* 100; (2) *Eger. Gos.* 2. 3ac; (3) Mark 12:13–17 = Matt. 22:15–22 = Luke 20:20–26; **(88) 106. Fasting and Wedding:** (1) *Gos. Thom.* 104; (2) Mark 2:18–20 = Matt. 9:14–15 = Luke 5:33–35; **(89) 322. A Harlot's Son:** (1) *Gos. Thom.* 105; **(90) 323. From My Mouth:** (1) *Gos. Thom.* 108; **(91) 108. The Treasure:** (1) *Gos. Thom.* 109; (2) Matt. 13:44; **(92) 324. Finding the World:** (1) *Gos. Thom.* 110; **(93) 325. Finding Oneself:** (1) *Gos. Thom.* 111:3; **(94) 326. Flesh and Soul:** (1) *Gos. Thom.* 112; **(95) 327. Peter and Mary:** (1) *Gos. Thom.* 114.

B. Particular Sayings Tradition in the *Q Gospel* but Not in the *Gospel of Thomas*

63% (64 out of 101 units) of the *Q Gospel* does not have parallels in the *Gospel of Thomas*.

(1) **137. John's Warning:** (1) Q²: Luke 3:7–9a = Matt. 3:7–10a; (2) **115 [& 138]. John's Message:** (1a) Q²: Luke 3:15–18= Matt. 3:11–12 = Matt. 7:19; (1b) Acts 13:24–25; (1c) John 1:24–31; (2) Mark 1:7–8; (3) **116 [& 139]. Jesus Tempted Thrice:** (1a) Q³: Luke 4:1–13 = Matt. 4:1–11; (1b) *Gos. Naz.* 3; (4) **56. Blessed the Sad:** (1) Q¹: Luke 6:21= Matt. 5:4; (2) *Dial. Sav.* 13–14; (3) John 16:20, 22; (5) **114. Love Your Enemies:** (1) P. Oxy. 1224, 2 r i, lines 1–2a; (2a) Q¹: Luke 6:27–28, 35a = Matt. 5:43–44; (2b) Pol. *Phil.* 12:3a; (3) *Did.* 1:3ac; (6) **140. The Other Cheek:** (1) Q¹: Luke 6:29 = Matt. 5:38–41; (2) *Did.* 1:4b; (7) **117. Better than Sinners:** (1a) Q¹: Luke 6:32–35 = Matt. 5:45–47; (1b) 2 *Clem.* 13:4a [from Luke 6:32]; (2) Ign. *Pol.* 2:1; (3) *Did.* 1:3b; (8) **14. As Your Father:** (1a) Q¹: Luke 6:36 = Matt. 5:48; (1b) Pol. *Phil.* 12:3b; (9) **118. Judgment for Judgment:** (1a) Q¹: Luke 6:37a = Matt. 7:1–2a; (2a) 1 *Clem.* 13:2e; (2b) Pol. *Phil.* 2:3a; (10) **57. Measure for Measure:** (1a) Q¹: Luke 6:38bc = Matt. 7:2b; (2) Mark 4:24b; (3a) 1 *Clem.* 13:2g; (1a/3b) Pol. *Phil.* 2:3d; (11) **58. Disciple and Servant:** (1) Q¹: Luke 6:40 = Matt. 10:24–25; (2) *Dial. Sav.* 53c; (3a) John 13:16; (3b) John 15:20; (12) **111. Invocation without Obedience:** (1) *Eger. Gos.* 3; (2a) Q¹: Luke 6:46 = Matt. 7:21; (2b) 2 *Clem.* 4:2; (13) **142. Rock or Sand:** (1) Q¹: Luke 6:47–49 = Matt. 7:24–27; (14) **119. Distant Boy Cured:** (1) Q²: Luke 7:1–2[3–6a]6b–10 = Matt. 8:5–10, 13; (2) John 4:46b–53; (15) **143. Reply to John:** (1) Q²: Luke 7:18–23 = Matt. 11:2–6; (16) **144. Wisdom Justified:** (1) Q²: Luke 7:31–35 = Matt. 11:16–19; (17) **145. Leave the Dead:** (1) Q²: Luke 9:59–60 = Matt. 8:21–22; (18) **147. Lambs Among Wolves:** (1a) Q¹: Luke 10:3 = Matt. 10:16a; (1b) 2 *Clem.* 5:2; (19) **148. Cities of Woe:** (1) Q²: Luke 10:12–15 = Matt. 11:15, 20–24; (20) **10. Receiving the Sender:** (1) Q¹: Luke 10:16 = Matt. 10:40; (2) Mark 9:36–37 = Matt. 18:2, 5 = Luke 9:47–48a; (3) *Did.* 11:4–5; (4a) John 5:23b; (4b) John 12:44–50; (4c) John 13:20; (5) Ign. *Eph.* 6:1; (21) **66. Wise and Understanding:** (1) 1 Cor. 1:19; (2a) Q²: Luke 10:21 = Matt. 11:25–26; (2b) *Gos. Naz.* 9; (22) **120 [& 27]. The Lord's Prayer :** (1a) Q¹: Luke 11:(1)2–4 = (!) Matt. 6:9–13; (1b) *Gos. Naz.* 5; (1c) Pol. *Phil.* 7:2a; (2) *Did.* 8:2b; (23) **149. Good Gifts:** (1) Q¹: Luke 11:11–13 = Matt. 7:9–11; (24) **121. Beelzebul Controversy:** (1a) Q²: Luke 11:14–15, 17–18 = Matt. 12:22–26; (1b) Matt. 9:32–34; (2) Mark 3:22–26; (25) **150. By Whose Power:** (1) Q²: Luke 11:19–20 = Matt. 12:27–28; (26) **57. For and Against:** (1) P. Oxy. 1224, 2 r i, lines 2b–5; (2) Q²: Luke 11:23 = Matt. 12:30; (3) Mark 9:40 = Luke 9:50b; (27) **151. The Returning Demon:** (1) Q²: Luke 11:24–26 = Matt. 12:43–45; (28) **122. Request for Sign:** (1a) Q²: Luke 11:29–30 = Matt. 12:38–40; (1b) Matt. 16:4a; (1c) *Gos. Naz.* 11; (2a) Mark 8:11–13 = Matt. 16:1, 4 = Luke 11:16; (29) **152. Judgment by Pagans:** (1) Q²: Luke 11:31–32 = Matt. 12:41–42; (30) **123. The Body's Light:** (1) Q²: Luke 11:34–36 = Matt. 6:22–23; (2) *Dial. Sav.* 8 [125:18–126:4]; (31) **153. Tithing and Justice:** (1) Q²: Luke 11:42 = Matt. 23:23; (32) **124. Honors and Salutations:** (1) Q²: Luke 11:43 = Matt. 23:6b–7a; (2) Mark 12:38–40 = Matt. 23:5–7 = Luke 20:45–46; (33) **154. Like Graves:** (1) Q²: Luke 11:44 = Matt. 23:27–28; (34) **155. Helping with Burdens:** (1) Q²: Luke 11:45–46 = Matt. 23:4; (35) **156. The Prophets' Tombs:** (1) Q²: Luke 11:47–48 = Matt. 23:29–31; (36) **157. Wisdom's Envoys:** (1a) Q²: Luke 11:49–51 = Matt. 23:34–36; (1b) *Gos. Naz.* 17; (37) **158. Whom To Fear:** (1a) Q¹: Luke 12:4–5 = Matt. 10:28; (1b) 2 *Clem.* 5:4; (38) **159. God and Sparrows:** (1) Q¹: Luke 12:6–7 = Matt. 10:29–31; (39) **28. Before the Angels:** (1a) Q²: Luke 12:8–9 = Matt. 10:32–33; (1b) 2 *Clem.* 3:2 [from Matt. 10:32]; (2) Mark 8:38 = Matt. 16:27 = Luke 9:26; (3) Rev. 3:5; (4) 2 Tim 2:12b; (40) **59. Spirit Under Trial:** (1) Q²: Luke 12:11–12 = Matt. 10:19–20; (2) Mark 13:11 = Matt. 10:19–20 = Luke 21:14–15; (3) John 14:26; (41) **160. Heart and Treasure:** (1) Q¹: Luke 12:34 = Matt. 6:21; (42) **161. Master and Steward:** (1) Q²: Luke 12:42–46 = Matt. 24:45–51a;

(43) 162. *Before the Judgment:* (1) Q²: Luke 12:57–59 = Matt. 5:25–26; (2) *Did.* 1:5c; (44) 163. *The Narrow Door:* (1) Q¹: Luke 13:23–24 = Matt. 7:13–14; (45) 164. *The Closed Door:* (1) Q²: Luke 13:25 = Matt. 25:1–12; (46) 165. *Depart from Me:* (1a) Q²: Luke 13:26–27 = Matt. 7:22–23; (1b?) 2 *Clem.* 4:5; (1c?) *Gos. Naz.* 6; (47) 166 [& 125]. *Patriarchs and Gentiles:* (1) Q²: Luke 13:28–29 = Matt. 8:11–12; (48) 167. *Jerusalem Indicted:* (1) Q²: Luke 13:34–35 = Matt. 23:37–39; (49) 379. *Exaltation and Humiliation:* (1) Q¹: Luke 14:11 = Luke 18:14 = Matt. 23:12; (50) 60. *Saving One's Life:* (1) Q¹: Luke 17:33 = Matt. 10:39; (2) Mark 8:35 = Matt. 16:25 = Luke 9:24; (3) John 12:25–26; (51) 126. *Salting the Salt:* (1) Q¹: Luke 14:34–35a = Matt. 5:13; (2) Mark 9:50a; (52) 168. *Kingdom and Violence:* (1a) Q²: Luke 16:16 = Matt. 11:12–14; (1b) *Gos. Naz.* 8; (53) 169. *Not One Iota:* (1) Q²: Luke 16:17 = Matt. 5:18; (54) 15. *Against Divorce:* (1) 1 Cor. 7:10–11; (2) Q²: Luke 16:18 = Matt. 5:31–32; (3) Mark 10:10–12 = Matt. 19:9; (4) *Herm. Man.* 4.1:6b, 10; (55) 170. *Woe for Temptation:* (1) Q²: Luke 17:1–2 = Matt. 18:6–7; (56) 171. *Reproving and Forgiving:* (1) Q²: Luke 17:3 = Matt. 18:15; (57) 172. *Unlimited Forgiveness:* (1a) Q²: Luke 17:4 = Matt. 18:21–22; (1b) *Gos. Naz.* 15ab; (58) 173. *Faith's Power:* (1) Q²: Luke 17:5–6 = Matt. 17:20; (59) 174. *As with Lightning:* (1) Q²: Luke 17:24 = Matt. 24:27; (60) 175. *As with Noah:* (1) Q²: Luke 17:26–27 = Matt. 24:37–39a; (61) 176. *As with Lot:* (1) Q²: Luke 17:28–30 = Matt. 24:39b; (62) 177. *Corpse and Vultures:* (1) Q²: Luke 17:37 = Matt. 24:28; (63) 178. *The Entrusted Money:* (1a) Q²: Luke 19:(11)12–24, 27 = Matt. 25:14–28, 30; (1b) *Gos. Naz.* 18; (64) 179. *On Twelve Thrones:* (1) Q²: Luke 22:28–30 = Matt. 19:28.

Appendix 3

Gospel of Thomas, Q Gospel, and Mark

This appendix is based on Crossan 1991: Appendix 1B, but see changes given in Preliminary Note to Appendix 1 above.

A. Sayings Tradition Common to the *Gospel of Thomas*, the *Q Gospel*, and Mark

30% (11 out of 37 units) of what is common to the *Gospel of Thomas* and the *Q Gospel* has parallels in Mark.

(1) **4. Ask, Seek, Knock:** (1a) *Gos. Thom.* 2 = P. Oxy. 654.5–9; (1b) *Gos. Thom.* 92:1; (1c) *Gos. Thom.* 94; (2) *Gos. Heb.* 4ab; (3) Q¹: Luke 11:9–10 = Matt. 7:7–8; (4) Mark 11:24 = Matt. 21:22; (5a) *Dial. Sav.* 9–12; (5b) *Dial. Sav.* 20d; (5c) *Dial. Sav.* 79–80; (6a) John 14:13–14; (6b) John 15:7; (6c) John 15:16; (6d) John 16:23–24; (6e) John 16:26; **(2) 8. When and Where:** (1a) *Gos. Thom.* 3:1 = P. Oxy. 654.9–16; (1b) *Gos. Thom.* 51; (1c) *Gos. Thom.* 113; (2) Q²: Luke 17:23 = Matt. 24:26; (3) Mark 13:21–23 = Matt. 24:23–25; (4?) *Dial. Sav.* 16; (5) Luke 17:20–21; **(3) 32. Hidden Made Manifest:** (1a) *Gos. Thom.* 5:2 = P. Oxy. 654.29–30; (1b) *Gos. Thom.* 6:4 = P. Oxy. 654.38–40; (2) Q¹: Luke 12:2 = Matt. 10:26; (3) Mark 4:22 = Luke 8:17; **(4) 1. Mission and Message:** (1a) 1 Cor. 9:14; (1b) 1 Cor. 10:27; (2) *Gos. Thom.* 14:2; (3) Q¹: Luke 10:(1), 4–11 = Matt. 10:7, 10b, 12–14; (4) Mark 6:7–13 = Matt. 10:1, 8–10a, 11 = Luke 9:1–6; (5) *Dial. Sav.* 53b[139:9–10]; (6) *Did.* 11:(3)4–12; (7) 1 Tim 5:18b; **(5) 35. The Mustard Seed:** (1) *Gos. Thom.* 20:1–2; (2) Q¹: Luke 13:18–19 = Matt. 13:31–32; (3) Mark 4:30–32 = Matt. 13:31–32; **(6) 336. Lamp and Bushel:** (1) *Gos. Thom.* 33:2; (2) Q²: Luke 11:33 = Matt. 5:15; (3) Mark 4:21 = Luke 8:16; **(7) 81. Strong One's House:** (1) *Gos. Thom.* 35; (2) Q²: Luke 11:21–22 (= Matt. 12:29); (3) Mark 3:27 = Matt. 12:29 (= Luke 11:21–22); **(8) 40. Have and Receive:** (1) *Gos. Thom.* 41; (2) Q²: Luke 19:26 = Matt. 25:29; (3) Mark 4:25 = Matt. 13:12 = Luke 8:18b; **(9) 23. All Sins Forgiven:** (1) *Gos. Thom.* 44; (2) Q²: Luke 12:10 = Matt. 12:32; (3) Mark 3:28–30 = Matt. 12:31; (4) *Did.* 11:7; **(10) 44. Carrying One's Cross:** (1) *Gos. Thom.* 55:2b; (2) Q¹: Luke 14:27 = Matt. 10:38; (3) Mark 8:34 = Matt. 16:24 = Luke 9:23; **(11) 51. Into the Desert:** (1) *Gos. Thom.* 78; (2) Q²: Luke 7:24–27 = Matt. 11:7–10; (3) Mark 1:2–3 = Matt. 3:3 = Luke 3:4–6 = (?) John 1:19–23.

B. Sayings Tradition Common to the *Gospel of Thomas* and Mark but Not in the *Q Gospel*

17% (16 of 95 units) of what is particular to the *Gospel of Thomas* has parallels in Mark.

(1) **31. First and Last:** (1) *Gos. Thom.* 4:2–3 = P. Oxy. 654.25–27 (2) Mark 10:31 = Matt. 19:30; (3) Matt. 20:16; (4) Luke 13:30; **(2) 9. Who Has Ears:** (1a) *Gos. Thom.* 8:4; (1b) *Gos. Thom.* 21:10; (1c) *Gos. Thom.* 24:2; (1d) *Gos. Thom.* 63:4; (1e) *Gos. Thom.* 65:8; (1f) *Gos. Thom.* 96:3; (2a) Mark 4:9 = Matt. 13:9 = Luke 8:8b; (2b) Mark 4:23 = Matt. 13:43b; (3) Matt. 11:15; (4) Luke 14:35b; (5) Rev. 2:7, 11, 17, 29; 3:6, 13, 22; 13:9; **(3) 34. The Sower:** (1) *Gos. Thom.* 9; (2)

Mark 4:3–8 = Matt. 13:3b–8 = Luke 8:5–8a; (3) *1 Clem.* 24:5; (4) **73. *Who Is Jesus?*** (1) *Gos. Thom.* 13; (2a) Mark 8:27–30 = Matt. 16:13–20 = Luke 9:18–21; (2b) *Gos. Naz.* 14; (2c) John 6:67–69; (5) **19. *What Goes In:*** (1) *Gos. Thom.* 14:5; (2) Mark 7:14–15; (3) Matt. 15:10–11; (4a) Acts 10:14b; (4b) Acts 11:8b; (6) **75. *The Harvest Time:*** (1) *Gos. Thom.* 21:8–9; (2) Mark 4:26–29; (7) **20. *Kingdom and Children:*** (1) *Gos. Thom.* 22:1–2; (2) Mark 10:13–16 = Matt. 19:13–15 = Luke 18:15–17; (3) Matt. 18:3; (4) John 3:1–5, 9–10; (8) **22. *Prophet's Own Country:*** (1) *Gos. Thom.* 31 P. Oxy. 1.30–35; (2) Mark 6:1–6a = Matt. 13:53–58; (3) Luke 4:16–24; (4) John 4:44; (9) **88. *Patches and Wineskins:*** (1) *Gos. Thom.* 47:4–5; (2) Mark 2:21–22 = Matt. 9:16–17 = Luke 5:36–38 (10) **92. *Knowing the Mystery:*** (1) *Gos. Thom.* 62:3b; (2a) *Secret Mark* f2r10; (2b) Mark 4:10–12 = Matt. 13:10–11, 13–15 = Luke 8:9–10; (11) **46. *The Tenants:*** (1) *Gos. Thom.* 65:1–7; (2) Mark 12:1–9, 12 = Matt. 21:33–41, 43–46 = Luke 20:9–16, 19; (3) *Herm. Sim.* 5.2:4–7; (12) **47. *The Rejected Stone:*** (1) *Gos. Thom.* 66; (2) Mark 12:10–11 = Matt. 21:42 = Luke 20:17–18; (3) *Barn.* 6:4; (13) **49. *Temple and Jesus:*** (1) *Gos. Thom.* 71; (2a) Mark 14:55–59 = Matt. 26:59–61; (2b) Mark 15:29–32a = Matt. 27:39–43 =(!) Luke 23:35–37; (2c) Acts 6:11–14; (3) John 2:18–22; (14) **105. *Jesus' True Family:*** (1) *Gos. Thom.* 99; (2a) Mark 3:19b–21, 31–35 = Matt. 12:46–50 = Luke 8:19–21; (2b) *2 Clem.* 9:11; (2c) *Gos. Eb.* 5; (15) **55. *Caesar and God:*** (1) *Gos. Thom.* 100; (2) *Eger. Gos.* 2. 3ac; (3) Mark 12:13–17 = Matt. 22:15–22 = Luke 20:20–26; (16) **106. *Fasting and Wedding:*** (1) *Gos. Thom.* 104; (2) Mark 2:18–20 = Matt. 9:14–15 = Luke 5:33–35.

C. Sayings Tradition Common to the *Q Gospel* and Mark but Not in the *Gospel of Thomas*

19% (12 out of 64 units) of what is particular to the *Q Gospel* has parallels in Mark.

(1) **115 [& 138]. *John's Message:*** (1a) Q²: Luke 3:15–18 = Matt. 3:11–12 = Matt. 7:19; (1b) Acts 13:24–25; (1c) John 1:24–31; (2) Mark 1:7–8; (2) **57. *Measure for Measure:*** (1a) Q¹: Luke 6:38bc = Matt. 7:2b; (2) Mark 4:24b; (3a) *1 Clem.* 13:2g; (1a/3b) Pol. *Phil.* 2:3d; (3) **10. *Receiving the Sender:*** (1) Q¹: Luke 10:16 = Matt. 10:40; (2) Mark 9:36–37 = Matt. 18:2, 5 = Luke 9:47–48a; (3) *Did.* 11:4–5; (4a) John 5:23b; (4b) John 12:44–50; (4c) John 13:20; (5) Ign. *Eph.* 6:1; (4) **121. *Beelzebul Controversy:*** (1a) Q²: Luke 11:14–15, 17–18 = Matt. 12:22–26; (1b) Matt. 9:32–34; (2) Mark 3:22–26; (5) **57. *For and Against:*** (1) P. Oxy. 1224, 2 r i, lines 2b–5; (2) Q²: Luke 11:23 = Matt. 12:30; (3) Mark 9:40 = Luke 9:50b; (6) **122. *Request for Sign:*** (1a) Q²: Luke 11:29–30 = Matt. 12:38–40; (1b) Matt. 16:4a; (1c) *Gos. Naz.* 11; (2a) Mark 8:11–13 = Matt. 16:1, 4 = Luke 11:16; (7) **124. *Honors and Salutations:*** (1) Q²: Luke 11:43 = Matt. 23:6b–7a; (2) Mark 12:38–40 = Matt. 23:5–7 = Luke 20:45–46; (8) **28. *Before the Angels:*** (1a) Q²: Luke 12:8–9 = Matt. 10:32–33; (1b) *2 Clem.* 3:2 [from Matt. 10:32]; (2) Mark 8:38 = Matt. 16:27 = Luke 9:26; (3) Rev. 3:5; (4) 2 Tim 2:12b; (9) **59. *Spirit Under Trial:*** (1) Q¹: Luke 12:11–12 = Matt. 10:19–20; (2) Mark 13:11 = Matt. 10:19–20 = Luke 21:14–15; (3) John 14:26; (10) **60. *Saving One's Life:*** (1) Q¹: Luke 17:33 = Matt. 10:39; (2) Mark 8:35 = Matt. 16:25 = Luke 9:24; (3) John 12:25–26; (11) **126. *Salting the Salt:*** (1) Q¹: Luke 14:34–35a = Matt. 5:13; (2) Mark 9:50a; (12) **15. *Against Divorce:*** (1) 1 Cor. 7:10–11; (2) Q²: Luke 16:18 = Matt. 5:31–32; (3) Mark 10:10–12 = Matt. 19:9; (4) *Herm. Man.* 4.1:6b, 10.

Appendix 4

Gospel of Thomas and Some Other Sources

This appendix is based on Crossan 1991: Appendix 1B, but see changes given in Preliminary Note to Appendix 1 above.

A. Sayings Tradition Common to the *Gospel of Thomas* and Special Matthew

12% (16 out of 132 units) of the *Gospel of Thomas* has parallels in Special Matthew.

(1) **31. First and Last:** (1) *Gos. Thom.* 4:2–3 = P. Oxy. 654.425–427; (2) Mark 10:31 = Matt. 19:30; (3) Matt. 20:16; (4) Luke 13:30; (2) **71. The Fishnet:** (1) *Gos. Thom.* 8:1–3; (2) Matt. 13:47–48; (3) **9. Who Has Ears:** (1a) *Gos. Thom.* 8:4; (1b) *Gos. Thom.* 21:10; (1c) *Gos. Thom.* 24:2; (1d) *Gos. Thom.* 63:4; (1e) *Gos. Thom.* 65:8; (1f) *Gos. Thom.* 96:3; (2a) Mark 4:9 = Matt. 13:9 = Luke 8:8b; (2b) Mark 4:23 = Matt. 13:43b; (3) Matt. 11:15; (4) Luke 14:35b; (5) Rev. 2:7, 11, 17, 29; 3:6, 13, 22; 13:9; (4) **20. Kingdom and Children:** (1) *Gos. Thom.* 22:1–2; (2) Mark 10:13–16 = Matt. 19:13–15 = Luke 18:15–17; (3) Matt. 18:3; (4) John 3:1–5, 9–10; (5) **21. The World's Light:** (1) *Gos. Thom.* 24:1+3 = P. Oxy. 655, fr. d.1–5; (2) Matt. 5:14a; (3a?) *Dial. Sav.* 14; (3b?) *Dial. Sav.* 34; (4a) John 8:12; (6) **77. Two or Three:** (1) *Gos. Thom.* 30 = P. Oxy. 1.23–27; (2) Matt. 18:20; (7) **78. The Mountain City:** (1) *Gos. Thom.* 32 = P. Oxy. 1.36–41; (2) Matt. 5:14b; (8) **38. Serpents and Doves:** (1) *Gos. Thom.* 39:3 = P. Oxy. 655, col. ii.19–23; (2a) Matt. 10:16b; (2b) *Gos. Naz.* 7; (3) Ign. *Pol.* 2:2; (9) **39. Plant Rooted Up:** (1) *Gos. Thom.* 40; (2) Matt. 15:12–13; (3a) Ign. *Trall.* 11:1b; (3b) Ign. *Phld.* 3:1b; (10) **41. Trees and Hearts:** (1) *Gos. Thom.* 45; (2a) Q¹: Luke 6:43–45 = Matt. 7:16–20; (2b) Matt. 12:33–35; (3) Ign. *Eph.* 14:2b; (11) **90. The Planted Weeds:** (1) *Gos. Thom.* 57; (2) Matt. 13:24–30; (12) **93. On Secrecy:** (1) *Gos. Thom.* 62:2; (2) Matt. 6:3b; (13) **98. The Pearl:** (1) *Gos. Thom.* 76:1–2; (2) Matt. 13:45–46; (14) **52. Yoke and Burden:** (1) *Gos. Thom.* 90; (2) Matt. 11:28–30; (3) *Dial. Sav.* 65–68; (15) **54. Dogs and Swine:** (1) *Gos. Thom.* 93; (2) Matt. 7:6; (3) *Did.* 9:5; (16) **108. The Treasure:** (1) *Gos. Thom.* 109; (2) Matt. 13:44.

I have not counted **53. Knowing the Times:** (1) *Gos. Thom.* 91; (2) Luke 12:54–56; (3?) Matt. 16:2–3; (3b?) *Gos. Naz.* 13; (4?) John 6:30.

B. Sayings Tradition Common to the *Gospel of Thomas* and Special Luke

8% (10 out of 132 units) of the *Gospel of Thomas* has parallels in Special Luke.

(1) **31. First and Last:** (1) *Gos. Thom.* 4:2–3 = P. Oxy. 654.25–27; (2) Mark 10:31 = Matt. 19:30; (3) Matt. 20:16; (4) Luke 13:30; (2) **9. Who Has Ears:** (1a) *Gos. Thom.* 8:4; (1b) *Gos. Thom.* 21:10; (1c) *Gos. Thom.* 24:2; (1d) *Gos. Thom.* 63:4; (1e) *Gos. Thom.* 65:8; (1f) *Gos. Thom.* 96:3; (2a) Mark 4:9 = Matt. 13:9 = Luke 8:8b; (2b) Mark 4:23 = Matt. 13:43b; (3) Matt. 11:15; (4) Luke 14:35b; (5) Rev. 2:7, 11, 17, 29; 3:6, 13, 22; 13:9; (3) **72. Fire on Earth:** (1) *Gos. Thom.* 10; (2) Luke 12:49; (4) **22. Prophet's Own Country:** (1) *Gos. Thom.* 31 = P. Oxy. 1.30–35; (2) Mark 6:1–6a = Matt. 13:53–58; (3) Luke 4:16–24; (4) John 4:44; (5) **87. Drinking Old Wine:**

(1) *Gos. Thom.* 47:3; (2) Luke 5:39; **(6) 94. *The Rich Farmer:*** (1) *Gos. Thom.* 63:1–3; (2) Luke 12:16–21; **(7) 97. *The Disputed Inheritance:*** (1) *Gos. Thom.* 72; (2) Luke 12:13–15; **(8) 24. *Blessed the Womb:*** (1) *Gos. Thom.* 79:1–2; (2) Luke 11:27–28 [Q¹?]; (3?) John 13:17; (4?) James 1:25b; **(9) 100. *Jerusalem Mourned:*** (1) *Gos. Thom.* 79:3; (2) Luke 23:27–31; **(10) 53. *Knowing the Times:*** (1) *Gos. Thom.* 91; (2) Luke 12:54–56; (3?) Matt. 16:2–3; (3b?) *Gos. Naz.* 13; (4?) John 6:30.

C. Sayings Tradition Common to the *Gospel of Thomas* and John

9% (12 out of 132 units) of the *Gospel of Thomas* has parallels in John.

(1) 205. *Not Taste Death:* (1) *Gos. Thom.* 1 = P. Oxy. 654.3–5; (2) John 8:51–52; **(2) 4. *Ask, Seek, Knock:*** (1a) *Gos. Thom.* 2 = P. Oxy. 654:5–9; (1b) *Gos. Thom.* 92:1; (1c) *Gos. Thom.* 94; (2) *Gos. Heb.* 4ab; (3) Q¹: Luke 11:9–10 = Matt. 7:7–8; (4) Mark 11:24 = Matt. 21:22; (5a) *Dial. Sav.* 9–12; (5b) *Dial. Sav.* 20d; (5c) *Dial. Sav.* 79–80; (6a) John 14:13–14; (6b) John 15:7; (6c) John 15:16; (6d) John 16:23–24; (6e) John 16:26; **(3) 20. *Kingdom and Children:*** (1) *Gos. Thom.* 22:1–2; (2) Mark 10:13–16 = Matt. 19:13–15 = Luke 18:15–17; (3) Matt. 18:3; (4) John 3:1–5, 9–10; **(4) 21. *The World's Light:*** (1) *Gos. Thom.* 24:1 + 3 = P. Oxy. 655, fr. d.1–5; (2) Matt. 5:14a; (3a?) *Dial. Sav.* 14; (3b?) *Dial. Sav.* 34; (4a) John 8:12; (4b) John 11:9–10; (4c) John 12:35–36; **(5) 22. *Prophet's Own Country:*** (1) *Gos. Thom.* 31 = P. Oxy. 1.30–35; (2) Mark 6:1–6a = Matt. 13:53–58; (3) Luke 4:16–24; (4) John 4:44; **(6) 83. *Seeking Too Late:*** (1) *Gos. Thom.* 38:2; (2) John 7:34a, 36b; **(7) 42. *Scriptures and Jesus:*** (1) *Gos. Thom.* 52; (2) *Eger. Gos.* 2.1; (3) John 5:39–47; **(8) 45. *Father and Son:*** (1) *Gos. Thom.* 61:4; (2) Q²: Luke 10:22 = Matt. 11:27; (3a) John 3:35b; (3b) John 13:3a; **(9) 49. *Temple and Jesus:*** (1) *Gos. Thom.* 71; (2a) Mark 14:55–59 = Matt. 26:59–61; (2b) Mark 15:29–32a = Matt. 27:39–43 = (!) Luke 23:35–37; (2c) Acts 6:11–14; (3) John 2:18–22; **(10) 50. *Harvest Is Great:*** (1) *Gos. Thom.* 73; (2) Q¹: Luke 10:2 = Matt. 9:37–38; (3) John 4:35; **(11) 24. *Blessed the Womb:*** (1) *Gos. Thom.* 79:1–2; (2) Luke 11:27–28 [Q¹?]; (3?) John 13:17; (4?) James 1:25b **(12) 53. *Knowing the Times:*** (1) *Gos. Thom.* 91; (2) Luke 12:54–56; (3?) Matt. 16:2–3; (3b?) *Gos. Naz.* 13; (4?) John 6:30.

Appendix 5

Multiple Versions of *Gospel of Thomas* Sayings

There are 8 cases involving 18 or maybe 19 out of 132 units (14%). Note that in all cases except #6 there are also *Q Gospel* parallels.

(1) 4. Ask, Seek, Knock: (1a) *Gos. Thom.* 2 = P. Oxy. 654:5–9; (1b) *Gos. Thom.* 92:1; (1c) *Gos. Thom.* 94; (2) *Gos. Heb.* 4ab; (3) Q¹: Luke 11:9–10 = Matt. 7:7–8; (4) Mark 11:24 = Matt. 21:22; (5a) *Dial. Sav.* 9–12; (5b) *Dial. Sav.* 20d; (5c) *Dial. Sav.* 79–80; (6a) John 14:13–14; (6b) John 15:7; (6c) John 15:16; (6d) John 16:23–24; (6e) John 16:26; **(2) 8. When and Where:** (1a) *Gos. Thom.* 3:1–3 = P. Oxy. 654.9–16; (1b) *Gos. Thom.* 51; (1c) *Gos. Thom.* 113; (2) Q²: Luke 17:23 = Matt. 24:26; (3) Mark 13:21–23 = Matt. 24:23–25; (4?) *Dial. Sav.* 16; (5) Luke 17:20–21; but see also (as 1d?) **285. Beginning and End:** (1) *Gos. Thom.* 18:1–3; **(3) 32. Hidden Made Manifest:** (1a) *Gos. Thom.* 5:2 = P. Oxy. 654.29–30; (1b) *Gos. Thom.* 6:5–6 = P. Oxy. 654.38–39; (2) Q¹: Luke 12:2 = Matt. 10:26; (3) Mark 4:22 = Luke 8:17; **(4) 12. Knowing the Danger:** (1a) 1 Thess. 5:2; (1b) 2 Pet 3:10; (2a) *Gos. Thom.* 21:5–7; (2b) *Gos. Thom.* 103; (3) Q²: Luke 12:39–40 = Matt. 24:43–44; (4a) Rev. 3:3b; (4b) Rev. 16:15a; **(5) 84. On Hindering Others:** (1a) *Gos. Thom.* 39:1–2 = P. Oxy. 655, col. ii.11–19; (1b) *Gos. Thom.* 102; (2) Q²: Luke 11:52 = Matt. 23:13; **(6) 298. Unity and Mountain:** (1a) Gos. Thom. 48; (1b) Gos. Thom. 106; & 173 **(7) 89. Hating One's Family:** (1a) Gos. Thom. 55:1–2a; (1b) Gos. Thom. 101; (2) Q¹: Luke 14:25–26 = Matt. 10:37; **(8) 48. Blessed the Persecuted:** (1a) Gos. Thom. 68; (1b) Gos. Thom. 69:1; (2a) Q¹: Luke 6:22–23 = Matt. 5:11–12 [except for 6:23c = 5:12c]; (2b) Matt. 5:10; (2c) Pol. *Phil.* 2:3f; (3a) 1 Pet 3:14a; (3b) 1 Pet 4:14.

Appendix 6

Kingdom Sayings

The following statistics are intended to be as secure as possible. For the *Q Gospel* and the Common Sayings Tradition, the kingdom must be present in *both* extant versions to be counted. In those cases, therefore, there may have originally been more instances than we can now count. But here, at least, are the most secure cases.

(1) *Gospel of Thomas*. The "kingdom of Heaven" is found 3 times: (1) 20:1; (2) 54; (3) 114:3. The "kingdom of the Father" is found 7 times: (4) 57:1; (5) 76:1; (6) 96:1; (7) 97:1; (8) 98:1; (9) 99:3; (10) 113:4. The "kingdom" without any specification is found 7 times: (11) 3:1, 3; (12) 22:1, 3, 7; (13) 27:1; (14) 46:1; (15) 107:1; (16) 109:1; (17) 113:1. That counts repetitions within the same saying (3:1, 3; 22:1, 3, 7) as single instances and gives 17 instances out of 132 sayings, or about 13%.

(2) *Q Gospel*. The "kingdom," usually as the "kingdom of God" in Luke but the "kingdom of the heavens" in Matthew, is found as follows: (1) Luke 6:20b = Matt. 5:3; (2) Luke 7:28 = Matt. 11:11; (3) Luke 10:9, 11 = Matt. 10:7; (4) Luke 11:2 = Matt. 6:10; (5) Luke 11:20 = Matt. 12:28; (6) Luke 12:31 = Matt. 6:33; (7) Luke 13:18 = Matt. 13:31; (8) Luke 13:20 = Matt. 13:33; (9) Luke 13:28, 29 = Matt. 8:11, 12; (10) Luke 16:16 = Matt. 11:12. That counts repetitions within the same saying (Q 10:9, 11 & 13:28, 29) as single instances and gives 10 instances out of 101 sayings, or about 10%.

(3) Common Sayings Tradition. The "kingdom" is found 4 times: (1) *The Mustard Seed* in *Gos. Thom.* 20 = Q 13:18–19 or Luke 13:18–19 = Matt. 13:31–32; (2) *Greater Than John* in *Gos. Thom.* 46 = Q 7:23 or Luke 7:28 = Matt. 11:11; (3) *Blessed the Poor* in *Gos. Thom.* 54 = Q 6:20 or Luke 6:20 = Matt. 5:3; (4) *The Leaven* in *Gos. Thom.* 96:1–2 = Q 13:20–21 or Luke 13:20–21 = Matt. 13:33. That gives 4 out of 37 instances, or about 11%.

Appendix 7

The Synoptic Independence of *Didache* 1:3b–2:1

In Appendix 1 of *The Historical Jesus,* I inventoried *Didache* 1:3b–2:1 as dependent on a harmonized version of Matthew and Luke (Layton). I have now changed that position to one of complete synoptic independence. This changes the multiple independent attestation of the following five sayings from that section of the *Didache* in my earlier inventory:

(1) **114. *Love Your Enemies:*** (1) P. Oxy. 1224, 2 r i, lines 1–2a; (2a) Q¹: Luke 6:27–28, 35a = Matt. 5:43–44; (2b) Pol. *Phil.* 12:3a; (3) *Did.* 1:3ac; (2) **117. *Better Than Sinners:*** (1a) Q¹: Luke 6:32–35 = Matt. 5:45–47; (1b) 2 *Clem.* 13:4a [from Luke 6:32]; (2) Ign. *Pol.* 2:1; (3) *Did.* 1:3b; (3) **140. *The Other Cheek:*** (1) Q¹: Luke 6:29 = Matt. 5:38–41; (2) *Did.* 1:4b; (4) **103. *Give Without Return:*** (1) *Gos. Thom.* 95; (2) Q¹: Luke 6:30 = Matt. 5:42; (3) *Did.* 1:4c, 5a; (5) **162. *Before the Judgment:*** (1) Q²: Luke 12:57–59 = Matt. 5:25–26; (2) *Did.* 1:5c.

Bibliography

Abbreviations

AB = Anchor Bible; AF = *The Apostolic Fathers* (see Lake below); ANET = *Ancient Near Eastern Texts Relating to the Old Testament* (see Pritchard below); ANF = *Ante-Nicene Fathers* (see Roberts, Donaldson, and Coxe below); ANRW = *Aufstieg und Niedergang der römischen Welt* (see Temporini and Haase below); BA = *Biblical Archaeologist*; BAR = *Biblical Archaeology Review*; BASOR = *Bulletin of the American Schools of Oriental Research*; BASP = *Bulletin of the American Society of Papyrologists*; BETL = Bibliotheca Ephemeridum Theologicarum Lovaniensium; BLE = *Bulletin de littérature ecclésiastique*; CBQ = *Catholic Biblical Quarterly*; CBQMS = Catholic Biblical Quarterly Monograph Series; DSSP = Dead Sea Scrolls Project of Princeton Theological Seminary (see Charlesworth et al. below); DSST = *The Dead Sea Scrolls Translated* (see García Martínez below); ETL = *Ephemerides Theologicae Lovanienses*; GLAJJ = *Greek and Latin Authors on Jews and Judaism* (see Stern below); HR = *History of Religions*; HTR = Harvard *Theological Review*; HTS = Harvard Theological Studies; IEJ = *Israel Exploration Journal*; IQP = International Q Project (see Robinson et al. below); JBL = *Journal of Biblical Literature*; JECS = *Journal of Early Christian Studies*; JSNT = *Journal for the Study of the New Testament*; JSOT = *Journal for the Study of the Old Testament*; JTS = *Journal of Theological Studies*; LCL = Loeb Classical Library; NDIEC = *New Documents Illustrating Early Christianity* (see Horsley, Llewelyn, and Kearsley below); NHLE = *The Nag Hammadi Library in English* (see Robinson 1988 below); NHS = Nag Hammadi Studies; NTA = *New Testament Apocrypha* (see Schneemelcher and Wilson below); NTS = *New Testament Studies*; OTP = *The Old Testament Pseudepigrapha* (see Charlesworth below); PEQ = *Palestine Exploration Quarterly*; SBLDS = Society of Biblical Liberative Dissertation Series; SBLRBS = Society of Biblical Literature Resources for Biblical Study; SNTSMS = Society for New Testament Studies Monograph Series; TS = *Theological Studies*; TU = Texte und Untersuchungen; TYNB = *Tyndale Bulletin*; WMANT = Wissenschaftliche Monographien zum Alten und Neuen Testament; ZNW = *Zeitschrift für die Neutestamentliche Wissenschaft*; ZPE = *Zeitschrift für Papyrologie und Epigraphik*; ZTK = *Zeitschrift für Theologie und Kirche*.

Sources

Adan-Bayewitz, David. 1992. *Common Pottery in Roman Galilee: A Study of Local Trade*. Bar-Ilan Studies in Near Eastern Languages and Culture. Ramat-Gan, Israel: Bar Ilan Univ. Press. Revised, expanded, and updated version of "Manufacture and Local Trade in the Galilee of Roman-Byzantine Palestine: A Case Study." Ph.D. diss., Hebrew University, Jerusalem (under Isadore Perlman and Daniel Sperber), 1985.

Adan-Bayewitz, David, and Isadore Perlman. 1990. "The Local Trade of Sepphoris in the Roman Period." *IEJ* 40:153–172.

Alcock, Susan E. 1993. *Graecia Capta: The Landscapes of Roman Greece*. Cambridge, UK: Cambridge Univ. Press.

Alexiou, Margaret. 1974. *The Ritual Lament in Greek Tradition*. New York: Cambridge Univ. Press.

Alföldy, Géza. 1985. *The Social History of Rome*. Translated by David Braund and Frank Pollock. London: Croom Helm.

Anderson, Øivind. 1992. "Oral Tradition." In *Jesus and the Oral Gospel Tradition*, edited by Henry Wansbrough, pp. 17–58. *JSNT* Supplement Series, 64. Sheffield, UK: Sheffield Academic Press (JSOT Press).

Applebaum, Shimon. 1977. "Judaea as a Roman Province: The Countryside as a Political and Economic Factor." *ANRW* 2.8.355–396.

————. 1989. "Josephus and the Economic Causes of the Jewish War." In *Josephus, the Bible, and History*, edited by Louis H. Feldman and Gohei Hata, pp. 237–264. Detroit, MI: Wayne State Univ. Press.

Arnal, William. E. 1995. "The Rhetoric of Marginality: Apocalypticism, Gnosticism, and Sayings Gospels." *HTR* 88:471–494.

Arnold, Dean E. 1985. *Ceramic Theory and Cultural Process*. Cambridge, UK: Cambridge Univ. Press.

Attridge, Harold W. 1979. "The Original Text of Gos. Thom., Saying 30." *BASP* 16:153–157.

————. 1984. "Josephus and His Works." In *Jewish Writings of the Second Temple Period: Apocrypha, Pseudepigrapha, Qumran Sectarian Writings, Philo, Josephus*, edited by Michael E. Stone, pp. 185–232. Vol. 2 of Section II, *The Literature of the Jewish People in the Period of the Second Temple and the Talmud* (3 vols.), in *Compendia Rerum Iudaicarum ad Novum Testamentum* (10 vols.), edited by M. de Jonge and Schmuel Safrai. Assen: Van Gorcum; and Philadelphia: Fortress Press, 1974–.

————. 1989. "The Gospel According to Thomas. Appendix: The Greek Fragments." In *Nag Hammadi Codex II,2–7*, 2 vols., edited by Bentley Layton, vol. 1, pp. 95–128. NHS 20–21 (The Coptic Gnostic Library). Leiden: Brill.

————. 1990. "Liberating Death's Captives: Reconsideration of an Early Christian Myth." In *Gnosticism and the Early Christian World* ("In Honor of James M. Robinson"), edited by James E. Goehring, Charles W. Hendrick, and Jack T. Sanders with Hans Dieter Betz, pp. 103–115. Forum Fascicles, 2. Sonoma, CA: Polebridge Press.

Audet, Jean-Paul. 1958. *La Didachè: Instructions des apôtres*. Études Bibliques. Paris: Gabalda.

Avi-Yonah, Michael. 1950. "The Foundation of Tiberias." *IEJ* 1:160–169.

Bar-Ilan, Meir. 1992. "Illiteracy in the Land of Israel in the First Centuries C.E." In *Essays in the Social Scientific Study of Judaism and Jewish Society*, 2 vols., edited by Simcha Fishbane and Stuart Schoenfeld with Alain Goldschläger, vol. 2, pp. 46–61. Hoboken, NJ: KTAV.

Barnes, Timothy D. 1981. *Constantine and Eusebius*. Cambridge, MA: Harvard Univ. Press.

Bartchy, S. Scott. 1991. "Community of Goods in Acts: Idealization or Social Reality?" In *The Future of Early Christianity: Essays in Honor of Helmut Koester*, edited by Birger A. Pearson, in collaboration with A. Thomas Kraabel, George W. E. Nickelsburg, and Norman R. Petersen, pp. 309–318. Minneapolis: Fortress Press.

Bartlett, Sir Frederic C. 1964. *Remembering: A Study in Experimental and Social Psychology*. Cambridge, UK: Cambridge Univ. Press. Originally published in 1932.

Batey, Richard A. 1991. *Jesus and the Forgotten City: New Light on Sepphoris and the Urban World of Jesus*. Grand Rapids, MI: Baker.

Beall, Todd S. 1988. *Josephus' Description of the Essenes Illustrated by the Dead Sea Scrolls*. SNTSMS 58. New York: Cambridge Univ. Press.

Beames, Michael. 1983. *Peasants and Power: The Whiteboy Movements and Their Control in Pre-Famine Ireland*. New York: St. Martin's Press.

Bell, Harold Idriss, and Theodore Cressy Skeat. 1935a. *Fragments of an Unknown Gospel and Other Early Christian Papyri*. London: Oxford Univ. Press. ("Unknown Gospel," pp. 1–41; see also plates I and II.)

————. 1935b. *The New Gospel Fragments*. London: Oxford Univ. Press.

Benko, Stephen. 1980. "Pagan Criticism of Christianity During the First Two Centuries A.D." *ANRW* 2.23.1055–1118.

Betz, Hans Dieter. 1994. "Jesus and the Cynics: Survey and Analysis of a Hypothesis." *Journal of Religion* 74:453–475.

Boas, Franz. 1901. *Kathlamet Texts*. Smithsonian Institution, Bureau of American Ethnology, Bulletin 26. Washington, D.C.: Government Printing Office.

Bohannon III, John Neil, and Victoria Louise Symons. 1992. "Flashbulb Memories: Confidence, Consistency, and Quantity." In Winograd and Neisser (eds.), pp. 65–91.

Borg, Marcus J. 1994. *Jesus in Contemporary Scholarship*. Valley Forge, PA: Trinity Press International.

————. 1997. "The Historical Study of Jesus and Christian Origins." In *Jesus at 2000*, edited by Marcus J. Borg, pp. 121–147. Boulder, CO: Westview Press.

Bouriant, Urbain. 1892. "Fragments du texte grec du livre d'Enoch et de quelques écrits attribués a Saint Pierre." In *Mémoires publiés par les membres de la Mission archéologique française au Caire*, vol. 9, fascicle 3, edited by Urbain Bouriant, pp. 91–147. Paris: Leroux (Libraire de la Société asiatique). (*Gospel of Peter* is on pp. 137–142.)

Boyarin, Daniel. 1993. *Carnal Israel: Reading Sex in Talmudic Culture*. The New Historicism: Studies in Cultural Poetics, 25. Berkeley: University of California Press.

————. 1994. *A Radical Jew: Paul and the Politics of Identity*. Contraversions: Critical Studies in Jewish Literature, Culture, and Society, 1. Berkeley: University of California Press.

Brewer, William F. 1992. "The Theoretical and Empirical Status of the Flashbulb Memory Hypothesis." In Winograd and Neisser (eds.), pp. 274–305.

Broshi, Magen. 1978. "Estimating the Population of Ancient Jerusalem." *BAR* 4(2/June):10–15.

Brown, Peter. 1982. "Response" (to Robert M. Grant's, "The Problem of Miraculous Feedings in the Graeco-Roman World"). In *Protocol of the Forty-Second Colloquy* (Mar. 14, 1982), pp. 16–24. Berkeley: Center for Hermeneutical Studies in Hellenistic and Modern Culture (The Graduate Theological Union and the University of California at Berkeley).

————. 1988. *The Body and Society: Men, Women, and Sexual Renunciation in Early Christianity*. Lectures on the History of Religions Sponsored by the American Council of Learned Societies. New Series, 10. New York: Columbia Univ. Press.

Brown, Raymond E. 1962–1963. "The Gospel of Thomas and St. John's Gospel." *NTS* 9:155–177.

————. 1987. "The *Gospel of Peter* and Canonical Gospel Priority." *NTS* 33:321–343. Presidential address delivered at the 41st general meeting of SNTS, Atlanta, GA, Aug. 1986.

————. 1994. *The Death of the Messiah: From Gethsemane to the Grave. A Commentary on the Passion Narratives in the Four Gospels*. 2 vols. The Anchor Bible Reference Library. New York: Doubleday.

Brown, Roger, and James Kulik. 1977. "Flashbulb Memories." *Cognition* 5:73–99.

Brown, Schuyler. 1970. "Concerning the Origin of the *Nomina Sacra*." *Studia Papyrologica* 9:7–19.

Burford, Alison. 1972. *Craftsmen in Greek and Roman Society*. Aspects of Greek and Roman Life. Ithaca, NY: Cornell Univ. Press.

Byatt, Anthony. 1973. "Josephus and Population Numbers in First Century Palestine." *PEQ* 105:51–60.

Cameron, Ron, ed. 1982. *The Other Gospels: Non-Canonical Gospel Texts*. Philadelphia: Westminster.

Cancian, Frank. 1989. "Economic Behavior in Peasant Communities." In *Economic Anthropology*, edited by Stuart Plattner, pp. 127–170, 443–446. Stanford, CA: Stanford Univ. Press.

Cannon, Lou. 1991. *President Reagan: The Role of a Lifetime*. New York: Simon & Schuster.

Caraveli, Anna. 1986. "The Bitter Wounding: The Lament as Social Protest in Rural Greece." In *Gender and Power in Rural Greece*, edited by Jill Dubisch, pp. 169–194. Princeton, NJ: Princeton Univ. Press.

Caraveli-Chaves, Anna. 1980. "Bridge Between Worlds: The Greek Women's Lament as Communicative Event." *Journal of American Folklore* 93:129–157.

Carney, Thomas F. 1975. *The Shape of the Past: Models and Antiquity*. Lawrence, KS: Coronado Press.

Charlesworth, James H., ed. 1983–1985. *The Old Testament Pseudepigrapha*. 2 vols. Garden City, NY: Doubleday.

Charlesworth, James H., et al., eds. 1994–. *The Dead Sea Scrolls: Hebrew, Aramaic, and Greek Texts with English Translations*. 10 vols. Vol. 1: *Rule of the Community and Related Documents* (1994). Vol. 2: *Damascus Document, War Scroll, and Related Documents* (1995). Louisville, KY: Westminster/John Knox Press.

Charlesworth, James H., and Craig A. Evans. 1994. "Jesus in the Agrapha and Apocryphal Gospels." In Chilton and Evans, pp. 479–533.

Chilton, Bruce D., and Craig A. Evans. 1994. *Studying the Historical Jesus: Evaluations of the State of Current Research*. New Testament Tools and Studies, 19. Leiden: Brill.

Clanchy, M. T. 1979. *From Memory to Written Record: England, 1066–1307*. Cambridge, MA: Harvard Univ. Press.

Cohen, Shaye J. D. 1979. *Josephus in Galilee and Rome. His Vita and Development as a Historian*. Columbia Studies in the Classical Tradition, 8. Leiden: Brill.

Coles, R. A., G. M. Browne, J. R. Rea, J. C. Shelton, and E. G. Turner. 1972. *The Oxyrhynchus Papyri*, vol. 41. Cambridge: Cambridge Univ. Press. (R. A. Coles edited Oxy P 2949 [*Gos. Pet.* 2], pp. 15–16; see also plate II.)

Collins, Adela Yarbro. 1992. "Apocalypse and Politics." In *The Looking Glass: Essays in Celebration of a Precursor* ("For Robert W. Funk"), edited by Bernard Brandon Scott and John L. White with Lane C. McGaughy, pp. 297–312. Santa Rosa, CA: Polebridge Press. Also published in *Forum* 8(1992):297–312.

Comfort, Philip W. 1995. "Exploring the Common Identification of Three New Testament Manuscripts: $\mathfrak{P}^4$, $\mathfrak{P}^{64}$, and $\mathfrak{P}^{67}$." *TynB* 46:43–54.

Corbier, Mireille. 1991. "City, Territory, and Taxation." In Rich and Wallace-Hadrill (eds.), pp. 211–239.

Corley, Kathleen E. Forthcoming. *Gender and Jesus: History and Lament in Gospel Tradition*. New York: Oxford Univ. Press.

Coser, Lewis A. 1956. *The Functions of Social Conflict*. Glencoe, IL: Free Press.

Crossan, John Dominic. 1973. *In Parables: The Challenge of the Historical Jesus*. New York: Harper & Row. Reprinted in 1992 (Sonoma, CA: Polebridge Press).

———. 1983. *In Fragments: The Aphorisms of Jesus*. San Francisco: Harper & Row.

———. 1985/1992. *Four Other Gospels: Shadows on the Contours of Canon*. Minneapolis: Winston/Seabury, 1985. Reprinted in 1992 (Sonoma, CA: Polebridge Press).

———. 1988. *The Cross That Spoke: The Origins of the Passion Narrative*. San Francisco: Harper & Row, 1988.

———. 1991. *The Historical Jesus: The Life of a Mediterranean Jewish Peasant*. San Francisco: HarperSanFrancisco.

———. 1994a. *Jesus: A Revolutionary Biography*. San Francisco: HarperSanFrancisco.

———. 1994b. *The Essential Jesus: Original Sayings and Earliest Images*. San Francisco: HarperSanFrancisco.

———. 1995. *Who Killed Jesus? Exposing the Roots of Anti-Semitism in the Gospel Story of the Death of Jesus*. San Francisco: HarperSanFrancisco.

———. 1996. "Why Christians Must Search for the Historical Jesus." *Bible Review* 12(2/Apr.):34–38, 42–45.

———. 1997. "Jesus and the Kingdom: Itinerants and Householders in Earliest Christianity." In *Jesus at 2000*, edited by Marcus J. Borg, pp. 21–51. Boulder, CO: Westview Press, 1997.

Danby, Herbert. 1967. *The Mishnah*. London: Oxford Univ. Press.

Danforth, Loring M. 1982. *The Death Rituals of Rural Greece*. Photos by Alexander Tsiaras. Princeton, NJ: Princeton Univ. Press.

Daniels, Jon B. 1990. "The Egerton Gospel: Its Place in Early Christianity." Ph.D. diss., Claremont Graduate School. Ann Arbor, MI: University Microfilms International.

Danker, Frederick W. 1982. *Benefactor: Epigraphic Study of a Graeco-Roman and New Testament Semantic Field*. St. Louis, MO: Clayton Publishing House.

Davids, Stacy. 1995. "Appearances of the Resurrected Jesus and the Experience of Grief." Unpublished paper presented at the spring meeting of the Jesus Seminar, Santa Rosa, CA.

Davies, Stevan L. 1983. *The Gospel of Thomas and Christian Wisdom*. New York: Seabury Press.

———. 1992. "The Christology and Protology of the *Gospel of Thomas*." *JBL* 111:663–682.

———. 1993. "Whom Jesus Healed and How." *The Fourth R* 6(2/Mar.–Apr.):1–11.

———. 1995. *Jesus the Healer: Possession, Trance, and the Origins of Christianity*. New York: Continuum.

Denaux, Adelbert, ed. 1992. *John and the Synoptics*. BETL 101. Leuven: Leuven Univ. Press. 39th Colloquium Biblicum Lovaniense, Aug. 7–9, 1990.

Denker, Jürgen. 1975. *Die theologiegeschichtliche Stellung des Petrusevangeliums*. Ein Beitrag zur Frühgeschichte des Doketismus. *Europäische Hochschulschriften* 23:36. Bern/Frankfurt: Lang.

de Solages, Bruno. 1979. "L'Évangile de Thomas et les Évangiles canoniques: L'ordre des péricopes." *BLE* 80:102–108.

Dessau, Hermann. 1979. *Inscriptiones Latinae Selectae*. 5 vols. Chicago: Ares. Originally published in 1892–1916 as 3 vols.

de Ste. Croix, G.E.M. 1975. "Karl Marx and the History of Classical Antiquity." *Arethusa* 8:7–41.

Dever, William G. 1981. "The Impact of the 'New Archaeology' on Syro-Palestinian Archaeology." *BASOR* 242:15–29.

Dewey, Arthur J. 1989. "'And an Answer Was Heard from the Cross . . .': A Response to J. Dominic Crossan." *Forum* 5:103–111.

———. 1990. "Time to Murder and Create: Visions and Revisions in the Gospel of Peter." *Semeia* 49:101–127.

———. 1995. "Four Visions and a Funeral: Resurrection in the Gospel of Peter." *Journal of Higher Criticism* 2(2/Fall):33–51.

Dickinson, Emily (1830–1886). 1955. *Poems: Including Variant Readings Critically Compared with All Known Manuscripts.* 3 vols. Edited by Thomas Herbert Johnson. Cambridge, MA: Harvard Univ. Press (Belknap Press).

Dobrowolski, Kazimiertz. 1971. "Peasant Traditional Culture." In *Peasants and Peasant Society: Selected Readings,* edited by Teodor Shanin, pp. 277–298. Baltimore, MD: Penguin Books. Originally published in 1958.

Donahue, John R. 1973. *Are You the Christ? The Trial Narrative in the Gospel of Mark.* SBLDS 10. Cambridge, MA: SBL.

Douglas, Mary. 1966. *Purity and Danger: An Analysis of Concepts of Pollution and Taboo.* London: Routledge & Kegan Paul.

————. 1970. *Natural Symbols: Explorations in Cosmology.* New York: Random House (Pantheon Books).

Draper, Jonathan. 1985. "The Jesus Tradition in the Didache." In *The Jesus Tradition Outside the Gospels,* edited by David Wenham, pp. 269–287, vol. 2 of *Gospel Perspectives.* Sheffield, UK: JSOT Press.

Duling, Dennis C., and Norman Perrin. 1994. *The New Testament: Proclamation and Paranesis, Myth and History.* 3rd ed. New York: Harcourt Brace Jovanovich.

Duncan-Jones, Richard. 1982. *The Economy of the Roman Empire: Quantitative Studies.* 2nd ed. Cambridge, UK: Cambridge Univ. Press.

Dunn, James D. G. 1992. "John and the Oral Gospel Tradition." In *Jesus and the Oral Gospel Tradition,* edited by Henry Wansbrough, pp. 351–379. JSNT Supplement Series, 64. Sheffield, UK: Sheffield Academic Press (JSOT Press).

Dyson, Stephen L. 1971. "Native Revolts in the Roman Empire." *Historia* 20:239–274.

————. 1975. "Native Revolt Patterns in the Roman Empire." *ANRW* 2.3.138–175.

————. 1981. "A Classical Archaeologist's Response to the 'New Archaeology.'" *BASOR* 242:7–13.

Eddy, Paul Rhodes. 1996. "Jesus as Diogenes? Reflections on the Cynic Jesus Thesis." *JBL* 115:449–469

Edwards, James R. 1989. "Markan Sandwiches: The Significance of Interpolations in Markan Narratives." *Novum Testamentum* 31:193–216.

Eisenberg, Leon. 1977. "Disease and Illness: Distinctions Between Professional and Popular Ideas of Sickness." *Culture, Medicine, and Psychiatry* 1:9–23.

Eisenstadt, Shauel Noah. 1993. *The Political Systems of Empires.* New ed. New Brunswick, NJ: Transaction Publishers. Originally published in 1963 (New York: Free Press of Glencoe).

Emmel, Stephen, Helmut Koester, and Elaine Pagels. 1984. *Nag Hammadi Codex III,5: The Dialogue of the Savior.* NHS 26 (The Coptic Gnostic Library). Leiden: Brill.

Epsztein, Léon. 1986. *Social Justice in the Ancient Near East and the People of the Bible.* London: SCM Press. Originally published in 1983 as *La justice sociale dans le Proche-Orient ancien et le peuple de la Bible* (Paris: Cerf).

Etienne, Mona, and Eleanor Leacock. 1980. "Introduction." In *Women and Colonization: Anthropological Perspectives,* edited by Mona Etienne and Eleanor Leacock, pp. 1–24. New York: Praeger.

Fager, Jeffrey A. 1993. *Land Tenure and the Biblical Jubilee: Uncovering Hebrew Ethics Through the Sociology of Knowledge.* JSOT Supplement Series, 155. Sheffield, UK: Sheffield Academic Press (JSOT Press). Based on "Land Tenure and the Biblical Jubilee: A Moral World View." Ann Arbor, MI: University Microfilms International, 1987.

Fagles, Robert, trans. 1990. *Homer: The Iliad.* New York: Viking.

Farb, Peter, and George Armelagos. 1980. *Consuming Passions: The Anthropology of Eating.* Boston, MA: Houghton Mifflin.

Fentress, James, and Chris Wickham. 1992. *Social Memory: New Perspectives on the Past.* Cambridge, MA: Blackwell.

Fermor, Patrick Leigh. 1984. *Mani: Travels in the Southern Peloponnese.* New York: Harper & Row.

Fiensy, David A. 1991. *The Social History of Palestine in the Herodian Period: The Land Is Mine.* Studies in the Bible and Early Christianity, 20. Lewiston, PA: Mellen.

Finley, Moses I. 1974. "Aristotle and Economic Analysis." In *Studies in Ancient Society,* edited by Moses I. Finley, pp. 26–52. Past and Present Series [article is from 1970]. London: Routledge and Kegan Paul.

———. 1977. "The Ancient City: From Fustel de Coulanges to Max Weber and Beyond." *Comparative Studies in Society and History* 19:305–327.

Fitzgerald, Robert, trans. 1983. *Virgil: The Aeneid.* New York: Random House.

Fitzmyer, Joseph A. 1970. "The Priority of Mark and the 'Q' Source in Luke." *Perspective* 11:131–170.

———. 1974. "The Oxyrhynchus Logoi of Jesus and the Coptic Gospel According to Thomas." In his *Essays on the Semitic Background of the New Testament,* pp. 355–433. SBLSBS 5. Missoula, MT: Scholars Press. Originally published in 1971 (London: Chapman). Updated from *TS* 20(1959):505–560.

———. 1981–1985. *The Gospel According to Luke.* 2 vols. with continuous pagination. *AB* 28–28a. Garden City, NJ: Doubleday.

Foster, George M. 1967. "Introduction: What Is a Peasant?" In *Peasant Society: A Reader,* edited by Jack M. Potter, May N. Diaz, and George M. Foster, pp. 2–14. Boston, MA: Little, Brown.

Francis, James A. 1995. *Subversive Virtue: Asceticism and Authority in the Second-Century Pagan World.* University Park: Pennsylvania State Univ. Press.

Fredriksen, Paula. 1988. *From Jesus to Christ: The Origins of the New Testament Images of Jesus.* New Haven, CT: Yale Univ. Press.

———. 1991. "Judaism, The Circumcision of Gentiles, and Apocalyptic Hope: Another Look at Galatians 1 and 2," *JTS* 42:532–564.

———. 1995a. "What You See Is What You Get: Context and Content in Current Research on the Historical Jesus." *Theology Today* 52:75–97.

———. 1995b. "Did Jesus Oppose the Purity Laws?" *Bible Review* 11(3/June):18–25, 42–47.

Frost, Robert. 1979. *The Poetry of Robert Frost: The Collected Poems, Complete and Unabridged,* edited by Edward Connery Lathem. New York: Holt.

Funk, Francis Xavier. 1905. *Didascalia et Constitutiones Apostolorum.* 2 vols. Paderborn, Germany: Schoeningh.

Gamble, Harry W. 1995. *Books and Readers in the Early Church: A History of Early Christian Texts.* New Haven, CT: Yale Univ. Press.

García Martínez, Florentino. 1996. *The Dead Sea Scrolls Translated: The Qumran Texts in English.* Translated by Wilfred G. E. Watson. 2nd ed. Brill: Leiden; and Grand Rapids, MI: Eerdmans. Originally published in 1994.

Gardner-Smith, P. 1925–1926a. "The Gospel of Peter." *JTS* 27:255–271.

———. 1925–1926b. "The Date of the Gospel of Peter." *JTS* 27:401–407.

Garitte, Gérard. 1957. "Le premier volume de l'édition photographique des manuscrits gnostiques coptes et l'"Évangile de Thomas.'" *Muséon* 70:59–73.

Garnsey, Peter, Keith Hopkins, and C. R. Whittaker, eds. 1983. *Trade in the Ancient Economy.* Berkeley: University of California Press.

Garrison, Roman. 1993. *Redemptive Almsgiving in Early Christianity.* JSNT Supplement Series, 77; Sheffield, UK: Sheffield Academic Press (JSOT Press).

Genovese, Eugene D. 1974. *Roll, Jordan, Roll: The World the Slaves Made.* New York: Random House (Pantheon Books).

Georgi, Dieter. 1992. "The Interest in Life of Jesus Theology as a Paradigm for the Social History of Biblical Criticism." *HTR* 85:51–83.

Germani, Gino. 1980. *Marginality.* New Brunswick, NJ: Transaction Books.

Gibbon, Edward. n.d. *The Decline and Fall of the Roman Empire.* 2 vols. The Modern Library. New York: Random House. Originally published in 1776–1788.

Glover, Richard. 1958–1959. "The *Didache*'s Quotations and the Synoptic Gospels." *NTS* 5:12–29

Goldschmidt, Walter, and Evalyn Jacobson Kunkel. 1971. "The Structure of the Peasant Family." *American Anthropologist* 73:1058–1076.

Goodman, Martin. 1987. *The Ruling Class of Judaea: The Origins of the Jewish Revolt Against Rome A.D. 66–70.* Cambridge, UK: Cambridge Univ. Press.

———. 1991. "Who Was Jesus?" Review of John P. Meier, vol. 1 (see below). *The New York Times Book Review,* Dec. 22, pp. 3, 23.

Goodspeed, Edgar J. 1950. *The Apostolic Fathers: An American Translation.* New York: Harper.

Goody, Jack 1977. *The Domestication of the Savage Mind.* Cambridge, UK: Cambridge Univ. Press.

———. 1986. *The Logic of Writing and the Organization of Society.* Studies in Literacy, Family, Culture, and the State. New York: Cambridge Univ. Press.

———. 1987. *The Interface Between the Written and the Oral.* Studies in Literacy, the Family, Culture, and the State. Cambridge, UK: Cambridge Univ. Press.

Gordon, Barry. 1982. "Lending at Interest: Some Jewish, Greek, and Christian Approaches, 800 B.C.–A.D. 100." *History of Political Economy* 14:406–426.

Gottwald, Norman K. 1985. *The Hebrew Bible: A Socio-Literary Introduction.* Philadelphia: Fortress Press.

———. 1993. "Social Class as an Analytic and Hermeneutical Category in Biblical Studies." *JBL* 112:3–22.

Green, Joel B. 1987. "The Gospel of Peter: Source for a Pre-Canonical Passion Narrative?" *ZNW* 78:293–301.

Grenfell, Bernard Pyne, and Arthur Surridge Hunt. 1897. LOGIA IHCOU: *Sayings of Our Lord from an Early Greek Papyrus.* London: Frowde (for the Egypt Exploration Fund).

———. 1898. *The Oxyrhynchus Papyri.* Part I, nos. 1–207. London: Egypt Exploration Fund. See no. 1, LOGIA IHCOU, pp. 1–3.

———. 1904a. *The Oxyrhynchus Papyri.* Part IV, nos. 654–839. London: Egypt Exploration Fund. See no. 654, "New Sayings of Jesus," pp. 1–22; no. 655, "Fragment of a Lost Gospel," pp. 22–28.

———. 1904b. *New Sayings of Jesus and Fragment of a Lost Gospel from Oxyrhynchus.* London: Frowde (for the Egypt Exploration Fund).

————. 1922. *The Oxyrhynchus Papyri*. Part XV, nos. 1780–1828. London: Oxford Univ. Press. See no. 1782, *Didache* 1–3, pp. 12–15.

Guillaumont, A., et al., eds. 1959. *The Gospel According to Thomas*. Leiden: Brill; and New York: Harper & Row.

Haas, N. 1970. "Anthropological Observations on the Skeletal Remains from Givʿat ha-Mivtar." *IEJ* 20:38–59, plates 18–24.

Habel, Norman C. 1995. *The Land Is Mine: Six Biblical Land Ideologies*. Overtures to Biblical Theology. Minneapolis: Fortress Press.

Hamel, Gildas H. 1983. "Poverty and Charity in Roman Palestine, First Three Centuries C.E." Ph.D. diss., University of California, Santa Cruz. Ann Arbor, MI: University Microfilms International. Later published in University of California Publications, Near Eastern Studies, 23. Berkeley: University of California Press. 1990.

Harris, William V. 1989. *Ancient Literacy*. Cambridge, MA: Harvard Univ. Press.

Harrison, Tony. 1990. *The Trackers of Oxyrhynchus: The Delphi Text 1988*. London: Faber & Faber.

Hartin, Patrick J. 1995. "'Yet Wisdom Is Justified by Her Children' (Q 7:35): A Rhetorical and Compositional Analysis of Divine Sophia in Q." In *Conflict and Invention: Literary, Rhetorical, and Social Studies on the Sayings Gospel Q,* edited by John S. Kloppenborg, pp. 151–164. Valley Forge, PA: Trinity Press International.

Henaut, Barry W. 1993. *Oral Tradition and the Gospels: The Problem of Mark 4. JSNT* Supplement Series, 82. Sheffield, UK: Sheffield Academic Press (JSOT Press).

Henderson, Ian H. 1992. "*Didache* and Orality in Synoptic Comparison." *JBL* 111:283–306.

Hengel, Martin. 1977. *Crucifixion in the Ancient World and the Folly of the Message of the Cross*. Philadelphia: Fortress Press.

Hills, Julian Victor. 1985. "Tradition and Composition in the *Epistula Apostolorum.*" Th.D diss., Harvard University. Ann Arbor, MI: University Microfilms International.

————. 1990. *Tradition and Composition in the* Epistula Apostolorum. Harvard Dissertations in Religion, 24. Minneapolis: Fortress Press. From Ph.D. diss., Harvard University, 1985.

Hoffmann, R. Joseph. 1987. *Celsus: On the True Doctrine: A Discourse Against the Christians*. New York: Oxford Univ. Press.

Holst-Warhaft, Gail. 1992. *Dangerous Voices: Women's Laments and Greek Literature*. New York: Routledge.

Hopkins, Keith. 1978. "Economic Growth and Towns in Classical Antiquity." In *Towns in Societies: Essays in Economic History and Historical Sociology,* edited by Philip Abrams and E. A. Wigley, pp. 35–77. Cambridge, UK: Cambridge Univ. Press.

————. 1983. "Introduction." In Garnsey, Hopkins, and Whittaker, pp. ix–xxv.

Horsley, G. H. R. (ed. for vols. 1–5), S. R. Llewelyn with R. A. Kearsley (eds. for vols. 6–7). 1981–1994. *New Documents Illustrating Early Christianity: A Review of the Greek Inscriptions and Papyri Published in 1976–83*. 7 vols. North Ryde, Australia: The Ancient History Documentary Research Centre, Macquarie University.

Horsley, Richard A. 1989. *Sociology and the Jesus Movement*. New York: Crossroad.

————. 1994. "The Historical Jesus and Archaeology of the Galilee: Questions from Historical Jesus Research to Archaeologists." In *Society of Biblical Literature 1994 Seminar Papers,* edited by Eugene H. Lovering, Jr., pp. 91–135. SBLSP 33. 130th annual meeting, Nov. 19–22 , 1994, Chicago. Atlanta: Scholars Press.

Horsley, Richard A., and John S. Hanson. 1985. *Bandits, Prophets, and Messiahs: Popular Movements in the Time of Jesus*. New Voices in Biblical Studies. Minneapolis: Winston

Press (Seabury Books).

Hunter, Ian M. L. 1985. "Lengthy Verbatim Recall: The Role of Text." In *Progress in the Psychology of Language,* edited by Andrew W. Ellis, vol. 1, pp. 207–235. London and Hillsdale, NJ: Erlbaum.

Hutton, Delvin D. 1970. "The Resurrection of the Holy Ones (Mt 27:51b–53): A Study of the Theology of the Matthean Passion Narrative." Th.D. diss., Harvard University.

Jackson, John, et al., trans. 1914–1937. *Tacitus.* 5 vols. Loeb Classical Library. Cambridge, MA: Harvard University

Jacobson, Arland Dean. 1978. *Wisdom Christology in Q.* Ann Arbor, MI: University Microfilms International.

———. 1992. *The First Gospel: An Introduction to Q.* Sonoma, CA: Polebridge Press. Completely revised version of Ph.D. diss., Claremont Graduate School, 1978.

James, Montague Rhodes. 1953. *The Apocryphal New Testament.* Oxford: Clarendon Press. Originally published in 1924; corrected edition published in 1953.

Jarrett, Janice Carole. 1977. "The Song of Lament: An Artistic Women's Heritage (A Study of the Modern Greek Lamenting Tradition and Its Ancient West Asian and Mediterranean Prototypes)." Ph.D. diss. (ethnomusicology), Wesleyan University. Ann Arbor, MI: University Microfilms International.

Jefford, Clayton N. 1989. *The Sayings of Jesus in the Teaching of the Twelve Apostles.* Supplements to *Vigiliae Christianae.* Texts and Studies of Early Christian Life and Language, 11. Leiden: Brill.

Jefford, Clayton N., ed. 1995. *The* Didache *in Context: Essays on Its Text, History, and Transmission.* Supplements to *Novum Testamentum,* 77. Leiden: Brill.

Jewett, Robert. 1993. "Tenement Churches and Communal Meals in the Early Church: The Implications of a Form-critical Analysis of 2 Thessalonians 3:10." *Biblical Research* 38:23–43.

———. 1994. "Tenement Churches and Pauline Love Feasts." *Quarterly Review* 14:43–58. A less technical version of the preceding article.

Johnson, Benjamin A. 1965. "Empty Tomb Tradition in the Gospel of Peter." Th.D. diss., Harvard University.

———. 1984–1985. "The Gospel of Peter: Between Apocalypse and Romance." In *Papers Presented to the Seventh International Conference on Patristic Studies Held at Oxford 1975,* 2 vols., edited by Elizabeth Livingstone, vol. 2, pp. 170–174. Studia Patristica 15–16 and TU 128. Berlin: Akademie.

Johnson, Luke Timothy. 1996. *The Real Jesus: The Misguided Quest for the Historical Jesus and the Truth of the Traditional Gospels.* San Francisco: HarperSanFrancisco.

Jones, F. Stanley. 1982. "The Pseudo-Clementines: A History of Research, Parts I and II." *Second Century* 2:1–33, 63–96.

———. 1995. *An Ancient Jewish Christian Source on the History of Christianity: Pseudo-Clementine Recognitions* 1:27–71. SBL Texts and Translations, 37: Christian Apocrypha Series, 2. Atlanta: Scholars Press.

Jones, F. Stanley, and Paul A. Mirecki. 1995. "Considerations on the Coptic Papyrus of the *Didache* (British Library Oriental Manuscript 9271)." In Jefford (ed.) 1995, pp. 47–87 and plates I–II.

Josephus, Flavius. See Thackeray et al. below.

Junger, Sebastian. 1997. *The Perfect Storm.* New York: Norton.

Jungmann, Josef A. 1959. *The Early Liturgy: To the Time of Gregory the Great.* Translated by

Francis A. Brunner. Notre Dame, IN: University of Notre Dame Press.

Kahl, Werner. 1992. *New Testament Miracle Stories in Their Religious-Historical Setting: A* Religionsgeschichtliche *Comparison from a Structural Perspective*. Ph.D. diss., Emory University. Ann Arbor, MI: University Microfilms International.

Kautsky, John H. 1982. *The Politics of Aristocratic Empires*. Chapel Hill, NC: University of North Carolina Press.

Kelber, Werner H. 1978. "Concepts and a Model for the Comparison of Medical Systems as Cultural Systems." *Social Science and Medicine* 12(2B):85–94.

———. 1983. *The Oral and the Written Gospel: The Hermeneutics of Speaking and Writing in the Synoptic Tradition, Mark, Paul, and Q*. Philadelphia: Fortress Press.

———. 1994. "Jesus and Tradition: Words in Time, Words in Space." *Semeia* 65:139–167.

King, Karen L. 1987. "Kingdom in the Gospel of Thomas." *Forum* 3:48–97.

———. 1994. "The Gospel of Mary Magdalene." In *Searching the Scriptures: A Feminist Commentary*, 2 vols., edited by Elisabeth Schüssler Fiorenza with Ann Brock and Shelly Matthews, vol. 2, pp. 601–634. New York: Crossroad.

Kirk, Alan. 1994. "Examining Priorities: Another Look at the *Gospel of Peter*'s Relationship to the New Testament Gospels." *NTS* 40:572–595.

Kleinman, Arthur. 1980. *Patients and Healers in the Context of Culture: An Exploration of the Borderland Between Anthropology, Medicine, and Psychiatry*. Comparative Studies of Health Systems and Medical Care. Berkeley: University of California Press.

———. 1988. *The Illness Narratives: Suffering, Healing, and the Human Condition*. New York: Basic Books.

Kleinman, Arthur, and Lilias H. Sung. 1979. "Why Do Indigenous Practitioners Successfully Heal?" *Social Science and Medicine* 13B/1:7–26.

Klijn, A.F.J. 1962. "The 'Single One' in the Gospel of Thomas." *JBL* 81:271–278.

Kloppenborg, John S. 1987a. *The Formation of Q: Trajectories in Ancient Wisdom Collections*. Studies in Antiquity and Christianity. Philadelphia: Fortress Press.

———. 1987b. "Symbolic Eschatology and the Apocalypticism of Q." *HTR* 80:287–306.

———. 1990. "'Easter Faith' and the Sayings Gospel Q." *Semeia* 49:71–99.

———. 1991. "Literary Convention, Self-Evidence, and the Social History of the Q People." *Semeia* 55:77–102.

———. 1996. "The Sayings Gospel Q and the Quest of the Historical Jesus." *HTR* 89:307–344.

Kloppenborg, John S., Marvin W. Meyer, Stephen J. Patterson, and Michael G. Steinhauser. 1990. *Q Thomas Reader*. Sonoma, CA: Polebridge Press. (Introduction to the *Q Gospel* by Steinhauser; translation by Kloppenborg. Introduction to the *Gospel of Thomas* by Steinhauser; translation by Meyer.)

Koester, Helmut. 1957. *Synoptische Überlieferung bei den Apostolischen Vätern*. TU 65. Berlin: Akademie.

———. 1971. "One Jesus and Four Primitive Gospels." In James M. Robinson and Helmut Koester, *Trajectories Through Early Christianity*, pp. 158–204. Philadelphia: Fortress Press. Originally published in 1968.

———. 1980a. "Apocryphal and Canonical Gospels." *HTR* 73:105–130.

————. 1980b. "Gnostic Writings as Witnesses for the Development of the Sayings Tradition." In *The School of Valentinus*, edited by Bentley Layton, pp. 238–256 (discussion: pp. 256–261), vol. 1 of *The Rediscovery of Gnosticism*. Proceedings of the International Conference on Gnosticism at Yale, New Haven, CT, Mar. 28–31, 1978. Studies in the History of Religions: Supplements to Numen XLI/1. Leiden: Brill.

————. 1982. *Introduction to the New Testament*. 2 vols. Vol. 1: *History, Culture, and Religion of the Hellenistic Age*. Vol. 2: *History and Literature of Early Christianity*. Hermeneia Foundations and Facets. Philadelphia: Fortress Press. Translated from *Einführung in das Neue Testament*. Berlin: de Gruyter, 1980.

————. 1989. "The Text of the Synoptic Gospels in the Second Century." In *Gospel Traditions in the Second Century: Origins, Recensions, Text, and Transmission*, edited by William L. Petersen, pp. 19–37. Christianity and Judaism in Antiquity, 3. Notre Dame, IN: University of Notre Dame.

————. 1990a. *Ancient Christian Gospels: Their History and Development*. London: SCM Press; and Philadelphia: Trinity Press International.

————. 1990b. "Q and Its Relatives." In *Gospel Origins and Christian Beginnings* ("In Honor of James M. Robinson"), edited by James E. Goehring, Charles W. Hedrick, and Jack T. Sanders with Hans Dieter Betz, pp. 49–63. Forum Fascicles, 1. Sonoma, CA: Polebridge Press.

————. 1992. "Jesus the Victim." *JBL* 111:3–15.

————. 1994a. "Jesus' Presence in the Early Church." *Cristianesimo nella Storia* 15:541–557.

————. 1994b. "The Historical Jesus and the Historical Situation of the Quest: An Epilogue." In *Studying the Historical Jesus: Evaluations of the State of Current Research*, edited by Bruce D. Chilton and Craig A. Evans, pp. 535–545. New Testament Tools and Studies, 19. Leiden: Brill.

————. 1995. "The Historical Jesus and the Cult of the *Kyrios Christos*." *Harvard Divinity Bulletin* 24:13–18.

————. 1996. "The Sayings Gospel Q and the Q of the Historical Jesus: A Response to John S. Kloppenborg." *HTR* 89:345–349.

Kraemer, Ross S. 1988–1989. "Monastic Jewish Women in Greco-Roman Egypt: Philo Judaeus on the Therapeutrides." *Signs: Journal of Women in Culture and Society* 14:342–370.

Kretschmar, Georg. 1964. "Ein Beitrag zur Frage nach dem Ursprung frühchristlicher Askese." *ZTK* 61:27–67.

Kuhn, Heinz-Wolfgang, and Rami Arav. 1991. "The Bethsaida Excavations: Historical and Archaeological Approaches." In *The Future of Early Christianity: Essays in Honor of Helmut Koester*, edited by Birger A. Pearson in collaboration with A. Thomas Kraabel, George W. E. Nickelsburg, and Norman R. Petersen, pp. 77–106. Minneapolis: Fortress Press.

Kyrtatas, Dimitris J. 1987. *The Social Structure of the Early Christian Communities*. New York: Verso. Revised version of 1980 Ph.D. diss., Brunel University (under Keith Hopkins).

Lake, Kirsopp, trans. and ed. 1912–1913. *The Apostolic Fathers*. 2 vols. LCL. Cambridge, MA: Harvard Univ. Press.

Landsberger, Henry A. 1973. "Peasant Unrest: Themes and Variations." In *Rural Protest: Peasant Movements and Social Change*, edited by Henry A. Landsberger, pp. 1–64. New York: Barnes & Noble.

Layton, Bentley. 1968. "The Sources, Date, and Transmission of *Didache* 1.3b–2.1." *HTR* 61:343–383.

———. 1987. *The Gnostic Scriptures*. New York: Doubleday.

Layton, Bentley, and Thomas O. Lambdin. 1989. "Critical Edition and Translation of the Gospel According to Thomas." In *Nag Hammadi Codex II,2–7*, 2 vols., edited by Bentley Layton, vol. 1, pp. 52–93. NHS 20–21 (The Coptic Gnostic Library). Leiden: Brill.

Leacock, Eleanor. 1980. "Montagnais Women and the Jesuit Program for Colonization." In *Women and Colonization: Anthropological Perspectives*, edited by Mona Etienne and Eleanor Leacock, pp. 25–42. New York: Praeger.

Lenski, Gerhard E. 1966. *Power and Privilege: A Theory of Social Stratification*. New York: McGraw-Hill.

Lenski, Gerhard E., and Jean Lenski. 1974. *Human Societies: An Introduction to Macrosociology*. 3rd ed. New York: McGraw-Hill. See "Agrarian Societies," pp. 177–230.

Levi, Carlo. 1947. *Christ Stopped at Eboli: The Story of a Year*. Translated by Frances Frenaye. New York: Farrar, Straus.

Levi, Peter. 1984. *"The Lamentation of the Dead" with "The Lament for Arthur O'Leary" by Eileen O'Connell*, translated by Eilís Dillon. Inaugural lecture by the Professor of Poetry in the University of Oxford, Oct. 25, 1984. Poetica, 19. London: Anvil Press Poetry.

Levine, Amy-Jill. 1994. "Second Temple Judaism, Jesus, and Women: Yeast of Eden." *Biblical Interpretation* 2:8–33.

Lewis, Naphtali, and Meyer Reinhold. 1951. *Roman Civilization: Selected Readings*. 2 vols. Records of Civilization, Sources and Studies. New York: Columbia Univ. Press.

LiDonnici, Lynn R. 1995. *The Epidaurian Miracle Inscriptions: Text, Translation, and Commentary*. SBL Texts and Translations, 36; Graeco-Roman Religion Series, 11. Atlanta: Scholars Press.

Linebaugh, Peter. 1975. "The Tyburn Riot Against the Surgeons." In *Albion's Fatal Tree: Crime and Society in Eighteenth-Century England*, edited by Douglas Hay, pp. 63–117. New York: Random House (Pantheon Books).

Lods, Adolphe. 1892. *Evangelii secundum Petrum et Petri Apocalypseos quae supersunt*. Paris: Leroux.

———. 1893. "Reproduction en héliogravure du manuscrit d'Enoch et des écrits attribués a Saint Pierre." In *Mémoires publiés par les membres de la Mission archéologique française au Caire*, Vol. 9, Fascicle 3, edited by Urbain Bouriant, pp. 217–235 (232–235 are mispaginated as 332–335) and plates I–XXXIV. Paris: Leroux (Librairie de la Société asiatique). (*Gospel of Peter* is on pp. 219–224 and plates II–VI.)

Loftus, Elizabeth F. 1979. *Eyewitness Testimony*. Cambridge, MA: Harvard Univ. Press.

———. 1980. *Memory: Surprising New Insights into How We Remember and Why We Forget*. Reading, MA: Addison-Wesley.

Loftus, Elizabeth F., and James M. Doyle. 1987. *Eyewitness Testimony: Civil and Criminal*. Kluwer Evidence Library. New York: Kluwer Law Book Publishers. Updated with a 1990 *Cumulative Supplement*. Charlottesville, VA: Michie, 1990 (in pocket at back of 1987 volume).

Loftus, Elizabeth F., and Katherine Ketcham. 1991. *Witness for the Defense: The Accused, the Eyewitness, and the Expert Who Puts Memory on Trial*. New York: St. Martin's Press.

———. 1994. *The Myth of Repressed Memory: False Memories and Allegations of Sexual Abuse*. New York: St. Martin's Press.

Longstaff, Thomas R. W. 1990. "Nazareth and Sepphoris: Insights into Christian Origins." *Anglican Theological Review* 11:8–15.

Lord, Albert Bates. 1971. *The Singer of Tales*. New York: Atheneum. Originally published as Harvard Studies in Comparative Literature, 24. Cambridge, MA: Harvard Univ. Press, 1960. Based on a 1949 Ph.D. diss., Department of Comparative Literature, Harvard University.

Lührmann, Dieter. 1969. *Die Redaktion der Logienquelle*. WMANT, 33. Neukirchen-Vluyn: Neukirchener Verlag.

———. 1981. "POx 2949: EvPt 3–5 in einer Handschrift des 2./3. Jahrhunderts." *ZNW* 72:216–226.

Maccoby, Hyam. 1982. "The Washing of Cups." *JSNT* 14:3–15.

Mack, Burton L. 1993. *The Lost Gospel: The Book of Q and Christian Origins*. San Francisco: HarperSanFrancisco.

MacMullen, Ramsay. 1974. *Roman Social Relations. 50 B.C. to A.D. 384*. New Haven, CT: Yale Univ. Press.

MacRae, George W. 1978. "Nag Hammadi and the New Testament." In *Gnosis* ("Festschrift für Hans Jonas"), edited by B. Aland et al., pp. 144–157. Göttingen: Vandenhoeck & Ruprecht.

Malina, Bruce J., and Jerome H. Neyrey. 1988. *Calling Jesus Names: The Social Value of Labels in Matthew*. Sonoma, CA: Polebridge Press.

Malina, Bruce, and Richard L. Rohrbaugh. 1992. *Social Science Commentary on the Synoptic Gospels*. Minneapolis: Fortress Press.

Mandler, Jean M., and Nancy S. Johnson. 1977. "Remembrance of Things Parsed: Story Structure and Recall." *Cognitive Psychology* 9:111–151.

Mara, Maria G. 1973. *Évangile de Pierre: Introduction, texte critique, traduction, commentaire, et index*. Sources Chrétiennes, 201. Paris: Cerf.

Marcovich, M. 1969. "Textual Criticism on the Gospel of Thomas." *JTS* 20:53–74.

Marxsen, Willi. 1970. *The Lord's Supper As a Christological Problem*. Translated by Lorenz Nieting. Philadelphia: Fortress.

———. 1992. "The Meals of Jesus and the Lord's Supper of the Church." In *Jesus and the Church*, translated by P. I. Devenish, pp. 137–146. New York: Trinity Press International.

Mason, Steve. 1991. *Flavius Josephus on the Pharisees: A Composition-Critical Study*. Studia Post Biblica, 39. Leiden: Brill.

Mathews, Thomas F. 1993. *The Clash of Gods: A Reinterpretation of Early Christian Art*. Princeton, NJ: Princeton University Press.

McCant, Jerry Walter. 1978. "The Gospel of Peter: The Docetic Question Re-examined." Ph.D. diss., Emory University (under Leander Keck). Ann Arbor, MI: University Microfilms International.

———. 1984. "The Gospel of Peter: Docetism Reconsidered." *NTS* 30:258–273.

McCourt, Frank. 1996. *Angela's Ashes: A Memoir*. New York: Scribner.

McKenna, Margaret Mary. 1981. "'The Two Ways' in Jewish and Christian Writings of the Greco-Roman Period: A Study of the Form of Repentance Parenesis." Ph.D. diss., University of Pennsylvania. Ann Arbor, MI: University Microfilms International.

Meeks, Wayne A. 1974. "The Image of the Androgyne: Some Uses of a Symbol in Earliest Christianity." *hr* 13:165–208.

———. 1983. *The First Urban Christians: The Social World of the Apostle Paul*. New Haven, CT: Yale Univ. Press.

Meier, John P. 1990. "Jesus in Josephus: A Modest Proposal." *CBQ* 52:76–103.

————. 1991–. *A Marginal Jew: Rethinking the Historical Jesus*. 3 vols. Vol. 1: *The Roots of the Problem and the Person* (1991). Vol. 2: *Mentor, Message, and Miracles* (1994). The Anchor Bible Reference Library. New York: Doubleday.

Mellor, Ronald. 1993. *Tacitus*. New York: Routledge, Chapman, & Hall.

Metzger, Bruce M. 1971. *A Textual Commentary on the Greek New Testament*. New York: United Bible Societies.

————. 1981. *Manuscripts of the Greek Bible: An Introduction to Greek Palaeography*. New York: Oxford Univ. Press.

Meyer, Marvin. 1992. *The Gospel of Thomas: The Hidden Sayings of Jesus*. San Francisco: HarperSanFrancisco.

Meyers, Eric M. 1975–1976. "Galilean Regionalism as a Factor in Historical Reconstruction." *BASOR* 220/221:93–101.

————. 1979. "The Cultural Setting of Galilee: The Case of Regionalism and Early Judaism." *ANRW* 2.19.686–702. Later published as "The Cultural Setting of Galilee: The Case of Regionalism and Early Palestinian Judaism," pp. 31–47, in Meyers and Strange.

————. 1985. "Galilean Regionalism: A Reappraisal." In *Approaches to Ancient Judaism*, edited by William Scott Green, vol. 5, pp. 115–131. Atlanta: Scholars Press.

————. 1992. "Roman Sepphoris in Light of New Archeological Evidence and Recent Research." In *The Galilee in Late Antiquity*, edited by Lee I. Levine, pp. 321–338. New York and Jerusalem: The Jewish Theological Seminary of America. Papers from the First International Conference on Galilean Studies in Late Antiquity, Kibbutz Hanaton, Lower Galilee, Israel, Aug. 13–15, 1989.

Meyers, Eric M., Ehud Netzer, and Carol L. Meyers. 1986. "Sepphoris: 'Ornament of All Galilee.'" *BA* 49:4–19.

————. 1992. *Sepphoris*. Winona Lake, IN: Eisenbrauns.

Meyers, Eric M., and James F. Strange. 1981. *Archaeology, the Rabbis, and Early Christianity: The Social and Historical Setting of Palestinian Judaism and Christianity*. Nashville, TN: Abingdon.

Milavec, Aaron. 1989. "The Pastoral Genius of the Didache: An Analytical Translation and Commentary." In *Christianity*, edited by Jacob Neusner, Ernest S. Frerichs, and Amy-Jill Levine, pp. 89–125, vol. 2 of *Religious Writings and Religious Systems: Systemic Analysis of Holy Books in Christianity, Islam, Buddhism, Greco-Roman Religions, Ancient Israel, and Judaism*. Brown Studies in Religion, 2. Atlanta: Scholars Press.

————. 1994. "Distinguishing True and False Prophets: The Protective Wisdom of the Didache." *JECS* 2:117–136.

Miller, Barbara Butler. 1994. "Women, Death, and Mourning in the Ancient Eastern Mediterranean World." Ph.D. diss., University of Michigan (under Pamela Milne and Brian Schmidt). Ann Arbor, MI: University Microfilms International.

Millett, Martin. 1991. "Roman Towns and Their Territories: An Archaeological Perspective." In Rich and Wallace-Hadrill, pp. 169–189.

Mintz, Sidney W. 1973. "A Note on the Definition of Peasantries." *Journal of Peasant Studies* 1:91–106.

Moore, Jr., Barrington. 1966. *Social Origins of Dictatorship and Democracy: Lord and Peasant in the Making of the Modern World*. Berkeley: University of California Press.

Morris, Charles R. 1997. *American Catholic: The Saints and Sinners Who Built America's Most Powerful Church*. New York: Random House (Times Books).

Morris, Ian. 1992. *Death-Ritual and Social Structure in Classical Antiquity.* Key Themes in Ancient History. Cambridge, UK: Cambridge Univ. Press.

Neirynck, Frans. 1972. *Duality in Mark: Contributions to the Study of the Markan Redaction.* BETL 31. Leuven: Leuven Univ. Press.

———. 1974. *The Minor Agreements of Matthew and Luke Against Mark with a Cumulative List.* BETL 37. Gembloux: Duculot.

———. 1982. *Evangelica [I: 1966–1981]. Collected Essays by Frans Neirynck,* edited by F. Van Segbroeck. BETL 60. Leuven: Leuven Univ. Press.

———. 1989. "The Apocryphal Gospels and the Gospel of Mark." In *The New Testament in Early Christianity: La réception des écrits néotestamentaires dans le christianisme primitif,* edited by Jean-Marie Sevrin, pp. 123–175. BETL 86. Leuven: Leuven Univ. Press.

———. 1991. *Evangelica II: 1982–1991. Collected Essays by Frans Neirynck,* edited by F. Van Segbroeck. BETL 99. Leuven: Leuven Univ. Press.

———. 1994a. "The Historical Jesus: Reflections on an Inventory." *ETL* 70:221–234.

———. 1994b. "Gospel Issues in the Passion Narratives: Critical Note on a Recent Commentary." *ETL* 70:406–416.

———. 1995a. "Q: From Source to Gospel." *ETL* 71:421–430.

———. 1995b. "Title." Review of John Dominic Crossan, *Who Killed Jesus? ETL* 71:455–457.

Neisser, Ulric, ed. 1982. *Memory Observed: Remembering in Natural Contexts.* San Francisco: Freeman.

Neisser, Ulric. 1982a. "Memory: What Are the Important Questions?" In Neisser 1982, pp. 3–19, reprinted from 1978.

———. 1982b. "Literacy and Memory." In Neisser 1982, pp. 241–242.

———. 1982c. "John Dean's Memory: A Case Study." In Neisser 1982, pp. 139–159, reprinted from 1981.

Neisser, Ulric, and Nicole Harsch. 1992. "Phantom Flashbulbs: False Recollections of Hearing the News About *Challenger.*" In Winograd and Neisser (eds.), pp. 9–31.

Neusner, Jacob. 1990. *The Economics of the Mishnah.* Chicago Studies in the History of Judaism. Chicago: University of Chicago Press.

Nickelsburg, Jr., George W. E. 1972. *Resurrection, Immortality, and Eternal Life in Intertestamental Judaism.* HTS 16. Cambridge, MA: Harvard Univ. Press.

———. 1980. "The Genre and Function of the Markan Passion Narrative." *HTR* 73:153–184.

———. 1981. *Jewish Literature Between the Bible and the Mishnah.* Philadelphia: Fortress Press.

Niederwimmer, Kurt. 1989. *Die Didache: Ergänzungsreihe zum Kritisch-exegetischen Kommentar über das Neue Testament: Kommentar zu den Apostolischen Vätern,* vol. 1. Göttingen: Vandenhoeck & Ruprecht.

Oakman, Douglas E. 1986. *Jesus and the Economic Questions of His Day.* Studies in the Bible and Early Christianity, 8. Lewiston, NY, and Queenston, Ontario: Edwin Mellen Press.

O'Collins, Gerald, and Daniel Kendall. 1994. "Did Joseph of Arimathea Exist?" *Biblica* 75:235–241.

Oldfather, W. A. 1925–1928. *Epictetus: The Discourses as Reported by Arrian, the Manual, and Fragments.* 2 vols. LCL. Cambridge, MA: Harvard Univ. Press.

Olrik, Axel. 1965. "Epic Laws of Folk Narrative." In *The Study of Folklore,* edited by Alan Dundes, pp. 129–141. Englewood Cliffs, NJ: Prentice-Hall. Originally published in 1909.

Ong, Walter J. 1982. *Orality and Literacy: The Technologizing of the Word.* New Accents. London and New York: Methuen.

Osiek, Carolyn. 1983. *Rich and Poor in the Shepherd of Hermas: An Exegetical-Social Investigation*. CBQMS 15. Washington, D.C.: Catholic Biblical Society of America.

———. 1994. "An Early Tale That Almost Made It into the New Testament." *BR* 10(5/Oct.):48–54.

Overman, J. Andrew. 1988. "Who Were the First Urban Christians? Urbanization in Galilee in the First Century." In *Society of Biblical Literature 1988 Seminar Papers,* edited by David J. Lull, pp. 160–168. SBLSP 27. 124th annual meeting, Nov. 19–22, 1988, Chicago. Atlanta: Scholars Press.

———. 1993. "Recent Advances in the Archaeology of the Galilee in the Roman Period." *Currents in Research: Biblical Studies* 1:35–57.

Paap, Anton Herman Reiner Everhard. 1959. *Nomina Sacra in the Greek Papyri of the First Five Centuries* A.D.: *The Sources and Some Deductions*. Papyrologica Lugduno-Batava, 8. Leiden (Lugdunum Batavorum): Brill.

Packer, James E. 1967. "Housing and Population in Imperial Ostia and Rome." *Journal of Roman Studies* 57:80–95.

———. 1971. *The Insulae of Imperial Ostia*. Memoirs of the American Academy of Rome. Rome: American Academy of Rome.

Pagels, Elaine H. 1980. "Gnostic and Orthodox Views of Christ's Passion: Paradigms for the Christian's Response to Persecution." In *The School of Valentinus,* edited by Bentley Layton, pp. 262–283 (discussion: 283–288), vol. 1 in *The Rediscovery of Gnosticism*. Proceedings of the International Conference on Gnosticism at Yale, New Haven, CT, Mar. 28–31, 1978. Studies in the History of Religions: Supplements to Numen XLI/1. Leiden: Brill.

Park, Robert E. 1928. "Human Migration and the Marginal Man." *American Journal of Sociology* 33:881–893.

———. 1931. "Personality and Cultural Conflict." *Publication of the American Sociological Society* 25:95–110.

Parry, Adam, ed. 1971. *The Making of Homeric Verse: The Collected Papers of Milman Parry*. Oxford: Clarendon Press.

Parry, Milman, coll. 1974. *The Wedding of Smailagić Meho* (Avdo Međedović), vol. 3 of *Serbo-Croatian Heroic Songs*. Collected by Milman Parry. Translated and edited by Albert B. Lord and David E. Bynum. Cambridge, MA: Harvard Univ. Press.

Patterson, John R. 1991. "Settlement, City, and Elite in Samnium and Lycia." In *City and Country in the Ancient World,* edited by John Rich and Andrew Wallace-Hadrill, pp. 146–168. New York: Routledge.

Patterson, Stephen John. 1988. "The Gospel of Thomas Within the Development of Early Christianity." Ph.D. diss., Claremont Graduate School. Ann Arbor, MI: University Microfilms International.

———. 1990. "The Gospel of Thomas and the Historical Jesus: Retrospectus and Prospectus." In *Society of Biblical Literature 1990 Seminar Papers,* edited by David J. Lull, pp. 614–636. SBLSP 29. 126th annual meeting, Nov. 17–20, 1990, New Orleans. Atlanta: Scholars Press.

———. 1991. "Paul and the Jesus Tradition: It Is Time for Another Look." *HTR* 84:23–41.

———. 1992. "The Gospel of Thomas and the Synoptic Tradition." *Forum* 8:45–97.

———. 1993a. *The Gospel of Thomas and Jesus*. Foundations and Facets Reference Series. Sonoma, CA: Polebridge Press. A "much revised version" of Patterson 1988, with pp. 215–241 added.

————. 1993b. "Wisdom in Q and Thomas." In *In Search of Wisdom: Essays in Memory of John G. Gammie,* edited by Leo G. Perdue, Bernard Brandon Scott, and William Johnston Wiseman, pp. 187–221. Louisville, KY: Westminster/John Knox Press.

————. 1995. "*Didache* 11–13: The Legacy of Radical Itinerancy in Early Christianity." In Jefford (ed.) 1995, pp. 313–329.

Pearson, Birger, A., in collaboration with A. Thomas Kraabel, George W. E. Nickelsburg, and Norman R. Petersen, eds. 1991. *The Future of Early Christianity: Essays in Honor of Helmut Koester.* Minneapolis: Fortress Press.

Perkins, Pheme. 1980. *The Gnostic Dialogue: The Early Church and the Crisis of Gnosticism.* New York: Paulist Press.

Piaget, Jean. 1962. *Plays, Dreams, and Imitation in Childhood.* Translated by C. Gattegno and F. M. Hodgson. New York: Norton. Originally published as *La formation du symbole chez l'enfant.*

Piper, Ronald A. 1989. *Wisdom in the Q-Tradition: The Aphoristic Teaching of Jesus.* SNTSMS 61. New York: Cambridge Univ. Press.

Pixner, Bargil. 1997. "Jerusalem's Essene Gateway: Where the Community Lived in Jesus' Time." *BAR* 23 (3/May–June):22–31, 64, 66.

Polanyi, Karl. 1957. "Aristotle Discovers the Economy." In *Trade and Market in the Early Empires: Economies in History and Theory,* edited by Karl Polanyi, Conrad M. Arensberg, and Harry W. Pearson, pp. 64–94. New York: Free Press.

Pritchard. James B., ed. 1955. *Ancient Near Eastern Texts Relating to the Old Testament.* 2nd ed. Princeton, NJ: Princeton Univ. Press.

Pucci, Giuseppe. 1983. "Pottery and Trade in the Roman Period." In Garnsey, Hopkins, and Whittaker, pp. 105–117, 199–201.

Rackham, H., W.H.S. Jones, and D. E. Eichholz. 1938–1963. *Pliny: Natural History.* 10 vols. LCL. Cambridge: Harvard Univ. Press.

Radice, Betty, trans. 1963. *The Letters of the Younger Pliny.* Baltimore, MD: Penguin Books.

————. 1969. *Pliny the Younger: Letters and Panegyricus.* 2 vols. LCL. Cambridge, MA: Harvard Univ. Press.

Redfield, Robert. 1953. *The Primitive World and Its Transformation.* Ithaca, NY: Cornell Univ. Press.

Reed, Jonathan L. 1992. *The Population of Capernaum.* Occasional Papers of the Institute for Antiquity and Christianity, 24. Claremont, CA: Institute for Antiquity and Christianity.

————. 1994a. "Places in Early Christianity: Galilee, Archaeology, Urbanization, and Q." Ph.D. diss., Claremont Graduate School. Ann Arbor, MI: University Microfilms International.

————. 1994b. "Population Numbers, Urbanization, and Economics: Galilean Archaeology and the Historical Jesus." In *Society of Biblical Literature 1994 Seminar Papers,* edited by Eugene H. Lovering, Jr., pp. 203–219. SBLSP 33. 130th annual meeting, Nov. 19–22, 1994, Chicago. Atlanta: Scholars Press.

————. 1995. "The Social Map of Q." In *Conflict and Invention: Literary, Rhetorical, and Social Studies on the Sayings Gospel Q,* edited by John S. Kloppenborg, pp. 17–36. Valley Forge, PA: Trinity Press International.

Reisberg, Daniel, and Friderike Heuer. 1992. "Remembering the Details of Emotional Events." In Winograd and Neisser (eds.), pp. 162–190.

Renan, Ernest. 1972. *The Life of Jesus.* New York: Random House (Modern Library). Originally published in 1863.

Rich, John, and Andrew Wallace-Hadrill, eds. 1991. *City and Country in the Ancient World.* New York: Routledge.

Riggs, John W. 1984. "From Gracious Table to Sacramental Elements: The Tradition-History of *Didache* 9 and 10." *Second Century* 4:83–101.

———. 1995. "The Sacred Food of *Didache* 9–10 and Second-Century Ecclesiologies." In Jefford (ed.) 1995, pp. 256–283.

Riley, Gregory John. 1995. *Resurrection Reconsidered: Thomas and John in Controversy.* Minneapolis: Fortress.

———. 1998. *One Jesus, Many Christs: How Jesus Inspired Not One True Christianity, but Many.* San Francisco: HarperSanFrancisco.

Roberts, Alexander, James Donaldson, and A. Cleveland Coxe, eds. 1926. *The Ante-Nicene Fathers.* American reprint of the original Edinburgh edition. 10 vols. New York: Scribner.

Roberts, Colin H. 1953. "An Early Papyrus of the First Gospel." *HTR* 46:233–237.

———. 1962. "Complementary Note." In R. Roca-Puig, pp. 58–60.

———. 1979. *Manuscript, Society, and Belief in Early Christian Egypt.* The Schweich Lectures of the British Academy 1977. London: Oxford Univ. Press.

Roberts, Colin H., and Theodore Cressy Skeat. 1983. *The Birth of the Codex.* London: Oxford Univ. Press (for the British Academy). Complete revision of Colin H. Roberts, *The Codex,* in *Proceedings of the British Academy* 40(1954):169–204.

Robinson, J. Armitage. 1892. "The Gospel According to Peter." In J. Armitage Robinson and Montague Rhodes James, *The Gospel According to Peter, and the Revelation of Peter* ("Two Lectures on the Newly Discovered Fragments Together with the Greek Texts"), pp. 11–36 (lecture) and 82–88 (Greek text). London: Clay.

Robinson, James M. 1971. *"LOGOI SOPHON:* On the Gattung of Q." In James M. Robinson and Helmut Koester, *Trajectories Through Early Christianity,* pp. 71–113. Philadelphia: Fortress Press. From "ΛΟΤΟΙ ΣΟΦΩΝ: Zur Gattung der Sprachquelle Q." In *Zeit und Geschichte: Dankesgabe an Rudolf Bultmann,* pp. 77–96. Tübingen: Mohr/Siebeck, 1964.

———. 1979. "The Discovery of the Nag Hammadi Codices." *BA* 42:206–224.

Robinson, James M., et al. 1990–1995. "The International Q Project." *JBL* 109(1990):499–501; 110(1991):494–98; 111(1992):500–508; 112(1993):500–506; 113(1994):495–500; 114(1995):501–511.

Robinson, James M., gen. ed. 1988. *The Nag Hammadi Library in English.* 3rd (completely revised) ed. Leiden: Brill.

Roca-Puig, Ramon. 1962. *Un papiro griego del Evangelio de San Mateo.* 2nd ed. Barcelona: Grafos.

Rogers, Benjamin Bickley, trans. 1924. *Aristophanes.* 3 vols. LCL. Cambridge: Harvard Univ. Press.

Rogers, Susan Carol. 1975. "Female Forms of Power and the Myth of Male Dominance: A Model of Female/Male Interaction in Peasant Society." *American Ethnologist* 2:727–756.

———. 1978. "Woman's Place: A Critical Review of Anthropological Theory." *Comparative Studies in Society and History* 20:123–162.

Rolfe, John C., trans. 1979. *Suetonius.* 2 vols. LCL. Cambridge: Harvard Univ. Press.

Rordorf, Willy. 1981. "Le probleme de la transmission textuelle de *Didachè* 1,3b–2,1." In *Überlieferungsgeschichtliche Untersuchungen,* edited by Franz Paschke, pp. 499–513. TU 125. Berlin: Akademie.

———. 1992. "Does the Didache Contain Jesus Tradition Independently of the Synoptic Gospels?" In *Jesus and the Oral Gospel Tradition,* edited by Henry Wansbrough, pp. 394–423. *JSNT* Supplement Series, 64. Sheffield, UK: Sheffield Academic Press (JSOT Press).

Rordorf, Willy, and André Tuilier. 1978. *La doctrine des douze apôtres (Didachè)*. Sources Chrétiennes, 248. Paris: Cerf.

Roseberry, William. 1989. "Peasants and the World." In *Economic Anthropology*, edited by Stuart Plattner, pp. 108–126, 441–443. Stanford, CA: Stanford Univ. Press.

Rose-Gaier, Deborah. 1996. "The Didache: A Community of Equals." Paper presented at the session on "Women and the (Search for the) Historical Jesus," Society of Biblical Literature annual meeting, Nov. 25, 1996, New Orleans.

Rudolph, Kurt. 1983. *Gnosis*. Translated by R. McL. Wilson, P. W. Coxon, and K. H. Kuhn. Edited by R. McL. Wilson. San Francisco: Harper & Row. Translated from the German 2nd ed., 1980; first German ed. published in 1977.

Sabbe, Maurits. 1991. *Studia Neotestamentica. Collected Essays*. BETL 98. Leuven: Leuven University Press, 1991.

———. 1994. "The Johannine Account of the Death of Jesus and Its Synoptic Parallels (Jn 19, 16b–42)." *ETL* 70:34–64.

———. 1995. "The Denial of Peter in the Gospel of John." *Louvain Studies* 20:219–240.

Saldarini, Anthony J. 1988. *Pharisees, Scribes, and Sadducees in Palestinian Society: A Sociological Approach*. Wilmington, DE: Glazier, 1988.

Sanders, E. P. 1985. *Jesus and Judaism*. Philadelphia: Fortress Press.

———. 1992. *Judaism: Practice and Belief 63 B.C.E.–66 C.E.* London: SCM Press; Philadelphia: Trinity Press International.

———. 1993. *The Historical Figure of Jesus*. London: Allen Lane / The Penguin Press.

Sawicki, Marianne. 1994a. *Seeing the Lord: Resurrection and Early Christian Practices*. Minneapolis: Fortress.

———. 1994b. "Archaeology as Space Technology: Digging for Gender and Class in Holy Land." *Method and Theory in the Study of Religion* 6:319–348.

Sayers, Dorothy L. 1943. *The Man Born to Be King: A Play-Cycle on the Life of Our Lord And Saviour Jesus Christ*. San Francisco: Ignatius Press.

Sayre, Farrand. 1948. *The Greek Cynics*. Baltimore, MD: Furst.

Schacter, Daniel L. 1996. *Searching for Memory: The Brain, the Mind, and the Past*. New York: HarperCollins (Basic Books).

Schaeffer, Susan E. 1991a. "The Gospel of Peter, the Canonical Gospels, and Oral Tradition." Ph.D. diss., Union Theological Seminary (under Raymond E. Brown). Ann Arbor, MI: University Microfilms International.

———. 1991b. "The Guard at the Tomb (Gos. Pet. 8:28–11:49) and Matt. 27:62–66; 28:2–4, 11–16): A Case of Intertextuality?" In *Society of Biblical Literature 1991 Seminar Papers*, edited by Eugene H. Lovering, Jr., pp. 499–507. SBLSP 30. 127th annual meeting, Nov. 23–26, 1991, Kansas City, MO. Atlanta: Scholars Press.

Schaff, Philip. 1889. *The Oldest Church Manual Called the Teaching of the Twelve Apostles*. 3rd ed. Ann Arbor, MI: University Microfilms International. Originally published in 1885; 2nd ed. published in 1886.

Schiffman, Lawrence H. 1994a. "The *Temple Scroll* and the Nature of the Law: The Status of the Question." In *The Community of the Renewed Covenant: The Notre Dame Symposium on the Dead Sea Scrolls*, edited by Eugene Ulrich and James VanderKam, pp. 37–55. Christianity and Judaism in Antiquity Series, 10. Notre Dame, IN: University of Notre Dame.

———. 1994b. *Reclaiming the Dead Sea Scrolls: The History of Judaism, the Background of Christianity, the Lost Library of Qumran*. Philadelphia: The Jewish Publication Society.

Schneemelcher, Wilhelm, ed., and R. McL. Wilson, trans. and ed. 1991–1992. *New Testament Apocrypha.* 2 vols. Rev. ed. Philadelphia: Westminster/John Knox Press.

Schumpeter, Joseph Alois. 1954. *History of Economic Analysis.* Edited from manuscript by Elizabeth Boody Schumpeter. New York: Oxford Univ. Press. (The manuscript was unfinished at the author's death in 1950 [after nine years of work]; even so, the book contains 1,260 closely printed pages.)

Schüssler, Fiorenza, Elisabeth. 1994. *Jesus: Miriam's Child, Sophia's Prophet.* New York: Continuum.

Schwartz, Daniel R. 1990. *Agrippa I: The Last King of Judaea.* Texte und Studien zum antiken Judentum, 23. Tübingen: Mohr (Siebeck). Originally published in Hebrew, 1987.

Schweitzer, Albert. 1933. *Out of My Life and Thought: An Autobiography.* Translated by Charles Thomas Campion. New York: Holt.

———. 1969. *The Quest of the Historical Jesus: A Critical Study of Its Progress from Reimarus to Wrede.* Translated by William Montgomery. Introduction by James M. Robinson. New York: Macmillan. Originally published in 1906.

Scott, James C. 1976. *The Moral Economy of the Peasant: Subsistence and Rebellion in Southeast Asia.* New Haven, CN: Yale Univ. Press.

———. 1977. "Protest and Profanation: Agrarian Revolt and the Little Tradition." *Theory and Society* 4:1–38, 211–246.

———. 1985. *Weapons of the Weak: Everyday Forms of Peasant Resistance.* New Haven, CN: Yale Univ. Press.

———. 1990. *Domination and the Arts of Resistance: Hidden Transcripts.* New Haven, CT: Yale Univ. Press.

Seeley, David. 1996. "Futuristic Eschatology and Social Formation in Q." In *Reimagining Christian Origins: A Colloquium Honoring Burton L. Mack,* edited by Elizabeth A. Castelli and Hal Taussig, pp. 144–153. Philadelphia: Trinity Press International.

Seeman, Christopher. 1993. "The Urbanization of Herodian Galilee as an Historical Factor Contributing to the Emergence of the Jesus Movement." M.A. thesis, Graduate Theological Union, Berkeley (San Francisco Theological Seminary, under Robert Coote).

Seremetakis, Constantina-Nadia. 1990. "The Ethics of Antiphony: The Social Construction of Pain, Gender, and Power in the Southern Peloponnese." *Ethos* 18:481–511.

———. 1991. *The Last Word: Women, Death, and Divination in Inner Mani.* Chicago: University of Chicago Press.

Setzer, Claudia. 1997. "Excellent Women: Female Witness to the Resurrection." *JBL* 116:259–272.

Shanin, Teodor. 1971a. "Peasantry as a Political Factor." In *Peasants and Peasant Society: Selected Readings,* edited by Teodor Shanin, pp. 238–263. Baltimore, MD: Penguin Books. "Revised and somewhat extended" from the original 1965 edition.

———. 1971b. "Peasantry: Delineation of a Sociological Concept and a Field of Study." *European Journal of Sociology* 12:289–300.

Shanks, Michael, and Christopher Tilley. 1987. *Re-Constructing Archaeology: Theory and Practice.* New Studies in Archaeology. Cambridge, UK: Cambridge Univ. Press.

———. 1988. *Social Theory and Archaeology.* Albuquerque: University of New Mexico Press. Originally published in 1987 (Polity Press and Basil Blackwell).

Shaw, Brent D. 1996. "Body/Power/Identity: Passions of the Martyrs." *JECS* 4:269–312.

Shepherd, Tom. 1995. "The Narrative Function of Markan Intercalation." *NTS* 41:522–540.

Shipley, Frederick William. 1924. *Velleius Paterculus: Compendium of Roman History and Res Gestae Divi Augusti*. LCL 152. Cambridge, MA: Harvard Univ. Press.

Sieber, John H. 1966. "A Redactional Analysis of the Synoptic Gospels with Regard to the Question of the Sources of the Gospel According to Thomas." Ph.D. diss., Claremont Graduate School. Ann Arbor, MI: University Microfilms International.

Silone, Ignazio. 1934. *Fontamara*. Translated by Michael Wharf. New York: Smith & Haas.

Silver, Morris. 1983. *Prophets and Markets: The Political Economy of Ancient Israel*. Social Dimensions of Economics. Boston, MA: Kluwer-Nijhoff.

Simmel, Georg. 1955. *Conflict* and *The Web of Group-Affiliations*. Translated, respectively, by H. Wolff and Reinhard Bendix. Glencoe, IL: Free Press. Originally published, respectively, in 1908 and 1922.

Sjoberg, Gideon. 1960. *The Preindustrial City: Past and Present*. New York: Free Press.

Skeat, Theodore Cressy. 1969. "Early Christian Book-Production: Papyri and Manuscripts." In *The West from the Fathers to the Reformation*, edited by G.W.H. Lampe, pp. 54–79, vol. 2 of *The Cambridge History of the Bible*. Cambridge, UK: Cambridge Univ. Press.

———. 1994. "The Origin of the Christian Codex." *ZPE* 102:263–268.

———. 1995. "Was Papyrus Regarded as 'Cheap' or 'Expensive' in the Ancient World?" *Aegyptus* 75:75–93.

———. 1997. "The Oldest Manuscript of the Four Gospels?" *NTS* 43:1–34.

Smith, Dwight Moody. 1979–1980. "John and the Synoptics: Some Dimensions of the Problem." *NTS* 26:425–444.

———. 1992a. *John Among the Gospels: The Relationship in Twentieth-Century Research*. Minneapolis: Fortress Press.

———. 1992b. "The Problem of John and the Synoptics in the Light of the Relation Between Apocryphal and Canonical Gospels." In *John and the Synoptics*, edited by Adelbert Denaux, pp. 147–162. BETL 101. Leuven: Leuven Univ. Press. 39th Colloquium Biblicum Lovaniense, Aug. 7–9, 1990.

Smith, Jonathan Z. 1965–1966. "The Garments of Shame." *HR* 5:217–238.

———. 1975. "Wisdom and Apocalyptic." In *Religious Syncretism in Antiquity: Essays in Conversation with Geo. Widengren*, edited by Birger A. Pearson, pp. 131–156. Missoula, MT: Scholars Press.

———. 1977. "The Temple and the Magician." In *God's Christ and His People: Studies in Honour of Nils Alstrup Dahl*, edited by J. Jervell and Wayne A. Meeks, pp. 233–247. Oslo: Universitetsforlaget.

———. 1982. "Sacred Persistence: Toward a Redescription of Canon." In his *Imagining Religion: From Babylon to Jonestown*, pp. 36–52, 141–143. Chicago Studies in the History of Judaism. Chicago: University of Chicago Press.

Smith, Morton. 1956. "Palestinian Judaism in the First Century." In *Israel: Its Role in Civilization*, edited by Moshe Davis, pp. 67–81. New York: Harper & Row.

Sperber, Daniel. 1965–1966. "Costs of Living in Roman Palestine." *Journal of the Economic and Social History of the Orient* 8:248–271 and 9:182–211.

Stambaugh, John E. 1988. *The Ancient Roman City*. Baltimore, MD: Johns Hopkins Univ. Press.

Stanton, Graham N. 1997. "The Fourfold Gospel." *NTS* 43:317–346.

Stark, Rodney. 1996. *The Rise of Christianity: A Sociologist Reconsiders History*. Princeton, NJ: Princeton Univ. Press.

Stegemann, Wolfgang. 1984. "Vagabond Radicalism in Early Christianity? A Historical and Theological Discussion of a Thesis Proposed by Gerd Theissen." In *God of the Lowly: Socio-Historical Interpretations of the Bible*, edited by Willy Schottroff and Wolfgang Stegemann, translated by Matthew J. O'Connell, pp. 148–168. Maryknoll, NY: Orbis. Originally published in German, 1979.

Stern, Menahem. 1976–1984. *Greek and Latin Authors on Jews and Judaism*. 3 vols. Publications of the Israel Academy of Sciences and Humanities, Section of Humanities. Fontes Ad Res Judaicas Spectantes. Jerusalem: The Israel Academy of Sciences and Humanities.

Stock, Brian. 1983. *The Implications of Literacy: Written Language and Models of Interpretation in the Eleventh and Twelfth Centuries*. Princeton, NJ: Princeton Univ. Press.

Stonequist, Everett V. 1937. *The Marginal Man: A Study in Personality and Culture Conflict*. New York: Scribner.

Strange, James F. 1992a. "Some Implications of Archaeology for New Testament Studies." In *What Has Archaeology to Do with Faith?* edited by James H. Charlesworth and Walter P. Weaver, pp. 23–59. Faith and Scholarship Colloquies. Philadelphia: Trinity.

———. 1992b. "Six Campaigns at Sepphoris: The University of South Florida Excavations, 1983–1989." In *The Galilee in Late Antiquity*, edited by Lee I. Levine, pp. 339–355. New York and Jerusalem: The Jewish Theological Seminary of America. Papers from the First International Conference on Galilean Studies in Late Antiquity, Kibbutz Hanaton, Lower Galilee, Israel, Aug. 13–15, 1989.

———. 1994. "First-Century Galilee from Archaeology and from the Texts." In *Society of Biblical Literature 1994 Seminar Papers*, edited by Eugene H. Lovering, Jr., pp. 81–90. SBLSP 33. 130th annual meeting, Nov. 19–22, 1994, Chicago. Atlanta: Scholars Press.

Street, Brian V. 1984. *Literacy in Theory and Practice*. Cambridge Studies in Oral and Literate Culture, 9. Cambridge, UK: University of Cambridge Press.

Stroker, William Dettwiller. 1970. "The Formation of Secondary Sayings of Jesus." Ph.D. diss., Yale University. Ann Arbor, MI: University Microfilms International.

———. 1989. *Extracanonical Sayings of Jesus*. SBLRBS 18. Atlanta: Scholars Press.

Suggs, M. Jack. 1972. "The Christian Two Ways Tradition: Its Antiquity, Form, and Function." In *Studies on New Testament and Early Christian Literature: Essays in Honor of Allen P. Wikgren*, edited by David Aune, pp. 60–74. *Novum Testamentum* Supplements, 33. Leiden: Brill.

Swete, Henry Barclay. 1893. EYAGGELION KATA PETRON: *The Akhmîm Fragment of the Apocryphal Gospel of St. Peter*. London: Macmillan.

Talmon, Shemaryahu. 1992. "Oral Tradition and Written Transmission, or the Heard and Seen Word in Judaism of the Second Temple Period." In *Jesus and the Oral Gospel Tradition*, edited by Henry Wansbrough, pp. 121–158. JSNT Supplement Series, 64. Sheffield, UK: Sheffield Academic Press (JSOT Press).

Temporini, Hildegard, and Wolfgang Haase, eds. 1972–. *Aufstieg und Niedergang der römischen Welt*. Geschichte und Kultur Roms im Spiegel der neueren Forschung. 3 parts. Berlin and New York: Walter de Gruyter.

Thackeray, Henry St. John, et al., trans. 1926–1965. *Josephus*. 10 vols. LCL. Cambridge: Harvard Univ. Press.

Theissen, Gerd. 1978. *Sociology of Early Palestinian Christianity*. Translated by John Bowden. Philadelphia: Fortress Press. Originally published in German, 1977.

————. 1982. *The Social Setting of Pauline Christianity: Essays on Corinth.* Translated by John H. Schütz. Philadelphia: Fortress Press. Originally published in German, 1974–1975.

————. 1991. *The Gospels in Context: Social and Political History in the Synoptic Tradition.* Minneapolis: Fortress Press. Originally published in German, 1989.

————. 1992. *Social Reality and the Early Christians: Theology, Ethics, and the World of the New Testament.* Translated by Margaret Kohl. Minneapolis: Fortress Press. Originally published in German, 1982.

Treat, Jay C. 1990. "The Two Manuscript Witnesses to the Gospel of Peter." In *Society of Biblical Literature 1990 Seminar Papers,* edited by David J. Lull, pp. 391–399. SBLSP 29. 126th annual meeting, Nov. 17–20, 1990, New Orleans. Atlanta: Scholars Press.

Tuckett, Christopher M. 1989. "Synoptic Tradition in the *Didache.*" In *The New Testament in Early Christianity: La réception des écrits néotestamentaires dans le christianisme primitif,* pp. 197–230. Louvain: Louvain Univ. Press.

Turner, Eric G. 1952. "Roman Oxyrhynchus." *Journal of Egyptian Archaeology* 38:78–93.

————. 1971. *Greek Manuscripts of the Ancient World* (plates 1–73). Princeton, NJ: Princeton Univ. Press.

————. 1977. *The Typology of the Early Codex.* Haney Foundation Series, 18. Philadelphia: University of Pennsylvania Press.

————. 1987. *Greek Manuscripts of the Ancient World.* 2nd ed. revised and enlarged by Peter J. Parsons (plates 1–88). University of London Institute of Classical Studies, Bulletin Supplement 46. Oxford, UK: Oxford Univ. Press.

Vaage, Leif Eric. 1987. *Q: The Ethos and Ethics of an Itinerant Intelligence.* Ph.D. diss., Claremont Graduate School. Ann Arbor, MI: University Microfilms International.

————. 1994. *Galilean Upstarts: Jesus' First Followers According to Q.* Valley Forge, PA: Trinity Press International. Vaage 1987 "forms part of the substance of a number of chapters in this book."

Vaganay, Léon. 1930. *L'Évangile de Pierre.* 2nd ed. Études Bibliques. Paris: Gabalda.

Vale, Ruth. 1987. "Literary Sources in Archaeological Description: The Case of Galilee, Galilees, and Galileans." *Journal for the Study of Judaism* 18:210–227.

VanderKam, James C. 1994. *The Dead Sea Scrolls Today.* Grand Rapids, MI: Eerdmans.

van Haelst, Joseph. 1976. *Catalogue des Papyrus Littéraires Juifs et Chrétiens.* Série Papyrologie, 1. Paris: Publications de la Sorbonne.

————. 1989. "Les Origines du Codex." In *Les débuts du codex: Actes de la journée d'étude organisée à Paris les 3 et 4 juillet 1985 par l'Institut de Papyrologie de la Sorbonne et l'Institut de Recherche et d'Histoire des Textes,* pp. 13–35. Bibliographia: Elementa ad Librorum Studia Pertinentia, 9. Edited by Alain Blanchard. Turnhout, Belgium: Brepols.

Van Voorst, Robert E. 1989. *The Ascents of James: History and Theology of a Jewish-Christian Community.* SBLDS 112. Atlanta: Scholars Press. From Ph.D. diss., Union Theological Seminary (under J. Louis Martyn), 1988.

————. 1995. "Extracanonical Passion Narratives." In *The Death of Jesus in Early Christianity,* John T. Carroll and Joel B. Green, pp. 148–161. Peabody, MA: Hendrikson.

Vermes, Geza. 1981. *Jesus the Jew: A Historian's Reading of the Gospels.* Philadelphia: Fortress Press. Originally published in 1973 (London: Collins).

————. 1984. *Jesus and the World of Judaism.* Philadelphia: Fortress Press. London: Collins, 1983.

————. 1985. *The Dead Sea Scrolls: Qumran in Perspective.* With Pamela Vermes. Rev. ed. Philadelphia: Fortress Press.

———. 1993. *The Religion of Jesus the Jew*. Minneapolis: Fortress Press.

Vermes, Geza, and Martin D. Goodman. 1989. *The Essenes: According to the Classical Sources*. Oxford Centre Textbooks, 1. Sheffield, UK: Sheffield Academic Press (JSOT Press).

Vidal-Naquet, Pierre. 1980. "Interpreting Revolutionary Change: Political Divisions and Ideological Diversity in the Jewish World of the First Century A.D" (translated by Maria Jolas). *Yale French Studies* 59:86–105.

Vielhauer, Philipp. 1964. "ΑΝΑΡΑΥΣΙΣ: Zum gnostischen Hintergrund des Thomasevangeliums." In *Apophoreta* ("Festschrift für Ernst Haenchen zu seinem siebzigsten Geburtstag am 10. Dezember 1964"), edited by W. Eltester and F. H. Kettler, pp. 281–299. BZNW 30. Berlin: Töpelmann.

Viviano, Benedict T. 1992. "Beatitudes Found Among Dead Sea Scrolls." *BAR* 18 (6/Nov–Dec):53–55, 66.

von Harnack, Adolf. 1893. *Bruchstücke des Evangeliums und der Apokalypse des Petrus*. TU 9. Leipzig: Hinrichs.

Wallace-Hadrill, Andrew. 1991. "Introduction" and "Elites and Trade in the Roman Town." In Rich and Wallace-Hadrill, pp. ix–xviii, 241–272.

Weinfeld, Moshe. 1995. *Social Justice in Ancient Israel and in the Ancient Near East*. Publications of the Perry Foundation for Biblical Research in the Hebrew University of Jerusalem. Jerusalem: Magnes Press of Hebrew University; and Minneapolis: Fortress Press.

Whyte, Martin King. 1978. *The Status of Women in Preindustrial Societies*. Princeton, NJ: Princeton Univ. Press.

Williamson, G. A., trans. 1965. *Eusebius: The History of the Church from Christ to Constantine*. Penguin Classics. New York: Penguin Books.

Winograd, Eugene, and Ulric Neisser, eds. 1992. *Affect and Accuracy in Recall: Studies of "Flashbulb" Memories*. Emory Symposia in Cognition, 4. Cambridge, UK: Cambridge Univ. Press.

Wolf, Eric Robert. 1966. *Peasants*. Foundations of Modern Anthropology Series. Englewood Cliffs, NJ: Prentice-Hall.

Wright, Nicholas Thomas. 1992–. *Christian Origins and the Question of God*. 2 vols. to date. Vol. 1: *The New Testament and the People of God* (1992). Vol. 2: *Jesus and the Victory of God* (1996). Minneapolis: Fortress Press.

Yonge, Charles Duke, trans. 1993. *The Works of Philo*. New updated ed. Peabody, MA: Hendrikson. Originally published in 1854–1855.

Zahn, T. 1893. *Das Evangelium des Petrus*. Erlangen: Deichert.

Zias, Joseph, and Eliezer Sekeles. 1985. "The Crucified Man from Givʿat ha-Mivtar: A Reappraisal." *IEJ* 35:22–27.

SUBJECT INDEX

AUTHOR INDEX

TEXT INDEX

Jewish Texts